D0323618

THE ROMANTIC MOVEMENT

GARLAND REFERENCE LIBRARY
OF THE HUMANITIES
(VOL. 219)

THE ROMANTIC MOVEMENT
A Selective and Critical Bibliography for 1984

Edited by
David V. Erdman

with the assistance of
Brian J. Dendle
Robert R. Mollenauer
Augustus Pallotta
James S. Patty

Z
6514
.R6
E73
1985

GARLAND PUBLISHING, INC. • NEW YORK & LONDON
1985

© 1985 Garland Publishing, Inc.
All rights reserved

Library of Congress Cataloging-in-Publication Data
Main entry under title:

The Romantic movement.

(Garland reference library of the humanities ;
vol. 219)
    1. Romanticism—Bibliography. I. Erdman, David V.
II. Dendle, Brian J., 1936–   III. Series: Garland
reference library of the humanities ; v. 219.
Z6514.R6R647 1985 [PN603] 016.809′9145   84-48854
ISBN 0-8240-9505-7 (alk. paper)

INDIANA
UNIVERSITY
NORTHWEST

LIBRARY

Printed on acid-free, 250-year-life paper
Manufactured in the United States of America

This bibliography is compiled by a joint bibliography committee of the Modern Language Association representing groups General Topics II (now Comparative Studies in Romanticism and the Nineteenth Century), English 9 (English Romantic Period), French 6 (Nineteenth-Century French Literature), German 4 (Nineteenth- and Early Twentieth-Century German Literature), Italian 2 (Italian Literature, Seventeenth Century to the Present), and Spanish 4 (Eighteenth- and Nineteenth-Century Spanish Literature). It is designed to cover a "movement" rather than a period; though the English section, for example, is largely limited to the years 1789–1837, other sections extend over different spans of years.

It is our intent to include, with descriptive and, at times, critical annotation, all books and articles of substantial interest to scholars of English and Continental Romanticism. Studies of American Romanticism that relate to this interest are selectively included. We also make note of items of minor but scholarly interest, except those which may be expected to appear in the annual *MLA International Bibliography*. Major and controversial works are given what is intended to be judicious if necessarily brief review.

The approximate size of a book is indicated by report of the number of pages. Book prices are noted when available.

We continue the practice of including available current (1985) reviews of listed books.

The editorial committee gratefully acknowledges the help of its collaborators, whose names are given at the heads of the respective sections.

To ensure notice in the next issue of the bibliography, authors and publishers are invited to send review copies of relevant books or monographs and offprints of articles to: David V. Erdman, 58 Crane Neck Road, Setauket, N.Y. 11733.

CONTENTS

JOURNALS SEARCHED

All journals regularly searched are listed here. The editor welcomes notice of omissions, to be made good in the next annual.

AANL	*Atti dell'Accademia Nazionale dei Lincei*
ABC	*American Book Collector* (new series)
ABI	*Accademie e Bibliotheche d'Italia*
	Académie d'Angers. Mémoires
AConf	*Les Annales, Conferencia*
ActaG	*Acta Germanica* (Capetown)
	Acta Musicologicae
ActaN	*Acta Neophilologica*
	Adam: International Review
ADPh	*Arbeiten zur deutschen Philologie*
	Aevum: Rassegna di Scienze Storiche, Linguistiche, Filologiche
AFLSHA	*Annales de la Faculté des Lettres et Sciences Humaines d'Aix*
AG	*Anglica Germanica*
AHR	*American Historical Review*
AHRF	*Annales Historiques de la Révolution Française*
AI	*American Imago*
AION-SG	*Annali Istituto Universitario Orientale, Napoli, Sezione Germanica*
AJ	*Art Journal*
AJES	*Aligarh Journal of English Studies*
AJFS	*Australian Journal of French Studies*
AKG	*Archiv für Kulturgeschichte*
	Akzente: Zeitschrift für Literatur
AL	*American Literature*
	Albion
ALittASH	*Acta Litterarica Academiae Scientiarum Hungaricae. Magyar Tudomanyos Akademia. Budapest*
	Allegorica
ALM	*Archives des Lettres Modernes*
	American Art Journal
	American Art Review
	American Journal of Sociology

```
    ASch  American Scholar
   ASLHM  American Society Legion of Honor Magazine
          Association des Amis d'Alfred de Vigny.  Bulletin
    ASSR  Archives de Sciences Sociales des Réligions
     AUB  Analele Universitatü, Bucuresti
   AUMLA  Journal of the Australasian Universities Language
          and Literature Association
  Aurora  Aurora: Eichendorff-Almanach
          L'Avant-Scène
     AWR  Anglo-Welsh Review
    BAAD  Bulletin de l'Association des Amis d'Alexandre
          Dumas
    BAGB  Bulletin de l'Association Guillaume Budé
    BAWS  Bayerische Akademie der Wissenschaften.  Philo-
          sophischhistorisch Klasse, Sitzungsberichte
    B&BM  Books & Bookmen
      BB  Bulletin of Bibliography
   BBaud  Bulletin Baudelairien
    BBMP  Bulletin de la Biblioteca Menéndez Pelayo
      BC  Book Collector
    BCLF  Bulletin Critique du Livre Français
    BduB  Bulletin du Bibliophile
          Belfagor: Rassegna di Varia Umanità
          Bennington Review
          Berkshire Review (Williams College)
      BF  Book Forum
     BFE  Boletín de Filología Española
   BGDSL  Beiträge zur Geschichte der deutschen Sprache
          und Literatur
      BH  Bulletin Hispanique
     BHR  Bibliothèque d'Humanisme et Renaissance
     BHS  Bulletin of Hispanic Studies
          Bibliothèque de l'Ecole des Chartres
          Biblos
    BIHR  Bulletin of the Institute of Historical Research
          (London)
    BioC  Biologia Culturale
     BIQ  Blake: An Illustrated Quarterly
     BJA  British Journal of Aesthetics
    BJHS  British Journal for the History of Science
    BJRL  Bulletin of the John Rylands Library
      BL  Beiträge zur Literaturkunde
          Blackwood's Magazine
    BLAM  Bulletin de la Librairie Ancienne et Moderne
     BLE  Bulletin de Littérature Ecclesiastique
     BLR  The Bodleian Library Record
      BM  The Burlington Magazine
   BMMLA  Bulletin of the Midwest MLA
          Boletín de la Académia Argentina de Letras
```

	Cahiers Internationaux du Symbolisme
	Les Cahiers Naturalistes
CahiersS	Cahiers Staëliens
CAIEF	Cahiers de l'Association Internationale des Etudes Françaises
CalSS	California Slavic Studies
CamR	Cambridge Review
CAN	Cahiers Gerard de Nerval
	Canadian Journal of Research in Semiotics
CB	Cuadernos Bibliográficos
CE	College English
CentR	Centennial Review
CeS	Cultura e Scuola
CG	Colloquia Germanica
CH	Crítica Hispanica
CHA	Cuadernos Hispanoamericanos (Madrid)
ChLB	Charles Lamb Bulletin
CHR	Catholic Historical Review
CimR	Cimarron Review
CJC	Cahiers Jean Cocteau
CJG	Cahiers Jean Giraudoux
CJH	Canadian Journal of History
CJIS	Canadian Journal of Italian Studies
CL	Comparative Literature
CLAJ	College Language Association Journal
ClaudelS	Claudel Studies
	Clio
CLQ	Colby Library Quarterly
CLS	Comparative Literature Studies
CMen	Cahiers Mennaisiens
CML	Classical and Modern Literature: A Quarterly
CMLR	Canadian Modern Language Review
CollL	College Literature
	Colloquio (Lisbon)
	Commentary
	Commonweal
	Comparatist: Journal of the Southern Comparative Literature Association
	Comparative Criticism: A Yearbook (Cambridge)
	Comparative Literature Symposium Proceedings (Texas Tech University)
CompD	Comparative Drama
CompLB	Comparative Literature Bulletin Commentary
	Computers and the Humanities
	Computer Studies in the Humanities
	Connaissance des Arts
	The Connoisseur
	Contemporary French Civilization

EAS   *Essays in Arts and Sciences* (University of New Haven)
E&S   *Essays and Studies*
ECent   *The Eighteenth Century: Theory and Interpretation*
EcHR   *Economic History Review*
ECLife   *Eighteenth-Century Life*
ECl   *Etudes Classiques*
    L'Ecole des Lettres Lendemains
ECr   *L'Esprit Créateur* (Minneapolis)
    Ecrits de Paris
ECS   *Eighteenth Century Studies*
EDH   *Essays by Divers Hand*
EdL   *Etudes de Lettres*
EG   *Etudes Germaniques*
EHR   *English Historical Review*
EIA   *Estudos Ibero-Americanos*
EiC   *Essays in Criticism* (Oxford)
    Eire
EL   *Esperienze Letterarie*
ELH   *Journal of English Literary History*
ELit   *Etudes Littéraires*
ELLF   *Etudes de Langue et Littérature Françaises* (Tokyo)
ELN   *English Language Notes*
ELWIU   *Essays in Literature* (Western Illinois University)
EM   *English Miscellany*
    Encounter
    English
EnlE   *Enlightenment Essays*
EP   *Etudes Philosophiques*
ES   *English Studies*
ESA   *English Studies in Africa* (Johannesburg)
ESC   *English Studies in Canada*
    Esprit
ESQ   *Emerson Society Quarterly*
ESR   *European Studies Review*
    Essays in French Literature
    Essays in Literature
EstF   *Estudios Filosóficos*
ETR   *Etudes Théologiques et Réligieuses*
    Etudes
    Etudes Bernanosiennes
    Etudes Françaises
    Etudes Gobiniennes
    Etudes Nervaliennes et Romantiques
    Euphorion: Zeitschrift für Literaturgeschichte
    Europe
    Explicator
ExTL   *Explicación de Textos Literarios*

The Hebrew University Studies in Literature
HeineJ *Heine Jahrbuch*
HisJ *Hispanic Journal*
 Hispania
Hispano *Hispanófila*
 Historia
 The Historian
 History and Theory
 History of Religions
 Historical Methods
HJ *Historical Journal*
HLB *Harvard Library Bulletin*
HLQ *Huntington Library Quarterly*
HöJb *Hölderlin Jahrbuch*
 Horizon
HPE *The History of Political Economy*
HR *Hispanic Review*
HSL *Hartford Studies in Literature*
HT *History Today*
HudR *Hudson Review*
Hum *Humanities*
 Humanities Association Review
 The Humanities Review (New Delhi)
IASL *Internationales Archiv für Sozialgeschichte der deutschen Literatur*
I&L *Ideologies and Literature*
Ibero *Iberomania*
IdS *Idealistic Studies*
IHA *L'Information d'Histoire de l'Art*
IL *L'Information Littéraire*
 L'Information Historique
 Inti: Revista de Literature Hispánica
 International Fiction Review
 Interpretations (Memphis State University)
IPQ *International Philosophical Quarterly*
IQ *Italian Quarterly*
IS *Italian Studies*
 Italica
 Italianistica
IUB *Indiana University Bookman*
JAAC *Journal of Aesthetics and Art Criticism*
JAF *Journal of American Folklore*
JBS *Journal of British Studies*
JDH *Jahresverzeichnis der deutschen Hochschulschriften*
JDSG *Jahrbuch der deutschen Schiller-Gesellschaft*
JEGP *Journal of English and Germanic Philology*
JEH *Journal of Ecclesiastical History*
JES *The Journal of European Studies*
JFDH *Jahrbuch der Freien deutschen Hochstifts* (Tübingen)

LE&W	*Literature East and West*
LenauA	*Lenau-Almanach* (Wien)
LenauF	*Lenau-Forum. Vierteljahresschrift für vergleich-ende Literaturforschung* (Wien)
	Leonardo
LetN	*Lettres Nouvelles*
	Letras
LHR	*Lock Haven Review* (Lock Haven State College, Pa.)
LI	*Lettere Italiane*
	Library
	The Library Quarterly
	La Licorne (Faculté des Lettres et des Langues de l'Université de Poitiers)
LiLi	*Zeitschrift für Literaturwissenschaft und Linguistik*
	Lingua e Stile
	Literature and Ideology
LitR	*Literary Review*
	Littérature
	Littératures
LJ	*Library Journal*
LJGG	*Literaturwissenschaftliches Jahrbuch. Im Auftrage der Littérature Gorres-Gesellschaft. N.F.*
LMFA	*Literature, Music and Fine Arts*
LNL	*Linguistics in Literature*
LR	*Les Lettres Romanes*
LSoc	*Language in Society*
LuK	*Literatur und Kritik*
	Lumière et Vie
LWU	*Literatur in Wissenschaft und Unterricht*
LY	*Lessing Yearbook*
MA	*Le Moyen Age*
M&L	*Music and Letters* (London)
	Marche Romane
	Master Drawings
MC	*Misure Critiche*
McNR	*McNeese Review* (McNeese State University, Louisiana)
MD	*Modern Drama*
Merkur	*Merkur: Deutsche Zeitschrift für europäisches Denken*
MFS	*Modern Fiction Studies*
MGS	*Michigan Germanic Studies*
MHG	*Mitteilungen der E.T.A. Hoffmann-Gesellschaft*
MichA	*Michigan Academician*
MidH	*Midlands History*
MiltonQ	*Milton Quarterly*

	Mime, Mask, and Marionette: A Quarterly Journal of Performing Arts
	Minerva
MinnR	*Minnesota Review*
ML	*Modern Languages* (London)
MLJ	*Modern Language Journal*
MLN	*Modern Language Notes*
MLQ	*Modern Language Quarterly*
MLR	*Modern Language Review*
MLS	*Modern Language Studies*
MMM	*Mélanges Malraux Miscellany*
	Modern Age
	Modern Australian Literature
Monatshefte	*Monatshefte: A Journal Devoted to the Study of Germanic Language and Literature*
	Mosaic
MP	*Modern Philology*
MQ	*Midwest Quarterly* (Pittsburg, Kansas)
MQR	*Michigan Quarterly Review*
MR	*Massachusetts Review*
MSE	*Massachusetts Studies in English*
MSpr	*Moderna Språk*
MuK	*Maske und Kothurn*
	Mundus Artium
MusQ	*Musical Quarterly*
MV	*Minority Voices: An Interdisciplinary Journal of Literature and the Arts*
NA	*Nuova Antologia*
	Names
N&Q	*Notes & Queries*
NARG	*Nuovi Argumenti*
NCF	*Nineteenth Century Fiction*
NCFS	*Nineteenth-Century French Studies*
NCM	*Nineteenth-Century Music*
NDEF	*Notre Dame English Journal*
NDH	*Neue deutsche Hefte*
NDL	*Neue deutsche Literatur*
NDQ	*North Dakota Quarterly*
	Neohelicon
Neophil	*Neophilologus* (Groningen)
NEQ	*New England Quarterly*
	New Left Review
	New Statesman
	New York Times Book Review
NFS	*Nottingham French Studies*
NGC	*New German Criticism*
NGS	*New German Studies*
NL	*Nouvelles Littéraires*

NLB	*The Newberry Library Bulletin*
NLH	*New Literary History*
NM	*Neuphilologische Mitteilungen*
	Le Nouvel Observateur
	Novel: A Forum on Fiction
NR	*New Republic*
NRev	*The New Review* (London)
NRF	*Nouvelle Revue Française*
NRFH	*Nueva Revista de Filología Hispánica*
NRRS	*Notes and Records of the Royal Society of London*
NRs	*Neue Rundschau*
NS	*Die Neueren Sprachen*
NUQ	*New Universities Quarterly*
NY	*New Yorker*
NYRB	*New York Review of Books*
O&C	*OEuvres et Critiques*
	L'OEil
ÖGL	*Österreich in Geschichte und Literatur*
OGS	*Oxford Germanic Studies*
OHis	*Ottawa Hispanica*
OL	*Orbis Litterarum*
OLR	*Oxford Literary Review*
ON	*Otto-Novecento*
	Opera
	Opera News
OPL	*Osservatore Politico Letterario*
OUR	*Ohio University Review*
	Oxford Art Journal
P&L	*Philosophy and Literature*
	Pantheon
	Parliamentary History: A Yearbook
P&P	*Past and Present*
PAPS	*Proceedings of the American Philosophical Society*
	Parnasse (Oxford)
P&R	*Philosophy and Rhetoric*
	Paragone: Rivista Mensile di Arte Figuritiva e Letteratura
PBSA	*Papers of the Bibliographical Society of America*
PCL	*Perspectives on Contemporary Literature*
PEGS	*Publications of the English Goethe Society*
	Pensiero Politico
Person	*The Personalist*
PFSCL	*Papers on French Seventeenth Century Literature*
	Philobiblon
	Philologica Pragensis
PhJ	*The Philosophical Journal*
PhJb	*Philosophisches Jahrbuch*
	Phoebus
	Pisa: Annali della Scuola Normale Superiore di Pisa

RDM   *Revue des Deux Mondes*
RdS   *Revue de Synthèse*
RE   *Revue d'Esthetique*
       Réalités
       Recherches de Sciences Religieuses
RecL   *Recovering Literature*
REE   *Revista de Estudios Extremenos*
REG   *Revue des Etudes Grecques*
REH   *Revista de Estudios Hispanicos*
REI   *Revue des Etudes Italiennes*
REL   *Review of English Literature* (Leeds)
       représentations
RES   *Review of English Studies*
RevEH *Revue d'Histoire Ecclésiastique*
       Review
       Reviews in European History
RevR   *Revue Romane*
       Revue Belge de Musicologie
       Revue d'Esthétique
       Revue d'Histoire et de Philosophie Religieuses
       Revue d'Histoire Moderne et Contemporaine
       Revue de la Bibliothèque Nationale
       Revue de l'Art
       Revue de l'Histoire des Religions
       Revue de Louisiane (Louisiana Review)
       Revue de l'Université de Bruxelles
       Revue de Metaphysique et de Morale
       Revue de Théologie et de Philosophie
       Revue des Etudes Juives
       Revue des Etudes Slaves
       Revue des Sciences Religieuses
       Revue du Louvre et des Musées de France
       Revue du Monde Russe et Soviétique
       Revue du Pacifique
       Revue Française d'Histoire de Livre
       Revue Française de Psychanalyse
RF   *Romanische Forschungen*
RFE   *Revista de Filologia Española*
RFNS   *Revista di Filosophia Neo-Scolastica*
RG   *Revue Générale*
RGer   *Recherches Germaniques*
RH   *Revue Historique*
RHEF   *Revue d'Histoire de l'Eglise de France*
RHL   *Revue d'Histoire Littéraire de la France*
RHM   *Revista Hispánica Moderna*
RHT   *Revue d'Histoire du Théâtre*
RHV   *Revue Historique Vaudoise*
RI   *Revista Iberoamericana*
RIE   *Revista de Ideas Estéticas*
RiLI   *Rivista di Letteratura Italiana*

Scheidewege	*Scheidewege: Vierteljahresschrift für skeptisches Denken*
SchM	*Schweitzer Monatshefte für Politik, Wirtschaft, Kultur*
ScHR	*Scottish Historical Review*
SCR	*South Carolina Review*
SCr	*Strumenti Critici*
SECC	*Studies in Eighteenth-Century Culture* (University of Wisconsin)
SEEJ	*Slavic and East European Journal*
SEL	*Studies in English Literature, 1500-1900* (Rice University)
	Seminar: A Journal of Germanic Studies
	Semiolus
	Semiotext
	Semiotica: Revue Publiée par l'Association Internationale de Sémiotique
SFI	*Studi di Filologia Italiana*
SFR	*Stanford French Review*
SFr	*Studi Francesi*
SGr	*Studi Germanici*
ShawR	*The Shaw Review*
	Shenandoah
SHPS	*Studies in the History and Philosophy of Science*
SHR	*Southern Humanities Review*
ShS	*Shakespeare Survey*
	Signs
SiR	*Studies in Romanticism* (Boston University)
SJP	*Southern Journal of Philosophy*
SJW	*Shakespeare Jahrbuch* (Weimar)
SlavR	*Slavic Review*
SLIm	*Studies in the Literary Imagination*
SLJ	*Scottish Library Journal*
SN	*Studia Neophilologica*
SNNTS	*Studies in the Novel* (North Texas University)
SÖAW	*Sitzungsberichte der Österreichischen Akademie der Wissenschaften im Wien, Philosophisch-historisch Klasse*
	Société Chateaubriand, Bulletin
	Société de Linguistique de Paris. Bulletin
	Société des Amis de Montaigne. Bulletin
	Société Paul Claudel. Bulletin
SoR	*Southern Review* (Louisiana State University)
SoRA	*Southern Review* (Adelaide, Australia)
	Soundings: A Journal of Interdisciplinary Studies
	Soviet Studies in Literature
	Source
SovL	*Soviet Literature*

WZUH	Wissenschaftliche Zeitschrift der Martin-Luther-Universität Halle-Wittenberg
WZUJ	Wissenschaftliche Zeitschrift der Friedrich-Schiller-Universität Jena
WZUL	Wissenschaftliche Zeitschrift der Karl-Marx-Universität Leipzig
YCGL	Yearbook of Comparative and General Literature
YES	Yearbook of English Studies
YFS	Yale French Studies
YR	Yale Review
YULG	Yale University Library Gazette
YWMLS	Year's Work in Modern Language Studies
ZAA	Zeitschrift für Anglistik und Amerikanistik
ZDA	Zeitschrift für deutsches Altertum und deutsche Literatur
ZDP	Zeitschrift für deutsche Philologie
	Zeitschrift des deutschen Vereins für Kunstwissenschaft
	Zeitschrift für Adthetik und allgemeine Kunstwissenschaft
	Zeitschrift für Kirchengeschichte
	Zeitschrift für Kunstgeschichte
ZFSL	Zeitschrift für französische Sprache und Literatur
ZG(Korea)	Zeitschrift für Germanistik (Korea)
ZG(Leipzig)	Zeitschrift für Germanistik (Leipzig)
ZPhF	Zeitschrift für Philosophische Forschung
ZRG	Zeitschrift für Religions- und Geistegeschichte
ZRL	Zagadnienia Rodzajów Literackich
ZRP	Zeitschrift für Romanische Philologie (Halle)
ZS	Zeitschrift für Slawistik
ZV	Zeitschrift für Volkskunde

THE ROMANTIC MOVEMENT

GENERAL

(Compiled by David V. Erdman with the assistance of
Thomas L. Ashton, Irene H. Chayes, Bishop C. Hunt,
Robert R. Mollenauer, Augustus Pallotta, James S.
Patty, Jeffrey C. Robinson, Robert Michael Ryan, and
Mark T. Smith)

1. BIBLIOGRAPHY

See the respective "Bibiliography" and "General" sections for
each language, below. *The Romantic Movement Bibliography* has
been published in its present form beginning with the *Bibliography* for 1979, in 1980. For previous years, see the "Bibliography of the Romantic Movement" in *English Language Notes* (*ELN*),
September supplements, 1965-79. In 1973 a cumulative reprint
since 1936 was published in seven volumes by the Pierian Press
and R.R. Bowker, New York. For the most extensive general listing, in all languages, without commentary, see the annual *MLA
International Bibliography*, Volumes I and II.

Diderot/D'Alembert. *Encyclopédie.* Elmsford, N.Y.: Pergamon
Press, 1984.

Five-volume reprint of the 35 volumes of 1751-80. Weight
60 pounds. $150.00 plus shipping ($14.50; overseas $38.50).

Frank, Frederick S. *Guide to the Gothic: An Annotated Bibliography of Criticism.* Metuchen, N.J.: Scarecrow, 1984.

Not seen.

Frye, Northrop; Sheridan Baker; and George Perkins. *The Harper
Handbook to Literature.* New York: Harper & Row, 1984. Pp.
608. Paper.

For undergraduate English majors and graduate students.
Essays on "major topics" followed by bibliographies; a

3

"Chronology of Literature and World Events," by Barbara M.
Perkins.
   Not seen.

Gephart, Ronald M., comp. *Revolutionary America, 1763-1789:*
A Bibliography. 2 vols. Washington, D.C.: Historical
Publications Office, Manuscript Division, Library of Congress,
1984. $38.00.

Hanak, Miroslav John, ed. *Romantic Poetry on the European*
Continent. (An English Language Anthology, Vol. I.)
University Press of America, 1983. Pp. xxii+592. Paper
$20.75.

   After a five-page Preface tracing the career of the Romantic
ego, there are selections from Schlegel, Hölderlin, Tieck,
Novalis, Brentano, Arnim, Chamisso, Uhland, Eichendorff,
Müller, Rückert, Platen, Heine, Lenau; then Lamartine, Vigny,
Hugo, Gautier, Musset, Nerval; then Saavedra, Espronceda,
Zorrilla, Tenorio, Bécquer, all in English translation.
   Offered in the cheapest possible format: faintly printed
typewriting, no line numbers, no names of translators, no
dates, no annotation, no index.
   No announcement about Vol. II.

Harris, Lauri Lanzen, and Sheila Fitzgerald, eds. *Nineteenth-*
Century Literature Criticism: Excerpts from Criticism of ...
Creative Writers Who Died Between 1800 and 1900. Vols. 6 &
7. Detroit: Gale Research, 1984. Pp. 600 & 625; $80.00 &
$82.00.

   Vol. 6 includes Constant, Lockhart, Mérimée, and Ann Radcliffe among its 15 authors. Vol. 7 includes Andersen,
Dostoevski, de Musset, Pater, Thoreau, and de Toqueville, among
its 13 authors.
   On vols. 1-3, see *RMB* for 1982; on vols. 4-5, see *RMB* for
1983. Each selection of excerpts is extensive; each excerpt
ample.
   And since vols. 8 and 9 will be off the press before we are,
we may as well list the relevant authors they include:
Charlotte Brontë, William Cowper, Eichendorff, Foscolo, Herder,
Keats, Maginn, and Southey in vol. 8; and in remaining vols.:
Arnim, Blake, Carlyle, Clare, Cobbett, Coleridge, Crabbe,
Godwin, Hazlitt, Hölderlin, Hood, Lamb, Landor, Leopardi,
Nodier, Novalis, Paine, Peacock, Rogers, Schiller, Scott,
Shelley (M. and P.B.), Stendhal, and Wordsworth.

Heitman, K., ed. *Neues Handbuch der Literaturwissenschaft:*
Europäische Romantik. Vol. I. Wiesbaden: Akademisch Ver-

lagsgesellschaft Athenaion, 1982. Pp. 382.

Rev. by Elda Tapparelli in *SFr* 28 (1984): 370-71.

Hoffman, Herbert H. and Rita L. *International Index to Recorded Poetry*. New York: H.W. Wilson Co., 1983. Pp. 529. $70.00.

Analyzes more than 1,700 phonodiscs, tapes, cassettes, and films of spoken poetry recorded anywhere, through 1980.

Redman, Harry, Jr. "A Few More Nineteenth-Century French Treatments of the Don Juan Theme." *WVUPP* 28 (1982): 29-40.

These items were included in the "Fifth Supplement" to Armand E. Singer's bibliography of the Don Juan theme (see *RMB* for 1980, p. 4).

Taubert, Sigfred, and Peter Weidhaas, eds. *The Book Trade of the World*. Vol. 4: *Africa*. New York: Bowker, 1984. Pp. 392; maps; index of complete set. $70.00 each vol.

Vol. 1: *Europe and International* (1973); vol. 2: *The Americas, Australia, and New Zealand* (1977); vol. 3: *Asia* (1982).

Urdang, Laurence, ed. *Historical and Literary Names and Allusions*. Detroit: Gale Research Co., 1984. About 3,100 pp. in 4 vols. $240.00 the set.

2. ENVIRONMENT: ART, PHILOSOPHY, POLITICS, RELIGION, SOCIETY

Abrahm, Gerald, ed. *The New Oxford History of Music*, viii: *The Age of Beethoven 1790-1830*. Oxford University Press, 1982. Pp. xix+747. $49.95.

Rev. by Julian Rushton in *M&L* 65 (1984): 51-55.

Aldridge, A. Owen. *Thomas Paine's American Ideology*. University of Delaware Press, 1984. Pp. 327. $38.50.

A richly documented examination of the sources and influence of Paine's intellectual career between 1775 and 1787, at home and abroad. A valuable component of the discussion is a pamphlet not hitherto identified as Paine's called *Four Letters on Interesting Subjects*. This study will increase our awareness of Paine's role in the Enlightenment. (D.V.E.)

Allison, Henry E. *Kant's Transcendental Idealism: An
Interpretation and Defense.* Yale University Press, 1984.
Pp. ix+390. $32.50.

For the specialist as well as the philosophical layman who
can take his Kant straight, here is an energetic and stimulating defense of the *Critique of Pure Reason* and of transcendental idealism against accusations of confusion and self-
contradiction. Allison argues (with a pleasant lack of academic acerbity) that many of Kant's critics have simply failed
to understand some of his subtler distinctions, particularly
those involving the *a priori* epistemic conditions that determine what can properly be considered as an object for the
human mind. Following Kant's abstruser musings is not easy
even for the professionals, but Allison has succeeded in
clarifying much obscurity, not least by the precision and
grace of his writing. (R.M.R.)

Aron, Jean-Paul, and Roger Kempf. *La Bourgeoisie, le sexe et
l'honneur.* (Histoire.) Paris: Presses universitaires de
France, 1984. Pp. 306. Fr. 35.00.

"... Jean-Paul Aron et Roger Kempf scrutent ici, sans
distance et avec verdeur, la mise en place d'une morale qui
régit le discours du XIXe siècle.... De ce discours fou,
de ces obsessions ... Kempf et Aron font un livre savant
et drôle. Un livre à mettre entre--presque--toutes les
mains." (Christian Descamps, *Le Matin*)

Badura-Skoda, Eva, and Peter Branscombe, eds. *Schubert
Studies: Problems of Style and Chronology.* Cambridge
University Press, 1982. Pp. 350. $37.50.

Rev. by John Reed in *M&L* 65 (1984): 74-77.
Essays of interest to non-specialists include Walter Durr's
"Schubert's Songs and Their Poetry: Reflections on Poetic
Aspects of Song Composition"; Peter Branscombe's "Schubert
and the Melodrama"; and Elizabeth Norman McKay's "Schubert
as a Composer of Operas."

Bann, Stephen. *The Clothing of Clio: A Study of the Representation of History in Nineteenth-Century Britain and
France.* Cambridge University Press, 1984. Pp. 196. $37.50.

Rev. by Eugen Weber in *TLS*, Sept. 28, 1984, p. 1072, as a
good, suggestive "read": "The historian as taxidermist ...
is evidence 'of the extreme ... value which our culture places
upon the myth of recreating the real....' But history is
not reality."

Berlin, Ira, and Ronald Hoffman, eds. *Slavery and Freedom in the Age of the American Revolution.* University Press of Virginia, 1983. Pp. 314. $15.95.

Rev. by Claude Levy in *ECS* 18 (1984-85): 275-78.

Best, Geoffrey. *War and Society in Revolutionary Europe, 1770-1870.* New York: St. Martin's, 1982. Pp. 336. $27.50.

Rev. by William H. McNeill in *JMH* 56 (1984): 322-24.

Binney, Edwin, 3rd. "Longing for the Ideal: Images of Marie Taglioni in the Romantic Ballet." *HLB* 32 (1984): 105-48.

She conquered London in 1831. (T.L.A.)

Blakemore, Steven. "Burke and the Fall of Language: The French Revolution as Linguistic Event." *ECS* 17 (1984): 284-307.

Bouloiseau, Marc. *The Jacobin Republic 1792-1794.* (The French Revolution 2: Editions de la Maison des Sciences de l'Homme.) Cambridge University Press, 1984. Pp. xvi+251. $39.50; paper $13.95.

The second of a three-volume series on the French Revolution, which "aims to provide an up-to-date synthesis of the latest research and to highlight recent controversies." Instructive; judicious. (D.V.E.)
For Volume 1, see Vovelle below. Volume 3 is yet to be announced.

Brown, John L. "Revolution and the Muse: The American War of Independence in Contemporary French Poetry." *WMQ* 41 (1984): 592-614.

"Contemporary" means late eighteenth century.

Cameron, David R. "The Hero in Rousseau's Political Thought." *JHI* 45 (1984): 397-419.

Concentrates on Machiavelli as understood by Hobbes as a major influence. Useful. (T.L.A.)

Cameron, Kenneth Neill. *Marxism: The Science of Society: An Introduction.* Mass.: Bergin & Garvey, 1985. Pp. xvi+ 222. $25.95.

"The Marxist world-view is no easier to grasp than are the complex realities it attempts to reflect" (149). But this sage explication of that world-view, including its ideas in

relation to the realities of "Class, Ideas, and Art"
(Chapter 7), supplies a lucid *and* documented account of the
origins, development, and present-day illumination of the
central thought of Marx and Engels.

"The Roots" (Chapter 1) are located in the economic Industrial Revolution that followed the political French Revolution; an evolution of thought traced from Godwin (and
Condorcet and Erasmus Darwin) to Owen (and Chartism) to
Marx. Modern bourgeois historians are chided for neglecting
the evolutionary dynamics of social history, the subject of
Chapters 4 and 5 ("Capitalism" and "Communism").

Chapter 6, "Women and Society," begins with Godwin--
and "his wife, Mary Wollstonecraft" who "in some respects
went further than he did," and concludes with the "bold new
ways" of the contemporary "women's liberation" movement:
"Marx and Engels would certainly have rejoiced in this movement even as they would wish that it had greater proletarian
and Marxist components."

Chapter 7, with a warning against anachronism--"no group
of thinkers, writers or artists can develop beyond the con-
fines of the social forces that produce them"--introduces
Shelley and Byron as responding to "a new cultural phenomenon,
... the first stirrings of working class thought" (146). And
it is suggested why Marx and Engels seemed to prefer Balzac
and Shelley, among early nineteenth-century writers, a
"sharply contrasting" pair (156).

A concluding section on "Modern Science and Nature" points
out how "Marx's view of the inherently materialistic and
dialectical nature of reality has been further confirmed by
modern scientific discoveries, indeed to a greater degree
than most Marxists today [or any others] seem to realize"
(170). Indeed, those of us who have read Cameron's books
and watched his mind at work--getting into the deepest
scientific scholarship about the history of life (e.g., the
evolution of the universe and of animal life; the development
of consciousness "apparently some 200,000 years ago," the
subsequent "basic socioeconomic interaction of productive
forces ... and inherited behavior patterns")--will not be
surprised at the range of his wisdom but only delighted at
his ability to communicate so much of it. (D.V.E.)

Chan, Victor. "Rebellion, Retribution, Resistance, and Re-
     demption: Genesis and Metamorphosis of a Romantic Giant
     Enigma." *Arts Magazine* 58,x (1984): 80-95.

     A fascinating, heavily documented survey and analysis
of the imagery of giants in the eighteenth century and the
Romantic period. Precursors Dante and Bunyan lead to discussions of Blake, Byron, Goya, Flaxman. Important. (J.C.R.)

Chessex, Pierre. "A Swiss Painter in Rome: A.L.R. Ducros."
   Apollo 119 (1984): 430-37.

Chissell, Joan. *Clara Schumann: A Dedicated Spirit*. London:
   Hamish Hamilton, 1983. Pp. xvi+232.

   Rev. by Ronald Taylor in *M&L* 65 (1984): 378-79: "the
   sad fact is that Clara Schumann was a dull person ... and
   a biographer can do little about it."

Clouatre, Dallas L. "The Concept of Class in French Culture
   Prior to the Revolution." *JHI* 45 (1984): 219-44.

Davis, David Brion. *Slavery and Human Progress*. Oxford
   University Press, 1984. Pp. 374. $25.00.

   Rev. by J. Morgan Jousser, "Ironies of Abolition," *TLS*,
   Feb. 1, 1985, pp. 123-24, as representing great advances which
   have been made in the study of slavery--yet as vitiated by
   a "creed of inconsistency and complexity" which allows Davis
   to offer a great number of "scattered, if brilliant, insights"
   yet fail to "push the study of the history of slavery very
   far forward."
   Not seen.

Delano, Sterling F. *"The Harbinger" and New England Transcendentalism: A Portrait of Associationism in America*.
   Cranbury, N.J.: Associated University Presses, 1983. Pp.
   217. $27.50.

   Rev. by Jayme A. Sokolow in *NEQ* 57 (1984): 467-69.
   The influence of Charles Fourier is well detailed. (T.L.A.)

Dutton, H.I. *The Patent System and Inventive Activity during
   the Industrial Revolution 1750-1852*. Manchester University
   Press, 1984. Pp. 232. £22.50.

   This is the first general study of the patent system and of
   how patents related to inventive activity, hitherto "a wide
   uncultivated space" in historiography. Dutton does not
   quote François Furet's remark that the "industrial revolution" was only "a bourgeois invention," but the thrust of
   his industrious documentation seems to be to scotch any such
   legend by demonstrating that "the net economic effect" of the
   activity of inventors was to propel an actual revolution
   in industry. (D.V.E.)

Edmunds, Bill. "A Jacobin Debacle: The Losing of Lyon in
   Spring 1793." *H* 69,ccxxv (1984): 1-14.

"The Jacobins won impressive political victories in Paris
in 1793 but against this should be set costly failures in
the provinces caused by their inflexibility and narrow
Parisian focus."

Erdman, David V.   "Citizen Stanhope and the French Revolution."
   TWC 15 (1984):   8-17.

   Charles Mahon, third Earl Stanhope: Erdman thinks he may
   have visited Paris incognito in December, 1791, and that he
   was not the genial buffoon that history has taken him for.
   A mine of information and ingenious speculation.   (B.C.H.)

Frängsmyr, Tore, ed.   Linnaeus, the Man and His Work.   University of California Press, 1983.   Pp. xii+203. $25.00.

   Rev. by James Larson in ECS 18 (1984-85):   272-74.

Gassier, Pierre.   Léopold Robert.   Editions Idées et Calendes
   Neuchâtel, 1983.   £58.00

   Rev. ("A Swiss Romantic") by David Wakefield in Apollo
   119 (1984):   386.

Gillispie, Charles C.   The Montgolfier Brothers and the Invention of Aviation, 1783-1784.   Princeton University Press,
   1983.   Pp. xii+210. $35.00.

   Rev. by Martin S. Staum in JMH 56 (1984):   729-31.

Greene, David B.   Temporal Processes in Beethoven's Music.
   New York, London, and Paris: Gordon and Breach, 1984.
   Pp. ix+192. $28.00.

   Rev. by Wilfred Mellers in TLS, June 29, 1984, p. 723, as
   an "analysis of the timeless temporality of Beethoven's music
   [that] reveals his wisdom and, unlike most books about music
   (or anything else), leaves us wiser as well as more knowledgeable."
   The chapter titles describe the processes: Living from
   the Past/Living toward the Future; Heroism Prevailing/
   Heroism Falling Short; Creating Several Futures at Once;
   Disparate Shapes Confirming One Another/Disparate Shapes
   Contradicting One Another.   An immense debt is acknowledged
   to Kant, Hegel, Husserl, Heidegger, Bergson, Poulet, and
   McLuhan.   Joseph Kerman and Charles Rosen are frequently
   cited and differed from.

Hathaway, Thomas.   "Beethoven's Biographers."   QQ 91 (1984):
   140-52.

Hellerstein, Erna Olafson; Leslie Parker Hume; and Karen W.
   Offen.   Victorian Women.   A Documentary Account of Women's

Lives in Nineteenth-Century England, France, and the United States. Stanford University Press, 1981. Pp. 534. $27.50; paper $11.95.

"A wonderfully useful book, as much so for the casual reader as for the professional: the historian, the religious studies, women's studies, sociology, or literature student or teacher. The sources are organized according to the ages of women, starting with girlhood and ending with old age. Coverage of the situation of women in the three countries is very broad; all classes and many points of view are represented.... [About] women ranging from slave girls to George Sand." (Claudette K. Columbus, Hobart and William Smith Colleges)

Helsted, Dyveke. "Christian VIII: An Intelligent Amateur." *Apollo* 120 (1984): 418-25.

Prince Christian Frederik (1786-1848), who was a patron of the arts and succeeded to the Danish throne in 1839.

Higman, B.W. *Slave Populations of the British Caribbean, 1807-1834.* The Johns Hopkins University Press, 1984. Pp. 832. $65.00.

Hornsley, Peter R.G. *Pewter of the Western World, 1600-1850.* Exton, Pa.: Schiffer, 1983. $60.00.

Rev. by Geoffrey Wills in *Apollo* 119 (1984): 306.

Hudspeth, Robert N., ed. *The Letters of Margaret Fuller.* Vol. I: 1817-38 (374 pp.); Vol. II: 1839-41 (276 pp.). Cornell University Press, 1983. $25.00.

Rev. by David M. Van Leer in *PMHB* 108 (1984): 241-43.

Hunt, Lynn. *Politics, Culture, and Class in the French Revolution.* University of California Press, 1984. Pp. 251. $19.95.

Rev. by Robert Darnton in *NYRB*, Jan. 31, 1985, pp. 21-23, analytically and sympathetically, as an account which the revolutionaries would not have recognized; abounding in abstractions but failing "to communicate the sense of men struggling to create some meaningful order...."
"The new textualism has many advantages over the old social science, but it does not free historians from the constraints of evidence." Nevertheless, "Lynn Hunt's ... failures are more instructive than her successes.... The shifting ground of scholarship has produced more questions than answers. But they are important questions...."
Valuable on Wordsworth's favorite, Grégoire. (D.V.E.)

Jones, Collin. *Charity and Bienfaisance: The Treatment
of the Poor in the Montpellier Region, 1740-1815.* Cambridge
University Press, 1982. Pp. xvi+317. $44.50.

   Rev. by Cissie Fairchilds in *JMH* 56 (1984): 363-65.

Jones, John A. "The 'Reconciliation of Opposites' in Romantic
Poetry and Classical Style Music: Some Relations." *CentR*
28 (1984): 159-84.

   The "possibilities for conflict and resolution" inherent
in structure itself are used for dramatic effect in both
Classical music and Romantic lyric, prior to 1825.

Journal of Modern History 56,4 (1984): 579-697, "Political
Practice in the French Revolution."

   A special number, contents as follows: Mona Ozouf, "War
and Terror in French Revolutionary Discourse, 1792-1794"
(579-97), which is particularly excellent on the role of
Benjamin Constant; Vivian R. Gruder, "A Mutation in Elite
Political Culture: The French Notables and the Defense of
Property and Participation, 1787" (598-634); Michael L.
Kennedy, "The Best and the Worst of Times: The Jacobin
Club Network from October 1791 to June 2, 1793" (635-66);
and Ted W. Margadent, "Tradition and Modernity in Rural
France during the Nineteenth Century" (667-97), which reviews
some two dozen studies all with a rural focus. All in all
a useful bit of background, particularly for those with
Wordsworth's Beaupuy in mind. (T.L.A.)

Kain, Philip J. *Schiller, Hegel, and Marx: State, Society
and the Aesthetic Ideal of Ancient Greece.* McGill-Queen's
University Press, 1982. Pp. xii+179. $25.00.

   Rev. by Joseph J. O'Malley in *JHP* 22 (1984): 127-28, as
"a serious and thought-provoking contribution to Marxology."

Krejcí, Jaroslav. *Great Revolutions Compared: The Search for
a Theory.* Assisted by Ann Krejcová. New York: St. Martin's
Press, 1984. Pp. xxi+251. $27.50.

   Each of six revolutions is studied as a prolonged process
of political and social change; study of the French "Bourgeois"
Revolution as beginning in 1778 (after a 30-year period of
mental ferment) and ending in 1884 (with legalization of
trade unions)--by which time it had become truly "bourgeois"--
can prove liberating to those of us who have been bewildered
by the historians' battles about just what kind of revolution
"it" was in 1789-93. (Krejcí even supplies chronologies as

well as graphs, marking the periods of "institutionalized
presence" of political-economic groupings and the moments of
shifts in power or policy.) In all the struggles, after its
first stage, "for the heritage of the revolution there is a
contradiction which invites both a Marxian and an Aristotelian
interpretation" (76). In the chapter of "Conclusions" comparing all six revolutions, the observation is made that "there
has been no successful revolution in which the revolutionary
leadership has not been to a substantial extent recruited
from the cultural elite of the *ancien régime*" (195). (The
role of poets and pamphleteers is not separately discussed.)
"During the revolutionary process each of the main revolutionary factions has a chance, at least for a limited period,
to play a leading role; only the extreme left is denied this
opportunity--owing to the decisive action of its next of kin,
the main left" (214). In Graph 3 these are identified as,
respectively, the Democrats (Sans-culottes) and Radicals
(Jacobins).
   The "Pattern of the English Revolution" (Graph 2; Chronology
pp. 79-81, 1628-89) is equally illuminating. In short,
this compact comparative study will help us all. (D.V.E.)

Lantz, Pierre. "Malthus-Sismondi-Darwin: populations et
   concurrence vitale." *EP* (1984): 385-98.

Levi, Albert William. "Hegel's *Phenomenology* as a Philosophy
   of Culture." *JHP* 22 (1984): 445-70.

Liss, Peggy K. *Atlantic Empires: The Network of Trade and
   Revolution, 1713-1826*. The Johns Hopkins University Press,
   1983. Pp. xiii+386. $29.95.

   Rev. by James C. Bradford in *NEQ* 57 (1984): 142-44, as
   "ambitious."

Makkreel, Rudolf. "Imagination and Temporality in Kant's
   Theory of the Sublime." *JAAC* 42 (1983-84): 303-15.

Marichal, Juan. "Bolívar and the Age of Constitutions." *HLB*
   32 (1984): 176-89.

   Strong on his acquaintance with Enlightenment thought.
   (T.L.A.)

Meister, Peter Wilhelm, and Horst Reber. *European Porcelain
   of the Eighteenth Century*. Oxford: Phaidon, 1983. £60.00.

   Rev. by Geoffrey Wills in *Apollo* 119 (1984): 306.

Mellers, Wilfrid. *Beethoven and the Voice of God.* London:
Faber; New York: Oxford University Press, 1983. Pp. viii+453
$49.95.

    Rev. with strong reservations by Lionel Pike in *M&L* 65
(1984): 78-79.

Miller, James. *Rousseau: Dreamer of Democracy.* Yale
University Press, 1984. Pp. xii+272. $25.00.

    "I hope to show that Rousseau, in however problematic a
fashion, did help awaken a new desire for democracy, at the
same time that he defined and defended it in a new way; and
moreover, that he was well aware of what he had done. If
this much can be established, it will entail revising the
iconoclastic conservativism of some recent interpretations.
It will also restore Rousseau's work as a crucial document--
arguably the decisive one--for anyone interested in modern
democracy."

Miller, L.B., ed. *Charles Willson Peale: Artist in Revolu-
tionary America.* (The Selected Papers of Charles Willson
Peale and His Family--Vol. I.) Yale University Press.
Pp. liii+673. $50.00.

    Rev. by Edward M. Cifelli in *PMHB* 108 (1984): 517-20.

Perrot, Philippe. *Les Dessus et les dessous de la bourgeoisie.
Une Histoire du vêtement au XIXe siècle.* Paris: Fayard,
1981. Pp. 344. Fr. 40.00.

    "Fascinante et amusante analyse des attitudes sociales
à travers une histoire du vêtement." (Phillipe Thody, *TLS*)

Perrot, Philippe. *Le Travail des apparences ou les transformations du corps féminin XVIIIe-XIXe siècle.* Paris: Editions
du Seuil, 1984. Pp. 284. Fr. 79.00.

Pestelli, Giorgio. *The Age of Mozart and Beethoven.* Trans.
Eric Cross. Cambridge University Press, 1984. Pp. 311.
$34.00.

    Rev. by Julian Rushton in *M&L* 65 (1984): 412-12: "this
book deserves to appear on innumerable reading-lists."
    Haydn, Mozart, and Beethoven examined in cultural and
literary and professional contexts.

Polasky, Janet L. "Traditionalists, Democrats, and Jacobins
in Revolutionary Brussels." *JMH* 56 (1984): 227-62.

Pollock, Linda A. *Forgotten Children: Parent-Child Relations from 1500 to 1900.* Cambridge University Press, 1984. Pp. 334. £25.00; paper £9.50.

Rev. by Linda Colley in *TLS*, June 8, 1984, p. 629, as lacking in subtlety and historical sense.

Richardson, E.P.; B. Hindle; and L.B. Miller. *Charles Willson Peale and His World.* New York: Abrams, 1983. Pp. 272. $45.00.

Rev. by Edward M. Cifelli in *PMHB* 108 (1984): 517-20.

Ritter, Joachim. *Hegel and the French Revolution: Essays on the "Philosophy of Right."* (Studies in Contemporary Social Thought.) MIT Press, 1982. Pp. xii+191. $22.50.

Rev. by Kenneth L. Schmitz in *JHP* 22 (1984): 493-94.

Robertson, Priscilla. *An Experience of Women: Pattern and Change in Nineteenth-Century Europe.* With an Appendix by Steve Hochstadt. Temple University Press, 1982. Pp. xii+ 673. Paper $14.95.

Drawing on a wide range of sources, Robertson concisely surveys the roles of bourgeois married and unmarried women in England, France, Germany, and Italy. Provides undergraduates with an engrossing and informative comparative survey of nineteenth-century women's history. (M.F.)

Rocke, Alan J. *Chemical Atomism in the Nineteenth Century: From Dalton to Carnnizzaro.* Ohio State University Press, 1984.

Not seen.

Russell, Charles C. "The Libertine Reformed: 'Don Juan' by Gluck and Angiolini." *M&L* 65 (1984): 17-27.

The 1761 ballet emphasized the heroic and tragic aspects of the legend, using "music of great dignity and a kind of heroic grandeur."

Russell, Colin. *Science and Social Change in Britain and Europe 1700-1900.* New York: St. Martin's Press, 1983. Pp. xvii+307. $25.00.

Rev. by David Philip Miller in *Albion* 16 (1984): 430-31, as filling "a long-standing lacuna on our text-book shelves" but to be used "with caution." The "centerpiece" of the Enlightenment section of the book "is a lucid, critical

discussion of the ideological and political uses of
'Newtonianism.'"
Not seen.

Ryan, Alan. *Property and Political Theory*. Oxford: Blackwell,
1984. Pp. 198. £15.00.

   Rev. by Harold Perkin in *TLS*, Jan. 18, 1985, p. 59, as useful history but inapplicable to the present world.

Salmen, Walter, ed. *The Social Status of the Professional
Musician from the Middle Ages to the 19th Century*. Trans.
Herbert Kaufman and Barbara Reisner. New York: Pendragon,
1983. Pp. 240. $45.00.

   Rev. by Alice M. Hanson in *M&L* 65 (1984): 402.

Stafford, Barbara Maria. *Voyage into Substance: Art, Science,
Nature and the Illustrated Travel Account, 1760-1840*. MIT
Press, 1984. Pp. 645. $39.95.

   Rev. by Chloe Chard, in *TLS*, March 8, 1985, p. 250, as
"heroically encyclopaedic" but weak in its theorizing.

Stagg, J.C.A. *Mr. Madison's War: Politics, Diplomacy, and
Warfare in the Early American Republic, 1783-1830*. Princeton
University Press, 1983. Pp. xiii+517. $50.00.

   Rev. by Drew R. McCoy in *PMHB* 108 (1984): 383-84; by
Robert A. Rutland in *NEQ* 57 (1984): 155-56.

Stapleton, Darwin H., and Edward C. Carter II. "'I have the itch
of Botany, of Chemistry, of Mathematics ... strong upon me':
the Science of Benjamin Henry Latrobe." *PAPS* 128 (1984):
173-92.

Sussman, George D. *Selling Mother's Milk: The Wet-Nursing
Business in France, 1715-1914*. University of Illinois Press,
1983. Pp. xii+210. $16.95.

   Rev. by Olwen Hufton in *JMH* 56 (1984): 365-66.
   Emile-inspired breast feeding reached only the aristocracy.
(T.L.A.)

Taylor, R.J., ed. *Papers of John Adams*. Vol. V: Aug. 1776-
March 1778 (xliii+410 pp.); Vol. VI: March-Aug. 1778 (x+
465 pp.). Harvard University Press, 1983. $60.00.

   Rev. by John L. Bullion in *PMHB* 108 (1984): 237-39; by
Paul Nagel in *NEQ* 57 (1984): 264-67.

Thoreau, Henry D. *The Illustrated A Week on the Concord and
  Merrimack Rivers.* Eds. Carl F. Hovde, William L. Howarth,
  and Elizabeth Hall Witherell. With Photographs from the
  Gleason Collection. Princeton University Press, 1983. Pp.
  xxxvi+415. $25.00.

  Thoreau's *A Week* took ten years to write but sold only 400
  copies in four years. The brief historical introduction by
  Linck Johnson includes Thoreau's hilarious description of
  lugging the unsold copies up his stairs, after which he
  flippantly but mournfully observed: "I have now a library
  of nearly nine hundred volumes, over seven hundred of which
  I wrote myself."
  Omitting the textual apparatus of the 1980 edition, this
  beautiful edition of a neglected masterpiece, approved by the
  MLA's Center for Editions of American Authors, is illustrated
  with 48 photographs taken by Herbert Wendell Gleason between
  1899 and 1937. A thorough index, including all the poetry
  quoted (whether Thoreau's or other's), aids the browser in
  refinding favorite passages. (M.T.S.)

Troyat, Henri. *Alexander of Russia: Napoleon's Conqueror.*
  Trans. J. Pinkham. New York: Dutton, 1983. Pp. 320.
  $17.95.

  Rev. by Eric Christiansen in *S*, Feb. 25, 1984, pp. 26-27,
  as polished and readable, though not a work of original scholarship.

Tytler, Graeme. *Physiognomy in the European Novel: Faces and
  Fortunes.* Princeton University Press, 1982. Pp. 384.
  $28.50.

  Rev. by Ellen Z. Lambert in *SiR* 22 (1983): 636-39: "At
  the center of Tytler's study stands ... Johann Caspar Lavater."

Vovelle, Michel. *The Fall of the French Monarchy 1787-1792.*
  (The French Revolution 1: Editions de la Maison des Sciences
  de l'Homme.) Cambridge University Press, 1984. Pp. xv+247.
  $39.50; paper $14.95.

  A narrative yet critical history, sufficiently detailed to
  tell the story yet judiciously attending to the various histo-
  rians' interpretations, from Jaures to Soboul and from
  Mathiez to Furet. Valuable for beginners--and oldtimers.
  (D.V.E.)
  (For the second volume, see Bouloiseau, above.)

Walker, Alan. *Franz Liszt*, i: *The Virtuoso Years, 1811-1847.*
  London: Faber: New York: Knopf, 1983. Pp. xxiii+481.
  $25.00.

Rev. by Alexander Main in *M&L* 65 (1984):   402-06:   "In sum, the volume is a disappointment."

Weber, William.   "La Musique Ancienne in the Waning of the Ancien Régime."   *JMH* 56 (1984):   58-88.

"The repertory changed fast after the death of Louis XV.... The audacious nineteen-year-old queen [Marie Antoinette] would have nothing to do with the old [opera] repertory: let them eat Gluck, she all but said." Wins the prize for the best insight of the year, while also establishing the revolution as the beginning of the connection between young girls and rock stars. (T.L.A.)

Wolf, Bryan Jay.   *Romantic Re-Vision: Culture and Consciousness in Nineteenth-Century American Painting and Poetry*. University of Chicago Press, 1982. Pp. xx+272; 62 illus. $27.50.

Rev. by Elizabeth Johns in *ArtB* 66 (1984):   705-07; and enthusiastically by Joy S. Kasson in *AQ* 36 (1984):   310-14. Not seen.

Youens, Susan.   "Poetic Rhythm and Musical Metre in Schubert's 'Winterreise.'"   *M&L* 65 (1984):   28-40.

Discusses the composer's response to metric subtleties in the poems of Wilhelm Müller ("the German Lord Byron").

Yolton, Jean S., and John W. Yulton.   "Locke's Suggestion of Thinking Matter and Some Eighteenth-Century Portuguese Reactions."   *JHI* 45 (1984):   303-07.

Reviews of books previously listed:

CRANSTON, Maurice William, *Jean-Jacques: The Early Life and Work of Jean-Jacques Rousseau, 1712-1754* (see *RMB* for 1983, p. 7), rev. by Malcolm Jack in *ECS* 18 (1984-85):   267-70; DAHLHAUS, Carl, *Between Romanticism and Modernism: Four Studies in the Music of the Later Nineteenth Century* (see *RMB* for 1983, p. 8), rev. by Allan Keiler in *SiR* 23 (1984): 277-85; DARNTON, Robert, *The Literary Underground of the Old Regime* (see *RMB* for 1982, p. 6), rev. by Giles Barber in *Library* 6 (1984):   302-05, with praise; by Ronald C. Rosbottom in *BCS* 18 (1984):   76-81; FLIEGELMAN, Jay, *Prodigals and Pilgrims: The American Revolution Against Patriarchal Authority 1750-1800* (see *RMB* for 1982, p. 7), rev. by Isaac Kramnick in *ECS* 18 (1984-85): 251-54, as a "model of interdisciplinary study"; HAMPSON, Norman, *Will and Circumstance: Montesquieu, Rousseau and the French Revolution* (see *RMB* for

1983, p. 10), rev. by Robert Darnton (with Daniel Roche,
ed., *Journal de ma vie: Jacques-Louis Ménétra, compagnon
vitrier au 18e siècle*, as "Working-Class Casanova") in *NYRB*,
June 28, 1984, pp. 32-37; HASKELL, Francis, and Nicholas
Penny, *Taste and the Antique: The Lure of Classical Sculpture
1500-1900* (see *RMB* for 1981, p. 10), rev. by L.D. Ettlinger
in *ArtB* 66 (1984): 527-28; KENNEDY, Michael L., *The Jacobin
Clubs in the French Revolution: The First Years* (see *RMB*
for 1982, p. 11), rev. by Ran Halévi in *JMH* 56 (1984): 158-
60; ROSE, R.B., *The Making of the Sans-culottes: Democratic
Ideas and Institutions in Paris, 1789-92* (see *RMB* for 1983,
p. 16), rev. approvingly by Gwynne Lewis in *TLS*, July 15,
1983, p. 758; THOMAS, Keith, *Man and the Natural World: A
History of the Modern Sensibility* (see *RMB* for 1983, p. 17),
rev. by Harriet Ritvo in *YR* 73 (1983-85): 439-46.

Composite reviews:

Carp, E. Wayne. *PMHB* 108 (1984): 367-75.

Reviews Jerry Grundfest, *George Clymer: Philadelphia
Revolutionary, 1739-1813* (New York: Arno Press, 1982; pp.
554; $60.00); J.R. Pole, *The Gift of Government: Political
Responsibility from the English Restoration to American
Independence* (University of Georgia Press, 1983; pp. xiv+185;
$16.00); and Thomas O. Hanley, *Revolutionary Statesman:
Charles Carroll and the War* (Loyola University Press, 1983;
pp. x+448; $15.95), all reinforcing and restoring the con-
tribution of Lockean thought. (T.L.A.)

Jordan, Marc. *S*, May 26, 2984, pp. 23-24.

Reviews Robert Rosenblum and H.W. Janson, *Art of the Nine-
teenth Century: Painting and Sculpture* (London: Thames
& Hudson; New York: Abrams, 1984; pp. 528; $45.00); and
Charles Rosen and Henri Zerner, *Romanticism and Realism:
The Mythology of Nineteenth-century Art* (New York: Viking,
1984; $22.50).

Popkin, Jermey. *ECS* 17 (1984): 358-63.

Covers three books: William Doyle, *Origins of the French
Revolution* (see *RMB* for 1981, p. 7); George Armstrong Kelly,
*Victims, Authority and Terror: The Parallel Deaths of
d'Orleans, Custine, Bailly, and Malesherbes* (see *RMB* for
1983, pp. 12-13); and Patrice Higonnet, *Class, Ideology and
the Rights of Nobles during the French Revolution* (see *RMB*
for 1982, p. 9).

Porter, Ray. *LRB* 6, xxi (1984): 12-14.

Reviews John Lesch, *Science and Medicine in France: The Emergence of Experimental Physiology 1790-1855* (Harvard University Press, 1984; pp. 276; £20.00); and Dorinda Outram, *Georges Cuvier: Vocation, Science and Authority in Post-Revolutionary France* (Manchester University Press, 1984; pp. 299; £25.00).

Scott, William. "Whom to Commemorate." *TLS*, Aug. 3, 1984, p. 873.

A judicious and informative review of six new books on the French Revolution, mostly on the Thermidorean era and beyond.

3. CRITICISM

Baker, Carlos. *The Echoing Green: Romanticism, Modernism, and the Phenomena of Transference in Poetry*. Princeton University Press, 1984. Pp. xiii+377. $32.50.

Carlos Baker's book is divided into two parts: first, short essays on each of the major Romantic poets except Blake, and second, slightly longer essays on each of "the" major Modernist poets--Yeats, Frost, Pound, Eliot, Stevens, and Auden. "Transference" refers neither to psychoanalysis nor to the anxiety of influence but simply to the visible remains (usually verbal but sometimes philosophical or atmospheric) of the Romantics in the work of the Moderns. Baker modestly says: "Anyone interested in the overlap of the past upon the present should emerge from a reading of these pages with useful information...."
Yet the book is also beautifully written. The essays are models of the no-longer-practiced genre of the "appreciation," which means, in this instance, that the criticism industry is largely passed by. In its place the author gives us the distillation of a lifetime of thinking upon his subjects. When, however, one reads about the "transference" from Shelley and Blake to Yeats without mention of the opposing politics of the earlier poets and the later one, one is recalled to the limitations of Baker's tradition.
The title of the book describes very well its tone and vision. "Echoes" occur in a pastoral literary history, not in a history of "mental fight." Of Frost's poetry he says: "Each work glinted with its native fervors, like fireflies in a Vermont dusk, and part of the pleasure in reading him was to find the patterns they made on the blanket of the dark." The book has the familiarity of one who grew up with

the early recognitions of these poets, and he draws for his insights on the atmosphere from their first fame. At times the point about Romanticism seems to disappear from the intensity of the recollection of that atmosphere, but one always senses that whenever Romanticism vanishes from view it is because Baker is measuring its relative unimportance. Part of the book's fine modesty lies in the refusal to grant Romanticism the most formative place in the works of the Moderns. But after reading Baker, we know precisely that when it was there, it was really there. (J.C.R.)

Beddow, M. *The Fiction of Humanity: Studies in the Bildungsroman from Wieland to Thomas Mann.* Cambridge University Press, 1982. Pp. x+325.

   Rev. by D. Roberts in *AUMLA* 61 (1984): 101-02.

Beer, John. "Nature and Liberty: The Linking of Unstable Concepts." *TWC* 14 (1983): 201-13.

Bromwich, David. "The Uses of Biography." *YR* 73 (1983-84): 161-76.

   Appeals for an opening of the border between biography and criticism since it is an artificial and ineffective one. Biography is inevitably influenced by criticism, since it creates its heroes in accordance with current critical taste (the 1890s Keats is quite a different person from the 1960s Keats), and it affects criticism in turn by limiting the range of plausible interpretations, and occasionally by forcing critics toward an entirely new evaluation of an artist (e.g., Lawrance Thompson's biography of Frost).

Brown, Marshall. "'Errours Endless Traine': On Turning Points and the Dialectical Imagination." *PMLA* 99 (1984): 6-25.

   "As turning points occur, they are always moments of confusion, not moments of clarification.... Spenser's Mutability Cantos and poems of Keats, Yeats, and Stevens attempt responses to this universal turning; they suggest that we aim not at discovering the truth of outcomes but at comprehending the historical processes in movement."

Bryson, Norman. *Vision and Painting: The Logic of the Gaze.* Yale University Press, 1983. Pp. xvi+189; 39 illus. $17.95.

   Rev. by Michael Podro ("Misconceived Alternatives") in *Art History* 7 (1984): 243-47.
   In contrast to Bryson's earlier *Word and Image: French*

Painting of the Ancien Régime (see *RMB* for 1983, p. 164),
which includes perceptive discussions of specific painters
and paintings, its successor remains largely on the level
of theory, expository and polemical. Among the few artists
whose works are directly though briefly mentioned, and the
only ones from "our" period, are David, Ingres, Gérard, Gros,
and Géricault.
    Bryson's main dispute is with E.H. Gombrich, in the matter
of naturalism and "illusion"; his interpretation is disputed
in turn by Michael Podro in the review cited above. (See
also below, Kemp, under "Review articles.") There are also
critiques of Saussure and the Russian linguist N.Y. Marr,
in the light of Bryson's own sign theory, and discussions of
such topics as the stereotype, or the "body of labour" in
Oriental painting, that are fascinating in themselves. What
is perhaps most noteworthy, considering the scope of this
book, is that Bryson is not a professional art historian but
Director of English Studies at King's College, Cambridge.
(I.H.C.)

Chan, Victor. "Rebellion, Retribution, Resistance, and
    Redemption: Genesis and Metamorphosis of a Romantic Giant
    Enigma." *Arts Magazine* 58,x (June, 1984): 80-95.

    Caption: "The Giant looms large as a Romantic image
serving both to represent the world and to transcend the
world."

Darnton, Robert. "The Origin of Modern Reading." *NR*, Feb.
    27, 1984, pp. 26-33.

    On the changes in reading that took place in the later
eighteenth century. The witness is Jean Ranson, an "ordinary
bourgeois" in provincial France during the last two decades
before the Revolution, whose correspondence reveals that,
by his "Rousseauistic" manner of reading, he embodied both
Rousseau's "ideal" reader and the book-buying "real" reader.

de Man, Paul. *The Rhetoric of Romanticism.* Columbia Univer-
    sity Press, 1984. Pp. ix+327. $22.50.

    This posthumous collection (assembled, however, before
the author's death) brings together essays written between
1956 and 1983, two new, most previously published; one,
"Image and Emblem in Yeats," was originally part of de Man's
doctoral dissertation at Harvard in the 1950s. The differences in style, tone, technique, and of course terminology
are striking; yet it is possible to see now that, for all
its change in orientation, the later critical method grew

not only away from but also out of de Man's early practice of what was known as close reading. From his own standpoint, he notes in the Preface that at the time it was written the Yeats essay "was already a rhetorical analysis of figural language *avant la lettre*." In addition to Yeats, the writers considered in major and minor ways, some more than once, are Rousseau, Hölderlin, Wordsworth, Shelley, Keats, Kleist, Baudelaire, and Mallarmé. Except perhaps for the essay on *The Triumph of Life*, in which de Man earns his own triumph over a difficult and resistant text, the study of Kleist's *Über das Marionettentheater* is the most outstanding, a subtle "pedagogical" and ideological as well as rhetorical analysis. The closing sentences, warning against the "trap" of extreme aesthetic fomalization ("an aesthetic education which inevitably confuses dismemberment of language by the power of the letter with the gracefulness of a dance"), stand as the last in the book and hence as the critic's enigmatic parting words. He himself may have been thinking of "formalism." Some readers may be reminded of the more recent effort to elevate criticism to the status of art. (I.H.C.)

Ellison, Julie. *Emerson's Romantic Style*. Princeton University Press, 1984. Pp. xii+256. $25.00.

In this exceptionally fine study, Ellison develops a way of analyzing Romantic prose that, like the Emerson she recovers for us, ought to find an audience among all students of Romanticism and of literary theory.

The self-conscious critical and philological mentality of the higher biblical criticism opened a way for Emerson to shift the balance of power and authority from the author-text dyad to the reader-text dyad. By implication the critic became the authority for the text while the authors became previous readers. Emerson thus reduced formerly intimidating texts to tissures of quotation, repetitions, and transformation of previous texts. Emerson thus discovered what Ellison calls a reader's sublime, becoming himself a circumspect critic and evader of its dangers. Result: a remarkable and frequently baffling Emersonian kind of ironic humor. Previous generations' misreadings of Emerson have involved a deafness to what might be called Emersonian comedy--now to be seen as central to what Emerson is all about.

One of Emerson's "hermeneutic episodes" involved his having "confronted literature impersonated," by visits to Coleridge and Wordsworth and Carlyle; whereupon he was "ready to make a career of showing how its influence may be overcome" (72).

Ellison's analyses of selected essays and structural units within essays make a clear case for Emerson as a major practitioner and theorist of Romantic irony. (David E. Laurence)

Feagin, Susan L. "Some Pleasures of Imagination." *JAAC* 43 (1984-85): 41-55.

"The greater effect of imaging in comparison with sensing is a specific case of the more general phenomen that what art expresses is incommunicable by any other means. The role of imaging in appreciating (some) metaphors, for example, explains why they cannot be paraphrased to the same effect. Metaphor can never be identical with its paraphrase any more than art is identical with interpretation." Rings the death knell on phenomenological flatulence--doesn't it? (T.L.A.)

Fingesten, Peter. "Delimiting the Concept of the Grotesque." *JAAC* 42 (1983-84): 419-26.

Much on Fuseli's *Nightmare* (reproduced) and Goya.

Flax, Neil. "Fiction Wars of Art." *Representations* no. 7 (Summer 1984): 1-25.

An important contribution to both general critical theory and the history of Romantic criticism, which begins from and moves beyond Michael Fried's *Absorption and Theatricality: Painting and Beholder in the Age of Diderot* (see *RMB* for 1981, p. 163). Arguing that works of art are "constructed" by the critical language used to discuss them, Flax devotes much of his essay to Goethe's "Über Laokoon" (1798), "the first systematic application of formal or Kantian esthetics to practical art criticism," which was provoked by Goethe's opposition to the literary and "fabulating" method of Diderot in the *Salon of 1765*. Thus, although Flax does not quite say so, Goethe was in effect the first "formalist" or "modernist" critic of art. The polarities of the two methods and of the two traditions of subsequent art criticism that developed in their wake are illustrated from the contemporary debates in Germany over the early paintings of Caspar David Friedrich; to represent the "Diderotian" school, Flax quotes Heinrich von Kleist. (I.H.C.)

Grabowicz, George G. *The Poet as Mythmaker: A Study of Symbolic Meaning in Taras Sevcenko*. Harvard University Press, 1982. Pp. x+170. $12.50.

Rev. by Michael M. Naydan in *SiR* 23 (1984): 285-89, as "welcome and thought-provoking" and "an instructive model"

of "the proper application of structural anthropology as a
critical methodology."

Grob, Alan. "The Uses of Northrop Frye: 'Sunday Morning'
and the Romantic Topocosm." *SiR* 22 (1983): 587-615.

The topocosm of Wallace Stevens's "Sunday Morning" taken
as a demonstration model. Frye's archetypes are not really
"informing structures," but they are "observable and
authentic phenomena." There is a danger, at the present
critical moment, that we may "lose sight of Frye and thus
deny ourselves the benefits of his undeniable strengths....
He deserves a place at the very forefront of those who shape
contemporary literary discourse" (615).

Gunn, J.V. *Autobiography: Towards a Poetics of Experience.*
University of Pennsylvania Press, 1982. Pp. x+154. $16.50.

Rev. by C.D.E. Tolton in *CRCL* 11 (1984): 114-17.
I agree with the negative review in *CRCL* that one cannot
discuss Wordsworth in this context by "bypassing" the *Prelude*
so that a biography squeezed out of *Tintern Abbey* and
Resolution and Independence can be used to explain *Black
Elk Speaks*. Wordsworth in feathers! (T.L.A.)

Hartman, Geoffrey. "The Interpreter's Freud." *Raritan* 4,ii
(1984): 12-28.

Hernadi, Paul, ed. *The Horizon of Literature.* University of
Nebraska Press, 1982. Pp. 373. $29.95.

Rev. by Martin Steinmann in *JAAC* 42 (1983-84): 347-50,
who finds the collection of *BMWMLA* essays choked by establishment thinking.

Hume, Althea. *Edmund Spenser: Protestant Poet.* Cambridge
University Press, 1984. Pp. 202. £18.50.

Rev. by H.R. Woodhuysen in *TLS*, April 20, 1984, p. 438,
concluding that this "is a very fine and scholarly book which
cuts through much recent, arid, critical debate and interpretation...."

Huray, Peter le, and James Day, eds. *Music and Aesthetics in
Eighteenth and Early-Nineteenth Centuries.* (Cambridge
Readings in the Literature of Music.) Cambridge University
Press, 1981. £35.00.

Rev. by Morse Peckham in *KSMB* 34 (1983): 91-94.

Jacobus, Mary. "'That Great Stage Where Senators Perform':
   Macbeth and the Politics of Romantic Theatre." *SiR* 22
   (1983): 353-87.

   Wordsworth, Burke, Coleridge, DeQuincey.... What if it's
   all idiotic, "signifying nothing"?
   "Wordsworth's actual powerlessness to be anything other
   than a spectator of the French Revolution resulted in a
   play." "Coleridge's distinction between absolute and
   commanding genius proves to have the same structure as the
   relation between 'theory' and 'practice,' between the
   theatre of desire and the political arena, or the Shakes-
   pearean page and the stage" (386-87).

Jay, Paul. *Being in the Text: Self-Representation from
   Wordsworth to Roland Barthes*. Cornell University Press,
   1984. Pp. 189. $22.50.

   This book analyzes the autobiographical writings of
Wordsworth, Carlyle, Joyce, Proust, Adams, Valery, Eliot,
and Barthes. Augustine's *Confessions* is the Ur-text;
Hegel's observations about self-representation and production, Nietzsche's questionings of the traditional assumptions
of the unified self, and Freud's narrative of the therapeutic reconstruction of the self define the book's theoretical limits. The analysis of *The Prelude* takes almost one-
third of the space, thus defining Jay's Romantic orientation.
Conspicuously absent are Enlightenment autobiography (e.g.,
Rousseau, Gibbon), Victorian autobiography (e.g., Mill,
Gosse), autobiographies from other cultures (e.g., Gorki,
Pasternak), and autobiographies by members of other races
and by women.
   The past of the autobiographer undergoes reconstruction,
often involving the anatomization of narrative itself, in the
process of "healing" the "shattered" state in which the
autobiographer finds himself. After Wordsworth autobiographers question the truth of the eighteenth-century autobiographical narrative model of *Bildung*. In Wordsworth one
can see both the traditional pull toward the transcendental
vision of a unified self and hints of future autobiographers'
preoccupation with a deconstructed narrative of self. The
mosaic of compositional history of *The Prelude* anticipates
Carlyle's retailoring of autobiographical narrative; the
process continues apace to Barthes's alphabetical and
photographic arrangement of autobiographical shards.
   But so much, as I said, is left out. Jay, for example,
does not consider (what critics more and more have begun
to consider) that Wordsworth's "restoration" is a restoration *from history*, in particular his history with the

French Revolution and with passionate love (Annette Vallon).
The absence of such material in the Wordsworth section and on
the larger scale the absence of autobiographies that find
historical involvement less aversive and more nourishing
makes *Being in the Text* a less than satisfying study of
autobiography. (J.C.R.)

Johnson, W.R. *The Idea of Lyric: Lyric Modes in Ancient and
Modern Poetry.* University of California Press, 1983. Pp. 214.
$22.50; paper $7.95.

 Rev. by Diane L. Ostrom in *CP* 17,i (1984): 108-11.

Johnston, Mary S. "In Quest of Highest Truth: Journeys in
Romantic Poetry." Ann Arbor, Mich.: University Microfilms
International, 1984.

 Dissertation.

Kipperman, Mark. "Fichtean Irony and Some Principles of
Romantic Quest." *SiR* 23 (1984): 223-36.

 Romanticism in the arts and in Schlegel's theory of irony
"drew special inspiration from Fichte and his circle." But
only in 1970 was a reliable translation published, enabling
us to see that "as much as Wordsworth, Coleridge, Keats, or
Shelley had in their long poems, Fichte [had] explored ...
the question: What does it mean to live in a world where
man is his own creator and defense?" (223). "Never before,
one feels, had a whole generation of poets felt so vitally
expectant--or so alone" (236). The quest from p. 223 to
p. 236 is much less lonely. (D.V.E.)

Krieger, Murray. "The Ambiguities of Representation and Illusion:
An E.H. Gombrich Retrospective." *CritI* 11 (1984): 181-94.
Reply by E.H. Gombrich, "Representation and Misrepresentation,"
ibid., pp. 195-201.

 Krieger expresses disappointment with Gombrich's most recent
book, *The Image and the Eye: Further Studies in the Psychology
of Pictorial Representation* (1982), for what he understands
is Gombrich's retreat from his early view of art as convention
in favor of revived imitation theory and pictorial naturalism,
which Krieger calls "anticonventionalist theoretical conservatism" and, in a footnote, compares to the Western
"imperialism of spirit" condemned by Edward Said. In his
vigorous reply, Gombrich maintains that his early work was
misunderstood and reaffirms his interest in the scientific
study of visual perception. (I.H.C.)
 See also above, Bryson, and below (under "Review articles"),
Kemp.

Leighton, Lauren G. "The Great Soviet Debate over Romanticism: 1957-1964." *SiR* 22 (1983): 41-64.

"Romanticism has not yet been fully defined in Soviet scholarship, and romanticism remains a controversial subject, but by 1964 the most basic questions were resolved and an official view established." The notion that "the romantic" survived in the continuum of literary history provided "the needed connection between romanticism and socialist realism."

Loving, Jerome. *Emerson, Whitman, and the American Muse.* University of North Carolina Press, 1982. Pp. 220. $22.00.

Rev. by Albert Gelpi in *NEQ* 57 (1984): 137-40.

Lüchinger, Rita. *Salomon Gessner in Italien: Sein literarischer Erfulg im 18. Jahrhunderts.* Bern: Peter Lang, 1981. Pp. 226. Sw.Fr. 45.00.

Rev. by F. Meregalli in *CRCL* 11 (1984): 127-28, as a useful door-opener on the Italian reception.

Macpherson, Jay. *The Spirit of Solitude: Conventions and Continuities in Late Romance.* Yale University Press, 1982. $27.50.

Rev. by Ronald Hatch in *CL* 102 (1984): 82-83, under the rubric of "Romantic."

McGann, Jerome J. *The Romantic Ideology: A Critical Investigation.* University of Chicago Press, 1983. Pp. x+172. $15.00.

Rev. by Paul Fry in *YR* 73 (1984): 603-16; by Anthony H. Harrison in *SAR* 49,ii (1984): 123-27; by Peter L. Thorslev, Jr., in *KSJ* 33 (1984): 205-08.
Never received. Here are notes from a copy borrowed as we go to press: McGann's call for "a radical revisionary reading of Romanticism" draws critical power from Heine and Marx and what *their* critique of post-Marxism Marxists would have been. "Marx's indictment of the radical Hegelians ... carries an application and warning" for Adorno, Althusser, Macherey, and Eagleton (and presumably McGann): "Literary criticism today is practiced under the aegis of very particular sorts of Ideological State Apparatuses" which criticism must take into account (158-59).
One can see from the index that the texts upholding this superstructure are, in descending order of quantity: Coleridge's, Byron's, Shelley's, Wordsworth's, Keats's, and Blake's. (D.V.E.)

McGann, Jerome J. "Rome and Its Romantic Significance."
Pp. 83-104 in Annabel Patterson, ed., Roman Images.
(Selected Papers from the English Institute, 1982.) The
Johns Hopkins University Press, 1984. $10.00.

"The obsession of Napoleon and Chateaubriand, the grave of
Keats, Rome attracted to herself ... nearly all the great
figures of the Romantic movement.... Even Wordsworth would
eventually visit Rome...." McGann watches Goethe, Chateaubriand, Staël, Byron, Stendhal ("a Byron with no faith at
all in the political ideal of ... 'the North'...").

McLaverty, James. "The Concept of Authorial Intention in
Textual Criticism." Library 6 (1984): 121-38.

Meregalli, Franco. "Venice in Romantic Literature." Arcadia
18 (1983): 225-39.

Short summaries of the image of Venice as seen in the works
of Chateaubriand, Mme de Staël, Wordsworth, Byron, Sand,
Musset, Gautier, Ruskin, and Taine.

Mersereau, John. Russian Romantic Fiction. Ann Arbor, Mich.:
Ardis, 1984. Pp. 336. $29.50; paper $10.00.

Rev. by Richard Freeborn in TLS, June 8, 1984, p. 635, as
a welcome contribution to the fuller understanding of
European Romanticism.

Mitchell, W.J.T. "The Politics of Genre: Space and Time in
Lessing's Laocoon." Representations no. 6 (Spring 1984):
98-115.

An illuminating reexamination of the famous treatise, in
which Lessing's argument for the distinction between the
"spatial" and "temporal" arts is shown to be less cogent
and less systematic than has been assumed, as well as inadequate to a resolution of the broad aesthetic problem it
raised. Mitchell points out that the breaching of the
supposed spatial-temporal boundaries has been "a fundamental
impulse" in both theory and practice in the arts, and proposes
that the problem be reconceived as "a dialectical struggle
in which the opposed terms take on different ideological
roles and relationships at different moments in history."
Mitchell's own argument for the "politics of genre" is
rather less persuasive than his critique of Lessing because
of its complicated ingenuity, turning on gratuitous word-play
("adulterous" as "adulteration," "genre" as "gender")
apparently suggested originally by Blake's personifications
of Time and Space as male and female. Blake also is brought

on at the conclusion to exemplify the blurring of the
genres in his "mixed art of poetry and painting." (I.H.C.)

Mitchell, W.J.T. "What Is an Image?" *New Literary History*
15 (1984): 503-37.

In this ambitious and widely ranging essay, a companion
to his "The Politics of Genre" (see preceding entry),
Mitchell sets out "to examine some of the ways we use the
word *image* in a number of institutionalized discourses ...
and to criticize the way each of these disciplines makes use
of notions of imagery borrowed from its neighbors."
Especially relevant to current interdisciplinary concerns
are the last four sections, on the relations of image and
word, pictures and texts. (I.H.C.)

Moynihan, Robert. "Interview with Paul de Man." Intro.
J. Hillis Miller. *YR* 73 (1983-84): 576-602.

The interview was taped in 1980.

Muenzer, Clark S. *Figures of Identity: Goethe's Novels and
the Enigmatic Self.* Pennsylvania State University Press,
1984. Pp. 256; illus. $19.50.

Natella, Arthur, Jr. "Towards a Definition of Latin American
Modernism--Debate and Reconciliation." *RP&P* 8,ii (1984):
23-38.

"Both modernism and post-modernism are varieties of neo-
romanticism."

Meufeldt, Leonard N. "Henry David Thoreau's Political
Economy." *NEQ* 57 (1984): 359-83.

Parker, Hershel. *Flawed Texts and Verbal Icons: Literary
Authority and American Fiction.* Northwestern University
Press, 1984. Pp. xv+242.

No examples drawn from the Romantics, but a very important
critical manifesto of the new "biographico-textico-aesthetico
'movement'" which insists on biographical and textual
scholarship as the base for sound criticism and literary
theory and criticism. And Parker points not only to specific
textual evidence and critical pratfalls but boos and cheers
villains and heroes of "the new scholarship." (D.V.E.)

Patterson, Annabel. *Censorship and Interpretation: The Conditions of Writing and Reading in Early Modern England.*
University of Wisconsin Press, 1984. Pp. 283. $27.50.

Early Modern England ends in the seventeenth century, but
the questions raised, defined as "the hermeneutics of
censorship," are brought together in a concluding chapter
of "Afterwords: Three Sidneys, John Dryden, and Jean-
Jacques Rousseau." "For if there were ever a paradigmatic
figure in which the story of censorship connects with the
story of self-definition, that figure is Rousseau," the
study of whom has been "central to the development of postmodernist criticism" (237). And it turns out that the
censorship that prevails in the modern academy, postmodernist
textuality it may be called, is what Patterson wishes to
evade. "This book of mine ... is written in defense" of
values recognized in the careers and principles of Rousseau
and the early modern writers discussed. She does "not wish
to challenge" de Man, or Foucault, or Derrida, directly
or totally (see 164, 237, 238); yet, defining these values
"under the title of liberal humanism ... recently much under
attack, even within our own profession," she gently pleads
that "if we in the academy do not defend the tradition of
liberal humanism," no one may, in time. Hear! Hear!
(D.V.E.)

Porte, Joel, ed. *Ralph Waldo Emerson: Essays and Lectures.*
New York: Viking Press, 1983. Pp. 321. $27.50.

   Rev. by David M. Van Leer in *PMHB* 108 (1984): 522-24.

Rapp, Carl. "Philosophy and Poetry: The New Rapprochement."
HSL 16 (1984): 58-67.

   "Poetry in the modern period has declared its independence";
yet "philosophy remains as vigorous as ever behind the
scenes." "In the period ... from Blake and Wordsworth
to the present day, something like a poetic reformation has
been under way...."

Rawson, Claude, ed., with Jenny Mezciems. *English Satire and
the Satiric Tradition.* London and New York: Blackwell,
1984. Pp. xiii+289. $24.95; paper $12.95.

   Published first in the *Yearbook of English Studies* (*YES*,
1984) and then in book form, this "Special Satire Number"
in memory of Robert C. Elliott and his enduring book of
1960, *The Power of Satire: Magic, Ritual, Art*, is a proper
and effectual ritual extension of Elliott's power of opening
questions for scholarship.
   After an Introduction by Claude Rawson and an essay on
Robert Elliott by Alvin Kernan, there are 17 essays that
range from Aristophanes to Borges, including "The Satirical

Game at Cards in Pope and Wordsworth" by Howard Erskine-
Hill (183-95); "Hogarth's 'County Inn Yard at Election
Time': A Problem in Interpretation" by Ronald Paulson
(196-208); "Satire and the Images of Self in the Romantic
Period: The Long Tradition of Hazlitt's *Liber Amoris*" by
Marilyn Butler (209-25); several discussions of Restoration
and Augustan satire; and Martin Price on Conrad and Hugh
Kenner on Wyndham Lewis. (D.V.E.)

Reed, Arden. *Romantic Weather: The Climates of Coleridge
and Baudelaire.* Hanover, N.H.: The University Press of
New England, 1983. Pp. xiii+338. $33.00.

    Rev. by Lachlan Mackinnon in *TLS*, June 15, 1984, p. 678,
with examples that certainly sound absurd. What Coleridge
sees at the end of "Frost at Midnight" is his own face in
the window; the Mariner appears in a "Rime" because he is
a snowman; etc. (See below, p. 87.)
    The pattern of chapter epigraphs in *Romantic Weather* gives
a clue to the point of the book and to the experience one has
reading it. All the Coleridge chapters have epigraphs by
Baudelaire and all the Baudelaire chapters have epigraphs by
Coleridge. An Interchapter, attempting to connect Coleridge
to Baudelaire through De Quincey's Pirenesian cloudy architectural (or architecturally cloudy) imagery, has an epigraph
by Derrida, and the long opening theoretical introduction-
summary has an epigraph from Proust (i.e., autobiography as
fiction). The book is about various poetic displacements
from or movements beyond Enlightenment stabilities in early
and late European Romantic poetry as filtered through or
contained in the pervasive presence of weather imagery (in
the broadest sense). The reader is not allowed any of the
traditional stabilities of literary history or poetic explication. One thinks of such a phenomenologist of the image as
Bachelard whose writing and conception, however, are far
purer--that is, the authenticating frame of the study is
the freedom of the image from historical or aesthetic contexts:
the image really is an archetype. In Reed's book, however,
the imagery of the weather (meteor, wind, heat-cold, and,
above all, mist) clings tenaciously if warily to poems and
prose, to history (Aristotle, Enlightenment, Romanticism),
and to modern deconstruction. One reads uneasily, not only
often feeling "mist"ified but--to shift the metaphor--as if
the tail is wagging the dog.
    The imagery of the weather serves as an occasion to explore
some of the contrary impulses in post-Enlightenment poetry,
such as the Enlightenment drive for "truth" and openness vs.
the recognition of obscurity and mystery, the wish for

domestication of drives and passions vs. the drives or
passions themselves. Reed is particularly interesting on
Coleridge's early poems leading up to "Frost at Midnight."
(J.C.R.)

Reish, Joseph G. "'Those Who See God' in Flaubert's *Trois
Contes.*" *Renascence* 36 (1984): 219-29.

Riffaterre, Michael. "Intertextual Representation: On Mimesis
as Interpretive Discourse." *CritI* 11 (1984): 141-62.

One of the illustrative texts examined (under "Second
Type, Negating the Intertext") is Wordsworth's "Composed
Upon Westminster Bridge." In the critic's summary paraphrase,
"the spectacle [i.e., of the non-realistic Thames] therefore is born not of a spectator's delusion but of a cancella-
tion of sociolectic conventions: this is enough to make it
a coded sign, the self-sufficient icon of a truth deeper than
conventional representation."

Sauer, Thomas G. *A.W. Schlegel's Shakespearian Criticism in
England, 1811-46.* Bonn: Bouvier, 1981. Pp. xii+219.
DM 45.00.

Rev. by Ernest Behler in *CRCL* 11 (1984): 311-13.

Schleifer, Ronald, and Robert Con Davis, eds. *Deconstruction
at Yale.* (*Genre* Special Topics: 9.) *Genre* 17 (Spring/
Summer 1984).

Ronald Schleifer and Robert Con Davis, "Introduction: The
Ends of Deconstruction"; J. Hillis Miller, "The Search for
Grounds in Literary Study"; Juliet Flower MacCannell,
"Portrait: de Man"; Barbara Johnson, Louis Mackey, and J.
Hillis Miller, "Marxism and Deconstruction: Symposium";
Barbara Johnson, "Gender Theory and the Yale School";
Barbara Foley, "The Politics of Deconstruction"; Robert Con
Davis, "Error at Yale"; Geoffrey Hartman, "Psychoanalysis
and Deconstruction"; Herman Rapaport, "Geoffrey Hartman
and the Spell of Sounds"; Robert Markley, "*Tristram Shandy*
and 'Narrative Middles': Hillis Miller and the Style of
Deconstructive Criticism"; Christopher Norris, "Some Version
of Rhetoric: Empson and de Man"; Ronald Schleifer, "The
Anxiety of Allegory: de Man, Greimas, and the Problem of
Referentiality"; Richard Macksey, "Paul de Man: Siste Viator."
See also Hartman ("English 4. Wordsworth").

Shiff, Richard. "Representation, Copying, and the Technique
of Originality." *NLH* 15 (1984): 333-63.

Sircello, Guy. "The Poetry of Theory: Reflections on *After
the New Criticism.*" *JAAC* 42 (1983-84): 387-96.

Essentially a hymn to Lentricchia (see *RMB* for 1980,
p. 22). (T.L.A.)

Slater, J.; A.R. Ferguson; and J.F. Carr, eds. *The Complete
Works of Ralph Waldo Emerson.* Vol. III: *Essays Second
Series.* Harvard University Press, 1983. Pp. lxi+305. $25.00.
$25.00.

Rev. by David M. Van Leer in *PMHB* 108 (1984): 522-24.

Stecker, Robert. "Expression of Emotion in (Some of) the
Arts." *JAAC* 42 (1983-84): 409-18.

Wordsworth's "A slumber did my spirit seal" is an example.
(T.L.A.)

Strelka, Joseph P. *Literary Criticism and Philosophy.*
Pennsylvania State University Press, 1983. Pp. 259. $17.95.

Rev. by John Hospers in *JAAC* 42 (1983-84): 461-63, as
displaying no light at the end of the tunnel.

Strelka, Joseph P., ed. *Literary Theory and Criticism.*
(Festschrift in Honor of René Wellek.) *Part I: Theory;
Part II: Criticism.* Bern, Frankfurt, and New York: Peter
Lange, 1984. Pp. 1462. $83.00.

In the "Theory" volume, Romanticists will take note of
Ernst Behler's essay on Romantic hermeneutics; in the second
volume they will note Emerson R. Marks's "Meter in English
Romantic Poetics," Anthony Thorlby's "Is Romanticism a Kind
of Literature or a Kind of Criticism?" and Jacques Voisine's
"William Hazlitt as a Literary Critic in *The Spirit of the
Age.*"

Sussman, Henry. *The Hegelian Aftermath: Readings in Hegel,
Kierkegaard, Freud, Proust, and James.* The Johns Hopkins
University Press, 1982. Pp. 260. $22.50.

Rev. by Russell A. Berman in *Criticism* 26 (1984): 203-06.

Thomas, D.M., trans. *The Bronze Horseman: Selected Poems
of Alexander Pushkin.* New York: Viking, 1982. Pp. 261.
$15.95.

Rev. by Leslie O'Bell in *MLJ* 68 (1984): 185-86.

Thorslev, Peter L., Jr. *Romantic Contraries: Freedom versus
Destiny.* Yale University Press, 1984. Pp. 256. $21.50.

   Treats of freedom and destiny in the late Enlightenment
and the Romantic period (relating them to the themes of
theodicy and optimism, as in Pope, and to the scientific
Necessitarianism of Hartley and Godwin). Then analyzes three
hypothetical universes, the teleological, the gothic, and
the open.
   Not seen.

Thurley, Geoffrey. *The Romantic Predicament*. London:
   Macmillan, 1983; New York: St. Martin's, 1984. Pp. 215.
   $22.50.

   A pithy, impressive, and extremely valuable contribution--
top of my list this year--from a writer on Dickens, Hardy,
Yeats, and current critical theory (who, alas, died while
this work was in press). It will help us to get on top of
the problems of "Defining Romanticism" and "Romantic Subjectivity" (titles of the two last chapters) and to see the
value of recognizing Wordsworth and Byron (and later Baudelaire) in the main roles--not to belittle Blake, Coleridge,
Keats, Shelley, or Proust.
   Thurley defines what is clearly NOT his position by describing Harold Bloom as taking literary criticism, outside
"any socio-historical context," about as far as it can go (86).
   The nature of the Romantic predicament is described as a
"shift in contents," seen, for example, in the transformation of the quest-motif in changing historical contexts.
Teleological clarity gave Spenser's poem a hard contour;
the point of Byron's *Pilgrimage* is that it consists of a
voyage from nowhere to nowhere, and that the hero finds
nothing as, in effect, he looks for nothing. (The going is
the message.) "Shelley's 'Alastor' merely takes this to
its conscious conclusions: Death, welcomed and accepted,
is the logical end to this quest for nothing, as it was to
be for Proust." (Browning's "Child Roland" takes this into
the realm of the inchoate: a quest *for* nothing, into a
deformalizing darkness that "almost convinces us that there
is something there.")
   But it was Wordsworth who "penetrated to the heart of the
writer's predicament in the new world" (120-31). Whither
is fled gleam, glory, dream? "The real poignancy of these
marvellous stanzas is that Wordsworth's vision was never
more limpid--the world never appeared more wonderfully alive
and joyous to his mind." Yet the "principle" of the second
part of the Ode is "really given in Coleridge's sixth and
seventh stanzas" (123). Coleridge "stitches his antithesis
to Wordsworth's thesis." It was Byron, however, with a poetic
methodology comparable to Wordsworth's who achieved "a logical

continuation of the Wordsworthian preoccupation with role."
He gives the quest a "daring and important literalness: it
is not some parabolic quest of the Soul in search of God
or Grail ... but the wanderings of a poet in a world to
which he himself must bring the meaning."
But the message of this study is not easy to summarize.
(D.V.E.)

Tuveson, Ernest Lee. *The Avatars of Thrice Great Hermes:*
An Approach to Romanticism. Bucknell University Press,
1982. Pp. xiv+264. $27.50.

   Rev. by Michael Fixler in *SiR* 23 (1984): 132-38; by G.S.
Rousseau in *ECS* 18 (1984-85): 263-67; and by L.J. Swingle
in *MLQ* 44 (1983): 80-91. Rousseau praises Tuveson's
previous thought and works but protests that this "Approach"
is "eclectic, eccentric, and ultimately inchoate." His
being "out of touch with the current history of science"
keeps him from distinguishing empirical science from "its
hermetic or esoteric milieu." And if his aim was to correct
Romantic historiography, "then Tuveson ought to have rewritten Harold Bloom's *Visionary Company* with a decidedly
hermetic Wordsworth as its centerpiece."

Vijn, J.P. *Carlyle and Jean Paul: Their Spiritual Optics.*
(Utrecht Publications in General and Comparative Literature,
18.) Philadelphia: John Benjamins, 1982. Pp. xii+284.

   Rev. by Ian Campbell in *SLJ* 11 (1984) supp. 20: 21-22.

Wald, Alan M. *The Revolutionary Imagination: The Poetry*
and Politics of John Wheelwright and Sherry Mangan. University of North Carolina Press, 1983. Pp. xix+288. $28.00.

   Rev. by Jack Salzmann in *NEQ* 57 (1984): 118-20, as
"frustrating."

Waldinger, Ellen S. *Acts of Recovery: Wordsworth, Keats,*
Baudelaire, and the Task of the Imagination. Ann Arbor,
Mich.: University Microfilms International, 1984.

   Dissertation.

Watkins, Floyd C. "Sex and Art on Tour: Warren's 'Flaubert
in Egypt.'" *PLL* 20 (1984): 326-38.

   Robert Penn Warren went beyond Steegmuller for his
sources. Was he shocked by what he found? (T.L.A.)

Wellberry, David E. *Lessing's Laocoon: Semiotics and Aesthetics in the Age of Reason.* Cambridge University Press, 1984. Pp. 288. $49.50.

Analyzes the emergence of aesthetic theory in eighteenth-century German in relation to contemporary theories of the nature of language and signs.
Not seen.

Zheleznova, Irina, ed. *Russian 19th-Century Verse: Selected Poems by Pushkin, Baratynsky, Tyutchev, Koltsov, Lermontov, Tolstoy, Fet, Nekrasov.* Moscow: Raduga, 1983. Pp. 368. $9.95.

Rev. by Victoria A. Babenko-Woodbury in *MLJ* 68 (1984): 423-24.

Reviews of books previously listed:

AARSLEFF, Hans, *From Locke to Saussure: Essays on the Study of Language and Intellectual History* (see *RMB* for 1982, p. 20), rev. by Robert Mankin in *EiC* 34 (1984): 164-69; BLOOM, Harold, *Agon: Towards a Theory of Revisionism* (see *RMB* for 1981, p. 22) and *The Breaking of the Vessels* (see *RMB* for 1982, p. 21); rev. by Steven Gould Axelrod in *MP* 81 (1984): 290-97; by Charles Molesworth ("Promethean Narcissism") in *PR* 51 (1984): 155-58; the latter only, by P. Van Rutten in *CRCL* 11 (1984): 91-94, unfavorably; GARBER, Frederick, *The Autonomy of the Self from Richardson to Huysmans* (see *RMB* for 1983, p. 22), rev. by Virgil Nemoianu in *CRCL* 11 (1984): 128-32, who finds an exemplary and Proustian study; MILLER, D.A., *Narrative and Its Discontents* (see *RMB* for 1982, p. 27), rev. by Mark Boulby in *CRCL* 11 (1984): 135-37; by Erling B. Holtsmark in *CLS* 20 (1983): 466-67 as "well worth knowing"; MITCHELL, W.J.T., ed., *The Language of Images* (see *RMB* for 1980, pp. 23-24), rev. by Stephen Leo Carr in *BIQ* 18 (1984): 35-38; PAULSON, Ronald, *Representations of Revolution (1789-1820)* (see *RMB* for 1983, p. 24), rev. by David Carrier in *JAAC* 42 (1983-84): 223-25; by Regenia Gagnier in *Criticism* 26 (1984): 201-03; TEYSSANDIER, Hubert, *Les Formes de la création romanesque à l'époque de Walter Scott et de Jane Austen 1814-1820* (see *ELN* 17, Supp., 57), rev. by Rolf P. Lessinich in *Anglia* 102 (1984): 546-48; ZIFF, Larzer, *Literary Democracy: The Declaration of Cultural Independence in America* (see *RMB* for 1982, p. 32), rev. by Edwin Sill Fussell in *SiR* 22 (1983): 146-50.

Composite Reviews:

Buell, Lawrence. *NEQ* 57 (1984): 435-39.

Reviewing the collections: Joel Myerson, ed., *Studies
in the American Renaissance, 1983* (University Press of
Virginia, 1983; pp. ix+417; $30.00), and Harry R. Garvin,
ed., *The American Renaissance: New Dimensions* (Bucknell
University Press, 1983; pp. 169; $15.00)--both suggestive
of the early stages of a major reevaluation. (T.L.A.)

Sitter, John. *ECS* 17 (1983-84): 189-93.

Discusses the following: Stephen D. Cox, *"The Stranger
Within Thee: Concepts of the Self in Late-Eighteenth-
Century Literature* (University of Pittsburgh Press, 1980;
pp. 185; $14.95); Frederick Garber, *The Autonomy of the Self
from Richardson to Huysmans* (see *RMB* for 1983, p. 22); and
Arnold Weinstein, *Fictions of the Self: 1550-1800* (Princeton University Press, 1981; pp. 301; $27.00; paper $13.50).

Review articles:

Barrell, John. "Oedipal Conflicts." *Art History* 7 (1984):
120-26.

Careful, detailed criticism of Ronald Paulson, *Representations
of Revolution* (see *RMB* for 1983, p. 24), with objections to
Paulson's method but praise for his learning.

Johnson, W.R. "The Refusal of Grandeur." *ASch* 53 (1984):
562-65.

A review-essay on the late Robert Fitzgerald's translation
of *The Aeneid* (Random House, 1983), with interesting remarks
on Wordsworth's unfinished version as potentially the finest
Aeneid in English--better than either Dryden or Fitzgerald.

Kemp, Martin. "Seeing and Signs: E.H. Gombrich in Retrospect."
Art History 7 (1984): 228-43; 12 figs.

A thoughtful consideration of Gombrich's art theory and its
critics, taking off from his *The Image and the Eye: Further
Studies in the Psychology of Pictorial Representation* (Oxford:
Phaidon Press, 1982). See also above, Bryson, Krieger.

ENGLISH

(Compiled by Thomas L. Ashton, University of Massachusetts; Robert A. Brinkley, University of Maine; Irene H. Chayes, Kensington, Maryland; Moira Ferguson, University of Nebraska; Peter J. Garside, University College, Cardiff; Bishop C. Hunt, College of Charleston; John E. Jordan, University of California, Berkeley; Mark Minor, Westmar College; Charles E. Robinson, University of Delaware; Jeffrey C. Robinson, University of Colorado; Robert M. Ryan, Rutgers University, Camden, New Jersey; Mark T. Smith, Southwest Missouri State University)

1. BIBLIOGRAPHY

Bataille, Robert. "Arthur Young and the *Universal Museum* of 1762." *Library* 6 (1984): 279-85.

Studies a minor periodical to find a translation of Gessner's *Abel*, and much on American tensions. (T.L.A.)

Baylen, Joseph O., and Norbert J. Grossman, eds. *Biographical Dictionary of Modern British Radicals.* Vol. II: 1830-1870. Sussex: Harvester Press; Atlantic Highlands, N.J.: Humanities Press, 1984. Pp. 600. $66.00.

Written by 82 contributors, and bound to be uneven, as was the first volume. But often correcting the *DNB*, and supplementing its list. (D.V.E.)

Butler, Marilyn, ed. *Burke, Paine, Godwin, and the Revolution Controversy.* (Cambridge English Prose Texts.) Cambridge University Press, 1984. Pp. xii+260. $39.50; paper $13.95.

Selections from all of the above, plus Tooke, Price, Wollstonecraft, Helen Maria Williams, Priestley, Mackintosh, Young, Cobbett, Horsley, Watson, Hannah More, Eaton, Spence, Coleridge, Ritson, Thelwall, *The Antijacobin*, Wakefield, and Wordsworth.

Judiciously selected, with a pithy introduction and brief
introductions to each work; annotated. Yes, as the jacket
says, "a vital sourcebook for students of English Romantic
literature, history, and political theory." (D.V.E.)

Carter, John; Graham Pollard; Nicolas Barker; and John
Collins. *An Enquiry into the Nature of Certain Nineteenth
Century Pamphlets and a Sequel. The Forgeries of H. Buxton
Forman and T.J. Wise.* Second Edition with Corrections.
2 vols. London and Berkeley: Scolar Press, 1983. £65.00.

    Rev. by Arthur Freeman in *Library* 6 (1984): 415-16.
    A lasting memorial. (T.L.A.)

Clubbe, John. "The W. Hugh Peal Collection at the University
of Kentucky." *KSJ* 33 (1984): 16-17; also *TWC* 15 (1984):
73-74.

    Announcing deposit of this collection of over 15,000 items,
    with many books and manuscripts by major and minor Romantic
    writers, including unpublished letters by Coleridge, Words-
    worth, Southey, and especially Lamb.

Cross, Nigel. *The Royal Literary Fund 1790-1918: An Introduction to the Fund's History and Archives with an Index
of Applicants*; with a Foreword by Janet Adam Smith.· London:
World Microfilms Publication, 1984. (Address: 62 Queen's
Grove, London NW8 6ER.) Pp. 72. Free with the £3000.00/
c. $5275.00 microfilm collection; otherwise £15.00/c. $26.00.

    Rev. by Christine Duff Stewart in *VPR* 17 (1984): 114-15.
    This slim volume is quite expensive by itself--but as the
    door to a £3000 microfilm collection of the archives of the
    RLF, it is indispensable for the study of over 3000 nine-
    teenth-century writers who applied to the Fund for money
    during their years of poverty. Those who have not worked
    at the RLF or with photocopies of their holdings will be
    amazed by the factual materials and autograph letters in this
    collection. Because each applicant to this charity fund
    had to file the nineteenth-century equivalent of an NEH
    application (listing publications, dates of birth, marriage,
    etc.), Walter Houghton was able to use these files to make
    scores of attributions for his *Wellesley Index to Victorian
    Periodicals* after exhausting all other printed and archival
    sources of information. The volume accompanying this micro-
    film collection contains Nigel Cross's brief "Introduction
    to the History of the Fund" (10-24), a general description
    of the archives and of the catalogues and indices he compiled
    over an eight-year period (26-29), a list of RLF's principal

officers and committee members (30-32), and an alphabetical
index of all 3060 applicants to the Fund between 1790 and
1918 (the RLF is still in operation but the post-1918 files
are not yet made public). Early nineteenth-century writers
whose files are micro-filmed include Thomas Haynes Bayly,
Robert Bloomfield, Egerton Brydges, Chateaubriand, Coleridge,
Amos Cottle, Cowper, John Galt, Anne Grant, William Hone,
Thomas Hood, Leigh Hunt, Charles Lloyd, Charles Maturin,
Charles Ollier, Peacock, Cyrus Redding, and Cornelius Webbe.
(Many other contemporaries are represented by letters of
sponsorship.) Each file contains the writer's application,
letters of support from his literary friends, committee
correspondence, and ephemera (printed advertisements, press
cuttings, etc.). No other single archive contains such a rich
collection of information on so many Romantic and Victorian
writers—over 47,000 manuscripts, mainly letters from the
3060 applicants and from their 10,000 sponsors. In addition
to indices and catalogues for the applicants and sponsors,
this microfilm contains indices to and the minutes of the RLF
Committees' actions. Nigel Cross has been very generous to
those who sought information from him during the past few
years; he now graciously lays bare the riches that he has
superintended. (C.E.R.)

Crossan, Greg. "John Clare: A Bibliography of Commentary
on the Poems, to 1982." *BB* 41 (1984): 185-200.

Existing bibliographies of Clare criticism are organized
chronologically and indexed largely by topic; the value of
Crossan's is that it is arranged chronologically by poem
title. The brevity of most of the entries is a sobering
reminder of how often Clare has been discussed in very general
terms, and how seldom even his best poems have been given
detailed, systematic explication.

Cruickshanks, Eveline, ed. *Parliamentary History*. (A Yearbook.)
Vol. 1. Gloucester: Alan Sutton; New York: St. Martin's
Press, 1984. Pp. 281. $22.50.

This first "Yearbook" reached us in 1985; its jacket reads
"1982"; title page "1983"; imprint page G.B. 1982; U.S.A.
1984. Published for "The Parliamentary History Yearbook
Trust." Not to trust in printers.
The *Yearbook* will cover the history of parliamentary
institutions in the British Isles (including the Scottish
and Irish Parliaments) from the Middle Ages to the present.
The first seven articles range from 1509 to 1846 (the last
two relating to the Great Reform Act); three review articles
are followed by reviews of 27 books. Among these are McDowell

on Ireland, Hinde's *Castlereagh*, and Vols. II and V of
The Writings and Speeches of Edmund Burke (see below under
"Burke").
We look foward to Volume 2--in 1986?

Dixon, Diana. "The Provincial Press: A Decade of Writings,
1972-1981." *VPR* 17 (1984): 103-07.

Over 100 entries in this bibliography.

Ford, Jill. "Ackermann's *History of the Colleges*: The
Identification of Its Authors and Notes on Its Publishing
History." *Library* 6 (1984): 61-71.

Much on the contribution of William Combe. Byronians will
find details of Henry Drury's Harrow contributions of interest.
(T.L.A.)

Gandy, Clara I., and Peter J. Stanlis. *Edmund Burke: A
Bibliography of Secondary Studies to 1982*. (With a forword
by William B. Todd.) New York: Garland Publishing, Inc.,
1983. Pp. xxx+357. $49.00.

Only listed last year (p. 35).
Todd surveys "Burke's Historical Reputation: 1797-1981"--
and in a Foreword explains how the belated release of Burke
papers for scholarly use, in 1948, has made possible Thomas
Copeland's *Checklist of the Correspondence* (1955), the
definitive edition of the *Writings and Speeches* which has
begun appearing, and also, as an essential adjunct, this
Bibliography. It is arranged under 13 categories, with author
and subject indexes. More of us can get things right, now.
(D.V.E.)

Jackson, J.R. de J. *Annals of English Verse, 1770-1835: A
Preliminary Survey of the Volumes Published*. New York:
Garland Publishing, Inc., 1985. Pp. xiv+709. $76.00.

A comprehensive list covering the Romantic period. Over
10,000 citations are organized by year, then alphabetically
by title, with an author index.
The sort of curious information that might be helpful in
source identification is the listing for 1796 of three
translations of Burger's *Lenore*, one in four editions. (D.V.E.)

Khan, Mofakhkhar Hussain. "The Printer of the Earliest Calcutta
Calendar: Hicky or Kiernander." *Library* 6 (1984): 174-76.

Argues for Kiernander in 1777, and is challenged in a
letter (*Library* 6 [1984]: 284-85) by Graham Shaw, who thinks

the printer was John Andrews. Shaw is a well-known Hicky man (see *RMB* for 1983, p. 53). (T.L.A.)

Kline, Sims, ed. *Literary Criticism Register (LCR). A Monthly Listing of Studies in English & American Literature.* PO Drawer CC, DeLand, Fla. 32720. Annual subscription $34.00; institutional rate $48.00.

Begun in 1984, indexed by subject and author, this new journal surveys all journals in the field, also the *American Book Publishing Record* and *Dissertation Abstracts International.* It helps us cover journals not received. (D.V.E.)

Mack, Douglas S. "Scottish Literary Manuscripts at Stirling University Library." *SLJ* 11 (1984), supp. 20: 44-45.

Notes new Hogg donations from New Zealand. (T.L.A.)

McGill's Critical Survey of Poetry. (English Language Series.) 8 vols. Englewood Cliffs, N.J.: Salem Press, 1984. $350.00.

Contents: one treatise on Explicating Poetry; 20 Exhaustive Essays; 340 All-Encompassing articles on Great Poets. Not seen.

Myers, Robin, ed. *Records of the Stationers' Company 1554-1920.* Chadwyck-Healey, 1984-86. 115 reels of microfilm, with printed guide. $5,500.00.

Descriptive brochure in preparation.

Palmer, Gregory, ed. *A Bibliography of Loyalists Source Material in the United States, Canada, and Great Britain.* London: Meckler, 1984. Pp. 1, 064. £103.50.

Rev. by Peter Marshall in *TLS*, July 13, 1984, p. 795: "Future research on the Loyalists must begin by reference to this work. It cannot, however, be regarded as either a complete or perfectly organized assembly of Loyalist materials."

Rosenbaum, Barbara, and Pamela White, comps. *Index of English Literary Manuscripts. Vol. IV, 1800-1900. Part I: Arnold-Gissing.* London and New York: Mansell, 1982. £90.00.

Rev. by Ian Jack in *RES* 35 (1984): 278-80.

Savory, Jerold J. "An Uncommon Comic Collection: Humorous Victorian Periodicals in the Newberry Library." *VPR* 17 (1984): 94-102.

Among those listed are *The Ass* (1826), Hood's *Comic Almanack, The English Spy* (1825-26), *The Literary Humbug* (1832), *The*

Pic-Nic (1803), *The Satirist* (1807-14), *The Tickler* (1818-22),
and *The Wasp* (1826).

Sherbo, Arthur. "John Coleridge and the *Gentleman's Magazine.*"
BRH 86 (1983[84]): 86-93.

Some attention to the poet's father--and a checklist of
his contributions: nine certain, in 1750-63; eight possible,
in 1748-80.

Uffelman, Larry K., ed. "Victorian Periodicals 1983: A Checklist of Scholarship and Criticism." *VPR* 17 (1984): 169-72.

This annual bibliography often contains entries on the major
English Romantics and related periodicals.

Viscomi, Joseph. *Blake at Cornell: An Annotated Checklist
of Works by and about William Blake in the Cornell University
Libraries and the Herbert F. Johnson Museum.* Cornell University, 1984. Pp. 35.

There is also a separate pamphlet, of 20 pages, 8 illus.,
of the Cornell exhibition, "William Blake: Illustrator &
Poet," of spring 1983.

Wellens, Oskar. "The Colliers of London: Early Advocates of
Wordsworth, Lamb, Coleridge, and Other Romantics." *BRH* 86
(1983[84]): 105-25.

Includes checklists of John Payne Collier's contributions
to the *Critical Review* and to the *Critical's* "Bibliotheca
Antiqua," in 1816-17; and of John Dyer Collier's to the
Critical Review in the same period.

Wellens, Oskar. "Thomas Barnes's and John Payne Collier's
Contributions to the *British Lady's Magazine* (1815-1818)."
N&Q 31,i (March 1984): 62-63.

Contributions hitherto unnoticed.

Willey, Edward P. "The Works of Alexander Chalmers, Journalist,
Editor, Biographer." *BRH* 86 (1983[84]): 94-104.

Survey and bibliography of the career of Alexander Chalmers
(1759-1834).

See also Bentley, Essick, Minnick and Dörrbecker ("English 4.
Blake"); Spector ("English 4. The Gothic"); Rhodes ("English
4. Keats"); Glut ("English 4. Shelley, M.").

Reviews of books previously listed:

BROGAN, T.V.F., *English Versification, 1570-1980: A Reference Guide with a Global Appendix* (see *RMB* for 1981, p. 35), rev. by Anne Elliott in *RES* 35 (1984): 419-20; CRUMP, M., and M. Harris, eds., *Searching the Eighteenth Century* (see *RMB* for 1983, p. 34), rev. by Giles Barber in *Library* 6 (1984): 410-12; KUIST, James M., *The Nichols File of "The Gentleman's Magazine": Attributions of Authorship and Other Documentation in Editorial Papers at the Folger Library* (see *RMB* for 1983, p. 35), rev. by James Ogden in *VPR* 17 (1984): 64-67; SULLIVAN, Alvin, ed., *British Literary Magazines, I: The Augustan Age and the Age of Johnson, 1698-1788; II: The Romantic Age, 1789-1836* (see *RMB* for 1983, pp. 37-39), rev. by G.E. Bentley, Jr., in *VPR* 17 (1984): 109-13; by Phyllis J. Guskin in *Albion* 16 (1984): 428-29; by David E. Latane, Jr., in *SHR* 18 (1984): 355.

2. ENVIRONMENT: ART, PHILOSOPHY, POLITICS, RELIGION, SOCIETY

Adams, Bernard. *London Illustrated 1604-1851: A Survey and Index of Topographical Books and Their Plates*. London: Library Association, 1983. Pp. 620. $110.00 or £68.00 (cased); £160.00 (leatherbound).

Rev. by Antony Griffiths in *Library*, Sixth Series, 6 (1984): 297-98; by John Martin Robinson in *Apollo* 119 (1984): 467.
A bibliography and catalogue of prints, with 50 illustrations.

Adams, Thomas R. *The American Controversy: A Bibliographical Study of the British Pamphlets about the American Disputes, 1764-1783*. 2 vols. Brown University Press, 1980. Pp. xxx+ 1,102. $60.00.

Rev. by John L. Bullion in *PBSA* 78 (1984): 95-97.

Bahmueller, Charles F. *The National Charity Company: Jeremy Bentham's Silent Revolution*. University of California Press, 1981. Pp. xii+272. $25.00.

Rev. by Gertrude Himmelfarb in *JMH* 56 (1984): 138-40.
Pauper Management Improved (1798) is the centerpiece. (T.L.A.)

Beckett, J.V. "The Pattern of Landownership in England and Wales, 1660-1880." *EcHR* 37,i (1984): 1-22.

Belcham, John. "English Working-Class Radicalism and the Irish, 1815-1850." *Eire* 19,iv (1984): 78-93.

What were the "political attitudes and allegiances of the growing numbers of Irish immigrants in early industrial England"? What was "the attitude of the English radicals to the Irish?"

Bell, Susan Groag, and Karen M. Offen, eds. *Women, the Family, and Freedom: The Debate in Documents*. Vol. I: 1750-1880; Vol. II: 1880-1950. Stanford University Press, 1983. Pp. xiv+561. Vol. I: $32.50; paper $14.95. Vol. II: $30.00; paper $13.95.

Rev. by Theresa McBride in *Albion* 16 (1984): 60-62, with praise for the comprehensiveness and balance of the collection of documents.

Boening, John, ed. *The Reception of Classical German Literature in England, 1760-1860: A Documentary History from Contemporary Periodicals*. 10 vols. New York: Garland Publishing, Inc., 1977. $120.00 each vol.

Rev. by Peter Boener in *ECS* 18 (1984): 134-37.

Bohstedt, John. *Riots and Community Politics in England and Wales 1790-1810*. Harvard University Press, 1983. Pp. viii+ 310. $37.50.

Rev. by Victor Bailey in *Albion* 16 (1984): 192-93, as "lucidly written, convincingly argued, and based on extensive archival research"; by John Stevenson, in *TLS*, April 19, 1985, p. 443, as "one of the most detailed attempts we have had to examine the level and role of riot ... during the critical years of the revolutionary and Napoleonic wars."
Not seen.

Boucé, Paul-Gabriel, ed. *Sexuality in Eighteenth-Century Britain*. Manchester University Press; Totowa, N.J.: Barnes & Noble, 1982. Pp. iii+262. $25.00.

Rev. by John H. O'Neill in *ECS* 18 (1984-85): 261-63, as a collection of essays ranging from the primarily factual to the theoretical and interpretative--all valuable in their different ways. "Two of the most imaginative essays," by G.S. Rousseau and Ruth Perry, "seek analogues of the present in the anomalies of the past."
Not seen.

Bourne, Kenneth. *Palmerston: The Early Years, 1784-1841*. New York: Macmillan, 1982. Pp. xiv+749. $24.95.

Rev. by J.E. Cookson in *VS* 27 (1984): 239-41; by D.C. Moore in *JMH* 56 (1984): 142-44.
Not seen.

Breihan, John R. "William Pitt and the Commission on Fees, 1785-1801." *HJ* 27,i (1984): 59-81.

Burns, R.M. *The Great Debate on Miracles from Joseph Glanvill to David Hume.* London and Toronto: Associated University Presses; Bucknell University Press, 1981. Pp. 305. $28.50.

Rev. by James Noxon in *JHP* 22 (1984): 207-27, as "the final definitive word on the subject."

Butler, Marilyn, ed. *Burke, Paine, Godwin, and the Revolution Controversy.* (Cambridge Prose Texts.) Cambridge University Press, 1984. Pp. xii+260. $39.50; paper $13.95.

Rev. by D.A.N. Jones in *LRB* 6, xvi (1984): 18-19.
Texts include short pieces by Hannah More, Thomas Spence, and William Cobbett.
Not received.

Campbell, R.H., and A.S. Skinner. *Adam Smith.* New York: St. Martin's Press, 1982. Pp. 231. $25.50.

Rev. by Malcolm Jack in *ECS* 17 (1984): 378-80.

Canovan, Margaret. "The Un-Benthamite Utilitarianism of Joseph Priestley." *JHI* 45 (1984): 435-50.

And the value of Bentham's. (T.L.A.)

Cardwell, Donald, and Joan Mottram. "Fresh Light on John Dalton." *NRRS* 39 (1984): 29-40.

Dalton (1766-1844) was president of the Manchester Literary and Philosophical Society, the "father of Manchester science as well as the author of the atomic theory."

Charlesworth, Andrew, ed. *An Atlas of Rural Protest in Britain, 1548-1900.* London: Croom Helm; University of Pennsylvania Press, 1982. Pp. 224. $25.00.

Rev. by T.C. Smout in *ScHR* 63 (1984): 195-96: "the emphasis is on the spatial distribution of the riots, though the interpretive text is also extensive."

Chilton, C.W. *Early Hull Printers and Booksellers: An Account of the Printing, Bookselling, and Allied Trades from Their Beginnings to 1840.* Kingston-upon-Hull City Council, 1982. Pp. lxxxiv+274. £3.50.

Rev. by Elizabeth A. Swaim in PBSA 78 (1984):   245-
47.

Christie, Ian. Stress and Stability in Late Eighteenth-Century Britain: Reflections on the British Avoidance of
   Revolution. Oxford University Press, 1984. Pp. 226.
   $34.50.

   Rev. by William Thomas in TLS, April 19, 1985, p. 443.
   A firm and determined effort to reestablish Pitt's view,
   that the French Revolution was "a species of tyranny" utter-
   ly alien to British tradition and British experience. Whatever happened in France, says Christie, "it is doubtful
   if British history in the late eighteenth century should
   be viewed in a context of an 'age of revolution'" (25).
   Consider the "factors of social cohesion," the social
   support in the Poor Law; the "defence of the interests
   of working men" in the tradition of food riots, non-revolutionary; the "positive element in the conservatism of the
   evangelical movement"--these are themes of the chapter
   titles.
   People who write of "the contagion of revolution" forget
   that contagion "creates fear and revulsion" (218). Inevitably
   E.P. Thompson's reading of history creates fear in Christie--
   exhibited passim, most extremely in a "scientific" effort
   to overthrow Thompson's reliance on crowd statistics of
   1795, based on a variety of contemporary estimates (100,000
   to 200,000), from a single piece of "direct evidence" from
   a bystander giving "a total of 8,000" (50n.). The British
   would surely never have been slaves to notions of Liberty,
   Equality, or--with Frenchmen--Fraternity; hence we must not
   be surprised that they "escaped" and "avoided" Revolution.
   (D.V.E.)

Copley, Stephen, ed. Literature and the Social Order in
   Eighteenth-Century England. (World and Word Series.)
   London: Croom Helm, 1984. Pp. 202. $31.00; paper $15.50.

   Over 50 excerpts from Steele, Addison, Defoe, Goldsmith,
   Johnson, Berkeley, Mandeville, Hume, Smith, Swift, Young,
   Fielding, and a few others, on "The Social Establishment,"
   "Commerce and Industry," "The Economy and the Social Order,"
   "The Poor," and "Crime." Few later than 1751.

Corfield, P.J. The Impact of English Towns, 1700-1800. Oxford
   University Press, 1982. Pp. viii+206. $23.95.

   Rev. by Joseph O'Brien in JMH 56 (1984):   528-31.

Cox, Alwyn, and Angela Cox. *Rockingham Pottery and Porcelain 1745-1842.* London: Faber, 1983. £35.00.

Rev. by Geoffrey Wills in *Apollo* 119 (1984): 306.

Craddock, Patricia B. *The Young Edward Gibbon: Gentleman of Letters.* The Johns Hopkins University Press, 1982. Pp. xvi+380. $25.00.

Rev. by David P. Jordan in *JMH* 56 (1984): 136-38.

Dekker, H.T. Douwes. "Anglica Kauffmann imitatrice de Madame Vigée Lebrun?" *GBA* 104 (Nov. 1984): 195; 2 illus.

Kauffmann's "The Marquise of Bristol and Her Daughter" and Vigée Lebrun's "La tendresse maternelle."

Derry, Warren, ed. *The Journals and Letters of Fanny Burney (Madame d'Arblay). Vol. IX, Bath 1815-1817, Letters 935-1085A. Vol. X., Bath 1817-1818, Letters 1086-1179.* Oxford: Clarendon Press, 1982. Vol. IX: pp. xxii+466; Vol. X: pp. viii+467-1,062. £80.00 the set.

Rev. by R.L. Brett in *RES* 35 (1984): 555-56.

Donaldson, William. "The Glencairn Connection: Robert Burns and Scottish Politics, 1786-1796." *SSL* 16 (1981): 61-79.

"Why then, when he possessed sympathies which should have made him very much *persona grata* to the Scottish establishment in 1786 did he find himself in the hands of an impotent and penurious Opposition clique? It was a simple accident of geography."

Duffy, Ian P.H., ed. *Women and Society in the Eighteenth Century.* Bethlehem, Pa.: The Lawrence Henry Gipson Institute of Lehigh University, 1983. Pp. vii+38. $3.95.

Rev. by Barbara J. Harris in *Albion* 16 (1984): 303-04.
Three essays: Patricia Spacks on "The Talent of Ready Utterance: Eighteenth-Century Female Gossip" (gossip used as a source of energy in Burney's *Evelina* and Austen's *Emma*); Linda Kerber on American women "in the Revolutionary Era"; Lawrence Stone, on a tale of "Money, Sex and Murder" in an upper-class family, documenting women's vulnerability to male violence, "a reality only hinted at in ... *Evelina* and entirely repressed in ... *Emma.*"

Dunkley, Peter. *The Crisis of the Old Poor Law in England 1795-1834.* New York: Garland Publishing, 1982. Pp. vi+217. $31.00.

Rev. by Mark Neuman in *Albion* 16 (1984): 433-34, as a
welcome "endeavor to get to the very heart of paternalism,
its motives and effects, and to link the poor laws, old
and new, to that mentality and system."
As laissez-faire ideology seemed to prevail in this epoch,
were not the functions of government diminished to a minimum?
Dunkley enters the debate on this question with the help
of neglected evidence about "the social relationships which
gave the poor law problem its urgency." E.g.: "Samuel
Whitbread's 1807 bill was the last general measure for the
reform of the poor laws presented to Parliament by a private
member, and by 1817 speakers in the House of Commons were
declaring reform to be a govenment responsibility" (117).

du Prey, Pierre de la Ruffinière. *John Soane: The Making of
an Architect*. University of Chicago Press, 1982. Pp.
xxiv+408. 8 col. pls., 256 illus. $37.50.

Rev. by Roger Lewis in *ASch* 53 (1984): 406-10; by Rhodri
Windsor Liscombe in *QQ* 91 (1984): 425-27, as containing
much new material: the young Soane's "persistent desire for
orginality" masked a persistent habit of plagiarism from
"the folios of mentor and colleague alike to satisfy his
intense ambition," making him a kind of "Artful Dodger" of
the Neoclassical era; by Thomas J. McCormick in *ECS* 18 (1984):
143-44.

Edwards, David L. *Christian England*. Vol. 3: *From the 18th
Century to the First World War*. Grand Rapids, Mich.: Eerd-
mans, 1984. $8.95.

Rev. by James Bentley in *New Statesman*, Aug. 24, 1984, p.
22, as "usually very bright about the poets."

Egerton, Judy. "George Stubbs and the Landscape of Creswell
Crags." *BM* 126 (Dec. 1984): 738-43; 4 illus.

Elliot, Bridget J. "The Scottish Reformation and English
Reform: David Willkie's *Preaching of Knox* at the Royal
Academy Exhibition of 1832." *Art History* 7 (1984): 313-
28; 6 illus.

Investigates the reception, interpretation, and assessment
of the painting by groups with conflicting positions on
political and social questions of the time. The painting
"provided a space where crucial ideological cracks would be
filled in and papered over thus helping the establishment ...
to resist growing external pressure on the existing forms
and institutions of cultural domination."

Ferguson, Frances. "Reading Morals: Locke and Rousseau on Education and Inequality." *Representations* no. 6 (Spring 1984): 66-84.

Finlay, Nancy. "Thomas Stothard's Illustrations for Parnell's 'Hermit.'" *PULC* 45 (1984): 174-77.

> Princeton has acquired the 24 drawings.

Force, James E. "Hume and the Relation of Science to Religion among Certain Members of the Royal Society." *JHI* 45 (1984): 517-36.

> Hume against miracles while the Society is still bridging the gap between science and providence. (T.L.A.)

Frew, John. "Gothic in Transition: Wyatt and Bernasconi at New College Chapel, Oxford, 1788-94." *BM* 126 (Nov. 1984): 683089; 3 illus.

Fryckstedt, Monica Correa. "The Hidden Rill: The Life and Career of Maria Jane Jewsbury: I." *BJRL* 66,ii (1984): 177-203.

> The obscure novelist.

Garrett, Clarke. "Swedenborg and the Mystical Enlightenment in Late Eighteenth-Century England." *JHI* 45 (1984): 67-81.

> On the apostles Mather, Duché, and Rainsford, and much else of interest. (T.L.A.)

Gash, Norman. *Lord Liverpool: The Life and Political Career of Robert Banks Jenkinson, Second Earl of Liverpool, 1770-1828.* London: Weidenfeld & Nicolson, 1984; Harvard University Press, 1985. Pp. 296. $20.00.

> Rev. by Robert Stewart in *S*, Aug. 18, 1984, p. 20: "for the most part, an account of what governments did between 1790 and 1827."

Gaston, Robert W. "British Travellers and Scholars in the Roman Catacombs, 1450-1900." *JWCI* 46 (1983): 144-65; 1 illus.

> A few late eighteenth- and early nineteenth-century travelers and authors are mentioned.

Gingerich, Owen. "William Herschel's Autobiography of 1784." *HBL* 32 (1984): 73-82.

> Neatly elucidating the brief sketch transcribed herein. (T.L.A.)

Glen, Robert. *Urban Workers in the Early Industrial Revolution.*
New York: St. Martin's Press, 1984. Pp. 348. $30.00.

 Rev. by Malcolm I. Thomis in *Albion* 16 (1984): 434-35,
as a contribution to the debate about the "Making of the
English Working Class" within "the context created by
Hobsbawn, Thompson, Perkin, Foster, and later scholars."
As a local history, of Stockport, and perhaps an exceptional
sample, the evidence presented here finds a class-conscious
"working class" still unmade in the 1830s.

Gooch, Bryan N.S., and David S. Thatcher, comps. *Musical
Settings of British Romantic Literature: A Catalogue.*
2 vols. New York: Garland Publishing, Inc., 1982. Pp.
lxxxiii+1,768. $150.00.

 Rev. by Alice Levine in *KSJ* 33 (1984): 239-41.

Grant, Kerry S. *Dr. Burney as Critic and Historian of Music.*
(Studies in Musicology, 62.) University of Michigan Research
Press, 1983. Pp. xiv+381. $59.95.

 Rev. by Peter LeHuray in *M&L* 65 (1984): 360-61, as
providing "general insights into the ways that informed
eighteenth- and early nineteenth-century people experienced
music."

Green, London. "Edmund Kean's Richard III." *TJ* 36 (1984):
505-24.

 A vivid reconstruction of Kean's performance in his most
popular role (Colley Cibber's simplification of Shakespeare),
based on accounts by Hunt, Hazlitt, and a surprising number
of other contemporary witnesses. This is a remarkable exercise in theatrical archeology. (R.M.R.)

Griffiths, D.N. "Prayer-Book Translations in the Nineteenth
Century." *Library* 6 (1984): 1-24.

 The endless tide exposed in scholarly text and accompanying
tables. Some translations to set one thinking: Acawoio,
Bullom, Chopi, Grebo, Igala, Kaguru, Mota, Nupe, Pashto,
Soso, Telugu, and Vaturange. (T.L.A.)

Gudeman, Stephen. "Ricardo's Representations." *Representations*
no. 5 (Winter 1984): 92-114.

 Examination of the ways in which Ricardo's economic model
was a "cultural representation."

Halstead, John P. *The Second British Empire: Trade,
Philanthropy, and Good Government, 1820-1890.* (Contribu-
tions in Comparative Colonial Studies, No. 14.) Westport,
Conn.: Greenwood Press, 1983. Pp. xiii+261. $35.00.

Rev. by Robert O. Collins in *Albion* 16 (1984): 70-72,
as "a delightful book," an "attempt to liberate imperialism
from the confinement of ideology ... and the inclusive theory
seeking to explain all."

Hemingway, Andrew. "Meaning in Cotman's Norfolk Subjects."
Art History 7 (1984): 57-77; 8 illus.

Reconstruction of the various "meanings" (political, social,
historical, agricultural) particular drawings would have had
for contemporary and local audiences, in the light of
Associationist theory. The author opposes the accepted
view that Cotman was anticipating post-Impressionist
"formalism."

Hendricks, Ella. "The First Patron of John Flaxman." *BM* 126
(Oct. 1984): 618-25; 3 illus.

The patron is identified as Edward Knight (1734-1812)
of Wolverley House, Worcestershire.

Himmelfarb, Gertrude. *The Idea of Poverty: England in the
Early Industrial Age.* New York: Knopf, 1983; Random House
(Vintage Books), 1985. Pp. 596. $25.00; Vintage, paper
$12.95.

Rev. by Noel Annan ("Fable of the Poor") in *NYRB*, March 1,
1984, pp. 12-15; by George Szamuely in *S*, Aug. 4, 1984, pp.
24-25.
A fascinating historical digest, with a running critique
of all critiques. By Chapter V we get to a summary of "the
Legacy of Malthus"; Chapter VIII is given to Carlyle;
Chapter IX to Cobbett. And a footnote on p. 406 overturns
the idea that "any novel written between roughly 1780 and the
1850s is necessarily an expression of and a response to ...
the Industrial Revolution" (as declared in a recent book)--
"if only," cautions Himmelfarb, "because in the early part
of that period in many parts of the country, the industrial
revolution had neither industrialized nor revolutionized
the economy, still less social relations, social sensi-
bilities, or the social consciousness." For any period
"the relationship between a novel and the economic and social
environment of the author is never ... mechanical, reduc-
tivistic, and determinate...."
And the same can be said of poetry. (D.V.E.)

Hont, Istvan, and Michael Ignatieff, eds. *Wealth and Virtue:*
The Shaping of Political Economy in the Scottish Enlighten-
ment. Cambridge University Press, 1984. Pp. 371. $59.50.

Symposium papers on "Scottish political economy and the
civic humanist tradition," rev. by D.D. Raphael in *TLS*,
June 25, 1984, p. 672, with praise and criticism.
Not seen.

Housum, Mary E. "Boswell's Account of Bonnie Prince Charlie
and the *Journal of a Tour to the Hebrides.*" *SSL* 16 (1981):
135-47.

Jacques, David. *Georgian Gardens: The Reign of Nature.*
London: Batsford, 1983. £25.00.

Rev. by Kenneth Woodbridge in *Apollo* 119 (1984): 466-67.

Jenkins, Ian. "'G.F. Watts' Teachers': George Frederic Watts
and the Elgin Marbles." *Apollo* 120 (1984): 176-81.

Jenkins, Philip. *The Making of a Ruling Class: The Glamorgan*
Gentry 1640-1790. Cambridge University Press, 1983. Pp.
xxvi+353; 7 maps; 23 tables. $44.50.

Rev. by Anthony Fletcher in *Albion* 16 (1984): 184-85, as
"many-sided, rich, and rewarding."
Not seen.

Johnson, Dale A. *Women in English Religion 1700-1925.*
(Studies in Women and Religion 10.) Lewiston, N.Y.:
The Edwin Mellen Press, 1983. Pp. x+353. $49.95.

Rev. by Martha Vicinus in *Albion* 16 (1984): 436, as an
anthology of primary sources that deserves a wide audience.
Not seen.

Jouve, Michel. *L'Âge d'or de la caricature anglaise.* Paris:
Presses de la Fondation Nationale des Sciences Politiques,
1983. Pp. 278. Fr. 128.00.

Rev. by Cecelia J. Hynes-Higman in *BJA* 24 (1984): 274-75.
Not seen.

Kenyon, John. *The History Men: The Historical Profession in*
England Since the Renaissance. London: Weidenfeld and
Nicolson, 1983; University of Pittsburgh Press, 1984. Pp.
xi+324. Paper $14.95.

Rev. by Michael G. Finlayson in *Albion* 16 (1984): 296-
98, as "an enjoyable, gossipy study" which "tends to de-

scribe too much while explaining too little."

Carlyle and Buckle, "the prophets," share a chapter on
"The High Victorians," and since Carlyle's "sources were
highly selective, and all of them printed" (101), Kenyon
cannot take him seriously as a historian and is "surprised
to find" his books still in print--in America! Kenyon
seems unaware that most of the sources that survived the
Revolution *are* the printed ones--and that Carlyle used
them well. He does admit, reluctantly, that Carlyle's
"wild and disordered vocabulary often hits the mark with
amazing felicity" and even at times "advances our understanding" (107). (D.V.E.)

King, Peter. "Decision-makers and Decision-making in the
English Criminal Law, 1750-1800." *HJ* 27,i (1984):   25-28.

"This paper focuses on a central component of the
eighteenth-century judicial system, the treatment of
property offenders."

Law, Alexander. "Scottish Schoolbooks of the Eighteenth and
Nineteenth Centuries." *SSL* 18 (1983):   1-32.

The old school *was* a hard school. (T.L.A.)

Lerski, Hanna Hryniewecka. *William Jay, Itinerant English
Architect, 1792-1837.* Lanham, Md.: University Press of
America, 1983. Pp. 376; 101 illus. $25.25.

Rev. by Roderick O'Donnell in *BM* 126 (April 1984):   240-
41.

Liesenfeld, Vincent J. *The Licensing Act of 1737.* University
of Wisconsin Press, 1984. xiv+259. $27.50.

A thorough account of the issues that engendered the
controversial licensing act of 1737. Decides there is no
conclusive proof that Walpole enforced the act to suppress
dissent, although the importance of political drama,
particularly Fielding's, to its passage is clear. Concludes
that Jacobinism and satire were clear influences, but the
case is not proven. The act was as much "a product of particular social, legal, economic, and political conditions
as a reaction to literary works." A very informative work.
(M.F.)

Lister, Raymond. *Samuel Palmer and "The Ancients."* Cambridge:
Fitzwilliam Museum and Cambridge University Press, 1984.
Pp. xvi+100, 149 illus. $49.50.

Foreword by Michael Jaffe. Introduction by Lister, who
selected and catalogued the exhibition. (This involved a
careful elimination of several "fakes" that had got into
earlier compilations.)
Lister clears up some misconceptions about "The Ancients"
(i.e., Samuel Palmer, Edward Calvert, and George Richmond--
also Finch, Tatham, Walter, and Sherman). It has only
recently been realized "that the Ancients' early 'visionary'
experience lasted little more than six years"; that "their
work was based securely on the traditions of Western art";
and, therefore, that their own influence on artists and
writers was "powerful."

MacLaren, I.S. "David Thompson's Imaginative Mapping of the
Canadian Northwest 1784-1812." *ArielE* 15, no. 2 (1984):
89-106.

Marshall, P.J., and Glyndour Williams. *The Great Map of
Mankind: Perceptions of New Worlds in the Age of Enlightenment.* Harvard University Press, 1982. Pp. 314. $22.50.

Rev. by Regina Janes in *ECS* 17 (1984): 354-57.

Mays, James O. *Mr. Hawthorne Goes to England: The Adventures
of a Reluctant Diplomat.* Ringwood, Eng.: New Forest
Leaves, 1983. Pp. 222. $24.00.

Rev. by Joseph Flibbert in *NEQ* 57 (1984): 455-58.

McCahill, Michael W. *Order and Equipoise: The Peerage and
the House of Lords 1783-1806.* London: Royal Historical
Society, Studies in History No. 11. Swift Printers, 1978.
Pp. x+256. £15.00.

Rev. by G.M. Ditchfield in *Parliamentary History* 1 (1983):
260-63.

McEvoy, John G. "Joseph Priestley, Scientist, Philosopher
and Divine." *PAPS* 128 (1984): 193-99.

McKendrick, Neil; John Brewer; and J.H. Plumb. *The Birth of
a Consumer Society: The Commericialization of Eighteenth-
Century England.* London: Hutchinson, 1984. Pp. 345.
Paper £8.50.

Rev. by Pat Rogers in *TLS*, June 15, 1984, p. 668.
"The most representative essay in the book is McKendrick's
intriguing account of 'The Commercialization of Fashion.'"
Not seen.

Meisel, Martin. *Realizations: Narrative, Pictorial, and Theatrical Arts in Nineteenth-Century England.* Princeton University Press, 1983. Pp. xx+471. $45.00.

Rev. by Alan Donovan in *JAAC* 43 (1984): 93-96.

Meranze, Michael. "The Penitential Ideal in Late Eighteenth-Century Philadelphia." *PMHB* 108 (1984): 419-50.

Useful on the influence of John Howard's *The State of the Prisons in England and Wales* (1777). (T.L.A.)

Mills, John A. "Thomas Brown's Theory of Causation." *JHP* 22 (1984): 207-27.

Brown (1778-1820) shared the chair of Moral Philosophy at Edinburgh with Dugald Stewart. This article compares his ideas on causation with those of Thomas Reid and David Hume.

Mokyr, Joel. "New Developments in Irish Population History, 1700-1850." *EcHR* 37,iv (1984): 473-88.

Morley, John. *The Making of the Royal Pavilion, Brighton.* Pp. 352; 111 col. pls., 197 b/w illus. £47.50.

Rev. by Nicholas Penny in *BM* 126 (Dec. 1984): 792.

Morris, Kevin L. *The Image of the Middle Ages in Romantic and Victorian Literature.* London: Croom Helm, 1984. Pp. 259. £18.95.

Rev. by Elizabeth Archibald in *TLS*, Dec. 14, 1984, p. 1450, as dealing more with "religious medievalism" than with literature: the last word in the title should be "*Thought.*"
Not seen.

Morris, R.J. "Voluntary Societies and British Urban Elites, 1780-1850: An Analysis." *HJ* 26,i (1983): 95-118.

"Whilst it would be wrong to claim that voluntary societies in Britain were new in the period 1780 to 1850, the growth of large industrial and urban populations was accompanied by an increase in the foundation and prosperity of such societies." They include "mechanics institutes, literary societies, circulating libraries," etc.

Mullett, Michael. "From Sect to Denomination? Social Developments in Eighteenth-Century English Quakerism." *Journal of Religious History* 13 (1984): 168-91.

Helpful for reconstructing the religious atmosphere of the late eighteenth century.

Mulvey, Christopher. *Anglo-American Landscapes: A Study of Nineteenth-Century Anglo-American Travel Literature.* Cambridge University Press, 1983. Pp. xv+293. $27.50.

Rev. by Robert E. Streeter in *NEQ* 57 (1984): 144-47.

Norton, David Fate. *David Hume: Common-Sense Moralist, Sceptical Metaphysician.* Princeton University Press, 1982. Pp. xii+329. $25.00.

Rev. by Alexander Rosenberg in *QQ* 91 (1984): 213-14.

Norton, David Fate, and J.C. Stewart-Robertson. "Thomas Reid on Adam Smith's Theory of Morals." *JHI* 45 (1984): 309-21.

Continues *JHI* 41 (1980): 381-98, and see *RMB* for 1980, p. 43.

O'Gorman, Frank. "Electoral Deference in 'Unreformed' England, 1760-1832." *JMH* 56 (1984): 391-429.

Counting fewer sheep than Namier, O'Gorman takes us to the verge of an important rethinking of British attitudes. (T.L.A.)

Oram, Hugh. *The Newspaper Book: A History of Newspapers in Ireland, 1649-1983.* Dublin: MO Books, 1983. Pp. 357. IR £8.50.

Rev. by Josef L. Altholz in *VPR* 17 (1984): 168.

Ormond, Richard, with contributions by Joseph Rishel and Robin Hamlyn. *Sir Edwin Landseer.* New York: Rizzoli International Publications in assoc. with The Philadelphia Museum of Art and The Tate Gallery, 1981. Pp. 224; 44 text illus., 158 figs. $45.00.

Rev. by Susan P. Casteras in *ArtB* 66 (1984): 344-46.

Pearson, Bill. *Rifled Sanctuaries: Some Views of the Pacific Islands in Western Literature.* (The Macmillan Brown Lectures 1982.) Oxford University Press, 1984. Pp. 93. $12.95.

Europe and Tahiti made their first reported contact in 1767; the terms in which Europe judged Tahitian society, "and by which it came to destroy it, were inadequate to understanding it in the way that Tahitians must have understood themselves." Defoe established the strongest myth about the islanders; Byron saw pre-missionary Tahiti as a happy place free from "the sordor of civilization." But to many the pagans of the Islands were sinfully degenerate, i.e., too lazy to work. Coleridge suggested to Southey that "extirpating the bread-fruit from their island" would make them learn to "live by the sweat of their brows"--in 1803; 27 years later Southey read that the missionaries had made the Tahitians so meek as to be vulnerable to raids from still heathen natives, "and he urged that the missionaries give them military training."

Toward the end of Pearson's survey, D.H. Lawrence arrives at the Southeyan position of hostility to the idyllic myths. (D.V.E.)

Peterson, Susan Rae. "The Compatibility of Richard Price's Politics and Ethics." *JHI* 45 (1984): 537-47.

Price (1723-1791) is refuted by Burke in *Reflections on the Revolution.* (T.L.A.)

Playfair, Giles. *The Flesh of Lightning: A Portrait of Edmund Kean.* London: William Kimber, 1983. Pp. 188.

Rev. by Raymund FitzSimons in *TN* 38 (1984): 147-48. A third, condensed edition of the 1939 biography.

Pointon, Marcia. "Portrait-Painting as a Business Enterprise in London in the 1780s." *Art History* 7 (1984): 187-205.

Written in "the conviction that considerations of ideology, aesthetics and artistic tradition are meaningful only if taken within the context of the means and constraints of production ... [and] within social organizations of various kinds." Artists whose careers provide documentation include Reynolds, Romney, Gainsborough, Opie, Northcote, and Gilbert Stuart.

Rashid, Salim. "Malthus' Theology: An Overlooked Letter and Some Comments." *HPE* 16,i (1984): 135-38.

The letter raises the question of whether war, as a means of controlling the population, is justifiable.

Reed, Michael. *The Georgian Triumph 1700-1830.* (The Making of Modern Britain 1066-1939.) Boston: Routledge & Kegan Paul, 1983. Pp. xvi+250.

Rev. by Kenneth L. Campbell in *Albion* 16 (1984): 306-07, as a fairly successful attempt to provide "a snapshot of Britain" (while a century and a half of history stand still?) showing us "how politics, society, religion, technology,

leisure, thought, and [yes] literature are all interrelated...."
Not seen.

Richardson, Joanna, ed. *Letters from Lambeth: The Correspon-*
dence of the Reynolds Family with John Freeman Milward
Dovaston, 1808-1815. London: Published for The Royal
Society of Literature by the Boydell Press, 1981. Pp. iv+
212. $30.00.

Rev. by Donald H. Reiman in *SiR* 22 (1983): 470-74.
Not seen. Reiman observes that this is "both a labor of
love and done hastily" and that when the dates and names in
this correspondence are more fully recovered it "will ultimately yield considerable ... evidence about the milieu
of Keats and other poets of his generation."

Robinson, John Martin. "Dalmeny House, West Lothian." *Apollo*
119 (1984): 400-405.

The design of William Wilkins. Three other articles (pp.
406-20) detail the furniture, paintings, and Napoleon room
at Dalmeny House.

Robinson, John Martin. *Georgian Model Farms: A Study of*
Decorative and Model Farm Buildings in the Age of Improve-
ment, 1700-1846. Oxford: Clarendon, 1983. Pp. xiv+190.
$69.00.

Rev. by Gavin Stamp in *S*, Aug. 11, 1984, p. 23: "No
building type tells us more about the preoccupations of
late 18th-century Britain."

Rosenfeld, Sybil. *Georgian Scene Painters and Scene Painting.*
Cambridge University Press, 1981.

Rev. by Edward Craig in *TN* 37 (1983): 41-43.

Roworth, Wendy Wassyng. "Angelica Kauffmann's 'Memorandum of
Painting.'" *BM* 126 (Oct. 1984): 629-30; 4 illus.

A chronological list of works, beginning in December 1781
in Venice, providing an "invaluable account" of the artist's
years in Italy. The actual authorship is ascribed to
Kauffmann's husband, Antonio Zucchi.

Russell, Colin A. *Science and Social Change in Britain and*
Europe 1700-1900. New York: St. Martin's Press, 1983. Pp.
xvii+307. $25.00.

An entertaining but misleadingly titled book, since it
mostly discusses how science was organized and pursued rather

than how related to social change. Only Chapters 6 ("Science in the Early Industrial Revolution"), 7 ("Change and Continuity in French Science, 1789-1815"), and 8 ("Radical Science in Britain, 1790-1830") concern our period. However, the early chapters are worth reading for their discussion of the non-scientific influence of Newtonianism during the eighteenth century. (M.M.)

Saunders, Ann. *The Art and Architecture of London.* London: Phaidon, 1984. £22.50.

Rev. by John Martin Robinson in *Apollo* 120 (1984): 78.

Semmel, Bernard. *John Stuart Mill and the Pursuit of Virtue.* Yale University Press, 1984. Pp. xii+212. $17.50.

Rev. by Bruce L. Kinzer in *Albion* 16 (1984): 438-40, as arguing, less from conclusive evidence than as a tract for the times, that Mill's *On Liberty* is a defense of the "positive liberty" of self-realization advocated by German transcendentalism and its English sponsors, Coleridge and Carlyle.
This episodic intellectual biography traces Mill's progress away from his father's and Bentham's determinist emphasis on material happiness toward a concept of liberty centered on individual virtue and a definition of happiness transcending material comfort. The book is a welcome reminder of the manifold interests and talents of the earnest Victorian and offers the additional pleasure of a guided tour around the intellectual map of mid-century Europe, with stops at Bentham, Carlyle, Saint-Simon, and Tocqueville, as well as some forgotten backwaters like Whewall and Buckle. Semmel is good at resuscitating old controversies, although his fascination with exploded theories (like Comte's phrenological anti-feminism) occasionally slows the progress. The mounting critique of determinism and materialism on behalf of "humanism" does not quite prepare one for the concluding attack on contemporary disciples of Marx, Freud, Keynes, and Skinner and on the "hubristic, utopian claims" of social science in general, or for the discovery that the primary intent of the book is to capture the idol of the liberals and establish his cult among the avatars of the right. Semmel has usefully illustrated Mill's political complexities but may have forgotten some of them en route to his conclusion. (R.M.R.)

Shapiro, Fred R. "The French Revolution and the English Language." *ELN* 22,ii (1984): 38-48.

Siebert, Donald T. "Hume on Idolatry and Incarnation." *JHI*
45 (1984): 379-96.

   The *Dialogues Concerning Natural Religion* remind us that
   Blake's anti-Druidism had a precursor. (T.L.A.)

Smith, Bernard. "Captain Cook's Artists and the Portrayal
of Pacific Peoples." *Art History* 7 (1984): 295-312; 29 illus.

   On the difficulties faced by Cook's artists--Alexander
   Buchan, Sydney Parkinson, William Hodges, John Webber--when
   they tried to depict the inhabitants of the Pacific. The
   author concludes that as a result "individualism" was
   promoted in the island societies and that at the same time
   the discovery of the native arts and crafts by the English
   artists "provided a threshold for the development of the
   European taste for primitive art" in the nineteenth and
   twentieth centuries.

Stone, Lawrence, and Jeanne C. Fautier Stone. *An Open Elite?*
England 1540-1880. Oxford University Press, 1984. Pp. 566.
$29.95.

   Rev. by Jeremy Black in *New Statesman*, Sept. 7, 1984,
   p. 30; by Rosalind Mitchison in *LRB* 6,xxi (1984): 11-12;
   by Ferdinand Mount in *S*, Oct. 6, 1984, pp. 25-27, as "an
   attempt to demolish the 'hoary myth' that for centuries
   English landed society has been uniquely open to newcomers."

Sutton, Denys. "Aspects of British Collecting, Part III."
Apollo 119 (1984): 312-72.

   Five separate articles on art collecting in the eighteenth
   and early nineteenth centuries: "The Lure of the Antique";
   "Amateurs and Scholars"; "Paris-Londres"; "A Wealth of Pictures"; "The Orleans Collection."

Sutton, Denys. "The History of British Art--A Growth Area."
Apollo 119 (1984): 394-99.

Sutton, Denys. "Revaluations in Nineteenth-Century Art."
Apollo 120 (1984): 84-85.

Sutton, Denys. "The Satiric Spirit in British Art." *Apollo*
120 (1984): 304-11.

   On "English Caricature 1620 to the Present," at the Library
   of Congress, with an exhibition catalogue edited by John
   Riely.

Tansey, E.M. "The Life and Works of Sir Alexander Crichton, F.R.S. (1763-1856): A Scottish Physician to the Imperial Russian Court." *NRRS* 38 (1984): 241-59.

Taylor, George, ed. *Plays by Samuel Foote and Arthur Murphy: The Minor, The Nabob, The Citizen, Three Weeks After Marriage, Know Your Own Mind.* Cambridge University Press, 1984. Pp. xi+233; 4 illus. $44.50; paper $15.95.

   A long introduction, on the playwrights and performances; biographical records; bibliography. The pre-Romantic stage-play.

Thompson, M.W., ed. *The Journeys of Sir Richard Colt Hoare Through Wales and England 1793-1810.* London: Allan Sutton.

   Rev. by George Clive in *S*, April 7, 1984, p. 31, as "the reactions of an exceptionally cultivated and inquiring man to what were then ... the principal sites of Wales and England."

Thornton, A.P. "Scotland, 1789-1832: Problems of a Political Satellite." *QQ* 91 (1984): 100-13.

   First presented at a symposium on Romanticism and Revolution at the University of Toronto, Jan. 18, 1983. Let us hope for a volume of these essays. (T.L.A.)

Trench, Charles Chenevix. *The Great Dan: A Biography of Daniel O'Connell.* London: Jonathan Cape, 1984.

   Rev. by Stan Gebler Davies in *S*, Oct. 13, 1984, pp. 27-28.

Tuman, Myron C. "'Irritant Poison': Idealism and Scientific History in Late-Victorian England." *SiR* 22 (1983): 407-19.

   There are difficulties of terminology, but this discussion of the "scientific" departure from the idealism of the "romantic historian" such as Carlyle, who "saw history as a veiled form of theology," to the professional historicism which disdained ideas as "irritant poison," to the reassertion of the Romantic tradition in the twentieth century, mulls over a matter of great importance. (D.V.E.)

Twitchell, James B. *Romantic Horizons: Aspects of the Sublime in English Poetry and Painting, 1770-1850.* University of Missouri Press, 1983. Pp. xii+232; 13 black-and-white illus. $23.50.

   Rev. by Matthew C. Brennan in *RP&P* 8,ii (1984): 45-49. A study of the changing significance of the horizon-line

in Romantic poetry and painting, with some consideration of
later developments, especially in painting. Poets are paired
with specific paintings by the artists named in the chapter
headings: "Blake: The Anti-Sublime" (paired with himself);
"Wordsworth and Wright: The Natural Sublime"; "Coleridge
and Turner: The Sublime at the Vortex"; "Byron and Martin:
The Daemonic Sublime"; "Keats and Cozens: The Systematic
Sublime"; "Shelley and Constable: The Empyreal Sublime."
The Conclusion ranges forward to modern painters like Mondrian
and Mark Rothko, and there is a valuable 11-page bibliography
at the end. As an example of the author's approach, the
chapter on Wordsworth and Joseph Wright of Derby draws a
detailed parallel between *Yew Trees* and *A Cavern: Evening*
(1774). *Yew Trees* is based, according to the author, on a
subliminal image of a cave (the argument is convincing in
context), and both works take the mind of artist and observer
alike to the brink of a transcendental experience; in
Riffaterre's phrase, both works constitute a "mimesis of a
visionary act" (quoted on p. 82). Wordsworth's contribution,
not surprisingly, is to locate the sublime in the perceiving
mind rather than in some arbitrary category of external objects as in earlier formulations in Burke *et al.* In the
Snowdon episode the poet "finally attempts to go still
farther"; "this pushing past the aperture, moving over the
horizon" is what "characterizes the direction of the romantic
vision from Wordsworth onward" (84). Not always convincing,
but often suggestive in a valuable way. (B.C.H.)

Vaughan, Frederick. *The Tradition of Political Hedonism from
    Hobbes to J.S. Mill.* New York: Fordham University Press,
    1982. Pp. ix+271. $25.00.

    Rev. by Timothy Fuller in *JHP* 22 (1984): 499-501.

Vignoles, K.H. *Charles Blacker Vignoles: Romantic Engineer.*
    Cambridge University Press, 1982. Pp. xii+187. $44.50.

    Rev. by R.A. Buchanan in *VS* 28 (1984): 200-01.

Walker, Ian C. "Scottish Nationalism in *The Weekly Magazine.*"
    SSL 16 (1981): 1-13.

    Published in the 1770s.

Wallech, Steven. "The Elements of Social Status in Hume's
    Treaties." *JHI* 45 (1984): 207-18.

    The *Treatise of Human Nature* contra Rousseau. (T.L.A.)

Waszek, Norbert. "Two Concepts of Morality: A Distinction
   of Adam Smith's Ethics and Its Stoic Origin." *JHI* 45 (1981):
   591-606.

Wiener, Joel H. *Radicalism and Freethought in Nineteenth-*
   Century Britain: The Life of Richard Carlile. (Contributions
   in [sic] Labor History, 13.) Westport, Conn., and London:
   Greenwood Press, 1983. Pp. x+285. $29.85.

   Rev. by Joseph Hamburger in *VPR* 17 (1984): 73-75.
   Includes a valuable "Bibliographical Essay" (269-75) which
   covers the whole century. No illustrations.
   A student of Romanticism who reads this grim personal tale
   of a determined provoker of radical controversy who was
   somehow "one of the most important British working-class
   reformers" of the century, and then reads carefully some
   of his writings--here quoted only in thematic bits, to indicate his theoretical evolution in its twists and turns--should
   be able to shed a good deal of retrospective light on the
   "science" of the Romantic poets--not only Byron and Shelley
   (whom Carlile quoted and admired) but perhaps also Blake and
   Coleridge.
   (The index is spotty, giving, e.g., no "Byron" entries and
   only five for "Shelley," to which four more should be added:
   62, 76, 92, 159.) (D.V.E.)

Wills, Garry. "Washington's Citizen Virtue: Greenough and
   Houdon." *CritI* 10 (1984): 420-42; 15 illus.

   On the problems of representing in sculpture both "republican grandeur" and George Washington's personal simplicity,
   exemplified in the statues by Horatio Greenough and Jean-
   Antoine Houdon. Includes an interesting discussion of the
   Neoclassical conventions within which the contemporary sculp-
   tors worked or which they had to revise.

See also Butlin and Joll ("English 4. Turner").

Review of books previously listed:

BERRIDGE, Virginia, and Griffith Edwards, *Opium and the*
   People: Opiate Use in 19th-Century England (see *RMB* for
   1982, p. 39), rev. by Andrew Scull in *JMH* 56 (1984): 724-
   26; CAVE, Kathryn, ed., *The Diary of Joseph Farington*, vols.
   XI-XII (see *RMB* for 1983, p. 41), rev. by Luke Herrmann in
   BM 126 (April 1984): 240; DOZIER, Robert R., *For King,*
   Constitution, and Country: The English Loyalists and the
   French Revolution (see *RMB* for 1983, pp. 42-43), rev. by
   J.R. Dinwiddy in *Albion* 16 (1984): 308-09, as begging

important questions and strewn with errors; EHRMAN, John,
The Younger Pitt (see *RMB* for 1983, p. 43), rev. by Donald
E. Ginter in *Albion* 16 (1984): 190-91 as monumental though
flawed; GANZEL, Dewey, *Fortune and Men's Eyes: The Career
of John Payne Collier* (see *RMB* for 1983, p. 45), rev. by Alan
Bell in *Library* 6 (1984): 413-14, who joins other negative
evaluators; by Scott Bennett in *VS* 27 (1984): 260-62; by
Kenneth Muir in *SR* 92 (1984): 270-73; GARLICK, Kenneth,
and Angus MacIntyre, eds., and Cave, Kathryn, ed., *The Diary
of Joseph Farington*, vols. I-X (see *RMB* for 1980, p. 38, for
1982, p. 41, and for 1983, p. 41), rev. by Anne Tennant
("Editorial Impressions") in *Art History* 7 (1984): 375-78;
GUNN, J.A.W., et al., eds., *Benjamin Disraeli Letters* (see
RMB for 1983, p. 46), rev. by Stephen Koss in *JMH* 56 (1984):
534-35; HAWES, Louis, *Presences of Nature: British Land-
scape, 1780-1830* (see *RMB* for 1983, p. 46), rev. by Luke
Herrmann in *BM* 126 (May 1984): 301-02; HAYES, John, *The
Landscape Paintings of Thomas Gainsborough: A Critical Text
and Catalogue Raisonné* (see *RMB* for 1983, p. 46), rev. by
Edward J. Nygren in *ECS* 18 (1984-85): 239-42; HELENIAK,
Kathryn, *William Mulready* (see *RMB* for 1981, p. 43), rev. by
Sarah Symmons in *SiR* 22 (1983): 467-69; HINDE, Wendy,
Castlereagh (see *RMB* for 1981, p. 43), rev. by P.J. Jupp
in *Parliamentary History: A Yearbook* 1 (1983): 263-65,
raising several questions; HONE, J. Ann, *For the Cause of
Truth: Radicalism in London, 1796-1821* (see *RMB* for 1983,
p. 48), rev. by Gary S. De Krey in *JMH* 56 (1984): 140-42,
as finding greater unity than the reviewer [and T.L.A.];
McDOWELL, R.B., *Ireland in the Age of Imperialism and
Revolution, 1760-1801* (see *RMB* for 1981, p. 45), rev. by
E.M. Johnston in *Parliamentary History* 1 (1984): 254-56,
as clear and valuable, but a bit disappointing in its biases;
MUNSCHE, P.B., *Gentlemen and Poachers: The English Game
Laws, 1671-1831* (see *RMB* for 1982, pp. 49-50), rev. by J.H.
Baker in *JMH* 56 (1984): 135-36, favorably; PAULSON, Ronald,
Literary Landscape: Turner and Constable (see *RMB* for 1982,
p. 50), rev. by John Gage in *BM* 126 (June 1984): 362-63,
who does not believe the book "will persuade historians of
landscape art that they have anything to learn from their
literary critics"; by Anne K. Mellor in *RP&P* 8,1 (1984):
51-55; PICKERING, Samuel F., Jr., *John Locke and Children's
Books in Eighteenth-Century England* (see *RMB* for 1982, p.
51), rev. by Mary V. Jackson in *ECS* 17 (1984): 367-69;
PRESSLY, William L., *The Life and Art of James Barry* (see
RMB for 1981, p. 47), rev. by Peter Funnell in *Oxford Art
Quarterly* 4,ii (1981): 47; ROYLE, Edward, and James Walvin,
English Radicals and Reformers, 1760-1848 (see *RMB* for 1982,
p. 53), rev. by James Epstein in *SAQ* 83 (1984): 476-77, as

well-informed but without E.P. Thompson's fixation on class-structure; STOCK, R.D., *The Holy and the Daemonic from Sir Thomas Browne to William Blake* (see *RMB* for 1982, p. 54), rev. by Patricia Meyer Spacks in *MP* 82 (1984): 206-09, who finds that Stock "knows a great deal: but not, apparently, how to read poetry"; THALE, Mary, *Selections from the Papers of the London Corresponding Society 1792-1799* (see *RMB* for 1983, p. 53), rev. by Joel H. Weiner in *Albion* 16 (1984): 191-92; WEBB, Timothy, *English Romantic Hellenism 1700-1824* (see *RMB* for 1983, p. 68), rev. by Peter J. Manning in *SiR* 23 (1984): 401-09.

Composite reviews:

Colley, Linda. *LRB* 6,xx (1984): 18.

Reviews Robert Dozier, *For King, Constitution and Country* (see *RMB* for 1984, pp. 42-43); Margaret and James Jacobin, *The Origins of Anglo-American Radicalism* (London: Allen and Unwin, 1984; pp. 333; £18.50); Roger Wells, *Insurrection: The British Experience 1795-1803* (Allan Sutton, 1983; pp. 312; £16.00); and Joel H. Wiener, *Radicalism and Freethought in Nineteenth-Century Britain* (see above).

Cunliffe, Marcus. "Gorgeous George." *NYRB*, Oct. 11, 1984, pp. 47-50.

Two books are reviewed: John R. Alden, *George Washington: A Biography* (Louisiana State University Press, 1984; pp. 326; $19.95), and Garry Wills, *Cincinnatus: George Washington and the Enlightenment* (Garden City, N.Y.: Doubleday, 1984; pp. 272; $18.95).

Gifford, Henry. "Lermontov's Demon." *NYRB*, May 31, 1984, pp. 28-30.

The books reviewed are two translations: *Mikhail Lermontov: Major Poetical Works*, trans. with introd. and comm. by Anatoly Liberman (University of Minnesota Press, 1984; pp. 635; $39.50), and *Narrative Poems by Alexander Pushkin and by Mikhail Lermontov*, trans. Charles Johnston, introd. Kyril FitzLyon (New York: Random House, 1984; pp. 144; $12.95, paper $5.95).

Keates, Jonathan. "Superior Lakes." *TLS*, June 22, 1984.

Reviews Bicknell's edition of *The Illustrated ... Guide to the Lakes*; and McCracken's related book (see p. 184), dwelling on the *Guide*'s "continuing fascination" as lying

in its serving as "a companion to the Wordsworthian
aesthetic."

Porter, Roy. *Albion* 16 (1984): 425-28.

Review of two books by John W. Yolton: *Thinking Matter:
Materialism in Eighteenth-Century Britain* (University of
Minnesota Press, 1983; pp. iv+238; $29.50, paper $12.95) and
Perceptual Acquaintance from Descartes to Reid (University
of Minnesota Press, 1984; pp. x+248; $32.50, paper $13.95).
Porter welcomes these "400 pages of lucid and penetrating
analysis of many of the key issues confronting the philosophical mind in the era after the collapse of formal Scholasti-
cism." *Thinking Matter* explores "the repercussions of Locke's
suggestion that there would be nothing inconsistent in be-
lieving that God could superadd thought to the powers of
matter." *Perceptual Acquaintance* argues that "the successful philosophy is ... the one that achieves a holding
operation, and, possibly, the invention of 'psychology' was a
bolt-hole to escape to when literal and physical explanation
seemed to fail."
Not seen.

Rocher, Rosane. *ECS* 18 (1984): 118-24.

Reviewing Richard B. Barnett, *North Indian between Empires:
Awadh, the Mughals, and the British, 1720-1801* (University
of California Press, 1980; pp. xviii+276; $25.00), and Frank
Lequin, *Het personeel van der Verenigde Oost-Indische
Compagnie in Azië in der achttiende eeuw, meer in het bijzonder
in de vestiging Bengalen* (Leiden, 1982; 2 vols.; pp. xii+653;
Fl. 70.00).

Stone, Lawrence. "The New Eighteenth Century." *NYRB*, March
29, 1984.

Among the 14 books discussed, the following by their dates
are relevant to the Romantic period: R.S. Neale, *Bath 1680-
1850: A Social History* (Boston: Routledge & Kegan Paul,
1982; pp. 466; $45.00); Penelope J. Corfield, *The Impact of
English Towns, 1700-1800* (Oxford University Press, 1982; pp.
206; $25.95, paper $9.95); Michael Reed, *The Georgian Triumph,
1700-1830* (Boston: Routledge & Kegan Paul, 1983; pp. 240;
$19.95).

Vaughan, William. "British Landscapes: Views and Reactions."
Art History 7 (1984): 368-74.

The following books are discussed: Louis Hawes, *Presences
of Nature: British Landscape 1780-1830* (see *RMB* for 1983, p.

46); Ronald Paulson, *Literary Landscape: Turner and Constable* (see *RMB* for 1982, p. 50); Edward J. Nygren, *James Ward's Gordale Scar: An Essay in the Sublime* (London: Tate Gallery, 1982; pp. 64; 60 illus.; £2.95); David H. Solkin, *Richard Wilson: The Landscape of Reaction* (London: Tate Gallery, 1982; pp. 251; 146 illus., 14 col. pls.; £9.95); Graham Reynolds, *Constable's England* (New York: The Metropolitan Museum of Art; London: Weidenfeld & Nicolson, 1983; pp. 2-5; 175 illus., 95 col. pls.; £18.50); Michael Rosenthal, *Constable: The Painter and His Landscope* (see *RMB* for 1983, p. 109); Katharine S. Crouan, ed., *John Linell: A Centennial Exhibition* (see *RMB* for 1983, p. 42).

White, John Charles. *ECS* 17 (1983-84): 210-14.

Reviewing Alan Forrest, *The French Revolution and the Poor* (see *RMB* for 1982, p. 7), and Clive H. Church, *Revolution and Red Tape: The French Ministerial Bureaucracy, 1770-1850* (see *RMB* for 1983, p. 7).

Review article:

Teichgraeber, Richard F., III. *ECS* 18 (1984-85): 242-47.

Reviews two recent volumes in the wake of completed publication of the *Glasgow Edition of the Works and Correspondence of Adam Smith* (6 vols., Oxford, 1976-83). Knud Haakonssen's *The Science of a Legislator: The Natural Jurisprudence of David Hume & Adam Smith* (Cambridge University Press, 1981) "provides the first detailed and systematic examination of the views of law and government that underlay Smith's economic doctrines." *Wealth and Virtue: The Shaping of Political Economy in the Scottish Enlightenment*, edited by Istvan Hont and Michael Ignatieff (Cambridge University Press, 1983; pp. ix+371; $59.50) presents 13 colloquium papers, seen as of great value yet some at times "ingenious to the point of implausibility."

3. CRITICISM

Abrams, M.H. *The Correspondent Breeze: Essays on English Romanticism.* With a Foreword by Jack Stillinger. New York and London: Norton & Co., 1984. Pp. xii+296. $22.50.

A collection of Abrams's essays written over three decades, handily made available since they will always be needed. Coleridge and Wordsworth have received by far the greatest attention, then Shelley; few, but valuable, essays treat of

Blake, Schelling, Keats, Kant, and Hazlitt, in that descending order.
    Abrams is represented symbolically on the front cover by a
Turner "tree in a storm" and on the back by his own grinning
face. (D.V.E.)

Agress, Lynne. *The Feminine Irony: Women on Women in Early*
    Nineteenth-Century English Literature. Lanham, Md.; New
    York; and London: University Press of America, 1984. (Ori-
    ginally published in 1978 by Fairleigh Dickinson University
    Press--see *RMB* for 1979, p. 50.) Pp. 190; $11.50.

    Argues that women writers affirmed social discrimination
against women with abundant proof from many works, including
those of Hannah More, Maria Edgeworth, the less well-known
Ann Taylor and Jane West, and even Mary Wollstonecraft.
At the same time these writers forged a popular and
autonomous place in society in contrast to the roles for
women that they encouraged and perpetuated. (M.F.)

Anderson, Wayne C. "The Rhetoric of Silence in the Discourse
    of Coleridge and Carlyle." *SAR* 49 (1984): 72-90.

Barnard, Robert. *A Short History of English Literature.* Oxford:
    Basil Blackwell, 1984. Pp. vii+218. $24.95; paper $9.95.

    Efficient, clear, mainstream; 23 pages divided between
"The Birth of Romanticism" and "Romantics and Anti-Romantics."
Serviceable for first assignment--or opening lectures.
(D.V.E.)

Barrell, John. *English Literature in History 1730-80: An*
    Equal, Wide Survey. New York: St. Martin's Press, 1984.
    Pp. 228. $22.50.

    Textual events leading up to the "crisis of social knowl-
edge" which the mid-century authors "bequeathed to the
Romantics."
    The works examined are the poems of Thomson and Dyer,
Johnson's *Dictionary,* and Smollett's *Roderick Random,* all
having in common their response to the organizing principles
of the polity. They all attempt "to represent a wide range
of social knowledge and experience, and thus to exhibit
society as a various and complex organization" while concerned
to suggest that "the gentleman" is "still adequate to the
task of comprehending that organization."
    A shrewd and widely suggestive scrutiny. (D.V.E.)

Bassill, Veronica. "Eros and Psyche in 'The Artist of the Beautiful.'" *ESQ* 30 (1984): 1-21.

Touches on the myth of Keats in a useful examination of Hawthorne's tale. (T.L.A.)

Bidney, Martin. "The Exploration of Keatsian Aesthetic Problems in Browning's 'Madhouse Cells.'" *SEL* 24 (Autumn 1984): 671-81.

Bligh, John. "Shakesperian Character Study to 1800." *ShS* 37 (1984): 141-53.

How much better is S.T.C. than the minor critics discussed here? Very much. (T.L.A.)

Brantley, Richard E. *Locke, Wesley, and the Method of English Romanticism.* University of Florida Press, 1984. Pp. xi+300. $30.00.

In this contribution toward a "unified field theory of British Romanticism," Brantley declares, "I announce a program for studies in Romanticism whereby one finds, *mirabile dictu*, that Romantic tension in England at least is both partially reconcilable and fully understandable along clear lines of Wesley's philosophical theology." Brantley wants domestic and contemporary influences on Romanticism rather than, for example, Germanic and Miltonic. "John Wesley's dialectic of philosophy and faith ... provides a ready means of understanding the 'religious' empiricism and the English 'transcendentalism' of British Romantic poetry."

Brantley's main argument is that Wesley developed a theology based on an analogy between Lockean sense perception and the apprehension of revelation and grace. He sees a "fundamental point common to evangelicalism and empiricism alike: experience provides criteria for deciding what is true."

Most of the book is a persuasive demonstration of the breadth of John Wesley's influence, religious, intellectual, and cultural. If the evidence does not quite convince that "Wesley's intellectual influence surpassed that of all other intellectuals of his century" (even in the field of biology), it nevertheless leaves no doubt that the Methodism of Wesley was heavy in the air which the Romantics breathed.

Byron is largely omitted (although hinted at for two pages), and Keats and Shelley must make do with rather oblique evidence, but the sections on Blake and on Coleridge, and especially on Wordsworth, reveal a Lockean Wesleyanism which must be acknowledged. Unfortunately, Brantley's method often

relies on insinuation which leads to speculation rather than
firm foundations. Thus, Blake's "self-disclosing God ...
almost necessarily the God of immediate revelation, could
hardly be more reminiscent of Wesley's," and "at least by
1816, an uncannily Blakean terminology entered into evangelical
language." At times this kind of indirection, especially
for Blake and Keats, undermines the entire approach.

The strongest evidence for Brantley's case is of course
Wordsworth and nature: e.g., "The 'mystical' moments in
Wordsworth's "Natural Methodism" (1975). He agrees with
Colin Clarke that Wordsworth's struggles with the strangeness
of perception caused some of his finest poetry. Especially
effective is Clarke's insistence on the reciprocity between
Wordsworth and nature: e.g., "The 'mystical moments in
Tintern Abbey ... are validated by, and find their primary
analogue in, quite ordinary sensory experiences in which the
visible scene and the observer's mind at once confront each
other (preserving their distinctions) and interpenetrate
deeply." Brantley shows in some detail how the center of
Tintern Abbey is "fully consistent with and sharply reminiscent
of the Wesleyan and quintessentially English form of natural
religion whereby God is seen to be present in, but not
equivalent to, the text and texture of his second book."

Almost we are persuaded that "Wesley is the one figure who
comes near being the model for Wordsworth's ability to convey
to an increasingly widespread audience a complex message
creative in its tension between 'the language of the sense' ...
and otherworldly glimpses of 'the light that never was, on
sea or land.'"

Brantley's book is both precise in its detail and provocative in its assertions, or as Brantley himself says he is
trying to be, "both judicious and creative." However, a
unified field theory will need to be more inclusive than
this. (M.T.S.)

Buckley, Jerome Hamilton. *The Turning Key: Autobiography and
the Subjective Impulse Since 1800.* Harvard University Press,
1984. Pp. x+191. $15.00.

Rev. by Albert E. Stone in *Genre* 17 (1984): 316-18.

An exploration of "the subjective impulse" as it develops,
after a great leap from St. Augustine to Rousseau and Wordsworth, appearing in different literary genres, before it
emerges in the "subjective novel" of modern times.

With Rousseau it first assumes a literary form, serving
both as "calculated self-portraiture and unintentional
self-betrayal" (42). "The major spiritual autobiographies
in English are ... records of becoming different persons,

narratives of conversion, of recovering ... or discovering
a ... self" (53).
    Wordsworth is frequently invoked, also DeQuincey, Carlyle,
and Byron—of the Romantics. A treatise that widens our
perspective. (D.V.E.)

Burnham, R. Peter. "The Social Ethos of Mackenzie's *The Man
of Feeling*." *SSL* 18 (1983): 123-37.

Cantor, Paul A. *Creature and Creator: Myth-making and English
Romanticism*. Cambridge University Press, 1984. Pp. xxi+223.
$34.50.

    Rev. by Iain McGilchrist in *TLS*, Aug. 3, 1984, p. 862, as
at first unpromising but then rewarding.
    Focuses on Blake's *The Book of Urizen* and *The Four Zoas*,
Shelley's *Prometheus Unbound*, Mary Shelley's *Frankenstein*,
Byron's *Cain*, and Keats's *Hyperion* poems.

Chandler, James. "The Pope Controversy: Romantic Poetics and
the English Canon." *CritI* 10 (1984): 481-509.

    The Romantic challenge to Pope is seen as "almost inevitable
in light of the movement and the motives [i.e., nationalistic]
for forming a native English canon." Chandler's extended account of the controversy includes the contributions, on one
side or the other, of Joseph Warton, Cowper, Southey,
Wordsworth, Keats, Thomas Campbell, Hazlitt, and
Isaac D'Israeli, as well as of the better-known antagonists
William Lisle Bowles and Byron.

Chavkin, Allan. "Bellow and English Romanticism." *SLIm* 17,ii
(1984): 7-18.

    "Like Wordsworth and most of the other ... English Romantics,
Bellow calls for the liberation of the mind ..." (18).

Cockshut, A.O.J. *The Art of Autobiography in 19th- & 20th-
Century England*. Yale University Press, 1984. Pp. 222.
$20.00.

    Rev. by Brian Martin in *New Statesman*, Oct. 26, 2984, p. 33.
    Brief mentions of Byron (about his idea of himself),
DeQuincey, Haydon, Leigh Hunt—and Harriet Wilson. In an
interesting context, however, in which questions of truth and
quality in autobiographical writing are examined with great
care. (D.V.E.)

Collins, Richard W. "A Toy of Double Shape: The Hermaphrodite
as Art and Literature in Nineteenth-Century Britain." Ann

Arbor, Mich.:   University Microfilms International, 1984.
Dissertation.

Cook, Eleanor; Chaviva Hosek; Jay Macpherson; Patricia Parker;
and Julian Patrick, eds.   *Centre and Labyrinth: Essays in
Honour of Northrop Frye.*   University of Toronto Press, 1983.
Pp. x+346. $30.00; paper (1985) $15.95.

Rev. (with Frye's *The Myth of Deliverance: Reflections on
Shakespeare's Problem Comedies*, 1983), by Dan O'Hara in
Criticism 26 (1984):   91-95.

Paul Ricoeur, in "*Anatomy of Criticism* or the Order of
Paradigms" (1-13), suggests that "the phenomena of deviance,
schism, and the death of paradigms constitute the inverse
side of the problem posed by" Frye's book "of an order of paradigms constituting the schematism of narrative understanding."
In "The Riddle of Katharsis" (14-37) Francis Sparshott argues
that "the weakness of Frye's theory is its strength."   In
"Anagogic Metaphor: Breaking Down the Wall of Partition"
(38-58) Patricia Parker examines the "copular or anagogic
metaphor" in Shakespeare--and its Gothic emergence in *Wuthering
Heights*.   Michael Dolzani discusses "The Infernal Method:
Northrop Frye and Contemporary Criticism" (59-68).

John Freccero, in "Manfred's Wounds and the Poetics of the
'Purgatorio'" (69-82), resists any temptation to compare Dante's
Manfred with Byron's.   In "'Paradise Regained' by One Greater
Man: Milton's Wisdom Epic as a 'Fable of Identity'" (83-114)
James Nohrnberg stays with Milton and his ambience.

Thomas Willard writes on "Alchemy and the Bible" (115-27);
James Carscallen on "Three Jokers: The Shape of Alice Munro's
Stories" (128-45); David Staines on "The Holistic Vision of
Hugh of Saint Victor" (147-61).   Julian Patrick, in "'The
Tempest' as Supplement" (162-77), finds that play's end in
its whole.

Helen Vendler introduces "The Golden Theme: Keats's Ode
'To Autumn'" (181-96) as, in effect, a theme of Frye's own
teaching that illuminates subsequent criticism.

Milton Wilson investigates "Bodies in Motion: Wordsworth's
Myths of Natural Philosophy" (197-209); Geoffrey H. Hartman
proposes "Reading Aright: Keats's 'Ode to Psyche'" (210-26).

Subsequent essays deal with Victorians and Moderns, from
Tennyson to Stevens and Joyce--with occasional glances at
the Romantics.   Harold Bloom treats the ambivalences of
"Reading Freud: Transference, Taboo, and Truth" (309-28),
and Angus Fletcher concludes a discussion of "The Image of
Lost Direction" (329-46)--Frye's *Anatomy* definition of the
labyrinth--with an unexpected "exit into light."

The whole collection is a challenging "read," with that kind
of unexpectedness.   (D.V.E.)

Cooksey, Thomas L. "Dante's England, 1818: The Contribution
of Cary, Coleridge, and Foscolo to the British Reception of
Dante." *PLL* 20 (1984): 355-81.

Finds a turning point in appreciation from 1818 on, but of
course with the completion of the Cary translation in 1814,
and it is nice to know that Walpole called Dante a Methodist
parson in Bedlam, but with Byron coming in for a sentence
that misunderstands his work, and too much else scanted,
the essay has a ways to go. (T.L.A.)

Culviner, Thomas P. "The Style of Change: Historical Attitudes
in the Prose of Scott, Carlyle, Macaulay, and Thackeray."
Ann Arbor, Mich.: University Microfilms International, 1984.

Dissertation.

Daiches, David. *Literature and Gentility in Scotland*. Edinburgh University Press. Pp. i+105.

Rev. by A. Porteous in *AUMLA* 61 (1984): 87-89.
Not seen.

Dingley, R.J. "The Ending of Gray's *Elegy*." *AUMLA* 61 (1984):
29-36.

Just like Keats's *Urn*. (T.L.A.)

Dowling, Linda. "Nero and the Aesthetic of Torture." *VN* 66
(1984): 1-5.

Passing through De Quincey on the way to Pater's *Marius*.
(T.L.A.)

Ellis, Steve. *Dante and English Poetry: Shelley to T.S.
Eliot*. Cambridge University Press, 1984. Pp. 280. £20.00.

Rev. by C.H. Sisson in *TLS*, July 13, 1984, p. 798: "A
main theme ... is the distortions the poet and the poem
underwent as seen through the eyes of Shelley, Byron,
Browning, Rossetti and Yeats." As to literary influence, "it
is perhaps the Shelley of *The Triumph of Life* who comes out
most brilliantly...."

Ellison, Julie. "The Laws of Ice: Emerson's Irony and 'The
Comic.'" *ESQ* 30 (1984): 73-82.

Passing reference to Emerson's meeting with Wordsworth.
(T.L.A.)

Epstein, Julia L., and Mark L. Greenberg. "Decomposing Newton's
Rainbow." *JHI* 45 (1984): 115-40.

"While the scientifice poets of the eighteenth century
have been interpreted traditionally as glorifiers of the new
science and deifiers of Newton ... they are more nearly
precursors to Romantic attitudes and aesthetics than the
Romantics themselves would admit." This conclusion is
followed by a careful survey of the image as used by the
English Romantics, and their manipulation of eighteenth-
century sources. Altogether an excellent piece of work,
reminiscent of the best of *PMLA* before it took up other
causes. Not to be missed. (T.L.A.)

Figes, Eva. *Scx and Subterfuge: Woman Writers to 1850*.
London: Macmillan, 1982. Pp. 178. £12.00.

Rev. by Janet Horowitz Murray in *VS* 27 (1984): 257-58 as
"quite useful."
Not seen.

Flanders, Jane. "Other Lives of the Romantics." *Shenandoah*
34 (1984) 4: 29-30.

A poem consisting of 21 sentences, each beginning with a
year, as in the sample below:
1818--Byron teaches Shelley to Swim.
1840--Shelley dies while leading uprising of croupiers in
Monaco.
Worth it. (T.L.A.)

Gaull, Marilyn. "Romantic Theater." *TWC* 14 (1983): 255-63.

A swift but encyclopedic survey of the kinds of drama and
audiences in the unlicensed theaters, from juvenile drama
to "penny gaffs" or "blood tubs" (offering "lurid representations of local crimes, burlesques of middle class manners,
sentimental pieces, bawdy songs, and twenty-minute versions
of Shakespeare), to the Eidophusikon, to the "pantomime"
behind *Don Juan*--"an adult entertainment giving audiences
legally sanctioned access to a body of literature, of en-
chantment and erotic allegory"--and melodrama, and more.
We need to know these phantoms of off-limits culture, and
Gaull will bring it all to us: this is "a chapter ... in
my forthcoming book on the backgrounds of English Romanticism,"
she warns. Let's clap in anticipation! (D.V.E.)

Gittings, Robert. *The Nature of Biography*. University of
Washington Press, 1984. Pp. 96. $10.00; paper $4.95.

Hardbound published 1978; listed in *RMB* for 1980, p. 56.
Still not seen.

Green, Catherine S. "The Courtesy Novel (1740-1820): Women Writing for Women." Ann Arbor, Mich.: University Microfilms International, 1984.

Dissertation.

Gunn, J.A.W. *Beyond Liberty and Property: The Process of Self-Recognition in Eighteenth Century Political Thought.* McGill-Queen's University Press, 1983. Pp. xi+331. $35.00.

Rev. by Eldon John Eisenach in *Albion* 16 (1984): 55-56, as effectively drawing on pamphlets rather than great books to document "the complexity of those forms of political language which mark and help to guarantee non-revolutionary eras."

Haefner, Joel E. "The Shaper of the English Romantic Essay and the Spirit of the Age: Hazlitt, Lamb, and the *London Magazine*." Ann Arbor, Mich.: University Microfilms International, 1984. No. 2153A.

Dissertation.

Hodnett, Edward. *Images and Text. Studies in the Illustration of English Literature.* London: Scolar Press, 1982. Pp. viii+272. £17.50.

Rev. by Nicholas Pickwoad in *RES* 35 (1984): 272-75.

Hollander, John. "Poems That Talk to Themselves: Some Figurations of Modes of Discourse." *Shenandoah* 34 (1984) 3: 3-83.

Three subtle and rich meditations touching often on Blake and Keats in the course of understanding poetry. (T.L.A.)

Honnigshausen, Lothar. *Grundprobleme der englischen Literaturtheorie des neunzehnten Jahrhunderts.* (Erträge der Forschung, 71.) Darmstadt: Wissenschaftliche Buchgesellschaft, 1977. Pp. xiv+347. DM 48.00.

Rev. by Rudiger Ahrens in *Anglia* 102 (1984): 543-46. Not seen, and not previously listed.

Jack, Ian. *The Poet and His Audience.* Cambridge University Press, 1984. Pp. 198. £20.00; paper £6.95.

Rev. by Denis Donoghue as a surprisingly limited venture, sticking to "the external considerations, worldly procedures of buying and selling, a poet's promotion of his wares." The poets discussed are Dryden, Pope, Byron, Shelley, Tennyson, and Yeats.

Jack, R.D.S., and Andrew Noble, eds. *The Art of Robert Burns.*
London: Vision, 1984. Pp. 240. £13.95.

> Rev. by Emma Letley in *TLS*, April 6, 1984, p. 383.
> One of the essays, by Noble, takes up "a largely unremarked
> link with Blake," showing both "to be products of the Romantic
> insurrectionist impulse."

Jacobus, Mary. "The Art of Managing Books: Romantic Prose
and the Writing of the Past."

> See Reed, below.

Jarrett-Kerr, Martin. "Indian Religion in English Literature
1675-1967." *E&S* 37 (1984): 87-103.

> The main focus is on the Romantics, particularly Southey
> and Shelley.

Johnson, Mary Lynn, and Seraphia D. Leyda, eds. *Reconcilia-
tions: Studies in Honor of Richard Harter Fogle.* (SSEL,
Romantic Reassessment, 96. University of Salzburg.)
Atlantic Highlands, N.J.: Humanities Press, 1983. Pp. ix+
26. $25.00.

> Essays running from Shakespeare to Bellow (with a list of
> Professor Fogle's publications) include two on Blake, one on
> Coleridge, two on Keats.
> Mary Lynn Johnson, in "Blake's Judgment on the Book of
> Judges: The Watercolor Designs as Biblical Commentary"
> (41-71a; 5 illus.), shows that when Blake's Samson illustra-
> tions "are compared with their texts and placed within their
> iconographic traditions," they "take shape as an obique
> pictorial commentary on the Bible." Richard E. Johnson,
> in "Blake as Audience: The Designs to Gray's 'Ode on the
> Death of a Favourite Cat'" (72-94; 4 illus.), guided by
> Morris Eaves's expressivist theory of art, reads Blake as
> establishing "a whole series of re-readings that play off
> and undermine each other" and then turning upon himself
> "to examine self-consciously his own responses as an audience."
> Daniel M. McVeigh, in "Reconciliations in Coleridge's
> Politics" (95-110), reads Coleridge's "growing obsession
> with religious truth" as "a natural evolution in his thought,
> rather than an indication of its failure."
> Seraphia D. Leyda, in "The Structure of Keats's 'I stood
> tip-toe upon a little hill'" (111-28), impressively over-
> throws "the concensus [sic] opinion," argued by Fogle him-
> self, that this poem lacks coherent structure.
> W. Paul Elledge (129-52) investigates Keats's range "From
> Sonship to Fatherhood: Procreative and Paternal Imagery
> in Keats's 'Sleep and Poetry.'"

Kestner, Joseph. "Charlotte Brontë and Charlotte Elizabeth
  Tonna: A Possible Source for *Jane Eyre*." *PLL* 20 (1984):
  96-98.

  Tonna's (1790-1846) *The Museum* (1832), written for the
  Irish Religious Tract and Book Society, has a Jane and Edward
  in like circumstance. (T.L.A.)

Kincaid, James R., and Albert J. Kuhn, eds. *Victorian
  Literature and Society*. (Essays Presented to Richard D.
  Altick.) Ohio State University Press, 1983. Pp. viii+374.
  $25.00.

  Most essays are on Victorian fiction, but two touching the
  Romantics are "Genre and the Integration of Gender: From
  Wordsworth to George Eliot to Virginia Woolf," by U.C.
  Knoepflmacher (94-117), which begins with Wordsworth "as a
  reminder that male poets see themselves as possessing an
  imagination composed of interacting male and female elements"
  and ends with Woolf, "the daughter of a man who misread both
  Wordsworth and George Eliot" (111); and "Carlyle as Epic
  Historian" by John Clubbe (reviewed below, under "Carlyle").
  The index shows that most of the Romantics are cited, only
  Wordsworth and Scott and Carlyle heavily. Godwin and Woll-
  stonecraft of course get into Jerome Beaty's discussion of
  "Jane Eyre at Gateshead: Mixed Signals in the Text and
  Context" (168-96).

Klancher, John. "Reading the Social Text: Power, Signs, and
  Audience in Early Nineteenth-Century Prose." *SiR* 23 (1984):
  183-204.

  Examines the unsystematic and systematic attempts of the
  British magazines to revamp the "interpretive identity" of
  the middle-class audience, especially the self-conscious
  efforts of the *Edinburgh*, the *Examiner*, the *Quarterly*, the
  New Monthly, *Blackwood's*, the *London*, the *Westminster*, the
  Athenaeum, *Fraser's*, and the *Metropolitan* (a range from 1802
  to 1831).

Knight, G. Wilson. *Poets of Action*. Lanham, Md.: University
  Press of America, 1982. Pp. 320. $27.00; paper $14.24.

  Discusses Spenser, Milton, Swift, and Byron, as narrative
  artists deeply concerned with action.
  (Based on two earlier Knight books, *The Burning Oracle* and
  Chariot of Wrath.)
  Not seen.

Lease, Benjamin. *Anglo-American Encounters: England and the Rise of American Literature.* Cambridge University Press, 1981. Pp. xv+299. $29.95.

> Rev. by Robert E. Streeter in *NEQ* 57 (1984): 144-47.

Lehman, John. *Three Literary Friendships.* London: Quartet.

> Rev. by Alan Bold in *New Statesman*, Jan. 27, 1984, p. 26; by Peter Quennell in *S*, Jan. 14, 1984, p. 21.
> The three are Shelley-Byron, Verlaine-Rimbaud, and Frost-Thomas.
> Not seen; date and price not discovered.

Lloyd, Pamela. "Some New Information on Jane West." *N&Q* 31,iv (1984): 468-70.

> New biographical information on Jane West, who influenced Austen's and Scott's novels.

MacLaren, I.S. "Samuel Hearne & the Landscapes of Discovery." *CL* 103 (1984): 27-40.

Macovski, Michael St. "Failed Auditors: The Rhetoric of Romantic Colloquy, Coleridge to Conrad." Ann Arbor, Mich.: University Microfilms International.

> Dissertation. Includes Mary Shelley and Wordsworth.

Marshall, David. "Adam Smith and the Theatricality of Moral Sentiments." *Speculum* 59 (1984): 592-613.

McCormack, Kathleen. "The Sybil and the Hyena: George Eliot's Wollstonecraftian Feminism." *DR* 63 (1983-84): 602-14.

> The complaint of her lack of liberation is answered when Wollstonecraft is taken as the model. (T.L.A.)

Meisel, Martin. *Realizations: Narrative, Pictorial, and Theatrical Arts in Nineteenth-Century England.* Princeton University Press, 1983. Pp. xx+471. $45.00.

> Rev. by R.A. Donovan in *JAAC* 43 (1984-85): 93-96.
> Serial pictures, narrative painting, "pictorial" descriptions in fiction, *tableaux vivants*, dioramas, engravings, print shops, scene drops, book illustrations that were served by rather than served the text--these and other forms of popular art are studied in their interrelationships in this lavishly illustrated book that argues that each art "realized" the others: e.g., "the nineteenth century revealed a power-

ful bent in whole classes of fiction to assimilate themselves
with drama, while drama itself was under a compuslion to
make itself over as picture" (64). Although Meisel's extensive researches illuminate primarily Victorian fiction,
theater, and painting (and engraving), this book not in-
frequently deals with the Romantics. One will find, e.g., a
stray suggestion (197n) that Shelley's "pictorial" fragment
"A Vision of the Sea" could be profitably studied in the context of paintings of shipwrecks; or an analysis (Chapter
15) of the relations (by way of paintings) between Byron's
"Caritas Romana" stanzas in *Childe Harold* IV and Dickens's
Little Dorrit. In the excellent chapter "The Material Sublime: John Martin, Byron, and Turner," Meisel interrelates
Martin's paintings with Byron's *Sardanapalus* and *Manfred*,
productions of which by Alfred Bunn in 1834 "realized" some
of Martin's well-known paintings. The influences are many
and complex: Byron's verse dramas have a "pictorial" as well
as a "theatrical" sense of scene, Martin's paintings were
probably influenced by Byron's dramas, and the designer
brothers Grieve copied Martin's illustrations to *Paradise
Lost* in order to stage parts of *Manfred*. Martin informs us
that the nineteenth-century audiences were aware of such
exchanges among the sister arts, and he helps us to share
in that knowledge. (C.E.R.)

Mengel, Ewald. (Der englische historische Roman im 19. und
20. Jahrhundert: Aspekte der neueren Forschung." *Anglia*
102 (1984): 108-31; 437-55.

Useful survey. (B.C.H.)

Mintz, Samuel I.; Alice Chandler; and Christopher Mulvey, eds.
*From Smollett to James. Studies in the Novel and Other
Essays Presented to Edgar Johnson*. University Press of
Virginia, 1981. Pp. xiv+302. $24.95.

Rev. by Rosemary Ashton in *RES* 35 (1984): 269-70.
Not seen.

Mudge, Bradford K. "On Tennyson's The Princess: Sara Coleridge
in the *Quarterly Review*." *TWC* 15 (1984): 51-54.

Needham, John. *"The Competest Mode": I.A. Richards and the
Continuity of English Literary Criticism*. Edinburgh University Press, 1982. Pp. vii+210.

Rev. by J.S. Ryan in *AUMLA* 61 (1984): 103-04.
The Coleridgean influence is sustained everywhere.
(T.L.A.)

Newey, Vincent. *Cowper's Poetry: A Critical Study and Reassessment.* Totowa, N.J.: Barnes and Noble, 1982. Pp. 358.
$29.50.

   Rev. by Verlyn Klinkenberg in *ECS* 18 (1984): 89-92.

Oxenhorne, Harvey. "Water Music: Wordsworth, MacDiarmid,
and Frost." *SR* 20 (1984): 265-78.

Parker, Reeve. "Oh' Could You Hear His Voice!': Wordsworth,
Coleridge, and Ventriloquism."

   See Reed, below.

Peltason, Timothy. "Tennyson, Nature, and Romantic Nature
Poetry." *PQ* 63 (1984): 75-93.

Pelton, Marvin L. "Tennyson's Romantic Revisionism: A Study
of the Romantic Heritage in Tennyson's Early Poems, 1827-
42." Ann Arbor, Mich.: University Microfilms International,
1984.

   Dissertation.

Pereira, E. "The Poetic Image in English Romantic Poetry."
Unisa 22 (1984): 6-16.

   Concerns Byron, Hunt, Keats, Shelley.

Pinion, F.B. *A Tennyson Companion: Life and Works.* New York:
St. Martin's Press, 1984. Pp. 267; 17 illus. $27.50.

   At various stages of his intellectual journey, Tennyson's
reactions or relations to the Romantics, particularly Keats
and Wordsworth, are indicated.

Poovey, Mary. *The Proper Lady and the Woman Writer: Ideology
as Style in the Works of Mary Wollstonecraft, Mary Shelley,
and Jane Austen.* University of Chicago Press, 1984. Pp.
xxii+287. $20.00. (Inaugural volume in the new interdis-
ciplinary series *Women in Culture and Society,* ed. Catharine
R. Stimpson.)

   Rev. by Laurie A. Finke in *Genre* 17 (1984): 337-40; by
Deborah Kaplan in *Novel* 17,i (Fall 1983): 81-84 (with
Rachel Brownsten, *Becoming a Heroine: Reading about Women
in Novels*).
   What do you write if you are a female creative artist
living in a society that demands conformity to a constrictive
ideal--that of the proper lady who constantly embodies
feminine propriety in her behavior? This is the question

Mary Poovey sets out to explore in the lives and works of
Mary Wollstonecraft, Mary Shelley, and Jane Austen. With
its textual readings thoroughly grounded in biographical,
social, and literary reality, the book complements the rich
text-oriented reinterpretations of nineteenth-century women's
literature in *The Madwoman in the Attic* and brilliantly
displays another important strand in contemporary feminist
literary criticism.

Beginning with Mary Wollstonecraft, Poovey demonstrates
the different yet overlapping narrative strategies each
writer devised to reconcile the need to conform with the
desire to create politically and imaginatively. Since the
second *Vindication* scarcely permitted Wollstonecraft the
expression of her "finer sensations," she turned to the
novel. In *Maria*, it became clearer that Wollstonecraft's
political beliefs contradicted those "sensations" that
were so deeply related to the bourgeois values that she
sought to criticize. Textual hesitations and contradictions
reflect that tension: the narrator continually falls into
a "susceptibility to romantic expectaions which ... society
annexed to female sexuality." Wollstonecraft's own feelings
prevented her from resolving the paradox although she perceived the gap between her political realism and her sentimental idealism. Nonetheless, she could not relinquish the
old values.

Her attempt to construct a myth of the autonomous self
is faulty but determined and courageous. Sentimentalism
cannot work as a solution to spiritual impoverishment in
bourgeois society nor, in its denial of systemic oppression,
can it confront injustice.

Poovey concludes that a genre that promotes feeling and
expression--inevitable traps for women--will always be an
inadequate genre for any writer bent on asserting female
autonomy.

Mary Shelley tackled the problem differently, assuming the
pose of the "proper lady," yet consistently exploring the
imagination's quest for self-actualization. Through authorial
identification with more than one character in *Frankenstein*,
for example, Shelley avoided taking a "single definitive
position on her unladylike subject."

Exploring Jane Austen's texts, Poovey clarifies a central
tension between the heroine's independence and orthodox
endings. From *Pride and Prejudice* Poovey deduces that Austen
used the idea of propriety to introduce a necessary check
on female energy and passion. Her irony enabled her to
dramatize and reward individual desire and establish critical
distance from individualism. Simultaneously, then, she
endorsed individual rights and authoritarian structures.

Poovey's exposition of the relationship between gender,
social expectation, and literary style will help to relocate
contemporary feminist criticism--lately so exclusively focused
on the text--within a secure historical and cultural framework. An exemplary volume worth everyone's while. (M.F.)

Rapaport, Herman. *Milton and the Postmodern*. University of
Nebraska Press, 1983. Pp. xiv+270. $18.95.

No Romantics are named in the index, but Northrop Frye
gets bloodied for "thinking of Blake" and "Spenser's Saint
George's dragon" (229) when he should see that Milton is not
writing archetypal poetry. The busiest name in the index
is "Derrida," with "Foucault" and "Freud" and "Nietzsche"
trailing at some distance. (D.V.E.)

Reed, Arden, ed. *Romanticism & Language*. Cornell University
Press, 1984. Pp. 327. $39.50; paper $12.95.

Many approaches to Romanticism omit Byron because he
won't fit; many in the past omitted Blake. Strangely,
although apparently accidentally, this collection omits
both, even though they would have fit. As the title implies,
language is in the foreground in each essay, and deconstruction, although not dominant, is always lurking. All of the
essays emphasize the disappointments and frustrations, and
less frequently the joys, of language which is self-referen-
tial or otherwise meaningless. "Language is the neatest
trick" (Chase) might be the motto for the collection.
Because of the intricacy and specificity of the essays, any
summarizing below is strictly provisional and suggestive.
I can only hint at some of the labyrinths this book beckons
us to enter.

    For various reasons, it is convenient to consider the ten
essays in pairs. The two essays on Shelley emphasize the
necessity to acknowledge interpenetrating contraries within
the limits of language. Frances Ferguson, in "Shelley's
Mont Blanc: What the Mountain Said," follows Earl Wasserman
in emphasizing an "elaborate schema of reciprocity" in the
poem. She insists that the material world cannot be taken
as merely material because of the inevitability of humans'
seeing in terms of relationship. After some playing with
the puns in "Ravine" and "Arve," she makes her serious
point: "just as one can see the letters that go together
to make up 'Arve' and 'Ravine of Arve' as an example of the
material aspects of language but cannot see them as language
without seeing them as implying something more than matter,
so one can see the mountain as an example of materiality
but cannot see it even as a mountain without seeing it as

involving more than matter." She convincingly traces the
language of the poem in its movement from epistemological
questions to "love language in which all the questions are
of [the poet's] being understood."

Leslie Brisman's "Of Lips Divine and Calm: Swinburne
and the Language of Shelleyan Love" begins with Ruskin's
distinction between imagination contemplative (which con-
templates with the eye of God) and imagination penetrative
(which penetrates into the heart of man). It seems that
Swinburne and Shelley practice the former, which is more
abstract, and Shakespeare the latter, which is more concrete.

Brisman uses Ruskin's terms as a way of considering the
limits of language: "The limit of imagination penetrative
is the point beyond which song expressing desire for human
presence would actualize the godlike power of creating
another soul under the ribs of death. The limit of imagination contemplative is the bourn beyond which lies the realm
of the gods.... These are the limits of language in relation to which any actual poetic language must define itself."

Two sophisticated essays explore the rhetoric of Wordsworth. In "The Ring of Gyges and the Coat of Darkness:
Reading Rousseau with Wordsworth," Cynthia Chase brilliantly
explores ways in which Wordsworth's comments on invisibility
help to explain Rousseau's self-deception. Her texts are the
Sixth Promenade in which Rousseau wishes to be invisible
because he hates the ways that everyone misunderstands him
and the passage in *The Prelude* in which Wordsworth describes
a play with one character wearing the word "invisible" written
on his chest.

Chase leads us into the labyrinths of intention. Rousseau's
wish for invisibility is a reaction against the assigning
of intention to him by others, but supposes intentions in
others. "Such a motivation to find motives is the cause
or condition of the very predicament of which Rousseau
complains, the subversion of the correlation between intention and meaning.... The motive to establish motives is
the very condition of their ruin.... Hence the only possible
motive, for Rousseau, must be the avoidance of motivation."

But even that formula is not exact enough for Chase. Later
in the essay she finds her way beyond it: "We were wrong ...
to think that the identification of an utterance as fictional
could be adequately accounted for in terms of a motive to
deny motivation in order to defend the integrity of the
speaker. The loss of control evoked by such a claim can in
no way be motivated. Rather the claim itself repeats the
unmotivated gesture of the fiction 'Marion'" [referring to
her excellent discussion of the incident in which Rousseau
blames a servant girl for stealing a ribbon which he himself

had stolen].

She then uses Wordsworth's passage to explain what is
missing, repressed, or accidental in Rousseau. "Wordsworth's
irony embraces the fact that any work of poetry ... depends
for its effects on rhetorical devices requiring the compli-
city of the reader. That reading effect is magically
efficient in presenting the idea of invisibility, not so
much despite as because of the very paradox that when invisibility is made visible (by becoming readable) its
invisibility becomes invisible. Language is the neatest
trick."

In "Wordsworth's Rhetorical Theft," Timothy Bahti treats
the theft scenes of *Prelude* I as "prolegomenon to further
interpretation of the textual character and strategy of
Wordsworth's autobiography." As the self becomes itself,
explains Bahti, it appropriates objects to itself, and
therefore the objects become improper to themselves insofar
as they are property. Thus the self is dependent on render-
ing objects improper.

The relation between the mind of the poet and nature
becomes extremely problematic. When Wordsworth is hanging
over a bird's nest to steal eggs, the "sky seem'd not a
sky / Of earth." Bahti asks, "What does it mean for reality
to *seem*? And what does it mean for reality, in this mode
of semblance, to have *unreal* properties?" Later he continues
the idea: "For the forms neither *are* nor *are not* some
literal thing, but, like the cliff again, only appear like
or unlike something else." It turns out that "rhetorical
structure ... is the text's allegory of theft--of the attempt
to get from properties to *the proper* (self or understanding)
by ways of dispossession, transfer, and appropriation."

Two essays concentrate explicitly and simply on the ways
that writers become trapped in their language. Reeve Parker,
in "'Oh Could You Hear His Voice!': Wordsworth, Coleridge,
and Ventriloquism," sees *The Borderers* as displaying the
lives of Coleridge and Wordsworth, especially their quarrels.
Parker's thesis is threefold: (1) character is shaped in
response to narrative; (2) characters reenact the tales they
hear and become images of the teller; and (3) characters
become tragically bound to repeated actions. Thus also
Coleridge and Wordsworth.

Mary Jacobus, in "The Art of Managing Books: Romantic
Prose and the Writing of the Past," traces the fear "that
it is not we that write, but writing that writes us" in
several Romantic prose writers. De Quincey's prose, for
example, reveals him to be a "helpless passenger on an out-
of-control vehicle that threatens death to what he holds
dear."

Two essays brilliantly explore Coleridge's word traps.
Arden Reed's "The Mariner Rimed" is an entertaining and
illuminating meditation on the pun "rime." It seems that
rime may be either a delusion (like fog) or a sanctification
(like a halo). Reed maintains that it is both/and, not
either/or. When Life-in-Death rimes (freezes the blood
of) the Mariner, the paradoxial transformation at once
curses and saves him. "She freezes or rimes him precisely
so that he can go on rhyming indefinitely." The blessing
scene continues this doubleness: the "blessing is insepara-
ble from his curse ... he is simultaneously saved and
damned." The duplicity of "bless" and "be blessed ...
effectively unhinges them from their referents and reveals
them to be rhetorical figures deployed by the rime." Thus,
"language precedes and constitutes the Ancient Mariner's
selfhood."

Jerome Christensen, in "The Mind at Ocean: The Impropriety of Coleridge's Literary Life," rewrites Chapter 4
of his brilliant *Coleridge's Blessed Machine of Language*
(see *RMB* for 1981, pp. 57-58). The basis of his approach
is the pun property/propriety: "What is property? is so
nearly the same question as what is propriety? that for
Coleridge the answer to one is involved in the solution of
the other. The solution of both involves the question of
meaning itself."

Beginning with Coleridge's comparison between a ship
image in *The Merchant of Venice* and Gray's "imitation" of
it, which lacks propriety, Christensen carries us on to the
man of the letter who interrupts the *Biographia Literaria*.
This interruption is crucial "because it is without any
genealogy whatsoever. The man of the letter is a man of
the text he interrupts."

Two essays treat Keats as the ultimate poet in dealing
with these problems of language. In "The Language of
Interpretation in Romantic Poetry: 'A Strong Working of
the Mind,'" Susan Wolfson traces a problem from "The Rime
of the Ancient Mariner" through "The Thorn" and "La Belle
Dame sans Merci" to "Ode on a Grecian Urn" in which Keats
"not only makes a premise of the problems of interpretation
all these lyrical ballads trace with increasing intensity,
but extends that negotiation with uncertainty to the
reader's engagement with the play of his rhyme."

She begins by emphasizing the "ambiguity of signs" as
exemplified by the albatross, "that is, the ambiguity
with which the external world vexes a desire for interpretive certainty." In "The Thorn," Wordsworth invites the
reader to ask, "What manner of mind is this?" and does
not solve the question for us with his interpretive authority.

When Wolfson arrives at the Odes, she especially focuses
on one line: "The teetering syntax of 'All breathing human
passion far above'--first promoting, then subverting, a
coordination between the 'happy love' on the urn and the
highest promise of 'human passion'--becomes significant not
only for what it would describe, but for the way it behaves.
Just as the urn's art resists decisive interpretation, so
that one line entangles nearly every reader who has studied
Keats's Ode." Similarly, "Urn and aphorism [Beauty is
truth ...] together go round and round, each serenely
self-enclosed, endlessly circular, resonating with mysterious
promise, but 'still unravish'd' at last."
    Finally, Richard Macksey ends the collection with that
most famous of Romantic closures in his "'To Autumn' and
the Music of Mortality: 'Pure Rhetoric of a Language
without Words,'" one of the best essays I have seen on this
ode. Keats practiced a "progressive unselving as the means
of achieving the absolute. In this manner he sought to resolve the Romantic division of the human and the ideal."
Because Keats was too honest, Macksey finds him doomed to
failure except through imaginative evasion.
    Macksey points out that no one has adequately "accounted
for the paradoxically *rhetorical* character of this poem....
The three 'moments' figured by the three strophes correspond,
in fact, to the three major rhetorical strategies, early
and late, of Romantic nature poetry. The progression is,
simply stated, from symbolic to allegorical to ironic. The
last stanza, however, points the way to a new landscape
whose music has displaced the more familiar linguistic disjunctions of subject and object, of inside and outside, of
simultaneity and succession. If Keats is supremely a liminal
poet, he crosses here three thresholds, the last of which
admits of no return." (M.T.S.)

Rignall, J.M. "The Historical Double: *Waverley, Sylvia's
    Lover, The Trumpet-Major.*" *EiC* 34 (1984): 14-32.

Robertson, P.J.M. "Criticism and Creativity." *QQ* 91 (1984):
    66-72, 336-46, 665-78, 941-53.

    While we may not agree with this continuing essay's
initial premise, "that criticism is [not] necessarily
inferior to imaginative literature," we are soon lured to
its argument because of thorough grounding in the works of
the English Romantic poets who figure throughout as a central
subject. With two segments yet to be published, it appears
that the poetic masterpieces encountered result in a far
more serious argument than that suggested initially. (T.L.A.)

Scheuermann, Mona. "Redefining the Filial Tie: Eighteenth-
Century English Novelists from Brooke to Bage." *EA* 37,iv
(1984): 385-98.

"By the 1790s reason is the rule by which all human
beings are to be judged; parents are to be judged no
differently from others." Parents in these novels are
assessed or evaluated according to their ability to educate
and not oppress their children. An excellent survey of
progressive or radical novels. (J.C.R.)

Streatfield, David C., and Alistair M. Duckworth. *Landscape
in the Gardens and the Literature of Eighteenth-Century
England. Papers Read at a Clark Library Seminar 18 March
1978.* Los Angeles, 1981. Pp. viii+138.

Rev. by April London in *RES* 35 (1984): 89-90.

Thesing, William B. *The London Muse: Victorian Poetic
Responses to the City.* University of Georgia Press, 1982.
Pp. xviii+230. $20.00.

Rev. by Emily Auerbach in *WHR* 38 (1984): 82-84; said to
contain discussion of Blake and Wordsworth.

Van Anglen, Kevin P. "Emerson, Milton, and the Fall of Uriel."
ESQ 30 (1984): 139-53.

Very good on the change in consciousness leading from
Locke to Coleridge. (T.L.A.)

Venis, Linda. "The Problem of Broadside Balladry's Influence
on the *Lyrical Ballads*." *SEL* 24 (Autumn 1984): 617-32.

Voorhees, Richard J. "Chesterton the Romantic." *QQ* 91 (1984):
17-26.

Watson, Ian. *Song and Democratic Culture in Britain: An
Approach to Popular Culture in Social Movements.* New York:
St. Martin's Press, 1983. Pp. 247. $25.00.

Rev. by Roy T. Matthews in *Albion* 16 (1984): 203-04, as
valuable if not altogether theoretically convincing.
Not seen.

Williams, Merryn. *Women in the English Novel 1800-1900.*
London: Macmillan; New York: St. Martin's, 1984. Pp.
xiv+201. $20.00.

Rev. as "hopelessly timid" by Oliver Harris in *New Statesman*, Aug. 3, 1984, p. 26.

The opening chapter usefully scans the situation of women
in society and the novel. Chapter 2 outlines beliefs about
the influence of ideology on women's lives. After that,
single chapters on Austen, the Brontës, Eliot, and Gaskell
are interspersed with chapters on Scott and Dickens. The
sexist attitudes of male novelists are exposed in a somewhat
old-fashioned, schematized approach, classified as "Male
Images of Women."
    One potentially interesting chapter on Edgeworth, Ferrier,
Gore, Martineau, and Frances Trollope succumbs to an evaluation of their "real contribution" to the early nineteenth-
century novel. The last chapter addresses the emergence
of the "New Women" in Meredith and the like. (M.F.)

Wolfson, Susan. "The Language of Interpretation in Romantic
    Poetry: 'A Strong Working of the Mind.'"
        See Reed, above.

Reviews of books previously listed:

AERS, David; Jonathan Cook; and David Punter, *Romanticism
    and Ideology: Studies in English Writing 1765-1830* (see
    RMB for 1981, p. 55), rev. by Mark Roberts in *RES* 35 (1984):
    385-88; by Clifford Siskin in *CLS* 21 (1984): 227-28 as
    "relentlessly aggressive" but "very valuable"; ASHTON,
    Rosemary, *The German Idea: Four English Writers and the
    Reception of German Thought 1800-1860* (see *RMB* for 1981,
    p. 56), rev. by Paul Hamilton in *RES* 35 (1984): 397-98;
    BUTLER, Marilyn, *Romantics, Rebels, and Reactionaries* (see
    RMB for 1981, pp. 56-57), rev. by Frederick W. Shilstone in
    SHR 18 (1984): 178-80; CHURCHILL, Kenneth, *Italy and English
    Literature 1764-1930* (see *RMB* for 1982, p. 59), rev. by
    Silvia Albertazzi in *RES* 35 (1984): 270-71; COOKE, Michael G.,
    *Acts of Inclusion: Studies Bearing on an Elemental Theory
    of Romanticism* (see *RMB* for 1979, p. 52), rev. by Marshall
    Brown in *CRCL* 11 (1984): 132-35; HART, Francis R., *The
    Scottish Novel* (see *RMB* for 1979, p. 54), rev. by Cairns
    Craig in *SSL* 15 (1980): 302-10; HARVEY, A.D., *English
    Poetry in a Changing Society, 1780-1825* (see *RMB* for 1981,
    p. 61), rev. by E.B. Murray in *RES* 35 (1984): 96-98; KEITH,
    W.J., *The Poetry of Nature: Rural Perspectives in Poetry from
    Wordsworth to the Present* (see *RMB* for 1980, pp. 58-59),
    rev. by April London in *RES* 35 (1984): 89-90; KING, Everard
    H., *James Beattie* (see *RMB* for 1979, p. 55), rev. by Robert
    T. Eberwein in *SSL* 15 (1980): 286-88; LEVINE, George, *The
    Realistic Imagination: English Fiction from Frankenstein to
    Lady Chatterley* (see *RMB* for 1982, pp. 63-64), rev. by Robert

O'Kell in *QQ* 91 (1984): 448-49; LIPKING, Lawrence, *The Life of the Poet: Beginning and Ending Poetic Careers* (see *RMB* for 1982, p. 64), rev. by Stuart Curran in *SAR* 49 (1984): 109-111; LIPKING, Lawrence, ed., *High Romantic Argument: Essays for M.H. Abrams* (see *RMB* for 1981, pp. 63-64), rev. by James H. Averill in *SiR* 22 (1983): 632-36; by Mark Roberts in *RES* 35 (1984): 558-60; McFARLAND, Thomas, *Romanticism and the Forms of Ruin: Wordsworth, Coleridge, and Modalities of Fragmentation* (see *RMB* for 1981, p. 64), rev. by Michael G. Cooke in *SiR* 22 (1983): 617-23; by Lucy Newlyn in *RES* 35 (1984): 388-89; MELLOR, Anne K., *English Romantic Irony* (see *RMB* for 1980, p. 60), rev. by Ian Donaldson in *YES* 14 (1984): 331-32; by Janice Haney-Peritz in *SiR* 22 (1983): 111-19; MORGAN, Peter F., *Literary Critics and Reviewers in Early Nineteenth-Century Britain* (see *RMB* for 1983, p. 63), rev. by Kenneth Curry in *VPR* 17 (1984): 67-68; by Philip Flynn in *ES* 65 (1984): 581-82; MORSE, David, *Perspectives on Romanticism* (see *RMB* for 1982, p. 72), rev. by David Simpson in *SiR* 22 (1983): 462-67, quite severely, as full of "very winning minute particulars ... subsumed within a shaky transformational analysis" and often dependent simply on what the author "happens to have read"; NUSSBAUM, Felicity A., *The Brink of All We Hate: English Satires on Women 1660-1750* (see *RMB* for 1983, p. 64), rev. by Douglas Brooks-Davies in *TLS*, June 15, 1984, p. 678, as "thorough and tactful, perhaps too tactful"; PRICKETT, Stephen, ed., *The Romantics* (see *RMB* for 1981, p. 66), rev. by Mark Roberts in *RES* 35 (1984): 385-88; SALES, Roger, *English Literature in History 1780-1830: Pastoral and Politics* (see *RMB* for 1983, pp. 65-66), rev. by Mitzi Myers in *KSJ* 33 (1984): 231-34; SCHAPIRO, Barbara A., *The Romantic Mother: Narcissistic Patterns in Romantic Poetry* (see *RMB* for 1983, pp. 66-67), rev. by Thomas R. Frosch in *KSJ* 33 (1984): 208-09; WENDORF, Richard, ed., *Articulate Images* (see *RMB* for 1983, p. 29), rev. by Graham Reynolds in *TLS*, May 25, 1984, p. 578, emphasizing Robert Wark's condemnation of the methods of contributors who "shut their eyes when discussing pictures"; WOLF, Bryan J., *Romantic Re-Vision: Culture and Consciousness in Nineteenth-Century American Painting and Literature* (see *RMB* for 1983, p. 68), rev. (with Karen Halttunen, *Confidence Men and Women: A Study of Middle-Class in America, 1830-1870*) by Eric J. Sundquist in *Criticism* 26 (1984): 277-81; YOUNG, Howard T., *The Line in the Margin: Juan Ramon Jimenez and His Readings in Blake, Shelley, and Yeats* (see *RMB* for 1983, pp. 68-69), rev. by Dario Fernández-Morera in *CRCL* 11 (1984): 317-19.

Composite review:

Auerbach, Nina. "Recent Studies in the Nineteenth Century."
  SEL (Autumn 1984): 769-94.

  The first ten pages of the journal's regular annual survey
  are devoted to books on the following Romantic writers,
  individually and in selected groupings: Hazlitt, Blake,
  Clare, Wordsworth, Coleridge, Byron, the Shelleys, Scott,
  Wollstonecraft, and Austen. This year's reviewer also has
  kind words to say about *RMB* for 1982.

Review essays:

Bloom, Harold. "Inescapable Poe." *NYRB*, Oct. 11, 1984, pp.
  23-37.

  Although the critical view is Bloom's own, two books serve
  as the point of departure: Patrick F. Quinn, ed., *Edgar
  Allan Poe: Poetry and Tales* (The Library of America, 1984;
  pp. 1,408; $27.50), and G.R. Thompson, ed., *Edgar Allan Poe:
  Essays and Reviews* (The Library of America, 1984; pp. 1,544;
  $27.50).

Fry, Paul H. "Literature and Our Discontents." *YR* 73 (1983-
  84): 603-16.

  Exigent criticism of Jerome McGann's *The Romantic Ideology*
  (see above, "General 3. Criticism"), Terry Eagleton's
  Literary Theory: An Introduction (University of Minnesota
  Press, 1983), and Helen Vendler's *The Odes of John Keats*
  (see *RMB* for 1983, pp. 120-21). Being reviewed by Paul Fry
  is like being mugged by the Pope--something between a mis-
  fortune and an honor. He is at his best here: smart, funny,
  trendy, yet serious about culture and criticism, and admirable
  for the precise elegance of his prose. (R.M.R.)

Jackson, Mary. *ECS* 17 (1984): 367-69.

  Reviews Samuel Pickering's *John Locke and Children's Books
  in Eighteenth-Century England* (see *RMB* for 1982, p. 51), as
  a "learned and graceful book" that is "hard to put down."
  The reviewer manages to do that by calling attention to
  "many matters" overlooked. The book and the review together
  suggest both a theory and a syllabus.

4. STUDIES OF AUTHORS

AUSTEN

Andersen, Walter E. "From Northanger to Woodston: Catherine's Education to Common Life." *PQ* 63 (1984): 493-509.

Boyd, Zelda. "Jane Austen's 'Must': The Will and the World." *NCF* 39 (1984): 127-43.

Cerny, Lothar. "Das gute Ende des Romans: Jane Austens *Persuasion*." *Anglia* 102 (1984): 80-100.

Gilson, David. "Jane Austen's Verses." *BC* 33 (1984): 25-37.

Records the whereabouts of the manuscripts of 15 Austen poems (two still unfound) and of five others, not hers, in her hand.

Halperin, John. "The Novelist as Heroine in *Mansfield Park*: A Study in Autobiography." *MLQ* 44 (1983): 136-56.

Hardy, John. *Jane Austen's Heroines: Intimacy in Human Relationships*. London, Boston, Melbourne, and Henley: Routledge & Kegan Paul, 1984. Pp. xvi+133. $25.00.

In the first sentence of this study Hardy quotes Elizabeth Hardwick's warning that Austen "is much more fun to read than to read about"--but is not deterred. Using the loose link that for all Austen's heroines "an essential element is the potential, at least, that exists for the kind of intimacy which involves a mutual recognition of the other parties and leads to a shared privacy" (xii), Hardy offers a short chapter on each of the six major heroines. Since the heroines are central to the stories, analyses of their human relationships inevitably skirt the edge of becoming plot summaries. Hardy does this adroitly, producing what is in effect a variant on the theme of the education of Austen's heroines. (J.E.J.)

Honan, Park. "Jane Austen and Marriage." *ContR* 245 (Nov. 1984): 253-59

Provides the details of Austen's brief engagement in 1802.

Hopkinson, David. "A Niece of Jane Austen." *N&Q* 31,iv (1984): 470-71.

Mrs. Hubback, Austen's niece, was a prolific writer whose works are now almost unknown. Hopkinson provides some biographical data.

Johnson, Claudia L. "The 'Operations of Time, and the
    Changes of the Human Mind': Jane Austen and Dr. Johnson
    Again." *MLQ* 44 (1983): 23-38.

Keener, Frederick M. *The Chain of Becoming: The Philosophical
    Tale, the Novel, and a Neglected Realism of the Enlightenment:
    Swift, Montesquieu, Voltaire, Johnson, and Austen.*
    Columbia University Press, 1983. Pp. 344.

    Rev. by Carol Blum in *RR* 75 (1984): 112-12.

Lane, Maggie. *Jane Austen's Family through Five Generations.*
    U.K.: Hale, 1984.

    Rev. by Peter Quennell in *S*, Sept. 29, 1984, p. 30, as
    "an informative and illuminating book."
    Not seen.

Leavis, Q.D. *Collected Essays. 1. The Englishness of the
    English Novel.* Ed. G. Singh. Cambridge University Press,
    1984. Pp. ix+352. $44.50; paper $15.95.

    Half the volume consists of Q.D. Leavis's essays on Jane
    Austen; the rest of "A fresh approach to Wuthering Heights,"
    her introductions to the novels of Charlotte Brontë and
    George Eliot, and her 1980 lecture which gives this volume
    its subtitle. A very brief Introduction; pithy notes.

Le Fay, Deirdre. "The Nephew Who Missed Jane Austen." *N&Q*
    31,iv (1984): 471-72.

    An attempt to identify a nephew mentioned but unnamed in
    James Edward Austen-Leigh's *Memoir* of Jane Austen.

McDonnell, Jane. "'A Little Spirit of Independence': Sexual
    Politics and the Bildungsroman in *Mansfield Park.*" *Novel:
    A Forum on Fiction* 17 (1984): 197-214.

Richards, Bill. "Jane Austen Birthday to Be Noted Proudly,
    Without Prejudice." *Wall Street Journal*, Nov. 27, 1984,
    pp. 1, 20.

    For the right kind of girl anything is possible. (T.L.A.)

Rosmarin, Adena. "'Misreading' *Emma*: The Powers and Per-
    fidies of Interpretive History." *ELH* 51 (1984): 315-42.

Searle, Catherine R. "Prose Style in the Works of Jane
    Austen." Ann Arbor, Mich.: University Microfilms Inter-
    national, 1984. No. 2155A.

    Dissertation.

Sense and Sensibility. With an afterword by Patricia Meyer Spacks. New York: Bantam Books, 1983. Pp. 346. Paper $2.50.

The "afterword" (333-46) points out the complexities beneath the apparent simplicity, the clarity beneath the ironies of concealment, and offers a current "Bibliography" (344-46).

Siskin, Clifford. "A Formal Development: Austen, the Novel, and Romanticism." *CentR* 28,iv--29,i (1984-85): 1-28.

Austen's novels are a means for "examining the problem of literary change ... to clarify both how we can identify innovative activity and how such literary innovation inter-relates with change in other forms of discourse."

Wiesenfarth, Joseph. "The Case of *Pride and Prejudice.*" *SNNTS* 16 (1984): 261-73.

Yeazell, Ruth Bernard. "The Boundaries of Mansfield Park." *Representations* no. 7 (Summer 1984): 133-52.

See also Duffy ("English 2. Environment"); Lloyd, Poovey, Williams ("English 3. Criticism"); Nollen ("Radcliffe").

Reviews of books previously listed:

DE ROSE, Peter, and S.W. McGuire, *A Concordance to the Works of Jane Austen* (see *RMB* for 1982, p. 72), rev. by G.E. Bentley, Jr. ("Jane Austen's Range of Language") in *UTQ* 54 (1984): 119-23; by David Gilson in *Library* 6 (1984): 195-96, who, as biographer and bibliographer, worries about the textual basis; GILSON, David, ed., *A Bibliography of Jane Austen* (see *RMB* for 1982, p. 73), rev. by Andrew Wright in *NCF* 39 (1984): 95-99; WALLACE, Robert K., *Jane Austen and Mozart: Classical Equilibrium in Fiction and Music* (see *RMB* for 1983, p. 73), rev. by Claudia Johnson in *NCF* 39 (1984): 336-39.

BECKFORD

Orlando, Francesco. "Vathek, o la dannazione dell' 'enfant gâté.'" *Saggi e Ricerche di Letteratura Francese* 23 (1984): 277-303.

Sichère, Bernard. "Je, Beckford." *L'Infini* 8 (Autumn 1984): 64-70.

Interview with Sichère, mainly on Beckford's sexual life.

Sichère, Bernard. *Je, William Beckford.* Paris: Lenoël, 1894.
   Pp. 364.
      Rev. by Christine Jordis in *QL* 428 (Nov. 16-30, 1984): 12.

BEDDOES

See Priestman ("Coleridge").

BENTHAM

Goldworth, Anmon, ed. *Deontology together with a Table of
   the Springs of Action and the Article on Utilitarianism.*
   (Collected Works of Bentham.) Oxford University Press,
   1983. Pp. xxxvi+394. $79.00.
      See review essay, on the importance of acquaintance with
   some of Bentham's texts—although both "fascinating and disappointing, brilliant and naive, wonderfully skeptical and
   not skeptical enough"—by Robert Maniquis in *RP&P* 9,i (1985):
   83-89.

BLACKWOOD'S EDINBURGH MAGAZINE

Alexander, J.H. "*Blackwood's*: Magazine as Romantic Form."
   TWC 15 (1984): 57-68.

See also Klancher ("English 3. Criticism").

BLAKE

Adlard, John. "Blake and Wimbledon." *N&Q* 31,iv (1984): 468.
      The first telegraph system, which crossed Wimbledon,
   reminded Blake of his relay of messenger larks.

Alford, Steven E. *Irony and the Logic of the Romantic Imagination.* (American University Studies. Series III, Comparative
   Literature, 13.) New York: Peter Lang, 1984. Pp. 177.
   Paper $19.45.
      This book would make a good companion to Howard (see review
   in this section). This is weak where that is strong, and
   vice versa. The conception here is exciting, but the execu-

tion is disappointing. Of course part of the problem is the
resistance of Alford's ideas to simple summary so that they
can be grasped. In some ways, that is the whole point.
Alford equates "romantic irony with the modern notion of
the performative (language whose intention is a 'force' toward
an effect rather than a reference to a meaning)." "Romantic
irony appears mainly as a dialectic, except for those epiphantic moments of Unity, when it comes into its own as the
performative." The way that Alford sees Romantic irony
working is provocative but somehow unsatisfying: "in an
attempt to understand a work we assume that there is a content
to the work.... [T]hat leads to the error that the content
of the work is its *meaning*." The ironist sets up "a dilemma
that will throw our attempts at understanding into an endless
negative dialectical spiral." The writer will "exhaust the
understanding in order to make way for an imaginative, unifying 'spiritual' completion of the work."
     The first five chapters explore Schlegel's irony, especially
in *Über die Unverständlichkeit*. According to Alford, the
German Romantics saw irony "neither as a technical rhetorical
trope nor as a stylistic device, but as a metaphysical term
which best embodied their epistemology, and for some of the
German Romantics, 'irony' was of cosmological significance."
     Alford's discussion of Schlegel gives us hints toward his
final three chapters on Blake. "For our purposes, Schlegel's
most important assumption is the literal existence of, or
continuous spiritual access to, 'infinity' ... and the romantic necessity to 'bind' infinitude with finitude." According
to Alford, Schlegel's writing performs rather than argues
or narrates unity: "The assent of a reader who has 'understood' Schlegel's writing is not a nod of the head, or a sense
of completion following a well structured argument, but more
likely a laugh."
     When Alford comes to apply his method to a text, *The Marriage
of Heaven and Hell*, it is again exciting in conception but
disappointing in execution. He begins by setting out three
possible levels of irony: (1) Blake may be the voice of the
Devil, but that reading is too oversimplified; (2) Blake may
be both Angel and Devil, but that reading reconciles the
contraries too easily; (3) "An imaginative reading of the
MHH would assert both heaven and hell at once.... [W]hat
we need to do is to cointend heaven and hell, but not attempt
to reconcile them."
     Despite the problems in clarity, I think that Alford has
something very valuable here, an insistence on contraries
which do not always submit themselves to logic. "A proper
reading of the prophecies ... consists in the irreducibly
dualistic (or contrary) activity of an unending Generational,

discursive attempt to grasp the 'meaning' of the text ... combined with the epiphantic, performative affect of a 'dialectical,' Edenic reading of the text." Whatever its flaws, this book deserves the attention of every Blake scholar. (M.T.S.)

Anderson, Mark R. "Apollyon's Bow: Perspective, Reading, and Meaning in the Illuminated Works of William Blake." Ann Arbor, Mich.: University Microfilms International, 1984. No. 2475A.

   Dissertation.

Anderson, Mark. "Oothoon, Failed Prophet." *RP&P* 8,ii (1984): 1-21.

Baine, Rodney M. "Blake's Sons of Los." *PQ* 63 (1984): 239-54.

Beer, John. *William Blake. 1757-1827.* (Writers & Their Work.) Windsor, Berks.: Profile Books, 1982. Pp. 52. Paper £15.0.

   An excellent, lively introduction, with a well-chosen "Select Bibliography."
   "Blake might seem in his later years to have shut himself off deliberately from the world about him. But as one penetrates further into his life and work, one comes to see that his firm independence" sustained his capacity for "serving the cause of human freedom" (46).

Bentley, G.E., Jr. "The 1821 Edwards Catalogue." *BIQ* 17 (1984): 154-56.

Bentley, G.E., Jr. "The Felpham Rummer: A New Angel and 'Immoral Drink' Attributed to William Blake." *BIQ* 18 (1984): 94-99; illus.

   If Blake inscribed these lines of "ANGUISH" on a drinking cup in "AUG 1803," they could tell of his feelings during the Scolfield business.

Berninghausen, Thomas F. "The Marriage of Contraries in 'To Tirzah.'" *CLQ* 20 (1984): 191-98.

Borges, Jorge Luis, and Gert Schiff. "Blake in Heaven and Hell." *FMR* 3 (1984): 67-94; illus.

   Extracts from Borges's commentary on *The Divine Comedy.* Schiff deals (88-90) with Blake and Dante. (Many reproductions of Blake's Dante designs.)

Bracher, Mark. "The Metaphysical Grounds of Oppression in Blake's *Visions of the Daughters of Albion*." *CLQ* 20 (1984): 164-76.

A closely reasoned and convincing explication of the moral and philosophical perspectives represented by Bromion (empiricism/hedonism), Theotormon (idealism/religion), and Oothoon (organicism/process metaphysics). A very condensed preview of Bracher's book now in the press--from which we may all expect insight and comfort: or the challenge to attain these. (D.V.E.)

BRH: Bulletin of Research in the Humanities 84,iii (Autumn 1981--actually 1984).

"Blake and the Night Sky": articles by David Worrall, "The 'Immortal Tent'" (276-95); David V. Erdman, "Art against Armies" (296-304); and Paul Miner, "Visionary Astronomy" (305-36; 15 illus.).
The star charts of Blake's day had many now-forgotten constellations, from pump and printing-press and hot-air balloon to the Harp of George II, to the Lynx or Tiger (Tigris). Familiar with those charts, Miner and Worrall are able to identify numerous particulars in Blake's fiery songs.
Erdman discusses Blake's use of the night sky as a staging area for a war of images anticipating modern media.
In the same issue Patrick J. Keane turns to Blake's successor, Yeats: "The Human Entrails and the Starry Heavens: Some Instances of Visual Art as Patterns for Yeats's Mingling of Heaven and Earth" (366-91).
Christopher Heppner concentrates, not on the heavens, but on "Reading Blake's Designs: *Pity* and *Hecate*" (337-65; illus.). The relation between *Pity* and the images of the text (in *Macbeth*) is shown to be that Blake has taken a group of "partly alternative, partly conflated images and visualized them quite separately, putting them into dynamic relationship with each other." As for the so-called *Hecate* (not Blake's title) the challenge Heppner meets--impressively-- is to read a picture whose only "text" is its own visual signs. (D.V.E.)

Chayes, Irene H. "Blake's Ways with Art Sources: Michelangelo's *The Last Judgment*." *CLQ* 20 (1984): 60-89; 13 illus.

Here is much valuable instruction in the suitable "ways" to make critical use of what we can discover of "Blake's use of the work of other artists for purposes of his own"-- a subject upon which "art historians have had little to say."

After some careful refinement of the distinction between
copying and borrowing, eight Blake designs are shown to
have drawn closely upon figures and details in Michelangelo.
Much of this is convincing and helpful. Unhappily Chayes
is too quick to dismiss the possibility of Blake's own
purposes in *America*, plate 6, as discoverable in the text
or even the prophetic context. Reading *America* as a prophecy
published soon after the beheading of the King of France,
most of us see a revolutionary tribunal with flaming sword
weighing a king in the balance, finding him wanting, and
delivering him to flames and the Serpent's coils. Chayes
sees the little king in three positions as three people--
thus freezing the action and the significance. Even so,
her close attention to detail leads her to find an analogue
to the posture of the third figure--in the "pseudo-headless
pose" of the trumpeter in Blake's *Night Thoughts* 38--which
is precisely helpful as strengthening the idea that the
America picture is prophetic, that it shows what *has*
happened to King Louis and what *will* happen to King George.
He has not *yet* lost his head, but we see that he *will* lose
it if he *does* (pun). (D.V.E.)

Author's comment: My point about *America* 5 (noted only
incidentally) is simply that the figures adapted from
Michelangelo's angels and falling sinners, together with
the attributes of the Archangel Michael--the defender of
Heaven, of course, not one of the rebels himself--serve to
evoke the rebellion, defeat, and expulsion of Lucifer and
thereby to supplement thematically the cryptic allusion to a
lost leader ("our center") in the text on the same plate.
The serpent coils are symbolic or diagrammatic, as elsewhere in Blake, not a means of punishment. If the design
is "prophetic," it predicts defeat and fall for the later
avatars of Lucifer, including (if Erdman insists on
historical analogy) the revolutionary movement in Europe.
The descending figure with head strained back (it was
Erdman who originally saw him as "headless") recurs often
in Blake; see my p. 77. As for the *Night Thoughts* trumpeter,
he would be a Judgment Day angel summoning the shrouded
skeleton to literal or metaphorical resurrection even without reference to the two different Michelangelo scenes I
cite. Finally, in indubitable political "cartoons" Blake
is almost as broad as Gillray; why would he conceal a
gratifyingly Oedipal threat to King George in a picture
that most plausibly shows, in recognizable, traditional
terms, the *defeat* of rebellion? (I.H.C.)

Connolly, Thomas E. "Point of View in Interpreting 'The Fly.'"
    ELN 22 (1984): 32-37.

Cramer, Patricia. "The Role of Ahania's Lament in Blake's
  Book of Ahania: A Psychological Study." *JEGP* 83 (1984):
  522-33.

Crehan, Stewart. *Blake in Context*. Dublin: Gill and
  Macmillan, 1984. Pp. 364; 15 illus. £25.00; $47.50.

  Rev. by Paul Hamilton (see composite review, below) with
  this summarizing comment: "What Blake saw with biblical
  assurance in the class-struggle of his day is now clearly
  applicable to the Third World where Stewart Crehan teaches.
  His admiration for Blake could not be more apt."
  All of us who study and teach Blake will benefit from
  this book--our students especially. Crehan, for instance,
  goes beyond previous historical readings of "The Tyger" by
  going more thoroughly into the "*relative*, not *absolute*"
  social and political meanings "embedded in the poem's basic
  symbolism" (125). And in Book I of *Milton*, the imagery of
  work and different work processes, "too often ... treated
  by critics as secondary to a philosophic or autobiographical
  scheme, whose meaning lies above or outside the social
  process," is seen as functioning in a narrative which is "a
  kind of allegory of the whole social order: what it is,
  how it has been upset and how it can be restored, as well as
  the artist's place within it" (171). As for Los who was
  Urthona, "Blake's mythical smith has many qualities that
  lie not in the poet's head but in those social and historical
  realities of which the poet felt himself intuitively to be
  a part: the smith is of ancient origin ... he is ... indispensable to society; he is a fierce rebel (as were the
  Jacobin blacksmiths of Paris); his role as a kind of founder
  of industrial and economic progress connects him with ...
  progressive energies ... and his 'eternal' nature has a
  connection with real life [for] the blacksmith's skills were
  some of the last to be extinguished by the industrial revolution" (174-75).
  Minute social particulars are brought to bear upon each
  text examined. (D.V.E.)

Davies, William. Review of *Blake*, a two-act opera by Andrew
  Gant. *Opera* 35 (1984): 692.

Essick, Robert N. "Blake in the Marketplace, 1982-1983."
  BIQ 18 (1984): 68-93.

Essick, Robert N. "Some Unrecorded States, Printings, and
  Impressions of Blake's Graphic Works." *BIQ* 17 (1984): 130-
  38; illus.

Essick, Robert N. "A Supplement to *The Separate Plates of*
    William Blake: A Catalogue." *BIQ* 17 (1984):   139-44;
    1 illus.

Glen, Heather. *Vision and Disenchantment: Blake's Songs and*
    Wordsworth's Lyrical Ballads. Cambridge University Press,
    1983. Pp. ix+399. $44.50; paper $9.95.

>   Rev. by Susan Matthews in *English* 33 (1984):   66-71.
    This book explores the ways in which the early poems of
    Blake and Wordsworth refused to conform to the expectations
    of readers who were accustomed to poems about children and
    rustics.
>   Two examples should demonstrate Glen's point clearly. In
    "A Shepherd's Song" Blake "refuses to engage with [the
    eighteenth-century reader] in the expected way.... Blake
    offers a vision that could not without distortion be
    assimilated to a moral lesson at all--a vision of a self-
    sufficient, reciprocally satisfying way of life in which
    expressive freedom and ordered security are held in perfect
    balance."
>   In "Old Man Traveling: Animal Tranquility and Decay"
    Wordsworth shows the "shock with which the otherness of even
    the least articulate can assert itself. This old man is not
    an edifying object: he is a separate individual, with his
    own voice and history and point of view.... [R]efusing to
    assume what eighteenth-century readers would most fundamentally
    have expected--the central controlling viewpoint which would
    direct their responses and draw general conclusions--this
    whole poem questions the validity of such a viewpoint."
>   In a series of detailed readings Glen demonstrates that
    Blake and Wordsworth "seem to be foregrounding and exploring
    the problematic nature of that process whereby men seek to
    categorize and label experience." (M.T.S.)

Greenberg, Mark L. "William Michael Rossetti's Transcription
    and William Bell Scott's Tracings from Blake's Notebook."
    Library 6 (1984):   254-70.

>   In 1981 Greenberg, after a solid year's search, located
    the Scott tracings at Brigham Young University--having seen
    the words "Not in Scott" in the Rossetti transcription he
    described two years ago (see *RMB* for 1982, p. 87). The new
    Rossetti transcript gives the text of nearly 100 poems.
    (T.L.A.)

Heppner, Christopher. (See above, under *BRH*.)

Hoagwood, Terence Allan. "'God Blessing the Seventh Day':
William Blake's Visions of God and His Biblical Watercolors."
Studia Mystica 7,ii (1984):   65-77; 1 illus.

A closely argued demonstration that Blake's "visionary
theology is embodied in his visual art as well as his writing."
A Manichean framework is inadequate for understanding
Blake's theology, since Blake's God and Satan "are not
exclusive forces at a distance, engaged in a contest that
one might win" but "both powerful realities enclosed within
a unitary and mentalistic ontology." (D.V.E.)

Howard, John. *Infernal Poetics: Poetic Structures in Blake's
Lambeth Prophecies*. Fairleigh Dickinson University Press;
London and Toronto: Associated University Press, 1984.
Pp. 259. $34.00.

This book would be an excellent companion to Alford (see
review in this section), for that is strong where this is
weak, and vice versa. The strength of this book is in its
details and its simple ideas. It would serve as a useful
guide for any student wishing help through the Lambeth
prophecies and a little bit of *The Four Zoas*. Howard is
especially good at pointing out Blake's major influences
and allusions, from Erdman's historical discoveries through
Swedenborg, the Bible, Joel Barlow, and others. However,
in his desire to oversimplify, to domesticate, to find the
easy answer, he often performs a disservice to Blake and
to his readers.

The analysis of *The Book of Thel* is typical. The details
are an excellent guide through the movement of the poem,
but Howard ignores the last two lines, preferring instead to
find the "message" in the illustration of the children
riding on the serpent's back. "Thel discovers that one must
be ready to ride a serpent and to accept the ambivalence of
the sensual experience of life with faith in him who smiles
on all." Of course such a reading is possible, but Thel's
shrieking retreat must also be acknowledged.

Howard's main idea is that Blake employs a dual strategy,
first giving the reader a sense of "reality" through using,
for example, observable human behavior and references to
the Bible. This familiarity "functions as a point of
departure for the process of expanding reader awareness, the
second prong of Blake's dual strategy." Howard concentrates
on several of Blake's techniques: elaborating the familiar
by analogy, uniting the physical and mental, analogizing
the material and spiritual, and intensifying defamiliariza-
tion by ironic devices. (M.T.S.)

James, G. Ingli, ed. *William Blake: Annotations to Richard Watson: An Apology for the Bible in a Series of Letters Addressed to Thomas Paine* 8th ed. *1797.* (Regency Reprints III.) University College Cardiff Press, 1984. Pp. viii+ [170]. Paper $8.00.

A photographic copy, page for page, and diagrammatic transcript of Blake's marginalia, with detailed notes, plus a reproduction of the ten-page Conclusion to Paine's *Age of Reason,* thoroughly transpose the command Blake received "from Hell not to print this." The introduction and notes are pithy but meaty. The proper command to all Blakists is to add this to their shelves.

One quibble. Note 61 confuses the words and context of four lines from *The Everlasting Gospel* (to be found not on "p. 18" but pp. 52 and 98 of the *Notebook*) and gives confused endorsement to a misconstruction of what Blake is saying. (D.V.E.)

Kauvar, Elaine M. "Blake's Interpretation of Dreams." *AI* 41 (1984): 19–46.

"I propose to show that because Blake's and Freud's conception of the psyche's dynamics is so remarkably similar, they should be read together," insists Kauvar, making much use of the Angels' dream and taking Raine by storm. (T.L.A.)

Keane, Patrick J. "Times Ruins and the Mansions of Eternity: or, Golgonooza and Jerusalem, Yes; Bloomusalem and Beulah, No; Ithaca, Yes and No: Another Joyce-Blake Parallel at the End of Bloomsday." *BRH* 86 (1983[84]): 33–66; illus.

For another Keane essay, see *BRH,* above.

Kestner, Joseph. "Legend of Lovers." *Opera News* 48 (March 31, 1984): 12.

Article about the legend of Paolo and Francesca includes a reproduction of Blake's illustration to Dante, "The Circle of the Lustful."

Keynes, Geoffrey. "An Unpublished Poem by William Blake." *TLS,* Sept. 14, 1984, pp. 1021-22.

Twelve iambic tetrameter couplets, "The Phoenix to Mrs Butts," a manuscript now in the family of a great grandson of Mrs. Butts, and signed by an authenticated Blake signature, are now first published. The late Sir Geoffrey was confident of the signature and made an impressively biographical interpretation of the poem—in which a Phoenix (Blake) is happy to be "Mrs Butt's Bird," as long as she is not too

fairy-like: "Seem a Child & be a Child / And the Phoenix
is beguild / But if thou seem'st a Fairy thing / Then it
flies on glancing wing."
The Phoenix to Mrs Butts is to be published as a book by
Cygnet Press for the Blake Trust. (D.V.E.)

Lamberton, Robert. Porphyry on the Cave of the Nymphs.
Translation and Introductory Essay. Barrytown, N.Y.:
Station Hill Press, 1983. Pp. 48. (Blake's painting on
the cover.) $4.95.

That Porphyry's Neoplatonic interpretation of Homer was
known to Blake, and that Kathleen Raine finds its influence
pervading Blake are known to Blake scholars. "What we do
not yet know ... is what Blake may have thought of the
relationship of his own epic to Homer's." A useful discussion. (D.V.E.)

Latané, David E. "'Energetic Exertion'--Reading the
Romantic Long Poem: Blake's Jerusalem and Browning's
Sordello." Ann Arbor, Mich.: University Microfilms Inter-
national, 1984.

Dissertation.

Lima, Marcelo. Hommage à William Blake. (Poème-objet bilingue
brésilien-français en quatre lithotriptyques en couleurs.
Tirage limité.) Paris: Les Enfants de la Balle (Diffusion:
Trinckuel), 1984. Fr. 400.00.

Not seen.

Maheux, Anne. "An Analysis of the Watercolor Technique and
Materials of William Blake." BIQ 17 (1984): 124-29; illus.

Identifies the pigments used in eight paintings, an admittedly small sample.

McCord, James. "Historical Dissonance and William Blake's
The Song of Los." CLQ 20 (1984): 22-35.

McCord, James. "John Butler Yeats, 'The Brotherhood,' and
William Blake." BRH 86 (1983[84]): 10-32; illus.

A report on "one of the earliest and most devoted circles
of admirers" of Blake: Edwin Ellis, John Butler Yeats,
John Trivett Nettleship, and George Wilson, first formed
in 1869.

Middleton, Peter. "The Revolutionary Poetics of William
    Blake: Part II--Silence, Syntax, and Spectres." *OLR* 6,i
    (1983): 35-51.

    Part I was published in the proceedings of the Essex con-
    ference on "1789." "... perhaps Blake's failure to ... use
    completed utterances can be explained as a further way of
    evading the reproduction of ideology." Similarly, through-
    out, Middleton sees Blake's poetics as an attempt to evade
    absolutist positions. These are helpful speculations.
    (J.C.R.)

Minnick, Thomas L., and Detlef W. Dörrbecker. "Blake and His
    Circle: A Checklist of Recent Publications." *BIQ* 18 (1984):
    100-15.

    Seems always to include some items we have missed.

Mitchell, Orm. "Blake's Subversive Illustrations to Wollstone-
    craft's *Stories*." *Mosaic* 17,iv (1984): 17-34.

    "Blake saw her emphasis on rationality and her use of the
    object lesson as destructive of the child's innate visionary
    capacity...." An excellent article. (J.C.R.)

Nanavuty, Piloo. "Blake and Gnostic Imagery: A Note." *AJES*
    9 (1984): 43-55.

    "Not only are the commonplaces of gnostic doctrine woven
    into Blake's poetry, but the feeling of being forlorn ... in
    a world of loneliness, expressed with great pathos in several
    gnostic texts, also finds its way in Blake's poems" (46).
    Some gnostic texts, only recently translated, sound close
    to Blake. The conclusion, that it remains "difficult to
    assess Blake's indebtedness to gnostic imagery" until more
    gnostic poems are gathered and translated, almost implies
    that Blake knew the originals--in Heaven? (D.V.E.)

Ott, Judith. "Iris & Morpheus: Investigating Visual Sources
    for *Jerusalem* 14." *BIQ* 17 (1984): 149-54; illus.

Peterfreund, Stuart. "Blake, Freemasonry, and the Builder's
    Task." *Mosaic* 17,iii (1984): 35-57.

    After surveying the allusions in Blake to Freemasonry,
    Peterfreund "suggests the manner in which Blake's intellectual
    struggle with Freemasonry led to a clarification of that
    part of the prophetic undertaking here referred to as 'the
    builder's task.' It is through the 'builder's task' that
    visionary wrath seeks form...."

Piquet, François. "'Techniques infernales': Blake et le livre." *Romantisme* 43 (1984): 3-18.

Punter, David. *Blake, Hegel and Dialectic*. Amsterdam: Rodopi, 1982. Pp. 268. $23.00.

Rev. by Nelson Hilton in *BIQ* 17 (1984): 164-69, as displaying "a breadth of reading equal to that of any serious dissertation" yet neglecting to "write" adequately about "each of its terms" (i.e., Blake, Hegel, and dialectic) but "dominating them, instead, with academic idealization"; by François Piquet in *EA* 37 (1984): 208-09. Not seen.

Punter, David. "Blake, Trauma and the Female." *NLH* 15 (1984): 475-90.

A quasi-sociological attempt to explain Blake's "anguished treatment of the 'Female Will'": it seems that he was one of the eighteenth-century Englishmen "traumatized" by the increased movement of women away from the home and into the labor force.

Punter, David. "A Response to Nelson Hilton's Review." *BIQ* 18 (1984): 58-63.

Here Punter challenges Hilton--challenges us all--with a workmanlike reconstruction of "The Tyger." The book sounds worth going after. (D.V.E.)

Robertson, P.J.M. "Criticism and Creativity IV: Blake and Keats." *QQ* 91 (1984): 941-53.

Part III, on Pope and Coleridge, is listed below under Coleridge.

Shabetai, Karen. "Blake's Perception of Evil." Ann Arbor, Mich.: University Microfilms International, 1984.

Dissertation.

Staudt, Kathleen Henderson. "The Text as Material and Sign: Poetry and Incarnation in William Blake, Arthur Rimbaud, and David Jones." *MLS* 14,iii (Summer 1984): 13-30.

Stemmler, Joan K. "Cennino, Cumberland, Blake and Early Painting Techniques." *BIQ* 17 (1984): 145-49; 1 illus.

Storch, Margaret. "The 'Spectrous Fiend' Cast Out: Blake's Crisis at Felpham." *MLQ* 44 (1983): 115-35.

VanSchaik, Pamela. "Blake's Vision of the Fall and Redemption
  of Man: A Reading Based on the Contrary Images of Innocence
  and Experience." Ann Arbor, Mich.: University Microfilms
  International, 1984.

  Dissertation.

Warner, Janet A. *Blake and the Language of Art.* McGill-Queen's
  University Press; Gloucester: Alan Sutton, 1984. Pp. xx+
  211; 106 illus. $29.95.

  Previously published articles on Blake's art are revised
and supplemented by several new essays on loosely related
topics. All vary in the degrees of their persuasiveness
as well as in their coherence with each other. "The Visual
Languages of the Passions" is illuminating on the influences
current in the eighteenth-century--from the theories of
LeBrun and Lavater to theatrical practice--which would
account for certain of the facial expressions, gestures, and
attitudes in Blake's designs. That he may also have been influenced by the decorative arts of the time is less likely,
on the evidence offered. The information given on social
culture in Blake's England is always interesting, but
Warner's slighting of more traditional art history is
puzzling, especially since she includes in her Introduction
her promising note of a few years ago on the pose of the
Sleeping Ariadne.

  In her theoretical formulations, Warner is on less secure
ground. She equates with the "language" of her title terms
pertaining to images--"archetype," "symbol," "allegory,"
"emblem," "iconography"--which in accepted usage differ
markedly. Similarly, the recurring figures she cites as
bearers of intentionally codified meanings are not always
enough alike to be categorized together (e.g., those with
bowed heads are not necessarily "huddled," and vice versa),
or enough like the sources suggested to justify comparison
(it is not certain that the figure in "Albion Rose" is
dancing at all, much less engaged in an identifiable ballet
step). The meanings she proposes for the specimen figures
considered under "Blake's Visionary Forms" are general
concepts, so broad that sometimes, in order to satisfy her
thesis, verse passages as well as the designs referring to
them must be translated into capitalized abstractions (Despair, Energy), as though the method of visual allegorical
personification used in Ripa's *Iconologia* (a favorite with
Blakeists and not overlooked here) were to be turned back
upon itself. A better answer is needed to the questions
raised by the combination of recurrence and variation among
Blake's human figures.

Yet "Blake's Metaphors of Form," based mainly on his
texts, is a sensitive discussion, the first and best in
the collection, and the commentaries on the *Comus* designs
and the watercolor "The Fall of Man" are superior examples
of their kind. These might have been the core of a different,
perhaps more conventional but better integrated critical
study. (I.H.C.)

Webster, Brenda S. *Blake's Prophetic Psychology.* University
of Georgia Press, 1983. Pp. xiv+325; 76 illus. $27.50.

Rev. by Dan Miller in *BMWMLA* 17,ii (1984): 37-39.
Blake is about the last major writer whose view of himself and of his career has been accepted at face value
in most formal criticism and commentary. Now a nonspecialist
(apparently; she is identified only as the author of a
psychoanalytic study of Yeats) comes forward to examine and
give names to the aspects of his work which, separately
rather than in the aggregate, are more often noticed than
mentioned, and even when mentioned are likely to be ration-
alized and explained away without being openly acknowledged.
With minimal appeal to Blake's external biography and to
"classic" Freudian writings (her citations are most often
to present-day studies in infant psychology), Webster is
concerned with archaic, but persisting, infantile patterns
of Oedipal rivalry in his works themselves, ranging from
An Island in the Moon through *Jerusalem.* Her evidence is
impressive: obsessive imagery of devouring, mutilation,
disease, and defilement; manifestations of such psychoanalytic staples as the primal scene and the phallic mother;
hints of castration fears, sadism, anality, masturbation,
homosexuality; and always, as the main themes, aggression
toward the father and father surrogates, accompanied by
rage, guilt and anxiety, and ambivalence toward woman,
the original object of frustrated incestuous desire.
Studies like this are usually, and usually with justice,
found to be "reductive." In the case of Blake, however,
there is no substantial body of criticism of his texts as
such to offer a damaging contrast; Webster is one of the
very few writers who have tried in any systematic way to
explore the language of his verse and the larger import of
his narrative situations. The weaknesses of the book she
has written are of a more elementary kind, which could have
been remedied by revision. There are misreadings of some
of the texts quoted; uncertainties about how to treat the
designs; interpretations that might be disputed on her own
premises, or retreats to received interpretations in the
face of unexpected complexities. The argument is not helped

by her chosen method of poem-by-poem commentary, which
becomes needlessly repetitious and leaves her only a few
pages at the end to sum up what she sees as Blake's lifelong
struggle with impulses he could neither renounce nor defend
against, and the effects of that struggle on his poetry.

Nevertheless, Brenda Webster deserves the greatest credit
for having had the courage to break a taboo which has pre-
vailed for too long in Blake studies and actually does no
honor to its object. (The taboo seems to have reached into
publishers' offices. The manuscript of this book was
finished by 1978 [see p. 310] and its belated publication
is by a minor university press, not one of the familiar
dissertation outlets.) Even for those who may regret the
loss of an illusion, the fuller view of both the man and the
work that has been made possible can only benefit Blake
criticism in the long run. (I.H.C.)

Whitmarsh-Knight, David E. "Structure as a Key to Meaning in
William Blake's *The Four Zoas*." Ann Arbor, Mich.: University
Microfilms International, 1984.

    Dissertation.

See also Chan ("General 2. Environment"); McGann, Mitchell,
Thurley ("General 3. Criticism"); Viscomi ("English 1.
Bibliography"); Lister, Siebert, Wiener ("English 2. Environ-
ment"); Abrams, Cantor, Hollander, Jack, Johnson and Leyda,
Thesing ("English 3. Criticism").

Reviews of books previously listed:

BEHRENDT, Stephen, *The Moment of Explosion: Blake and the
Illustration of Milton* (see *RMB* for 1983, pp. 74-75), rev.
by Joseph Wittreich, enthusiastically, in *MiltonQ* 18 (1984):
92-94; BERTHOLF, Robert J., and Annette S. Levitt, eds.,
William Blake and the Moderns (see *RMB* for 1982, pp. 77-80),
rev. by Paul Mann in *BIQ* 17 (1984): 169-72, who suggest that
the title should have been "Imaginative Form and the Moderns";
BOGAN, James, and Fred Goss, eds., *Sparks of Fire: Blake in
a New Age* (see *RMB* for 1982, p. 81), rev. by Jenijoy La Belle
in *BIQ* 18 (1984): 48-49; BUTLIN, Martin, *The Paintings and
Drawings of William Blake* (see *RMB* for 1981, pp. 78-79), rev.
by Jonathan Wordsworth in *RES* 35 (1984): 92-95; COX, Stephen
D., *"The Stranger With Thee": Concepts of the Self in Late
Eighteenth-Century Literature* (see *RMB* for 1982, p. 60), rev.
by David Worrall in *BIQ* 18 (1984): 31-32; DAMROSCH, Leopold,
Jr., *Symbolic Truth in Blake's Myth* (see *RMB* for 1981, p. 79),
rev. by J.M.Q. Davis in *DUJ* 45 (1984): 300-03; DEEN, Leonard,

Conversing in Paradise: Poetic Genius and Identity-as-Community in Blake's Los (see *RMB* for 1983, p. 77), rev. by Charlene Werner in *MiltonQ* 18 (1984): 35-36; DOSKOW, Minna, *William Blake's Jerusalem: Structure and Meaning in Poetry and Picture* (see *RMB* for 1983, pp. 79-80), rev. by V.A. De Luca in *BIQ* 18 (1984): 56-58, politely but severely, as "almost certainly incorrect" in a schematic reading that produces frequent straying from the text; DUNBAR, Pamela, *William Blake's Illustrations to the Poetry of Milton* (see *RMB* for 1980, p. 74), rev. by Bette Charlene Werner in *BIQ* 18 (1984): 33-34; by Joseph Wittreich in *YES* 14 (1984): 329-31; EAVES, Morris, *William Blake's Theory of Art* (see *RMB* for 1982, p. 83), rev. by Peter A. Taylor in *QQ* 91 (1984): 719-22; ERDMAN, David V., ed., *Complete Poetry and Prose of William Blake* (see *RMB* for 1982, p. 84), rev. by Peter A. Taylor in *QQ* 91 (1984): 719-22; ESSICK, Robert N., and Morton D. Paley, *Robert Blair's The Grave, Illustrated by William Blake: A Study with Facsimile* (see *RMB* for 1982, p. 85), rev. by Jonathan Wordsworth in *RES* 35 (1984): 547-48; GLECKNER, Robert F., *Blake's Prelude: Poetical Sketches* (see *RMB* for 1983, pp. 81-83), rev. by Thomas J. Corr in *CollL* 11 (1984): 286-89; by Nelson Hilton in *SiR* 23 (1984): 409-13; HILTON, Nelson, *Literal Imagination: Blake's Vision of Words* (see *RMB* for 1983, p. 83), rev. by Brian Wilkie in *JEGP* 83 (1984): 566-68 as "one of the three or four most seminal" books on Blake ever written; LEADER, Zachary, *Reading Blake's Songs* (see *RMB* for 1981, p. 84), rev. by Hazard Adams in *SiR* 22 (1983): 458-62, with praise but some misgivings; by Thomas A. Vogler in *BIQ* 18 (1984): 39-47, as "a mixture of religion and politics masquerading as literary criticism"; SINGH, Charu Sheel, *The Chariot of Fire: A Study of William Blake in the Light of Hindu Thought* (see *RMB* for 1981, p. 88), rev. by Mary V. Jackson in *BIQ* 18 (1984): 121-25, as so inaccurate as to be "a model of botched research offered in support of half-thought-through ideas"; TANNENBAUM, Leslie, *Biblical Tradition in Blake's Early Prophecies: The Great Code of Art* (see *RMB* for 1982, pp. 90-91), rev. by Jerome J. McGann in *BIQ* 18 (1984): 120-21.

Composite reviews:

Gassenmeier, Michael. *Anglia* 102 (1984): 248-59.

Examines G.E. Bentley, Jr., *Blake Books* (see *ELN* 16, Supp., 27-28) and Bentley's two volumes of *William Blake's Writings* (see *RMB* for 1979, pp. 69-70).

Hamilton, Paul. "From the Position of Dissent." *TLS*, June
15, 1984, p. 674.

A swift review of Gleckner (*Blake's Prelude*), Paley (*The
Continuing City: William Blake's "Jerusalem"*), Doskow
(*William Blake's "Jerusalem"*), Webster (*Blake's Prophetic
Psychology*), and Crehan (*Blake in Context*: see above).

Review vendetta:

The Santa Cruz Blake Study Group (anon.). *BIQ* 18 (1984):
4-22.

A review of *The Complete Poetry and Prose of William Blake*,
ed. David V. Erdman; Commentary by Harold Bloom (see *RMB*
for 1982, p. 84).

Treats Erdman as the autocrat responsible for all format
and production decisions, as well as editorial choices, and
the Committee on Scholarly Editions as an officious blight
(quite unaware that if it had not been for CSE support, a
seriously flawed text might have been put on the market).

I can be grateful, however, for the Study Group's detection
of one howling typo ("The petrific abdominable chaos" in
Urizen 3:26).

Actually some 75 errata emendata, discovered by careful
readers unashamed of their names, have been reported to the
two publishers to be corrected in the next printing--or the
next (at this point I wish I *were* the autocrat who seems
required). (D.V.E.)--P.S.: They *were* corrected in the
Doubleday.

BLOOMFIELD

Means, James A. Untitled Note. *SSL* 16 (1981): 240.

Prints an unpublished Bloomfield verse on Burns from a
manuscript bound in the Clement Shorter copy of *The Farmer's
Boy* (London, 1800). The similarities with Keats are cultural-
ly, not textually, suggestive. (T.L.A.)

BURKE

Blakemore, Steven. "Burke and the Fall of Language: The
French Revolution as Linguistic Event." *ECS* 17 (1984): 284-
307.

Burke's "probing semantic analysis" in the *Reflections* was
a "linguistic effort to reestablish the semantic links between

the old world and its language," threatened by the altered meanings given familiar words by "English hacks and French philosophes." Finally, it is Burke's own language that sustains his "linguistic worlds of order and grace" and "'presents' his reflections on the French Revolution as the last, great flowering statement of the old eighteenth century."

Browning, Reed. "The Origin of Burke's Ideas Revisited." *ECS* 18 (1984): 57-71.

The origin was in "Court Whiggery," as expounded by defenders of Walpole and the Pelhams.

Lambert, Elizabeth R. "The History and Significance of the Relationship of Edmund Burke and James Boswell." Ann Arbor, Mich.: University Microfilms International, 1984.

Dissertation.

Langford, Paul, gen. ed. *The Writings and Speeches of Edmund Burke.* Vol. II: *Party, Parliament and the American Crisis 1766-1774.* Ed. Paul Langford. Oxford University Press, 1981. Pp. xviii+508. $120.00. Vol. V: *India: Madras and Bengal 1774-1785.* Ed. P.J. Marshall, 1981. Pp. xv+667. $130.00.

Continuing the great project of T.W. Copeland, who completed the *Correspondence* volumes in 1978.
Rev. by Ian R. Christie in *Parliamentary History* 1 (1984): 256-58, who notes that of Burke's 230 speeches between the dates of Vol. II only 39 have been selected for inclusion; only 11 of the 84 speeches between the dates of Vol. V.

Palmer, William. "Edmund Burke and the French Revolution: Notes on the Genesis of the *Reflections.*" *CLQ* 20 (1984): 181-90.

Priestley, F.E.L. "Reflections on Burke." *DR* 63 (1983-84): 13-22.

How the old whig became a new whig. (T.L.A.)

See also Jacobus ("General 3. Criticism"); Butler, Peterson ("English 2. Environment"); Bromwich ("Hazlitt").

Benson, Nancy A. "Hero and Narrator in Byron's *Don Juan*:
A Piagetian Approach." *CentR* 28:4 (1984)/29:1 (1985)
[double number]: 48-57.

    "Juan carries his merely tenuous identity as hero ...
with him throughout the action. Because he possesses no
central core of self to be true to, he is restricted to an
accommodative mode. In contrast, the poet-narrator offers
us the world he has assimilated in all of its problematic
ambiguity and deceptive theatricality, achieving literary
play that is a human triumph of the highest order. Thus,
Piaget's theory of accommodation and assimilation provides
a model for the two modes in which Byron's satiric imagination finds its greatest possibilities." *Thus* is made to
stand on a review of the play theory of Piaget, Huizinga,
Caillois, Groos, and Jerome S. Bruner--peppered with a pinch
of West, Cooke, Ridenour, and Manning (called "less satisfactory"). But the essay nowhere distinguishes word play and
foreplay. (T.L.A.)

Bold, Alan, ed. *Byron: Wrath and Rhyme*. London: Vision
Press; Totowa, N.J.: Barnes & Noble, 1983. Pp. 216.
£13.95; $26.50.

    Rev. by Erik Frykman in *SLJ* 11 (1984) supp. 20: 19-21,
who calls it "a mixed bag"; and by Malcolm Kelsall in
Byron Journal 12 (1984): 86-87.
    Contents: J.F. Hendry, "Byron and the Cult of Personality";
J. Drummond Bone, "The Rhetoric of Freedom"; Geoffrey
Carnall, "Byron as Unacknowledged Legislator"; Ronald
Stevenson, "Byron as Lyricist: The Poet among the Musicians";
Jenni Calder, "The Hero as Lover: Byron and Women"; Edwin
Morgan, "Voice, Tone, and Transition in *Don Juan*"; Philip
Hobsbaum, "Byron and the English Tradition"; Walter Perrie,
"The Byronic Philosophy"; Tom Scott, "Byron as a Scottish
Poet." I find limitations throughout, particularly because
Byron is often tortured on the rack of modern or personal
causes. One Scots poet (Morgan) does bring a poet's sense
to *Don Juan*, but the other (Scott) translates stanzas into
Scots to demonstrate loss. Hobsbaum is more concerned with
Pope and Frere than with any new conception, and Perrie
will not go beyond *Childe Harold* in discussing Calvinism
and modernity. In Jenni Calder the poet exemplifies the
double standard; in Hendry he is as general as his culture is
reductive. Carnall and Drummond Bone are best, along with
Morgan, particularly for their political emphasis--but the
totality of that interest needs greater recognition. (T.L.A.)

Byron Journal 12 (1984).

Victor Luftig, "Auden and Byron" (17-30) is a very useful, detailed review of Auden's writings on Byron, supporting the modern poet's early evaluation in verse against his later prose comments; L.M. Findlay, "'Perpetual Activity' in Byron's Prose" (31-47) turns a deconstructionist tour through Byron's letters and journals into a tour de force and sometimes farce that ends on an apt note: "The conjugal is constantly imperilled by the need to conjugate"; Mary Clapinson, "A Rejected Suitor of Lady Byron" (48-56) follows; Gordon Spence, "Moral and Sexual Ambivalence in *Sardanapalus*" (59-69) finds "masculine and feminine tendencies in irreconcilable conflict" and distances himself from McGann's criticism of the poem; Gwen Beaumont, "Byron's Nottingham" (70-72) follows; Itsuyo Higashinaka, "Gulbeyaz and Joseph Andrews" (74-75) is a note on *Don Juan* V:131, 139; a newly discovered letter from T. Morton to Lord Lansdowne concerning payment to Moore for Byron's destroyed memoirs is reprinted next (76); Frederic Raphael, "The Byronic Myth" (77-83) is a 1982 talk to the Byron Society reminiscent of Raphael's longer mythicizing (see *RMB* for 1982, p. 101); significant book reviews are listed under their respective subjects.

The best of this year's *Byron Journal* I have saved for last: John Clubbe, "Byron's Lady Melbourne" (4-16). In 1966 I learned that Lady Melbourne's letters to Byron for the 1812-15 period were on deposit in what was then called the British Museum; because they had been restricted until 1980 I was unable to scan them for my work on *Byron's Hebrew Melodies*, nor to learn from them what I hoped might bear on Byron's relationship with Augusta. They came to mind as I was reviewing John Chapman's *Byron and the Honourable Augusta Leigh* in these pages. Chapman wrote: "It is curious and interesting that of the many letters and notes Lady Melbourne must have sent to Byron, ... very few ... have been preserved," and later, "Whatever may be true of other evidence and its interpretation, the charge of incest derives its best support from Byron's letters to Lady Melbourne." I responded at the time: "Clearly Lady Melbourne's half of the correspondence will prove all the putative pudding. Let us hope that those letters, which do in fact exist, go first to Leslie Marchand when they are released from their legal restrictions" (*ELN* 14 [1976]: 34). So I am pleased that John Clubbe has taken up my hint made nine years ago, but all this remains a disappointment. As Clubbe's liberal quotation shows, the released correspondence, some 15 items, does not add to our knowledge of Byron's relations with Augusta. The letters do however show Byron flirting much with Lady Melbourne, and this may account for the Countess of Airlie's desire to hold them back for so long. At this point, the best we can hope for is a full transcription to accompany Clubbe's excellent elucidation of their contents. (T.L.A.)

Coldwell, Patricia C. "Allusion in Byron's *Don Juan*." Ann Arbor, Mich.: University Microfilms International, 1984.

Dissertation.

Ferguson, Robert I. "The Responsible Dream: A Study of Political Thought in the Work of Lord Byron." Ann Arbor, Mich.: University Microfilms International, 1984. No. 2477A.

Dissertation.

Fleming, Anne. *Bright Darkness: The Poetry of Lord Byron Presented in the Context of His Life & Times.* London: Nottingham Court Press, 1983. Pp. 288. £9.95.

Rev. by Elizabeth Longford in *Byron Journal* 12 (1984): 87-88, favorably.
Not seen.

Gatti, Hilary. "Byron and Giorgione's Wife." *SiR* 23 (1984): 237-43.

This is a gem of an essay, particularly for those caught up in the obsession of identifying just what painting Byron refers to in *Beppo*. As it turns out, what Byron saw was a triple portrait by Titian, now hanging in Northumberland's Alnwick Castle; after its removal from the Manfrin Palace, and in consideration of the *Beppo* attribution to Giorgione, that painter's *La Tempesta* was falsely identified. (Reproductions of both works are included.) E.H. Coleridge and Prothero are both corrected, and the record finally set right. Nor does my concern with this issue mean to ignore the greater point of the essay, that the changes reflected in *Beppo* have more to do with what he took from all of Italian culture past and present than what he learned from Hookham or Frere. (T.L.A.)

Gatton, John Spalding. "Squaring Accounts: An Unpublished Byron Letter." *N&Q* 31 (1984): 474.

December 7, 1819, to Hoppner, Byron stalling on the final payment of the lease for Palazzo Mocenigo because of a debt run up by an owner-engaged servant. (T.L.A.)

Graham, Peter W., ed. *Byron's Bulldog: The Letters of John Cam Hobhouse to Lord Byron*. Ohio State University Press, 1984. Pp. ix+364. $25.00.

Graham has given us one of the most useful studies of Byron produced in several years by means of his edition of Hobhouse's letters to the poet. He has first salvaged Hobhouse from the stuffy editing of his daughter, Lady Dorchester, familiar to those of us who have wallowed through the six volumes of *Recollections of a Long Life*. Second, by collecting only Hobhouse's letters to Byron for the 17 years of their friendship, he allows us to measure the growth and development of Hobhouse against a continuing standard. For the first time we see his changes and the shaping of his character. Then, because Graham has been apt in his notes, it is possible to read in this one volume the dialogue of the friendship, which in turn makes clear fresh aspects of Byron's own personality and development. Graham has worked with what he terms 80 percent of the Hobhouse letters; still missing are some nine letters from the La Mira period, and the 1821 letter containing Hobhouse's criticism of *Cain*. But Graham has made up well for these deficiencies, by judicious quoting from Marchand's edition of Byron's letters which allows us to sense what Hobhouse must have written. Finally, it is good to have Hobhouse's understanding of Byron's complexity. Though we know that Byron held back at times, the honesty of Hobhouse's vision of the poet is worth a dozen of the rose-colored variety. (T.L.A.)

Haley, Bruce. "The Sculptural Aesthetics of *Childe Harold* IV." *MLQ* 44 (1983): 251-66.

Hayden, John O. "An Uncollected Poem (Probably) by Lord Byron." *KSJ* 33 (1984): 18-24.

Three quatrains "To Barbara" from the Cambridge period that are probably not Byron's. (T.L.A.)

Hoefnagel, Dick. "Lord Byron's Letters to J.J. Coulmann." *N&Q* 31 (1984): 63-64.

Dates Byron's reply to Coulmann's interview request to January 6, 1823, using his *Réminiscences* (1862-69). Byron's better-known letter to Coulmann was prompted when the Frenchman sent him the *Essai sur le Génie et le Caractère de Lord Byron*. (T.L.A.)

Hoffmeister, Gerhart. *Byron und der europäische Byronismus*. (Erträge der Forschung, 188.) Darmstadt: Wissenschaftliche Buchgesellschaft, 1983. Pp. 177. DM 45.00.

Rev. by Erik Frykman in *SLJ* 11 (1984) supp. 20: 19-21;
by Lilian Furst in *CRCL* 11 (1984): 308-10.

"To seek out so called 'Byronesque' traits in either real
or literary figures inevitably leads to drift and slippage,"
writes Furst, "dangers which Hoffmeister has not entirely
avoided." The book is called "particularly discerning" on
the relationship of Goethe and Byron, "but [has] somehow
missed the essential core, at least as far as literature
is concerned." Claimed for Byron the culture hero--not
poet--are Rochester, Heathcliff, Steerforth, Carton, Wray-
burn, Emma Bovary, and Mme. de Rênal from Stendhal--among
others. (T.L.A.)

Huber, Werner, and Rainer Schöwerling, eds. *Byron Symposium:
Mannheim 1982*. University of Paderborn, 1983.

    Not seen.

Kelsall, Malcolm, ed. *John Cam Hobhouse: A Trifling Mistake,
and Reform of Parliament*. (Regency Reprints II.) University
College Cardiff Press, 1984. Pp. xiv+[63]. Paper $8.00.

    A Trifling Mistake sent Byron's Hobhouse to prison at
the tag end of 1819, and *Reform of Parliament* was written
in Newgate prior to Hobhouse's release on February 28, 1820.
Byron scholars will be particularly pleased with the photographic reprinting of these rare pamphlets, and equally so
with Kelsall's short and erudite introduction and notes.
All in all it is a treat to see just how much of a fire-eater
John Cam becomes as Peterloo fills his sails. Also of
interest are several references to classical satire that will
cause a few Byron scholars to wonder. (T.L.A.)

Lamb, Lady Caroline (Ponsonby). *Glenarvon* ... *with Original
Introduction*. 3rd ed. London, 1816. Reprint. 3 vols.
New York: AMS Press, 1984. $97.50.

Latané, David E., Jr. "'See You?'": Browning, Byron, and the
Revolutionary Deluge in *Sordello*, Book I." *VP* 22 (1984):
85-91.

    Sordello I:213-37 ascribed (but by conjecture) to Byron's
famous journal entry of January 9, 1821, on revolution,
selfhood, tide, and ocean--as Byron wrote, "*sea-weed* is
manure." (T.L.A.)

Martineau, Gilbert. *Lord Byron: La malédiction du genie*.
(Figures de Proue.) Paris: Tallandier, 1984. Pp. 400.
Fr. 98.00

    Not seen.

Matzneff, Gabriel. *La Diététique de Lord Byron.* Paris:
La Table Ronde, 1984.

Not seen.

McVeigh, D.M. "'In Caines Cynne': Byron and the Mark of
Cain." *MLQ* 43 (1982): 337-51.

Mellown, Muriel J. "Francis Jeffrey, Lord Byron, and *English
Bards and Scotch Reviewers.*" *SSL* 16 (1981): 80-90.

Good on the paradox "that the very virulence of Byron's
attack on Jeffrey and the *Edinburgh Review* was occasioned
by his real approval of the periodical." (T.L.A.)

Pahl, Dennis. "Recovering Byron: Poe's 'The Assignation.'"
Criticism 26 (1984): 211-29.

"The question of Byron's 'presence' in the text becomes
not simply a matter of his being nominated in Poe's fictional
work, but of his being as such.... to what Harold Bloom
refers to as a 'relation between texts' (in which case we
must regard 'The Assignation' as Poe's *reading* of Byron) ...
a play on Poe's part to reinterpret, if not reinvent, Byron
in Poe's own image." (T.L.A.)

Pitcher, E.W. "Byron's 'The Deformed Transformed' Transformed:
A Short Fiction Adaptation in 1825." *KSJ* 33 (1984): 24-30.

In *Endless Entertainment; or Comic Terrific and Legendary
Tales,* June 10, 1825, where Byron is only a pinched source
used to draw attention to the volume. (T.L.A.)

Pujols, Esteban. "Lord Byron en Andalucía (verano de 1809)."
ArH No. 196 (May 1981): 85-91.

Includes identification of Byron's lodgings. Illustrated.

Shilstone, Frederick W. "The Dissipated Muse: Wine, Women,
and Byronic Song." *CLQ* 20 (1984): 36-46.

Stillman, Mira T. *The Byronic Hero: A Revision of Traditional
Views.* Ann Arbor, Mich.: University Microfilms International, 1984.

A dissertation--that without much revision should be made
available as a book. Stillman with shrewd insight argues--
and nicely demonstrates--a greater satiric presence in Byron
than most critics like to see. She will make you want to
reread "Werner" (even). (D.V.E.)

Vassallo, Peter. *Byron: The Italian Literary Influence.*
New York: St. Martin's, 1984. Pp. x+192. $21.95.

We can learn something of Byron's Italian study from this
volume, but we shall not learn what its title promises
misleadingly. "The study concentrates largely but not
exclusively on Byron's debt to Casti and Pulci for the
satirical mode of *Beppo*, *Don Juan*, and *The Vision of
Judgement* [sic]," writes the author, and later the focus
is narrowed: "It is my purpose ... to demonstrate that
it was mainly Casti's style in the *Novelle Galanti* which
was responsible for Byron's new satirical technique in
Beppo and not, as is commonly supposed, that of *Mr. Whistle-
craft* or Frere's Italian models, Pulci and Berni." In
several senses we can benefit from this narrow focus: it
teaches us that Byron took his Italian study seriously;
it offers numerous quotations from Casti and others of his
time, providing for direct comparison on the reader's part.
Also to the good are the work's emphasis on William Stewart
Rose's influence on Byron's taste, and its discussion of
the impact of *Corinne* on Byron's evolving style. But that
is where the benefits run out, and they nowhere make up
for the silent assumption in which they are grounded: the
tired saw that *Don Juan* emerges as a fluke, that Byron's
poetic development did not lead him to it unerringly. Put
it this way, can one discuss the Italian literary influence
on Byron without discussing his dramas?--for that is what
goes on here. To approach Byron in Italy, we need to
understand first and foremost that Byron looked at Italy
as Rome in the way he looked at modern Greece as fallen.
Then we must do away with another great misunderstanding--
that "La Guiccioli" was no more than a demimondaine. In
fact Teresa shows herself a keen student of her cultural
heritage, one ever anxious to direct Byron's attention to
it. Then we need to understand that in the *salon* of the
period, Byron was exposed to a level of cultural discourse
he found intriguing and stimulating. And of course there
was the theatre of Alfieri, attended, discussed, and used
by the English poet writing plays out of Italian history.
Alfieri is only a sonneteer in this study. The historians
Ginguené and Sismondi are referenced here, but their
influence is scanted, as is that of Sanuto, who goes
unmentioned. Each and all of these influences had their
effect on Byron's consciousness as he left *Hints from
Horace* behind and took up *The Vision of Judgment*, passed
from *The Prisoner of Chillon* to *The Lament of Tasso*,
finished with *Childe Harold* and began *Don Juan*. His Italian
study was broad and deep, so too his actual experience of

Italy; these far more than any one poet or one model
account for his last gift to those who read him from the
start. (T.L.A.)

Vicario, Michael. "The Implications of Form in *Childe
Harold's Pilgrimage*." *KSJ* 33 (1984): 103-29.

"Although Byron saw fit to subtitle *Childe Harold's
Pilgrimage* 'A Romaunt,' criticism has not investigated
the implications of Byron's generic subtitle for the
structure of the poem as a whole, nor has the poem been
inadequately set within the context of late eighteenth-
century speculation on the origin, rise, and progress
of an important medieval form.... Yet to ignore the
tradition of eighteenth-century Spenserian imitation is
at least in part to deprive the initial cantos of their
admittedly tenuous coherence." A contribution is made by
studying the influence of Thomson's *Castle of Indolence*.
(T.L.A.)

Vitale, M. "The Domesticated Heroine in Byron's *Corsair*
and William Hone's Prose Adaptation." *L&H* 10 (1984):
72-94.

Byron's complexity is watered down twice. (T.L.A.)

Wilson, Milton. "Byron and Occupied Countries: The Double
Agent as Revolutionary." *DR* 63 (1983-84): 207-16.

Concentrates on the tales and *Childe Harold* I & II with
much flash and the same old patrician/plebeian dichotomy.
The author seems to have ingested Herb Philbrick of *I
Led Three Lives*. (T.L.A.)

See also Redman ("General 1. Bibliography"); Chan, Russell
("General 2. Environment"); McGann, Thurley ("General 3.
Criticism"); Wiener ("English 2. Environment"); Cantor,
Chandler, Cockshut, Ellis, Jack, Knight, Lehman, Meisel,
Pereira, van Anglen ("English 3. Criticism"); Bromwich
("Hazlitt"); Shaaban ("Shelley, P.B."); Pujols ("Spanish
2. General").

Reviews of books previously listed:

BURNETT, T.A.J., *The Rise and Fall of a Regency Dandy:
The Life and Times of Scrope Berdmore Davies* (see *RMB*
for 1981, p. 92), rev. by Todd K. Bender in *SHR* 17 (1983):
390-91; by Marilyn Butler in *KSMB* 34 (1983): 80-85;
CLUBB, John, *Byron's Natural Man: Daniel Boone &
Kentucky* (see *RMB* for 1981, p. 93), rev. by Eric Frykman

in *SLJ* 11 (1984) supp. 20: 19-21; CLUBBE, John, and
Ernest Giddey, *Byron et la Suisse: Deux études* (see *RMB*
for 1982, p. 96), rev. by Frederick L. Beaty in *KSJ* 33
(1984): 210-14; by Michael Rees in *Byron Journal* 12 (1984):
84; CUNNINGHAM, John, *The Poetics of Byron's Comedy in
Don Juan* (see *RMB* for 1982, pp. 96-97), rev. by Michael
Rees in *Byron Journal* 12 (1984): 87; HOWELL, Margaret J.,
*Byron Tonight: A Poet's Plays on the Nineteenth-Century
Stage* (see *RMB* for 1982, p. 98), rev. by Frederick L.
Beaty in *KSJ* 33 (1984): 210-14; by Gilbert B. Cross in
VS 27 (1984): 244-45; by William Ruddick in *TN* 38 (1984):
43; MARCHAND, Leslie A., ed., *Byron's Letters and Journals*
(see *RMB* for 1982, p. 98), rev. by John Buxton in *KSMB*
34 (1983): 73-79; by Doucet Devin Fischer in *KSJ* 33 (1984):
214-16; MARTIN, Philip W., *Byron: A Poet Before His Public*
(see *RMB* for 1982, p. 98), rev. by Frederick L. Beaty in
KSJ 33 (1984): 210-14; by Peter J. Manning in *SiR* 23
(1984): 401-09; by Frederick W. Shilstone in *SAR* 49
(May 1984): 127-30; McGANN, Jerome J., ed., *Lord Byron:
The Complete Poetical Works* (see *RMB* for 1982, p. 100),
rev. by Donald H. Reiman in *KSMB* 34 (1983): 66-72. This
is a mature assessment of the first three volumes, which
adds corrections but, more important, knows what went
right and what went wrong: "If this edition of Byron's
Complete Poetical Works has thus far been slightly less
than an *unqualified* scholarly success, it remains a personal triumph."

Review essay:

Buxton, John. *KSMB* 34 (1983): 73-79.

   Byron as letter-writer in a review of Vols. I-XI of
   Marchand's *Byron's Letters and Journals* (1973-82) and
   Selected Letters and Journals (1982).

CARLYLE, J.

Froude, James Anthony, ed. *Letters and Memorials of Jane
   Welsh Carlyle*, 1883. Reprint. 2 vols. in 1. New York:
   AMS Press, 1984. $67.50.

CARLYLE, T.

Bidney, Martin. "Diminishing Epiphanies of Odin: Carlyle's
   Reveries of Primal Fire." *MLQ* 44 (1983): 51-64.

Carlyle, Alexander, ed. *New Letters and Memorials of Jane
   Welsh Carlyle: Annotated by Thomas Carlyle*, 1903. Reprint.
   2 vols. New York: AMS Press, 1984. $87.50.

Clubbe, John. "Carlyle as Epic Historian." Pp. 119-45 in
   Kincaid and Kuhn, eds., *Victorian Literature and Society*
   (see above, "English 3. Criticism").

   Carlyle's "discovery" of Homer in 1834 made him almost as
   influential as Goethe in Carlyle's thought--and prepared
   him for the epic style of *The French Revolution*.

Frye, Lowell T. "Chaos and Cosmos: Carlyle's Idea of History."
   VN 65 (1984): 19-21.

   The essays "On History" (1830) and "On History Again"
   (1833) show diminished expectations for history pure and
   simple--at a glance. (T.L.A.)

Kaplan, Fred. *Thomas Carlyle: A Biography*. Cambridge University Press; Cornell University Press, 1984. Pp. 640.

   Rev. by John Clive ("Missionary of Unconsciousness") in
   TLS, April 20, 1984, pp. 419-20, strongly praising Kaplan
   for a biography that "makes sense" of Carlyle; by Michael
   Goldberg in *Albion* 16 (1984): 316-19, as "both the most
   ambitious biographical study of Carlyle undertaken in this
   century and the most successful"; by Brian Martin in *New
   Statesman*, March 9, 1984, p. 26; by Peter Quennell in *S*,
   Feb. 4, 1984, pp. 25-26, as "most comprehensive."
   Not seen; will review next year.

Mulderig, Gerald P. "The Rhetorical Design of Carlyle's
   Life of John Sterling." *JNT* 14 (1984): 142-50.

   Whatever its inadequacies as biography, Carlyle's reshaping
   of Sterling's life successfully rebutted Julius Hare's
   ecclesiastical emphasis, and, particularly by his contrast
   of Sterling's vitality with Coleridge's inertia, presented
   forcefully his own view of life as an exploratory pilgrimage.
   (R.M.R.)

Surtees, Virginia. *The Ludovisi Goddess: The Life of Louisa
   Lady Asburton*. Wiltshire: Michael Russell, 1984. Pp.
   xiii+210.

   Rev. by Peter Quennell in *S*, Sept. 1, 1984, p. 21.
   She was the object of Carlyle's middle-aged passion.

Tennyson, G.B., ed. *A Carlyle Reader: Selections from the
    Writings of Thomas Carlyle.* Cambridge University Press,
    1984. Pp. xlvi+497. $44.50; paper $9.95.

    A reprint of the Random House edition of 1969. Wide
    selection; judicious Introduction. Good to see it kept in
    print.

See also Ellison, Vijn ("General 3. Criticism"); Himmelfarb,
    Kenyon, Semmel, Tuman ("English 2. Environment"); Buckley,
    Culviner, Kincaid and Kuhn ("English 3. Criticism"); Anderson
    ("Coleridge").

Reviews of books previously listed:

    SANDERS, Charles, *Carlyle's Friendships* (see *ELN* 17, Supp.,
    77), rev. by K.J. Fielding in *SSL* 15 (1980): 296-98; SANDERS,
    Charles Richard, and Kenneth J. Fielding, eds., *The Collected
    Letters of Thomas and Jane Welsh Carlyle*, Vols. 8-9 (see *RMB*
    for 1980, p. 92), rev. by Graham Storey in *RES* 35 (1984):
    251-52.

CLARE

Deacon, George. *John Clare and the Folk Tradition.* Sinclair
    Browne, 1984. Pp. 397. £15.00.

    Not seen.

Grainger, Margaret, ed. *The Natural History Prose Writings of
    John Clare.* Oxford University Press, 1983. Pp. lxii+397.
    $69.00.

    Natural history is such an integral part of Clare's poetry
    that having his prose writings on the subject at last in a
    complete and textually reliable edition should mark an impor-
    tant step forward in the study of his work. In her introduc-
    tion Grainger sets Clare's natural history prose in the
    context of the burgeoning popularity of such writing during
    the late eighteenth and early nineteenth centuries, while
    carefully distinguishing his methods from those of many other
    naturalists; she finds him most like Dorothy Wordsworth in
    that he did not "shoot, stuff, dissect or arrange," but made
    observations that "are intimately linked with his poems and
    his biography." While the editor's apparatus sometimes
    threatens to overwhelm the text, by and large her exhaustive
    annotations and indexing will prove helpful to all readers.
    (M.M.)

The John Clare Society Journal 1 (1982).

Contents: Edward Storey, "Editorial" (304); Ronald Blythe, "A Message from the President" (5); Eric Robinson, "Clare and Nature" (7-24); Trevor Hold, "The Composer's Debt to John Clare" (25-29); R.K.R. Thornton, "The Flower and the Book: The Gardens of John Clare" (31-45); George E. Dixon, "Clare and Religion" (47-50); Rodney Lines, "John Clare's 'The Skylark'" (53-56).

This first issue of the *Journal* illustrates the strengths and weaknesses of societies devoted to authors. The best pieces are by professionals of one kind or another: Robinson and Thornton (academics) and Hold (composer); the worst by amateur enthusiasts such as Dixon, whose essay on Clare's religion is superficial, misleading, and factually inaccurate. (M.M.)

The John Clare Society Journal 2 (1983).

Contents: John Barrell, "John Clare's 'The Lane'" (3-8); Eric Robinson, "Editorial Problems in John Clare" (9-24); E. Barbara Dean, "John Clare at Lolham Bridges" (24-27); Cecil Scrimgeour, "John Clare and the Price of Experience" (28-39); Trevor Hold, "John Clare's Birds" (40-44); Pauline Buttery, "John Clare and the Folk Tradition" (45).

Barrell provides a brilliant explication of a Clare poem, Robinson a forthright and informative look at the complexities of editing Clare. Dean discusses briefly a Clare inscription on a stone not hitherto noticed, while Scrimgeour, Hold, and Buttery all review recent books about and editions of Clare.

The John Clare Society Journal 3 (1984).

Contents: Mark Storey, "Clare in His Letters" (5-16); Greg Crossan, "The Godfrey Collection of Clare Items in the Peterborough Museum" (17-25); Richard Lessa, "John Clare's Voice, and Two Sonnets" (26-33); Timothy Brownlow, "A Moment's Monument" (34-37); Edward Storey, "John Clare Moves House" (39); Lynn Banfield-Pierce, "John Clare and Peter DeWint" (40-48); Joe Goddard, "A Formative Influence of John Clare" (49-52); reviews of the new *Later Poems* by Ronald Blythe, of the *Autobiographical Writings* by Robert Gittings, and of *John Clare and Picturesque Landscape* by R.K.R. Thornton.

Of those items whose titles are not self-evident, Brownlow's is an explication of Clare's "The Magic of Beauty"; Storey's is a poem. While these essays are not up to the critical standards found in the two previous issues of the *Journal*, all are at least informative and interesting. (M.M.)

Rankin, Paula C. "John Clare's Quest for Identity." Ann Arbor,
Mich.: University Microfilms International, 1984.

Dissertation.

Robinson, Eric, and David Powell, eds. *John Clare.* (The
Oxford Authors.) Oxford University Press, 1984. Pp. xxix+
530. $24.95; paper $8.95.

Selections of Clare's poetry and prose have been appearing
regularly since 1901 and frequently in the last two decades.
Yet this volume in the new "Oxford Authors" series (replacing
the venerable "Oxford Standard Authors") can be called the
first truly satisfactory selection of Clare ever published
because it combines textual reliability with extensive annotation and the length necessary to capture something of Clare's
enormous and varied output. Regrettably, small failings
in the volume which the specialist can overlook may mislead
the "student and general reader" for whom the series is
designed. The selection of poems does less than justice to
Clare's infrequent but important ones on social literary
subjects; the notes on the prose writings provide insufficient
identification of social and political dates and issues; and
the guide to further reading is unreliable. But if there
ever was a text of Clare suitable for the classroom and the
undergraduate library, this is it. (M.M.)

Robinson, Eric; David Powell; and Margaret Grainger, eds.
The Later Poems of John Clare, 1837-1864. 2 vols. Oxford
University Press, 1984. Pp. xxiv+1165. $135.00.

Because there has never been anything approaching a complete
and reliable edition of Clare, and very few competently
edited selections, Romanticists have had to limp along with
texts seriously compromised by bowdlerization or by careless-
ness born of too much enthusiasm and too little editorial
training. No anthology of Romantic writers now or recently
in print contains reliable texts of all the Clare poems it
prints. Since the early 1960s Eric Robinson and various
co-editors have been preparing a definitive edition of Clare.
The present two volumes will be followed by perhaps four others
of the earlier poems, plus a new edition of the letters; the
Autobiographical Writings (see *RMB* for 1983, p. 98) and
the *Natural History Prose Writings* (see above under Grainger)
have already appeared. The editing task for the later poems,
all written in asylums, must have been a daunting one. For
many of the poems only transcripts exist which on occasion
appear to depart from now lost manuscripts. For others,
Clare's darkening mind left a muddle of partly revised drafts

and occasional intermingling of several different works in
one manuscript. The editors have conquered these and other
obstacles to such an extent that it is difficult to imagine
this edition needing to be replaced except as new manuscripts
may turn up. They have established a chronological order
for most of the poems (an important accomplishment, for
Clare continued to develop as a poet in the asylum), and
have provided all known variants to their chosen texts.
Although there is an understandable sameness about many of
these poems, in some Clare managed to transcend the limitations of his condition to produce a handful of lyrics that
rank with the best written in the century, and dozens of
others with powerful individual stanzas and lines even where
the poem as a whole may falter. Robinson's introduction
lays out the variety of Clare's verse forms and his indebtedness to the folk tradition, and argues the need for redefining
Romanticism to make more room for Clare. Robinson, Powell,
and Grainger's presentation of the text will not only add
greatly to our knowledge of Clare, but is also likely to
alter permanently the way he is read. (M.M.)

Strickland, Edward. "Approaching 'A Vision.'" *VP* 22 (1984):
229-45.

Searches out ambiguities in Clare's poem from "biographical
and generic perspectives."

See also Crossan ("English 1. Bibliography").

Composite reviews:

Lucas, John. "More Poet Than Peasant." *TLS*, July 27, 1984,
pp. 845-46.

Surveys the textual career of Clare's poems in a review of
Robinson and Powell (above) and Deacon (above).
Response by Mark Storey, in *TLS*, Aug. 24, 1984, p. 943,
remarks upon "the inadequacies of John Lucas's review" and
its "warmth that springs from ignorance shared."

Pigrome, Stella. "John Clare Books." *ChLB* 46 (1984): 114-
24.

A full review, including choice quotations, of *The Journal,
Essays and Journey from Essex* and *The Midsummer Cushion* (see
RMB for 1980, p. 94), both ed. by Anne Tibble; *The Rural
Muse*, ed. R.K.R. Thornton (see *RMB* for 1983, p. 99); *John
Clare's Birds*, ed. Eric Robinson and Richard Fitter (see
RMB for 1982, p. 107); and a notice of H.O. Dendurent's

Reference Guide (see *RMB* for 1981, p. 105) and of the first
issue of the *John Clare Society Journal* (see above).

COBBETT

Green, Daniel, ed. *Cobbett's Tour in Scotland*. Foreword by
Lord Grimond. Aberdeen University Press; Atlantic Highlands,
N.J.: Humanities Press, 1985. Pp. 232. $23.75.

The *Tour*, a continuation of his series of *Rural Rides*,
first appeared in the *Political Register* in 1832.

Knight, Denis, ed. *Cobbett in Ireland: A Warning to England*.
London: Lawrence and Wishart, 1984. Pp. 302. £12.50.

Rev. by Charles Townshend in *TLS*, Oct. 19, 1984, p. 1184.
A collection of Cobbett's reports and admonitions during
his Irish tour of 1834.
Not seen.

Townsend, Molly. *Not by Bullets and Bayonets: William Cobbett
and the Irish Question, 1795-1835*. New York: Sheed & Ward,
1982. Pp. 160. $40.00.

Not seen.

See also Butler, Himmelfarb, Wiener ("English 2. Environment");
Anderson ("English 3. Criticism").

Reviews of book previously listed:

SPATER, George, *William Cobbett: The Poor Man's Friend* (see
RMB for 1982, p. 108), rev. by John Clive in *WMQ* 41 (1984):
171-74; by William Thomas in *RES* 35 (1984): 557-58; by
David A. Wilson in *QQ* 91 (1984): 174-76, who finds the
achievement magnificent but Spater too generous.

COLERIDGE

Anderson, Wayne C. "The Prince of Preparatory Authors: The
Problem of Conveying Belief in Coleridge's *The Statesman's
Manual*." *TWC* 15 (1984): 28-32.

Anderson, Wayne C. "The Rhetoric of Silence in the Discourse
of Coleridge and Carlyle." *SAR* 49, No. 1 (Jan. 1984):
72-90.

Omissions, pauses, avoidances, and blank spaces function
rhetorically to evoke mystery, show the limits of language,
and invite reader participation. The discussion of how this
"rhetoric of the ineffable" makes the wordless present in
a text contributes usefully to the deconstructionist-logo-
centrist debate on language. (R.M.R.)

Bacigalupo, Massimo. "An Unnoticed Borrowing from the
   Odyssey in Coleridge's 'The Ancient Mariner.'" *N&Q* 31,iv
   (1984): 468-69.

   The Mariner's supernatural trip home is like Odysseus's
   return to Ithaca.

Bidney, Martin. "The Structure of Epiphanic Imagery in Ten
   Coleridge Lyrics." *SiR* 22 (1983): 20-40.

Chambers, Jane. "Leoline's Mastiff Bitch: Functions of a
   Minor Figure in *Christabel*." *ELN* 22,i (1984): 38-43.

Christensen, Jerome. "The Mind at Ocean: The Impropriety
   of Coleridge's Literary Life."

   See Reed ("English 3. Criticism").

DePaolo, Charles. "Coleridge and the Idea of a University."
   RP&P 8,i (1984): 17-34.

DePaolo, Charles. "Coleridge on Child-Labour Reform." *ChLB*
   47-48 (1984): 187-94.

   An explication of his 1818 work to suggest that Coleridge
   "was a significant child-labour reformer."

Engell, James, and W. Jackson Bate, eds. *Biographia Literaria,*
   Or Biographical Sketches of My Literary Life and Opinions.
   The Collected Works of Samuel Taylor Coleridge, 7. (Bollin-
   gen Series 75.) 2 vols. London: Routledge & Kegan Paul;
   Princeton Unversity Press, 1983. Vol. I: Pp. cxxxvi+306;
   3 illus. Vol. II: Pp. vii+409; 2 illus. $65.00; paper
   (2 vols. in one) $19.95.

   Rev. by R.L. Brett in *CritQ* 26,iii (1984): 83-85; by
   Lawrence Buell in *ELN* 22,ii (1984): 74-75; by Donald H.
   Reiman in *RP&P* 8,ii (1984): 39-44; by K.M. Wheeler in *EiC*
   34 (1984): 87-95, who protests that the editorial account
   of the distinction between primary and secondary imagination
   is a "complete falsity," "misguided," and "leads readers
   into regrettable misunderstandings about the dynamic nature
   of Coleridge's philosophy in general and of his theory of

imagination in particular," being accurate "only at the level of the history of ideas."

Coleridge's major work at last takes its place in the monumental series of his Collected Works now in progress. The high editorial standards of the preceding volumes continue to be upheld in an edition which undoubtedly will not be superseded for a long time to come. In their nearly 100-page introductory essay, Engell and Bate discuss *Biographia* exhaustively, from the circumstances (expectably troubled) of its composition and original publication, to its peculiar unity as a whole of many parts, "multeity in unity," calling on the "life of the whole man" who was its author. Sections of particular value are those on the background of Coleridge's concepts of Imagination and Fancy and the distinction between them, and "The German Borrowings and the Issue of Plagiarism." In the latter and in their annotations to the actual chapters in question, without taking a position of their own the editors make clear it is impossible to assert flatly that Coleridge was a plagiarist, even when he incorporated paraphrases or translated words and phrases in his expositions, because he was at one with his German authors in their knowledge of each other's writings and their use of earlier sources, some of which he shared, and because of his method of composition, which reflected the complex processes of his thought in reaction to his reading. These sections of the Introduction should be a final corrective to the hasty accusations that have persisted for a century and a half. (I.H.C.)

Flavin, James. "Paragraph One of *Biographia Literaria*: Coleridge on Structure." *N&Q* 31,i (March 1984): 56-57.

Supports Shawcross's editorial note in the Oxford edition that the opening paragraph was written after the work was largely completed. A point ignored by Engell and Bate.

Gleckner, Robert F. "Coleridge and Wordsworth Together in America." *TWC* 15 (1984): 17-19.

Unrecorded appearances of poems in early American publications.

Gravil, Richard. "Coleridge's Wordsworth." *TWC* 15 (1984): 38-46.

Harding, Anthony John. "Mythopoeic Elements in 'Christabel.'" *MLQ* 44 (1983): 39-50.

Havens, Michael Kent. "Tolkien's Green Earth: Coleridge's *Natura Naturans* Realized." *WVUPP* 28 (1982): 127-31.

Asserts a connection between Tolkien's fantasy world and Coleridge's ideas on art and nature, but the presentation of Coleridge is inadequate to establish the point. (R.M.R.)

Hill, John Spencer. *A Coleridge Companion: An Introduction to the Major Poems and the Biographia Literaria.* London: Macmillan, 1983. Pp. xv+288; 18 pls.

A useful student guide; sensible and thorough. (D.V.E.)

Kitson, Peter. "Coleridge's *The Plot Discovered*: A New Date." *N&Q* 31,i (March 1984): 57-58.

This radical pamphlet, Kitson argues, must have been published between December 2 and 4, 1795, since the lecture it contains was given that November 26 and the latest possibility was December 10.

Lee, Sung-Won. "Hermes Bound: Coleridge's Reading of *Prometheus Bound*." *History and Mimesis* (Occasional Papers III, SUNY, Buffalo, Spring, 1983; Irving J. Massey and Sung-Won Lee, eds.): 30-51.

"Coleridge, in short, claims that there is a particular form of art which describes how God has revealed Himself through history and in different societies, that His plan can be described at many points in history, and that we see this truth clearly in great works of art, Aeschylus' Prometheus being one of them" (37).
While Coleridge, like Schleiermacher, "fosters a universal hermeneutics," in his *Prometheus* essay he employs it inversely, accommodating "literary texts in terms of theological meanings" (32). An impressive *applicatio*. (D.V.E.)

Leggett, B.J. "Why It Must Be Abstract: Stevens, Coleridge, and I.A. Richards." *SiR* 22 (1983): 489-515.

Little, Geoffrey. "Coleridge's Copy of *Lyrical Ballads*, 1800 and His Connection with the Irving Family." *BC* 33 (1984): 457-69.

This copy, now in the State Library of Victoria, Melbourne, was brought to Australia from London in 1856 by M.H. Irving, whose father, Edward Irving, received it from Coleridge. It contains Coleridge's addition of his name to his own poems. The handwritten notes to *The Ancient Mariner* suggest that Coleridge may have composed the marginal explanations soon after 1800 instead of just before they were published in 1817.

Memoir & Letters of Sara Coleridge. Edited by Her Daughter. New York, 1874. Reprint. New York: AMS Press, 1984. $42.50.

Miall, David S. "Guilt and Death: The Predicament of *The Ancient Mariner.*" *SEL* 24 (Autumn 1984): 633-53.

A modified psychoanalytic approach. The poem is found to present a "struggle for meaning" by the Mariner analogous to Coleridge's own lifelong struggle to explain the "misery of isolation and dread, the origin of which [i.e., in his father's death] was forever repressed in his memory."

Nye, Eric W. "Coleridge to Joseph Hughes: A Newly Identified Letter." *Library* 6 (1984): 376-80.

Griggs 1038 should be 1661A. To the Rev. Joseph Hughes [Spring or Summer 1829]. Neatly done. (T.L.A.)

O'Connor, Robert H. "'The Rime of the Ancient Mariner' and *Tales of the Devil*: A Note." *TWC* (15 (1984): 81-82.

Several stanzas of obvious parody in an anonymous 1801 spoof of "Gothic" poetry.

Potter, Stephen, ed. *Minnow Among Tritons: Mrs. S.T. Coleridge's Letters to Thomas Poole, 1799-1834.* Reprint. New York: AMS Press, 1984. $24.50.

Priestman, Donald G. "Lyrical Ballads and Variant, Ashley 2250." *ELN* 21,iv (1984): 41-48.

This variant copy of *Lyrical Ballads* in the British Library substitutes Thomas Beddoes's "Domiciliary Verses" for Coleridge's "Lewti."

Ray, Rhonda Johnson. "Geraldine as Usurper of Christ: An Un-Mystical Union." *PQ* 63 (1984): 511-23.

Raymond, M.B. "A Letter from Sara Coleridge." *TWC* 15 (1984): 55-56.

To John Kenyon, in or around 1846, concerned with defending Coleridge from the charge of plagiarism.

Reed, Arden. "The Mariner Rimed."

See Reed ("English 3. Criticism").

Reiman, Donald H. "The Beauty of Buttermere as Fact and
   Romantic Symbol." *Criticism* 26 (1984): 139-70.

   Recognizing that "little has been written about the
significance, either within the symbolic structure of *The
Prelude*, or to Wordsworth the human being and his contemporaries, of Mary Robinson," the "Beauty of Buttermere,"
Reiman has assembled the factual materials and made a
valuable and extensive examination of their symbolic significance. (D.V.E.)

Robertson, P.J.M. "Criticism and Creativity III: Pope and
   Coleridge." *QQ* 91 (1984): 665-78.

   Part IV, on "Blake and Keats," is listed above under
Blake.

Tave, Katherine Bruner. *The Demon and the Poet: An Interpretation of "The Rime of the Ancient Mariner" According
   to Coleridge's Demonological Sources*. (SSEL: Romantic
   Reassessment 99.) Atlantic Highlands, N.J.: Humanities
   Press, 1983. Pp. v+148. Paper $25.00.

   Tave so thoroughly applies to the minute particulars the
implicit and explicit logic of the pertinent demonology as
to have given us, at long last, a beautifully adequate
reading of Coleridge's "Rime"! The Wedding-Guest, as
reader, does grow to a sadder yet wiser humanity; the
Mariner as poet (Coleridge) is "not describing psychological
reactions, nor ... writing his autobiography" but illustrating
"the power of poetic truth to disorient and to change a
person completely" (poet and audience).
   This convincing study will make us all wise--yet not sad.
(D.V.E.)

Ting, Nai-Tung. "From Shangtu to Xanadu." *SiR* 23 (1984):
   205-22.

   Recent archeology reveals that Shangtu in the fourteenth
century was "actually" three walled cities: "the forbidden,
the imperial, and the outer, one enclosed within the other,"
with a moat outside the walls. (And there is much more:
with a map.)
   Through the genius of Coleridge, "an obscure Chinese city
in ruins has been transformed into Xanadu, a household word
in the English-speaking world and a fascinating challenge
to international scholarship." The leap from the diggers'
map to a pleasure dome also requires transformational genius.
   Ting is mistaken, however, in thinking that the Abyssinian
maid is imagined as in Xanadu; next challenge: explore the
sources of the Nile. (D.V.E.)

Ullrich, David W. "Distinctions in Poetic and Intellectual
    Influence: Coleridge's Use of Erasmus Darwin." *TWC* 15
    (1984): 74-80.

Vlasopolos, Anca. *The Symbolic Method of Coleridge, Baudelaire,
    and Yeats.* Wayne State University Press, 1983. Pp. 218.
    $18.95.
    Rev. by Thomas J. Corr in *CollL* 11 (1984): 286-89.

Whalley, George, ed. *The Collected Works of Samuel Taylor
    Coleridge: Marginalia* II. (Bollingen Series 75.) London:
    Routledge & Kegan Paul; Princeton University Press, 1984.
    Pp. xxxi+1,207. $90.00.

    From Camden's grammar to Hutton's epistemology, here we
    have all Coleridge's surviving annotations singled out and
    clarified; the final huge volume (from I to Z) to complete
    the late George Whalley's great labors will include a vast
    Index. I've enjoyed sampling the remarks on Defoe, Donne,
    Fichte, Fielding, Fuller, Godwin, Herbert, Herder, and
    Chapman's Homer: "What is stupidly said of Shakspere is
    really true & appropriate of Chapman--'mighty faults counter-
    poised by mighty Beauties.'" (D.V.E.)

Wylie, I.M. "How the Natural Philosophers Defeated the Whore
    of Babylon in the Thought of S.T. Coleridge, 1795-1796."
    RES 35 (1984): 494-507.

Zall, P.M. "The Cool World of Samuel Taylor Coleridge:
    William Ayrton's Rise." *TWC* 15 (1984): 22-25.

See also Ellison, Jacobus, Kipperman, McGann, Reed, Thurley
    ("General 3. Criticism"); Clubbe, Cross, Sherbo ("English
    1. Bibliography"); Semmel, Wiener ("English 2. Environment");
    Abrams, Anderson, Johnson and Leyda, Macovski, Mudge,
    Needham, Venis ("English 3. Criticism"); Mulderig ("Carlyle");
    Bromwich ("Hazlitt"); Parker, Roe ("Wordsworth, W.").

Reviews of books previously listed:

CHRISTENSEN, Jerome, *Coleridge's Blessed Machine of
    Language* (see *RMB* for 1981, p. 57), rev. by Arden Reed in
    SiR 22 (1983): 623-31; CORRIGAN, Timothy, *Coleridge,
    Language, and Criticism* (see *RMB* for 1983, p. 101), rev. by
    Frederick Burwick in *RP&P* 8,ii (1984): 58-64; by Kenneth
    Watson in *JAAC* 42 (1984): 227-30; DEKKER, George, *Coleridge
    and the Literature of Sensibility* (see *ELN* 17, Supp.), rev.

by Luther Tyler in *SiR* 22 (1983): 648-52; DOUGHTY, Oswald, *Perturbed Spirit: The Life and Personality of Samuel Taylor Coleridge* (see *RMB* for 1982, p. 109), rev. by Lucy Newlyn in *RES* 35 (1984): 564-66; JACKSON, J.R. de J., ed., *Logic*, No. 13 of *The Collected Works of Samuel Taylor Coleridge* (see *RMB* for 1981, p. 107), rev. by Paul Hamilton in *RES* 35 (1984): 246-48; LEVERE, Trevor H., *Poetry Realized in Nature: Samuel Taylor Coleridge and Early Nineteenth-Century Science* (see *RMB* for 1983, pp. 104-06), rev. by Martin K. Nurmi in *SiR* 23 (1984): 420-23; by Ian M. Wylie in *RES* 35 (1984): 394-96; MARKS, Emerson R., *Coleridge on the Language of Verse* (see *RMB* for 1982, p. 111), rev. by W.J.B. Owen in *RES* 35 (1984): 391-94; MILEUR, Jean-Pierre, *Vision and Revision: Coleridge's Art of Immanence* (see *RMB* for 1982, p. 111), rev. by Paul Magnuson in *MLQ* 44 (1983): 99-102; by Tilottama Rajan in *SiR* 23 (1984): 262-68; SULTANA, Donald, ed., *New Approaches to Coleridge: Biographical and Critical Essays* (see *RMB* for 1981, p. 109), rev. by Geoffrey Little in *RES* 35 (1984): 95-96; WHEELER, Kathleen M., *The Creative Mind in Coleridge's Poetry* (see *RMB* for 1982, p. 114), rev. by Paul Magnuson in *SiR* 22 (1983): 440-45 as occasionally rewarding but frequently self-contradictory; by W.J.B. Owen in *RES* 35 (1984): 391-94; WHEELER, Kathleen, *Sources, Processes and Methods in Coleridge's "Biographia Literaria"* (see *RMB* for 1980, pp. 97-98), rev. by Jerome Christensen in *SiR* 22 (1983): 126-35[sic]) in what reads like one continuous, troping sentence (of condemnation).

Composite review:

Dekker, George. *Modern Philology* 82 (1984): 106-10.

Reviews Jerome Christensen, *Coleridge's Blessed Machine of Language* (see *RMB* for 1981, p. 57), and Emerson R. Marks, *Coleridge on the Language of Verse* (see *RMB* for 1982, p. 111).

CONSTABLE

Fleming-Williams, Ian, and Leslie Parris. *The Discovery of Constable*. London: Hamish Hamilton, 1984. Pp. 276. £25.00.

Rev. by John Gage in *TLS*, Jan. 18, 1985, p. 56, along with Graham Reynolds's volumes (see below).

Reynolds, Graham. *The Later Paintings and Drawings of John Constable*. 2 vols. Yale University Press, 1984. 1,087 pls. (255 in color). $195.00.

Rev. by John Gage in *TLS*, Jan. 18, 1985, p. 56; by Denys
Sutton in *Apollo* 120 (1984): 435-36.

These are volumes III and IV of the complete catalogue
raisonné; volumes I and II, *The Earlier Paintings and Drawings*,
are being prepared by Charles Rhyne.

Constables and pseudo-Constables are still turning up,
and this catalogue is not what it would have been a few
decades ago. Beginning in 1817, these volumes cover the more
public part of Constable's career. Sketches are frequently
shown beside the paintings, and fully a quarter of the works
are here reproduced for the first time.

The bibliography shows exhibition catalogues and other
publications on Constable mounting from 12 between 1880 and
1946 to 23 in the 50s and 60s, to 33 in the 70s and 80s--
suggesting an exponential increase for the rest of the
century. Moreover, Reynolds's notes frequently correct
previous information and earlier interpretations of Constable's
biography as well as of his art; his hope seems well grounded
"that the body of Constable's work presented here is sufficiently comprehensive to provide a reliable survey of his
later years, and a structure into which the fruits of future
research can be fitted" (xii). (D.V.E.)

Reviews of book previously listed:

ROSENTHAL, Michael, *Constable: The Painter and His Landscape*
(see *RMB* for 1983, p. 109), rev. by Malcolm Cormack in *BM*
126 (June 1984): 361-62; by Graham Reynolds in *Apollo* 119
(1984): 387.

DARWIN, E.

Hassler, Donald M. "New Diggings in Old Mines: Erasmus
Darwin and Romantic Views on Evolution." *TWC* 15 (1984):
26-28.

See also Ullrich ("Coleridge").

DE QUINCEY

Blakemore, Steven. "De Quincey's Transubstantiation of Opium
in the *Confessions*." *MSE* 9,iii (1984): 32-41.

De Quincey (a) "metaphorically changes opium into the
Eucharist" and (b) "then transforms the paradisaical,
Eucharist opium into its anti-type: the 'forbidden' apple
of Eden...."

Dowling, Linda. "Nero and the Aesthetics of Torture." *VN* 66 (Fall 1984): 1-5.

Shapiro, Fred R. "Words for *OED* from DeQuincey." *AN&Q* 22 (1983): 49-50.

Snyder, Robert Lance. "A De Quinceyan Source for Poe's 'The Masque of the Red Death.'" *SSF* 21 (1984): 103-10.

Poe must have read *Klosterheim; or, The Masque* (1832) because it seems he took the "setting, plot, climactic incident, and expression" of his "Masque" from it.

Whale, John C. *Thomas De Quincey's Reluctant Autobiography.* Sydney: Croom Helm; Totowa, N.J.: Barnes & Noble, 1984. Pp. 245. $27.50.

Whale's study is welcome as the first serious effort to examine De Quincey as a working autobiographer, rather than a visionary opium eater. The title may be misleading: the "reluctant" refers chiefly to the resistance of the material, De Quincey's "reluctance" to simplify the complexities of his experience, his use of techniques of suspension and discontinuity which more created than reported experience, resulting in autobiography structured "around a gap between evaluation and enactment" (231). The study considers the relation of De Quincey's autobiographical writings to his other writings--finding many parallels and sometimes seeming to see nearly everything as autobiographical. Beginning with the reasonable assumption that De Quincey's autobiography is conditioned by his role as a periodical writer, Whale proceeds to a careful--if perhaps De Quinceyan, involuted, and repetitious--analysis of De Quincey's treatment of the reader, going on to discuss the Romantic elements in autobiography and the extent to which De Quincey adopts the role of the Victorian Sage.

This is a thorough, valuable work, knowledgeable about De Quincey scholarship. (Although it does not seem to make use of the contributions of De Luca, it does list his work in the "Select Bibliography," a substantial, useful updating of De Quincey materials.) (J.E.J.)

See also Jacobus, Reed ("General 3. Criticism"); Buckley, Cockshut ("English 3. Criticism"); Butler ("Hazlitt").

Reviews of book previously listed:

DE LUCA, V.A., *Thomas De Quincey: The Prose of Vision* (see *RMB* for 1980, p. 100), rev. by Robert M. Maniquis in *SiR*

23 (1984):   139-47, extensively and judiciously--and severely,
as a "fast shuffle" from Romanticism to Modernism, often
requiring "tone deafness"; by Stuart M. Tave in *YES* 4 (1984):
333-34.

EDGEWORTH

Atkinson, Colin B., and Jo Atkinson.   "Maria Edgeworth,
   Belinda, and Women's Rights." *Eire* 19,iv (1984):   94-118.

   Maria Edgeworth has a "comprehensive vision of woman's
   place in society."

See also Agress, Williams ("English 3. Criticism").

THE EDINBURGH REVIEW

See Klancher ("English 3. Criticism").

THE EXAMINER

See Klancher ("English 3. Criticism").

GALT

Waterston, Elizabeth.   "John Galt's Canadian Experience: The
   Scottish Strain." *SSL* 15 (1980):   257-62.

   Giving the background of *Bogle Corbet, or The Emigrants*
   (1831).   (T.L.A.)

GODWIN

Claey, Gregory.   "The Effects of Property on Godwin's Theory
   of Justice." *JHP* 22 (1984):   81-101.

   When revising *Political Justice* Godwin had to reconcile
   two conflicting concepts of justice, one based on the moral
   worth of the individual, the other on his need.   In resolving
   the conflict he developed an anti-revolutionary defense of
   property as stewardship, unequal wealth being justifiable
   if used to alleviate poverty and benefit society.   "Hence,
   though my mother may perish in the flames while Fenelon is

saved, she will, at least, not die of hunger in order that he shall be able to practice philosophy." An important essay for its clarifications and its demonstration of the utility of reading *Political Justice* (and more than one edition of it) closely. (R.M.R.)

DePorte, Michael. "The Consolations of Fiction: Mystery in *Caleb Williams*." *PLL* 20 (1984): 154-64.

"The problem of judgment is almost impossible because *Caleb Williams* has no normative characters" when mystery means reader anxiety. (T.L.A.)

Graham, Kenneth W. "The Gothic Unity of Godwin's *Caleb Williams*." *PLL* 20 (1984): 47-59.

Gothic structure bridges the gap between Godwin the novelist and Godwin the philosopher. "Simplified, the underlying meaning of *Caleb Williams* is that solipsism distorts perspective and sympathy counteracts solipsism." Thanks to Coleridge. (T.L.A.)

Kelly, Gary. "Convention and Criticism in William Godwin's Early Novels." *KSJ* 33 (1984): 52-69.

Marshall, Peter H. *William Godwin*. Yale University Press, 1984. Pp. xi+497; 34 illus. $30.00.

Rev. by Gertrude Himmelfarb in *NR*, Dec. 31, 1984, pp. 25-30; by D.A.N. Jones in *LRB* 6,xvi (1984): 18-19; by Nicolas Walter in *S*, Aug. 25, 1984, pp. 24-25, as "the best biography of Godwin for more than a century."
An excellent complement to Don Locke's recent *Life and Thought* (see *RMB* for 1980, p. 102). That probing portrait was painted deftly but swiftly. Marshall takes more time (given more space: though he is sometimes careless with details) to document and examine closely both life and thought; we travel with the chronicle of these, watching their evolution and also exploring and evaluating their philosophical and literary consequences--in Godwin's own works and in their influence. Marshall makes good use of the insights and evaluations offered by Don Locke and Burton Pollin, but he is right to place great importance, at this stage of such study, on chronology and historical context. (D.V.E.)

See also Butler ("English 1. Bibliography"); Bromwich ("Hazlitt").

Reviews of books previously listed:

PALACIA, Jean de, *William Godwin et son monde intérieur* (see
RMB for 1982, p. 118), rev. by Alice Green Fredman in *KSJ*
33 (1984): 229-31; by M. Paridon briefly in *Dix-Huitième
Siècle* 15 (1983): 532; TYSDAHL, B.J., *William Godwin as
Novelist* (see *RMB* for 1981, pp. 113-14), rev. by N.H. Roe
in *RES* 35 (1984): 242-43.

THE GOTHIC

Craig, R. "Beckford's Inversion of Romance in *Vathek.*"
Orbis Literarum 39 (1984): 95-106.

Mathews, John R. "Ghostly Language: A Theory of Gothic
Discourse." Ann Arbor, Mich.: University Microfilms International, 1984.

Dissertation.

Ringe, Donald A. *American Gothic: Imagination and Reason in
Nineteeneth-Century Fiction.* University Press of Kentucky,
1982. Pp. vii+215. $17.00.

Rev. by William Veeder in *NEQ* 57 (1984): 133-37.

Spector, Robert Donald. *The English Gothic. A Bibliographic
Guide to Writers from Horace Walpole to Mary Shelley.*
Westport, Conn., and London: Greenwood Press, 1984. Pp.
xiii+267. $35.00.

Another Gothic bibliography. Differs, however, by
offering continuous commentaries on select areas of Gothic
Criticism from the contemporary reviews to modern psychological and feminist studies. An introductory chapter is
followed by individual surveys of work to date on Horace
Walpole and Clara Reeve, Charlotte Smith and Ann Radcliffe,
M.G. Lewis and Beckford, Maturin and Mary Shelley. Spector
is dependent for much of his original material on reprints
such as the Arno series of Gothic novels, but his reading
in twentieth-century criticism is impressive. The focus
leads to slightly unbalanced reproof of critics who fail
to see the Gothic light (e.g., "sentiment" rather than the
sublime in Charlotte Smith). Some judgments are questionable:
The Monk's "introducing the Schauer-Romantik to England,"
or the automatically assumed "inferior" nature of Maturin's
Albigenses. Relentless summary of other people's judgments
can grate after a while, Spector's prose never rising above
the academically sound. On the other hand, a number of

surprising omissions are brought to light; the absence, for example, of scholarly "Monk" Lewis texts apart from *The Monk*. Each chapter ends with an impressive list of books and articles, where even the most practiced Gothicist is likely to find something new. Articles up to 1983 are included-- the net cast particularly wide in the 1970s. A useful reference and guide. (P.D.G.)

See also Frank ("General 1. Bibliography"); Frew ("English 2. Environment"); Cook et al. ("English 3. Criticism").

HAYDON

See Cockshut ("English 3. Criticism").

HAZLITT

Albrecht, W.P. "Hazlitt's 'On the Fear of Death': Reason Versus Imagination." *TWC* 15 (1984): 3-7.

Bromwich, David. *Hazlitt: The Mind of a Critic.* Oxford University Press, 1984. Pp. xviii+450. $35.00.

Rev. by M.H. Abrams in *NYRB*, May 10, 1984, pp. 37-40, as a complicated enterprise, successful in rescuing the acute critical mind of Hazlitt from neglect but undercut by an attempt to raise Hazlitt above Coleridge even as a theorist; by D.A.N. Jones in *LRB* 6,xvi (1984): 18-19; by Allan Massie in *S*, March 24, 1984, pp. 26-27, as "a decent bit of anatomising."

One picks up this long book about *Hazlitt: The Mind of a Critic* with scepticism: is there so much to add to the work of Baker, Albrecht, Park, Kinnaird, Wardle? One puts it down with lingering doubts but with-all a new appreciation of Hazlitt's power and influence. Bromwich has absorbed Hazlitt, sometimes writes with something of the master's wryness and gusto, seems to accept his politics, becomes so much involved that it is not always clear whether the ideas advanced are Hazlitt's or Bromwich's. Appropriately, Bromwich both defends and questions, calls attention to contradictions, frankly "cannot see how to reconcile" (298) Hazlitt's early and late positions.

Bromwich suggests his readers might fare more swimmingly if they start with his third chapter, returning later to Chap. I ("Imagination") and Chap. II ("Interest, Habit,

Association"). The early chapters lay the foundation for
the Hazlitt dear to Bromwich: the metaphysician; they
include such unexpected things as an account of Abraham
Tucker's chapter "The Vision" in *The Light of Nature Pursued*
and an analysis of the meaning of "disinterestedness" from
Godwin through Arnold to William James. The study, as
Bromwich says, falls in "a somewhat mixed genre"--it is not
a biography or an account of Hazlitt's critical career, but
a synchronic treatment of his critical ideas, their sources,
influence, and relation to the views of his contemporaries--
especially Burke, Hunt, Coleridge, Byron, Wordsworth, and
Keats. Most interesting is the analysis of Keats's development under Hazlitt's tutelage, conluding with critiques
of the odes. One is at least partly persuaded by, even
though finding overblown, the assertion that Hazlitt's "review of *The Excursion* was the incitement without which we
should hardly be reading Keats today" (372). (J.E.J.)

Butler, Marilyn. "Satire and the Images of Self in the
    Romantic Period: The Long Tradition of Hazlitt's *Liber
    Amoris.*" *YES* 14 (1984): 209-25.

    A provocative argument that the self-conscious Romantics
    self-consciously criticized (and satirized) their own self-
    consciousness. Too often, Butler argues, we (and sometimes
    the Romantics themselves) misread the Romantics' portrayal
    of solipsistic love as an aesthetic defense rather than an
    intellectual critique: thus Shelley's *Alastor* should be
    read as an indictment of Wordsworth's *Excursion* Book I;
    Keats's *Endymion*, of *Alastor*; De Quincey's *Confessions of an
    English Opium Eater*, of Rousseau's *Confessions*; and Hazlitt's
    Liber Amoris, of De Quincey's *Confessions*. Godwin's *Fleetwood*
    and *Mandeville*, Mary Shelley's *Frankenstein*, and other works
    are also invoked in this essay as essentially critical of
    the introverted individual who fails to love. As should be
    obvious from the above, Butler interprets "H--" in *Liber
    Amoris* as more than Hazlitt himself in an autobiography:
    "H--" is a character in a novel, in which Hazlitt "was de-
    fining his position in relation to some extreme contemporary
    versions of the doctrine of the Imagination, which, in
    Hazlitt's rendering, kills." (C.E.R.)

Haefner, Joel. "'The Soul Speaking in the Face': Hazlitt's
    Concept of Character." *SEL* 24 (Autumn 1984): 655-70.

See also Rawson, Strelka ("General 3. Criticism"); Green
    ("English 2. Environment"); Chandler, Haefner ("English 3.
    Criticism").

HOGG

Campbell, Ian. "Hogg's *Confessions* and the *Heart of Darkness*."
    SSL 15 (1980): 187-201.

    As analogue not influence, but a sensitive reading. (T.L.A.)

Groves, David. "Allusions to *Dr. Faustus* in James Hogg's
    A Justified Sinner." *SSL* 18 (1983): 157- 65.

    Marlowe helps us understand that "without discarding the
    moral and theological conflict of the Faust legend, James
    Hogg superimposes a more modern sense of epistemological and
    psychological complexity." (T.L.A.)

Hogg, James. *Anecdotes of Sir Walter Scott*. Ed. Douglas S.
    Mack. Edinburgh: Scottish Academic Press, 1984. Pp. 79.
    £5.50.

    Rev. by Neil Berry in *TLS*, Sept. 7, 1984, p. 987.
    The newly discovered original version of Hogg's *Familiar
    Anecdotes*, is less alarmingly different from the *Memoir* version
    (ed. by Mack in 1972) than Lockhart's effort to suppress it
    seemed to imply. That Lockhart "found it repugnant is
    further evidence of his snobbery and caste-consciousness,"
    observes Berry.

Oakleaf, David. "'Not the Truth': The Doubleness of Hogg's
    Confessions and the Eighteenth-Century Tradition." *SSL* 18
    (1983): 59-74.

    A significant contribution which finds that "the empirical
    perspective itself suggests the duality of man and raises
    the dilemma of different "selves" motivating the same
    'man.'" (T.L.A.)

HOOD

See Cross ("English 1. Bibliography").

HUNT

Allentuck, Marcia. "Leigh Hunt and Shelley: A New Letter."
    KSJ 33 (1984): 50.

    Hunt to Richard Westmacott, April 8, 1823.

Grigely, Joseph C. "Leigh Hunt and the *Examiner* Review of
    Keat's [sic] *Poems*, 1817." *KSJ* 33 (1984): 30-37.

Prints a letter of June 2, 1817, from John Hunt to Leigh
Hunt and argues that the latter's delay in reviewing Keats
probably resulted from his misplacement of the volume (but
couldn't he use the Shelleys' copy at Marlow?). The letter
also contains information on the profits and number of
copies printed of the *Examiner*. (C.E.R.)

O'Leary, Patrick. "John Scott and Leigh Hunt." *KSJ* 33 (1984):
51.

Brief remarks on the coincidence of two lives.

See also Cross ("English 1. Bibliography"); Green ("English
2. Environment"); Cockshut, Pereira ("English 3. Criticism").

JEFFREY

Pitrie, David W. "Francis Jeffrey and Religion: Excerpts from
His 1799-1800 Commonplace Book." *ECLife* 8,i (1982): 97-107.

Review of book previously listed:

FLYNN, Philip, *Francis Jeffrey* (see *ELN* 17, Supp., 87), rev.
by Peter Morgan in *SSL* 15 (1980): 292-93.

KEATS

Bayley, John. "Larkin and the Romantic Tradition." *CritQ*
26, Nos. 1 & 2 (Spring and Summer 1984): 61-66.

For Philip Larkin, as for Keats, "romanticism is the most
intense aspect of a common reality, an elsewhere conjured
up by soberly precise insistence on the banality of the here
and now." He is like Keats too in "the ability to bring
discrepant modes of feeling from other poets together and
make the result uniquely his own."

Bidney, Martin. "The Exploration of Keatsian Aesthetic
Problems in Browning's 'Madhouse Cells.'" *SEL* 24 (1984):
671-81.

Browning's two "mad aesthetes" validate in bizarre fashion
Keats's realization that one cannot immobilize reality to
preserve an aesthetically or emotionally intense moment.
Bidney could have reached the same conclusion without
straining to find in the "Ode on Melancholy" "the sado-
masochistic implications of aesthetic hedonism." (R.M.R.)

Fields, Beverly. "Keats and the Tongueless Nightingale: Some Unheard Melodies in 'The Eve of St. Agnes.'" *TWC* 14 (1983): 246-50.

The myth of Philomel provides the dark undersong of Keats's "fantasy of eroticized destructiveness." Porphyro, his reputation still slipping, is here a demonic descendant of Tereus representing the threat posed by violent unconscious impulses to the rational, controlled "daylight self." Even resisters of psychoanalytic criticism will find this session informative. It is an important essay by a very good reader of poetry. (R.M.R.)

Fisher, Peter. "A Museum with One Work Inside: Keats and the Finality of Art." *KSJ* 33 (1984): 85-102.

This is a brilliant (it really deserves the overused epithet, along with "dazzling") meditation on the "Ode on a Grecian Urn" as it illustrates the strategies of art in a situation of belatedness and historical crisis. Fisher's critical inventions, "emergency art" and "the aesthetics of the anthology," justify themselves by their usefulness, and his informed analogies between poetry and visual art illuminate the poem with repeated flashes of insight. The discussion is original, consistently intelligent, expressed in beautiful and energetic prose, and likely to become itself an anthology piece. Bravo! This is what the humanities are all about. (R.M.R.)

Goellnicht, Donald C. *The Poet-Physician: Keats and Medical Science.* University of Pittsburgh Press, 1984. Pp. xii+ 271. $26.95.

This is the latest and best study of Keats's medical background, more thorough than its predecessors in its investigation of the textbooks and lectures Keats was exposed to at the Borough School and in its attempt to connect his scientific knowledge with the poetry. We are reminded (again) how much chemistry is involved in Keats's concept of the creative process and how his apothecary's interest in botany helps to explain the precision of his descriptions of the natural world. But while Goellnight's exhaustive research has unquestionably produced a useful resource for students, one feels at times that his hard work has brought limited returns. Rather than enrich our sense of Keats, he tends to narrow it by insisting only on the medical origins or significance of the poet's words, on the vehicles of his metaphors at the expense of the tenors. On at least two occasions he complains that Keats "spoiled" a simile by deviating from literal medical observation. One is

finally left with the sense of having read 238 pages of
footnotes, none of which is absolutely essential to an
appreciation of the texts above.

This admitted reluctance "to stray from the realm of
medicine into that of aesthetics, which is beyond the
scope of this study," is probably wise, since Goellnicht
seems much less sure of himself in the latter area, relying
too often on routine and sometimes inaccurate literary
generalizations. One of his chief liabilities, in fact,
is his lack of familiarity with the contemporary literary
scene, which prevents him from knowing how precisely special
Keats's scientific knowledge really was. Keats knew that
laurel leaves were poisonous, but so did Blake, who as far
as we know never cracked a textbook in *materia medica*. The
architectural metaphors for the structure of the brain that
Goellnicht traces to an anatomy lecture can almost all be
found in one striking stanza of *Childe Harold* (II, vi),
which Keats read before going to medical school. Goellnicht's
scholarly blinders kept him from noticing that much of his
"medical" lore is common property or common sense. E.g.,
"[Keats] knew from his study of botany that a state of
dormancy is necessary ... before growth and renewed creativity can occur." The Hyperion poems "deal with the broad
subject of a healthy and balanced life--a concept Keats
developed from his medical training." If Keats didn't know
those things before he began his medical education, he was
even less precocious than we thought. (R.M.R.)

Graham-Campbell, Anugs. "John Keats and Marian Jeffery."
  KSJ 33 (1984): 40-50.

Examines a book of poems by Jeffery ("competent and
unexceptional in a minor romantic vein"), finding evidence
that she may have been Keats's mysterious benefactor "P.
Fenbank."

Hindin, Michael. "Reading the Painting, Seeing the Poem:
  Vermeer and Keats." *Mosaic* 17,iii (1984): 17-34.

"Both Vermeer's *An Artist in His Studio* and Keats's 'Ode
on a Grecian Urn' explore the role of the imagination in
the making and experience of art." In the case of each,
"its subject is the very process that it means to effect."

Hopkins, Brooke. "Keats' Negative Capability and Winnicott's
  Creative Play." *AI* 41 (1984): 85-100.

Lau, Beth. "Keats's Mature Goddesses." *PQ* 63 (1984): 323-41.

Sees Keats's poetry as progressing from its early fascination with alluring, demonic goddesses offering escape from
human limitations to a more resigned veneration of maternal
deities associated with earth-bound mutability. But Lau's
symmetry necessitates a number of simplifications and
elisions. The inconveniently late Lamia, for instance,
is blamed on a distracting Fanny Brawne, although the girl
doesn't seem to have interfered with the creation of Moneta.
Keats's goddesses are more complicated creatures than Lau
appears to realize. (R.M.R.)

Lee, Chong H. "The Fabric of Love and Death: Evolution of
the Feminine Principle in the Poems of John Keats." Ann
Arbor, Mich.: University Microfilms International, 1984.

Dissertation.

Macksey, Richard. "Keats and the Poetics of Extremity."
MLN 99 (1984): 845-84.

After eight pages of post-structuralist *vocalise*, Macksey
gets down to the business of presenting some strikingly fresh
perceptions of "To Autumn" relating to Keats's ideas on
negative capability. While his previous poems attempted to
reach the absolute by a canceling and transcending of self
through empathy, Keats succeeds in "To Autumn" "by turning
from his vain, dream-ridden striving for the transcendent
to the calm acceptance of the natural condition"--an acceptance reflected in his search for a simpler English idiom.
(R.M.R.)

Macksey, Richard. "'To Autumn' and the Music of Mortality:
'Pure Rhetoric of a Language without Words.'"

See Reed ("English 3. Criticism").

Pederson-Krag, Geraldine. *The Lurking Keats*. Lanham, Md.:
University Press of America, 1984. Pp. 98. $18.75;
paper $8.00.

Distinct from "the ostensible Keats" was the one that lurked
in his poetry disguised as Endymion, Lorenzo, Porphyro,
Lycius, and even Meg Merrilies and Bertha, with his family
and friends in various supporting roles. *Hyperion*'s Titans,
for example, "may represent all those relatives, ostlers and
customers with whom his family had dealings," while the
Beadsman and Angela seem to be Mr. and Mrs. Dilke. Since
in the poetry Keats was free to live out his fantasies,
"it is evident that he was happiest while lurking rather
than ostensible." Apart from that insight, this life of

Keats by a practicing psychoanalyst is little more than
a condensation of Gittings's biography, to which almost all
the footnotes refer. It has no scholarly pretensions.
(R.M.R.)

Powell, Margaret Ketchum. "Keats and His Editor: The Manuscript of *Endymion*." *Library*, 6th series, 6 (1984): 139-52.

An argument for using Keats's holograph fair copy as copy
text on the grounds that the printer made arbitrary changes
that the poet did not approve. Powell's scrupulously detailed
examination of John Taylor's editorial procedures is interesting enough almost to distract attention from the
slightness of her case against the printer. (R.M.R.)

Rhodes, Jack Wright. *Keats's Major Odes: An Annotated
Bibliography of the Criticism*. Westport, Conn.: Greenwood
Press, 1984. Pp. 224. $35.00

Although overlapping with other bibliographies, such as
Reiman's *The Romantics Reviewed* at one end and *RMB* and *KSJ*
at the other (the coverage goes from 1820 to 1980), this one
will be useful as a supplement, since it picks up a few
items that others have missed or ignored and offers lengthier,
sometimes more informative annotations (descriptive rather
than evaluative). Occasionally one detects signs of haste
in the gathering and reading of material; e.g., while scores
of less influential critics are represented by trivial
items, Paul de Man's name does not appear (his preface to
the Signet *Keats* should certainly have been listed). But
for the most part Rhodes has done his work intelligently
and conscientiously. His introductory essay describing
trends in critical response to the odes over 150 years is
successful enough as an overview, although it changes at
midpoint from a survey of Keats criticism to a more general
sociological study of the academic publishing industry--
provocative enough in its contention that most academic
criticism is motivated internally by a "romanticized" need
for original insight inspired by alienation and insecurity,
and externally by the economic sanctions of the profession.
(R.M.R.)

Rzepka, Charles J. "*Theatrum Mundi* and Keats's *Otho the
Great*: The Self in 'Saciety.'" *RP&P* 8, No. 1 (1984): 35-50.

This welcome addition to the limited *Otho* bibliography
makes a good case that the extravagance of the play's action
and diction is deliberate--a reflection of the self-con-
sciousness of Regency drama and an ironic commentary on the

role-playing that society demands of us in real life.
(R.M.R.)

Sitterson, Joseph C., Jr. "'Platonic Shades' in Keats's
Lamia." *JEGP* 83 (1984): 200-13.

Wonders what Keats knew about Platonists and Sophists and
concludes that the poem questions Apollonius's claim to know
reality from illusion, suggesting that the ideal world of
Platonic forms isn't any more real than Lamia's illusions,
since it is no less a projection of human desire. The
article strains a bit in tracing transmission of ideas
through Bailey, but its main point is effectively made.
(R.M.R.)

Spiegelman, Willard. "The 'Ode to a Nightingale' and
Paradiso, XXII." *KSJ* 33 (1984): 37-40.

Cary's translation joins Milton and Shakespeare as possible
source for "darkling" and "Queen Moon."

Ulmer, William A. "The Human Seasons: Arnold, Keats, and
'The Scholar-Gypsy.'" *VP* 22 (1984): 247-61.

Arnold's critique of inauthentic Victorian society also
includes a critique of Keats, whose sensuousness is
"inherently tragic" because "too devouring." Stanzas 14-
16, in particular, do not turn away from Keats, but correct
his deficiencies. "'The Scholar-Gypsy' contributes to that
process of assessment and assimilation by which the greatness of Keats was itself only gradually established."

Wentersdorf, Karl P. "The Sub-Text of Keats's 'Ode to a
Nightingale.'" *KSJ* 33 (1984): 70-84.

The sub-text, with its allusions to Dryads, Flora,
Provencal song, Cynthia, Ruth, etc., is a celebration of
love, the best consolation of those who resign themselves
to mortality. This is a graceful distillation of pains-
taking research. (R.M.R.)

Williams, Meg Harris. *Inspiration in Milton and Keats*.
London: Macmillan, 1982. Pp. xii+212. £17.50.

Rev. by Anne Elliott in *RES* 35 (1984): 541.

See also Bromwich, Brown, de Man, Kipperman, McGann, Thurley,
Waldinger ("General 3. Criticsm"); Abrams, Bassil, Bidney,
Cantor, Chandler, Cook, et al., Hollander, Johnson, and
Leyda, Pereira, Pinion ("English 3. Criticism"); Robertson

("Blake"); Bromwich, Butler ("Hazlitt"); Grigely ("Hunt");
Heffernan ("Shelley, P.B.").

Reviews of books previously listed:

HIRST, Wolf Z., *John Keats* (see *RMB* for 1981, pp. 120-21),
rev. by Stuart M. Sperry in *SiR* 23 (1984): 259-62, as
characterized throughout "by thoroughness and discrimina-
tion"; VAN GHENT, Dorothy, *Keats: The Myth of the Hero*
(see *RMB* for 1983, p. 120), rev. by Susan J. Wolfson in
KSJ 33 (1984): 221-25; VENDLER, Helen, *The Odes of John
Keats* (see *RMB* for 1983, p. 120), rev. by Marilyn Butler
("Reconstructing Keats") in *HudR* 37 (1984): 143-50;
WALSH, William, *Introduction to Keats* (see *RMB* for 1981,
p. 123), rev. by Vincent Newey in *RES* 35 (1984): 250-51.

LAMB, C.

Ades, John I. "Charles Lamb's Modest Proposal." *ChLB* 47-48
(1984): 143-47.

   His proposal of marriage to Fanny Kelly, her prompt reply,
and the vibrations in the air.

Beer, Gillian. "Lamb's Women." *ChLB* 47-48 (1984): 138-43.

   Charles Lamb "is one of those writers whom Virginia
Woolf wished for, as being 'man-womanly' and 'woman-manly':
his writing discloses his empathy with female experience...."

Coates, John. "'Damn the Age! I will write for antiquity':
Lamb's Style as Implied Moral Comment." *ChLB* 47-48 (1984):
147-58.

Flesch, William. "'Friendly and Judicious' Reading: Affect
and Irony in the Works of Charles Lamb." *SiR* 23 (1984):
163-81.

   Some ironic applications of the "Preface" to the *Last
Essays of Elia.* As the Preface suggests, "Lamb is quite
conscious that the affect in the *Essays* always comes from
the apparent refusal of affect, from the ironizing and
distancing of pathos."

Monsman, Gerald Cornelius. *Confessions of a Prosaic Dreamer:
Charles Lamb's Art of Autobiography.* Duke University Press,
1984.

   Not seen.

Nethery, Wallace, and Corry Nethery. *Charles Lamb's Town and Country Revisited.* Los Angeles: Dawson's Book Shop, 1983.

> Rev. by George L. Barnett in *ChLB* 46 (1984): 124-25.

Nethery, Wallace, and Corry Nethery. *Poetry for Children.* Los Angeles: Dawson's Book Shop, 1982.

> Rev. by George L. Barnett in *ChLB* 46 (1984): 125.

Ruddick, Bill. "'Beautiful Bare Narratives': Charles Lamb's Response to Eighteenth-Century Fiction." *ChLB* 47-48 (1984): 158-64.

> "Lamb's knowledge of the whole tradition of fiction, like his knowledge of contemporary literature, may surprise many readers still."

Woof, Robert. "John and Sarah Stoddart: Friends of the Lambs." *ChLB* 45 (1984): 93-109.

> Rich in documentation and insight. (D.V.E.)

See also Clubbe ("English 1. Bibliography"); Haefner ("English 3. Criticism"); Newlyn ("Wordsworth").

Reviews of books previously listed:

> CECIL, David, *A Portrait of Charles Lamb* (see *RMB* for 1983, p. 123), rev. by Bill Ruddick in *ChLB* 45 (1984): 110-11; COURTNEY, Winifred F., *Young Charles Lamb* (see *RMB* for 1982, p. 126), rev. by John O. Hayden in *ELN* 21,iii (1984): 69-72; by John R. Nabholtz in *KSJ* 33 (1984): 234-37; by Fred V. Randel in *SiR* 23 (1984): 413-16; PRANCE, Claude A., *Companion to Charles Lamb* (see *RMB* for 1983, p. 124), rev. by Peter Morgan in *ES* 65 (1984): 187-88.

LAMB, M.

Courtney, Winifred F. "*Mrs. Leicester's School* as Children's Literature." *ChLB* 47-48 (1984): 164-69.

LOCKHART

Milne, Maurice. "J.G. Lockhart and the Catholic Question." *VPR* 17 (1984): 49-51.

See also Klancher ("English 3. Criticism").

LONDON MAGAZINE

See Haefner, Klancher ("English 3. Criticism").

MATURIN

D'Amico, Diane. "Feeling and Conception of Character in
the Novels of Charles Robert Maturin." *MSE* 9,iii (1984):
42-54.

"... his heroes wander in a fallen world where man-made
prisons and cages and natural storms and chasms mirror their
own guilty state." "His paired characters, both male and
female, point to the fragmented nature of the human soul
and the need for each individual to journey inward, seeking
communion with his other self."
Melmoth on the (Jungian) couch. (T.L.A.)

See also Cross ("English 1. Bibliography"); Spector ("The
Gothic").

MOORE

Dowden, Wilfred S., ed., with Barbara Bartholomew and Joy L.
Linsley. *The Journal of Thomas Moore*. Vol. II. 1821-
1825. University of Delaware Press, 1984. Pp. 480.
$50.00.

Vol. I (see *RMB* for 1983, pp. 125-26) rev. by Leslie A.
Marchand in *KSJ* 33 (1984): 237-39.
There will be six volumes altogether, but each is
separately indexed; the notes are explicit and substantial.
Byron continues in the leading role, but there are numerous
references to Bonaparte, Bowles, Burke, Canning, Fox,
George IV, Hobhouse, the Hollands, Irving, Lady and Lord
Lansdowne, Longmans, Murray, Rogers, Scott, and Sheridan--
to note some prominent ones. (D.V.E.)

See also Murphy ("Spanish 3. Blanco White").

MORE, H.

Hess, Marlene A. "The Didactic Art of Hannah More." Ann Arbor, Mich.: University Microfilms International, 1984. No. 2153A.

Dissertation.

See also Butler ("English 2. Environment"); Agress ("English 3. Criticism").

NEW MONTHLY MAGAZINE

See Klancher ("English 3. Criticism").

OLLIER, C.

See Cross ("English 1. Bibliography").

PEACOCK

Harris, Anthony. "Peacock's Lord Littlebrain." *N&Q* 31 (1984): 474-75.

Identification of another figure in *Headlong Hall*.

Mulvihill, James D. "'The Four Ages of Poetry': Peacock and Historical Method." *KSJ* 33 (1984): 130-47.

See also Cross ("English 1. Bibliography"); Quinn ("Shelley, P.B.").

QUARTERLY REVIEW

See Klancher ("English 3. Criticism").

RADCLIFFE

Engel, Leonard. "The Role of the Enclosure in the English and American Gothic Romance." *EAS* 11 (1982): 59-68.

Nollen, Elizabeth. "Ann Radcliffe's *A Sicilian Romance*:   A
    New Source for Jane Austen's *Sense and Sensibility*."   *ELN*
    22,ii (1984):   30-37.

The Poetical Works of Ann Radcliffe.   London, 1834.   Reprint.
    2 vols.   New York: AMS Press, 1984. $36.00.

See also Spector ("The Gothic").

REYNOLDS

Jones, Leonidas M.   *The Life of John Hamilton Reynolds*.
    Hanover, N.H.:   University Press of New England, 1984.   Pp.
    371. $35.00.

    Rev. by David Bromwich in *TLS*, March 15, 1985, p. 276.

Review of book previously listed:

    RICHARDSON, Joanna, ed., *Letters from Lambeth: The
    Correspondence of the Reynolds Family with John Freeman
    Milward Dovaston 1808-1815* (see *RMB* for 1983, p. 126), rev.
    by Donald H. Reiman in *SiR* 22 (1983):   470-74, as "both a
    labor of love and done hastily."

See also Pointon ("English 2. Environment").

ROBINSON

Wickham, D.E.   "A Warning to the Curious with Regard to Henry
    Crabb Robinson."   *ChLB* 46 (1984):   134-35.

    Published versions of Robinson's diary and reminiscences
    are "far from reliable."   Originals are in Dr. Williams's
    Library.

ROGERS

Berry, Neil.   "Samuel Rogers's Anonymous Article."   *N&Q* 31,iv
    (1984):   472-73.

    The Wellesley Index does not cite Rogers as the coauthor
    of an *Edinburgh Review* article on Dante despite Rogers's own
    remark in his memoirs that he had helped write it.

SCOTT, John

Review of book previously listed:

O'LEARY, Patrick, *Regency Editor: Life of John Scott* (see *RMB* for 1983, p. 127), rev. by Ian Scott-Kilvert in *Byron Journal* 12 (1984): 85-86.

SCOTT, W.

Abrahamson, Robert L. "A Critical Edition of *The Lay of the Last Minstrel* by Sir Walter Scott." Ann Arbor, Mich.: University Microfilms International, 1984.

Dissertation.

Alexander, J.H. "The Year's Work in Scottish Literary and Linguistic Studies, 1981: Scott." *SLJ*, Supplement 19 (1983): 20-23.

Berkove, Lawrence. "Henry James and Sir Walter Scott: A 'Virtuous Attachment'?" *SSL* 15 (1980): 43-52.

Bold, Alan, ed. *Sir Walter Scott: The Long Forgotten Melody.* London: Vision Press; Totowa, N.J.: Barnes & Noble, 1983. Pp. 224. £13.95; $27.50.

Rev. by Graham McMaster in *SLJ*, Supplement 20 (1984): 15-18.
An odd patchwork, combining the scholarly and belletristic, placing Scott specialists awkwardly alongside interested (and not so interested) bystanders. Its editor puffs hard-- instead of taking "Scott apart," the endeavor will be to see his art as "whole"--and supplies a flashy apparatus (the essays are divided under two headings, "The Sounding Chords" and "The Full Tide of Song"). Underneath one senses something closer to book-making. The three most useful con- tributions are distinguishable by their academic profession- alism. Christopher Harvie ("Scott and the Image of Scot- land") takes a historian's bite at the Scott cherry, finding therein a shift from "unionist" optimism to a deeper Romantic Scottish conservatism in later years. (Nothing startlingly new; but interesting to see 1819 appearing again as the turning point.) David Hewitt's "Scott's Art and Politics" makes knowledgeable comments on Scott's political beliefs, arguing their general intrusiveness in his imaginative writing, and pointing to a parallelism (which I find exag- gerated) with Burke. Graham Tulloch, the most methodical

of all, demonstrates convincingly ("Scott and the Creation
of Dialogue in Scots") Scott's assimilation of specifically
literary and historical sources into the dialect speech in
the novels, and offers a plenitude of supportive evidence.
But from there it is mostly downhill. Owen Dudley Edwards
("Scott as a Contemporary Historian") fulsomely asserts the
importance of folklore in forming Scott's sense of social
history; lest we nodded, W.F.H. Nicolaisen ("Scott and the
Folk Tradition") celebrates folklore, particularly ballad,
as "a shaping force which never let him go." Allan Massie
("Scott and the European Novel"), hardly taking the initiated
by storm, turns to Scott's novelty as a medievalist and
wide-ranging influence on European literature; Robert
Giddings, striving for originality, writes interestingly
(in "Scott and Opera") on the Victorians' yen for grandiose
theatre productions, but leaves Scott's part in the plot
largely to inference. F.R. Hart ("Scott and the Idea of
Adventure") gives the impression of chasing a current hare
of his own, rather than advancing on previously-held views
on Scott. Iain Crichton Smith's offering ("Poetry in Scott's
Narrative Verse") is for the most part embarrassing: a sour
and bluff piece, the main import of which seems to be not to
read Scott's poetry. "It is easier to return to *Don Juan*,
for instance, than to these poems." The full tide of song?
(P.D.G.)

Clancy, Charles J. Untitled Note. *SSL* 16 (1981): 242-46.

Giving the background of Scott's *Halidon Hill*, "A Dramatic
Sketch, from Scottish History," perhaps written in 1822
for possible inclusion in a work to be edited for charity
by Joanna Baillie. (T.L.A.)

Criscuola, Margaret M. "Originality, Realism and Morality:
Three Issues in Sir Walter Scott's Criticism of Fiction."
SSL 16 (1981): 29-49.

Criscuola, Margaret Movshin. "The Porteous Mob: Fact and
Truth in *The Heart of Midlothian*." *ELN* 22 (1984): 43-50.

Useful comparison of the Porteous riots and aftermath in
the *Heart* with historical records known to Scott. Argues
convincingly that Scott exaggerated and conflated to highlight an intensity of Scottish feeling, first among the
mob, secondly (more efficaciously) in Jeanie Deans's resolve.
(P.D.G.)

Dale, Thomas. "The Jurists, the Dominie, and Jeanie Deans."
SLJ 11 (1984): 36-44.

Defends Jeanie Deans from the charge of inconsistency made by John C. Hayden (see *RMB* for 1979, p. 111). Jeanie's truth-telling satisfies both legalistic and moral dimensions in the narrative. Her alleged "lies" are either for self-survival or in obedience to larger moral imperatives. The result is a rounded picture of a Calvinistically influenced mind humanly and humanely in action. A sensible reply. (P.D.G.)

Davies, Rick A. "The Demon Lover Motif in *The Heart of Midlothian*." *SSL* 16 (1981): 91-96.

The demon is George Robertson/Staunton.

Gamerschlag, Kurt. "The Making and Un-Making of Sir Walter Scott's *Count Robert of Paris*." *SSL* 15 (1980): 95-123.

A careful and valuable correction of Lockhart. (T.L.A.)

Garside, Peter, ed. *The Visionary*. (Regency Reprint I.) University College Cardiff Press, 1984. Pp. xvii+56. $8.00.

First edited version of Scott's crucial pamphlet, taken from three newspaper articles written at the height of national crisis in 1819. Individual copies from Secretary, University College, Cardiff, U.K.

McMaster, Graham. "Lévi-Strauss in the Scottish Highlands: A Structuralist Account of Scott's *The Lady of the Lake*." *Studies in English Literature* (Tokyo: The English Literary Society of Japan), 61:1.

Linguistic analysis and sociological speculation. Seen only in offprint.

McMaster, Graham. "Who Really Was the Douglas in *The Lady of The Lake*?" *Scott Newsletter* 4 (Spring 1984): 11-15.

Half-identifies James Douglas of Bothwell with Archibald, sixth Earl of Angus. Speculates an incest motif, à la *Otrano*, displaced.

Millgate, Jane. *Walter Scott: The Making of the Novelist*. University of Toronto Press, 1984. Pp. xiv+223. $24.95.

Rev. by Lachlan Mackinnon in *TLS*, March 1, 1985, p. 240, as unjust to "the generosity of Scott's imaginative vision." Arguably the most polished book on Scott's fiction yet. Millgate combines scrupulous attention to detail, bibliographical and biographical, with cogently argued analyses of narrative strategies in the "Scottish" Waverley Novels to

A Legend of Montrose (1819). Honed down from the mass
of material at the author's command, the book is a masterpiece of concision, and deserves to become a classic not
only of Scott scholarship but criticism generally.

Scott's complicated use of narrative devices is seen in its
earliest form in the juxtaposition of annotation and ballad
in the *Minstrelsy of the Scottish Border.* Emphasis is also
placed on *Sir Tristram*, an almost obsessive concern of its
editor, in the almost imperceptible movement from antiquari-
anism to romance. Millgate offers excellent commentary on
the diverse "frames" in which the poems are set, and writes
with acumen on the process by which Scott moved from the
early draft chapters of *Waverley* (placed perhaps over-
confidently in 1805?) to committed novel authorship with
the publication of *Guy Mannering* (1815). A recurrent aim
is to liberate Scott's earlier novels from the artificial
"steadying" effect of the *Magnum Opus.* Millgate pointedly
uses first editions throughout, giving thereby a sense of
the original three- or four-deckers as they freshly appeared,
while at the same time recognizing Scott's sense of creating
sequences of fictions, and breaks in sequences, as he pro-
ceeded. Important shifts are noted with the completion of
The Antiquary--Scott changing not only publishers and
authorial personae, but narrative style--and *Montrose*,
effectively closing the "Scottish" series and at which point
Scott authorized the first collected edition of his fiction.
At both turning points, it is claimed, Scott had come close
to exposing aspects of himself in the shape of a protagonist.
Attention is also given to the contemporary audience's
growing awareness of a corpus of work by "the author of
Waverley" and its ability to find meanings through comparisons
with predecessors, Scott all the while revelling in a half-
involuntary process of semi-disclosure and withdrawal.

Commentary of this kind is bound to some extent to be speculative, and a number of interpretative links risk seeming far-
fetched or privately generated. But the reader's doubts
are generally quelled by the author's exceptional command
of significant minutiae, especially relating to textual
matters. Apposite facts are used with almost clinical precision to determine "motive" on Scott's part--an area never
unduly simplified--or to lay bare legendary accretions
emanating from Lockhart and other sources. Scotched forever,
one hopes, is the notion of Scott's "mercenary" motives in
adding a fourth volume to *The Heart of Midlothian.* In
restoring *The Bride of Lammermoor* to the fold, Millgate
also cuts through the all too easily accepted idea that
Scott composed using an amanuensis while in excruciating pain,
relieved only by laudanum. As she observes, the bulk of the

text can be found in Scott's neatly continuous hand in the
Edinburgh Signet Library. One less opium-eater in the Romantic
canon. Again, one might be tempted to query whether Scott
ended *The Antiquary* with such a conscious air of finality--
might not the shift to a new mode have been primarily financial in nature? But then Scott has written on the last page
of the manuscript, "Finis is is is." Professor Millgate
has been to look for herself!

The commentaries on individual novels are first rate,
several (e.g., those on *Guy Mannering* and *Rob Roy*) having
had an earlier airing elsewhere. The chapter on *Waverley*
is evidently new, and as good as anything there. Here Millgate
distinguishes limitations inherent in the *narrative* as well
as the hero's point of view, separated as it was temporarily
from the novel's original audience. Rather than being simply
rescued by chastening "history," Waverley finds knowledge
and a fount of sympathy in "romance." "In the ultimate
range of his sympathies Edward is more generous than the
narrator, and willing to take more risks; he is prepared to
acknowledge his feelings without benefit of protective irony;
he is ready to go to the end of the dark journey." Not
entirely unpredictable; but Millgate's strength is that
she is capable of taking even the most penetrating observations (Iser's, in the above instance) at least one sound
step further. The notes (regrettably, if inevitably, placed
at the end of the book) are testimony to the discerning
eye that has scanned so discriminatingly the mixed bag of
Scott criticism.

The book has been stylishly produced by its publishers,
with a minimum of perceptible errors. The placing of page
numbers alongside the running title gives it a somewhat
mannered appearance, and must be an irritation to the average
reader. (P.D.G.)

Morgan, Susan. "Old Heroes and a New Heroine in the Waverley
Novels." *ELH* 50 (1983): 559-85.

Listed in *RMB* for 1983, p. 131.
Scott's heroines embody central human values. A combative
counter-view. (P.D.G.)

Raleigh, John Henry. "*Ulysses* and Scott's *Ivanhoe*." *SiR* 22
(1983): 569-86.

"Joyce, who especially prized alogicalities, if he had
been told of the very large number of similarities between
Ivanhoe and *Ulysses* ... might have nodded an agreeable assent
and said, 'Yes, the world is like that.'"

Rignall, J.M. "The Historical Double: *Waverley, Sylvia's Lovers, The Trumpet-Major.*" *EiC* 34 (1984): 14-32.

Considers the shadowing of "passive" heroes by darker counterparts, and the related interplay of "fiction" and "history," as a point of entry into Scott's Victorian successors (notably Mrs. Gaskell and Trollope). Tightly argued and theoretically illuminating. (P.D.G.)

Shaw, Harry E. *The Forms of Historical Fiction: Sir Walter Scott and His Successors.* Cornell University Press, 1984. Pp. 257. $27.50.

Rev. by Emma Letley in *TLS*, June 15, 1984, p. 674, as an excellent book suggesting good ways of approaching historical fiction.

Sroka, Kenneth M. "Education in Walter Scott's *Waverley.*" *SSL* 15 (1980): 139-64.

For education read character development. (T.L.A.)

Whitmore, Daniel. "Scott's Indebtedness to the German Romantics: *Ivanhoe* Reconsidered." *TWC* 15 (1984): 72-73.

See also Thornton ("English 2. Environment"); Culviner, Lloyd, Williams ("English 3. Criticism"); Hogg ("Hogg").

Reviews of books previously listed:

ALEXANDER, J.H., and David Hewitt, eds., *Scott and His Influence* (see *RMB* for 1983, pp. 128-30), rev. by Graham McMaster in *SLJ* (1984) supp. 20: 30-34; ANDERSON, James, *Sir Walter Scott and History with Other Papers* (see *RMB* for 1982, pp. 129-30), rev. by Thomas Crawford in *SLJ*, supp. 19 (1983): 51-53; GAMERSCHLAG, Kurt, *Sir Walter Scott und die Waverley Novels* (see *ELN* 17, Supp., 94), rev. by Kurt Wittig in *SSL* 16 (1981): 301-04; HEWITT, David, ed., *Scott on Himself: A Selection of the Autobiographical Writings of Sir Walter Scott* (see *RMB* for 1982, p. 131), rev. by Donald A. Low in *RES* 35 (1984): 245-46; LAMONT, Claire, ed., *Sir Walter Scott. Waverley: Or, 'Tis Sixty Years Since* (see *RMB* for 1982, p. 132), rev. by Donald A. Low in *RES* 35 (1984): 245-46; McMASTER, Graham, *Scott and Society* (see *RMB* for 1982, pp. 133-34), rev. by Nelson S. Bushnell in *SSL* 18 (1983): 278-87; by Jane Millgate in *RES* 35 (1984): 562-63; by W. Ruddick in *L&H* 9 (1983): 120-21; SHAW, Harry E., *The Forms of Historical Fiction: Sir Walter Scott and His Successors* (see *RMB* for 1983, pp. 131-32), rev. by George

Dekker in *NCF* 39 (1984): 348-51; by Judith Wilt in *SNNTS* 16 (1984): 254-56; WEINSTEIN, Mark, ed., *The Prefaces to the Waverly Novels* (see *ELN* 17, Supp., 95), rev. by Thomas Dale in *SSL* 15 (1980): 284-86.

Composite reviews:

Ash, Marinell. *ScHR* 62 (1983): 194-96.

Reviews James Anderson, *Sir Walter Scott and History* (see *RMB* for 1982, pp. 129-30), and Paul Henderson Scott, *Walter Scott and Scotland* (see *RMB* for 1982, pp. 134-35).

Dale, Thomas. *SSL* 18 (1983): 272-78.

Reviews: Claire Lamont's edition of *Waverly* (see *RMB* for 1982, p. 132); David Brown, *Walter Scott and the Historical Imagination* (see *RMB* for 1980, p. 113); and James Anderson, *Sir Walter Scott and History* (see *RMB* for 1982, p. 129). Brown is knocked about, Anderson approved, and Lamont noted. (T.L.A.)

SHELLEY, M.

Ferguson, Frances. "The Nuclear Sublime." *Diacritics* 14 (1984): 4-10.

Includes a page about *Frankenstein* as "a kind of parable to be read into our thinking about the nuclear."

Glut, Donald F. *The Frankenstein Catalogue: Being a Comprehensive Listing of Novels, Translations, Adaptations, Stories, Critical Works, Popular Articles, Series, Fumetti, Verse, Stage Plays, Films, Cartoons, Puppetry, Radio & Television Programs, Comics, Satire & Humor, Spoken & Musical Recordings, Tapes, and Sheet Music Featuring Frankenstein's Monster and/or Descended from Mary Shelley's Novel.* Jefferson, N.C., and London: McFarland & Company, Inc., 1984. Pp. xiii+525; illus. $29.95.

This volume, as its long subtitle suggests, is designed for the popular culture market, the glut on which is astounding. Here we have 2,666 separate and frequently glossed entries (and scores of additionally named but "excluded" items given in prefatory remarks), over 2,500 entries in the name index, and well over 3,000 entries in the title index--a testament to what Mary Shelley hath wrought. Although most of the volume is devoted to more modern Frankensteiniana and therefore has little value for the nineteenth-century scholar, it does provide an education: did you know that in the late 1960s Paul McCartney was scheduled to play Percy Bysshe Shelley in a movie on the Diodati set; that in 1973 Jerry Lewis was to be cast in an unmade comedy, "Good Morning, Mr. Frankenstein"; or that Francis Ford Coppola announced a *Frankenstein* movie in 1972? Of greater scholarly use here are the lists of over 100 separate editions (including foreign ones), of the criticial books and articles on the novel, and of the stage adaptations. But even here there are problems: the list of literary criticism is incomplete; Lyles's *Mary Shelley* bibliography is not cited; reviews of the novel are omitted; and the list of plays (arranged alphabetically rather than chronologically) is thinly annotated for the nineteenth-century performances. But still worth a look. (C.E.R.)

Meneghelli, Pietro. "Frankenstein o dell'assenza del padre."
    Paragone 408-410 (Feb.-April 1984):   93-107.

O'Flinn, Paul. "Production and Reproduction: The Case of
    Frankenstein." *L&H* 9 (1983):   194-213.

Richter, Anne. "Mary Shelley et la création de Frankenstein."
    Revue générale, March 1984, pp. 60-69.

See also Cantor, Macovski, Poovey ("English 3. Criticism");
    Pitcher ("Byron"); Spector ("The Gothic"); Butler ("Haz-
    litt").

Reviews of book previously listed:

    BENNETT, Betty T., ed., *The Letters of Mary Wollstonecraft
    Shelley*, Vol. I (see *RMB* for 1980, pp. 118-19), rev. (with
    a few corrections) by P.M.S. Dawson in *YES* 14 (1984):   334-
    36; Vol. II (see *RMB* for 1983, pp. 133-34), rev. by Jack
    Stillinger in *KSJ* 33 (1984):   225-29.

SHELLEY, P.B.

Brisman, Leslie. "Of Lips Divine and Calm: Swinburne and
    the Language of Shelleyan Love."

    See Reed ("English 3. Criticism").

Brown, Nathaniel. "The 'Double Soul':   Virginia Woolf,
    Shelley, and Androgyny." *KSJ* 33 (1984):   182-204.

Woolf extensively read and praised and alluded to Shelley's works; yet for Woolf "androgyny ultimately resolves itself into psychosexual dualism and otherness; for Shelley into fusion and unity. The angelic body in Shelley is sexless; in Woolf it bears the attributes of woman."

Burling, William J. "Virginia Woolf's 'Lighthouse': An Allusion to Shelley's *Queen Mab*?" *ELN* 22,ii (1984): 62-65.

Butter, P.H. "Note on Freedom in Shelley." *KSMB* 34 (1983): 61-65.

Counters Philip Drew's argument in *The Meaning of Freedom* (Aberdeen University Press, 1982) that Prometheus's foreknowledge, rather than forgiveness or pity, leads to his unbinding.

Byrne, Lawrence J. "'Self-Destroying Swiftness': The Fictions of Language in Shelley's Poetry." Ann Arbor, Mich.: University Microfilms International, 1984.

Dissertation.

Duffy, Edward. "Where Shelley Wrote and What He Wrote For: The Example of 'The Ode to the West Wind.'" *SiR* 23 (1984): 351-77.

The best of the "Shelley" issue of *SiR* (Fall 1984), Duffy's article (albeit with a somewhat vague title) is excellent, and no summary can do it justice. Read it and be "driven" (i.e, shepherded) into the increasing flock of readers of Shelley who (with Reiman, Webb, Cronin, and others) represent the contexts and traditions of Shelley's artistry and humanity. Here semantics and semiotics, rather than being enfeebling clouds, serve as illuminating mirrors of what Shelley says and does as a lineal son of Athens and Jerusalem. A discourse on Shelley's various inflections of "the normally indicative mood of the Greek *logos* into a Biblical imperative which does not so much describe the world as command it into being" (i.e., truth or wisdom succeeds to virtue) precedes an extraordinarily good reading of *Ode to the West Wind* in terms of its Old and New Testament antecedents. Throughout the essay, very apt quotations demonstrate Duffy's mastery of Shelley. (C.E.R.)

Ferguson, Frances. "Shelley's *Mont Blanc*: What the Mountain Said."

See Reed ("English 3. Criticism").

Fraistat, Neil. "Poetic Quests and Questioning in Shelley's
    Alastor Collection." *KSJ* 33 (1984): 161-81.

   This essay bodes well for Fraistat's forthcoming book on
the purpose of and pattern among the poems in major English
Romantic volumes (e.g., *Lyrical Ballads* and *Prometheus
Unbound ... with Other Poems*). Here, although he does not
exhaust the relations among them, Fraistat profitably
studies the 12 poems making up the *Alastor* volume: "the
collection is polarized by the tensions between the opening
'Alastor' and the closing 'Daemon.' Just as the despair
of the former is countered by the limited hope of the latter,
the private cares and despondency ... in the first half of
the volume are subordinated to the public concerns and
vitality ... in the second. Throughout the 1816 collection ...
Shelley probes the limitations of human knowledge, questioning the nature of the world, the mind, and poetry itself."
(C.E.R.)

Freeman, John. "Shelley's Letters to His Father." *KSMB* 34
    (1983): 1-15.

   Shifts of tone and rhetorical strategies as Shelley seeks
his allowance in 1811 after his expulsion from Oxford and
his marriage to Harriet.

Friederich, Reinhard H. "The Apocalyptic Mode and Shelley's
    'Ode to the West Wind.'" *Renascence* 36 (1984): 161-70.

   With Curran in one hand and the *Revelation of John* in the
other. (T.L.A.)

Gervais, Ronald J. "Fitzgerald's 'Euganean Hills' Allusion
    in 'The Crack-Up.'" *AN&Q* 21 (1983): 139-41.

Hall, Jean. "The Socialized Imagination: Shelley's *The Cenci*
    and *Prometheus Unbound*." *SiR* 23 (1984): 339-50.

   Starting with Shelley's judgment that plays "are as mirrors
in which the spectator beholds himself, under a thin disguise
of circumstance," Hall sensibly compares the two dramas.
Although the circumstances of Prometheus acknowledging his
guilt differ from those of Beatrice denying her guilt, both
protagonists provide their audiences an opportunity to know
themselves in relation to society. (C.E.R.)

Heffernan, James A.W. "*Adonais*: Shelley's Consumption of
    Keats." *SiR* 23 (1984): 295-315.

With too much playfulness on the word "consumes,"
Heffernan argues that Shelley consciously misrepresented
the Keats of literary history (or at least the Keats he
knew): Shelley "invented the strange story of Keats's
death" at the hands of the *Quarterly Review*, overemphasized
Keats's weakness and powerlessness, and deprived him of an
identity by subsuming him into the burning fountain or the
colorless white light of Eternity. Shelley, of course,
was not writing biography; and Heffernan (and others) should
take note of Mary Russell Mitford's letters of July 5, 1820,
to Sir William Elford: "Poor John Keats is dying of the
'Quarterly Review.' This is a sad, silly thing, but it is
true. A young, delicate, imaginative boy--that withering
article fell upon him like an east wind. I am afraid he
has no chance of recovery.... He had a thousand faults
and a million of beauties; and he is struck to the earth
by the mere effect of worldly hardness and derision upon a
tender heart and a sensitive temper" (*The Life of Mary Russell
Mitford*, ed. Rev. A.G.K. L'Estrange [New York: Harper &
Brothers, 1870], I: 340-41). Mitford not only anticipates
Shelley's *later* judgments on the effect of the *Quarterly*'s
review of Keats, but she also may be reflecting what had
become a commonplace in London after June 1820, when a blood
vessel broke in Keats's lungs. (C.E.R.)

Hildebrand, Frederick L. "The Poet's Fiery Flight: A Study
of Unifying Patterns in Shelley's *Epipsychidion*." Ann Arbor,
Mich.: University Microfilms international, 1984. No. 2153A.

Dissertation.

Jacob, W.L., comp. *Sir Percy Shelley's Theatre, Boscombe
Manor (1866-1877)*. Available from Russell-Cotes Art Gallery
and Museum, East Cliff Hall, East Cliff, Bournemouth BH1
3AA, Dorset, England. Pp. 44. £2.00; $3.50.

Janowitz, Anne. "Shelley's Monument to Ozymandias." *PQ* 63
(1984): 477-91.

Keach, William. *Shelley's Style*. London and New York:
Methuen, 1984. Pp. xvii+269. $25.00.

Keach's book is a welcome addition to scholarship for it
thoughtfully examines the meaning and effects of Shelley's
artistic use of language. Chapter I ("The Mirror and the
Veil: Language in Shelley's *Defence*") explains with great
clarity the "antithetical impulses in Shelley's disposition
towards language" (whether Speech creates Thought or vice
versa--whether language and poetry are created by or are

constitutive of thought: Keach effectively uses eighteenth-
century philosophical and linguistic texts to advantage
here). Chapter II ("Imaging the Operations of the Human
Mind") repeats more than clarifies Shelley's phrase about
"imagery ... drawn from the operations of the human mind,"
but Keach does *extend* our understanding of what Shelley
means by such imagery; however, Keach might have used more
of his good close readings to deepen our understanding of
Shelley's judgment that "the difference is merely nominal
between thought and thing." Chapter III, a revised version
of Keach's 1975 *KSJ* article, illuminates the "reflexive
imagery" that is so central to Shelley's verse and thinking. In Chapter IV ("Evanescence: Melting, Dissolving,
Erasing") Keach is best when he glosses difficult passages
in such a way as to enlarge our understanding of a poem's
theme--see especially pp. 123-25 on "To a Skylark," 135-
39 on *Prometheus Unbound*, and 142-46 on "Lines Written
Among the Euganean Hills." Chapter V ("Shelley's Speed")
offers essentially correct analysis, although I would have
preferred more of the excellent appeal to Horne Tooke at
the end of the chapter and less of the risky judgments on
which line is speedier than others. Chapter VI on rhyme
accomplishes what it claims to do (show an artist at work
in control of the arbitrariness of language), and Keach is
especially good on Shelley's "Mont Blanc" when he shows
that rhyme is a function of the theme. The last chapter
("Shelley's Last Lyrics") departs from the formalistic
analysis in the other chapters and uses historical and
biographical information to assess Shelley's last lyrics
to and about Jane Williams. Although this last chapter
does not harmonize with the rest of the book, *Shelley's
Style* should be read by all serious students of Shelley;
it and Richard Cronin's *Shelley's Poetic Thoughts* (see *RMB*
for 1981, pp. 132-34) deepen our appreciation and understanding of Shelley's artistry. (C.E.R.)

Knerr, Anthony D. *Shelley's Adonais: A Critical Edition*.
Columbia University Press, 1984. Pp. x+292. $25.00.

    While not a variorum, Knerr's critical edition will prove
to be a useful book. Chapter I (1-9: "Background")
succinctly surveys the personal relations of Shelley and
Keats and does the same for the sources and antecedents of
Shelley's elegy. Chapter II (11-19: "Composition") provides specifics from Shelley's letters about the writing
of *Adonais* and describes the extant manuscripts that contain
drafts of the poem. Chapter III (21-54: "The Text") uses
the 1821 Pisa edition as copy-text and provides variants

from the 1829 Cambridge edition, the 1829 Galignani
edition, the 1834 Ascham edition, and Mary Shelley's 1839
edition (I note an error in transcription in stanza 44--*for*
"love and life content" *read* "love and life contend").
Chapter IV (55-104: "Notes and Commentary"), because it does
not offer the completeness of a variorum in its coverage
or in its representative commentary from other critics,
will not please everyone all of the time: Knerr, e.g.,
is good in interpreting the difficult stanza 29; he fails
to gloss Urania's important question "Who art thou?" in
stanza 34; and he misleads his audience by glossing "liquid"
in stanza 7 (not 8, as Knerr's notes have it) as "pure,
clear, undisturbed," thereby failing to link "liquid
rest" with the other water images of mortality and mutability. Chapter V (105-17: "Rejected Stanzas Associated
with *Adonais*") prints from Bodleian MS Shelley adds. e.9
the 16 fragments associated with *Adonais* (textual notes on
these stanzas reveal he modernized some spellings and printed
ampersand as "and," alterations that are incompatible with
Knerr's intent to provide manuscript evidence). Chapter VI
(119-35) offers a history of "Critical Opinion about *Adonais*."
A long appendix (137-248) provides transcriptions of all
extant manuscript drafts for the received poem, preface,
and rejected fragments. These transcriptions, the other
chapters, a bibliography, and finally an index make this
book a convenient starting place for subsequent research
on *Adonais*. (C.E.R.)

Leighton, Angela. *Shelley and the Sublime: An Interpretation
of the Major Poems*. Cambridge University Press, 1984.
Pp. x+195. $34.00; paper $12.95.

Shelley and the Sublime is an uneven book. In two good
introductory chapters, Leighton surveys empirical philosophy
(with its distrust of the sublime and suspicion of rhetorical
language) and opposes to it the demands of eighteenth-century theories of the sublime. She then, in a careful analysis
of Shelley's early letters, demonstrates his struggle to
overcome the limitations of empiricism by way of a theory of
creativity, an imaginative faith in a language that could
accommodate the sublime in human experience. Leighton uses
Shelley's famous passage on the "fading coal" to explain that
a sublime conception is often beyond expression (only a
skylark or ideal poet can simultaneously soar and sing) and
to prepare for her readings of *Hymn to Intellectual Beauty*
and *Mont Blanc*, *Prometheus Unbound*, *West Wind* and *Skylark*,
Adonais, *The Triumph of Life*. But the sublime and the fading
coal are not always at issue in the readings. Leighton is

best and most confident on *Adonais* ("The poem is concerned
with the twin problems of how to recapture the voice of the
dead as a living and eternal force, and how to recapture
the 'language *living*' of the heart in 'the *dead* letter' of
the poem"; "Personification ... is a fiction which obtrudes
itself as an unreal and rhetorical presence upon the elegist's
consciousness of death"), although I still prefer her earlier
version of this chapter in *Shelley Revalued*, where deconstruction rather than sublimity provided the immediate context
for her analysis. Her chapter on *West Wind* and *Skylark*
is the weakest, spending too much time on needless quotations
from other critics and on commonplaces about the poems. The
chapter on *Prometheus Unbound*, however, is better and yields
a conclusion that "in Acts I and II of *Prometheus Unbound*
Shelley is using his aesthetic of divided inspiration and
composition, voice and speech, or of the secret spell and
its speaker, in order to express a theory of political revolution which depends on the reconnection of the two."
(C.E.R.)

Mahoney, John L. "The Idea of Mimesis in Shelley's *A Defence
of Poetry*." *BJA* 24 (1984): 59–64.

Mathews, James W. "The Enigma of Beatrice Cenci: Shelley and
Melville." *SAR* 49, No. 2 (May 1984): 31–41.

An absorbing discussion of the unhistorical blondness of
Beatrice in Shelley's play and Melville's *Pierre*. Both
writers needed a fair heroine, one to emblematize bright
innocence, the other to suggest ironically that appearances
are deceptive. (R.M.R.)

Quinn, Mary A. "'Ozymandias' as Shelley's Rejoinder to Peacock's 'Palmyra.'" *ELN* 21 (1984): 48–56.

Quinn, Mary A. "Shelley's Philosophic Revel: *Alastor: and
Other Poems*." Ann Arbor, Mich.: University Microfilms
International, 1984.

Dissertation.

Quinn, Mary A. "Shelley's *Translation of Dante's Sonnet*."
Explicator 43 (1984): 23–26.

Rajan, Tilottama. "Deconstruction or Reconstruction: Reading
Shelley's *Prometheus Unbound*." *SiR* 23 (1984): 317–38.

Explores "the interpretive options opened up for romantic
literature by considering the disjunctions within a work
from a variey of theoretical perspectives."

Sacks, Peter. "Last Clouds: A Reading of 'Adonais.'" *SiR*
    23 (1984): 379-400.

Sacks, attempting to answer too many questions, provides
only partial answers about Shelley's mourning, his revisions
of elegiac fictions, his relation to Urania, his narcissism,
his ending of the poem, and his ambivalence toward figurative
language. (C.E.R.)

Shaaban, Bouthaina. "Shelley in the Chartist Press." *KSMB*
    34 (1983): 41-60.

With frequent and apt quotations, Shaaban argues that
Shelley (more than Byron or any other Romantic) was the most
popular poet in the Chartist press. (C.E.R.)

Strickland, Edward. "Transfigured Night: The Visionary
    Inversions of *Alastor*." *KSJ* 33 (1984): 148-60.

A controlled and confident essay with a number of insights
into *Alastor*: its Coleridgean landscape; its inversion of
Wordsworth's use of nature; a directionless quest that
abandons society and nature; a suggestion that the figure
by the well is the Spirit of Solitude; and a legitimate
question ("*when* did the Poet's blood ever beat in mystic
sympathy with nature's ebb and flow?"). But Strickland does
not convince me that "the maiden *is* found" at the conclusion
of the quest: even if the visionary has renounced all--
including life--that stood between him and the vision,
that's no guarantee that she is attained at the end. (C.E.R.)

Ulmer, William A. "Some Hidden Want: Aspiration in 'To a
    Sky-Lark.'" *SiR* 23 (1984): 245-58.

"Far less blithe and unreflecting than it may at first
appear, 'Sky-Lark' in fact demonstrates the impossibility
of either gratifying infinite desire or renouncing it....
But since Shelley establishes sadness as the necessary
condition for joy, concern with the sadness of 'To a Sky-
Lark' does not make it a less joyous poem ..." (246).

See also de Man, Kipperman, McGann, Thurley ("General 3.
    Criticism"); Wiener ("English 2. Environment"); Abrams,
    Cantor, Ellis, Jack, Jarrett-Kerr, Lehman, Meisel, Pereira
    ("English 3. Criticism"); Butler ("Hazlitt"); Allentuck
    ("Hunt").

Reviews of books previously listed:

ALLOTT, Miriam, ed., *Essays on Shelley* (see *RMB* for 1982,
pp. 139-40), rev. by Robert C. Casto in *RES* 35 (1984):   566-
67; by Jean Hall in *SiR* 23 (1984):   147-53; BROWN, Nathaniel,
Sexuality and Feminism in Shelley (see *RMB* for 1979, p.
117), rev. by Angela Leighton in *KSMB* 34 (1983):   86-90;
CRONIN, Richard, *Shelley's Poetic Thoughts* (see *RMB* for
1981, p. 132), rev. by Timothy Webb in *SiR* 22 (1983):   639-
47; DUFFY, Edward, *Rousseau in England: The Context for
Shelley's Critique of the Enlightenment* (see *RMB* for 1980,
p. 124), rev. by E.B. Murray in *SiR* 22 (1983):   474-84, as
"a good read but not good scholarship, a clever but not
successful exercise in structural and rhetorical gerry-
mandering"; EVEREST, Kelvin, ed., *Shelley Revalued: Essays
from the Gregynog Conference* (see *RMB* for 1983, p. 135),
rev. by Nathaniel Brown in *KSJ* 33 (1984):   216-18; HALL,
Jean, *The Transforming Image: A Study of Shelley's Major
Poetry* (see *RMB* for 1981, pp. 134-35), rev. by John Buxton
in *RES* 35 (1984):   98-99; by Anne McWhir in *ArielE* 14,ii
(1983):   92-94; by Timothy Webb in *SiR* 22 (1983):   639-47;
SCRIVENER, Michael Henry, *Radical Shelley: The Philosophical Anarchism and Utopian Thought of Percy Bysshe Shelley*
(see *RMB* for 1982, p. 143), rev. by Neil Fraistat in *KSJ*
33 (1984):   218-20.

Review essay:

Hall, Spencer. "Shelley, Skepticism(s), and Critical Dis-
course--A Review Essay." *SHR* 18 (1984):   65-74; 180-81.

Part one evaluates, in order of preference, Tilottama
Rajan's *Dark Interpreter: The Discourse of Romanticism*
(see *RMB* for 1980, pp. 24-25), Jean Hall's *The Transforming
Image: A Study of Shelley's Major Poetry* (see *RMB* for
1981, pp. 134-35), and Lloyd Abbey's *Destroyer and Preserver:
Shelley's Poetic Skepticism* (see *RMB* for 1980, pp. 121-22).
   Part two reviews *Essays on Shelley*, ed. Miriam Allott (see
RMB for 1982, pp. 139-40) and Richard Cronin's *Shelley's
Poetic Thoughts* (see *RMB* for 1981, pp. 132-34).

SOUTHEY

Curry, Kenneth. *The Contributions of Robert Southey to The
Morning Post.* University of Alabama Press, 1984. Pp. xii+
224. $19.75.

   Rev. by Peter Morgan in *VPR* 17 (1984):   70-72.

A valuable collection of all the poems Southey contributed
to the *Morning Post* (between January 1798 and December
1803)--except for about 80 that are merely listed (as having
been reprinted in the *Poetical Works* of 1837-38). There is
an appendix of conjectural attributions and of mistaken
attributions.

His most famous poems have long been available, but this
collection supplies their matrix--as well as a poetical and
political context for the writings of Coleridge and Wordsworth
in this period. Also, Curry helps us see that Southey "would
be far better known as a pioneer in the introduction of
Spanish poets and poetry to the British public" if he had
"ever collected his widely scattered translations [from
Spanish and Portuguese] into a volume--especially those
from the *Post*." (D.V.E.)

Holt, Rev. T.G. "Southey on Southwell." *N&Q* 31,i (March
    1984): 54.

A letter from W. Jos. Walter to Rev. Jos. Dunn concerning
Southey's opinion of Southwell as an artist.

Wellens, Oskar. "Robert Southey, *Critical* Reviewer: Some
    New Attributions." *TWC* 15 (1984): 68-71.

See also Clubbe ("English 1. Bibliography"); Chandler, Jarrett-
    Kerr ("English 3. Criticism").

SPENCE

See Butler ("English 2. Environment").

Review of book previously listed:

DICKINSON, H.T., ed., *The Political Works of Thomas Spence*
    (see *RMB* for 1982, pp. 146-47), rev. by G.E. Bentley, Jr.,
    in *BIQ* 17 (1984): 172-74.

TURNER

Butlin, Martin, and Evelyn Joll. *The Paintings of J.M.W.*
    Turner. Revised Edition. The Paul Mellon Centre for
    Studies in British Art and The Tate Gallery. 2 vols. Yale
    University Press, 1984. Vol. I (Text): pp. xliii+354.
    Vol. II (Plates): 243 black and white illus., 320 col. pls.
    $195.00 the set.

First published only in 1977, the Butlin-Joll catalogue
raisonné of Turner's paintings and sketches in oil has now
been issued in a revised and expanded edition, in response
(the compilers explain) to the acceleration in Turner
scholarhip in the intervening years. The changes incorporated
in the text include corrections in dating, attributions,
the identification of subjects, and current ownership,
along with up-to-date information on the physical condition
of the paintings, new works that have surfaced for the first
time, and old ones that have reappeared. The number of
color plates has been increased and the overall presentation
of the illustrations improved.

As in the original edition, many of the catalogue entries
amount to condensed scholarly articles, describing the subjects and occasions of the paintings and quoting generously
from contemporary reviews, most of which were hostile and
uncomprehending. The evidence of the critical attacks--
which were on the very fundamentals of his art, his choice
of colors and the nature of his brush strokes--may make it
seem that Turner was an avant-garde artist in the modern
sense; yet the overview we are given here of his work in
the major medium of the period demonstrates his affinities
were very nearly as much with his more distant predecessors
(Poussin, Claude, Rembrandt) and his mainly unlike contemporaries (Friedrich, Martin, even to some extent Fuseli and
Blake) as with the Impressionists of the future. (I.H.C.)

Shanes, Eric. "The True Subject of a Major Late Painting by
   J.M.W. Turner Identified." *BM* 126 (May 1984); 284-88;
   2 illus.

   "Inverary Pier. Loch Fyne. Morning," formerly misidenti-
   fied as a scene of Lake Maggiore.

See also Meisel ("English 3. Criticism").

WESTMINSTER REVIEW

See Klancher ("English 3. Criticism").

WOLLSTONECRAFT

Ferguson, Moira, and Janet Todd. *Mary Wollstonecraft.*
   (Twayne's English Authors Series.) Boston: Twayne Publishers, 1984. Pp. viii+158. $17.95.

Ferguson and Todd make efficient use of the Twayne format, giving a chapter to each of Wollstonecraft's works after a compact survey of her background and life and early writings on education. Each work or group of works is richly sampled and lucidly interpreted, with glances at their autobiographical subtexts and analyses of the shifting evolution of her assumptions and social and political messages. "Finally, she did achieve emotional rest in her life," and "her view of women in her last writings ... was more detached and more sympathetic than it had been in her earlier works" (123). (D.V.E.)

Hardt, Ulrich H., ed. *A Critical Edition of Mary Wollstonecraft's "A Vindication of the Rights of Women: With Strictures on Political and Moral Subjects."* Troy, N.Y.: Whitston, 1982. Pp. xvii+557. $45.00.

Rev. by Sara Hudson in *SHR* 19,ii (Spring 1984): 185-88; by Mitzi Myers in *KSJ* 33 (1984): 231-34.

Stewart, Sally N. "Mary Wollstonecraft's Contributions to the *Analytical Review*." *ELWIU* 11 (1984): 187-99.

Offers evidence that the reviews signed "M," "W," and "T" are Wollstonecraft's and makes some suggestions on determining authorship of unsigned reviews. Her count of 233 reviews by Wollstonecraft differs from the estimates of Derek Roper and Ralph Wardle. But see also Walter de Brouwer (*RMB* for 1983, p. 140). (R.M.R.)

See also Agress, McCormack, Poovey ("English 3. Criticism").

WORDSWORTH, D.

Bond, Alec. "Reconsidering Dorothy Wordsworth." *ChLB* 47-48 (1984): 194-207.

Bond approaches his subject "*not* from the usual context of Dorothy's being a useful and contributory member of a creative circle ... but rather from the traditions in which she works: the journal and travel book traditions especially." And he resists the common "notion" of Dorothy as "a blocked artist sacrificed to the ego and talent of William Wordsworth. She was an anchor for his imagination, and at times a sail as well...."

Liu, Alan. "On the Autobiographical Present: Dorothy Wordsworth's *Grasmere Journals*." *Criticism* 26 (1984): 115-37.

Shairp, J.C., ed. *Recollections of a Tour Made in Scotland*
A.D. 1803. Edinburgh, 1874. Reprint. New York: AMS Press,
1984. $37.00.

Taylor, Elisabeth R. "Dorothy Wordsworth: Primary and Secondary Sources." *BB* 40 (1983): 254-55.

Review of book previously listed:

HOMANS, Margaret, *Women Writers and Poetic Identity:*
Dorothy Wordsworth, Emily Bronte, and Emily Dickinson (see
RMB tor 1981, p. 145), rev. by Judith Wilt in *SiR* 22 (1983):
437-40, as a valuable contribution.

WORDSWORTH, W.

Averill, James. *"An Evening Walk" by William Wordsworth.*
Cornell University Press, 1984. Pp. xii+306. $38.50.

   There are now, counting Eric Birdsall's *Descriptive*
Sketches reviewed below, nine volumes in the Cornell series.
The chief contribution of this edition is that it presents
a "reading text" of the poem as revised in 1794, running
to more than 800 lines, *vs.* 446 in the first published version
of 1793. This text "reflects an effort to present this
second, 'lost' version of *An Evening Walk* in a form as close
as possible to that which Wordsworth would have published
had a second edition appeared in 1795 or 1796" (129). On
the evidence of the introduction (16), however, there is no
evidence at all to suggest that Wordsworth ever contemplated
publishing a revised version "in 1795 or 1796"; we have
another "poem" from Cornell that is, in a sense, a rabbit
pulled out of a hat. One must be grateful for the pains-
taking textual scholarship on the part of the editor, while
noting that the 1794 version, even though it reveals a
larger poetic world than *1793*, is a problematic and pro-
foundly confused work, much more so than the earlier text--
which is obviously why the poet did *not* offer it to the
public. (When he came to revise the poem many years later,
he went back to square one and apparently made no use at
all of *1794*.) The chief value of the new text, then, would
lie in what it could tell about the growth of Wordsworth's
mind between *1793* and *1794*--but to reveal *this*, the two texts
ought to be printed side by side. Instead, Cornell prints
1793 beside a version of 1836, with no apparatus enabling
the reader to check *1794*: you have to flip forward a hundred
pages. True, the reading text of 1794 has bracketed line

numbers that enable the reader to go back and dig out the
parallels for himself, but this is cumbrous. De Selincourt's
edition, in fact, remains more useful in this regard, even
if it is less textually sophisticated. He printed the
readings of 1794 at the foot of the page, and apparently
quite accurately, though he sometimes preferred readings from
Dove Cottage MS. 10 instead of MS. 9, the basis of reconstruction here. For a late text--unaccountably, it seems
to me--Cornell uses the edition of 1836 (Moxon's), instead
of the version of 1849 which De Selincourt used and which
embodies the poet's final thinking. The changes from 1836
on are few, but significant; e.g., the beautiful lines,
"There doth the twinkling aspen's foliage sleep,/And insects
clothe, like dust, the glassy deep" (Averill, p. 43, *app.
crit.*; De Selincourt, *PW* I, p. 15, ll. 116-17) do not appear
in this perfected form until the very end. We now, that is
to say, have four *Evening Walks*: 1793, 1794, 1836 (Cornell's),
and 1849 (Wordsworth's). You pays yer money and you takes
yer choice.

   The editor's introduction is admirable, and the notes useful, though many of these are matters of judgment. Averill
often helpfully expands De Selincourt's explanatory notes,
but some are omitted, including some calling attention to
echoes from Milton. De Selincourt also spotted an echo of
Langhorne's *Country Justice* (*PW* I, p. 322) which has been
dropped but ought to have been kept. Wordsworth's gloss
on his description of a rooster, *1793* ll. 129ff., which he
said came from a French poet named Rossuet (i.e., Pierre
de Rosset), is mentioned by all the editors I looked at
(De Selincourt, Hayden, Gill, and here) but not really
explained: Averill (46) says the lines Wordsworth refers
to appear in the "fourth *Chant*" of the 1782 edition of
Rosset's *L'Agriculture*. But no one gives the line numbers,
or quotes the actual passage. You have to go all the way
back to Legouis (*Early Life*, 1921, p. 143) to get the French
verses, which are very close to Wordsworth, and which
Legouis says come from the sixth, not fourth, *chapter*--the
word "Chant" appears on the same page in Legouis but identifies a citation from Delille's *Les Jardins*. I cannot verify
from an original French text who is right here, but the
editors, including De Selincourt, should have supplied a
direct quotation from *L'Agriculture* to make the note of
real use to scholars. (B.C.H.)

Bahti, Timothy. "Wordsworth's Rhetorical Theft."

   See Reed ("English 3. Criticism").

Bewell, Alan J. "The Discipline of Imagination: Empirical
    Discourse and the Poetry of William Wordsworth." Ann Arbor,
    Mich.: University Microfilms International, 1984. No. 2476A.
    Dissertation.

Bialostosky, Don H. *Making Tales: The Poetics of Wordsworth's
    Narrative Experiments.* University of Chicago Press, 1984.
    Pp. xii+208. Paper $12.50; library binding $25.00.

    A study of the role of narrators, and of narrative tech-
    nique, in *Lyrical Ballads,* based on distinctions which the
    author draws between Wordsworth's Platonic "poetics of
    speech" and the "Aristotelian" poetics of Coleridge. The
    theoretical discussion at the start of the book is very care-
    fully handled, but I confess to finding it hard going in
    some places and not always convincing. For example, the
    first chapter states that "when Coleridge says he thinks
    that poetic characters should be '*representatives* of a
    class,' he means social class" (32). But the rest of the
    quotation from Coleridge suggests, I think, just the opposite;
    the vicar and the shepherd-marine in "The Brothers," and
    the shepherd in "Michael" are, according to Coleridge, "per-
    sons of a known and abiding class, and their manners and
    sentiments the natural product of the circumstances common
    to the class." By "the class" he means simply "generic
    type"; the three person belong to wholly different *social*
    classes. The discussion, however, is a contribution to our
    growing awareness of the important *differences* between
    Wordsworth and Coleridge. The readings of individual poems
    that follow distinguish between works like "Michael," which
    convey stories or "tales," and poems like "We Are Seven,"
    which are called "dialogic personal anecdotes." These read-
    ings are very carefully worked out and show, once again,
    the poet's skill and literary tact even in works which were
    attacked, by Coleridge as well as others, as the ugly duck-
    lings of Romanticism. The book ends with an intriguing
    chapter on changes in narrative method between the earliest
    independent version of the Discharged Soldier passage and
    the same episode located in the larger context of the 1850
    Prelude. I hope the author will go on to do a full-scale
    study of the role of the narrator in *The Prelude,* which is
    obviously crucial but has never been worked out in detail.
    (B.C.H.)

Birdsall, Eric. *"Descriptive Sketches" by William Wordsworth.*
    Cornell University Press, 1984. Pp. xiv+301. $48.50.

As in Averill's edition of *An Evening Walk*, the "late"
reading text set up in parallel with the 1793 version is
based on Moxon's edition of 1836, even though Wordsworth
kept on revising the poem in still-later editions. In the
case of *Descriptive Sketches*, however, it proved possible
to arrange the apparatus more clearly, since no large trove
of manuscript revision has come to light to complicate
whatever scheme an editor chose to adopt. Here, variant
readings are given at the foot of the left-hand page,
below the 1793 text, for all changes through 1832; those
made from 1840-49 appear to the right, below the text of
1836. Apparently, and unlike *An Evening Walk*, the *Sketches*
"remained essentially similar to the original version
in every edition through the 1832 *Poetical Works*" (18).
The introduction gives a nicely complete account of the
origins of the poem, so far as these are known, and some
useful comments on the way Wordsworth's changing outlook
can be traced through the various, quite different, endings
of the poem in 1793, 1827, and again in 1836. Perhaps
the real highlight of this edition lies in the editor's
discovery, detailed in an appendix, that *The Old Man of
the Alps*, printed by Coleridge in March, 1798, was originally
part of some of the few early revisions to *Descriptive
Sketches* for which the evidence does survive. The first
letters of a number of lines can be detected on the stubs
of several pages torn out of the Racedown Notebook, and can
probably be dated to sometime in early 1794. "The work
grew too long for inclusion in *Descriptive Sketches*, where
the average section length is closer to 30 lines than 130.
Perhaps intending to publish it as a separate poem, Wordsworth let it lie until 1798, when his friend Coleridge was
pressed to meet his obligations to Stuart's newspaper. As
he did with some of the other material from Wordsworth,
Coleridge revised and supplemented Wordsworth's work, then
had it published over a pseudonym in *The Morning Post*"
(291). Dandy detective work! (B.C.H.)

Brennan, Matthew. "Wordsworth's *A Night-Piece*." *Explicator*
    42,iv (1984): 17-18.

Chandler, James K. *Wordsworth's Second Nature: A Study of
    the Poetry and Politics*. University of Chicago Press,
    1984. Pp. xxiv+313. $30.00; paper $14.95.

    A major and original study of the importance of "tradition"
in Wordsworth, with Burke as presiding genius. Chandler
sees the *L. to the Bishop of Llandaff* as a detailed attack
on Burke's *Reflections*, and the period of early 1797 through

early 1798 as the crucial one in Wordsworth's change from
radical to conservative. He finds that Wordsworth's politics
in the apparently "apolitical" years of the Great Decade are
expressed through his educational theory, which he sees not
as Rousseauistic but as a sustained attack on Rousseau and
the politics of the French "Committee on Public Instruction"
(Chapter V). One of the stated aims of the book is to
challenge "the received understanding of Wordsworth in American criticism"; the author believes "that M.H. Abrams,
Harold Bloom, and Geoffrey Hartman, for example, all miss
or misplot Wordsworth's position on the crucial intellectual
axes represented by Burke and Rousseau" (xx). A subsidiary
purpose is "to open up French intellectual history of the
1790's as an area of relevance to Wordsworth's thought and
writing. From where Wordsworth stood, English and Continental
intellectual history had everything to do with one another.
When we lose sight of this point of view, we misconstrue his
intellectual commitments both early and late" (xxiii).

This approach, which goes back to the work of Legouis,
Arthur Beatty, Basil Willey, and others, but reorients their
findings, has important consequences for the understanding
of Wordsworth (and, by implication, the English Romantics in
general): "A careful consideration of the major poetry in
the light of Burke's writings must lead one to challenge" the
prevailing interpretation "of Wordsworth's career.... *The
Prelude*, the magnum opus of the great decade and Wordsworth's
fullest attempt to deal with the French Revolution, is written
from an ideological perspective that is thoroughly Burkean....
If we understand 'conservative' to mean ideological proximity
to Burke, then the visionary and experimental writing for
which Wordsworth is revered, his program for poetry, is from
its very inception impelled by powerfully conservative motives"
(32). The author is referring specifically to the 1805
Prelude and not to "the later Wordsworth." To support his
claims, he includes a fascinating chapter on the "ideological"
content of the spots of time, the last place where recent
criticism would have us look for political vision. "The
structure of *The Prelude* requires that these passages stand
for 'psychological life' in a much broader sense than is to
be inferred from taking them as isolated lyric moments";
there is "powerful evidence linking the spots of time to
English nationalism" (198-99). Wordsworth, the author
concludes, "seemed to himself to have been for a time severed
from the national organism. The healing spots of time mark
his reunion. It is a reunion not only with the English coun-
tryside but also with the English mind and character, with
a way of thinking and feeling" (199-200). "If the personal
dimension of Wordsworth's 'personal epic' invites us to read

the poem as a 'crisis-autobiography,' then its epic dimension
invites us to see its crisis as national in scope" (203).
By "second nature" Chandler means what Burke meant by the
phrase--custom, tradition, discipline, almost Yeat's "custom
and ceremony." I expect, since "powerfully conservative
motives" have not found a happy home recently in the groves
of academe, that this book will be jumped on--on both sides
of the Atlantic; but I find its argument courageous and
almost wholly persuasive. (B.C.H.)

I agree, except to note that Chandler, for adversarial
reasons apparently, quite fails to notice how well Wordsworth's response to the educational theories of Tom Wedgwood
fits into the "second nature" approach. (D.V.E.)

Chase, Cynthia. "The Ring of Gyges and the Coat of Darkness:
Reading Rousseau with Wordsworth."

See Reed ("English 3. Criticism").

Cherney, Cynthia M. "'Fair Seed-Time': Beauty and Fear in
The Prelude and *The Excursion*." Ann Arbor, Mich.: University
Microfilms International, 1984.

Dissertation.

Cleary, Thomas R. "Wordsworth, Mrs. Morrison, MacLeish and
the Meanings of Robert Frost's 'A Silken Tent.'" *DR* 63 (1983-
84): 566-72.

The Excursion, IV:1295-99.

Colville, Derek. *The Teaching of Wordsworth*. New York,
Berne, and Frankfurt: Peter Lang Publishing, 1984.
Pp. 125. $12.55.

Not seen.

Davis, Norma S. "Stone as Metaphor: Wordsworth and Moore."
TWC 14 (1983): 264-68.

The sculptor Henry Moore.

Erskine-Hill, Howard. "The Satirical Game at Cards in Pope
and Wordsworth." *YES* 14 (1984): 183-95.

Galperin, William H. "'Then ... the Voice Was Silent': 'The
Wanderer' vs. The Ruined Cottage." *ELH* 51 (1984): 343-63.

Gill, Stephen, ed. *William Wordsworth*. (The Oxford Authors.)
Oxford University Press, 1984. Pp. xxxii+752. $29.95;
paper $9.95.

"This edition," the preface begins, must start "with what
may seem an immodest claim. Here for the first time a
selection of Wordsworth's work is offered in which the poems
are ordered according to the date of their composition, and
presented in texts which give as nearly as possible their
earliest completed state. That such a claim can be made
so long after Wordsworth's death in 1850 and in the face
of so many editions since then may seem amazing" (v). Not
only is it amazing; it is untrue--or, rather, only the second
half of the claim, about being the first to use the "earliest
completed state" of the text, is true. Knight printed in
the order of composition as early as 1882, and so did Hayden
for Penguin in 1977 (an edition that is available in this
country, by copyright fiddle, only in the much more costly
format of the Yale U.P.). The editor continues his argument
in a "Note on the Text" (xxx-xxxii): "In the belief that a
chronological presentation can best reveal the growth of
the poet's mind (the subject, after all, of his greatest
poem, *The Prelude*) and the unfolding of his imagination, this
volume is ordered according to date of composition. It
follows--and here I break with all of the editorial pioneers,
Dowden, Knight, Mutchinson, De Selincourt, Darbishire--that
one *must* print a text which comes as close as possible to the
state of a poem when it was first completed." What? Even
if the poem was terrible when it was first "completed" (itself an ambiguous term) and remains so in comparison with
later versions, some of them lovingly polished and perfected
through years of patient craftsmanship? "To place a poem
under 1795," the editor continues, "in a text encrusted with
the revisions of perhaps forty years--the practice of the
current Penguin edition--is, to say the least, confusing"
(xxxi). This edition, on the other hand--to say the least--
subjects the reader to a deal of what Coleridge in another
context called "damned bad poetry," for the sake of showing
us how Wordsworth's mind "grew." *Peter Bell* is a case in
point. The version printed here is just plain crude,
aesthetically, lacking almost all the truly great and memora-
ble passages--which, in fact, were added not very long after
the first text was "completed."

It is right--and inevitable--that an edition on the present
principle should be offered as a *scholarly* enterprise, part
of the continuing inquiry into how the poet's mind and art
developed. And this edition has a splendid introduction,
useful notes, a helpful selection of prose (including the
letter to Burns), and some useful suggestions for further
reading at the end. It has the 1805 *Prelude* complete, and
selections from the great blank-verse fragments of 1798 now
buried in the back of De Selincourt. As a readerly rather

than a scholarly book, however, it presents a picture of
Wordsworth that is far from complete, yet likely to be influential for many years. The book, incidentally, is beautifully printed--it resembles the Oxford English Novels
series--and makes the reader eager to dive in. (B.C.H.)

Gravil, Richard. "Wordsworth's Second Selves?" *TWC* 14 (1983):
191-201.

Hartman, Geoffrey H. "'Timely Utterance' Once More." *Genre*
17 (1984): 37-49.

The utterance may not be a specific poem but poetry itself,
which creates the bond between human feeling and mute nature.
But no summary can capture the subtleties of this display
of critical virtuousity. As Hartman says, "I have taken one
phrase as my starting point, and made many angels dance on
it." (R.M.R.)

Hay, Samuel H. "Wordsworth's Solitary: The Struggle with
Despondency." *TWC* 14 (1983): 243-45.

Hayden, John. "Wordsworth, Hartley, and the Revisionists."
SP 81 (1984): 94-118.

Sees the claims for Hartley's influence as unproved and
exaggerated.

Hinchliffe, Keith. "Wordsworth and the Kinds of Metaphor."
SiR 23 (1984): 81-100.

Holt, Ted, and John Gilroy. *A Commentary on Wordsworth's
"Prelude" Books I-V.* London, Boston, Melbourne, and Henley:
Routledge and Kegan Paul, 1983. Pp. xii+124. Paper $8.95.

A paragraph-by-verse-paragraph paraphrase and commentary
on the 1805 text, intended for readers coming to the poem
for the first time. More experienced readers will probably
find little of interest and be offended by the moralistic
fallout in the tone. For example, the comments on Bk. IV,
11. 288ff. leading up to the Poetic Dedication passage read
like this: "The stern phrase, 'these vanities/And how
they wrought' ... suggests that sin was actively working upon
him.... The 'stream of self-forgetfulness' (294) in classical myth was the river Lethe--the implication being that
Wordsworth *wished* to die to his old self (in the Pauline
sense) but could not." Furthermore, "'Slight shocks of
young love-liking' (325) lead on to priapic implications
in such phrases as 'Spirits upon the stretch' (322) and

'mounted up like joy' (326). Physical and visual titillation
are there in 'tingled through the veins' (327) and 'glancing
forms' (322)." This 'note of hollowness and irreligion"
is dispelled "in the emotional and spiritual plenitude expressed in the statement, 'to the brim/My heart was full'
(340-41)." The Dedication thus becomes a preacher-feature
instead of great poetry. (B.C.H.)

Johnston, Kenneth R. *Wordsworth and "The Recluse."* Yale
University Press, 1984. Pp. xxxii+397. $30.00.

Rev. by Keith Hanley, approvingly, in *TLS*, Aug. 3, 1984,
p. 862.

A learned, ambitious, and important study, to which no
short review can possibly do justice. The author sees
"Wordsworth's attachment to *The Recluse*" as "the heartbeat
of his creative life" (238), and by taking into account
virtually the whole body of textual and critical investigation accumulated during the past 20 years he is able to
throw new light on the project from beginning to end. This
is his conclusion: "Not only did [Wordsworth] write far
more of the poem itself than we have heretofore recognized,
a fragment large enough and good enough to stand with *The
Canterbury Tales* and *The Faerie Queene*, but it also provided
a motivational context for almost all of his greatest poetry"
(361). Baldly stated, Johnston's thesis is that Wordsworth
wrote well about himself and his own private, visionary
experience (*The Prelude*) but was unable to write successfully
about other people or about "Human Life" in general (*The
Recluse*). On this reading, his career becomes an almost
heroic effort to fulfill Coleridge's requirements for the
first "genuine" philosophical poetry. "Jonathan Wordsworth
and Stephen Gill," Johnston says, "assert that the objective
poetry implied by 'Human Life' was simply impossible for
Wordsworth; this has been the criticism of Wordsworth's
egotism from the beginning. Yet at each stage of *The
Recluse*'s development we see that Wordsworth's failure was
not simply in turning his eyes 'from half of human fate,' as
Arnold gibed, but turning *toward* 'the tribes and fellowships
of men' with a determination to make an 'authentic comment'
that was immediately undercut by his representation of general
human experience in terms of his own painful individual
experiences. His determination not to neglect Human Life
spelled the doom of his *Recluse*, but also gave it its fitful
glory" (98). Johnston sees Wordsworth's mind and art as
fundamentally "dialectical," and his set of contraries
develops logically from the "apocalyptic" *vs.* "humanizing"
tendencies that Hartman saw. The conflict between personal
and social experience provides a framework for the author

to examine the whole corpus of Wordsworth's verse from 1797
to 1815 (!), all of which he takes to be part of *The Recluse*.
This approach yields new insights into the structure of the
two-part *Prelude*, and the importance of the "social" books
of *1805*, as well as into the metaphors of locations, buildings, and "habitations" throughout. Wordsworth's architec-
tonic power has never been more clearly demonstrated.
(Johnston is mistaken, though, when he says, p. 119, that
the lines at the end of *1805* Bk. IV on "what rules govern"
the conduct of the poem were first printed in the Norton
text; they appear on p. 135 of the 1959 Darbishire edition.)
The discussion of "the *Recluse* poems of 1808," e.g., "St.
Paul's," and of *The Excursion* (Chapters 7-9), points the
way toward a major revaluation.

The least satisfactory chapters, to my mind, are the first
and last. Johnston reads the *O.C. Beggar* and *The Ruined
Cottage* as failed "social" poems, and he gets bogged down
at the end in the labyrinthine tensions between Wordsworth
and Coleridge that he detects in the *Biographia*, which he
reads as Coleridge's way of reappropriating the whole idea
of *The Recluse* once Wordsworth had failed to write it. There
is also a tendency to read provisional or fragmentary poems
like the two-part *Prelude* with more critical certainty than
seems wise--the very temptation which the marvellous Cornell
texts present. In summary: this book belongs centrally in
what James K. Chandler calls the "psychologizing interpretation" of Romantic poetry (*Wordsworth's Second Nature*, p.
185, reviewed above). The danger of the approach taken by
Johnston is that his central dialectic sometimes functions
as an *idée fixe*: by seeing everything as part of *The Recluse*,
we are sometimes blocked from seeing poems as individual
works of art. Wordsworth was interested in a whole range
of other concerns which do not make their presence felt in
Johnston's intensely focused study, and which are perhaps
not best approached through the idea of psychodrama. Even
his central thesis could be called into question, by noting
that in Wordsworth's greatest writing on Man, on Nature,
and on Human Life, "nature" serves as the reconciling medium
or midpoint for *both* the individual and society: a conception
based on a much older, triadic logic, descending from Neo-
platonism and Christianity, that would obviate the absolute
Hegelian antitheses on which this notable book is based.
(B.C.H.)

Jones, John A. "The 'Reconciliation of Opposites' in Romantic
Poetry and Classical Style Music: Some Relations." *CentR*
28 (1984): 159-84.

Kay, D.C. "Thomas, Donne, and Wordsworth's 'Monstrous Anthill.'"
    N&Q 31,i (March 1984): 55-56.

The anthill reference in *Prelude* II: 149-51.

Kelley, Theresa M. "Wordsworth and the Rhinefall." *SiR* 23
    (1984): 61-79.

Kelley, Theresa M. "Wordsworth, Kant, and the Romantic Sub-
    lime." *PQ* 63 (1984): 130-40.

By looking closely at Wordsworth's fragmentary essay on
the sublime, the author finds important differences rather
than similarities with Kant's ideas. "Because neo-Kantian
readings of Wordsworth's aesthetics have dominated much
recent discussion of the Romantic sublime, the misapplica-
tion of Kantian categories has distorted an understanding
of Romantic aesthetics in general." A fine article, and
a valuable corrective. (B.C.H.)

Kneale, Douglas. "The Rhetoric of Imagination in 'The
    Prelude.'" *Ariel* 15,iv (1984): 111-27.

La Cassagnere, Christian. "Histoire d'un regard: une lecture
    de 'The Thorn' de Wordsworth." *EA* 37,i (1984): 28-40.

"The Thorn" is "l'inscription de ce *voyage fantastique*,
de ce voyage du sujet au dedans et au bout de lui-même."

Lessa, Richard. "Wordsworth's *Michael* and the Pastoral
    Tradition." *UTQ* 53 (1984): 181-94.

Liu, Alan. "Wordsworth: The History in 'Imagination.'"
    ELH 51 (1984): 505-48.

Manning, Peter J. "Reading Wordsworth's Revisions: Othello
    and the Drowned Man." *SiR* 22 (1983): 3-28.

"In this textual history Othello occupies only a minuscule
space, but he stands at a point critical to Wordsworth's
formulation of his role as a poet" (27).

McCracken, David. *Wordsworth and the Lake District: A Guide
    to the Poems and Their Places.* Oxford University Press,
    1984. Pp. xviii+300; 18 black-and-white illus., 16 maps.
    $21.95.

A surprise and delight, not at all the glossy but actually
dreary Michelin-minus-the-restaurants-because-there-aren't-
any sort of thing the title suggested before I looked inside.

This guide is scholarly and even original in many small details, and it is refreshingly addressed to a general audience. It has two sections. The first, "Poems, and Places," takes the reader along the main road from Ambleside to Keswick, and then, on a different axis, to Wordsworthian places to the east and west. The text is a quiet and imaginative encyclopedia on the actual places connected with Wordsworth's poems, and well informed about earlier travelers as well as nineteenth-century Wordsworthians like Knight and Rawnsley. The engravings reproduced are probably rare and show what the Lake District must have looked like in the poet's lifetime. Geography is accompanied by generous quotations from the poetry, and both are cross-referenced to the second section, "In the Footsteps of Wordsworth," which has simple maps and drawings and is intended as an actual guide for exploring the region. *Vaut le voyage.* (B.C.H.)

McFarland, Thomas. "Wordsworth: Prophet of the Past." *TWC* 14 (1983): 251-55.

Miller, Judith D. "*The Excursion*: A Re-Evaluation." Ann Arbor, Mich.: Microfilms International, 1984.

   Dissertation.

Milstead, John. "Wordsworth's Non-Privileged Ungrammaticality: A Failed Semiosis." *TWC* 15 (1984): 32-35.

   A parody (I trust) of deconstructionist criticism, using "Lines Written in Early Spring" as colon-fodder. (B.C.H.)

Newlyn, Lucy. "Lamb, Lloyd, London: A Perspective on Book Seven of *The Prelude*." *ChLB* 47-48 (1984): 169-87.

   Finding "three different kinds of responses to the city" in the poetry of Cowper, Newlyn observes that "they recur (sometimes singly; sometimes in complicated juxtaposition) in the writings of Lamb, Lloyd, and Wordsworth."
   Charles Lloyd's "London" (quoted in full) is held up not merely as a "source" but as "The most remarkable treatment of London during the 1790's." All very illuminating. (D.V.E.)

Nichols, Ashton. "Towards 'Spots of Time': 'Visionary Dreariness' in *An Evening Walk*." *TWC* 14 (1983): 233-37.

Owen, W.J.B. "Wordsworth's Imaginations." *TWC* 14 (1983): 213-24.

Parker, Reeve. "'Oh Could You Hear His Voice!': Wordsworth,
Coleridge, and Ventriloquism." Pp. 125-43 in Arden Reed,
ed., *Romanticism & Language* (listed above in "English 3.
Criticism").

   A shrewd investigation of "the role tale-telling voices
play in art and life," finding that, more than generally
recognized, *The Borderers*, with its dramatization of strong
passion, repetition, and ventriloquism, gives form to the
passions and characters of Wordsworth and Coleridge "and
the ways in which these persons stood relative to each
other." A valuable contribution to the discussion of their
symbiosis. (D.V.E.)

Pittock, Malcolm. "Knowledge and Experience in Wordsworth
and Edward Thomas." *DUJ*, n.s. 45 (june 1984): 195-204.

   Passages from both poets are used to illustrate a situation common in Romantic poetry, when "its formal categories
of interpretation cannot contain the experience with which
it deals, and yet that experience breaks through in a series
of imaginative transformations all attempts to repress it."
Wordsworth's "stolen boat" episode, for example, cannot
entirely conceal "suppressed sexual desires and the guilt
associated with them." A subtle, persuasive analysis.
(R.M.R.)

Proffitt, Edward. "Book V in *The Prelude*: A Developmental
Reading." *RP&P* 8,i (1984): 1-16.

Radcliffe, Evan. "'In Dreams Begins Responsibility': Wordsworth's Ruined Cottage Story." *SiR* 23 (1984): 101-19.

Reiman, Donald H. "The Beauty of Buttermere as Fact and
Romantic Symbol." *Criticism* 26 (1984): 139-70.

Roe, Nicholas. "Who Was Spy Nozy?" *TWC* 15 (1984): 46-50.

   Identifies him as James Walsh, a Bow Street Officer and
informer, who spent much time tracking Thelwall.

Rogers, David. "Wordsworth's Late Echo of 'My Heart Leaps
Up.'" *Greyfriar* 24 (1983): 47-52.

Sampson, David. "Wordsworth and the 'deficiencies of language.'"
ELH 51 (1984): 53-68.

Sampson, David. "Wordsworth and the Poor: The Poetry of
Survival." *SiR* 23 (1984): 31-59.

Simpson, David. "Criticism, Politics, and Style in Wordsworth's
Poetry." *CritI* 11 (1984): 52-81.

Through their language and the attitudes of their speakers,
the poems "Alice Fell" and "Gipsies" are found to reflect
the great social and political debates of Wordsworth's
time, about "work and leisure, charity and relief, property
and vagrancy, rich and poor." Praising the work of "historical" writers on the period (e.g., E.P. Thomason, David Erdman, Carl Woodring), Simpson indicts Deconstruction as "discursive frustration," a gesture of "striving" imprisoned
within the limits of its own "received discourse." (I.H.C.)

Stevenson, Warren. "Wordsworth's Satanism." *TWC* 15 (1984):
82-84.

Thomas, Gordon K. "'The Thorn' in the Flesh of English Romanticism." *TWC* 14 (1983): 237-42.

Thomas, Gordon Kent, ed. *William Wordsworth's CONVENTION OF
CINTRA. A facsimile of the 1809 text.* Brigham Young University Press, 1983. Pp. xiii+216. Paper.

A helpfully precise and judicious Introduction, and a Note
on the Text. (D.V.E.)

Versluys, Kristiaan. "Western Wordsworthianism: Cities Re-
viled and Cities Idealized." *TWC* 15 (1984): 20-22.

"Western" in the sense of Californian: echoes of Wordsworth in West Coast anthologies of the 1860s.

Ward, J.P. *Wordsworth's Language of Men.* Brighton: Harvester Press; Totowa, N.J.: Barnes & Noble, 1984. Pp.
xii+235. $28.50.

According to a blurb on the dust-jacket from John Beer,
this is "A bold attempt to reinstate Wordsworth as the first
great figure in modern poetry by the use of recent theoretic
methods. The chapter on Wordsworth's favorite poetic sounds
is particularly fascinating and very persuasive." I was not
aware that Wordsworth needed reinstatement to that position--
by any method--and I find the book much less persuasive,
insofar as I understand it at all. The central section, on
"Characteristics of Wordsworth's Language," has its moments,
but the "Marxist" (I think) approach often seems heavy-
handed and curiously old-fashioned. This section contains
chapters on "Vibrancy and Motion," "Nominals," "The Copula,"
and "Speech to the Other." Perhaps it is fairest to let the
author summarize his own argument: "It would appear that

Wordsworth, and perhaps most of the romantics and Hegel, went
through the post-sacramental, post-stable stage of finding
how to express this new version of engagement with reality
generally, and that this successful expression helped pre-
dispose the later age of Freudian psychology and the bringing into the open of a universal awareness of the unconscious. But this in its turn has produced later still a
tendency for language to be seen as, first and foremost, the
constituting element in social interaction. It is through
language in a world of doubt and ontological insecurity,
and to many people a metaphysically purposeless world,
that we can now get and keep in touch with each other at
all. This is language's predominant use in our time, that
is, to communicate not just for information but for human
interaction's own sake and need. But language itself could
not have become this without developing into a mode of
interactive negotiation which took expected or noticed attitudes of others into account within the fabric of speech
itself. That is, the opening of the self to a merely subjective expression generally was first necessary for a con-
fessional, interactive discourse to evolve later. That in
itself was only possible, it is argued, because one major
poet did not merely replace old myths with new expressive
ones, or new expressions of the old. Rather he also grappled
with the language of his own mind and feelings, and did so
in a particular way. Wordsworth not only achieved the expression of engagement of self with reality. He also moved
toward a language which could be the foundation of the pre-
carious interaction between individuals in an era like ours
which had first achieved that earlier subjective expression.
This it seems is Wordsworth's achievement in making a
language of men" (103-04). He summarizes on p. 208: "If
in this later Marxist formulation ideology and its texts
are recognized as laced with contradictions, and if the
text's object (even if unconscious) is to rupture the ideology
that seems to hide them, then the language of metonymy in
its widest sense--Lacan's restlessness, desire, the language
of social interaction, the verbs and exclamations and non-
nominals made monimal--would seem to have to be the language
in which it is done. My contention is that Wordsworth
stamped English culture and literature with this language."
A new vision of the Distributor of Stamps. (B.C.H.)

Watson, J.R. *Wordsworth's Vital Soul: The Sacred and Profane
in Wordsworth's Poetry.* Atlantic Highlands, N.J.: Humanities Press, 1982. Pp. x+259. $30.00.

Rev. by Mark Casserley in *TLS*, April 6, 1984, p. 383, as of slight use, a problem being "that of relating what Watson has written, to Wordsworth"; by John A. Hodgson in *SiR* 23 (1984): 126-27, as "for the most part assimilating Wordsworth to Buber and the anthopologists, and not the reverse" but "at his best" in chapters on man's relation to men, "where he explores the relevance of *communitas* ... as a context...." Not seen.

Wedd, Mary R. "Light on Landscape in Wordsworth's 'Spots of Time.'" *TWC* 14 (1983): 224-32.

Wihl, Gary. "Empsonian Pregnancy and Wordsworth's Spousal Verse." *DR* 63 (1983-84): 555-65.

Only if you agree that "Wordsworth's poetry lack[s] the pregnancy that would make possible the third idea within a good mutual metaphor." Clearly the burthen of the mystery. (T.L.A.)

Williams, John. "Salisbury Plain: Politics in Wordsworth's Poetry." *L&H* 9 (1983): 164-93.

Wolfson, Susan J. "The Illusion of Mastery: Wordsworth's Revisions of 'The Drowned Man of Esthwaite.'" *PMLA* 99 (1984): 917-35.

Woodman, Ross. "Milton's Satan in Wordsowrth's 'Vale of Soulmaking.'" *SiR* 23 (1984): 3-30.

Wordsworth, Jonathan. "The Mind as Lord and Master: Wordsworth and Wallace Stevens." *TWC* 14 (1983): 183-91.

See also de Man, Ellison, Jacobus, Jay, Johnson, Kipperman, McGann, Meregalli, Rawson, Riffaterre, Thurley, Waldinger ("General 3. Criticism"); Clubbe ("English 1. Bibliography"); Abrams, Buckley, Chandler, Chavkin, Cook et al., Ellison, Kincaid, Macovski, Oxenhorne, Reed, Thesing, Venis ("English 3. Criticism"); Glen ("Blake"); Gleckner, Gravil, Priestman ("Coleridge"); Bromwich ("Hazlitt").

Reviews of books previously listed:

BAKER, Jeffrey, *Time and Mind in Wordsworth's Poetry* (see *RMB* for 1980, p. 135), rev. by Roger Sharrock in *ELN* 21,iv (1984): 76-82; BETZ, Paul F., ed., *"Benjamin the Waggoner" by William Wordsworth* (see *RMB* for 1981, pp. 145-47), rev.

by Stephen Gill in *RES* 35 (1984):   390-91; DARLINGTON, Beth,
ed., *The Love Letters of William and Mary Wordsworth* (see
RMB for 1981, p. 147), rev. by John R. Nabholtz in *MP* 82
(1984):   209-11; HODGSON, John A., *Wordsworth's Philosophical
Poetry, 1797-1814* (see *RMB* for 1981, pp. 149-50), rev. by
Roger Sharrock in *ELN* 21,iv (1984):   76-82; JOHNSON, Lee M.,
Wordsworth's Metaphysical Verse: Geometry, Nature, and Form
(see *RMB* for 1983, p. 150), rev. by Don H. Bialostosky in
MP 82 (1985):   328-30, as "a fine book" for "our most thoughtful and magnanimous moments"; by John A. Hodgson in *SiR* 23
(1984):   121-26 as valuable but claiming too much; by Thomas
A. Vogler in *RP&P* 8,ii (1984):   51-55; PIRIE, David B.,
*William Wordsworth: The Poetry of Grandeur and of Tender-
ness* (see *RMB* for 1983, p. 154), rev. by Theresa M. Kelley
in *SiR* 23 (1984):   128-32, as seriously flawed; by W.J.B.
Owen in *RES* 35 (1984):   560-62; by Edward Proffitt in *SHR* 18
(1984):   262-63; REHDER, Robert, *Wordsworth and the Beginnings
of Modern Poetry* (see *RMB* for 1981, p. 152), rev. by Lucy
Newlyn in *RES* 35 (1984):   243-44; SHERRY, Charles, *Wordsworth's Poetry of the Imagination* (see *RMB* for 1981, pp. 152-
53), rev. by Philip Drew in *YES* 14 (1984):   332-33; WORDS-
WORTH, Jonathan, *William Wordsworth: The Borders of Vision*
(see *RMB* for 1983, pp. 157-59), rev. by Michael Baron in
English 33 (1984):   71-78; scathingly, and with inimitably
Oxonian malice, by Stephen Logan in *EiC* 34 (1984):   254-62.

Composite reviews:

Arac, Jonathan. *SiR* 22 (1983):   136-46.

Discusses James H. Averill, *Wordsworth and the Poetry of
Human Suffering* (see *RMB* for 1980, pp. 133-34); John A.
Hodgson, *Wordsworth's Philosophical Poetry, 1797-1814* (see
RMB for 1981, pp. 149-50); and Charles Sherry, *Wordsworth's
Poetry of the Imagination* (see *RMB* for 1981, pp. 152-54).

Bialostosky, Don H. "Representing Wordsworth." *MLQ* 44 (1983):
305-10.

"The figures by means of which we have represented Wordsworth
and his poetry have generally, sometimes violently, taken a
part for the whole" (305). With introductory examples in
the criticism of Geoffrey Hartman and James H. Averill, of
selective preference for certain parts of the work or life
as "the ssential Wordsworth," Bialostosky reviews the work
of David B. Pirie, *William Wordsworth: The Poetry of Grandeur
and of Tenderness* (see *RMB* for 1983, p. 154) and David
Simpson, *Wordsworth and the Figurings of the Real* (see *RMB*
for 1983, p. 156).

Pirie "departs from previous representations of Wordsworth by replacing a preference for the poet's reconciliation of opposites" or variants of that position "with an admiration for his daring 'to face the impossibility of resolving ... incongruities'"; yet Pirie "remains among those critics who offer their representations of the poet as more true and worthy than his self-representations."

Simpson "offers the model of a critical enterprise capable of examining the fullness of human figurings without setting up 'standards' by which to exclude whole classes of former production or inhibit whole classes of future productivity.... It makes clear that the task of representing Wordsworth, as both Pirie and Simpson recognize, is far from complete" (310).

FRENCH

(Compiled by Mary Ellen Birkett, Smith College;
Alfred G. Engstrom, University of North Carolina;
Eugene F. Gray, Michigan State University; Jon B.
Hassel, University of Arkansas; Danielle Johnson-
Cousin, Vanderbilt University; James S. Patty,
Vanderbilt University; Albert B. Smith, Jr., Uni-
versity of Florida; Emile J. Talbot, University
of Illinois at Urbana-Champaign)

1. GENERAL

Albuquerque, Severino João. "A Brazilian Intermediary in the
Transmission of European Romantic Ideas: Alvares de Azevedo."
RomN 23 (1982-83): 220-26.

Amossy, Ruth, and Elisheva Rosen. *Les Discours du cliché*.
Paris: SEDES-C.D.U., 1982. Pp. 150. Fr. 78.00.

Rev. by Mireille Bossis in *SFr* 28 (1984): 169-70; by Ann
Jefferson in *FS* 38 (1984): 109-10.

Deals with Chateaubriand (*René*), Balzac (*Eugénie Grandet*),
Musset (*Confession*), and early Flaubert.

André, Jean-Marie. "La survie de Virgile dans le préromantisme
et dans le romantisme français." *Würzburger Jahrbücher für
die Altertumwissenschaft* 8 (1982): 149-59.

On Madame de Staël, Chateaubriand, Stendhal, Hugo, and
Lamartine.

Angenot, Marc. "La littérature populaire française au dix-
neuvième siècle." *CRCL* 9 (1982): 307-33.

For the relevant period, this article surveys such topics
as the *littérature de colportage*, *canards*, *complaintes*, the
melodrama, the sentimental novel, the *roman noir*, the Gothic
novel, and the *roman-feuilleton*. The Vicomte d'Arlincourt
and Sue are singled out to some extent.

Aron, Jean-Paul. *Misérable et glorieuse. La femme au XIXe siècle.* (Historiques.) Brussels: Editions Complexe, 1984. Pp. 256. Fr. 34.00.

This is a cheap reprint of a book originally published in 1980 (Paris: Fayard) but not so far listed in *RMB*. Contents: Jean-Paul Aron, "Préface" (7-24); Anne Martin-Fugier, "La bonne" (27-39); Alain Corbin, "La prostituée" (41-58); Madeleine Rebérioux, "L'ouvrière" (59-78); Jean-Pierre Peter, "Les médecins et les femmes" (79-97); Philippe Perrot, "Le jardin des modes" (101-16); Anne Martin-Fugier, "La maîtresses de maison" (117-34); Martine Segalen, "Femmes rurales" (137-52); Jean Borie, "Une gynécologie passionnée" (153-89); Laure Adler, "Flora, Pauline et les autres" (191-211); Béatrice Slama, "Femmes écrivains" (213-43).

Auzas, Pierre-Marie, ed. *Actes du Colloque international Viollet-le-Duc, Paris, 1980.* Paris: Nouvelles Editions Latines, 1982. Pp. 352. Fr. 180.00.

Rev. by Barry Bergdoll in *BM* 975 (June 1984): 363-64; by Emile Poulat in *ASSR* 55,ii (1983): 203.

Aymes, Jean-René, ed. *L'Espagne romantique.* (Témoignages de Voyageurs français.) Paris: A.M. Métailié, 1983. Pp. 214. Fr. 59.00.

Bailbé, J.-M. "L'orgue dans l'imaginaire romantique." *Etudes Normandes* 2 (1983): 25-73.

Bailbé, Joseph-Marc. "'Sémiramide' de Rossini." Pp. 161-70 in Robert Aubaniac, et al., *Les Opéras du Festival d'Aix-en-Provence.* Aix-en-Provence: Edisud, 1982. Pp. 232.

On the critical reaction to the early Paris productions (1823, 1860) of Rossini's opera by Balzac, Stendhal, et al., plus an evaluation of the work: its vocalism, its mixture of French and Italian styles, and its Orientalism.

Balmas, Enea. "Faust in Italia e la cultura francese." Pp. 196-234 in *Studi di letteratura francese*, IX. Florence: Leo S. Olschki, 1983. Pp. 274.

Focuses on an anonymous Italian opera, *Fausto* (given at the Théâtre royal italien in 1830), and, in fact, provides a facsimile of the complete libretto.

Bann, Stephen. *The Clothing of Clio: A Study of the Representation of History in Nineteenth-Century Britain and France.* Cambridge University Press, 1984. Pp. xii+196. £19.50.

Rev. by Eugen Weber in *TLS*, Sept. 29, 1984, p. 1072.

This interdisciplinary study, in which the names of Hayden White and Foucault are often invoked, aims at a "historical poetics" by a survey of various genres and media (historiography, museology, book illustrations, architecture, historical novels). Major French figures treated are Michelet, Barante, Daguerre (his diorama), the painter Delaroche, and the museum curators Alexandre Lenoir and Du Sommerard.

Bartlet, M. Elizabeth C. "A Newly Discovered Opera for Napoleon." *Acta Musicologica* 56 (1984): 266-96.

On Méhul's *Les Troubadours, ou la fête au château* (book by Alexandre Duval), intended to help celebrate Napoleon's marriage to Marie-Louise but never actually performed. The historical background is given in some detail, the plot outlined, the score analyzed.

Bassy, Alain-Marie. "Le livre mis en pièce(s). Pensées détachées sur le livre romantique." *Romantisme* 43 (1984): 19-27.

According to Bassy, around 1830 there is a rupture in the history of the book: no longer intended to preserve a text, it becomes a consumer object; where once it simulated interpersonal communication, now it simulates social communication. Illustrations invade the text. With the coming of the *roman-feuilleton* the book is fragmented, the chapter triumphing over the book. Various formats become technically possible; typography becomes a form of self-expression; illustration is individualized; wood pulp replaces rag, making the book obviously mortal. "La période romantique du livre est un moment d'explosion et de mort."

Beetem, Robert N. "Horace Vernet's Mural in the Palais Bourbon: Contemporary Imagery, Modern Technology, and Classical Allegory During the July Monarchy." *AB* 66 (1984): 254-69.

Emphasizes the compromising mixture of styles and motifs employed to present the theme of industrial progress during the age of Louis-Philippe.

Benge, Glenn F. *Antoine-Louis Barye: Sculptor of Romantic Realism*. Pennsylvania State University Press, 1984. Pp. 320. $42.50.

Berenson, Edward. *Populist Religion and Left-Wing Politics in France, 1830-1852*. Princeton University Press, 1984. Pp. 345. $35.00.

Berthier, Annie, et al. *Vers l'Orient*. Avant-propos par
Alain Gourdon. Paris: Bibliothèque Nationale, 1983. Pp.
104. Fr. 60.00.

Catalogue of an exposition at the Bibliothèque Nationale,
March 16–April 30, 1983.

Berthier, Patrick. "Autopsie d'un petit journal: *Chérubin*
(1834–1835)." *L'Année Balzacienne 1982*, pp. 211–23.

"Examen de *Chérubin* sous trois de ses aspects: la
littérature qu'il propose, celle qu'il critique, celle
qu'il aide à mieux lire."

Bertier de Sauvigny, Guillaume de. *La France et les Français
vus par les voyageurs américains, 1814–1848*. Paris:
Flammarion, 1982. Pp. 427. Fr. 120.00.

Listed without comment in *RMB* for 1982, p. 157, this is
the first of two volumes on the subject (the second will
deal with cultural and intellectual life, religion,
politics, etc.).
The author limits himself to printed sources and, usually,
to those published in book form. His organization is thematic
rather than by author or by chronology. A typical chapter,
e.g., "La traversée et l'arrivée en France," is divided
into a number of subsections: "La traversée de l'Atlantique,"
"Le passage de la Manche," "Le premier vapeur en Méditer-
ranée," "Les ports de la Manche," "Les rigueurs de la douane,"
"Débarquement à Boulogne et à Dieppe," "Quarantaines sani-
taires," "Sur les frontières terrestres," "Formalités
policières," "La fraude."
There is a helpful "Bio-bibliographie" (pp. 367–97),
arranged chronologically. On the other hand, there is no
index, with the result that it is hard to find all the
passages, for example, in which James Fenimore Cooper is
quoted. (J.S.P.)

Bertin, Claudie. "Un gouachiste oublié: Louis Bélanger
(1756–1816)." *GBA* 104 (July–Aug. 1984): 17–32; 12 illus.

Bertoni Del Guercio, Giuliana. *Thèmes romantiques*. Milan:
Principato, 1983. Pp. 246.

Boesche, Roger C. "The Strange Liberation of Alexis de
Tocqueville." *History of Political Thought* (Winter 1981):
495–524.

Bolster, Richard, ed. *Documents littéraires de l'époque
romantique*. (Situation, 43.) Paris: Minard (Lettres
modernes), 1984. Pp. 226. Fr. 95.00

Emphasizing the novel and moving through the decade of the
1830s, Bolster seeks to enlarge the picture usually given
of French Romanticism's critical stances (the theater has
generally had the spotlight).

The documents chosen are Jules Chopin, "Vers une réforme
dans les délassements littéraires" (*La Revue encyclopédique*,
Sept. 1829); Amédée Pichot, "*Le Rouge et le Noir*" (*ibid.*,
Feb. 1831); Charles de Bernard, "*La Peau de Chagrin*" (*La
Gazette de Franche-Comté*, Aug. 13, 1831); Sainte-Beuve,
"*Indiana*" (*Le National*, Oct. 5, 1832); Désiré Nisard,
"D'un commencement de réaction contre la littérature facile"
(*La Revue de Paris*, Dec. 1833); Jules Janin, "Manifeste de
la jeune littérature. Réponse à M. Nisard" (*ibid.*, Jan.
1834); Jules Janin, "*Un Grand Homme de province à Paris*"
(*ibid.*, July 1839); Arnould Frémy, "*La Chartreuse de Parme*"
(*ibid.*, May 1839).

Bolster's choice of documents is interesting, and his
annotations and analyses, as well as his introduction (5-
42), are solid. (J.S.P.)

Bordet, G. "Fête contre-révolutionnaire, néo-baroque ou
ordinaire? La grande mission de Besançon, janvier-février
1825." Pp. 183-345 in *La Fête, pratique et discours.
D'Alexandrie hellénistique à la mission de Besançon*. (Annales
littéraires de l'Université de Besançon, 267.) Paris:
Les Belles Lettres, 1981. Pp. 351.

A lavishly documented study of the mission, in which this
event is read as "politique événementielle," as *histoire à
longue durée*, and as an anthropological manifestation.

Bouscou, Franck. "La presse française à l'époque napoléonienne."
La Science Historique 4-5 (Summer-Autumn 1982): 49-59.

Brayer, Yves. "Louis Boilly et son temps." *L'OEil* 346
(May 1984): 22-27.

Inspired by a show at the Musée Marmottan, May 3-June 30,
1984. Brayer sees in the painter a "fidèle commentateur
de son temps." Nice illustrations.

Bressolette, Claude. *Le Pouvoir dans la société et dans
l'église. L'ecclésiologie politique de Mgr Maret au XIXe
siècle*. Préface de Jacques Gadille. (Histoire des
Doctrines ecclésiastiques.) Paris: Editions du Cerf, 1984.
Pp. 212. Fr. 99.00.

Brombert, Beth Archer. *Cristina Belgiojoso*. Milan: Dall'
Oglio, 1981. Pp. 481.

Rev. by Peter Byrne in *SFr* 28 (1984): 181-82.
On the original version of this 1977 book, see *ELN* 16,
Supp., 81.

Brown, Marilyn R. "Ingres's Pursuit of Perfection." *AJ* 44
(1984): 179-83.

Bryson, Norman. *Tradition and Desire: From David to Delacroix.* (Cambridge Studies in French.) Cambridge University
Press, 1984. Pp. 220. £27.50.

Applying structuralist and post-structuralist theories,
Bryson studies the personal reaction to tradition by David,
Ingres, and Delacroix.

Bucherie, Luoc. "Mise en scène des pouvoirs dans les graffiti
anciens (XV-XVIIIᵉ siècles)." *GBA* 103 (Jan. 1984): 1-10;
3 illus.

Includes specimens from the period of the French Revolution
and Napoleon.

Burney, John. "La Faculté des lettres de Toulouse de 1830 à
1875." *Annales du Midi*, July-Sept. 1982, pp. 277-99.

Changy, Hugues de. "La presse légitimiste sous la Monarchie
de juillet dans l'Est de la France." *La Science Historique*
4-5 (Summer-Autumn 1982): 61-70.

Charlton, D.G., ed. *The French Romantics.* Vols 1 & 2.
Cambridge University Press, 1984. Vol. 1. Pp. 224.
$44.50; paper $15.95; Vol. 2. Pp. 240. $44.50; paper $15.95.

Rev. by Victor Brombert in *TLS*, Jan. 4, 1985, pp. 15-16.
This work offers a most competent survey of French Romanticism, ranging over art, history, music, literature, and
religious and social thought. Each essay is followed by a
short critical bibliography. Contents of vol. 1: David
G. Charlton, "The French Romantic Movement" (1-32); David G.
Charlton, "Religious and Political Thought" (33-75); Frank
P. Bowman, "Illuminism, Utopia, Mythology" (76-112); J.C.
Ireson, "Poetry" (113-62); David G. Charlton, "Prose Fiction"
(163-203). Contents of vol. 2: W.D. Howarth, "Drama" (205-
47); Roger Fayolle, "Criticism and Theory" (248-73); Douglas
Johnson, "Historians" (274-307); William Vaughan, "The Visual
Arts" (308-52); Hugh Macdonald, "Music and Opera" (353-81);
Max Milner, "Romantics on the Fringe" (382-422). (E.F.G.)

Charpentier, Roger-Jean. "Incursion dans le monde des poètes varois du XIXe siècle (1832-1857)." *Bulletin de l'Académie du Var* (1982): 101-20.

Chisick, Harvey. *The Limits of Reform in the Enlightenment: Attitudes Toward the Education of the Lower Classes in Eighteenth-Century France.* Princeton University Press, 1981. Pp. 324. $29.50.

Rev. by Thomas E. Kaiser in *ECS* 18 (1984): 128-32.

Cohen, H. Robert. *Les Gravures musicales dans "L'Illustration."* 3 vols. Les Presses de l'Université Laval, 1983. Fr. 1600.00.

Rev. by François Lesure in *Fontes Artis Musicae* 31 (1984): 242; by Hugh Macdonald in *TLS*, Feb. 8, 1985, p. 141.
Covering the years from 1843 to the end of the century, these volumes offer over 3,000 reproductions (none larger than 6 x 9 cm., unfortunately), mostly of operative premieres, interior and exterior views of theaters, portraits and caricatures of composers and singers.

Colloque Franco-Allemand. *Paris au XIXe siècle. Aspects d'un mythe.* Presses universitaires de Lyon, 1984. Pp. 168. Fr. 80.00.

Proceedings of a symposium held at Frankfurt am Main June 22-24, 1982.

Conilleau, Roland, and Albert Ronsin. *Henri Valentin, illustrateur de la vie quotidienne en France de 1845 à 1855.* Barembach: Jean-Pierre Gyss, 1982. Pp. 220.

Rev. by Guy Cabourdin in *Annales de l'Est* 35 (1984): 152-53.
Valentin (d. 1855) did many illustrations for *L'Illustration* and the *London Illustrated News.* The authors divide his work into "Scènes de la vie de province" and "Scènes de la vie privée."

Coquillat, Michelle. *La Poétique du mâle.* Préface de Colette Audry. (Idées, 459.) Paris: Gallimard, 1982. Pp. 472.

Rev. by Aline Alquier in *SFr* 28 (1984): 371-72.
Colette Audry: "C'est une exploration ... des voies et moyens par lesquels la littérature opère sur les esprits ... d'une manière diffuse, à propos d'un sujet donné: le rapport du sexe à la création" (13). Pages relevant for Romantism: 113-384. Authors studied (passim): Rousseau, Chateaubriand, Stendhal, Vigny, Hugo, Musset, Balzac, Sand.

Corsi, Pietro.   "Lamarck en Italie."   *Revue d'Histoire des Sciences* 37 (1984):   47-64.

A reassessment of Lamarck's influence on Italian scientists in the nineteenth century.

Daniels, Barry V.   "A Footnote to Daguerre's Career as a Stage Designer."   *Theatre Survey* 24 (1983):   134-37.

Descriptions and engraved views of the curtains Daguerre painted for several Parisian theaters in the period 1815-19.   According to Daniels, they represent, not a throwback to the eighteenth century, "but rather an attempt to display the 19th century painter's illusionistic technique."

Daniels, Barry V.   *Revolution in the Theatre: French Romantic Theories of Drama.*   Westport, Conn.:   Greenwood Press, 1983.   Pp. xx+250. $29.95.

English translation of manifestoes, prefaces, etc., including Vigny's "Lettre à Lord * * *."

Dauzier, Martine.   "Troubadour de romance, troubadour de roman: la figure du troubadour des almanachs au *Journal du Dimanche.*"   Pp. 149-60 in *Iconographie et littérature. D'un art à l'autre.*   (Centre d'Etude et de Recherche d'Histoire des Idées et de la Sensibilité.)   Paris: Presses universitaires de France, 1983.   Pp. 224.   Fr. 220.00.

Delange, Yves.   *Lamarck, sa vie, son oeuvre.*   Arles: Actes Sud, 1984.   Pp. 228.   Fr. 85.00.

Delon, Michel.   "Combats philosophiques, préjugés masculins et fiction romanesque sous le Consulat."   *Raison Présente* 67 (June 1983):   67-76.

Deals with Sylvain Maréchal, Madame Gacon-Dufour, Albertine Clément, Madame Hémery, and Madame de Staël.

Delon, Michel.   "Rousseau et Voltaire à l'épreuve de 1848." *Lendemains* 7 (1982):   52-58.

On the ideology of the reading of Rousseau around 1848 (by Lamartine, Sand, and Saint-Marc Girardin) and on the presence of Voltaire and Rousseau in the evolution of the review *La Liberté de Penser.*

Delormes, Alain.   "Le roman populaire d'aventures sentimentales ou l'esthétique de la lisibilité."   *RSH* 190 (1983):   57-67.

"Des Allemagnes: Aspects of Romanticism in France." SiR 22 (1983).

Contents of this special issue on French Romanticism: Jeffrey Mehlman, "Introduction" (159-61); Maurice Blanchot, "The Athenaeum" (163-72); Andrzij Warminski, "Hölderlin in France" (173-97); Richard Sieburth, "Nerval's Lorely, or the Lure of Origin" (199-239); Cynthia Chase, "Getting Versed: Reading Hegel with Baudelaire" (241-66); James Hulbert, "Diderot in the Text of Hegel: A Question of Intertextuality" (267-91); Rodolphe Gasché, "The Stelliferous Fold: On Villiers de l'Isle-Adam's L'Eve Future" (293-327); Jeffrey Mehlman, "Literature and Hospitality: Klossowski's Hamann" (329-47).

d'Hulst, Lieven. "The Conflict of Translational Models in France (End of 18th-Beginning 19th Century)." Dispositio 7,xix-xx-xxi (1982): 41-52.

Diébolt, Evelyne. "Du roman populaire au roman policier." Le Français dans le Monde 187 (1984): 8-14.

Emphasis is on the period after 1850 (Le Petit Journal, Ponson du Terrail, Gaboriau, X. de Montépin).

Driskel, Michael Paul. "Painting, Piety, and Politics in 1848: Hippolyte Flandrin's Emblem of Equality at Nîmes." AB 66 (1984): 270-84.

According to the résumé, this study is the "social history" of a mural whose iconography is "a unique response to the revolutionary turmoil...." "... the ambiguous image served as a form of symbolic mediation between opposed concepts of the 'Christ humanitaire' and the 'Christ-roi,' and the conflicting ideologies which they represent."

Droulers, Paul. Cattolicesimo sociale nei secoli XIX e XX. Saggi di storia e sociologia. (Politica e Storia, 49.) Rome: Edizioni di Storia e Letteratura, 1982. Pp. xvi+540. L. 30,000.

Rev. by Owen Chadwick in JEH 35 (1984): 157-58.
This collection of Droulers's more important articles contains several dealing with the history of French Catholicism in the Romantic era and, in particular, with the conflicts between liberal and conservative Catholics.

Dufour, Gérard. Juan Antonio Llorente en France (1813-1822). Contribution à l'étude du libéralisme chrétien en France et en Espagne au début du XIXe siècle. Geneva: Droz, 1982. Pp. 375. Sw.Fr. 80.00.

Rev. by G. Cholvy in *RHE* 78 (1983): 549-53.

A Francophile and a liberal Catholic (he had to go into exile when the French were driven out of Spain), Llorente was the author of the *Histoire critique de l'Inquisition d'Espagne* (1817), which made him famous. In France, he was a protégé of the abbé Grégoire, wrote for the *Revue encyclopédique*, got involved in Charbonnerie, and joined the Société de la Morale chrétienne. In 1822, he was expelled from France because of his Charbonnerie activities.

The above review is rather negative, accusing the author of "interprétations fort discutables" and "flagrant délit d'anachronisme," pointing out that the book offers no bibliography, and calling the author a "chercheur consciencieux mais prisonnier des phantasmes de notre époque."

Echelard, Michel. *Histoire de la littérature française. XIXe siècle.* (Profil Formation, 366-367.) Paris: Hatier, 1984. Pp. 188. Fr. 29.20.

Einstein, Alfred. *La Musique romantique.* (Tel, 86.) Paris: Gallimard, 1984. Pp. 450. Fr. 45.00.

Eliel, Carol S. "Louis-Léopold Boilly's "The Galleries of the Palais-Royal.'" *BM* 126 (May 1984): 275-79; 6 illus.

Social background of Boilly's portrayal of prostitutes in his Salon painting of 1804.

Etlin, Richard A. *The Architecture of Death: The Transformation of the Cemetery in Eighteenth-Century Paris.* M.I.T. Press, 1983. Pp. 441. $37.50.

Rev. by Catherine Wilkinson in *NR*, May 28, 1984, pp. 34-36.

Felkay, Nicole. "Le *Musée encyclopédique* du libraire Documents inédits 1825-1845." *RHT* 35 (1983): 442-53; 36 (1984): 78-91.

Covering the years down to mid-1839, these articles are the fruit of a *dépouillement* of documents in the Archives de Paris; these documents rarely have literary implications.

Felkay, Nicole. "Le *Musée encyclopédique* du libraire Bossange." *BduB* 1984-I: 32-39.

On the literary salon *cum cabinet de lecture* established by Martin Bossange in 1824. (The word "encyclopédique" must have made the authorities nervous, for the project was blocked for a time.) There is also information on the Bossange publishing house on the rue de Richelieu (1785-1833; the *Musée* lasted till 1843).

Fortassier, Rose. *Le Roman français au XIXe siècle.* (Que sais-je?, 2040.) Paris: Presses universitaires de France, 1982. Pp. 128. Fr. 20.00.

Rev. by Arlette Michel in *IL* 36 (1984): 50.

Necessarily, a hop, skip, and jump through the history of the nineteenth-century French novel are about all this little manual can offer (less than 2 pages on *Adolphe*, less than 15 on Stendhal, slightly over 20 on Balzac, etc.).

Foucart, Bruno. "Saint François d'Assise et l'art français du XIXe siècle." *RHEF* 70 (1984): 157-66.

The cult of St. Francis was feeble in French art until near the end of the century. Granet was the only artist of some importance in the Romantic period who worked this vein.

Foucart, Jacques, et al. *Hippolyte, Auguste et Paul Flandrin: une fraternité picturale au XIXe siècle.* Paris: Musées nationaux, 1984. Pp. 302. Fr. 120.00.

The catalogue of the show given at the Orangerie du Luxembourg and the Musée des Beaux-Arts in late 1984 and early 1985. See Foucart's brief treatment of the subject in the *Revue du Louvre et des Musées de France* 34 (1984): 412-14. (Cf. the article by Driskel, *supra*.)

Furet, François. "Naissance d'un paradigme: Tocqueville et le voyage en Amérique (1825-1831)." *Annales* 39 (1984): 225-39.

Tocqueville's decision to travel in America is presented in the context of his dissatisfaction with England's aristocratic form of democracy as a model to set against French revolutionary democracy.

Gallet, Michel. *Claude-Nicolas Ledoux (1736-1806).* (Architectures.) Paris: A. et J. Picard, 1980. Pp. 320.

Rev. by Françoise Dierkens-Aubry in *RBPH* 62 (1984): 423-24.

Gayot, Gérard. *La Franc-maçonnerie française.* Paris: Gallimard, 1980. Fr. 43.80.

Rev. by Daniel Roche in *Annales* 39 (1984): 637-39.

Gilmore, Elizabeth. *The Triumph of Art for the Public, 1785-1848. The Emerging Role of Exhibitions and Critics.* (Documentary History of Art, 5.) Princeton University Press, 1984. Pp. 350.

Gossez, Rémi. *Un ouvrier en 1820. Manuscrit inédit de Jacques-Etienne Bédé.* (Centre de Correspondance du XIXe Siècle [Paris IV].) Paris: Presses universitaires de France, 1984. Pp. 408. Fr. 400.00.

Gridley, Roy E. *The Brownings and France: A Chronicle with Commentary.* London: The Athlone Press, 1982. Pp. xiv+321. $38.00.

    Rev. by Pierrette Daly in *FR* 57 (1983-84): 719-20.

Grossir, Claudine. *L'Islam des romantiques, 1811-1840.* (Islam et Occident, 3.) Paris: Maisonneuve et Larose, 1984. Pp. 176. Fr. 78.00.

    This is a somewhat disappointing book, because of the inadequate sample of literary texts examined. Chateaubriand's *Itinéraire* and *Aventures du dernier Abencérage*, Vigny's *Héléna*, Hugo's *Les Orientales*, Balzac's *Une Passion dans le désert*, Mérimée's *La Guzla*, Lamartine's *Voyage en Orient*, and Dumas's *Quinze jours au Sinaï* provide virtually all the quotations. The conclusions extracted from this material are valid as far as they go, it should be said, even if they are somewhat schematic. The salient ones are: (1) Chateaubriand's travel book reveals in him, not only a pilgrim to the Holy Land, but a *fils des croisés*, who, not surprisingly, reveals more of his *moi* than of the Islamic world which he visited; (2) the period of the 1820s produced primarily a superficial exoticism and pro-Greek militancy; (3) Lamartine's book reveals a surprising sympathy for Islam and the Arab world, but his thought is not without internal contradictions (e.g., he seems to foreshadow European colonialism). (J.S.P.)

Grunchec, Philippe. *Le Grand Prix de Rome de peinture. Les concours de 1797 à 1863.* Préface de Jacques Thuillier. Paris: Editions de l'Ecole nationale supérieure des Beaux-Arts, 1984. Pp. 448. Fr. 550.00.

    Rev. by Pierre-Louis Mathieu in *L'OEil* 345 (April 1984): 66.

    See also review article by Bernard Knox, *infra*.

Guccione, Eugenio. "Phillippe Buchez: una biografia intellettuale." *Storia e Politica*, June 1983, pp. 215-89.

Guérin, Denis. "La lecture publique à Paris au XIXe siècle." *Bulletin des Bibliothèques de France* 28 (1983): 143-53.

Guest, Ivor. *Jules Perrot: Master of the Romantic Ballet*. London: Dance Books, 1984. Pp. 380. £20.00.

  Rev. by Julie Hankey in *TLS*, Dec. 21, 1984, p. 1485.

Gury, Jacques. "Une Cancalaise à la découverte de la France au lendemain de la Révolution. Le journal de voyage de Marie-Jeanne Bougourd de Cancale à Mâcon pendant l'été 1802." *Annales de la Société d'Histoire et d'Archéologie de l'Arrondissement de Saint-Malo* (1982), pp. 189-211.

Gusdorf, Georges. *Les Sciences humaines et la pensée occidentale*. T. XI: *L'Homme Romantique* (Bibliothèque scientique.) Paris: Payot, 1984. Pp. 372. Fr. 180.00.

Hadjinicolaou, Nicos. "Art in a Period of Upheaval." *Oxford Art Journal* 6 (1983): 29-37.

  A survey of the criticism of the 1831 Salon as a reflection of society and especially of social change.

Harris, Dale. "Caught in the Act: Dancers Who Defined the Romantic Style Live on Gracefully in Prints." *Connoisseur*, Nov. 1984, pp. 138-43.

  On Taglioni, Cerrito, Elssler, et al.; several charming color illustrations are given.

Hartman, Elwood. *French Romantics on Progress: Human and Aesthetic*. (Studia Humanitatis.) Madrid: José Porrúa Turanzas, S.A., 1983. Pp. xiv-290.

Haskell, Francis. "The Death of Kings." *FMR* 1,v (1984): 116-32.

  An effort to rehabilitate Paul Delaroche and his once tremendously popular history paintings (e.g., *The Princes in the Tower*, *The Execution of Lady Jane Grey*, *The Assassination of the Duc de Guise*). "Delaroche specialized in the misfortunes of virtuous sovereigns and nobles sacrificed to the exigencies of destructive political forces...." Appended are several extracts from Théophile Gautier's criticism of the Delaroche retrospective in 1857.

Héraclès, Philippe. *Les Plus Beaux Poèmes romantiques*. Préface de Gonzague Saint-Bris. (Espaces.) Paris: Le Cherche-Midi, 1984. Pp. 192. Fr. 85.00.

  A selection of lyric poems from Rutebeuf to Guy-René Cadou, arranged in reverse chronological order.

Huard, Raymond, and Claire Torreilles. *Du Protestantisme au socialisme: un quarante-huitard occitan.* Toulouse: Privat, 1982. Pp. 268.

> Rev. by Jean Baubérot in *ASSR* 56,ii (1983): 268-69.
> On P.G. Encontre (1809-53), who began as a Protestant bookseller and polemicist of militant semi-rationalist persuasion but was radicalized by the Revolution of 1848 (he died in deportation in Algeria). A selection of extracts from Encontre's writing is included.

Hytier, Adrienne D. "The Eighteenth Century as Represented in Nineteenth-Century French Theater." Pp. 101-16 in O.M. Brack, Jr., ed., *Studies in Eighteenth-Century Culture,* Vol. 13. University of Wisconsin Press, 1984. Pp. ix+284.

> On the limited and simplistic view of the eighteenth century conveyed by the plays in question, which consistently presented "the elegant, frivolous, corrupt, aristocratic, impertinent, witty rococo side of life."

Iknayan, Marguerite. *The Concave Mirror: From Imitation to Expression in French Esthetic Theory, 1800-1830.* (Stanford French and Italian Studies, 30.) Saratoga, Calif.: ANMA Libri, 1983. Pp. 227. $20.00.

> This book is a welcome addition to the field but something less than a French counterpart to *The Mirror and the Lamp* (but, then, France did not have a Kant or a Coleridge). In any case, it goes beyond the usual dependence on such oft-cited texts as *Racine et Shakspeare* and the preface to *Cromwell.* Nearly every major French Romantic writer active in the period covered is invoked, but it is Quatremère de Quincy, Jouffroy, and Cousin who have pride of place.
> A few quibbles: the structure of the book is unsatisfactory, as the rapid, chronological survey of a large number of documents of very uneven quality leaves the reader a bit bewildered (a thematic arrangement would have been better, given the relative brevity of the period covered); the book's title really ought to feature the *topos* "imagination" as well as those of "imitation" and "expression"; the esthetics of the novel is rather neglected vis-à-vis that of poetry (but the author does well to de-emphasize dramatic theory, since it has been well covered in earlier studies). On the other hand, the attention given to such little-known figures as Ancillon, Kératry, and Magnin is a point in her favor, as is the exploitation of texts by painters and composers (David, Géricault, Girodet, Berlioz). In conclusion: a useful but not a definitive work. (J.S.P.)

Jardin, André. *Alexis de Tocqueville, 1805-1859.* Paris:
Hachette, 1984. Pp. 528. Fr. 150.00.

> Rev. by Bernard Cazes in *QL* 425 (Oct. 1-15, 1984): 22;
> by Pierre Gibert in *Etudes* 361 (Sept. 1984): 274-75; by
> Marcel Jullian in *Le Spectacle du Monde/Réalités* 269 (Aug.
> 1984): 74-77.

Jardin, André, and André-Jean Tudesq. *Restoration and Reaction, 1815-1848.* Trans. Elborg Forster. (The Cambridge
History of Modern France, 1.) Cambridge University Press,
1984. Pp. 431. $69.50.

Jean-Nesmy, Dom Claude. "La littérature et son apport chrétien.
La crise du romantisme et(est) la nôtre." *Esprit et Vie,*
March 17, 1983, pp. 167-75.

> Nerval, Nodier, Balzac, and Hugo are adduced as evidence.

Join-Diéterle, Catherine. "La monarchie, source d'inspiration de l'Opéra à l'époque romantique." *RHT* 35 (1983):
430-41.

> Under the Restoration, medieval monarchs furnished subjects
> (with political over- or undertones), but medieval stage sets
> did not appear until 1822 (*Alfred le Grand*). Under the July
> Monarchy there was the "opéra historico-romantique," be-
> ginning with *Robert le Diable* (1831). In this second phase,
> not royalty but the monarchical régime is celebrated, and
> there is great emphasis on spectacular scenery (thanks to
> Ciceri, Daguerre, et al.).

Jones, Louisa E. *Sad Clowns and Pale Pierrots: Literature
and the Popular Comic Arts in 19th-Century France.* Lexington, Ky.: French Forum Publishers, 1984. Pp. 296. Paper
$17.50.

Jordanova, L.J. *Lamarck.* (Past Masters Series.) Oxford
University Press, 1984. Pp. 750 (approx.). £7.95; paper
£1.95.

> Rev. by J.A. Secord in *TLS*, Jan. 18, 1985, p. 70.
> According to the above review, "Instead of viewing Lamarck
> as a pioneer of evolution, [the author] focuses on the con-
> text of the late Enlightenment.... Rather than making a
> strained case for a neglected precursor, the book recon-
> structs Lamarck's ideas in a form that Lamarck himself would
> have recognised."

Jullien, André and Renée. "Corot dans les montagnes de la
    Sabine." *GBA* 103 (May–June 1984): 179–97; 30 illus.

    Identifications of the places painted by Corot during his
    early visits to Italy, 1826-28.

Kaenel, Philippe. "Autour de J.-J. Grandville: les conditions
    de production socio-professionelles du livre illustré
    'romantique.'" *Romantisme* 43 (1984): 45-61.

    Devoted exclusively to Grandville's *Un Autre Monde*, in-
    terpreting the dialogue of "Crayon" and "Plume"--and espe-
    cially, of course, of the victory of the former over the
    latter--in economic and socio-professional terms: "les
    illustrations non seulement sont conçues pour faire vendre
    le livre ... mais elles visent encore, et surtout, à
    accroître le capital symbolique de leur auteur." Grand-
    ville's strange work, then, is not only a devious way around
    censorship but a protest against the domination of commerce,
    publicity, industry, and mechanization in the field of text-
    and image-production.

Kanceff, Emanuele, and Gaudenzio Boccazzi, eds. *Voyageurs
    étrangers à/Foreign Travellers in/Viaggiatori stranieri
    a/Venezia*. Actes du Congrès de l'Ateneo Veneto, 13-15
    octobre 1979. (Biblioteca del Viaggio in Italia, Studi,
    Bibliothèque du Voyage en Italie, Etudes, 9.) Geneva:
    Slatkine, 1981. Pp. 253.

    Rev. (in part) by Rosa Maria Grigo and Françoise Salnicoff
    in *SFr* 27 (1983): 569.
    For comment on the article in this symposium most relevant
    to this bibliography, see *RMB* for 1982, p. 170.

Kelley, Donald R., and Bonnie G. Smith. "What Was Property?
    Legal Dimensions of the Social Question in France (1789-
    1848)." *PAPS* 128 (1984): 200-30.

Kleinert, Annemarie. *Die frühen Modejournale in Frankreich.
    Studien zur Literatur der Mode von den Anfängen bis 1848*.
    (Studienreihe Romania, 5.) Berlin: Erich Schmidt, 1980.
    Pp. 372.

    Rev. by K. Baldinger in *RF* 99 (1983): 210-12; by H.
    Kröll in *Archiv* 220 (1983): 451-52.

Knapp-Tepperberg, Eva-Maria. *Literatur und Bewusstes*.
    (Freiburger Schriften zur romanischen Philologie, 39.)
    Munich: Wilhelm Fink, 1981. Pp. 178. DM 38.00.

    Rev. by David Bellos in *FS* 38 (1984): 110-11.

Knox, Bernard. "Visions of the Grand Prize." *NYRB*, Sept. 27,
1984, pp. 21-22, 24, 26, 28.

A review article based on two exposition catalogues (*Paris-
Rome-Athens: Travels in Greece by French Architects in the
Nineteenth and Twentieth Centuries* [Houston: Museum of Fine
Arts, 1984] and Philippe Grunchec, *The Grand Prix de Rome:
Paintings from the Ecole des Beaux-Arts 1797-1863* [Washington,
D.C.: International Exhibitions Foundation, 1984]) and the
book by Grunchec listed *supra*.

Krakovitch, Odile. "Les Romantiques et la censure au théâtre."
RHT 36 (1984): 56-68.

A sketch of the history and organization of censorship from
1830 to 1850. Essentially, it represented the attempt of
the triumphant bourgeoisie of the July Monarchy to shield
itself from criticism and to crush "subversive" ideas, e.g.,
the "anarchism" of Frédéric Lemaître's *Robert Macaire*. The
misadventures of Hugo, Dumas, Balzac, Sue, and Vigny are
emphasized. From her search in the Archives nationales, the
author has established, for example, that of 3825 plays sub-
mitted, 123 were forbidden in the period 1835-41. (The author
published a somewhat similar article in *Romantisme* 38 [1982]:
33-43, listed in *RMB* for 1982, pp. 167-68.)

Lacambre, Jean. "Un style international en 1850: à propos
de l'exposition Delaroche." *La Revue du Louvre et des Musées
de France* 34 (1984): 337-40.

The thrust of this article is to emphasize the international
scope of the genre which Delaroche inaugurated in France,
"l'anecdote historique."

La Condamine, Pierre de, ed. *Voyageurs pour Guérande à l'heure
du romantisme. Anthologie*. Guérande: Le Bateau Qui Vire
(diffusion: Breizh), 1984. Pp. 93. Fr. 55.00.

Pleasant, but not very consequential, evocations of the
literary life of this Breton locality in the Romantic era:
local personalities François-Auguste de Frénilly and Edouard
Richer are treated, as are the visits which Balzac (and Laure
de Berny) made there in June of 1830 and Flaubert (and Maxime
Du Camp) in 1847. The regionalistic work of Emile Souvestre,
as it related to Guérande, is briefly discussed. (J.S.P.)

Lamberti, Jean-Claude. *Tocqueville et les deux démocraties*.
Préface de François Bourricaud. (Sociologies.) Paris:
Presses universitaires de France, 1984. Pp. 328. Fr. 180.00.

Rev. by Bernard Cazes in *QL* 425 (Oct. 1-15, 1984): 22;
by Pierre Gibert in *Etudes* 360 (1984): 56.

Laufer, Roger. "L'espace graphique du livre au XIXe siècle."
Romantisme 43 (1984): 63-72.

A discussion, sometimes rather technical, of typographical
developments which emerged in the nineteenth century, e.g.,
the presentation of direct discourse through the use of the
dash, indentation, and quotation marks; contrast between the
title page or cover and the text (the latter in sober didot,
the former often in "caractères de fantaisie" taken from
various type faces); the rise of "typographical values"
(the possibility of exploiting the contrast between italic
and roman, large and small capitals, Arabic and Roman
numerals, the use of red ink for titles, revival of archaic
embellishment, especially in literary texts); the insertion
of vignettes right into the text; etc., etc.

Ledoux, Claude-Nicolas. *L'Architecture considérée sous le
rapport de l'art, des moeurs et de la législation.* 2 vols.
Nördlingen: Alfons Ulh (diffusion: Fischbacher [Paris]),
1981. Fr. 412.00.

Facsimile of the edition of Paris, 1804. (Cf. the book
by Gallet, *supra.*) Another facsimile of the same edition
was published by Georg Olms (in Hildesheim) in 1981 (DM
398.00).

Leflaive, Anne, ed. *Ce Merveilleux Troisième Âge: Madame
Swetchine.* Paris: Téqui, 1984. Pp. 102. Fr. 30.00.

Leigh, R.A. "Rousseau, His Publishers and the *Contrat Social.*"
BJRL 66,ii (1984): 204-27.

Lejeune, Philippe. "'La cote Ln[27].' Pour un répertoire des
autobiographies écrites en France au XIXe siècle." *ELit*
17,ii (1984): 213-37.

Lemaitre, Henri. *Du Romantisme au Symbolisme, 1790-1914.*
(Littérature.) Paris: Bordas, 1982. Pp. 752. Fr. 180.00.

An ambitious manual.

Le Men, Ségolène. "Calligraphies, calligramme, caricature."
Langages 19 (1984): 83-101.

A semiotic study of the political cartoons in *La Caricature*
and *Le Charivari*, with special attention to the famous
calligrams and calligraphs of Louis-Philippe as pear.

Lequin, Yves, ed. *Histoire des Français: XIXᵉ-XXᵉ siècles.*
3 vols. Paris: Armand Colin, 1983-84. Fr. 900.00.

Rev. (of T. II) by Philippe Lécrivain in *Etudes* 360 (1984):
849-50.
T. I: *Un Peuple et son pays*; T. II: *La Société*; T. III:
Les Citoyens et la démocratie. An attractively presented
history of modern France whose approach is somewhere between
that of Theodore Zeldin's famous *France: 1848-1945* and that
of the *Annales* school (in any case, it is not *de l'histoire
événementielle*).

LeQuire, Elise. "Jean Bart: The Fate of a Legendary Hero in
the Nineteenth Century." *NCFS* 12,iv; 13,i (1984): 33-42.

The literary references to the legendary sailor in Balzac
(*Le Lys dans la vallée*), Baudelaire ("Le mauvais vitrier"),
and Zola (*Germinal*) are fleeting or indirect, especially
in the first two, but the author deftly explores their implications, at the same time tracing the legend to its earliest
printed sources in the age of Louis XVI. Her point: "A
legend is not a static symbol...." (J.S.P.)

Lesky, Erna. *Franz Joseph Gall, 1758-1828, Naturforscher
und Anthropologe.* Bern, Stuttgart, and Vienna: H. Huber,
1979. Pp. 217. Sw.Fr. 28.00.

Rev. by Pierre Huard in *Revue d'Histoire des Sciences* 35
(1982): 89-90.
In the above review, Gall's influence on French authors
(among others) is brought out: Balzac, Sand, Baudelaire,
Comte, Flaubert.

Leuilliot, Bernard, ed. *Anthologie de la poésie française
du XIXᵉ siècle, de Chateaubriand à Baudelaire.* (Poésie/
Gallimard.) Paris: Gallimard, 1984. Pp. 504. Fr. 48.00.

A good selection, especially welcome for the poems by
secondary figures. Unfortunately, to make room for these
interesting *minores*, the major figures are somewhat squeezed.
The apparatus contains helpful "notices" on all the poets
represented. (J.S.P.)

Levitine, George. "Le 'Déluge' oublié de Michel-Honoré
Bounieu." *GBA* 103 (Jan. 1984): 44-50; 2 illus.

A lost and forgotten painting (first exhibited, 1783)
which "initiated the long series of catastrophe representations of the late eighteenth and the beginning of the nineteenth centuries."

Luciani, G. "La vie théâtrale à Chambéry sous l'Empire."
   Bulletin du Centre d'Etudes Franco-Italien, 1979, n⁰ 5, pp.
   14-33.

Malinowski, W.M. "La nouvelle historique en France à l'époque
   du romantisme." *Uniwersytet Imienia Adama Mickiewicza w
   Poznaniu. Seria Filogogia Românska* 9 (1983): 1-108.

Martin, Henri-Jean, and Roger Chartier, eds. *Histoire de
   l'édition française.* T. II.: *Le Livre triomphant, 1660-
   1830.* Paris: Promodis, 1984. Pp. 700. Fr. 797.00.

Mazzara, Richard A. "Machado de Assis (1839-1908): Francophile and Francophone." *KRQ* 31 (1984): 97-104.

   The Brazilian writer translated extracts from Lamartine's
   Histoire de la Restauration, and was influenced by various
   French Romantics, notably Chateaubriand, Hugo, and Musset.

McClellan, Andrew L. "The Politics and Aesthetics of Display:
   Museums in Paris 1750-1800." *Art History* 7 (1984): 438-64.

   On the side of aesthetics, the concern with "the process
   of restoration and with conditions of display, especially
   lighting, focussed attention on the surface of works of art
   and on the minutiae of technique."

McKee, George D. "The Publication of Bonaparte's Louvre:
   Illustrated Presentations before 1804." *GBA* 104 (Nov. 1984):
   165-72; 2 illus.

   On the series of prints with commentary illustrating the
   art works in the national collection.

*Mélanges à la mémoire de Franco Simone. France et Italie dans
   la culture européenne.* T. III: *XIXᵉ et XXᵉ siècle.*
   (Bibliothèque Franco-Simone, 8.) Geneva: Slatkine, 1984.
   Pp. 840. Fr. 473.00.

Mélonio, Françoise. "La religion selon Tocqueville: ordre
   moral ou esprit de liberté." *Etudes* 360 (1984): 73-89.

   Making use of the recently published volumes of Tocqueville's
   correspondence (as well as the usual sources), the author
   attacks the widely held view that, for Tocqueville, religion's
   role was a mere social function.

Mélonio, Françoise. "Tocqueville et la restauration du pouvoir
   temporel du pape (juin-octobre 1849)." *RH* 549 (1984): 109-23.

On Tocqueville's paradoxical part in the restoration of the Pope's temporal power, during his term as foreign minister.

Milner, Max. *La Fantasmagorie. Essai sur l'optique fantastique.* Paris: Presses universitaires de France, 1982. Pp. 261. After a brief introductory chapter tracing the development and the popularity of "fantasmagorie," or "l'art de faire apparaître des spectres ou des fantômes par des illusions d'optique" in the words of Bescherelle, the author examines the use of optical devices (mirrors, microscopes, telescopes, and the like) in fantastic literature from the eighteenth to the twentieth centuries. Among Romantic authors, Hoffmann and Gautier receive particular attention. Although parts of the book read like a catalogue, the reader will find in it information both unusual and useful. (E.F.G.)

Miscellanea di studi in onore di Vittore Branca. Vol. IV: *Tra illuminismo e romanticismo.* (Biblioteca dell'Archivum Romanicum, Serie I, Vol. 181.) 2 vols. Florence: Leo S. Olschki, 1983. Pp. xii+900. L. 95,000.00.

Mollier, Jean-Yves. *Michel et Calmann Lévy ou la naissance de l'édition moderne, 1836-1891.* Paris: Calmann-Lévy, 1984. Pp. 560. Fr. 149.00.

Moses, Claire Goldberg. *French Feminism in the Nineteenth Century.* State University of New York Press, 1984. Pp. 311. $39.50; paper $12.95.

Rev. by J.F. McMillan in *TLS*, Feb. 8, 1985, p. 153. The above review, which is moderately negative, nevertheless singles out Moses's treatment of the Utopian (i.e., Saint-Simonian and Fourierist) phase of French feminism.

Muray, Philippe. *Le Dix-neuvième Siècle à travers les âges.* Paris: Denoël, 1984. Pp. 684. Fr. 148.00.

Rev. by Jean Borie in *QL* 416 (May 1-15, 1984): 14-15; by Michel Delon in *Europe* 667-668 (1984): 227-28; by Bertrand Poirot-Delpech in *Le Monde*, May 11, 1984, pp. 29, 31. From the above reviews, it would appear that Muray's book is a right-wing polemic against the socialist, Utopian, progressive movement in French literature from the eve of the Revolution to the end of the nineteenth century.

Naudin, Marie. "La maladie dans le roman féminin du Consulat et du Premier Empire." *NCFS* 12,iv; 13,i (1984): 22-32.

Skillfully summarizes the medical element in the novels of
such writers as Mesdames de Genlis, Cottin, Gay, de Duras,
and, of course, de Staël. It turns out that illness plays
an important role in many plots. The author brings out the
novelistic justification for this, as well as the medical
philosophy implied. (J.S.P.)

Outram, Dorinda. *Georges Cuvier: Vocation, Science and
Authority in Post-Revolutionary France.* Manchester University Press, 1984. Pp. 299. £25.00.

   Rev. by Martin Rudwick in *TLS*, Nov. 2, 1984, p. 1263.

Palanque, Jean-Rémy, ed. *Une Catholique Libérale du XIXe
siècle: la marquise de Forbin d'Oppède d'après sa correspondance inédite.* (Bibliothèque de la Revue d'Histoire
ecclésiastique, 66.) Leuven: Nauwelaerts; Louvain-la-Neuve;
Bureau de la R.H.E., 1981. Pp. ix+469. Bel.Fr. 800.00.

   Rev. by Marvin L. Brown, Jr., in *CHR* 70 (1984):   488-89;
by Pierre Guiral in *RBPH* 62 (1984):   436-37.
   Montalembert figures prominently in the correspondence of
the marquise.

Parent-Lardeur, Françoise. "Lecture populaire? lecture
bourgeoise? les cabinets de lecture sous la Restauration."
Bulletin des Bibliothèques de France 28 (1983): 135-41.

Paulson, Ronald. *Representations of Revolution, 1789-1820.*
Yale University Press, 1983. Pp. xviii+398. $29.95.

   On the visual arts.

Paz, Maurice. *Un Révolutionnaire professionnel, Auguste
Blanqui.* Paris: Fayard, 1984. Pp. 320. Fr. 89.00.

Pelckmans, Paul. "Les derniers songes prémonitoires." *OL* 39
(1984): 324-37.

   Studying dream literature at the end of the eighteenth
and beginning of the nineteenth centuries (Ducis, *Abufar*;
Florian, *Gonsalve de Cordoue*; Balzac, *Annette et le criminel*),
the author seeks to show that the texts "comportent
quelquefois des fêlures qui, pour n'annoncer aucune réflexion vraiment originale sur l'onirisme, reflètent peut-
être ce qu'ils ne cherchent guère à révéler: dans ces
pages très oubliées, l'historien du rêve peut glaner quelques
précieux indices." They suggest "une *anomisation* de l'onirisme" (Pelckmans is thinking of Durkheim).

Perrot, Michelle. "Alexis de Tocqueville e le prigioni,
ovvero: il cattivo odore del liberalismo." *Aut Aut* 195-
196 (1983): 119-32.

Pich, Edgard. "La poésie française en 1850. Structures et
événements." *Lendemains* 28 (1982): 14-22.

"Etude des phénomènes poétiques de masse à la lumière
des renseignements fournis par la rubrique 'poésie' de la
Bibliographie de la France. Place importante de la chanson
et de la poésie populaire."

Poidevin, Raymond, and Jacques Bariéty. *Frankreich und
Deutschland. Die Geschichte ihrer Beziehung, 1815-1975.*
Munich: Beck, 1982. Pp. 498.

Rev. by Willerd R. Fann in *GSR* 7 (1984): 562-63.
German translation of a book originally published in France
as *Les Relations franco-allemandes, 1815-1975* (Paris: Armand
Colin, 1979 [second ed.]).

Poulat, Emile. "Nouveaux christianismes et religion de
l'humanité." *Note su Socialismo e Cristianesimo* 5 (March
1983): 3-20.

Poulat traces the "religion of humanity" primarily to
Pierre Leroux's *De l'humanité, de son principe · et de son
avenir où se trouve exposée la vraie définition de la religion*
(1840). See résumé by Peter Byrne in *SFr* 28 (1984): 168.

Pradier, James. *Correspondance*. T. I.: *1790-1833*; T. II:
1834-1842. Ed. Douglas Siler. Préface de Jacques de Caso.
(Histoire des Idées et Critique littéraire, 221.) Geneva:
Droz, 1984. Fr. 362.40.

The sculptor was a friend of Gautier and Hugo and (before
Hugo) the lover of Juliette Drouet; his wife--one of Flaubert's
models for Emma (?)--was the mistress of Flaubert, Dumas
fils, and Janin.

Przybos, Julia. "La conscience populaire et le mélodrame en
France dans la première moitié du dix-neuvième siècle."
FR 57 (1983-84): 300-08.

A study of the ideological underpinnings of French melodrama in the period 1800-50; they turn out to be "conservative if not reactionary." The genre consistently "exalte
le bonheur d'une société fondée sur l'ordre hiérarchique
familial, religieux et social et rejette les idéaux de

la Révolution...." How can one explain the success of such
a theater with the very people who, theoretically, cherished
these ideals? Przyboś turns to Durkheim for an answer: this
class suffered from the anomie produced by the Revolutionary
upheaval and the resulting social instability, and so clung
to the values of the past. Well done, but has the author
studied an adequate sample (only fourteen individual plays
are mentioned)? (J.S.P.)

Quemada, Bernard, ed. *Trésor de la langue française.* T. IX:
   G-Incarner; T. X: *Incartade-Losangique.* Paris: Editions
   du CNRS (diffusion: Gallimard-Sodis), 1981, 1983. Pp.
   xviii+1338; xxi+1381.

   Rev. by Veikko Väänanen in *NM* 85 (1984):   254.

Rachman, Odette-Adena. *Un Périodique Libéral sous la
   Restauration: Le Mercure du XIXe siècle (avril 1823-mars
   1826).* Suivi du *Répertoire daté et annoté.* Geneva and
   Paris: Slatkine, 1984. Pp. 504. Sw.Fr. 90.00.

Raser, Timothy. "Reference and Allegory in Romantic Description." *RR* 75 (1984): 35-50.

   Includes references to Barthes, Riffaterre, Leroux,
   Sainte-Beuve, and Chateaubriand.

Ravaisson, Félix. *La Philosophie en France au XIXe siècle.*
   Paris: Fayard, 1984. Pp. 256. Fr. 79.00.

   Ravaisson's book, originally published in 1868, emphasized
   Socialistic and Positivistic thought. (Another reprint of
   this work was published in 1983 [Paris: Vrin].)

Ravaisson, Félix. *Testament philosophique et fragments.*
   (Reprise.) Paris: Vrin, 1983. Pp. 162. Fr. 60.00.

   Ravaisson's book was originally published (posthumously,
   obviously) in 1933.

Real, Elena. "Caín: de la révolte au Nihilisme." *Cuadernos
   de Filología de la Universidad de Valencia* 3,iii (1983):
   119-44.

   Cain as a Romantic symbol of rebellion; the vision of a
   flawed creation in such poets as Nerval, Leconte de Lisle,
   Lamartine, Ludovic de Cailleux, and Hugo.

Richter, Noë. *La Lecture et ses institutions.* T. I: *Prélude,
   1700-1830.* Angers (?): Bibliothèque de l'Université du
   Maine, 1984. Pp. 95+xiii. Fr. 65.00

Rieger, Dietmar. *Diogenes als Lumpensammler. Materialen zu einer Gestalt der französichen Literatur des 19. Jahrhunderts.* Munich: W. Fink, 1983. Pp. 140. DM 28.00.

Roche, Daniel. *Le Peuple de Paris: essai sur la culture populaire au XVIIIe siècle.* Paris: Editions Aubier-Montaigne, 1981. Pp. 288.

    Rev. by Robert Darnton in *ECS* 18 (1984): 99-103.

Saisselin, Remy G. *The Bourgeois and the Bibelot.* Rutgers University Press, 1984. Pp. 240. $17.95.

Scaiola, Anna Maria. "La 'belle inconnue': sei occasioni d'una mancanza." Pp. 442-53 in *Scritti in onore di Giovanni Macchia*, Vol. I. Milan: Mondadori, 1982. L. 125,000.00.

Schamber, Ellie Nower. *The Artist as Politician: The Relationship Between the Art and the Politics of the French Romantics.* Lanham, Md.: University Press of America, 1984. Pp. 256. $23.50; paper $12.50.

Schiff, Gert. "The Sculpture of the 'Style Troubadour.'" *Arts Magazine* 58 (June 1984): 102-10.

    After a discussion of the troubadour style in painting, Schiff examines a number of sculptures that can be linked thematically to that genre; most of the examples are French: Jean-Auguste Barre, Jean-Pierre-Victor Huguenin, François-Frédéric, baron Lemot, Jean-François-Théodore Gechter, Félicie de Fauveau, Etex, Marie-Christine d'Orléans, Sébastien Delarue, Barye, Bosio, Rude, and Triqueti.

Schnitzler, Marion. *Die Kapitelüberschrift im französischen Roman des 19. Jahrhunderts. Formen und Funktionen.* (Studia Romanica, 50.) Heidelberg: Carl Winter, 1983. Pp. viii+352. DM 148.00.

Sewell, W.H. *Gens de métier et révolutions, le langage du travail de l'Ancien Régime à 1848.* Paris: Aubier-Montaigne, 1983. Pp. 425. Fr. 145.00.

    Rev. by Peter Byrne in *SFr* 28 (1984): 170.

Shedd, Meredith. "A Neo-Classical Connoisseur and His Collection: J.B. Giroud's Museum of Casts at the Place Vendôme." *GBA* 103 (May-June 1984): 198-206; 3 illus.

    On the contents and the influence of the museum, which opened in the early 1790s.

Sheon, Aaron. "Parisian Social Statistics: Gavarni, *Le Diable
à Paris*, and Early Realism." *Art Journal* 44 (1984): 139-48.

Gavarni's illustrations for *Le Diable à Paris* may well have
been the first images by a major French artist responding
to and reflecting the "grim statistical evidence about the
miserable lives of paupers in Paris." There is material on
the volume's publisher, Hetzel; on Adolphe Quetelet, a
Belgian statistician of Deterministic tendencies; and on
Alfred Legoyt, who did the statistical part of the volume.

Shiff, Richard. "The Original, the Imitation, the Copy, and
the Spontaneous Classic: Theory and Painting in Nineteenth-
Century France." *YFS* 66 (1984): 27-53.

On Quatremère de Quincy, Charles Blanc, Taine, and Zola

Simonin, Michel. "Réflexions sur un catalogue d'amateur."
Romantisme 44 (1984): 19-26.

On Viollet le Duc (the father of the architect) as bibliophile, focusing on his *Catalogue des livres composant la
bibliothèque poétique de M. Viollet-le-Duc* [sic], *avec des
notes bibliographiques, biographiques et littéraires sur
chacun des ouvrages catalogués* (1843-47). "La nouveauté
de la pratique du *catalogue d'amateur* tient à l'association
nécessaire et fondatrice entre l'objet et le texte." It
involves, then, a description of each book as merchandise
and as literature.

Stenzel, Hartmut, and Heinz Thoma. "De 'chants du Sacre'
des Jahres 1825--Uberlegungen zum Funktionswandel der
Lyrik in der Restaurationszeit." *Romanistische Zeitschrift
für Literaturgeschichte/Cahiers d'Histoire des Littératures
Romanes* 8 (1984): 565-90.

Treats Lamartine, Barthélemy, Baour-Lormian, Delphine
Gay, Amable Tastu, and Béranger.

Thomas, Jean-Jacques. "Contre-écriture (1830-1852)." *ECr*
23 (1983): 11-21.

On *engagement* (specifically, identification with *le peuple*)
or the lack of it among writers of the period studied. The
period 1848-1852 saw a permanent split between groups who
had previously made common cause: established writers and
humanitarians.

Thomasseau, Jean-Marie. *Le Mélodrame.* (Que sais-je?, 2151.)
Paris: Presses universitaires de France, 1984. Pp. 128.
Fr. 20.90.

Although, like all the books in this collection, this one
is very brief, it is unusually solid. Discussion of early
uses of the term *mélodrame* and the large variety of
theatrical genres to which it corresponded leads into a
chronological study of a very large number of nineteenth-
century plays, from Pixérécourt's landmark *Coelina* (1800)
on. The melodramas of the first half of the century,
rightly, receive the most attention. Thomasseau, perhaps
a little schematically, divides this period along political
lines, "le mélodrame classique" corresponding roughly to the
Napoleonic years (more precisely, 1800-23) and "le mélodrame
romantique" to the Restoration and July Monarchy. Dramatic
conventions, themes, character types, moral precepts, and
principal authors are neatly dealt with in surprising detail,
including summaries of a number of typical and/or important
plays. The approach is recapitulated for the succeeding
periods. The author insists on the non-literary character
of the melodrama and asks that it be judged accordingly;
the *mélodrame*, then, is essentially visual and "spectacular."
Several other key points emerge from his survey: the "classical" *mélodrame* promulgated a conventional morality and even,
at first, observed the unities; with the "romantic" *mélodrame*
a subversion of conventional morality is suggested (by, for
example, making criminals and brigands sympathetic); in the
1830s and 1840s, Romantic melodrama infused more "serious"
theater (Hugo, Dumas, et al.); in the Romantic period proper,
dramatic structures loosened, plays with multiple *tableaux*
replacing the three-act form; novel and melodrama inter-
penetrated one another, as works by Sue and like authors
appeared in both forms; "socialistic" tendencies began to
appear in the years just before the 1848 revolution, and
certain melodramas may have helped to create the revolutionary
situation. The period after 1848 is treated somewhat more
sketchily, since, despite what the author calls "diversifi-
cation," in most respects it prolonged what preceded. The
volume closes with some general considerations on the *esthétique
mélodramatique* and its survival in later drama, plus a
rather brief bibliography. A good book, then, despite its
brevity. (J.S.P.)

Thornton, Lynne. *The Orientalists. Painter-Travellers, 1828-
1908*. Paris and Courbevoie: ACR Editions internationales,
1983. Pp. 272. $65.00.

Rev. by M.D. Roullet in *GBA* 1388 (Sept. 1984), "La
Chronique des Arts," pp. 27-29.

Tocqueville, Alexis de. "Mémoire sur le paupérisme."
Commentaire 23 (Fall 1983): 630-36; 24 (Winter 1983-84):
880-88.

The editorial presentation is by Jean-Claude Casanova.

Trainar, Pierre. "Présence ou actualité du romantisme,
remerciement, 16-I-83." *Recueil de l'Académie des Jeux
Floraux* (1983), pp. 91-106.

Trousson, Raymond. "Jean-Jacques et les évêques de Mgr
Lamourette à Mgr Dupanloup." *Bulletin de l'Académie Royale
de Langue et de Littérature Françaises* 56 (1983): 278-303.

Under the Restoration, Church leaders, led by the abbé
Frayssinous (see his *Conférences*), sought to check the
publication of Rousseau's works and to counteract his influence. But there was some ambivalence: his religiosity
made him partly *récupérable*. By and large, however, he
was seen as Revolutionary and anti-Catholic.

Tulard, Jean. *Napoleon: The Myth of the Savior.* Trans.
Teresa Waugh. London: Weidenfeld and Nicolson, 1984. Pp.
470. £14.95.

Rev. by Norman Hampson in *TLS*, Oct. 5, 1984, p. 1122.
On the original French edition, see *ELN* 17, Supp., 119.

Vajda, György M., ed. *Le Tournant du Siècle des Lumières
(1760-1820). Les Genres en vers des Lumières au romantisme.*
Budapest: Akadémiai Kiadó (diffusion: Trismégiste), 1982.
Pp. 684. Fr. 828.00.

Rev. by A. Owen Aldridge in *Arcadia* 19 (1984): 183-92.
Vol. 3 of *A Comparative History of Literatures in European
Languages*, a project sponsored by the International Compara-
tive Literature Association. (Vol. 1 was on Expressionism,
Vol. 2 on European Symbolism.)

Van Holthe Tot Echten, C. Sophia. "L'envoi de jeunes artistes
Néerlandais à Paris pendant le règne de Louis Napoléon
Bonaparte, Roi de Hollande (1806-1810)." *GBA* 103 (Feb.
1984): 58-70; 6 illus.

Viollet le Duc, Eugène. *L'Eclectisme raisonné.* Ed. Bruno
Foucart. Paris: Denoël/Gonthier, 1984. Pp. 252. Fr.
88.00.

Voia, Vasile. "N.I. Apostolescu Comparatist." *Studia Universitatis Babeş-Bolyai. Philologia* 28 (1983): 34-40.

Treats the influence of French Romanticism on Rumanian poetry.

Welch, Cheryl B. *Liberty and Utility: The French Idéologues and the Transformation of Liberalism.* Columbia University Press, 1984. Pp. 209. $39.00.

Rev. by William Scott in *TLS*, Aug. 3, 1984, p. 873.

Weston, Helen. "Prud'hon in Rome: Pages from an Unpublished Sketchbook." *BM* 126 (Jan. 1984): 6-19; 29 illus.

On studies from the antique, made during the artist's stay in Rome, 1785-88.

Wick, Peter Arms. *French Illustrated Books of the Romantic School.* Boston: The Boston Athenaeum, 1983. Pp. 42. $5.00.

An exposition catalogue.

Williams, Huntingdon. *Rousseau and Romantic Autobiography.* (Oxford Modern Languages and Literatures.) Oxford University Press, 1983. Pp. 252. £20.00.

Rev. by Malcolm Jack in *ECS* 18 (1984-85): 269-70.

Wolfszettel, Friedrich, ed. *Der französische Sozialroman des 19. Jahrhunderts.* (Wege der Forschung, 364.) Darmstadt: Wissenschaftliche Buchgesellschaft, 1981. Pp. vi+511.

Rev. by Sieglinde Domurath in *Lendemains* 9 (1984): 133-35; by J. Thanner in *NCFS* 12 (1983-84): 215-17.
Contains articles on Balzac, Hugo, Sue, and Sand.

Wright, Beth S. "The Auld Alliance in Nineteenth-Century French Painting: The Changing Concept of Mary Stuart, 1814-1833." *Arts Magazine* 58,vii (1984): 97-107.

See also Brown ("General 2. Environment"); Bryson, Flax ("General 3. Criticism"); Dekker, Shapiro ("English 2. Environment").

Reviews of books previously listed:

AGULHON, Maurice, *The Republic in the Village* (see *ELN* 10, Supp., 71, and *RMB* for 1982, p. 155), rev. by Peter H. Amann in *The Historian* 46 (1983-84): 444-45; BAUDE, Michel, and Marc-Mathieu Münch, eds., *Romantisme et religion* (see *RMB* for 1981, pp. 158-60), rev. by G. Reiner in *EG* 38 (1983):

501; BERTIER DE SAUVIGNY, Guillaume de, *La France et les Français vus par les voyageurs américains (1814-1848)*, T. I. (see *RMB* for 1982, p. 157, and *supra*), rev. by John L. Brown in *CHR* 70 (1984): 486-87; by Georges Dethan in *Revue d'Histoire Diplomatique* 97 (1983): 173-74; by Maurice Ménard in *SFr* 27 (1983): 569-70; BROMBERT, Victor, *La Prison romantique* (see *ELN* 15, Supp., 83-84, and 17, Supp., 112), rev. by Vito Carofiglio in *Lectures* 12 (June 1983): 187-96; CASTEX, Pierre-Georges, *Horizons romantiques* (see *RMB* for 1983, pp. 164-65), rev. by Brian Juden in *FS* 38 (1984): 363-64; CASTRIES, duc de, *Monsieur Thiers* (see *RMB* for 1983, p. 165), rev. by Pierre de Boisdeffre in *RDM*, Feb. 1984, pp. 406-10; by Christian Brosio in *Le Spectacle du Monde/Réalités* 265 (1984): 97-101; by Eric Vatre in *RDM*, Jan. 1984, pp. 117-19; EITNER, Lorenz E., *Géricault: His Life and Work* (see *RMB* for 1983, p. 168), rev. by Norman Bryson in *FS* 38 (1984): 469-70; by Henri Zerner in *NYRB*, Jan. 17, 1985, pp. 36-39; in *Art and Artists* 213 (June 1984): 24-25; GASSIER, Pierre, *Léopold Robert* (see *RMB* for 1983, p. 168), rev. by M. Fremigier in *Le Monde*, July 21, 1983; by J.J.L. Whiteley in *BM* 975 (1984): 364; in *GBA* 1377 (1983): "La Chronique des Arts," pp. 19-20; GRASSION, Jean, and Frans Durit, eds., *The Journal of the Marquis de Bombelles* (see *RMB* for 1979, p. 145), rev. by C. Michaud in *DHS* 15 (1983): 477-78; GUSDORF, Georges, *Les Sciences humaines et la pensée occidentale*, T. IX (see *RMB* for 1982, p. 165), rev. by A. Montandon in *RHL* 84 (1984): 626-28; HELLER, Stephen, *Lettres d'un musicien romantique à Paris* (see *RMB* for 1981, p. 164), rev. by Francis Claudon in *SFr* 27 (1983): 578-79; HOWARTH, W.D., *Sublime and Grotesque* (see *ELN* 14, Supp., 63-64), rev. by Hana Jechová in *RBPH* 61 (1983): 736-37; HUMILIERE, Jean-Michel, *Louis-Blanc (1811-1882)* (see *RMB* for 1982, p. 166), rev. by Peter Byrne in *SFr* 28 (1984): 384; KENNEDY, Emmet, *A "Philosophe" in the Age of Revolution: Destutt de Tracy and the Origins of Ideology* (see *RMB* for 1979, p. 147), rev. by Terence Marshall in *Etudes Philosophiques* (1982): 455-59; LOUGH, John, *The Philosophes and Post-Revolutionary France* (see *RMB* for 1982, p. 169), rev. by Donald Schier in *ECS* 17 (1983-84): 241-43; LUBAC, Henri de, *La Postérité spirituelle de Joachim de Flore*, T. II (see *RMB* for 1982, p. 169), rev. by J.-P. Laurant in *RHR* 201 (1984): 104; MICHEL, Pierre, *Les Barbares, 1798-1848* (see *RMB* for 1981, p. 166), rev. by Peter France in *MLR* 79 (1984): 195-96; PARENT-LARDEUR, Françoise, *Les Cabinets de lecture* (see *RMB* for 1982, p. 173), rev. by Barbara T. Cooper in *NCFS*, 12,iv; 13,i (1984): 231; by Daniel Roche in *Annales* 39 (1984): 178-83; PARENT-LARDEUR, Françoise, *Lire à Paris au temps de Balzac* (see *RMB* for 1983, pp. 172-73), rev. by

Daniel Roche in *Annales* 39 (1984): 178-83; PORTER,
Laurence M., *The Literary Dream in French Romanticism* (see
RMB for 1979, pp. 151-52, 211, and *RMB* for 1980, p. 226),
rev. by P.J. Whyte in *PS* 38 (1984): 362-63; RENONCIAT,
Annie, *Gustave Doré* (see *RMB* for 1983, p. 175), rev. by
Jean Revel in *NRF* 371 (Dec. 1, 1983): 121-23; RICHARD,
Jean-Pierre, *Microlectures* (see *RMB* for 1979, p. 153),
rev. by Livius Ciocârlie in *CREL* 1982-II: 156-58; RINCÉ,
Dominique, ed., *La Poésie romantique* (see *RMB* for 1983,
p. 176), rev. by Arlette Michel in *IL* 36 (1984): 226;
STAMM, Therese Dolan, *Gaverni and the Critics* (see *RMB* for
1981, p. 170), rev. by Neil McWilliam in *Art History* 7
(1984): 119; STANTON, Domna C., *The Aristocrat as Art*
(see *RMB* for 1980, p. 164), rev. by J.M. Cocking in *FS* 38
(1984): 81-82; STAUM, Martin S., *Cabanis* (see *RMB* for
1980, p. 164), rev. by Michel Gourevitch in *Revue
d'Histoire des Sciences* 35 (1982): 367-69; SYDOW, Bronis-
lav-Edouard, ed., *Correspondance de Frédéric Chopin* (see
RMB for 1982, p. 177), rev. by Henri Musielak in *Revue
de Musicologie* 69 (1983): 237-38; TOCQUEVILLE, Alexis de,
*Correspondance avec Adolphe de Circourt et avec Madame
de Circourt* (see *RMB* for 1983, p. 179), rev. by Bernard
Cazes in *QL* 411 (Feb. 16-29, 1984): 24; TROUSSON, Raymond,
Voyages aux pays de nulle part (see *ELN* 16, Supp., 87),
rev. by Jindrich Veselý in *Philologica Pragensia* 27 (1984):
108-10; VIATTE, Auguste, *Histoire comparée des littératures
francophones* (see *RMB* for 1982, p. 180), rev. by Rosemarie
Jones in *FS* 38 (1984): 105-06; WALKER, Alan, *Franz Liszt:
The Virtuoso Years* (see *RMB* for 1983, p. 180), rev. by
Allan Keiler in *MQ* 70 (1984): 374-402; by Alexander Main
in *M&L* 65 (1984): 402-06; WECHSLER, Judith, *A Human Comedy*
(see *RMB* for 1982, pp. 180-81), rev. by Neil McWilliam in
Art History 7 (1984): 115-17.

Composite reviews:

Coleman, Patrick. *ECS* 18 (1984): 96-99.

Reviews Simon Harvey, Marian Hobson, et al., eds., *Reapprai-
sals of Rousseau: Studies in Honour of R.A. Leigh* (Manchester University Press and New York: Barnes & Noble,
1980; pp. viii+312; $27.50), and R.A. Leigh, ed., *Rousseau
After 200 Years: Proceedings of the Cambridge Biennial
Colloquium* (Cambridge University Press, 1982; pp. xv+299;
$59.95).

Merrick, Jeffrey. *ECS* 17 (1984): 333-35.

Discusses John A. Carey, *Judicial Reform in France Before the Revolution of 1789* (Harvard University Press, 1981; pp. xii+162; $22.50), and Bailey Stone, *The Parlement of Paris, 1774-1789* (University of North Carolina Press, 1981; pp. x+227; $19.00).

Sturzer, Felicia. *ECS* 18 (1984): 96-99.

A review of James F. Traer, *Marriage and the Family in Eighteenth-Century France* (Cornell University Press, 1980; pp. 208; $15.00), and Roderick Phillips, *Family Breakdown in Late Eighteenth-Century France: Divorces in Rouen, 1792-1803* (see *RMB* for 1981, p. 168).

Review article:

Knox, Bernard. "Visions of the Grand Prize." *NYRB*, Sept. 27, 1984, pp. 21-28.

On the Prix de Rome artists and their works, based on the study by Philippe Grunchec, *Le Grand Prix de Peinture: les concours des Prix de Rome de 1797 à 1863* (Paris: Ecole nationale supérieure des Beaux-Arts, and National Academy of Design, 1984; pp. 446; paper $55.00), and the catalogues of two recent traveling exhibitions: *Paris-Rome-Athens: Travels in Greece by French Architects in the Nineteenth and Twentieth Centuries* (Houston: Museum of Fine Arts, 1984; pp. 420; paper $45.00), and Philippe Grunchec, *The Grand Prix de Rome: Paintings from the Ecole Beaux-Arts* (Washington, D.C.: International Exhibitions Foundation, 1984; pp. 160; paper $18.00).

2.   Studies of Authors

AGOULT

De Lorenza, Antonio. "Luoghi e memorie francesi a Firenze: Marie d'Agoult." *Firme Nostre* 23,xc (March 1981): 11.

On the Countess's encounter with Florence and Florentines; it produced an essay entitled "Florence et Turin, études d'art et de politique."

Histoire de la révolution de 1848. Paris: Balland, 1985. Pp. 752. Fr. 169.00.

Originally published under her pen name, Daniel Stern.

ARLINCOURT

See Angenot ("French 1. General").

ASSOLANT

Mathé, R. "A. Assolant et le peuple de l'époque 1800."
   Trames ("Français") 3 (1981): 71-85.

AZAÏS

Bassan, Fernande. "Les démêlés de Chateaubriand avec Pierre-
   Hyacinthe Azaïs." *Société Chateaubriand, Bulletin* 27 (1984):
   74-77.

   A blow-by-blow account of the animosity between the two
   writers. (For Azaïs, Chateaubriand incarnated the *ultra*
   position.)

Baude, Michel. "La vie musicale sous la Restauration et la
   Monarchie de Juillet: le témoignage du journal inédit
   d'Azaïs." *Revue Internationale de Musique Française* 10
   (Feb. 1983): 55-86.

Rosso, Corrado. "Il filosofo e la montagna (Una villeggiatura
   di Azaïs)." Pp. 279-92 in *Lo Scrittore e la città. Saggi
   e studi di letteratura francese (miscellanea di studia in
   memoria di Dante Ughetti).* (Centre d'Etudes franco-italien.
   Universités de Turin et de Savoie. Bibliothèque Franco-
   Simone, 10.) Geneva: Slatkine, 1982. Pp. 333. Sw.Fr.
   50.00.

Review of book previously listed:

   BAUDE, Michel, *Pierre-Hyacinthe Azaïs, témoin de son temps*
   (see *RMB* for 1981, p. 175), rev. by A.J.L. Busst in *FS* 38
   (1984): 354-55.

BALLANCHE

Michel, Pierre. "Ballanche et le Sphinx de juillet." *Romantisme* 39 (1983): 166-68.

   One of several notes forming addenda to materials presented
   in a special issue of *Romantisme* devoted to the July Revolution (28-29: *Mille huit cent trente*). Ballanche saw the

Revolution as a crucial moment for the establishment of the
renewed human order which he had long envisioned.

Review of book previously listed:

La Ville des expiations (see *RMB* for 1981, p. 176), rev. by
Frank Paul Bowman in *RHL* 84 (1984):   632-33.

BALZAC

Andreoli, Max.   *Le Système balzacien.   Essai de description
synchronique.*   2 vols.   Paris: Aux Amateurs de Livres,
1984.   Fr. 250.00.

   "Une synthèse de la pensée de Balzac et une analyse de
l'univers du romancier.   Index.   Thèse d'Etat."

Barbéris, Pierre, ed.   *Le Colonel Chabert.   Le Contrat de
mariage.*   (Livre de poche, 5907.)   Paris, 1984.   Fr. 18.80.

Beizer, Janet L.   "Victor Marchand: The Narrator as Story
Seller in Balzac's *El Verdugo.*"   *Novel: A Forum on Fiction*
17 (1983-84);   44-51.

   Diffuse effort, largely successful, to link the two disᐟ
parate parts of the text into some kind of unified whole.
(J.B.H.)

Berthier, Philippe, ed.   *Gobseck.   Une Double Famille.*   (GF.)
Paris: Flammarion, 1984.   Pp. 256.   Fr. 21.00.

Berthier, Philippe, ed.   *La Muse du département.   Un Prince
de la bohème.*   (Folio, 1542.)   Paris: Gallimard, 1984.
Fr. 30.00.

Chambers, Ross.   "Seduction Denied: *Sarrasine* and the Impact
of Art."   Pp. 73-96 in Ross Chambers, *Story and Situation:
Narrative Seduction and the Power of Fiction.*   University
of Minnesota Press, 1984.   Pp. xxii+257. $29.59; paper
$14.95.

   Very interesting analysis of *Sarrasine* and the experiences
of Art, as seduction, a vehicle for desire, and a denial
of this seduction, an idealization of art as fiction capable
of producing meaning and, as such, prefiguring modern
aesthetics.   An earlier version of this study appeared in
French Forum 5 (1980):   220-38.   (J.B.H.)

Clark, Priscilla P.   "The Metamorphoses of Mentor: Fénelon
to Balzac."   *RR* 75 (1984):   200-15.

Argues convincingly that the educational novels of the
Comédie humaine do not satisfy our idea of *Bildungsroman*
because they more nearly approximate the *Erziehungroman*,
the novel of instruction, more associated with the eighteenth century. Balzac reveals his distrust of post-
Revolutionary France in his conception of education, both
as pedagogue-narrator and with the Mentors, the authori-
tative teachers of the *Comédie humaine*. Balzac combats
the disorder of the modern world by imposing the order
of fiction on the disorder of society. Interesting point
made that the Mentors are so bound to their pupils that
they cease to exist once the pupil is gone. (Potentially
interesting comparison with the fate of the geniuses;
see the article by Harari listed below.) (J.B.H.)

Cornille, Jean-Louis. "L'Assignation: analyse d'un pacte
épistolaire (Balzac)." Pp. 25-54 in Jean-Louis Bonnat
and Mireille Bossis, eds., *Ecrire, publier, lire les correspondances (problématique et économie d'un "genre
littéraire")*. Actes du colloque international: "Les
Correspondances." Nantes les 4, 5, 6, 7 octobre 1982.
Université de Nantes, 1982. Pp. 474. Fr. 120.00

Fassié, Pierre. "Interprétations du cryptogramme de la
Physiologie du mariage (Méditation XXV) de Balzac."
RomN 24 (1983-84): 249-53.

Rejecting the idea that the design (cryptogram) at the
beginning of the *Physiologie* has no sense, while not
interpreting it, nonetheless discusses its narrative function in terms of its effect on the reader.

Fischler, Alexander. "The Temporal Scale and the Natural
Background in Balzac's *Eugénie Grandet*." In Will L.
McLendon, ed., *L'Hénaurme siècle*. Heidelberg: Carl
Winter Universitätsverlag, 1984.

Gauthier, Henri. *L'Image de l'homme intérieur chez Balzac*.
Geneva: Droz, 1984. Pp. 352. Fr. 234.00.

Gray, Eugene F. "Balzac's Myth of Rejuvenation." Pp. 73-
83 in Laurel Porter and Laurence M. Porter, eds., *Aging
in Literature*. (Studies in Language and Literature.)
Troy, Mich.: International Book Publishers, 1984.

Interesting article on the theme of longevity, concerned
primarily with *La Peau de chagrin* but with reference to
Le Centenaire and several other works by Balzac. Shows
that Balzac clearly believed that while the human life

span is limited, immortality may be attained in the work
of art.

Harari, Josué. "The Pleasure of Science and the Pains of
Philosophy: Balzac's *Quest for the Absolute.*" *YFS* 67
(1984): 135-63.

Dense, extremely well-written discussion of *La Recherche*
which addresses and (re)solves many problems posed by this
text and others: what is the Absolute sought; why it is
that the Absolute, by definition, cannot be articulated in
social, sexual, and linguistic terms; why, finally, it must
be seen as desire without relation to the other. In more
general terms, why there are only "failed" geniuses in the
Etudes philosophiques. (J.B.H.)

Hubert, Renée Riese. "The Encounter of Balzac and Picasso."
Dalhousie French Studies 5 (1983): 38-54.

On Picasso's illustrations for *Le Chef-d'oeuvre inconnu.*

Jung, Willi. *Theorie und Praxis des Typischen bei Honoré
de Balzac.* Tübingen: Staufenber, 1983. Pp. 196.

Kadish, Doris Y. "Landscape, Ideology and Plot in Balzac's
Les Chouans." *NCFS* 12,i; 13,iv (1984): 43-57.

Important article discussing the narrative function of the
detailed landscape descriptions in *Les Chouans.* Sees the
descriptions as not merely ornamental or deterministic but
important in the production of narrative meaning. The often
confusing landscape descriptions evoke the obscure and
impure nature of the historical times Balzac was analyzing
and help establish the social and political meaning of the
novel. (J.B.H.)

Kashiwagi, Takao. *La Trilogie des célibataires d'Honoré de
Balzac.* Paris: Nizet, 1983. Pp. 245.

Study focusing on *Les Célibataires* (1832), *Pierrette*, and
La Rabouilleuse.

Le Men, Ségolène. "Balzac, Gavarni, Bertrall et *Les Petites
Misères de la vie conjugale.*" *Romantisme* 43 (1984): 29-44.

On the illustrations for this book in its various editions,
as exemplifying the history of Romantic book illustration
in general.

Lerner, Laurence. *The Literary Imagination: Essays on Litera-*
ture and Society. Totowa, N.J.: Barnes and Noble, 1982.
Pp. xi+204. $26.50.

Rev. by Ralph Albanese, Jr., in *Philosophy and Literature*
8 (1984): 135-36.

Manalan, Jo Ella. "Interior/Exterior Movement·in *La Comédie*
humaine." *Paroles Gelées* (UCLA) 1 (1983): 31-44.

Sketchy but suggestive study of the correlation between
exterior movement and a character's social, emotional,
and psychological situation. Establishes three categories:
inert, motion indecisive, and purposeful movement, and applies
idea to *Le Père Goriot* and *Illusions perdues*. (Mme Vauquer =
inert; Rastignac = indecisive but moving toward purposeful;
Mme de Beauséant = purposeful but falling out of role.)
(J.B.H.)

Miller, D.A. "Balzac's Illusions Lost and Found." *YFS* 67
(1984): 164-81.

Very good article dealing with the Vautrin cycle and
narrative closure, finding not a "problem" of closure but
a promise of further narration, a textual necessity in novels
predicated on the processes of circulation, exchange, money.
(J.B.H.)

Paulson, William. "Perceptors, Fathers, and Ideology: The
Strange Narrative of Balzac's *Le Médecin de campagne.*"
French Forum 9 (1984): 19-32.

Studies the interaction of the symbolic and ideological
strands of the novel, finding coherence not in the political
treatise but in the personal narratives of Benassis and of
Genestas and his boy. Some perceptive remarks on La Fosseuse.
Discusses, rather convincingly, the emergence of Balzac's
critical realism. (J.B.H.)

Preston, Ethel. *Recherches sur la technique de Balzac. Le*
Retour systématique des personnages dans la Comédie humaine.
Préface de Marcel Bouteron. Geneva: Slatkine, 1984. Pp.
304. Fr. 301.00.

Reprint of Paris, 1926, edition.

Rayfield, Donald. "Dostoyevsky's *Eugénie Grandet.*" *FMLS*
20 (1984): 133-41.

Article concerning Dostoyevsky's translation of the novel,
focusing primarily on his transformation of certain elements

of the text, but of interest nonetheless for Balzac *amateurs*.
(J.B.H.)

Schehr, Lawrence R. "The Unknown Subject: About Balzac's
Le Chef-d'oeuvre inconnu." *NCFS* 12,iv; 13,i (1984):   58-69.

   To be read by those interested in newer critical terminology applied to a Balzac text.

Schuerewegen, Franc. "Le docteur est un bon lecteur: à propos
d'*Autre étude de femme.*" *RBPH* 61 (1983):   563-70.

   Valuable article on *Autre étude*, stressing its "lisibilité,"
depending on the active participation of the reader. Could
profitably be read in conjunction with Lucienne Frappier-
Mazur's study in *MLN* 98 (1983):   712-27, and that of Peter
Lock, *MLN* 97 (1982):   872-89. (See *RMB* for 1983, p. 186,
and *RMB* for 1982, p. 189.) (J.B.H.)

Schuerewegen, Franc. "Pour effleurer le sexe. A propos
d'*Honorine* de Balzac.*" *SN* 55 (1983):   193-97.

Welsh, Alexander. "King Lear, Père Goriot, and Nell's Grand-
father." Pp. 1405-25 in Joseph P. Strelka, ed., *Literary
Theory and Criticism. Festschrift. Presented to René
Wellek in Honor of His Eightieth Birthday.* 2 vols. Bern,
Frankfurt on the Main, and New York: Peter Lang, 1984.
Pp. 1462. $80.00.

Zweig, Stefan. *Balzac.* Paris: Albin Michel, 1984.   Pp. 4-6.
Fr. 120.00.

   Reprint of his earlier study.

See also Amossy and Rosen, Bailbé, Bolster, Coquillat, Grossir,
   Jean-Nesmy, Krakovitch, La Condamine, LeQuire, Lesky, Pelckmans, Wolfszettel ("French 1. General"); Paradissis ("Spanish
   2. General"); Sayre and Löwy ("German 2. General"); Bech,
   Heinrich-Heine-Institut, Düsseldorf, ed. ("German 3. Heine").

Reviews of books previously listed:

ADAMSON, Donald, *Balzac* (see *RMB* for 1982, p. 187), rev. by
   P. Byrne in *SFr* 27 (1983):   372; by A. Finch in *FS* 38 (1984):
   73-74; BUTLER, Ronnie, *Balzac and the French Revolution* (see
   RMB for 1983, p. 185), rev. by D. Bellos in *MLR* 79 (1984):
   944-45; by W. Doyle in *HT* 24 (1984):   51-52; JAMESON, Frederic,
   Political Unconscious (see *RMB* for 1981, p. 179), rev. by
   R. Scholes in *Novel* 17 (1983-84):   266-78; LE HUENEN, Roland,
   and Paul Perron, *Balzac: Sémiotique* (see *RMB* for 1980, p.

173), rev. by D. Bellos in *FS* 38 (1984): 351-53; McCARTHY,
Mary Susan, *Balzac and His Reader* (see *RMB* for 1982, p. 189),
rev. by P. Byrne in *SFr* 28 (1984): 178; by W. Paulson in
French Forum 9 (1984): 122-24; MILEHAM, James W., *The Conspiracy Novel* (see *RMB* for 1983, p. 187), rev. by A. Finch
in *MLR* 79 (1984): 462-63; MOZET, Nicole, *La Ville de Province* (see *RMB* for 1982, p. 189), rev. by P. Berthier in
SFr 27 (1983): 576; by O. Heathcote in *NCFS* 12,iv; 13,i
(1984): 182-83; ROSSUM-GUYON, Françoise van, et al., *Balzac
et les parents pauvres* (see *RMB* for 1981, p. 180), rev. by
M. Tilby in *FS* 38 (1984): 211; STOWE, William, *Balzac,
James and the Realistic Novel* (see *RMB* for 1983, p. 188),
rev. by S. Daugherty in *AL* 55 (1983): 655-56; by M. Fried-
man in *Novel* 18 (1984-85): 92-94; TROUSSON, Raymond,
Balzac disciple (see *RMB* for 1983, p. 188), rev. by G.
Jacques in *LR* 38 (1984): 257-59; by G. Woolen in *MLR* 80
(1985): 171-72.

BARBEY D'AUREVILLY, J.-A.

Aynesworth, Donald. "The Telling of Time in *L'Ensorcelée*."
MLN 98 (1983): 639-56.

Bernheimer, Charles. "Female Sexuality and Narrative Closure:
Barbey's *La Vengeance d'une femme* and *A un dîner d'athées*.
RR 74 (1983): 330-41.

Berthier, Philippe. "Barbey d'Aurevilly et les malentendus du
réalisme." *LR* 37 (1983): 287-305.

Correspondance générale, III (1851-1853). (Annales littéraires
de l'Université de Besançon, 279.) Paris: Les Belles
Lettres, 1983. Pp. 313.

   Rev. by Jacques Landrin in *IL* 36 (1984): 231.

Moger, Angela S. "Gödel's Incompleteness Theorem and Barbey
d'Aurevilly: Raising Story to a Higher Power [Le dessous
de cartes d'une partie de whiste]." *Sub-Stance* 41 (1983):
17-30.

Oberlé, Gérard. "Communication au sujet d'un livre de Barbey
d'Aurevilly." *BduB* 1984-IV: pp. 559-60.

   Cites a letter of Barbey to Poulet Malassis that mentions
the printing of his *Du dandysme et de G. Brummel* (Caen:
Mancel, 1845) as limited to 250 copies. So the edition was
not so rare as suggested by Carteret and Clouzot and as
limited categorically by Vicaire at 30 copies.

Scott, M. "Sexual Ambivalence and Barbey d'Aurevilly's
  Le Chevalier des Touches." *FMLS* 19 (1983): 31–42.

BAUDELAIRE

Fried, Michael. "Painting Memories: On the Containment of
  the Past in Baudelaire and Manet." *CritI* 10 (1984): 510–
  42; 9 illus.

  The *Salon of 1846* and Baudelaire's claim for memory as "the
  great criterion of art" provide an approach to the problem
  of Manet's use of sources from museum art.

See also de Man, Reed, Thurley ("General 3. Criticism");
  Vlasopolos ("English 4. Coleridge"); Chase ("German 3. Hegel").

BÉRANGER

OEuvres complètes. T. I–II. (Les Introuvables.) Plan-de-
  la-Tour: Editions d'Aujourd'hui, 1982. Fr. 290.00.

  Reproduces the Perrotin edition (1847).

Quintus, Vera. *Karikatur als Wirkungsmittel im oppositionellen
  Chanson Bérangers.* (Trier Studien zur Literatur, 9.)
  Frankfurt am Main, Bern, and New York: Peter Lang, 1983.
  Pp. 238.

See also Stenzel and Thomas ("French 1. General").

BERLIOZ

Bailbé, Joseph-Marc. "Berlioz critique: à la recherche d'un
  art de vivre. Thème et variations sur le mot *cauchemar*
  (1842)." Pp. 9–34 in *La Critique artistique: un genre
  littéraire.* Préface par Jean Gaulmier. (Publications de
  l'Université de Rouen. Centre d'Art, Esthétique et Littérature, 94.) Paris: Presses universitaires de France, 1983.
  Pp. 284. Fr. 160.00.

Banks, Paul. "Coherence and Diversity in the *Symphonie
  Fantastique.*" *NCM* 8 (1984–85): 37–43.

  A study of Berlioz's revisions seeking to show that he
  achieved "a subtle interplay" of these two qualities.

Citron, Pierre, et al., eds. *Correspondance générale.* T. 4: *1851-1855.* Paris: Flammarion, 1983. Pp. 791. Fr. 240.00.

Rev. by John Warrack in *TLS*, March 16, 1984, p. 281.

Holoman, D. Kern. "The Berlioz Sketchbook Recovered." *NCM* 7 (1983-84): 282-317.

A description and analysis of the pocket-sized musical sketchbook which Berlioz kept from 1832 to 1836. A facsimile is include (the original is in the Musée Berlioz in La Côte-Saint-André).

Rushton, Julian. *The Musical Language of Berlioz.* Cambridge University Press, 1984. Pp. 303. £25.00.

Rev. by Hugh Macdonald in *TLS*, Feb. 24, 1984, p. 187; by Charles Rosen in *NYRB*, April 26, 1984, pp. 40-43. A strictly musical analysis.

Stearns, David Patrick, and Elizabeth Csicsery-Rónay. "Elusive Genius." *Opera News*, Feb. 18, 1984, pp. 18-20.

On the multifariousness of Berlioz's genius and of critical evaluations, obstacles eventually overcome, as evidenced by his ultimate success and influence.

Stone, Peter Eliot. "Inflamed by Love." *Opera News*, Feb. 18, 1984, pp. 12-14, 16-17.

In *Les Troyens*, Classicism and Romanticism, on the literary level (Virgil and Shakespeare) as well as on the musical level (Gluck and Weber), are fused. Stone follows Ernest Newman in discerning in the opera "a third, conversational style ... neither classic nor romantic but intimate and delicate, not restricted to set forms."

Reviews of books previously listed:

MACDONALD, Hugh, *Berlioz* (see *RMB* for 1983, p. 191), rev. by Pierre Citron in *Revue de Musicologie* 69 (1983): 127-30; RABY, Peter, *Fair Ophelia: A Life of Harriet Smithson Berlioz* (see *RMB* for 1982, p. 192), rev. by Elaine Brody in *NCFS* 12,iv; 13,i)1984): 210-12; by Cosette Thompson in *NCM* 8 (1984-85): 69-71.

Review article:

Rosen, Charles. "Battle over Berlioz." *NYRB*, April 26, 1984, pp. 40-43.

The book under review is Julian Rushton, *The Musical Language of Berlioz* (Cambridge University Press, 1984: pp. 303; $49.50).

BERTRAND, ALOYSIUS

Dhouailly, Jeanne. "Commentaire composé d'un poème en prose d'Aloysius Bertrand." *IL* 36 (1984): 165-68.

On "Le Maçon," Bertrand's favorite of his poems in prose, in which Dhouailly sees the figure of the mason as an allegory of the poet as architect and musician, erecting *dans l'azur* "his cathedral of words."

Review of book previously listed:

MILNER, Max, ed., *Gaspard de la Nuit* (see *RMB* for 1980, p. 179), rev. by Kathryn Slott in *NCFS* 12 (1983-84): 231-32.

BONALD

Chevallier, Jean-Jacques. "Louis-Ambroise de Bonald: un bloc de pensée contre-révolutionnaire." Pp. 587-95 in Claude Emeri and Jean-Louis Seurin, eds., *Religion, société et politique, mélanges offerts en hommage à Jacques Ellul.* Paris: Presses universitaires de France, 1983. Pp. xiv+866. Fr. 600.00.

Klinck, David M. "An Examination of the *notes de lecture* of Louis de Bonald: At the Origins of the Ideology of the Radical Right in France." *SVEC* 216 (1983): 18-19.

Bonald is shown to be, not a defender of feudalism (as usually supposed) but, rather, of "a relatively primitive rural, agrarian capitalism" at odds with "the centralised, rationalised, bureaucratic state," "large-scale capitalism," and "the essentially urban aristocratic-*haut bourgeois* élite" associated with the latter.

OEuvres. 15 vols. Geneva: Slatkine Reprints, 1982. Sw.Fr. 1350.00.

Reprint of the edition of Paris, 1814-43.

BONSTETTEN

Cahiers staëliens 33-34 (1983): "Actualité de Bonstetten.
Actes de la sixième Journée de Coppet (4 septembre 1982)
commémorant le cent-cinquanténaire de la mort de Charles-
Victor de Bonstetten (1745-1832)."

Contents: Jean-Daniel Candaux, "Introduction" (1-2);
François de Capitani, "L'éducation du patricien et Charles-
Victor de Bonstetten" (3-17); Raymond Chevallier, "Le
'Voyage sur la scène des six derniers livres de *l'Enéide*'
ou 'Voyage dans le Latium' (Genève, an XIII) à la lumière
des découvertes archéologiques récentes" (18-39); Norman
King, "Bonstetten correspondant de Madame de Staël" (40-47);
Jean Gaulmier, "Bonstetten intercesseur du romantisme de
l'imaginaire" (48-62); Lionello Sozzi, "Les illusions selon
Bonstetten" (63-83); Leo Neppi Modona, "Une polémique d'autre-
fois: Melchiorre Gioia contre Charles-Victor de Bonstetten"
(84-102).

BOREL

Scaiola, Anna-Maria. "La 'Belle inconnue': sei occasioni
d'una mancanza." Pp. 442-53 in *Discorsi e finzioni. Scritti
di litteraturologia in campo francese.* (Biblioteca di
Filologia Romanza della Facoltà di Lettere e Filosofia dell'
Università di Bologna, 2.) Bologna: Pàtron, 1982. Pp. 143.

Tondeur, Claire-Lise. "Pétrus Borel: l'univers carcéral de
Madame Putiphar. NCSF 12,iv; 13,i (1984): 70-80.

Borel's novel differs from the traditional Romantic novel
of imprisonment in which "la vie est régénérée par la
claustration." In *Madame Putiphar* there is no rite of passage
for the prisoner. For Borel the changing political regimes
after 1789 spared neither victims, executioners, nor avengers.
"Tous sont broyés inexorablement.... Chez Borel personne
n'échappe à l'engrenage destructeur."

CHARRIÈRE

Courtney, Cecil P. *Isabelle de Charrière (Belle de Zuylen):
A Secondary Bibliography.* Oxford: The Voltaire Foundation,
1982. Pp. 50. (Unpriced.)

Rev. by J. Vercruysse in *RHL* 84 (1984): 806-07.

Courtney, Cecil P. "*The Portrait of Zélide*: Geoffrey Scott
and Belle de Zuylen." *SVEC* 219 (1983): 281–88.

On the author (1884–1929) of the 1925 biography which
revealed Madame de Charrière to the English-speaking world
and on the genesis of the book.

Didier, Béatrice. "La nourriture dans les romans d'Isabelle
de Charrière." *DHS* 15 (1983): 187–97.

A mildly semiotic study aimed at revealing the link
between food and femininity, e.g., in the breast-feeding of
children. In her conclusion, the author is very modest as
to what she has actually revealed.

See also Wood ("Constant").

Reviews of book previously listed:

DEGUISE, Alix, *Trois femmes* (see *RMB* for 1981, p. 185), rev.
by Konrad Bieber in *CLS* 21 (1984): 237–38; by Elena Di
Pietro in *RLMC* 36 (1983): 279–82; by Dennis Wood in *FS* 38
(1984): 344–45.

CHATEAUBRIAND

Bassan, Fernande, ed. "*Moïse.*" *Tragédie en cinq actes en
vers.* Reproduction du texte de 1831. (Bibliothèque introuvable.) Paris: Minard (Lettres Modernes), 1983. Pp.
lxii+113–25.

Brocard, Dr. Raymond. "Henri V, avocat et poète langrois,
1827–1900. De Chateaubriand à Lacordaire et au Prince
impérial." *Bulletin de la Société Historique et Archéologique
de Langres,* 4e trimestre, 1983, pp. 162–69.

Buron, Pierre-Emile. "Le Donjuanisme de Chateaubriand."
*Annales de la Société d'Histoire et d'Archéologie de l'Arr^t
de St-Malo,* 1982 [1983], pp. 281–92.

Corciulo, M.S. "La polemica politica fra Chateaubriand e
Constant dopo lo scioglimento della 'Chambre introuvable'
(settembre-dicembre 1816)." *Critica Storica* 18 (1981):
74–88.

Rev. by Carlo Cordié in *SFr* 27 (1983): 159–60.

Crépin, A. "Chateaubriand et le Haut Moyen Age." *Licorne* 6
(1982): 255-63.

Cresci Marrone, Giovannella. "Chateaubriand epigrafista (in
margine alla dedica della cosiddetta di Pompeo)." *SFr* 27
(1983): 82-87.

Delhez-Sarlet, C. "Chateaubriand: scissions et rassemblement
du moi dans l'histoire." *Revue de l'Institut de Sociologie*
(Bruxelles), 1982--I-II: pp. 193-208.

Dubé, Pierre H. "Chateaubriand et Girodet." *RUO* 54 (1984):
85-94.

Gans, Eric. "*René* and the Romantic Model of Self-Centraliza-
tion." *SiR* 22 (1983): 421-35.

In the two novelettes, *Atala* and *René*, Chateaubriand
achieved the Romantic fusion of art and religion, ethics
and aesthetics.

Joseph, John. "I-tinerary: The Romantic Travel Journal after
Chateaubriand." *South Central Review* 1 (1984): 38-51.

Compares Washington Irving's "seeing a ruined Moorish
castle in an overgrown rock" in what is now Oklahoma with
Chateaubriand's ego-projections in the travel descriptions
in *Atala* and Stendhal's in his *Promenades dans Rome*--and
contrasts these Romantic accounts (I-tineraries or ego-
journeys) with the current travel material in the *National
Geographic* and Fodor's travel-guides.

King, Everard H. "Beattie's *The Minstrel* and the French
Connection." *SLJ* 11,2 (1984): 36-55.

A significant demonstration of Beattie's influence on
Chateaubriand's *Atala* and *René*. (T.L.A.)

Lauro, Carlo. "Chateaubriand o i Piombi svelati." *Lectures*
12 (1983): 139-50.

Martin, P. "Chateaubriand lecteur de Saint-Simon, ou la
cristallisation romanesque." *Cahiers Saint-Simon* (Paris)
10 (1982): 43-60.

Mémoires d'outre-tombe. Préface de J. Gracq. Paris: Flammarion,
1982. Pp. 233.

Rev. by Maria Rosaria Ansalone in *SFr* 27 (1983): 364.

Peltier, Michel. "Chateaubriand le polémiste." *Ecrits de Paris*, Dec. 1983, pp. 68-74.

Philippe, Paul. "La parenté malouine et lorientaise de la V^tesse de Chateaubriand." *Annales de la Société d'Histoire et d'Archéologie de l'Arr^t de Saint-Malo*, 1982, pp. 169-83.

Riberette, Pierre, ed. *Correspondance générale, t. IV: 1er janvier 1821-30 mars 1822.* (Collection Blanche.) Paris: Gallimard, 1983. Pp. 430. Fr. 210.00.

Rev. by Gilbert Comte in *Le Monde*, March 2, 1984, pp. 15, 20; by Raymond Lebègue in *RHL* 84 (1984): 973-74; by Fernand Letessier in *BAGB*, Oct. 1984, pp. 326-27; by George D. Painter in *TLS*, March 30, 1984, p. 324.

Société Chateaubriand. *Bulletin* 26 (1983).

Rev. by Arlette Michel in *IL* 36 (1984): 170.
Includes (along with the usual letters of Chateaubriand, review of autographs, notes, bibliography, etc.) the following entries (among others): Jean Marmier, "Un Malouin aux grands lacs en l'été 1791" (8-10); Lila Maurice-Amour, "Lettre inédite de Chateaubriand au chanteur Duprez, 1838" (11-17); Michel Lelièvre, "Chateaubriand, écrivain de combat" (20-24); Pierre Riberette, "Une erreur dans les *Mémoires d'outre-tombe*" (29-31); four papers from the Symposium Chateaubriand et l'Allemagne at Waldmünchen, 10 July 1983 (Leo Pullmann, "L'épisode de Waldmünchen dans les *Mémoires d'outre-tombe*" [40-45]; G. de Bertier De Sauvigny, "L'Allemagne dans la pensée politique de Chateaubriand" [46-50]; Michel Lelièvre, "Chateaubriand historien et polémiste en face de l'Allemagne" [51-57]; Pierre Riberette, "Une inspiratrice allemande de Chateaubriand: la duchesse de Cumberland" [59-66]); and among the "Notes et documents": Raymond Lebègue, "Questions de méthode (69-70); Harry Redman, Jr., "Jean Richepin, par la voix d'un Hollandais lettré, rend hommage à Chateaubriand (page retrouvée)" (71-72).

Tabart, Claude-André. *De René aux Mémoires d'outre-tombe, Chateaubriand.* (Profil d'une OEuvre.) Paris: Hatier, 1984. Pp. 80. Fr. 14.00.

Vita di Rancé. Pref. di R. Barthes. Trad. di G. Aventi, a cura di P. Ligorio. Milan: Bompiani, 1982. Pp. 214.

Rev. by Maria Rosaria Ansalone in *SFr* 27 (1983): 571-72.

See also Meregalli ("General 3. Criticism"); Cross ("English 1. Bibliography"); Amossy and Rosen, André, Coquillat, Grossir, Mazzara, Raser ("French 1. General"); Arboleda ("Spanish 3. Bécquer").

Reviews of books previously listed:

CLARAC, Pierre, ed., *Vie de Rancé* (see *ELN* 17, Supp., 129), rev. by Jacques-Louis Douchin in *Romantisme* 43 (1984): 115; ORMESSON, Jean d', *Mon dernier rêve sera pour vous* (see *RMB* for 1982, p. 195), rev. by Fernande Bassan in *NCFS* 12 (1983-84): 254-55; RIBERETTE, Pierre, ed., *Correspondance générale, III (1815-1820)* (see *RMB* for 1982, p. 195), rev. by Carlo Cordié in *SFr* 27 (1983): 159; by Charles A. Porter in *FR* 57 (1983-84): 879-80; *SOCIÉTÉ CHATEAUBRIAND. BULLETIN 25 (1982)* (see *RMB* for 1983, p. 196), rev. by Arlette Michel in *IL* 35 (1983): 228.

CHÊNEDOLLÉ

Nola, Jean-Paul de. *Chênedollé à la croisée des chemins et d'autres pages de littérature française.* Paris: A.-G. Nizet, 1983. Pp. 178. Fr. 75.00.

Five rather brief chapters, constituting less than half the book, form a very old-fashioned *vie et oeuvres* (one chapter for the life, four for the work) of this rather neglected figure. The poet's link with Romanticism is summarized thus: "il annonça le romantisme non par des audaces formelles, mais par son ton élégiaque, sa religiosité, son amour de la montagne helvétique et de la campagne normande, sa perméabilité aux littératures étrangères."

The "other pages on French literature" include "Treize lettres inédites de Julie Chenay à Tommaso Cannizzaro" (95-134) (Julie Chenay, née Foucher, was Victor Hugo's sister-in-law; Cannizzaro [1838-1921] visited the Hugo colony on Guernesey in 1863 and even asked for Adèle's hand in marriage; despite the rejection of his suit, he remained an admirer and literary disciple of Hugo) and reviews of the following books relevant to this bibliography: Robert Sabatier, *La Poésie du dix-neuvième siècle*, T. I: *Les Romantismes*; T. II: *Naissance de la poésie moderne* (Paris: Albin Michel, 1977); and Jacques Roos, *Etudes de littérature générale et comparée* (Paris: Ophrys, 1979 [three studies of Victor Hugo]). (J.S.P.)

COLET

Review of book previously listed:

BELLET, Roger, ed., *Femmes de lettres au XIXe siècle: autour de Louise Colet* (see *RMB* for 1982, p. 1974), rev. by Gianni Mombello in *SFr* 28 (1984): 387-88.

COMTE

Dezeuze, Guilhem. "Auguste Comte, le législateur rationnel." *Le Discours Psychanalytique*, Dec. 1983, pp. 20-24.

Trousson, Raymond. "Auguste Comte et les 'philosophes' de l'âge métaphysique." Pp. 23-41 in Roland Mortier and Hervé Hasquin, eds., *Etudes sur le XVIIIe siècle*, T. X. Brussels: Editions de l'Université de Bruxelles, 1983. Pp. 188. Bel.Fr. 485.00.

Vernon, Richard. "Auguste Comte and the Withering Away of the State." *JHI* 45 (1984): 549-66.

On Comte's decentralizing tendencies as revealed in the *Système de politique positive*. The paradox: "He was an authoritarian, a rationalist, a believer in hierarchy: his essential themes are those against which decentralizers have rebelled." Vernon claims that it was the evolution of his views on religion and woman which led him, in late life, toward an idealism reminiscent of Augustine.

See also Lesky ("French 1. General").

Review of book previously listed:

BERRÊDO CARNEIRO, Paulo E. de, and Paul Arbrousse-Bastide, eds., *Correspondance générale et confessions*, T. V (see *RMB* for 1982, p. 197), rev. by Annie Petitin in *Revue de Synthèse* 109 (Jan.-March 1983): 75-77.

CONSTANT

Barbier, Maurice. "Religion et politique chez Benjamin Constant." *Revue Française de Science Politique* 33 (1983): 14-40.

Delbouille, Paul. "Le texte d'*Adolphe*: notes supplémentaires." *FS* 38 (1984): 30-31.

In response to C.P. Courtney's article in *French Studies* on the text of *Adolphe* (see *RMB* for 1983, p. 198), the author summarizes the reasons which led him to prefer the text of third edition for his critical edition, rather than the text of the first edition, which Professor Courtney prefers.

Dentan, Michel. "Lire *Cécile.*" Pp. 13-32 in Michel Dentan, ed., *Le Texte et son lecteur: études sur Benjamin Constant, Villiers de l'Isle-Adam, Ramuz, Cendrars, Bernanos, Gracq.* (L'Aire critique.) Lausanne: Editions de l'Aire, 1983. Pp. 129. Fr. 95.00.

Fink, Beatrice. "Un inédit de Benjamin Constant." *DHS* 14 (1982): 199-218.

The text of part of *Du moment actuel et de la destinée de l'espèce humaine, ou histoire abrégée de l'égalité,* as well as a sketch of the projected work.

Furet, François. "Une polémique thermidorienne sur la Terreur. Autour de Benjamin Constant." *Passé Présent* 2 (1983): 44-55.

Holmes, Stephen. *Benjamin Constant and the Making of Modern Liberalism.* Yale University Press, 1984. Pp. 337. $27.50.

By placing great stress on the historical context surrounding Constant's writings, the author attempts to disentangle what he considers to be Constant's underlying arguments from his practical concessions of the moment. The discussion ranges from Constant's rejection of the ancient *res publica* as a foundation for the modern liberal state, to his attitude toward deceit and masks in public life, to his anti-Romantic concept of the state, to his ideas on progress and tyranny. A thoroughly reasonable and enlightening book. (E.F.G.)

Kloocke, Kurt. *Benjamin Constant: une biographie intellectuelle.* (Histoire des Idées et Critique littéraire, 218.) Geneva: Droz, 1984. Pp. xii+384. Sw.Fr. 80.00.

Rev. by D. Wood in *FS* 38 (1984): 468-69.

Lambert, Henri. "Le père de Benjamin Constant et les agents de la poste aux lettres à Dole." *Bulletin de la Société Littéraire des P.T.T.* 148 (1982): 20-25.

Lamberti, Jean-Claude. "De Benjamin Constant à A. de Tocqueville." *France Forum* (April-May 1983): 19-26.

Maurice, Marguerite. "Un ancêtre de Constant, le pasteur Antoine de Chandieu (1534-1591), originaire du Mâconnais." *Annales de l'Académie de Mâcon* (1980-81): 141-51.

Omacini, Lucia. *La Porta chiusa, lettere a Juliette Récamier (1814-1816).* (Biblioteca del Minotauro, 32.) Milan: Serra e Riva Editori, 1982. Pp. 120.

> Rev. by A. Borgheggiani in *SFr* 27 (1983): 571.

Pellegrini, Carlo. "L'edizione critica delle 'Lettres' di Benjamin Constant à Juliette Récamier." I: 369-75 in *Scritti in onore de Giovanni Macchia.* 2 vols. Milan: Arnoldo Mondadori, 1983. Pp. 1062+742.

Pizzorusso, Arnaldo. "Constant e Madame Récamier: la metamorfosi di un'immagine." *SFr* 27 (1983): 433-46.

> A comparative study of Constant's diaries and his letters to Madame Récamier.

Raynaud, Philippe. "Un Romantique libéral, Benjamin Constant." *Esprit*, March 1983, pp. 49-66.

Reymond, Claude, Mᵉ. "Benjamin Constant, de Lausanne à l'Europe." *L'OEil* 347 (1984): 42-47.

> In a special issue of this prestigious and world-famous monthly art review devoted to various aspects of artistic life in *le Pays de Vaud*, an introduction to Benjamin Constant's varied and original life and works by the President of the Committee for the Publication of Constant's *OEuvres complètes*, illustrated by photographs and art reproductions of houses and sites intimately connected with the man and his work.
>
> A glimpse into the vast enterprises, recently set up, of the publication of Constant's numerous works, voluminous correspondence, and countless manuscripts in general, by such specialists as C.P. Courtney, Pierre Deguise, Ephraïm Harpaz, and Etienne Hofmann, among others. (D.J.C.)

Riccioli, Giovanni. *"Bonheur" e società. Saggio su Samuel de Constant.* Bari: Adriatica, 1980.

> Rev. by P. Thompson in *RHL* 84 (1984): 628-29.

Roland, Patrice. "Equivoques du libéralisme. A propos de Benjamin Constant." *Commentaire* 4 (1981): 603-09.

Unwin, Timothy. "The Narrator and His Evolution in Constant's *Adolphe.*" *Swiss-French Studies* 3,ii (Nov. 1982): 60-86.

Vuillemin, Jules. "On Lying: Kant and Benjamin Constant." *Kant-Studien* 73 (1982): 413-24.

The author states Constant's and Kant's arguments in their
famous dialogue on the moral implications of lying.
Constant's statements imply: "I am free, therefore I have
rights; I have rights, therefore I have duties." Kant's
remarks imply: "I have duties, therefore I am free; I am
free, therefore I have rights. The first scheme allows
lying, the second seems to prohibit it."

Wood, Dennis. "Isabelle de Charrière, Benjamin Constant and
the Novel." *Lettre de Zuylen* 6 (Sept. 1981): 6.

Wood, Dennis. "Isabelle de Charrière et Benjamin Constant;
problématique d'une collaboration." *Lettre de Zuylen* 8
(Sept. 1983): 3-4.

See also Corciulo ("Chateaubriand"); Brunel et al., Delon
("Staël").

Reviews of books previously listed:

Annales Benjamin Constant 2 (see *RMB* for 1982, p. 198),
rev. by P. Delbouille in *RHL* 84 (1984): 286-87; *Annales
Benjamin Constant* 3 (see *RMB* for 1983, p. 198), rev. by
C.P. Courtney in *FS* 38 (1984): 468; COURTNEY, C.P., *A
Bibliography of the Writings of Benjamin Constant* (see *RMB*
for 1982, p. 200), rev. by J.-D. Candaux in *RHL* 84 (1984):
629-31; by D. Gilson in *The Library* 5 (1983): 193-97;
DELBOUILLE, Paul, "Une édition d'*Adolphe* à Vienne en 1817"
(see *RMB* for 1982, p. 200), rev. by C. Cordié in *SFr* 27
(1983): 364; FAIRLIE, Alison, *Imagination and Language*
(see *RMB* for 1981, p. 189), rev. by N. King in *MLR* 78 (1983):
926-27; HARPAZ, Ephraïm, ed., *Recueil d'articles (1820-
1824)* (see *RMB* for 1981, p. 189), rev. by L. Omacini in
SFr 27 (1983): 363; HOFMANN, Etienne, ed., *Benjamin Constant,
Madame de Staël et le Groupe de Coppet* (see *RMB* for 1982,
p. 261), rev. by C. Cordié in *SFr* 27 (1983): 570-71; by
A. Fairlie in *FS* 37 (1983): 469-70; by H. Grange in *RHL*
84 (1984): 968-73; by A. Ritchie in *RR* 75 (1984): 388-91;
by D. Wood in *MLR* 79 (1984): 193-95.

COTTIN

See Naudin ("French 1. General").

COURIER

Bernard, Camille. "Le crime de Paul-Louis Courier.--Paul-
Louis Courier et l'affaire d'Espagne en 1823.--Les dernières
pages de Paul-Louis Courier et la Grèce." *Cahiers Paul-
Louis Courier* 9 (1983): 11-40.

De Cesare, Raffaele. "Note bibliographiche sulla fortuna
italiana di Paul-Louis Courier nella prima metà del XIX
secolo." *Aevum* 57 (1983): 493-549.

A chronological arrangement of texts in Italian dealing
with Courier and his work, from 1808 to 1848, varying in
length from a few lines to a few pages. Among the Italian
authors represented are Cantù, Gioberti, Mazzini, Leopardi,
G. Montani, Foscolo, and D. Valeriani.

Viollet le Duc, Geneviève. "L'hellénisme de Paul-Louis
Courier: lettre ouverte à M. Jean-René Vieillefond."
Cahiers Paul-Louis Courier 9 (1983): 8-10.

COUSIN

Cotten, Jean-Pierre. "Démocratie et libéralisme dans
l'*Introduction à l'histoire de la philosophie*." *Cahiers de
Philosophie Politique et Juridique de l'Université de Caen*
2 (1982): 135-50.

See also Iknayan ("French 1. General").

CUSTINE

Brudo Madonia, Annie. "*Ethel* d'Astolphe de Custine." *Università di Palermo, Facoltà di Lettere....* *Quaderno 17*
(1983): 25-26.

Margerie, Diane de. *Aloys*. Paris: Fontaine, 1983. Pp. 158.
Fr. 55.00.

Rev. by Pierre Kyria in *Le Monde*, March 2, 1984, p. 20.

Sola, Jean. "Le Marquis de Custine ou les malheurs de
l'exactitude." *IL* 36 (1984): 153-55.

A résumé of the author's Sorbonne thesis, which attempts
a revision of the traditional portrait of Custine and presents a sympathetic view of his literary production.

DAVID

Bordes, Philippe. *Le Serment du Jeu de Paume de Jacques-Louis David*. Paris: Editions de la Réunion des Musées Nationaux, 1984. Pp. 260. Fr. 150.00.

Rev. by Francis Haskell (with two books on Watteau, as "The Voyage of Watteau") in *NYRB*, Dec. 20, 1984, pp. 25-30.

Wilson, Michael. "A New Acquisition for the National Gallery: Davis's Portrait of Jacobus Blauw." *BM* 126 (Nov. 1984): 694-98; 4 illus.

Biographic account of the Dutch patriot whose portrait was painted by David in 1795.

See also Bryson ("General 3. Criticism").

DELACROIX

Angrand, Pierre. "Les malheurs d'un Saint Sébastien." *GBA* 104 (Nov. 1984): 189-92.

Capsule history of the long series of contentions (1837-1902) over possession of the painting by Delacroix.

Brown, Roy Howard. "The Formation of Delacroix's Hero Between 1822 and 1831." *ArtB* 66 (1984): 237-54.

"... Delacroix's protagonist changed from a personality split between social concern, weak as it was, and egocentric detachment to one who was completely a-social, detached, and self-possessed. This is the 'heroism' of disengagement, in effect the basic ethic of the liberal journalists and financiers among whom were Delacroix's staunchest patrons."

Gervais, David. "Delacroix' 'Hamlet.'" *CQ* 13 (1984): 40-70.

Johnson, Lee. "A New Delacroix: 'Rebecca and the Wounded Ivanhoe.'" *BM* 974 (1984): 280-82.

"... of extraordinary interest, not only because it is the first painting by Delacroix of a subject from Scott (and probably the first in France from *Ivanhoe*), but also because it is the only painting of a literary or historical subject that he is known to have completed between the *Barque de Dante* of 1822 and the beginning of work on the *Massacres de Scio* in January 1824." A full-page color illustration is given.

Kliman, Eve Twose. "Delacroix's 'Jeune Tigre jouant avec sa
   mère.'" *GBA* 1388 (1984): 67-72.

   Stresses the unique realism of this early painting, which
   contrasts with Delacroix's usual emphasis, in his depiction
   of lions and tigers, on their power and ferocity.

Sérullaz, Arlette, ed. *Hamlet.* Trans. François-Victor Hugo.
   Paris: Marchal, 1984. Pp. 176. Fr. 150.00.

   Includes sixteen lithographs and twenty-one drawings by
   Delacroix inspired by Shakespeare's play.

Spector, Jack J. "Un rêve d'une main dans une lettre de
   Delacroix." Pp. 319-27 in Jean-Louis Bonnat and Mireille
   Bossis, eds., *Ecrire, publier, lire les correspondances
   (problématique et économie d'un "genre littéraire").* Actes
   du colloque international: "Les Correspondances." Nantes
   les 4, 5, 6, 7 octobre 1982. Université de Nantes, 1982.
   Pp. 474. Fr. 120.00.

Spector, Jack J. "Towards a Deeper Understanding of Delacroix
   and His Art: An Interpretation of *Michelangelo in His Studio.*"
   GBA 1380 (1984): 19-28.

   Spector surveys Delacroix's life-long interest in (and
   ambivalent feelings toward) Michelangelo, as a prelude to
   reading into the 1850-53 picture reflections of the painter's
   deep-seated anxieties (e.g., the fear of artistic sterility)
   and persistent need for a woman to serve as mistress, muse,
   and companion. This all leads up to a rather explicitly
   Freudian interpretation.

Steinke, William A. "An Archaeological Source for Delacroix's
   Death of Sardanapalus." *ArtB* 66 (1984): 318-20.

See also Bryson ("French 1. General").

Review of book previously listed:

   JOHNSON, Lee, *The Paintings of Eugène Delacroix* (see *RMB*
   for 1981, p. 193), rev. by Robert N. Beetem in *ArtB* 66
   (1984): 170-72.

DELAVIGNE

Girard, Marie-Hélène. "Le personnage de Marino Faliero dans le
romantisme français." Pp. 125-44 in Edouard Gaède, ed.,
*Trois figures de l'imaginaire littéraire: les odysées,
l'héroïsation de personnages historiques, la science et le
savant*. Actes du XVIIe congrès (Nice, 1981) de la Société
française de littérature générale et comparée. Préface
par Daniel-Henri Pageaux. (Publications de la Faculté
des Lettres et Sciences humaines de Nice, 22.) Paris:
Les Belles Lettres, 1982. Pp. 307. Fr. 135.00.

DELÉCLUZE

Review of book previously listed:

DELÉCLUZE, E.J., *Louis David, son école et son temps* (see
RMB for 1983, p. 204), rev. by Gilbert Lascault in *QL* 414
(April 1-15, 1984): 14.

DESBORDES-VALMORE

Moulin, Jeanine. *Marceline Desbordes-Valmore*. Edition revue
et mise au point. (Poètes d'Aujourd'hui, 46.) Paris:
Seghers, 1983. Pp. 219. Fr. 39.00.

First published in 1955.

Poésies. Précédées d'une notice par Sainte-Beuve. Avant-
propos de Pierre Lartigue. (Les Introuvables.) Plan-de-
la-Tour: Editions d'Aujourd'hui, 1983. Pp. 408. Fr. 86.00.

Facsimile of Charpentier edition (Paris, 1872).

Review of book previously listed:

Poésies, préface d'Yves Bonnefoy (see *RMB* for 1983, p.
204), brief rev. in *BCLF* 462 (June 1984): 738-39.

DESCHAMPS

Cohen, Henry. "An Adaptation of the Rey Rodrigo *romancero*:
Emile Deschamps, 'Le poème de Rodrigue, dernier roi des
Goths.'" *KRQ* 30 (1983): 15-28.

Cohen, Henry. "A French Romantic Poet's Adaptation of Medieval Spanish Romances." *Philological Papers* 27 (1981): 21-27.

On Deschamps's adaptation of the *romance* in drama.

Lambert, José. "How Emile Deschamps Translated Shakespeare's *Macbeth*, or Theatre System and Translational System in French Literature (1800-1850)." *Dispositio* 7,xix-xx-xxi (1982): 53-61.

Part of a longer study on translation theory and practice seeking "to elucidate the principles that guide the individual translator."

DIDIER

Springer, Carolyn. "*Rome souterraine*: The Classical Landscape in the Risorgimento from Didier to Garibaldi." *Stanford Italian Review* 3 (1983): 235-40.

"... his strategic focus on certain landmarks of the ancient city contributed to an Italian re-vision of the possibilities of Rome." "... Didier exploits the full subversive potential of the classical landscape by reclaiming it as the stage for the austere trials of republican virtue." The author draws parallels with Garibaldi's *Clelia: Il governo del monaco* (1870).

DU CAMP

Souvenirs littéraires. Préface de Michel Chaillou. Paris: Balland, 1984. Pp. 286. Fr. 84.90.

Rev. by David Coward in *TLS*, Feb. 1, 1985, p. 126.

DUMAS

Bäckvall, Hans. *Relations d'Alexandre Dumas père et fils avec la Suède*. (Kungl. Vitterhets Historie och Antikvitets Akademien. Filologiskt Arkiv, 28.) Stockholm: Almqvist & Wiksell, 1982. Pp. 39.

Bassan, Fernande. "*Napoléon Bonaparte* ou trente ans de l'histoire de France." *Bulletin de la Société des Amis d'Alexandre Dumas* 11 (1982): 10-13.

Campagnoli, Ruggero. "Il 'Voyage' come discorso specifico.
Dumas a Livorno." Pp. 57-95 in *Discorsi e finzioni. Scritti
di litteraturologia in campo francese.* (Biblioteca di
Filologia Romanza della Facoltà di Lettere e Filosofia
dell'Università di Bologna, 2.) Bologna: Pàtron, 1982.
Pp. 143.

Covensky, E. "Les débuts d'Alexandre Dumas père: *Henri III,
Antony* et *La Tour de Nesle.*" *RHT* 35 (1983): 329-37.

Dumas's heroes as victims of fate.

De Lorenzo, Antonio. "Luoghi e memorie francesi a Firenze:
Alexandre Dumas père." *Firme Nostre* 23,xcii (Sept. 1981):
4.

Les Garibaldiens: révolution de Sicile et de Naples.
Marseille: Jeanne Laffitte, 1982. Pp. 316.

Henry, Gille. *Le Secret de Monte Cristo ou les aventures des
ancêtres d'Alexandre Dumas.* Condé-sur-Noireau: Corlet,
1982.

A new, expanded version of the 1976 edition (see *ELN* 15,
Supp., 105).

Munro, Douglas. *Alexandre Dumas Pere: A Secondary Bibliography of French and English Sources to 1983; with Appendices.*
New York: Garland Publishing, Inc., 1984. Pp. 192.
$32.00.

Saurel, Renée. "Kean-Dumas-Sartre et Jean-Claude Drouot dans
le Palais des mirages." *TM* 39 (1983-84): 166-81.

Schifano, Jean-Noël, ed. *Le Corricolo.* (Les Chemins de
l'Italie.) Paris: Desjonquières, 1984. Pp. 517. Fr.
98.00.

Reprint of the 1843 edition, with a preface by the editor.
based on Dumas's visit to Naples in November 1835, the book
is, in Schifano's words, "le plus dumassien, le mieux
'dumassé' de ses livres, et sans nul doute l'un des plus
beaux." The editor compares it (favorably) to Stendhal's
Italian travel books: "Le génie de Stendhal est ailleurs.
Le génie de Dumas est là."

Schopp, Claude. "Les amours de Marie: dix lettres inédites
de Marie Dorval à Alexandre Dumas." *RHL* 84 (1984): 918-34.

Ten letters written during the short period between the
end of December 1833 and the end of April 1834.

Vingt ans après. 2 vols. Paris: France Loisirs, 1983.
Pp. 442, 441. Fr. 42.00.

See also Grossir, Krakovitch ("French 1. General"); Durnerin
("Spanish 3. Larra").

Reviews of book previously listed:

SCHOPP, Claude, ed., *Lettres à Mélanie Waldor* (see *RMB* for
1982, p. 208), rev. by C. Duchet in *Romantisme* 40 (1983):
175-76; by D.C. Spinelli in *NCFS* 12 (1983-94):   260-61.

DUPONT

Thoma, Heinz. "Pierre Dupont und das politische Lied 1848-
1851." *Lendemains* 28 (1982):   23-31.

On the variety of language forms and levels in the
political songs of the period in question, with particular
emphasis on Pierre Dupont, seen as "Porte-parole de la
Montagne."

DURAS

See Naudin ("French 1. General").

Review of book previously listed:

HERRMANN, Claudine, ed., *Edouard* (see *RMB* for 1983, p. 207),
rev. by Janine Aeply in *NRF* 371 (Dec. 1, 1983):   101-03.

ECKSTEIN

Le Guillou, Louis, ed. *Lettres inédites du baron d'Eckstein.*
Société et littérature à Paris en 1838-1840. (Centre de
Correspondances du XIXe Siècle, Paris IV.) Paris: Presses
universitaires de France, 1984. Pp. 256. Fr. 280.00.

Extracts from Eckstein's letters to the Comtesse Valérie
de Menthon (1813-39) and her husband (the "baron" had a
platonic affair with the lady during the last two years
of her short life). The present volume gives about a third

of the total material available--Le Guillou has entirely
omitted the purely personal and intimate side of the letters
in favor of texts that reveal the society of the time and
the literary world (the most frequently cited names are
Chateaubriand, Hugo, Lamartine, Lamennais, and Sand). Le
Guillou's annotation is discreet, succinct, and trustworthy.
(J.S.P.)

FAURIEL

See Trombatore ("Italian 3. Manzoni").

FLAUBERT

Douchin, Jacques-Louis. *Le Bourreau de soi-même. Essai
sur l'itinéraire intellectuel de Gustave Flaubert.* (Archives
des Lettres Modernes, 213.) Paris: Lettres Modernes/Minard,
1984. Pp. 115.

   A short, traditional biography of Flaubert, concentrating
on his intellectual development.

Ginsburg, Michal P. "Representational Strategies and the Early
Works of Flaubert." *MLN* 98 (1983): 1248-68.

   In *Mémoires d'un fou* and *Novembre* the narrator assumes
the existence of a unique self which gives birth to its
mirror image; in the first *Education sentimentale* the
narrator sees himself as dual from the beginning. These
differences in representation of the self form the essential
difference between the first two works and the third one.

Gothot-Mersch, Claudine, ed. *La Tentation de saint Antoine.*
(Folio, 1492.) Paris: Gallimard, 1983. Pp. 352.

   Rev. by A. Bourin in *RDM*, Oct.-Dec. 1983, pp. 425-29.

Jackson, Ernest A. "Flaubert in America. A Bibliographical
Review, 1857-1977." *The French-American Review* 6 (1982):
260-82.

Perrone-Moisés, Leyla. "L'autre Flaubert. *Quidquid Volueris*:
l'éducation scripturale." *Poétique* 53 (Feb. 1983): 109-22.

Robert, Marthe. *En haine du roman.* Paris: Balland, 1982.
Pp. 152.

Using a strictly Freudian approach and concentrating on Flaubert's youthful works (in particular "Un parfum à sentir," "Quidquid volueris," "Passion et vertu," *Mémoires d'un fou, Novembre, La Tentation de Saint Antoine* and the first *Education sentimentale*), Robert presents a coherent and cogent demonstration of the inner compulsions which led to Flaubert's mystical devotion to literature. The nucleus of her demonstration lies in her version of the young Gustave's "family romance," which he will never resolve and which thus will remain influential throughout his life. Along the way the author takes exception to many of Sartre's statements about Flaubert's early life. The treatment will especially interest those partial to psychological explanations. (E.F.G.)

Steegmuller, Francis. *The Letters of Gustave Flaubert.* Vol. I: *1830-1857.* Harvard University Press, 1980. Pp. 250.

Rev. by M.K. Lazarus in *NCFS* 11 (1982-83): 195-96.

Unwin, Timothy. "Flaubert's Early Philosophical Development: The Writing of *Smarh.*" *NFS* (Oct. 1982): 13-26.

See also Amossy and Rosen, La Condamine ("French 1. General").

Reviews of books previously listed:

BEM, Jeanne, *Désir et savoir dans l'oeuvre de Flaubert* (see *RMB* for 1981, p. 197), rev. by J. Neefs in *RHL* 84 (1984): 460-63; BERNHEIMER, Charles, *Flaubert and Kafka* (see *RMB* for 1983, p. 207), rev. by R. Denommé in *FR* 57 (1983-84): 558-59; CZYBA, Lucette, *Mythes et idéologie de la femme dans les romans de Flaubert* (see *RMB* for 1983, p. 207), rev. by D. Knight in *FS* 38 (1984): 213-14; UNWIN, Timothy A., ed., *Gustave Flaubert: trois contes de jeunesse* (see *RMB* for 1982, p. 209), rev. by A. Tooke in *FS* 38 (1984): 214.

FORNERET

Maya, Tristan. *X.F. humoriste noir blanc de visage.* Saint-Seine-l'Abbaye: Editions de Saint-Seine-l'Abbaye, 1984. Pp. 196. Fr. 70.00.

FOURIER

Bauwer, Bruce. "Guy Davenport: Fiction à la Fourier." *The New Criterion* 3,iv (1984): 8-14.

Davenport's *Apples and Pears* is dedicated to Fourier, and Bauwer claims that, "after lurking in the background of Davenport's previous books of fiction, Fourier, with *Apples and Pears*, takes center stage in Davenport's fiction." Davenport does not take Fourier's philosophy seriously *as* philosophy but "is nevertheless taken with his [Utopian] vision."

Beecher, Jonathan, and Richard Bienvenu, trans. and eds. *The Utopian Vision of Charles Fourier. Selected Texts on Work, Love, and Passionate Attraction.* University of Missouri Press, 1983. Pp. 448. $37.50; paper $14.50.

Cantagrel, Félix. *Le Fou du Palais-Royal. 1841.* (Corpus des OEuvres de Philosophie en Langue française.) Paris: Fayard, 1984.

Reproduces the 1841 set of philosophical dialogues on Fourier's ideas, which Cantagrel defends.

See also Milner, Moses ("French 1. General").

Reviews of book previously listed:

NATHAN, Michel, *Le Ciel des Fouriéristes* (see *RMB* for 1981, pp. 198-99), rev. by Frank Paul Bowman in *RHL* 84 (1984): 633-34; by Peter Byrne in *SFr* 27 (1984): 365-66.

GAUTIER

Bell, Ian F.A. "A Marginality of Context: Dobson's Gautier and Pound's Mauberley." *American Notes and Queries* 22,ix-x (1983-84): 141-43.

On the echo of Austin Dobson's translation of "L'Art" in the "Envoi" of *Hugh Selwyn Mauberley*.

Bulletin de la Société Théophile Gautier 5 (1983).

Contents: Alain Montandon, "Les neiges éboulies de Théophile Gautier" (1-4); Ruggero Campagnoli, "Eclats du *Capitaine Fracasse*" (15-40); David Graham Burnett, "Métaphore et signification architecturales dans les poésies de Gautier"

(41-52); Peter J. Edwards, "L'Opéra en 1847: un article
de Gautier et Nerval" (53-62); Jean-Yves Mollier, "Autour
du voyage de Théophile Gautier en Algérie" (63-88); Marie-
Louise Lentengre, "Un intertexte d'Apollinaire: 'Tristesse
en mer' de Gautier" (89-111); Pierre Miquel, "Sur trois
sortes de marques dans la vente Théodore Rousseau" (113-18);
Mariane Chermakian, "Le journal d'Eugénie Fort (suite)"
(119-53); Carmen Fernandez Sanchez, "Théophile Gautier en
Espagne" (155-57); society news (158-62).

Montandon identifies the rich connotative power of snow
imagery in Gautier, emphasizing the dynamics of the "snow
revery" in *Spirite*. Campagnoli's *éclats* (a first presentation of which appeared in *Théophile Gautier: l'art et
l'artiste* [Montpellier: Presses de l'Imprimerie de Recherche,
Université Paul Valéry, 1983], pp. 311-19) have to do here
with (1) Gautier's skillful use of corporeal imagery in
Le Capitaine Fracasse to underscore and clarify amorous
relationships and (2) his organization of the novel to move
Sigognac from Thanatos to Eros. Burnett focuses on the
semantic function of architectural images. Edwards argues
for Gautier's collaboration with Nerval on an unidentified
article in *L'Artiste* (Sept. 5, 1847) describing the redecora-
tion of the Opéra. Mollier presents the texts of two letters
and a newspaper account of Noël Parfait which evoke the
author's trip to Algeria with Gautier in 1845. Lentengre
challenges a view that Gautier's "Tristesse en mer" was a
source for Apollinaire's "Chanson du mal aimé"; she takes
the stand that both poets drew on a well-known motif (the
siren-fatal woman) to produce poems reflecting sharply
different intentions. Miquel considers the authentification
of paintings by Rousseau, an artist for whom Gautier regularly
expressed admiration. Chermakian continues to publish installments of Eugénie Fort's *journal*, covering here the period
Sept.-Dec. 1857. Sanchez sketches the (scanty) Spanish
interest in Gautier since the late nineteenth century.

Bulletin de la Société Théophile Gautier 6 (1984).

Acts of a colloquium, "Théophile Gautier et la narration,"
held at Bagni di Lucca, Italy, June 29-30, 1984. Contents:
Peter Whyte, "Du mode narratif dans les récits fantastiques
de Gautier" (1-19); Marcel Voisin, "Introduction à l'humour
narratif de Gautier" (21-41); Claudine Lacoste, "Le personnage du narrateur dans *Fortunio*" (43-50); Claude Senninger,
"*La Croix de Berny*, grand steeple-chase non académique"
(51-66); Nori Fornasier, "Pulsions et fonctions de l'idéal
dans les contes fantastiques de Gautier" (67-72); Andrew
Gann, "La musique élément structurant dans les récits fan-

tastiques de Gautier" (73-82); Carlo Pasi, "Le fantastique
archéologique de Gautier" (83-92); Luciana Grasso, "La
'Fantaisie pompéienne' de Gautier: *Arria Marcella*" (93-108);
Marie-Claude Schapira, "L'écriture de Narcisse: fiction et
réflexivité" (109-23); Jean-Claude Brunon, "Le pittoresque
et l'expression de la durée dans *Le Capitaine Fracasse*"
(125-33); Ruggero Campagnoli, "Eclats du *Capitaine Fracasse*:
la poétique du soleil bleu" (135-45); Bibliographie (of
recently published editions and secondary works) (147); news
of the society (148-50).

As the title of the colloquium indicates, the papers collected here focus on Gautier's narrative craftsmanship.
Whyte emphasizes the function of the narrator and narrative
devices. Gann underscores Gautier's sensitivity to music
and his use of music as a narrative catalyst for moving his
heroes from the real to the fantastic. Luciana Grasso compares *Arria Marcella* and Jensen's *Gradiva* (studied by Freud),
favoring the former for its richness, achieved through
ambiguity and suggestivity. Schapira's paper, a sort of
condensation of her new book (see below), brings out "specular"
elements in Gautier's work which give it, to use her term,
a narcissistic quality: auto-portraits, instances of self-
consciousness, mirror effects, doubling of personality,
mises en abyme, transpositions of art, etc. Senninger points
out traces of Gautier's character in *La Croix de Berny* and
uncovers allusions to his times, as well.

Critics here as elsewhere view Gautier's stories as
symbolic representations of the artist confronting the
problems of his art. Lacoste takes as her exemplar *Fortunio*.
Campagnoli continues his analysis of the *éclats* of *Le Capitaine Fracasse*, here studying the various messages of the
color blue and concluding that the novel is a statement on
the novelist's craft and a prime example of Gautier's craftsmanship.

It is noteworthy how many critics continue to look for the
"secret" Gautier within the works. In this collection,
Fornasier finds a Gautier at pains to resolve a conflict
between matter and spirit. One may question her inclusion
of *Le Roi Candaule* among Gautier's fantastic tales, and her
conclusion that peace for Gautier implies death. Voisin
argues that distanciation, parody, and verbal play permitted
Gautier to maintain his psychic equilibrium. Pasi advances
the notion that Gautier's stories reflect the author's own
incestuous desires. Brunon identifies behind certain narrative devices and patterns in *Le Capitaine Fracasse* a Gautier
attempting to escape his historicity by recapturing the
imaginative intensity of an earlier time.

Whatever the approach and whatever the relative success of

the individual papers, this collection demonstrates once
again that Gautier is a rich and complex author, well deserving
of the attention that he continues to receive.   (A.B.S.)

Cadot, Michel. "Les voyages en Russie de Théophile Gautier."
RLC 58 (1984): 5-25.

Material circumstances of the two trips, together with
details on Gautier's personal relationships: traveling
companions, artists, dancers, etc.

Caramaschi, Enzo. "1835: *Mademoiselle de Maupin.*" I, 432-
41 in Massimo Colesanti, Luigi di Nardis, Ferruccio Marotti,
and Arnaldo Pizzorusso, eds., *Scritti in onore di Giovanni
Macchia.* 2 vols. Milan: Arnoldo Mondadori, 1983.

Remarks on the structure of the novel and on its place
among French works of the mid-1830s. Caramaschi calls particular attention to Gautier's irony.

"Le drame en prose." *Cahiers Renaud-Barrault* 108 (1983):   3-5.

Text of an article by Gautier on Hugo's *Angelo*. The
article first appeared in *Le Monde Dramatique*, No. 7, on
July 5, 1835.

Eigeldinger, Marc, ed. *Mademoiselle Dafné*. (Textes Littéraires
Français, 324.) Geneva: Droz, 1984. Pp. 67. Fr. 66.30.

Gautier's story "dans la manière de Piranesi," first
published in Arsène Houssaye's *La Revue du XIXᵉ Siècle* on
April 1, 1866, pp. 17-40. In his introduction, Eigeldinger
studies the structure of the story, its mixture of humor and
oneirism, and its allusiveness. He also provides a history
of the text.

Girard, Marie-Hélène. "Théophile Gautier et Félix Ziem." Pp.
123-50 in *La Critique artistique: un genre littéraire.*
(Publications de l'Université de Rouen, Centre d'Art,
Esthétique et Littérature.) Paris: Presses universitaires
de France, 1983. Pp. 256+32 plates.

Useful for its confirmations as to Gautier's aesthetic
stance. As critic, he was concerned to bring the paintings
alive to the general public. As individual, he found appeal
in the picturesque and the vividly rendered.

Kapp, Volker. "Le bonheur de l'instant dans *Mademoiselle de
Maupin.*" *LR* 38 (1984):   77-97.

Laubriet, Pierre, and Claudine Lacoste, eds. *Correspondance
générale*. T. I: *1818-1843*. Geneva: Droz, 1984.

Lund, Hans Peter. "Contes pour l'art: la métaphorique picturale et théâtrale chez Gautier." *RevR* 18 (1983): 240-65.

   While possibly representing reactions to personal, even
existential, anguish, Gautier's shorter fictional works
reveal principally a concern with aesthetics. We should
all read these tales as allegories defining a poetics of
idealization. Lund rambles, but his basic point is well
taken. (A.B.S.)

Schapira, M[arie]-C[laude]. *Le Regard de Narcisse: romans
et nouvelles de Théophile Gautier*. Presses universitaires
de Lyon, 1984. Pp. 244. Fr. 95.00.

Voisin, Marcel. "Théophile Gautier, l'Italie et la 'rêverie
méditerranéenne.'" III: 411-24 in *Mélanges à la mémoire de
Franco Simone: France et Italie dans la culture européenne.*
(Bibliothèque Franco-Simone, 8.) 4 vols. Geneva: Editions
Slatkine, 1980-84.

   Gautier was compulsively drawn to Mediterranean locales
and cultures. After Spain, Italy occupied a dominant place
in his heart and mind. He saw in Italy the affirmation of
an aesthetic and moral ideal exalting life, passion, and
voluptuousness, all summed up in the art of Titian.

See also Meregalli ("General 3. Criticism"); Haskell, Pradier
("French 1. General").

Reviews of books previously listed:

BERCHET, Jean-Claude, ed., *Voyage en Espagne* (see *RMB* for
1981, p. 199), rev. by Mario Bensi in *SFr* 27 (1983): 375;
by Joy Newton in *FS* 38 (1984): 74-75; BERTHIER, Patrick,
ed., *Voyage en Espagne* (see *RMB* for 1981, p. 199), rev. by
Joy Newton in *FS* 38 (1984): 355-56; GOTHOT-MERSCH, Claudine,
ed., *Emaux et camées* (see *RMB* for 1981, p. 201), rev. by
H[arry] Cockerham in *FS* 37 (1983): 476; SAVALLE, Joseph,
Travestis, métamorphoses, dédoublements (see *RMB* for 1982,
p. 215), rev. by Hans Peter Lund in *RHL* 84 (1984): 637-38;
by P.J. Whyte in *FS* 38 (1984): 211-12; SMITH, Albert B.,
Gautier and the Fantastic (see *ELN* 16, Supp., 100), rev. by
Marcel Voisin in *RBPH* 60 (1982): 693-94; SNELL, Robert,
Théophile Gautier: A Romantic Critic (see *RMB* for 1982,
pp. 215-16), rev. by Robert Lethbridge in *FS* 38 (1984): 356;

by Albert B. Smith in *FR* 58 (1984-85): 292-93; by Thérèse
Dolan Stamm in *NCFS* 12,iv; 13,i (1984): 202-05; by Jon
Whitely in *Oxford Art Journal* 6 (1983): 83-84; VOISIN,
Marcel, *Le Soleil et la nuit* (see *RMB* for 1981, pp. 202-03),
rev. by Marc Eigeldinger in *RHL* 84 (1984): 636-37.

GENLIS

Deguise, Alix S., ed. *Mademoiselle de Clermont* suivie de
L'Histoire intéressante de Madame la Duchesse de C * *.
Geneva: Slatkine, 1982 (1983). Pp. 113. Fr. 196.00.

See also Naudin ("French 1. General").

GÉRICAULT

Johnson, Lee. "Géricault's 'Derby': An Equine Capriccio?"
BM 126 (March 1984): 159.

The Derby painted "is either a fantasy or an accurate
record of a race that has yet to be identified."

GIRARDIN

See Delon ("French 1. General").

GOBINEAU

Béziau, Roger, ed. *Etudes critiques (1842-1847)*. (Bibliothèque du XIXe Siècle, 11.) Paris: Klincksieck, 1984.
Pp. 368. Fr. 148.00.

Gobineau's literary criticism had been only very in-
completely published before (in 1927)--seven articles on
six writers (Balzac, Musset, Gautier, Heine, Janin, Sainte-
Beuve)--whereas the present volume offers twenty articles
on nineteen authors.

Béziau shows rather well in his introduction that the
young Gobineau was a literary critic of considerable powers,
inviting comparison with Sainte-Beuve's "impressionism,"
Villemain's "critique des beautés," the forward-lookingness
of a Chasles (and Gobineau, who read German, is, like Chasles,
important in the history of comparative literary criticism),
the historicism of Renan. A certain aristocratic aloofness

lifts him above most professional critics, however.
Béziau not only places Gobineau in the history of literary
criticism, but also analyzes the style of these essays,
pointing, in particular, to the imprint of Romanticism or,
rather, "ce goût de romanesque," and of Realism, although
his Realism is not that of the "plats copieurs de la plus
triviale réalité." Words that characterizes his style
are "fermeté," "vigueur," "goût du concret." His metaphors
are frequent, usually successful ("bien venues") and occasionally quite original, attaining effects suggestive of
Hugo, Sainte-Beuve, or Malraux.

The writers treated by Gobineau are Hoffmann, Quinet,
Musset, Gautier, Heine, Balzac, Laprade, Lady Georgianna
Fullerton, Adelphe Nouville, Stendhal, Francis Wey, Mignet,
Vitet, Villemain, Planche, Sainte-Beuve, Janin, Saint-Marc
Girardin, Charles Magnin. There are also two essays on
general topics, published in *La Revue Nouvelle*: "Une
littérature nouvelle est-elle possible?" and "Des buts
techniques de la littérature." (The other periodicals in
which Gobineau published were *L'Union Catholique*, *L'Unité*,
Le Commerce, and *La Quotidienne*.) (J.S.P.)

Dubant, Bernard. "Gobineau Fils de Roi." *Eléments pour la
Civilisation Européenne* 45 (1983): 55-59.

Jean-Nesmy, dom Claude. "Gobineau entre positivisme et
romantisme." *Revue Générale*, Jan. 1984, pp. 103-06.

Gobineau is proclaimed to be essentially a Romantic. The
(in)famous *Inégalité* should be judged accordingly, not as
a political statement ultimately leading to racism and
pangermanism but as something comparable to the "epic
legends" of Hugo, Lamartine, and Vigny, as a "'rêverie'
nostalgique sur un passé. " For Jean-Nesmy, Gobineau is one
of the great writers of the nineteenth century; his masterpieces are *Les Pléiades*, *Nouvelles asiatiques*, and *La
Renaissance*.

Murard, Léon, and Patrick Zylberman. "L'enfer tonique (Malthus et Gobineau)." *History of European Ideas* 2 (1983):
151-82.

Smith, Annette. *Gobineau et l'histoire naturelle*. (Histoire
des Idées et Critique littéraire, 219.) Geneva: Droz,
1984. Pp. 276. Sw.Fr. 60.00.

Reviews of book previously listed:

GAULMIER, Jean, and Jean Boissel, eds., *OEuvres* (see *RMB* for 1983, p. 214), rev. (T. I) by Michael D. Biddiss in *FS* 38 (1984): 75-76; by Jacques Landrin in *IL* 36 (1984): 232; by Mario Richter in *SFr* 28 (1984): 183-84; (T. II) by Peter Fawcett in *TLS*, March 30, 1984, pp. 323-24; JUIN, Hubert, ed., *Les Pléiades, Nouvelles asiatiques, Adélaïde, Mademoiselle Irnois* précédé de *Souvenirs de voyage* (see *RMB* for 1983, p. 214), rev. by Peter Fawcett in *TLS*, March 30, 1984, pp. 323-24.

GUÉRIN, EUGÉNIE AND MAURICE DE

Ambrière, Francis. "*L'Amitié Guérinienne* et la presse. Les cultes littéraires: les amis de Maurice de Guérin." *AmG* 54 (1984): 74-80.

Boussac, André-J. "Le nom des Guérin. (Extrait de l'*Almanach du Tarn Libre de 1954*)." *AmG* 54 (1984): 62-64.

Foutel, Joseph. "Interview posthume de Maurice de Guérin (1810-1839)." *AmG* 54 (1984): 11-24.

An imaginary interview, with material drawn from Maurice de Guérin's correspondence and from his famous journal, "le Cahier Vert."

Fumaroli, Marc, ed. *Le Centaure; La Bacchante; Le Cahier vert; Glaucus; Pages sans titre.* (Poésie/Gallimard, 183.) Paris: Gallimard, 1984. Pp. 288. Fr. 25.00

"La Garenne du Cayla. Sketch de circonstance radiodiffusé pour la première fois à Toulouse-Pyrénées le 20 juillet 1954." *AmG* 54 (1984): 65-71.

Text of a dramatic sketch broadcast by Toulouse-Pyrénées in memory of the 115th anniversary of the death of Maurice de Guérin (July 19, 1839). The scene is set in la Garenne du Cayla a few days before the poet's death.

Martineau. "Psychologie de la foi occitane chez Eugénie de Guérin." *AmG* 54 (1984): 58-59.

Souques, Mme Geneviève. "Lamennais vu par Maurice de Guérin." *AmG* 54 (1984): 25-44.

Vest, James. "Conférence du 15 juillet 1984 au Cayla. Les
vers de Maurice de Guérin." AmG 54 (1984): 87-94.

    Cites the gradually increasing interest in Maurice de
Guérin's verse after the early negative judgments of Sainte-
Beuve and Matthew Arnold, and urges the need for a complete
edition of all the available poems, some of which have never
been published, while others have been forgotten.

GUIZOT

*Des conspirations et de la justice politique. De la peine de
    mort en matière politique. 1822.* (Corpus des OEuvres de
    Philosophie en Langue française.) Paris: Fayard, 1984.
    Pp. 224. Fr. 75.00.

Review of book previously listed:

    HOEGES, Dirk, *François Guizot und die französische Revolu-
    tion* (see *ELN* 13, Supp., 91), rev. by Elda Tarrarelli in
    SFr 27 (1984): 369-70.

HUGO

A propos d'Angelo. Cahiers Renaud Barrault 108. Paris:
    Gallimard, 1984. Pp. 128.

    Contents: "Distribution" (2); Théophile Gautier, "Le
drame en prose" (3-5); Madame Victor Hugo, "Comment Hugo
fit représenter *Angelo*" (6-15); "*Angelo* en 1905" (16-28);
Louis Schneider, "Victor Hugo et la musique" (29-35);
"Quelques idées de Victor Hugo sur le théâtre" (36-40);
Gaëton Picon, "A propos des dessins de Victor Hugo, extrait
du *Soleil d'encre*" (41-43); "Quatre dessins de Victor Hugo"
(44-47); Joyce Mansour, "*Angelo Tyran de Padoue* ou Victor
Hugo versus la force majeure" (48-49); Dominique Desanti,
"Héroïnes hugoliennes en quête d'auteur" (50-63); "Hors-
texte: photos de Charles Hugo et Auguste Vacquerie" (64);
Jean-Louis Barrault, "1984: à propos d'*Angelo*" (65-72);
"Extraits de la préface de V. Hugo et des Statuts de l'Inquisition d'Etat (16 juin 1445)" (73-77); Jean-Louis Barrault
and Rudolf de Lippe, "Textes à propos du corps" (78-128).
    Gautier praises Hugo for elevating prose to higher
dramatic status than mere comedy and farce. Madame Hugo
recounts how Mademoiselle Mars and Madame Dorval gave character to rehearsals by their opposing viewpoints. Letters
of Sarah Bernhardt, Adolphe Mercier, and Mademoiselle Mars

suggest the atmosphere of enthusiasm and "la guerre des feuilletons" in which *Angelo* was presented in 1905. Schneider uses many examples to demolish the legend that Hugo did not like music. Picon introduces Hugo's work as "une histoire du regard." Mansour sees the feminine aspect of *Angelo* as the dominant one. Desanti finds the women of the Saint-Simonian movement and the activities of Flora Tristan to be worthy of portrayal--or invention--by Hugo. Barrault comments upon Hugo's prose style, presents an outline of his work as dramaturge, yet situates *Angelo* primarily as the work of a poet.

Achinger, Gerda. "Die Lyrik Victor Hugos im Urteil Puškins." *Arcadia* 18 (1983): 113-38.

Influence on Pushkin.

Ahearn, Edward J. "Confrontation with the City: Social Criticism, Apocalypse and the Reader's responsibility in City Poems by Blake, Hugo, and Baudelaire." *The Hebrew University Studies in Literature* 10 (1982): 1-22.

Alvarez-Borland, Isabel. "Victor Hugo, Gabriela Mistral y *l'intertextualité.*" *Revista de Estudios Hispánicos* 18 (1984): 371-80.

"Booz endormi" and Gabriela Mistral's "Ruth" (in her *Desolación* [1922]).

Avni, Abraham. "Heine and Hugo: The Biblical Connection." *Neophil* 68 (1984): 405-20.

In addition to disparagement and animosity, a kind of philosophical affinity prevails between the two poets, particularly where their creative responses to the Bible are concerned. After enumerating these points of juncture, Avni concludes that "'biblical' similarities between Hugo and Heine seem due to direct influence caused either by their reading of each other's work, which according to the evidence was sometimes possible, or by an exchange of views at their meetings" (418).

Azeyeh, Albert. "Excès et censure: une morale de l'écriture hugolienne à travers *Les Misérables.*" *Annales de la Faculté des Lettres et Sciences Humaines (Yaoundé)* 10 (1981): 59-71.

Barrère, Jean-Bertrand. "Victor Hugo et l'homme de Constantinople: le dossier François." Pp. 523-33 in Jean Jehasse, Claude Martin, Pierre Rétat, Bernard Yon, and René Pintard,

eds., *Mélanges offerts à Georges Couton.* Presses universitaires de Lyon, 1981. Pp. 640.

Letters to and from Joseph François.

Basile, Bruno. "D'Annunzio e Victor Hugo: Echi di *Notre Dame de Paris* in *Terra Vergine.*" *LI* 34 (1982): 260-73.

Blewer, Evelyn, and Jean Gaudon, eds. *La Fin de Satan.*
Préface de Jean Gaudon. (Poésie/Gallimard, 188.) Paris:
Gallimard, 1984. Pp. 336. Fr. 29.00.

Bony, Jacques. "Nerval et la Société des Gens de Lettres:
une lettre inédite à Victor Hugo." *Etudes Nervaliennes et Romantiques* 3 (1981): 95-103.

Text and explanatory material relating to a letter used
by Hugo as "brouillon" when composing *Les Jumeaux.*

Brody, Jules. "'Let There Be Night': Intertextuality in a
Poem of Victor Hugo." *RR* 75 (1984): 216-29.

Brody contends that Hugo uses components of the opening
lines of Genesis to cancel the Creation narrative in "Spes"
(*Les Contemplations*, VI, 21). Elements of Virgil's
description of the Cyclops further reinforce Hugo's representation of life as a godless creation. Borrowings from
the New Testament that effect the poem's transition from
darkness to light suggest the theme of the poet as the
pariah who comes to offer hope.

Brombert, Victor. "Hugo: l'édifice du livre." *Romantisme*
44 (1984): 49-56.

The recurring motif of the ruined Tower of Babel symbolizes
Hugo's obsession with language and his metaphysical malaise
about books as "works in progress," inexorably moving forward
in time yet destined to remain eternally incomplete.

Brombert, Victor. *Victor Hugo and the Visionary Novel.*
Harvard University Press, 1984. Pp. 286. $20.00.

Rev. by Frederick Brown in *NYRB*, Jan. 17, 1985, pp. 41-44;
by Angus Paul in *The Chronicle of Higher Education*, Sept.
26, 1984, p. 8; by Hayden White in *New York Times Book
Review*, Dec. 23, 1984, p. 7.

Brombert, Victor. "Victor Hugo: Revolution or the Hour of
Laughter." Pp. 719-28 in Joseph P. Strelka, ed., *Literary
Theory and Criticism. Festschrift. Presented to René Wellek*

in Honor of His Eightieth Birthday. 2 vols. Bern, Frankfurt on the Main, and New York: Peter Lang, 1984. Pp.
1462. $80.00.

Christ, Yvan. "La maison de Victor Hugo fait peau neuve."
Journal de l'Amateur de l'Art (Dec. 1983): 24-25.

Coats, John. "The Return to Hugo: A Discussion of the Intellectual Context of Chesterton's View of the Grotesque."
English Literature in Transition (1880-1920) 25 (1982): 86-
103.

Combes, Claudette. *Paris dans Les Misérables.* Nantes:
Editions CID, 1981.

Czarnecki, Marguerite. "Hugo misogyne?" *Comédie Française*
112 (Oct. 1982): 11-13.

    On *Marie Tudor.*

Debauve, Jean-Louis. "Une lettre de Victor Hugo à Elisa
Mercoeur." *Bulletin Mensuel de la Société Polymathique du
Morbihan* (July 1981): 21-22.

Delabroy, Jean. "'L'accident de l'histoire': Sur 1848 et
Les Misérables de Victor Hugo." *Lendemains* 28 (1982): 59-67.

de Man, Paul. "Hypogram and Inscription: Michael Riffaterre's
Poetics of Reading." *Diacritics* 11 (1981): 17-35.

    Treats Hugo's "Ecrit sur la vitre d'une fenêtre flamande."

Derigny, Colette. "A propos de Victor Hugo." *Comédie Française* 113 (Nov. 1982): 25-26.

Descotes, Maurice. *Victor Hugo et Waterloo.* (Archives des
Lettres Modernes, 214; Archives Victor Hugo, 10.) Paris:
Minard (Lettres Modernes), 1984. Pp. 78. Fr. 46.00.

"1985, année Hugo." *Le Monde,* May 11, 1984, p. 3.

    Announcement of activities organized in France to mark
the Hugo centennial.

Dotti, Ugo. "L'altra metà di Victor Hugo." *Belfagor* 39
(1984): 348-53.

    A study of Hugo's almost obsessive love of detail in his
evocation of Waterloo in *Les Misérables.*

Edelman, Frédéric. "Hugo dans ses meubles." *Le Monde Loisirs*, Jan. 28, 1984, p. 2.

Description of the newly restored Hugo museum at the Place des Vosges and announcement of the exposition of Hugo's drawings held at the Maison de Balzac.

Gale, John. "Where History and Fiction Meet: Napoleon Bonaparte and Jean Valjean." *French Literature Series* (Columbia, S.C.) 8 (1981): 65-75.

Garcin, Jérôme. "Quand Geneviève Dormann réhabilite la mère de Victor Hugo Sophie Trébuchet sort de l'oubli!" *NL*, Nov. 18, 1984, pp. 39-40.

Gasiglia, Danièle. *Victor Hugo, sa vie, son oeuvre*. Paris: F. Birr (Diffusion: L'Amateur), 1984. Pp. 128. Fr. 150.00.

Gaudon, Jean. "Sur *Hernani*." *CAIEF* 35 (1983): 101-20.

A study of the 148 notes Victor Hugo made in the margins of an original edition of *Hernani* during, or immediately following, one of the play's first performances. The notes themselves are given in an appendix.

Gaudon, Sheila. "La correspondance de Victor Hugo." *Romantisme* 40 (1983): 172-74.

Ginestier, Paul. "L'anti-théâtre de Victor Hugo." Pp. 165-87 in Cedric E. Pickford, ed., *Mélanges de littérature française moderne offerts à Garnet Rees par ses collègues et amis.* ("La Thésothèque": Réflexion et Recherche Univ. 7.) Paris: Minard, 1980. Pp. x+291.

Antidrama; influence on Ionesco and Beckett.

Gohin, Yves. "La plume de l'ange: analyse du manuscrit d'un poème des *Contemplations* (VI, 15)." *Littérature* 52 (Dec. 1983): 4-39.

Greenberg, Wendy. "Extended Metaphor in 'On Loge à la Nuit.'" *RR* 54 (1983): 441-54.

This reading of the poem's syntagmatic and paradigmatic structures demonstrates how the primary metaphor *auberge Louvre* takes on the metonymic function of describing, and thereby discrediting, the "greatness" of Napoleon III.

Greenberg, Wendy. "Symbolization and Metonymic Links in Three Poems from Hugo's *Les Rayons et les Ombres*." *DR* 62 (1982-83): 600-34.

Grimaud, Michel, ed. *Victor Hugo I: Approches critiques contemporaines.* (Revue des Lettres Modernes, 693-97.) Paris: Minard (Lettres Modernes), 1984. Pp. 224. Fr. 86.00.

Contents: Michel Grimaud, "Ouverture" (3-6); Victor Brombert, "Victor Hugo: la fin du héros ou l'éclipse du père" (9-23); Gilbert Chaitin, "Châtiment et scène primitive: le contre-sens de 'L'Expiation'" (25-37); Jeanne Bem, "*Châtiments* ou l'histoire de France comme enchaînement de parricides" (39-51); Jeanne-Marie Thomasseau, "Le jeu des écritures dans *Ruy Blas*" (55-80); Georges Combet, "Les parallélismes de 'Booz endormi'" (81-99); Claudie Bernard, "De l'architecture à la littérature: la topographie parisienne dans *Notre-Dame de Paris*" (103-38); Guy Talon, "Notre-Dame de Paris: la cathédrale dans l'univers hugolien" (139-55); Walter Secor, "Le credo d'Adèle" (159-6); Claire-Lise Rogers, "Bibliographie commentée de *Quatre-vingt-treize*" (165-88); Dorothy M. Betz, "Bibliographie commentée des études de l'edition Massin des *Oeuvres complètes* de Hugo" (189-223).
Each essay in this volume proposes to integrate theory with the actual practice of reading. Articles are grouped according to the critical genres of history and psychoanalysis (Brombert, Chaitin, Bem) and semiotics (Thomasseau, Combet). Studies of *Notre-Dame de Paris* and of Adèle Hugo and two bibliographies round out this diverse sampling of approaches to Hugo's work.

Gripari, Pierre. "Le sublime XIXe siècle." *Ecrits de Paris* 426 (July-Aug. 1982): 115-16.

On *Marie Tudor.*

Guérin, Jeanyves. "*Marie Tudor.*" *NRF* 354-55 (July 1-Aug. 1, 1982): 155-57.

Guest, Harry, trans. *Victor Hugo: The Distance, the Shadows: Selected Poems.* (Poetica, 10.) London: Anvil Press Poetry, 1981. Pp. 239. £6.95.

Rev. by Norma Rinsler in *FS* 38 (1984): 354.

Guibert, Noëlle. "*Marie Tudor* de Victor Hugo, l'histoire de la pièce." *Comédie Française* 109 (May 1982): 18-23.

Guille, Françoise Vernor. *Le Journal d'Adèle Hugo. III: 1854.* (Bibliothèque Introuvable, 12.) Paris: Minard (Lettres Modernes), 1984. Pp. 576. Fr. 220.00.

Heitmann, Klaus. "Mütterliches Deutschland: Zu Victor Hugos Heidelberg-Erlebnis." *Romanistische Zeitschrift für Literatur-*

geschichte/Cahiers d'Histoire des Littératures Romanes
8 (1984): 177-203.

Horn, Pierre L. "Victor Hugo's Theatrical Royalties During
His Exile Years." *ThR* 7 (1982): 132-37.

Inagaki, Naoki. "Fusion du livresque et du vécu: influence
de Ducray-Duminil sur la genèse de la structure double
de l'histoire d'amour dans *Han d'Islande* de Victor Hugo."
ELLF 44 (1984): 53-70.

  Hypothetical reconstruction of Hugo's mental drama during
the voyage to Dreux when he rediscovered Ducray-Duminil's
story of the kidnapping of virtuous, beautiful Adèle;
applications of this stereotype to Hugo's own obsessions
vis-à-vis his fiancée Adèle and their transposition into
the fictions of *Han d'Islande*.

Ionesco, Eugène; Gelu Ionescu, afterword; Dragomir Costineanu,
trans. *La Vie grotesque et tragique de Victor Hugo*. Paris:
Gallimard, 1982. Pp. 160.

Janc, John J., ed. *Les Deux Trouvailles de Gallus*. Lanham,
Md.: University Press of America, 1983. Pp. 259.

  Critical edition.

Jeronimidis, Elena D., and Keith Wren. "A One Way Ticket to
Heaven: History, Politics and Religion in the Theatre of
Manzoni and Victor Hugo." *Neophil* 66 (1982): 66-91.

Journet, René, and Guy Robert. *Contribution aux études sur
Victor Hugo VI. I. A propos du dossier de La Fin de Satan.
II. A propos des Reliquats et d'Océan. A. Questions de
texte. B. Regroupement des pièces*. Hors commerce, 1983.

Journet, René, and Guy Robert. *Fragments, tirés des manuscrits
Océan (vers et prose)*. Hors commerce, 1983.

Joyau, Auguste. *Adèle Hugo, la mal aimée: essai historique*.
Morne-Rouge, Martinique: Editions des Horizons Caraïbes,
1981.

Jumelais, Yann. "Hugo et les soldats de l'an II." Pp. 195-
302 in Edouard Gaède, ed., *Trois Figures de l'imaginaire
littéraire. Les Odysseys. L'Héroïsation de personnages
historiques. La Science et le savant*. Actes du XVIIe
congrès (Nice, 1981) de la Société française de Littérature
générale et comparée. (Publications de la Faculté des

Lettres et Sciences humaines, 22.) Paris: Les Belles
Lettres, 1982. Pp. 307. Fr. 135.00.

Kahn, Jean-François. "Le paradoxe sur Victor Hugo." *Comédie
Française* 111 (Sept. 1982): 5-7.

    On *Marie Tudor*.

Kapp, Volker. "Victor Hugos Konzeption des Welttheaters in
der 'Preface de Cromwell.'" Pp. 257-77 In Franz Link and
Günter Niggl, eds., *Theatrum Mundi: Götter, Gott und
Spielleiter im Drama von der Antike bis zur Gegenwart.*
Berlin: Duncker und Humblot, 1981. Pp. 417.

Kessler, Joan C. "Babelic Ruin, Babelic 'Ebauche': An
Introduction to a Hugolian Problematic." *SFR* 7 (1983):
285-99.

Knoepfler, Denis. "Le Diogène Laërce de M. Mabeuf dans *Les
Misérables* de Victor Hugo." *BAGB* (Oct. 1983): 319-25.

Lemarque, Danièle, and Emmanuel Fraisse. *Les Pyrénées.*
(La Découverte Illustrée.) Paris: La Découverte, 1984.
Pp. 224. Fr. 85.00.

    Contains Hugo's black and white illustrations.

Lanskin, Jean-Michel Charles. "*Ruy Blas*: héros romantique
ou amant courtois?" *Studies in Medievalism* 2,ii (1983):
27-33.

Laster, Arnaud. "Hugo, cet empereur de notre décadence
littéraire." *Romantisme* 42 (1983): 91-101.

Le Bris, Michel, ed. *Le Rhin.* (Réédition.) Paris: Bueb
et Reumaux (Diffusion: Ed. de l'Opale), 1984. Pp. 432.
Fr. 8.00.

Ledouppe, Christiane. *Victor Hugo et la création littéraire:
Guide systématique pour la connaissance des idées de l'écrivain.* (Mémoires, 3.) Liège: Association des Romanistes
de l'Université, 1980. Pp. 155.

Lemaître, Henri. "Hugo seul." Pp. 93-125 in *Du Romantisme
au Symbolisme: l'âge des découvertes et des innovations,
1790-1914.* (Collection Littérature.) Paris: Bordas, 1982.
Pp. 748.

Lentzen, Manfred. "Eminescu und Victor Hugo: Zu den Gedichten 'Maria Tudor,' 'Serenada' und 'Floare albastra.'" *CREL* (1982, i): 26-37.

Losito, Luigi. "Victor Hugo et les mystères Jersey." *Culture Française* (Bari) 29 (1982): 17-18.

Mambrino, Jean. *"Marie Tudor, drame en trois journées* de Victor Hugo au Théâtre Français." *Etudes* 361 (1982): 651-52.

Margot, Jean-Michel. "Une lettre de Victor Hugo." *Bulletin de la Société Jules Verne* 70 (1984): 70.

A short note of May 30, 1875, wherein Hugo asks for four tickets to *Le Tour du monde*.

Marquet, Jean-François. "Victor Hugo et l'infiniment petit." *Poésie* 31 (1984): 59-77.

Examination of how Hugo develops Lucretius's *imbris uti guttae* into a mythology embracing the world, the poem, and all humanity.

Maxwell, Richard. "Mystery and Revelation in *Les Misérables*. *RR* 73 (1982): 314-30.

Mende, Fritz. "Prüfstein und Gegenbild: Heinrich Heines Auseinandersetzung mit Victor Hugo." *WB* 27 (Nov. 1981): 114-29.

Minkov, Vladimir. "180 godini ot rozhdenieto na Viktor Iugo: Pronikni dobre vuv vzora mi, za da te zapomnia!" *Literaturen Front* (Sofia, Bulgaria) 38, Feb. 18, 1982, p. 7.

Les Misérables. 80 aquarelles et dessins de Berenice Cleev. 4 vols. Paris: André Sauvet (Diffusion: Trinckvel), 1984. Fr. 2400.00 (cloth) and 3600.00 (leather).

Moreau, Pierre. *Les Contemplations de Victor Hugo ou le temps retrouvé.* (Archives des Lettres Modernes, 41.) Paris: Lettres Modernes, 1982. Pp. 64.

Moreau, Thérèse. "La Faim [sic] de Satin, un membre de trop." Pp. 135-47 in Jean-Pierre Giusto, ed., *Langages poétiques.* (Cahiers de l'U.E.R. Froissart, 6.) Université de Valenciennes "Lez Valenciennes," 1981. Pp. 159.

Mourélos, Georges. "Poésie et métamorphoses." *Revue des Sciences Morales et Politiques* 4 (1982): 589-605.

Nicolas, Anne. "Le prix d'une virgule." *Langages* (March 1983): 85-96.

"Origine lorraine des ancêtres de Victor Hugo." *Généalogie Lorraine* (Spring 1983): 73-74.

Plunkett, Patric de. "Dorman(n), le roman des Hugo." *Le Figaro Magazine*, Nov. 27, 1982, pp. 154-55.

Pouilliart, Raymond. "Jeux d'intertextualité chez Hugo: la 'Préface' des *Burgraves*." *LR* (Nov. 1981): 343-51.

Régent, Roger. "*Les Misérables*." *RDM*, Oct. 1982, pp. 737-40.

   On the film by Robert Hosein.

Rosa, Guy. "Entre Cromwell et sa préface: du grand homme au génie." *RHL* 81 (1981): 910-18.

Rosenfeld, Micheline. "Baudelaire lecteur de Victor Hugo, 1837-66." *Etudes Baudelairiennes* 9 (1981): 75-178.

Salino, Brigitte. "Quand la reine subit les derniers outrages." *NL*, March 18, 1982, pp. 55-56.

   On *Marie Tudor*.

Savant, Jean. *La Vie sentimentale de Victor Hugo: les amants de Juliette, l'histoire de ses dettes et les personnages de sa vie.* Paris: L'Auteur (23-25 rue Louis-le-Grand, 75002), 1983.

Schaeffer, Gérald, ed. *L'Homme qui rit,* 2 vols, (Garnier-Flammarion.) Paris: Flammarion, 1982. Pp. 448 and 416.

Seebacher, Jacques. "Beaumarchais et Victor Hugo." *RHL* 84 (1984): 785-94.

   According to the author, Hugo found *Le Mariage de Figaro* to represent the invention of non-bourgeois drama and of popular gaiety that rose above the vulgar.

Spitéri, Gérard. "*Marie Tudor* pour la première fois à la Comédie Française: la dame sur un trône avec des amants et un échafaud." *NL*, March 18, 1982, pp. 54-55.

Ubersfeld, Anne. "Le rire noir de Victor Hugo." *Comédie Française* 108 (April 1982): 5-9.

On *Marie Tudor*.

Vadé, Yves. "Persée, Gilliatt, Oedipe." *SFR* 6 (1982): 147-73.

On *Les Travailleurs de la mer*.

Vargas Llosa, Mario. "El último clásico: a propósito de *Los Miserables*." *Quimera* 30 (April 1983): 50-57.

Wiegand, Horst Jürgen. *Victor Hugo und der Rhein: Le Rhin (1842-45), Les Burgraves (1843)*. (Abhandlungen zur Kunst-, Musik- und Literaturwissenschaft, 330.) Bonn: Bouvier, 1982.

Wilhelm, Frank. "Victor Hugo à/et Echternach." *Hémecht* 3 (1983): 411-58.

Wren, Keith. *Hugo: Hernani and Ruy Blas*. (Critical Guides to French Texts, 14.) London: Grant and Cutler, 1983. Pp. 91. £2.00.

Rev. by James J. Supple in *MLR* 79 (1984): 944; briefly in *FMLS* 20 (1984): 384.

See also André, Coquillat, Grossir, Jean-Nesmy, Krakovitch, Mazzara, Pradier, Real, Wolfszettel ("French 1. General"); Scaiola ("Borel"); Nola ("Chênedollé"); "Le drame en prose" ("Gautier"); Laserra ("Michelet"); Biermann ("Sand"); Espagne (German 3. Heine").

Reviews of books previously listed:

ALBOUY, Pierre, ed., *Odes et Ballades* (see *RMB* for 1981, p. 205), rev. by W.J.S. Kirton in *FS* 38 (1984): 74; GAUDON, Jean, ed., *Les Chansons des rues et des bois* (see *RMB* for 1983, p. 218), rev. by James S. Patty in *NCFS* 12,iv; 13,i (1984): 226-28.

INGRES

See Bryson ("General 3. Criticism").

JANIN

Kaiser, Gerhard R. "Baudelaire pro Heine contra Janin. Text, Kommentar, Analyse." *Heine-Jahrbuch* 22 (1983): 135-78.

Landrin, Jacques. "Jules Janin, témoin du théâtre romantique." *CAIEF* 35 (1983): 155-68.

> Landrin sees in Janin an evolution toward a comprehension of the orginality of Hugo's theater, and underscores the elements of fantasy and lyricism in his make-up (in which Classicism retained a certain hold).

See also Bolster, Pradier ("French 1. General"); Landrin ("Hugo").

JASMIN

Le Roy Ladurie, Emmanuel. *La Sorcière de Jasmin.* (L'Univers historique.) Paris: Les Editions du Seuil, 1983. Pp. 282. Fr. 79.00.

> Rev. by Peter Burke in *NYRB*, Feb. 28, 1985, pp. 33-34.
> Jasmin's poem *Françouneto* (1851) is reprinted in Occitan and in the poet's French translation. Le Roy Ladurie provides two essays on the historical background and on the nineteenth-century interest in witchcraft.

JOUBERT

Lettres à Pauline de Beaumont et Louise Angélique de Vintimille. Préface de Roger Judrin. Quimper: Calligrammes, 1984. Pp. 126. Fr. 79.00.

> Rev. by Serge Koster in *Le Monde*, March 2, 1984, p. 20.
> The letters are given without any annotation or scholarly apparatus. Judrin draws a pretty conclusion to his preface: "Mais ce qui nous rend différemment précieuse la correspondance qu'il entretint avec les deux femmes qu'il aima le mieux, c'est le subtile entrelacement, dans une prose tendre et sévère, de la rose et de l'épine. On ne fut jamais ni plus joli, ni moins fade. Ainsi sont drapées de nu, dans les fontaines innocentes, les nymphes de Jean Goujon."

Reviews of book previously listed:

TESSONNEAU, Rémy, ed., *Essais* (see *RMB* for 1983, p. 223), rev. by Jean Gaulmier in *Romantisme* 44 (1984): 120-21; by Marcel Lobet in *Revue Générale*, Nov. 1983, pp. 81-83.

JOUFFROY

See Iknayan ("French 1. General").

LACORDAIRE

Cabanis, José, ed. *Conférences de Toulouse.* (Les Introuvables.) Plan-de-la-Tour: Editions d'Aujourd'hui, 1984. Pp. 197. Fr. 74.00.

Reproduces the text of the 1911 edition.

Metz, J. de, o.p. "La fondation des dominicains enseignants par le Père Lacordaire." *Documents pour Servir à l'Histoire de l'Ordre de Saint Dominique* 18 (1983): A.I-A.16.

See also Brocard ("Chateaubriand").

Review of book previously listed:

CABANIS, José, *Lacordaire et quelques autres* (see *RMB* for 1982, p. 223), rev. by Louis Le Guillou in *RHL* 84 (1984): 809-11.

LA HARPE

Biaudet, Jean-Charles, and Marie-Claude Jequier, eds. *Correspondance de Frédéric-César de La Harpe sous la République Helvétique.* T. I.: *Le révolutionnaire, 16 mai 1796-4 mars 1798.* Neuchâtel: La Baconnière, 1982. Pp. 584. Sw.Fr. 66.00.

Rev. by Patrice Higonnet in *TLS*, Dec. 7, 1984, p. 1424. La Harpe's correspondence with the Russian imperial family, edited by Biaudet, appeared in 1979-80 and was reviewed in *TLS*, Sept. 19, 1980.

LAMARTINE

Ciocârlie, Livius. "Les masques du désir." *CREL* (1982,i):
48-56.

Domange, Michel. *Le Journal de Madame de Lamartine, mère
d'Alphonse de Lamartine (1801-1829)*. (Bibliothèque Introuvable, 13.) Paris: Minard (Lettres Modernes), 1983.
Pp. xxxii+380. Fr. 250.00.

  Brief rev. in *FMLS* 20 (1984): 376.

Godfrey, Sima. "Foules Rush In ... Lamartine, Baudelaire
and the Crowd." *RomN* 24 (1983-84): 33-42.

  Explores intertextual relationships of theme, dialectical
structure, and persona to show how the conditions of modern
urban life transform Lamartine's lonely, romantic dream of
love--epitomized in "L'Isolement"--into the more cynical
vision of love evoked in Baudelaire's "A une passante."

Jacques, Jean-Pierre, ed. *Histoire des Girondins*. (Les
Mémorables.) 2 vols. Paris: Plon, 1984. Pp. 896 and
976. Fr. 160.00 each.

  Rev. by André Bourin in *RDM*, June 1984, pp. 672-76.

Letessier, Fernand. "Lamartine et sa nièce Cécile de Cessiat:
documents inédits." *BAGB* (1982): 77-90.

Letessier, Fernand. "Marianne de Lamartine, née Birch, et sa
famille anglaise." *Annales de l'Académie de Mâcon* (1982):
45-63.

Magnien, Emile. *Lamartine: Gentilhomme de Bourgogne*. Saint-
Seine-l'Abbaye: Editions Saint-Seine-l'Abbaye, 1984. Pp.
125. Fr. 96.00.

See also André, Delon, Grossir, Mazzara, Real, Stenzel ("French
1. General").

Reviews of books previously listed:

  BIRKETT, Mary Ellen, *Lamartine and the Poetics of Landscape*
  (see *RMB* for 1982, p. 224), rev. by Peter Byrne in *SFr* 28
  (1984): 178; by J.C. Ireson in *MLR* 79 (1984): 459-60;
  by Joachim Schulze in *RF* 96 (1984): 189-91; FORTESCUE,
  William, *Alphonse de Lamartine: A Political Biography* (see
  RMB for 1983, p. 224), rev. by P.A. Ouston in *MLR* 79 (1984):
  710-11.

LAMENNAIS

Berenice 6 (Nov. 1982).   Special Issue on Lamennais.

   Contents: Peter Byrne, "Ecriture et anathème" (5-15);
Marie-Anne Rubat du Mérac, "Un premier 'Lamennais écrivain,'
celui de Yves Le Hir" (16-25) and "Lingua, stile e poesia
nell'*Esquisse d'une philosophie*" (26-40); Frank Paul Bowman,
"Surcharge et contradictions: l'introduction à l'*Essai sur
l'indifférence en matière de religion*" (41-56); Fernand Rude,
"Lamennais pamphlétaire" (57-75); Annarosa Poli, "*Le Lépreux
de la cité d'Aoste* de X. de Maistre nella versione di Olympe
Cottu, discepola di Lamennais" (76-105); Peter Byrne,
"Grégoire-homme et 'sor Padre Santo': deux portraits de
Mauro Capellari" (106-28); Muzio Mazzocchi Alemanni, "Gregorio
XVI fra storia e poesia" (129-37); Louis Le Guillou, "Bibli-
ographie mennaisienne" (138-45).

Bordet, Gaston.   "Emmanuel d'Alzon et la crise mennaisienne."
   Pp. 37-82 in René Remond and Emile Poulat, eds., *Emmanuel
   d'Alzon dans la société et l'Eglise du XIXe siècle*.   Paris:
   Editions du Centurion, 1982.   Pp. 336.   Fr. 130.00.

Foutel, Joseph.   "Un grand homme de chez nous.   Felicité de
   Lamennais (1782-1854)."   *Le Pays de Dinan* 2 (1982):   63-77.

Kenec'hdu, Tanguy.   "Les 200 bougies de 'Féli':   Mennaisiades
   1982."   *Contrepoint* 42-43 (1983):   123-29.

Le Guillou, Louis.   "Lamennais, la Pologne et les Polonais."
   *Annales de la Société d'Histoire et d'Archéologie de l'Arron-
   dissement de Saint-Malo* (1982 [1983]), pp. 243-53.

Petout, Pierre.   "L'hôtel natal de Lamennais."   *Annales de la
   Société et la Société d'Histoire et d'Archéologie de
   l'Arrondissement de Saint-Malo* (1982 [1983]), pp. 303-09.

Souques, Geneviève.   "Lamennais vu par Maurice de Guérin."
   AG 146 (1984):   25-44.

   An article by the same author and bearing the same title
was published in the same volume (*Annales*) as the two preceding items (pp. 267-80).

Reviews of books previously listed:

CAHIERS MENNAISIENS 14-15 (see *RMB* for 1982, p. 225), rev.
by Jean-René Derré in *RHL* 84 (1984):   809;   LE GUILLOU, M.J.,
and Louis Le Guillou, eds., *La Condamnation de Lamennais*

(see *RMB* for 1982, p. 226), rev. by Peter Byrne in *SFr* 27
(1983):   366; by Edward T. Gargan in *CHR* 70 (1984):   487-88;
by Jean Gaulmier in *RHL* 84 (1984):   807-09; by John W. Pad-
berg, S.J., in *Church History* 53 (1984):   263-64.

LAPRADE

Latta, Claude, et al.   "Centenaire de la mort de Victor de
   Laprade, 1883-1983." *Village de Forez* 13 (Jan. 1983):   3-28.

LEROUX

Rude, Fernand. "Le socialisme de Pierre Leroux." *Quaderno
   Filosofico* 6 (1982):   35-52.

   See résumé by Peter Byrne in *SFr* 28 (1984):   168.

See also Poulat ("French 1. General").

Reviews of book previously listed:

   VIARD, Jacques, *Pierre Leroux et les socialistes européens*
   (see *RMB* for 1983, p. 229), rev. by Jean Bastaire in *L'Amitié
   Charles Péguy* 7 (1984):   63-64; by Michèle Bertrand in *ASSR*
   56,ii (1983):   318-19; by Peter Byrne in *SFr* 27 (1983):   575-
   76.

LOAISEL DE TRÉOGATE

Review of book previously listed:

   BOWLING, Townsend Whelen, *The Life, Works, and Literary
   Career of Loaisel de Tréogate* (see *RMB* for 1981, p. 213),
   rev. by Patrick Coleman in *FR* 57 (1983-84):   879.

MAINE DE BIRAN

Isnard, Marcel. "Grandeur et servitude du moi: Maine de
   Biran." Pp. 315-21 in Robert Ellrodt, ed., *Genèse de la
   conscience moderne. Etudes sur le développement de la con-
   science de soi dans les littératures du monde occidental.*
   (Publications de la Sorbonne, "Littératures II," 14.) Paris:
   Presses universitaires de France, 1983. Pp. 424. Fr. 320.00.

Moore, F.C.T., ed. *OEuvres complètes de Maine de Biran.*
T. VI: *Rapports du physique et du moral de l'homme.* Paris:
Vrin, 1984. Pp. 226. Fr. 120.00.

MAISTRE, J. de

Fuchs, Michel. "Edmund Burke et Joseph de Maistre." *RUO* 54
(1984): 49-58.

Maistre's discovery of Burke and the story of their
relationship are told in some detail. The general thrust of
this study is concentrated in the item below by the same
author, although, in the present article, he manages to
spell out certain points more clearly (Maistre's unaware-
ness of economic realities, for instance).

Fuchs, Michel. "Edmund Burke vu par Joseph de Maistre."
SVEC 216 (1983): 14-15.

On the "décalage entre les deux pourfendeurs de la
Révolution" and the reasons for it (Burke lived in a post-
revolutionary society, whereas Maistre sought the regenera-
tion of the past through expiation of sins).

Guyon, Edouard-Félix. "Joseph de Maistre, diplomate sarde,
témoin et juge de son temps (1792-1817)." *Revue d'Histoire
Diplomatique* 97 (1983): 75-107.

Largely based on Maistre's official dispatches. They
reveal that, although he was the author of the mystical
and prophetic *Soirées de Saint-Pétersbourg*, he also possessed
"l'esprit d'observation" and "la faculté de juger avec
sang-froid et lucidité les événements et les hommes de son
temps."

OEuvres complètes. 14 vols. (in 7 tomes). Hildesheim:
Georg Olms, 1983. DM 1372.00.

Reprint of the edition of Lyon, 1884-86.

Revue des Etudes Maistriennes 8 (1982-83). Special Issue
entitled "Joseph de Maistre et la pensée catholique de son
temps, sous la direction de Louis Trenard."

Contents: Jacques Vier, "Apologétique des Lumières et
apologétique maistrienne" (9-28); Louis Trenard, "Joseph
de Maistre et ses amis lyonnais" (29-58); Mgr Bernard
Jacqueline, "Le Saint-Siège et la publication de *Du Pape*
d'après les archives du Vatican, 1818-1820" (59-82); Louis

Le Guillou, "Joseph de Maistre et Lamennais en 1820-21" [on
five unpublished letters of Lamennais] (83-100); Dom Louis
Soltner, o.s.b., "Joseph de Maistre et Dom Guéranger. *Du
Pape à* la *Monarchie pontificale*" (101-16); Richard Lebrun,
"Joseph de Maistre et la loi naturelle" [with an unpublished
text] (117-44).

Review of book previously listed:

DARCEL, Jean-Louis, ed., *Considérations sur la France* (see
RMB for 1982, p. 230), rev. by Claude Langlois in *ASSR* 55,ii
(1983): 254-55.

MAISTRE, X. de

Berthier, Alfred. *Xavier de Maistre. Etude biographique et
littéraire.* Geneva: Slatkine, 1984. Pp. 408. Sw.Fr. 100.00.

Lovie, Jacques, et al. *Nouvelles.* (Centre d'Etudes franco-
italien, Universités de Turin et de Savoie. Bibliothèque
Franco-Simone, 11.) Geneva: Slatkine, 1984. Pp. 262.
Sw.Fr. 40.00.

OEuvres complètes. Préface de Jules Claretie. (Les Introuvables.) Plan-de-la-Tour: Editions d'Aujourd'hui, 1984.
Pp. 326. Fr. 130.00.

   Reprint of the nineteenth-century edition.

*Voyage autour de ma chambre, 1794. Le Lépreux de la cité
d'Aoste.* Préface de Joseph de Maistre. (Romantique, 9.)
Paris: José Corti, 1984. Pp. 154. Fr. 75.00.

   The text of the 1839 edition.

MERCIER

Béclard, Léon. *Sébastien Mercier. Sa Vie, son oeuvre, son
temps. D'après des documents inédits avec un portrait en
héliogravure.* Hildesheim: Georg Olms, 1982. Pp. 8+810.
DM 138.00.

   Reprint of the edition of Paris, 1903.

Wilkie, Everett C., Jr. "Mercier's *L'An 2440*: Its Publishing
History During the Author's Lifetime. Part I." *HLB* 32
(1984): 5-35.

Topics treated are: the date of the first edition (here
pretty well proved to have come out in 1771, not in 1770
as Mercier said), Mercier's revisions, the novel's fame and
influence, its translations into foreign languages, and the
attribution to Mercier--and others. A list of libraries
holding copies is appended. (To be continued.)

MÉRIMÉE

Les Ames du purgatoire. (G.F., 263.) Paris: Garnier-Flammarion, 1983. Pp. 192. Fr. 11.50.

Also contains "Carmen."

Amprimoz, Alexandre. "*L'Abbé Aubain*: sémantique d'un récit."
RomN 24 (1983-84): 30-32.

On the symbolism of the bouquet of faded flowers.

Bertrand, Denis. "Les migrations de Carmen." *Le Français dans
le Monde* 18 (Nov.-Dec. 1983): 103-08.

Byers, Jane H. "The *Théâtre de Clara Gazul* and the Spanish
Comedia: A Case of Impudent Imitation." *Hispanófila* 81
(May 1984): 16-33.

Carmen. Paris: Encre, 1984. Pp. 206. Fr. 69.00.

Clancier, Anne, and Antonia Fonyi. "L'ours et la colombe.
Histoire d'un fantasme dans la correspondance et dans
l'oeuvre de Mérimée." Pp. 306-18 in Jean-Louis Bonnat and
Mireille Bossis, eds., *Ecrire, publier, lire les correspon-
dances (problématique et économie d'un "genre littéraire")*
Actes du colloque international: "Les Correspondances."
Nantes les 4, 5, 6, 7 octobre 1982. Université de Nantes,
1982. Pp. 474. Fr. 120.00.

By confronting remarks in Mérimée's correspondence about
the composition of "Lokis" with elements of the story as
published, the authors infer that the former represent
Mérimée's attempt to hide or repress certain fantasms which
come to the surface in the story itself.

Doran, Eva Maria Ceclia. "Stratégies de discours et de silence
dans le 'Vase étrusque.'" *MLS* 14 (1984): 56-64.

The spatial discontinuities of the story are linked to a
qualitative distinction: public versus private space.

Haller, Anne. "Mérimée et le mythe." *Dalhousie French Studies*
4 (Oct. 1982): 13-40.

H.B. Montréal: Dérives; Paris: Selin, 1983. Pp. 52. Fr.
34.00.

Rasson, Luc. "L'impossible disjonction: dit et non-dit dans
'Lokis' de Prosper Mérimée." *NCFS* 12,iv; 13,i (1984): 81-
94.

"Tamango," "Mateo Falcone" et autres nouvelles. (G.F., 392.)
Paris: Flammarion, 1983.

Ucherkowa, Urszula. "La projection du lecteur dans 'La
Vénus d'Ille' et 'Lokis' de Mérimée." Pp. 35-42 in *Le Lecteur et la lecture dans l'oeuvre.* Clermont-Ferrand: Faculté
des Lettres et Sciences humaines de l'Université de Clermont-
Ferrand, II, 1982. Pp. 206.

   Brief remarks on "le pacte de véracité" between the narrator
and the implied or virtual reader.

See also Grossir ("French 1. General").

Reviews of books previously listed:

   AUTIN, Jean, *Prosper Mérimée: écrivain, archéologue, homme
politique* (see *RMB* for 1983, p. 232), rev. by P. Byrne in
SFr 27 (1983): 377; by B. Cooper in *NCFS* 12,iv; 13,i (1984):
209-10; CHABOT, Jacques, *L'Autre moi. Fantasmes et fantastique
dans les "Nouvelles" de Mérimée* (see *RMB* for 1983, p. 232),
rev. by P.W.M. Cogman in *FS* 38 (1984): 471-72; FREUSTIE,
Jean, *Prosper Mérimée* (see *RMB* for 1982, p. 232), rev. by
B. Cooper in *NCFS* 12 (1983-84): 255-56.

MICHELET

Bucur, Marin. *Jules Michelet și revoluționarii românu in
documente și scrisori de epoca (1846-1874).* Cluj-Napoca:
Edituri Dacia, 1982.

Colesanti, Massimo. "Michelet o ipostasi della storia." Pp.
383-97 in Giorgetto Giorgi et al., eds., *Studi di cultura
francese ed europeo in onore di Lorenza Maranini.* Fasano:
Schena, 1983. Pp. 540. L. 30,000.00.

   See résumé by Pier Antonio Borgheggiani in *SFr* 27 (1983):
575.

Cordié, Carlo. "Michelet." *CeS* 88 (1983): 47-55.

Fauquet, Eric. "J. Michelet et l'histoire de l'architecture républicaine." *GBA* 1381 (1984): 71-79.

Grassin, Jean, ed. *La France. Le Peuple, par Jules Michelet.* (L'Encyclopédie poétique, 16.) Carnac: Jean Grassin, 1984. Pp. 384. Fr. 240.00.

Kaplan, Edward K., trans. and ed. *Mother Death: The Journal of Jules Michelete, 1815-1850.* University of Massachusetts Press, 1984. Pp. 192. $20.00.

Rev. by Eugen Weber in *TLS*, Sept. 28, 2984, p. 1072.
Extracts from the *Journal* for the years 1815-1850, i.e., from the death of Michelet's mother until the death of his infant son, selected to form a coherent story, that of the relationship between the man and the historian and accompanied by biographical and analytical commentaries using a psycho-analytical approach. In an epilogue, the chapter from *La Montagne* relating the historian's visit to the therapeutic mud baths at Acqui is given as a specimen of his literary prose. "Michelet's meticulous self-examinations allow readers to penetrate the turbulence beneath the optimistic philosophy of history," as the publisher's blurb explains.

Laserra, Annamaria. "Il polipo e la piovra (nell'evangelo romantico di Michelet, Verne, Hugo, Lautréamont)." *Micro-megas* 9,i-ii (1982): 49-76.

On the imagery and symbolism of the polyp and the octopus. See the résumé by Carlo Cordié in *SFr* 28 (1984): 378.

Leuilliot, Bernard. "Michelet 'en travail.' Genèse et alentours de l'*Histoire du XIX*^e *siècle*." *TLL* 19,ii (1981): 83-119.

See the résumé by Bernard Gallina in *SFr* 27 (1983): 369.

See also Aron, Bann ("French 1. General").

Reviews of books previously listed:

HAAC, Oscar, *Jules Michelet* (see *RMB* for 1982, pp. 233-34), rev. by Ceri Crossley in *MLR* 79 (1984): 196-97; MOREAU, Thérèse, *Le Sang de l'histoire* (see *RMB* for 1982, p. 234), rev. by Bernadette Chovelon in *SFr* 27 (1983): 575.

MILLEVOYE

Bulletin de la Société d'Emulation historique et littéraire d'Abbeville, T. XXV: *Travaux de 1982*. Special Issue on Millevoye.

Contents: Paul Rouët, "La famille du poète Millevoye" (87-90); Jean Macqueron, "Charles Hubert Millevoye, abbevillois et poète (texte de l'audiovisuel réalisé par Jean Macqueron) (91-100); Micheline Agache Lecat, "A propos d'une lettre de Millevoye à Mlle Duchesnois [17 août 1804]" (101-08); Louise Bercez, "Millevoye, précurseur du romantisme" (109-17); Philippe Camus, "Trois poèmes inédits de Millevoye" (119-23); Jean Lefebvre, "Contribution à l'étude de Millevoye: la langue de l'oeuvre poetique" (125-42).

MONTALEMBERT

See Palanque ("French 1. General").

MUSSET

Bishop, Lloyd. "Musset's First Sonnet: A Semiotic Analysis." *RR* 74 (1983): 455-60.

On "Que j'aime le premier frisson d'hiver! ..." (*Premières Poésies*).

Bishop, Lloyd. "Musset's 'Souvenir' and the Greater Romantic Lyric." *NCFS* 12,iv; 13,i (1984): 119-30.

"Souvenir" coincides perfectly with the "greater Romantic lyric," characterized by M.W. Abrams in "Structure and Style in the Greater Romantic Lyric," pp. 527-28 in *From Sensibility to Romanticism: Essays Presented to Frederick A. Pottle*, ed. Frederick W. Hilles and Harold Bloom (Oxford University Press, 1965).

Bourcier, Richard J. "Alfred de Musset: Poetry and Music." *The American Benedictine Review* 35 (1984): 17-24.

Evidence of Musset's strong interest in music.

Coulet, H[enri]. "Le *bateau* de Musset et l'*ancre* de Segalen." Pp. 171-75 in Louis Hay and Péter Nagy, eds., *Avant-texte, texte, après-texte*. Paris: Editions du CNRS; Budapest: Akadémiai Kiadó, 1982. Pp. 217.

Concerns less the writers than the general problems of *textologie*, or textual studies. Musset and Segalen serve as major examples of authors whose texts create problems for the production of critical editions. A fascinating paper, particularly useful as a cautionary document for inattentive editors and readers. (A.B.S.)

Erman, Michel. "Le récit d'Hermia: mise en abyme dans le théâtre de Musset." *Lendemains* 31-32 (1983): 120-24.

Ifri, Pascal. "Les techniques narratives dans l'autobiographie et le roman autobiographique: l'exemple de Stendhal et de Musset." *Neophil* 68 (1984): 353-64.

Focuses on point of view and (briefly) on structure to suggest that narrative techniques inevitably differ between autobiography and the autobiographical novel. Ifri thus attempts to cast doubt on the view that there are no distinctions between the two genres. He sidesteps, however, the question posed by Philippe Lejeune, viz., whether the novel *can* fully imitate autobiography. (A.B.S.)

Lehtonen, Maija. *Essai sur "La Confession d'un enfant du siècle."* (Suomalaisen Tiedeakatemian Toimituksia/Annales Academiae Scientiarum Fennicae, Ser. B, Tome 218.) Helsinki: Suomalainen Tiedeakatemia, 1982. Pp. 88.

Narratological analysis of the novel, plus study of major themes: the experience of time, the problem of identity, and man in society and in the world.

Machabéïs, Jacqueline. "Propositions sur la structure de *Lorenzaccio.*" *LR* 38 (1984): 99-116.

The failure of the various protagonists to effect a meaningful political change in Florence is reflected in Musset's arrangement of the elements comprising the different acts.

Maclean, Marie. "Cellini and Musset: The 'Reverse of the Medal' in *RLMC* 37 (1984): 41-52.

The "reversal of the medal" refers to Cellini's report of an episode in which Lorenzo promised to provide the goldsmith with a *revers* for a medallion honoring Duke Alexander. He was, of course, being ironic: the *revers* would be Alexander's murder. Musset takes his cue from Cellini in the number of doublings, repetitions, inversions, and reversals with which he structures *Lorenzaccio*.

See also Meregalli ("General 3. Criticism"); Amossy and Rosen, Coquillat, Mazzara ("French 1. General"); Tavernier ("Sand").

Review of book previously listed:

SIEGEL, Patricia Joan, comp., *Alfred de Musset: A Reference Guide* (see *RMB* for 1982, pp. 236-37), rev. by D.G. Charlton in *FS* 37 (1983): 350-51.

NERVAL, GERARD de

Béarez Caravaggi, Bernadette. "Signification de la poly-valence nervalienne." *SFr* 27 (1983): 280-86.

Sees Nerval's genius as being able to "allier la simplicité la plus pure à la densité la plus incandescente."

Blackman, Maurice. "Charles Dickens et *Les Nuits d'Octobre*: clés pour le réalisme nervalien." *AJFS* 19 (1982): 32-40.

Cites Nerval's reference to "La Clef de la rue," an article in the *Revue Britannique* translated from Charles Dickens, and compares passages in it with passages from *Les Nuits d'Octobre* and *Promenades et Souvenirs* and finds Nerval characteristically giving a *souvenir de lecture* as a *souvenir réel* and turning from a "réalisme trop absolu" to fuse dream and reality in *Aurélia*.

Bony, Jacques. *Le Dossier des "Faux Saulniers."* (Etudes Nervaliennes et Romantiques, VII.) Presses universitaires de Namur, 1984. Pp. 113.

Brings together reprints, and annotates all the documents on the abbé comte de Bucquoy consulted by Nerval as prepara-tion for *Les Faux Saulniers*, except for the *Evénement des plus rares ou Histoire du Sr. abbé comte de Bucquoy*, which will form a separate publication. The documents reprinted and amply commented upon here are: (1) *Pièces diverses de police*; (2) *L'Histoire d'Angélique de Longueval* (*Un enlève-ment en 1632*); (3) *Les Illuminés* (an article published in the *Revue Britannique*, Feb. 1839, which Bony thinks may be, not a translation from English, but an original work of Philarète Chasles); (4) two articles on the invention of printing and the Vente Motteley; (5) extracts from Constantin de Renneville's *L'Inquisition française* (1724); (6) the article on Bucquoy from Michaud's *Biographie universelle* (by Claude-Marie Pillet). (It was for reasons of space that these documents were not included in the recent Pléiade re-edition of Nerval's works.)

Bony, Jacques. "Encore *Le Monde dramatique*: un exemplaire
exceptionnel [Bibliothèque de l'Arsenal]." *BduB* 1983-IV:
pp. 433-47.

Buenzod, Jacques. "Nerval et le langage des oiseaux." *Romantisme* 45 (1984):   43-56.

   Notes that Nerval's "bestiary," which attracted the late
Léon Cellier, has still not been compiled. Sees the problem
of "le langage des oiseaux" as "d'autant plus important
qu'il débouche sur une aporie qui troubla Nerval tout au
long de son existence,--la relation profonde du sens et des
signes, la communication." The theme of the bird is linked
for Nerval with that of Time and, subsequently, death; and
the language of birds is related to "l'Unicité de la Parole
perdue."

Cahiers Gérard de Nerval 5 (1982):   "Nerval et les arts plas-
tiques."

   Rev. by Monique Streiff Moretti in *SFr* 27 (1983):   578.
   Contents: Jean Richer, "La recherche des formes signifi-
antes" (3-6); "[Gravures et graveurs (notes de Nerval)]"
with extensive notes by Jean Richer (8-16); Henry Bouillier,
"Nerval et la peinture orientaliste" (17-22); Monique Streiff
Moretti, "Portraits dans une bibliothèque: Nerval, Töpffer
et quelques autres" (23-36); Brian Juden, "Le Panthéon, ou
Le rêve de l'humanité: Paul Chenavard et Gérard de Nerval"
(37-47); Olivier Encrenaz, "L'énigme d'une lettre de Gérard
de Nerval à Franz Liszt. Les *Trois Mages* d'Ary Scheffer"
(48-63); Maria Luisa Belleli, "A propos de la *Judith* du
Musée de Naples: Nerval et les femmes blondes" (64-68);
Jean Richer, "Laurent *Le Penseur* et Gérard Laurent-Labrunie"
(69).
   There are many illustrations of unusual interest throughout
the issue, among them a beautiful miniature in color of
Jenny Colon by Jules Vernet (1823). One page (78) describes
the "Exposition Gérard de Nerval" (Dec. 18, 1981, to March
21, 1982) at the Maison de Balzac.

Cahiers Gérard de Nerval 6 (1983):   "Gérard de Nerval et les
genres littéraires: un dossier 'Pandora.'"

   Contents: Henri Bonnet, "Idyllique *Sylvie* ou 'L'astre
trompeur d'Aldébaran'" (2-7) and "A propos de la relation
de voyage: la 'grécité' de Nerval" (8-10); Jacques Huré,
"Nerval et le récit oriental" (11-18); Pierre-André Touttain,
"La nuit transfigurée: aspects du fantastique nervalien"
(19-23); Alice Planche, "Nerval ou la nostalgie des rythmes

anciens" (24-33); Roger Pierrot, "Nerval à la Bibliothèque
nationale" (34-39); Jean Richer, "En relisant la 'Généalogie
fantastique'" (40-41); Jean Senelier, "Une recherche: Nerval
à Crépy-en-Valois" (42-43); Joseph Suchy, "Une notation
d'Alexandre Herzen sur Gérard de Nerval" (44-45); "Lettre
de Nerval (30 mai, 1854) à Busquet" (46-48); Eric Buffetaud,
"*Pandora*, 'livre infaisable' (I-XXVIII)" (49-50) with many
illustrations of great interest; and Jean Senelier, "Bibliographie" (51-52). There are numerous fine illustrations
scattered through the whole issue, including a page for "La
mer d'airain et ses analogues."

Chambers, Ross. "Narrative as Oppositional Practice: Nerval's
  Aurélia.   *SFR* 8 (1984): 53-73.

  Using Michel de Certeau's definition of oppositional
practices as "defenses against alienation," author examines
Aurélia and concludes that, although Gérard is not the
narrator, writing the story "must have brought its alienated
author some oppositional success and satisfaction." His
suicide showed how fragile this was; but *Aurélia* stands as
an influence in favor of all alienated individuals and of
"the *continuity* of its oppositional practice."

Dunn, Susan. "Nerval: Transgression and the Amendement
  Riancey." *NCFS* 12 (1983-84): 86-95.

  On Nerval's recurrent humorous concern with the "amendement
Riancey," enacted in July 1851, which prohibited newspapers
from printing *romans-feuilletons*, but without a legal
definition of the genre. Underneath the humor there is a
serious and pervasive sense of guilt in Nerval about his
writing, for "the artist--creator, writer, or inventor--has
inherited the guilt of Cain ... the condemned artist, forever
outcast, forever guilty."

Guillaume, Jean, s.j. "Éléments scripuaires chez Nerval."
  EC1 52 (1984): 342-45.

  Suggested identification of a copy of the *Nouveau Testament*
mentioned in a manuscript found on Gérard's body at the time
of his suicide (Jan. 26, 1855) as the *édition stéréotype*
translated from the Vulgate by Le Maistre de Sacy and printed
by F. Didot in 1816.

Guillaume, Jean, and Claude Pichois. *Gérard de Nerval.*
  Chronologie de sa vie et son oeuvre, août 1850-juin 1852.
  (Études Nervaliennes et Romantiques, VI.) Presses universi-
  taires de Namur, 1984. Pp. 47.

Guillaume, Jean, and Claude Pichois, ed. *OEuvres complètes*,
T. II. (Bibliothèque de la Pléiade.) Paris: Gallimard,
1984. Pp. 1,904. Fr. 330.00.

A much enlarged and improved edition of the earlier version
by Albert Béguin and Jean Richer. The following texts by
Nerval are included: *Les Faux Saulniers*, *Voyage en Orient*,
Les Illuminés, and Nerval's journalism and letters for the
period Aug. 1850-June 1852. (A.G.E.)

Jouve, Pierre-Jean. *Folie et génie*. Fontfroide-le-Haut: Fata
Morgana (Distributeur: Distique), 1984. Pp. 70. Fr. 45.00.

Portraits of Tasso, Nerval, and Hölderlin: three *causeries*
of Jouve's radio broadcast.

Lebreton, Georges. *Nerval poète alchimique. La clef des
Chimères: le Dictionnaire mytho-hermétique de Dom Pernety*
Nouv. éd. Port-Laval: Curandera (Dedalus) (Distributeur:
Alternative Diffusion), 1982. Pp. 160. Fr. 65.00.

See description in *BCLF* 463 (1984): No. 127111 (p. 909).

Le Cocq, A. "Lecture d'*Aurélia* de Gérard de Nerval." *Cahiers.
Université d'Angers, UER des Lettres et des Sciences Humaines*
(Angers) 8 (1982): 27-41.

Lendemains 33 (1984): 5-63. "Gérard de Nerval."

Comprises an introduction by the editor, Bernard Dieterle
(5-6), with a strange little caricature of Nerval by Nadar,
and the following eight notes and articles: Claude Pichois,
"Aspects de la poétique nervalienne" (7-9); Jean Guillaume,
"Sur le sens des 'Chimères'" (10); Norbert Miller, "Sylvain
und ich. Anmerkungen zu Nervals 'Les faux saulniers'" (11-
19); Daniel Sangsue, "Proposition pour une lecture d' 'Angélique'" (20-31); Christoph Kunz, "Nervals poetische Identität"
(32-38); Jacques Geninasca, "Le plein, le vide et le tout.
Analyse des deux premiers alinéas de 'Sylvie'" (39-48);
Winfried Engler, "Bretons Nerval 1924" (49-54); and Bernard
Dieterle, "Le Watteau de Gérard de Nerval. A propos de
'Sylvie'" (55-63).

Malandain-Chamarat, Gabrielle. "Identité, voyage et écriture
dans l'oeuvre en prose de Gérard de Nerval." *IL* 36 (1984):
155-58.

Rauhut, Franz. "Nervals 'Antéros'--ein heidnischer Gott
rebelliert gegen Jehova." *Romanistische Zeitschrift für
Literaturgeschichte/Cahiers d'Histoire des Littératures Romanes*
7 (1983): 392-405.

Rosenfeld, Michel. "'De Paris à Pékin' ou 'La Nuit blanche'?:
une lettre inédite de Gérard de Nerval à Paul Bocage." *RHL*
84 (1984): 570-76.

Attempts to resolve some of the confusion concerning "la
pièce perdue" *Paris à Pékin*, supposedly written in collaboration by Paul Bocage, Joseph Méry, and Gérard de Nerval.

Thompson, Peter S. "*Sylvie*: The Method of Myth." *NCFS* 12
(1983-84): 96-104.

Suggests that "Nerval's story is not merely a myth-like
creation, but a story about such creative attempts" and
shows how Nerval employs fantasy and abstraction to provide
a timeless element for *Sylvie*--"colors in the mist, luminous
memories of Le Valois."

Versus. *Quaderni di Studi Semiotici* (Milan) 31-32 (1982).

Contains the following studies on *Sylvie*: D. Barbieri,
"Étapes de topicalisation et effet de brouillard" (97-116);
B. Cottafavi, "Micro-procès temporels dans le premier chapitre de *Sylvie*" (63-96); I. Pezzini, "Paradoxes du désir,
logique du récit" (35-61); M.P. Pozzato, "Le brouillard et
le reste" (117-39); P. Violi, "Du côté du lecteur" (3-33).

See also "*Des Allemagnes*," Jean-Nesmy, Real ("French 1. General");
Bulletin de la Société Théophile Gautier 5 ("Gautier").

Reviews of books previously listed:

DUNN, Susan, *Nerval et le roman historique* (see *RMB* for 1981,
p. 221), rev. by Bettina L. Knapp in *Symposium* 37 (1983):
324-25; SCHÄRER, Kurt, *Pour une poétique des "Chimères" de
Nerval* (see *RMB* for 1982, p. 242), rev. by Robert T. Denommé
in *FR* 58 (1984-85): 130; SENELIER, Jean, *Bibliographie
nervalienne 1968-1980 et Compléments antérieurs* (see *RMB* for
1982, p. 242), rev. by Carlo Cordié in *SFr* 27 (1983): 373-
74.

NISARD

See Bolster ("French 1. General").

NODIER

Castex, Pierre-Georges. "Le génie et l'asile." Pp. 35-48 in
Jean-Luc Marion, ed., *La Passion de la raison*. *Hommage à
Ferdinand Alquié*. Paris: Presses universitaires de France,
1983. Pp. 480. Fr. 450.00.

Crichfield, Grant. "Full Circle(s) in Nodier's *La Fée aux
miettes*." *French Forum* 9 (1984): 200-11.

 Another closely reasoned exploration of Nodier's tale by
this author (see *RMB* for 1983, p. 241). "In *La Fée aux
miettes*, narrative, temporal and spatial structures, metaphor
and symbol, even the philosophical and mythical underpinnings
are circular in nature and serve as a prefiguration at every
level of the unity and ulterior existence for which the
tale's central character strives." (J.S.P.)

Dictionnaire raisonné des onomatopées françaises. Précédé de
La Nature dans la voix, par Henri Meschonnic. Paris: T.E.R.,
1984. Pp. 403. Fr. 109.00.

Guérin, Claude. "I. 1834-1888." *BduB* 1984-IV: 451-74.

 Reprints the first part of the catalogue of "La Bibliophilie à travers cent cinquante ans du *Bulletin du Bibliophile*.
Exposition présentée à la Bibliothèque de l'Arsenal du 28
novembre au 29 décembre 1984." The show included several
manuscript letters of Nodier.

Hofer, Hermann. "Le(s) livre(s) de/chez Charles Nodier."
Romantisme 44 (1984): 27-34.

 On Nodier's cult of the book, as shown in his own collections, in his bibliophilia, in his career as librarian, but
especially in his literary works: "Cette bibliophilie fait
naître l'idée du Texte auquel aboutissent tous les efforts
de Nodier écrivain qui est hanté par l'idée de créer au-delà
de la fabrication purement matérielle d'un livre--due aux
efforts conjugués de l'écrivain, du typographe, du relieur
et de l'illustrateur--un livre qui se dérobe à la mortalité
et qui devienne l'idée pure d'un absolu, dont ses textes
préférés lui semblent être les témoins passagers mais aussi
les garants."

Kies, Albert. "La destruction du roman dans l'*Histoire du Roi
de Bohême et de ses sept Châteaux* de Charles Nodier." Pp.
141-51 in Claudine Gothot-Mersch, et al., eds., *Narration
et interprétation*. Actes du colloque organisé par la

Facultés de philosophie et lettres les 3, 4 et 4 avril
1984, à l'occasion du 125e anniversaire des Facultés
universitaires Saint-Louis. (Publications des Facultés
universitaires Saint-Louis, 32.) Brussels: Facultés
universitaires Saint-Louis, 1984. Pp. 260. Bel.Fr. 950.00.

A useful analysis of the "echo" of Sterne (*Tristram Shandy*)
in Nodier's book; both books raise the problem of "le récit
impossible" and use similar techniques in dealing with it.
(Nodier's title, moreover, comes directly from Sterne's
text.) (J.S.P.)

Lendemains 25-26 (1982). Special Issue on Nodier (Hermann
Hofer, ed.).

Contents: Hermann Hofer, "Der wiederentdeckte Charles
Nodier" (5-10); Jean Richer, "Le rituel d'incubation dans
La neuvaine de la Chandeleur" (11-14); Brian G. Rogers,
"Ecriture onirique dans *Thérèse Aubert*" (15-23); Edeltraut
Peters and Karl-Hans Borger, "*L'homme et la fourmi*" (24-28);
Hermann Hofer, "*Les Proscrits*. Der Roman als Revolution—
die Revolution als Roman" (29-33); Norbert Miller, "La
femme au collier de velours. Alexandre Dumas korrigiert
Charles Nodier" (35-51); Eckhart Schroeder-Buys, "Charles
Nodier und die Revolution" (56-62); Hans Peter Lund, "Note
sur Nodier face à l'histoire des historiens et des mémoria-
listes" (63-69); Jacques-Rémi Dahan, "Charles Nodier et les
'Méditateurs'" (71-82); Eduard Wiecha, "Die Entwicklung
des Regionalbewusstseins bei Charles Nodier" (83-94); Bernd
E. Scholz, "Charles Nodier im Russland" (95-110); Hans-
Ulrich Seifert, "Romantische Palingenesien: Charles Nodier
und Georg Friedrich Daumer" (111-114).

In his introduction, Hofer justifies the modern rehabilitation of Nodier and gives a brief *état présent*. Richer
relates *La Neuvaine de la Chandeleur* to the tradition of
incubation rituals. Rogers claims that the structure of
Thérèse Aubert is that of a dream. Peters and Borger seek
to find, in *L'Homme et la fourmi*, foreshadowings of modern
ecologism. Hofer makes a case for *Les Proscrits* as an
authentic novel about a young man ill at ease in the post-
Revolutionary world. (Without direct access to Norbert
Miller's article, this reviewer cannot even pretend to
comment on it.) Schroeder-Buys spells out Nodier's defense
of the Revolution in *Charlotte Corday* and *Le Dernier Banquet
des Girondins*. Lund studies Nodier's conception of history
as found in several of his historical works. Dahan relates
Nodier to the group of painters called "Méditateurs" and
gives biographies of its members. Wiecha marks out a
four-stage development in Nodier's regionalism. From Scholz's

account, it appears that Russian writers discovered Nodier in 1818 with *Jean Sbogar*, that Pushkin was much influenced by him, that he was unknown in the post-Romantic era (e.g., to Gogol and Dostoevsky), and that both academics and the general reading public have rediscovered him in the Soviet era. Finally, according to Seifert, the reading of Nodier's article on "La palingénésie humaine" was the point of departure for the philosopher Daumer (Kaspar Hauser's one-time teacher).

Vaulcher, Henri de. "Charles Nodier poète et savant." *Mémoires de la Société d'Emulation du Doubs* 24 (1982): 43-56.

See also Jean-Nesmy ("French 1. General").

Review of book previously listed:

LUND, Hans Peter, *La Critique du siècle chez Nodier* (see *RMB* for 1979, p. 213), rev. by R.A.G. Pearson in *FS* 38 (1984): 349-50.

OZANAM

Couzemius, Victor. *Frédéric Ozanam: Solidarität Statt Klassenkampf.* (Gelebtes Christentum.) Freiburg: Imba-Verlag; Hamburg: F. Wittig, 1983. Pp. 48. Fr. 5.00.

Des Rivières, Madeleine. *Ozanam, un savant chez les pauvres.* Paris: Cerf; Montreal: Bellarmin, 1984. Pp. 165. Fr. 95.00.

Maurin, J.M. "Les derniers jours de Frédéric Ozanam à Marseille." *Cahiers Ozanam* 1 (1983): 5-31.

PIXÉRÉCOURT

Tatu, Chantal. "Pixérécourt ou les malheurs du texte." Pp. 87-101 in *Sujet, texte, histoire (Colloque du 28 avril 1979).* (Annales littéraires de l'Université de Besançon, 259.) Paris: Les Belles Lettres, 1981. Pp. 113. Fr. 75.00.

PONSARD

Himmelsbach, Siegbert. *Un fidèle reflet de son époque: le théâtre de François Ponsard.* (Publications universitaires européennes, XIII/69.) Frankfurt am Main, Bern, and Las Vegas: Peter Lang, 1980. Pp. 162. Sw.Fr. 32.00.

Rev. by Jean Emelina in *RHL* 84 (1984): 635-36.

POTOCKI

Jean Potocki et le manuscrit trouvé à Saragosse. Warsaw: Université du Varsovie (diffusion: Trismégiste), 1984. Pp. 370. Fr. 120.00.

PROUDHON

Berti, G.D. *La Dimensione libertaria di P.J. Proudhon.* Rome: Città Nuova, 1982. Pp. 237. L. 8,000.00.

Vincent, K. Steven. *Pierre-Joseph Proudhon and the Rise of French Republican Socialism.* Oxford University Press, 1984. Pp. 352. $39.95.

Reviews of books previously listed:

HAUBTMANN, Pierre, *Pierre-Joseph Proudhon* (see *RMB* for 1982, p. 246), rev. by Peter Byrne in *SFr* 28 (1984): 383-84; RUBIN, James Henry, *Realism and Social Vision in Courbet and Proudhon* (see *RMB* for 1981, p. 226), rev. by Klaus Herding in *AB* 66 (1984): 533-35.

QUATREMÈRE DE QUINCY

See Iknayan, Shiff ("French 1. General").

QUINET

Aeschimann, W., and J. Tucoo-Chala, eds. *La Grèce moderne et ses rapports avec l'antiquité.* Suivi de: *Journal de voyage.* (Les Textes français.) Paris: Les Belles Lettres, 1984. Pp. 624. Fr. 550.00.

Le Christianisme et la Révolution française. (Corpus des
OEuvres de Philosophie en Langue française.) Paris: Fayard,
1984. Pp. 256. Fr. 79.00.

Crossley, Ceri. "La création d'Edgar Quinet." New Zealand
Journal of French Studies (Nov. 1982): 39-49.

Freydefond, Marcel. "Approche scénographique du premier acte
du Vercingétorix d'Edgar Quinet." Pp. 473-79 in Paul
Viallaneix and Jean Ehrard, eds., Nos Ancêtres les Gaulois.
Actes du colloque international de Clermont-Ferrand. (Faculté
des Lettres et Sciences Humaines de l'Université de Clermont-
Ferrand II, n.s., 13.) Clermont-Ferrand, 1982. Pp. 492.
Fr. 180.00.

Knecht, Edgar. "Le Moyen Age d'Edgar Quinet." La Licorne 6-I
(1982): 125-43.

See also Susini ("Sougey-Avisard").

Reviews of books previously listed:

CROSSLEY, Ceri, Edgar Quinet (1803-1875) (see RMB for 1983,
p. 243), rev. by Oscar A. Haac in NCFS 12,iv; 13,i (1984):
227-29; by Barbara Wright in FS 38 (1984): 470-71; FROMENTIN,
Eugène, and Paul Bataillard, Etude sur l'Ahasvérus d'Edgar
Quinet (see RMB for 1982, p. 247), rev. by Isa Agrisani
Guerrini in SFr 27 (1983): 579; by Bettina Knapp in NCFS
12 (1983-84): 228-29; by Arlette Michel in IL 36 (1984):
91-92.

REBOUL

Vier, Jacques. "La ville de Nîmes et le comte de Chambord."
La Pensée Catholique 204 (1983): 73-83.

SAINTE-BEUVE

Ciureanu, Petre. "La fortuna di Volupté del Sainte-Beuve in
Italia." III, 381-409 in Mélanges à la mémoire de Franco
Simone: France et Italie dans la culture européenne.
(Bibliothèque Franco-Simone, 8.) 4 vols. Geneva: Editions
Slatkine, 1980-84.

From 1834 to the 1960s. Interest in reactions both of
writers and of critic/scholars.

Dimić, Colette A.-M. "Les traits Biedermeier chez Sainte-
Beuve poète et romancier." *CRCL* 11 (1984): 39-60.

Evidence that Sainte-Beuve stands among writers introducing
a "Biedermeier" tendency into French letters. He is joined
by the George Sand of the rustic novels and the Fromentin
of *Dominique*. Biedermeier traits include a certain religious sentiment; love of a quiet, intimate nature; preference for the country over the city; the cult of home and
family; idealization of woman; fear of passion and excess;
attraction to simplicity and retirement; interest in humani-
tarian service; renunciation of fame and glory; and didacticism. Dimić finds these traits not only in Sainte-Beuve's
early poems and in *Volupté* but also in the man himself.

Madelenat, Daniel. "*Joseph Delorme* de Sainte-Beuve: émission,
réception, rétroaction." Pp. 229-42 in Józef Heistein, ed.,
La Réception de l'oeuvre littéraire. (Romanica Wratis-
laviensia, 20; Acta Universitatis Wratislaviensis, 635.)
Wroslaw: Wydawnistwo Universytetu Wroslawskiego, 1983. Pp.
314.

Madelenat, Daniel. "Le lecteur dans *Volupté* de Sainte-Beuve."
Pp. 69-78 in Alain Montandon, ed., *Le Lecteur et la lecture
dans l'oeuvre*. (Faculté des Lettres et Sciences Humaines
de l'Université de Clermont-Ferrand II, N.S. 15.) Clermont-
Ferrand: Association des Publications de la Faculté des
Lettres et Sciences Humaines de Clermont-Ferrand (France),
1982. Pp. 205.

Madelenat seeks the message behind Sainte-Beuve's insistent
emphasis on reading and readings in *Volupté*. Disoriented by
contradictions which he finds in the world--contradictions
revealed in his philosophical readings--Amaury achieves at
last a sense of unity and stability through the lessons of
sacred texts. The conclusion of the novel, however, is
scarcely plausible if we compare it with the career of
Sainte-Beuve himself. The critic was not able to effect
such a solution as that of his protagonist.

Regard, Maurice, ed. *Volupté* (suivi de) *Arthur*, *Livre d'amour*,
Madame de Pontivy. Illustrations de Marianne Clouzot.
(Lettres Françaises.) 2 vols. Paris: Imprimerie Nationale,
1984. Fr. 870.00.

Weber, Werner. "Sainte-Beuves 'Lundis' über Fromentin. In
individuellem Begegnen die Spur einer Epochenbewegung."
Pp. 1377-1403 in Joseph Strelka, ed., *Literary Theory and
Criticism*. *Festschrift*. *Presented to René Wellek in Honor*

of His Eightieth Birthday. 2 vols. Bern, Frankfurt on the
Main, and New York: Peter Lang, 1984. Pp. 1462. $80.00.

See also Raser ("French 1. General"); Scaiola ("Borel");
Susini ("Sougey-Avisard").

Review of book previously listed:

BONNEROT, ALAIN, ed., *Correspondance générale*, T. XIX (see
RMB for 1983, p. 244), brief rev. in *BCLF* 461 (May 1984):
591.

SAINT-SIMON

Frick, Jean-Paul. "Les détours de la problématique sociologique
de Saint-Simon." *Revue Française de Sociologie* 24 (April-
June 1983): 183-202.

Grappin, Pierre. "Lessing, Saint-Simon, Heine." *Tijdschrift
voor de Studie van de Verlichting en van het Vrije denken*
(1982), fasc. 1-3, pp. 203-12.

Moebus, Joachim, and Martin Blankenburg. "Die irdische Moral.
Saint-Simons Grundlegung des 'nouvel ordre des jouissances.'"
Lendemains 29 (1983): 98-106.

See also Moses ("French 1. General"); Bech ("German 3. Heine").

Reviews of book previously listed:

BULCIOLU, Maria Teresa, *L'Ecole saint-simonienne et la femme*
(see *RMB* for 1981, p. 229), rev. by Pierre Huard in *Revue de
Synthèse* 109 (Jan.-March 1983): 88-90; by Brian Rigby in
FS 38 (1984): 349.

SAND

Les Ailes de courage. Texte conforme à l'édition de Calmann-
Lévy de 1878. Illustrations d'Alain Durbec. Lyon: Ed. du
Chardon bleu, 1984. Pp. 202. Fr. 46.00.

   This tale (written between October and November 1872, at
the request of Aurore and Gabrielle Sand) is also reprinted
in the first series of *Contes d'une grand-mère*, edited by
Philippe Berthier with illustrations by Roland Figuière (Editions de l'Aurore, 1982), 175-256. (D.J.C.)

Les Amis de George Sand (1981).

    Contents: "Editorial" (1-2); Georges Lubin, "George Sand
et l'Académie française" (3-5); Christian Abbadie, "George
Sand et Guillery (II). Conclusion: le caractère gascon,
vu par George Sand" (6-14); Bernadette Chovelon, "George
Sand et Sarah Bernhardt" (15-18); J. Marillier, "Antoine-
Claude Delaborde, maître oyselier parisien, aïeul maternel
de George Sand (I)" (19-22); Georges Lubin, "Lettres de
George Sand et de Solange Clesinger [Solange Clesinger à
George Sand, 31 juillet 1858; George Sand à Solange
Clesinger, 18 août 1858]" (23-29).

Les Amis de George Sand (1982).

    Contents: "Nohant ... vu par des contemporains de George
Sand [Textes de J. Sandeau, E. Delacroix, E. Caro, T. Gautier,
J. Adam, A. Silvestre, Henri Amic, Aurore Sand]" (1-14);
Bernadette Chovelon, "La vie quotidienne à Nohant [en 1843]"
(18-21); Georges Lubin, "Quelques belles soirées de Nohant"
(25-36).

Les Amis de George Sand (1983).

    Contents: Georges Lubin, "Adieu à P. Salomon [1902-1983]"
(3); Pierre Salomon, "Les trois premières *Lettres d'un
voyageur* et la littérature de voyage" (4-13); Ruth Jordan,
"Une lettre inédite découverte en Angleterre [à Mme Dacher,
8 oct. 1838]" (14-19); Jean Gaulmier, "A propos de *Lavinia*"
(20-22); J. Marillier, "Antoine Claude Delaborde, maître
oyselier parisien, aïeul maternel de George Sand (II)"
(23-28); F. Gouron, "George Sand et les animaux" (29-31).

Armas, Isabel de. "Una George Sand salteña." *Cuadernos His-
    panoamericanos* 407 (May 1984): 171-74.

    Rev. of Martha Mercader, *Juana Manuela, mucha mujer*
(Barcelona: Planeta, 1983), a historical novel set in the
1830s in Argentina. The heroine has been compared to George
Sand by critics.

Autour de George Sand. Catalogue de lettres, ms. autographes
    et photographies de célébrités des XIXe et XXe siècles faisant
    partie des collections de famille de George Sand et de ses
    descendants. Gargilesse: Christiane Smeets-Sand, 1983.

Bergez, Daniel, ed. *La Mare au diable.* (Nouveaux classiques
    illustrés Hachette.) Paris: Hachette-Classiques, 1984.
    Pp. 176. Fr. 14.00.

Bergez, Daniel, ed. *La Mare au diable. Bibliographie
critique, commentaire littéraire et sujets de travaux.*
(Nouveaux classiques illustrés Hachette.) Paris: Hachette-
Classiques, 1984. Pp. 32. Fr. 14.00.

Biemann, Karlheinrich. "George Sand und die Soziale Republik
(1848-1851). Eine Schriftstellerin in der Revolution."
Lendemains 28 (1982): 45-51.

"Engagement politique de George Sand au début de la
deuxième République. Sa sympathie pour le peuple. Son
retrait après les journées de 1848."

Biemann, Karlheinrich. *Literarisch-politische Avantgarde in
Frankreich, 1830-1870. Hugo, Sand, Baudelaire und andere.*
Stuttgart: Kohlhammer, 1982. Pp. 256. DM 82.00.

Boisdeffre, Pierre de, ed. *La Mare au diable.* (Le Livre de
Poche, 3551.) Paris: Librairie générale française, 1973.
Pp. 160. Fr. 11.00.

Boisdeffre, Pierre de, ed. *La Petite Fadette.* (Le Livre de
Poche, 3550.) Paris: Librairie générale française, 1973.
Pp. 262. Fr. 15.70.

Bonnet, H. "Sand." Pp. 2103-14 in Jean-Pierre de Beaumarchais,
et al., eds., *Dictionnaire des littératures de langue
française*, T. III. Paris: Bordas, 1984. Pp. 2638. Fr.
340.00 le vol.

An 11-page introduction to George Sand and her *oeuvre*
(with a three-and-a-half-page "life and works" synopsis).
No place for misogyny here: Author-critic, thoroughly
knowledgeable and *au courant* of the Sandian state of scholarly
affairs ("capsule" bibliographies, and General Bibliography
at the end of "entry"), shows remarkable objectivity and
critical as well as intuitive understanding of both writer
and woman. Fits well into the rehabilitation movement of
Sand, originally started by Léon Cellier and L. Guichard
(1959). (D.J.C.)

Bossis, Mireille. "La correspondance comme figure de compromis."
Pp. 220-38 in Jean-Louis Bonnat and Mireille Bossis, eds.,
*Ecrire, publier, lire les correspondances (problématique et
économie d'un "genre littéraire").* Actes du colloque international: "Les Correspondances." Nantes les 4, 5, 6, 7
octobre 1982. Université de Nantes, 1982. Pp. 474. Fr.
120.00.

Bozon-Scalzitti, Yvette. "Vérité de la fiction et fiction de
la vérité dans *Histoire de ma vie*: le projet autobiographique
de George Sand." *NCFS* 12,iv; 13,i (1984):   95-118.

Brunel, Pierre; Claude Pichois; and André-M. Rousseau.
Qu'est-ce que la littérature comparée? Paris: Armand Colin,
1983. Pp. 172. Sw.Fr. 20.50.

   In the discussion of the "polygenesis" of the rustic novel
in Western Europe in the nineteenth century, George Sand
finds her place with her *romans champêtres*, after Jeremias
Gotthelf, and before George Eliot and Björnson (72).   (D.J.C.)

Busk-Jensen, Lise. *Frigφrelse eller selvrealisering. Analyser
i George Sands feministiske forfatterskab (1832-1844)*
[Analyse de l'oeuvre féministe de George Sand]. Copenhagen:
Ed. Reitzel, 1982.

Byrne, Peter. "George Sand e W.J. Linton, Lettere e documenti
inediti." *Note sul Socialismo e Cristianesimo* 4 (Sept. 1982):
11-32.

   See résumé by Peter Byrne in *SFr* 28 (1984):   168.

Carrabino, Victor. "George Sand's *Consuelo*: The Search for
a Soul." Pp. 79-85 in Josip Masteŝić and Erwin Wedel, eds.,
Festschrift für Nikola R. Pribić. (Selecta Slavica.)
Neuried: Hiëronymus Verlag, 1983. Pp. xxv+604.

   Stresses most convincingly archetypal symbolic importance
of Sand's best novel through a demonstration of Consuelo's
search for her own identity and purpose in life. In order
to complete what Jung calls the "individuation process"--
here the road to Art--author of article shows that Consuelo
must go down the labyrinth (here: archetypal metaphor), to
finally reach the center (of Hell), find Albert, and walk
back with him to the Castle of the Giants (Orpheus myth).
(D.J.C.)

Consuelo à Venise. Extraits de *Consuelo* lus par Madeleine
Robinson. (Collection "écrire, entendre.") Paris: Editions
des Femmes, 1984. 1 cassette-livre. Fr. 70.00.

   --Où le mot se fait parole.... Excerpts read are freely
adapted from original text used (editor not mentioned), and
pertain to Consuelo's Venetian period: Count Zustiniani's
courtship and his attempt at seducing Consuelo; Anzoleto's
unfaithfulness and his betrayal of Consuelo; la Corilla's
seduction of Anzoleto, woven into her rivalry with the young
girl of genius. With musical interludes (Pergolesi's

"Salve Regina" and "Stabat Mater," played by the Società
Camerista di Lugano, and Glück's "Orfeo," by the Chorus
and Orchestra of the Netherlands). (D.J.C.)

Cooper, Barbara T. "L'envers du décor: The Space of the Fantastic in George Sand's *Consuelo.*" *RomN* 24 (1983-84): 243-
48.

Courrier, Nicole, and Thierry Bodin, eds. *Horace.* Maquette
Roland Figuière. Meylan: Editions de l'Aurore, 1982. Pp.
400. Fr. 80.00.

Didier, Béatrice. "Rôles et figures du lecteur chez George
Sand." *ELit* 17 (1984): 239-59.

According to the "présentation" of this issue by Francine
Belle-Isle and Yvan Lévesque, "Béatrice Didier souligne ...
l'indispensable présence du narrataire dans *Histoire de ma
vie* de George Sand, un texte 'qui prétend ne pas appartenir
à la fiction'; par ailleurs, l'apparition de cette figure
dans *Indiana* coïncide curieusement avec les moments chargés
d'un 'poids autobiographique.'"
On the *problématique* of *auteur/lecteur (lectrice)*, *narrateur
(narratrice)/lecteur (lectrice)* or *narrataire* in George
Sand, in her first novel, *Indiana*; in her *Lettres d'un voyageur*;
and in *Histoire de ma vie.* Didier brilliantly reveals the
complexity of Sand's case, leading to a "blurring" of the
notion of literary *genre.* Stresses the necessity to refine
our understanding of the "autobiographical pact" (Philippe
Lejeune) between writer and reader, when a writer masks herself
behind a male pseudonym. (D.J.C.)

Didier, Béatrice, ed. *Indiana.* (Folio, 1604.) Paris: Gallimard, 1984. Pp. 400. Fr. 32.00.

Didier, Béatrice, ed. *Un Hiver à Majorque.* (Le Livre de Poche,
5897.) Paris: Librairie générale française, 1984. Pp. 285.
Fr. 18.00.

Dimić, Colette. "Les traits Biedermeier dans les romans champêtres de George Sand." *Neohelicon* 9,ii (1982): 123-62.

Friends of George Sand Newsletter 5,ii (Fall/Winter 1982).

Contents: Isabelle Naginski (Spec. ed. for this issue),
"Editorial" (3-5); Enid M. Standring, "Conference Report"
(6-7); Simone Vierne, "George Sand et l'imagination" (8-19);
Murray Sachs, "George Sand and Gustave Flaubert: French
Literature's Odd Couple" (20-25); Aaron Noland, "Henry James,

George Sand, and the 'Metaphysical Imagination'" (26-39);
Eve Sourian, "La femme dans les premières nouvelles de George
Sand" (40-46); Marie-Jacques Hoog, "Du rêve à l'écriture chez
George Sand" (47-50); Mireille Bossis, "Eléments pour une
formation de la dynamique romanesque en 1832 chez George
Sand" (51-56); V.Y. Mudimbe, "Invisible et catégorie du double
dans *Valentine* de George Sand" (57-62); Shoshana Knapp,
"'Un jeune Corse': Meditations on Napoleon's Cameo Appearance
in George Sand's *Spiridion*" (63-68); Peter G. Christensen,
"*Consuelo, Wilhelm Meister*, and the Historical Novel" (69-75);
Erika Ostrovsky, "*François le Champi* Reconsidered: A Mytho-
critical View" (76-81); Marie-Jacques Hoog, "Book Reviews"
(82-83); Janis Glasgow, "The George Sand Collection: A New
Home at the Musée Renan-Scheffer" (84); "Conferences, Conventions, Colloquia" (85-88).

Frier-Wantiez, Martine. "Analyse des demandes en mariage dans
La ville noire de George Sand." *Kodikas/Code. Ars Semiotica*
3-4 (1982): 283-303.

Godwin-Jones, Robert. "Where the Devil Leads: Peasant Super-
stitions in George Sand's *Petite Fadette* and Droste-Hülshoff's
Judenbuche." *Neohelicon* 12,i (1983): 221-38.

Herrmann, Claudine. *Les Voleuses de langue*. Paris: Editions
des Femmes, 1976. Pp. 180. Sw.Fr. 12.20.

   In this provocative, seminal work, George Sand (and Mme
de Staël) are mentioned among the first women who dared take
up the pen and live from it (economically or otherwise).
(D.J.C.)

Ives, G. Burnham, trans. *The Masterpieces of George Sand:
Now for the First Time Completely Translated into English*.
Philadelphia, [1900-1902]. Reprinted New York: AMS Press,
1984. 20 vols. $750.00 ($37.50 per vol.).

Jaton, Anne-Marie. "Energétique et féminité (1720-1820)."
Romantisme 46 (1984): 15-25.

Jean, Maurice. "Le séjour de George Sand à Tamaris en 1861."
Bulletin de la Société des Amis du Vieux Toulon 104 (1982):
47-98.

Karst-Matausch, Renate. "De la lettre aux lettres. Réflexions
sur la genèse de l'écriture épistolaire chez G. Sand." Pp.
146-64 in Jean-Louis Bonnat and Mireille Bossis, eds., *Ecrire,
publier, lire les correspondances (problématique et économie*

d'un "genre littéraire"). Actes du colloque international:
"Les Correspondances." Nantes les 4, 5, 6, 7 octobre 1982.
Université de Nantes, 1982. Pp. 474. Fr. 120.00.

Lacassagne, Jean-Pierre, ed. *Mauprat.* (Folio, 1311.) Paris:
Gallimard, 1981. Pp. 480. Fr. 25.10.

Laforge, François. "Structure et fonction du mythe d'Orphée
dans 'Consuelo' de George Sand." *RHL* 84 (1984): 53-66.

On George Sand's reworking ("remaniement") and alteration
("déplacement") of the classical versions of the Orpheus myth,
as a result of her deep concern for femininity in its relationship to virility, to desire, and to art.

Author's semiotic demonstration, interpretation, and conclusions are brilliant, with the exception, perhaps, of
page 65 (the notion of "l'art féminin de la stérilité"--the
unfortunate word is used at least six times), and 66 (conclusion on "l'art absolu"). *L'art féminin du sacrifice* or
du renoncement (author himself speaks of *l'art de la vir-
ginité* in one previous instance) would have been more fitting
to Consuelo-Consolation. (See Introduction to *Consuelo*,
by Simone Vierne and René Bourgeois, Editions de l'Aurore,
1983, I, 28-35, in particular.) (D.J.C.)

Lecherbonnier, Bernard, coord. With the collaboration of
Bernard and Jacqueline Cerquiglini, Fernand Egéa, Bernard
Lecherbonnier, Bernard Lehembre, and Jean-Jacques Mougenot.
Histoire de la littérature française. (Coll. Beaux Livres.)
Paris: Nathan, 1984. Pp. 240. Fr. 260.00.

L'Hôpital, M. "L'amitié de George Sand et de Delacroix.
Plaidoyer pour la tolérance." *Sévriennes d'Hier et d'Aujour-
d'hui* 112 (June 1983): 4-7.

Lubin, Georges. "Les débuts d'une femme de lettres en 1831
(avec des documents inédits)." *Revue de l'Académie du Centre*
(1980): 9-14.

Three undated letters from George Sand to Laure Decerfz.

Lubin, Georges. "Une lettre de George Sand à E. Souvestre
[12 June 1845]." *Les Cahiers de l'Iroise* (Jan.-March 1983):
4-5.

Lubin, Georges, ed. *Tamaris.* (Coll. Les OEuvres de George
Sand.) Illustrations de Maurice Sand et Vincent Courdouan.
Meylan: Editions de l'Aurore, 1984. Pp. 216. Fr. 82.00.

Naginski, Isabelle. "George Sand. Gynographie et androgynie."
Bulletin de la Société des Professeurs français en Amérique
1983-1984 (1984): 21-36.

A thought-provoking article on the crucial problem of
identity in George Sand and in her work. Most revealingly,
"androgynous disguise" in real life is the game George Sand
plays in fictional construction and narrative strategy.
Discusses Sand's epistolary and autobiographical androgyny
as well. From this "discours à double voix" (Elaine Showal-
ter), the author expands discussion to Sand's "polyphonic"
critical writings. The "game" is not gratuitous: it stems
from a deep personality need in Sand--a need for spatial,
mental, and aesthetic *élargissement*--and eventually reveals
Sand's "hermaphrodite" vision (ideal) and ideology. Interestingly enough, this thirst for "total" knowledge and
experience is not a woman writer's--or a woman's--exclusivity:
the author mentions "thematic androgyny" of, among others,
Latouche (*Fragoletta*), Gautier (*Mlle de Maupin*), and, of
course, Balzac (*Séraphita*). (D.J.C.)

Ninane de Martinoir, Francine. "Lecture dirigée. George
Sand, *Mauprat*." *L'Ecole des Lettres*, Sept. 15, 1983, pp.
5-16; Oct. 1, 1983, pp. 7-20.

Poli, Annarosa. "George Sand devant la critique, 1831-1833."
Pp. 355-61 in Giorgetto Giorgi, et al., eds., *Studi di*
cultura francese ed europea in onore di Lorenza Maranini.
Fasano: Schena, 1983. Pp. 540.

See résumé by Pier Antonio Borgheggiani in *SFr* 27 (1983):
577-578; *RLML* (1984): 82.

Recherches nouvelles sur George Sand sous la direction de
Françoise Van Rossum-Guyon. Groupe de recherches sur George
Sand de l'Université d'Amsterdam. *C.R.I.N.*, Institut de
Langues romanes, Groningen (1983). Pp. 264.

Contents: Françoise Van Rossum-Guyon, "Les enjeux d'*Indiana*
I, Méta-discours et réception critique" (1-35); Camille
Mortagne, "*Indiana* ou '*la langue*, cette reine prostituée.'
Rapports sociaux et maîtrise des significations" (36-61);
Arlette Béteille, "Où finit *Indiana*? Problématique d'un
dénouement" (62-73); Corrie Kruikemeier, "Fêtes et céré-
monies: la structure mythique de *Lélia*" (74-92); Jan Endel-
man, "*Le meunier d'Angibault*: symbolisme et poétique"
(93-119); Martine Frier-Wantiez, "Les demandes en mariage
dans *La ville noire*" (120-53); Elisabeth Milleman, "*Le*
château de Pictordu, du crépuscule à l'Aurore; Paysages"
(154-74); Ank Maas, "*Histoire de ma vie*: choix de l'auteur

et scrupules de la traductrice" (175-93); Bea Ikelaar-
Descamps, "Les préfaces de George Sand: fonctions et évolu-
tion" (194-220); Joop Stoelinga and Suzanne Van Dijk,
"*Mademoiselle La Quintinie* aux Pays-Bas. Une polémique
religieuse" (221-42); Anje Dik, "Juliette Adam et George Sand,
l'hommage d'une femme écrivain" (243-54); Joanne Boiten,
"George Sand en U.R.S.S., notes de voyage et bibliographie"
(255-64).

Rogers, Nancy. "Style, voix et destinataire dans les lettres
de George Sand avant 1837." Pp. 182-94 in Jean-Louis
Bonnat and Mireille Bossis, eds., *Ecrire, publier, lire les
correspondances (problématique et économie d'un "genre
littéraire")*. Actes du colloque international: "Les
Correspondances." Nantes les 4, 5, 6, 7 octobre 1982.
Université de Nantes, 1982. Pp. 474. Fr. 120.00.

Salvinien, Jean. "A propos du château de Valençay, demeure
princière des Talleyrand-Périgord dans le Bas-Berry [George
Sand à Valençay en 1834]." *Bulletin de l'Académie des
Sciences et Lettres de Montpellier* (1982): 167-77.

Sand, Christiane, ed. *Promenades autour d'un village*, suivies
du *Journal de Gargilesse*. Dessins inédits de G. Sand,
M. Sand, J. Véron, E. Grandsire et C. Sand. Nouvelle édition.
(Coll. Monts et Merveilles.) Saint-Cyr-sur-Loire: Christian
Pirot, 1984. Pp. 192. Fr. 99.00.

Rev. by Pierre de Boisdeffre in *RDM*, Sept. 1984, pp. 689-90.
This new edition of *Promenades* is an exact reproduction of
the text printed by Michel Lévy in 1866. The *Journal*
presents the twelve excursions made by Sand to Gargilesse,
between January 1858 and April 1864, in heretofore unpublished
notes, with a few changes made by her private secretary,
Alexandre Manceau. (D.J.C.)

Siganos, André. "Sur Hoffmann et George Sand: *L'Histoire
du véritable Gribouille et l'Enfant étranger*." *RLC* 56
(1982): 92-95.

Tavernier, René. "Sand et Musset, ou la leçon de Venise."
RG 12 (Dec. 1983): 21-27.

Moral defense of George Sand. While Musset never recovered
from the Venice affair, Sand gained a sense of personal
freedom, learned compassion and understanding, and developed
the will to teach these qualities to others.

Toesca, Maurice, ed. *François le Champi*. (Le Livre de Poche,
    4771.) Paris; Librairie générale française, 1976. Pp. 224.
    Fr. 15.70.

Tondeur, Claire-Lise. "Flaubert et Sand: une admiration piégée."
    RUO 54 (1984): 5-14.

    In adolescence, Gustave Flaubert greatly admired George
    Sand, but later he reacted against her "effusions lyriques"
    (Tondeur's word). He never mentioned her humanitarian novels
    or her *romans champêtres*. But he liked her personally--her
    simplicity, the fact that she was not a *bas-bleu*, her
    "virility," her blend of *force* and *douceur*.
    He reread *Histoire de ma vie*, *Consuelo*, and *La Comtesse
    de Rudolstadt* and spoke to her of them with (feigned?)
    enthusiasm. Whenever a new work of hers appeared, he wrote
    about his emotional reaction, but never analyzed it critically.
    (He never talked about her novels to other people.) Her
    death greatly saddened him, but he never mentioned her again
    in his letters. In *Bouvard et Pécuchet* he criticized her in-
    directly (by having Bouvard praise her), but he was kinder
    to her than to Dumas, Scott, and Rousseau.

Urien, Pierre. "George Sand et la Creuse en 1848." *Memoires
    de la Société des Sciences Naturelles et Archéologiques de la
    Creuse* 41 (1982): 407-08.

Vier, Jacques. "Considérations sur *Spiridion*." *Quaderno
    Filosofico* (Lecce) 6 (1982): 53-64.

    See résumé by Peter Byrne in *SFr* 28 (1984): 168.

Vier, Jacques. "Considérations sur *Spiridion*, roman de
    l'Evangile éternel." *La Pensée Catholique* 196 (1982): 93-
    101.

Vierne, Simone, and René Bourgeois, eds. *Consuelo; La Comtesse
    de Rudolstadt*. Vols. II-III. Meylan: Editions de l'Aurore,
    1983 and 1984. Pp. 408 and 480. Fr. 95.00 and 94.00,
    respectively.

Wingard, Kristina. "Correspondance et littérature épistolaire:
    George Sand en 1834." Pp. 165-81 in Jean-Louis Bonnat and
    Mireille Bossis, eds., *Ecrire, publier, lire les correspon-
    dances (problématique et économie d'un "genre littéraire")*.
    Actes du colloque international: "Les Correspondances."
    Nantes les 4, 5, 6, 7 octobre 1982. Université de Nantes,
    1982. Pp. 474. Fr. 120.00.

See also Meregalli ("General 3. Criticism"); Bolster, Coquillat,
Delon, Lesky, Wolfszettel ("French 1. General"); Bichsel
("German 3. Heine").

Reviews of books and periodicals previously listed:

COURRIER, Jean, and Jean-Hervé Donnard, eds., Le Péché de
Monsieur Antoine (see RMB for 1982, p. 250), rev. (briefly)
by René Bourgeois in SFr 27 (1983): 577; DATLOF, Natalie,
et al., eds., George Sand Papers: Conference Proceedings, 1978
(see RMB for 1982, pp. 252-53), rev. by Rena Feigenbaum-Knox
in NCFS 12,iv; 13,i (1984): 183-87; Présence de George
Sand 15 (1982) (see RMB for 1982, p. 255), rev. by René
Bourgeois in SFr 27 (1983): 577; VIERNE, Simone, ed., George
Sand, Colloque de Cerisy-la-Salle (1983) (see RMB for 1983,
pp. 252-53), rev. by Peter Byrne in SFr 28 (1984): 179-81.

SANDEAU

Dulmet, Florica. "Un romantique converti: Jules Sandeau
(1811-1883)." Ecrits de Paris, July-Aug. 1983, pp. 65-75.

SCHOELCHER

Review of book previously listed:

ALEXANDRE-DEBRAY, Janine, Victor Schoelcher ou la mystique
d'un athée (see RMB for 1983, p. 255), rev. by Bernard Plonge-
ron in Etudes 360 (1984): 130-31.

SCRIBE

Durnerin, James. "Larra, traducteur de Scribe et de Ducange."
Pp. 41-52 in Ecriture des marges et mutations historiques.
(Annales littéraires de l'Université de Besançon, 280.) Paris:
Les Belles Lettres, 1983. Pp. 120. Fr. 150.00.

Hofer, Hermann. "Scribe, Meyerbeer et la mise en scène du Moyen
Age. Essai sur le Diable à l'opéra en 1831." La Licorne 6-I
(1982): 65-87.

On Robert le Diable, presented at the Paris Opera in that
year.

Théâtre d'Eugène Scribe: opéras. (Les Introuvables.) Plan-
de-la-Tour: Editions d'Aujourd'hui, 1984. Pp. 312. Fr.
104.00.

Review of book previously listed:

KOON, Helene, and Richard Switzer, *Eugène Scribe* (see *RMB* for 1981, p. 238), rev. by H. Gaston Hall in *FS* 38 (1984): 71-72.

SÉNAC DE MEILHAN

Escoube, Pierre. *Sénac de Meilhan. De la France de Louis XV à l'Europe des émigrés.* Paris: Librairie académique Perrin, 1984. Pp. 416. Fr. 100.00.

This book does not add substantially to the spate of books on Sénac which appeared in 1968-70 (Henry A. Stavan, *Sénac de Meilhan* [1736-1803] [Paris: Minard, 1968]; G. de Monsembernard, *Sénac de Meilhan 1736-1803* [Auch: Imprimerie Th. Bouquet, 1969]; André Vielwahr, *La Vie et l'oeuvre de Senac de Meilhan* [Paris: A.-G. Nizet, 1970]), although a large number of archival documents are said to have been consulted. A few personal documents were made available to the author. The resulting work is more a popularization than those just cited, despite its greater length, and it is written in a rather old-fashioned style, not unpleasant to read but lacking in bite. Since Sénac's link to Romanticism is through his novel *L'Emigré*, the more detailed treatments of this work by Stavan and Vierwahl are still to be consulted. One clear advantage offered by the present book is the illustrations, one of which shows Sénac himself (it is the engraved version of a handsome lost oil portrait by Duplessis). Some extracts from Sénac's *Du gouvernement, des moeurs et des conditions en France avant la Révolution* (1795) are also included. (J.S.P.)

SENANCOUR

Gaxotte, Pierre. "Le coeur mélancolique de Senancour." *Le Spectacle du Monde/Réalites* 242 (May 1982): 85-87. Also pp. 47-53 in Pierre Gaxotte, *Le Purgatoire*. Paris: Fayard, 1982. Pp. 215.

Monnoyer, Jean-Marie, ed. *Obermann*. (Folio, 1566.) Paris: Gallimard, 1984. Pp. 544. Fr. 38.80.

Senancour's complete text and notes, introduced by a preface touching on biographical elements, the work's generic status and composition, the relationship between Obermann's illness and his superiority, and the ideological foundations of descriptive technique in the novel. This is augmented by a chronology, a bibliography, and a series of relevant contemporary documents including Senancour's "Du style dans les descriptions" and a thematic index to the 1804 edition.

Obermann, Roman in Briefen. Aus dem Französischen übertragen und mit einem Nachwort von Jürg Peter Walser. Frankfurt am Main: Insel-Verlag, 1982. Pp. 411.

Stempel, Ute. "Die passive Revolte." *Die Zeit*, Dec. 3, 1982, Literatur, p. 7.

SISMONDI

See Brunel et al. ("Staël").

SOUGEY-AVISARD

Susini, Eugène. "Varnhagen von Ense et Sougey-Avisard." *Francia* 9 (1981): 411-33.

SOUVESTRE

See La Condamine ("French 1. General").

STAËL

Bader, Wolfgang. "El pensamiento político de Madame de Staël. Contribución a una historia de la literatura comparada." *Sociedad Española de Literatura Comparada* 3 (1980): 7-26.

Balayé, Simone. "Une lettre de Madame de Staël à son ancienne femme de chambre, Madame Uginet." *Musées de Genève* 228 (Sept. 1982): 16-21.

Scholarly presentation of the only known letter (Dec. 16, 1815) written by Mme de Staël to Mme Uginet, her chambermaid and later intimate friend for many years. Shows closeness of both women; Mme de Staël's generosity, offering her room and board at Coppet; her concern for Olive Uginet's health. Discusses family matter.

Brunel, Pierre; Claude Pichois; and André-M. Rousseau. *Qu'est-ce que la littérature comparée?* Paris: Armand Colin, 1983. Pp. 172. Sw.Fr. 20.50.

Several references to Mme de Staël, Constant, and Sismondi
in Chapter 1, on the birth and growth of this "new" discipline.
The significance of the Coppet Group is also acknowledged
in passing. (D.J.C.)

Cahiers Staëliens 35 (1984). Madame de Staël: Lectures de
femmes.

Contents: Simone Balayé, "Hommage au Comte Victor de
Pange" (3-5); Simone Balayé, "Présentation" (6-8); Marie-
Claire Hoock-Demarle, "Madame de Staël et les femmes alle-
mandes, un malentendu positif" (9-40); Simone Balayé, "Destins
de femmes dans *Delphine*" (41-59); Claudine Herrmann, "Corinne
femme de génie" (60-76); Karl Ludwig von Knebel, "Un tableau
de la littérature allemande de Klopstock à Goethe, en 1804,"
translated and presented by Andrée Denis (77-94); "Table des
Matières" (95).

Castelot, André. *Napoléon Bonaparte*. Paris: Librairie
académique Perrin, 1984. Pp. 360. Fr. 330.00.

Corinne ou l'Italie. Extraits lus par Françoise Fabian.
(Collection "écrire, entendre.") Paris: Editions des
Femmes, 1984. 1 cassette-livre. Fr. 67.50.

    -- *Où le mot se fait parole*.... With musical interludes
by Ottorino Respighi ("Danses et airs anciens pour luth";
"Suite n° 1"), played by the Los Angeles Chamber Orchestra.
The excerpts chosen are adapted from the original text; it
was, therefore, a good idea to make a 46-page minibook from
them to accompany the cassette. (D.J.C.)

Delbouille, Paul. "Coppet (le groupe de) [vers 1803-1817]."
Pp. 536-37 in Jean-Pierre de Beaumarchais, et al., eds.,
Dictionnaire des littératures de langue française, T. I.
Paris: Bordas, 1984. Pp. 860. Fr. 340.00.

A nuanced and sensitive definition of Mme de Staël's group,
of its *raison d'être*; its political, literary, and aesthetic
goals; and its impact on the years 1803-17. With a short,
selective bibliography. A good starting point, by one of
the foremost Constant specialists. (D.J.C.)

Delon, Michel. "Madame de Staël, Benjamin Constant et le Groupe
de Coppet." Pp. 424-44 in Robert Mauzi, et al., eds.,
Littérature française. T. 6: *De l'Encyclopédie aux Médita-
tions*. (Littérature française/Poche.) Paris: Arthaud,
1984. Pp. 479.

Diesbach, Ghislain de. "L'histoire d'une colombe de proie."
Historia 443 (1984): 115-19.

Diesbach, Ghislain de. *Madame de Staël*. Paris: Librairie
académique Perrin, 1984. Reprinted as Presses Pocket n°
2269 (Coll. Histoire). Pp. 676. Fr. 30.00.

Rev. by Jacques Godechot in *AHRF* 55 (1983): 651-52;
by Danielle Johnson-Cousin in *NCFS* 12,iv; 13,i (1984):
208-09.

Escoffier, Françoise. "Madame de Staël: une *politologue*
intemporelle. *Considérations sur la Revolution française.*"
RDM, April 1984, pp. 95-100.

Essai sur les fictions. With: *De l'influence des passions
sur le bonheur des individus et des nations.* Paris: J.-P.
Ramsay (Editions Reliefs), 1979. Pp. 254. Fr. 57.00. env.

Gilbert, Sandra M. "From *Patria* to *Matria*: Elizabeth Barrett
Browning's Risorgimento." *PMLA* 99 (1984): 194-211.

In this excellent article, room is made for *Corinne ou
l'Italie* and its tacit influence on *Aurora Leigh*. Indeed,
Browning greatly admired Mme de Staël, and judged *Corinne*
to be "an immortal book" that "deserves to be read three
score and ten times--that is, once every year in the age of
man" (197). Links Aurora Leigh with Corinne (both the
daughters of Italian mothers and English fathers), and Browning with Staël, in their transformation of Italy into "a
land of free women, a female aesthetic utopia" (197). (D.J.C.)

Godechot, Jacques, ed. *Considérations sur la Révolution
française*. Paris: Tallandier, 1983. Pp. 693.

Rev. by Gilbert Comte in *Le Monde* (weekly selection of
Jan. 5-11, 1984); by Daniel Robert in *BSAPF* 130 (1984):
265-66; by J.-R. Suratteau in *AHRF* 55 (1983): 649-51.
First reprinting since 1881 of Mme de Staël's posthumous
work (first published in 1818 by Victor de Broglie and Auguste
de Staël in two editions). Text here reproduced dates from
April 1818.
With a substantial Introduction (7-41); a selective Bibliography (43-46); a Chronology of Mme de Staël's life and works
(47-55); and copious scholarly Notes, all by Godechot. A
welcome reprint. (D.J.C.)

Herold, J. Christopher. *The Horizon Book of the Age of Napoleon*
New York: American Heritage Publishing Co., Inc./Bonanza
Books, 1983. Pp. 432.

Hoog, Marie-Jacques. "L'improvisatrice ou la prise de la
parole féminine." *Bulletin de la Société des Professeurs
français en Amérique 1983-1984* (1984): 37-46.

Woman as improviser: brief historical sketch going back
to Antiquity's Pythia and Sybilla, but insistence upon the
emergence of this new literary type of female character
in nineteenth-century French literature: Corinne, of course,
followed by Lelia I and II, Colomba, and Consuelo. The
light is, however, on Mme de Staël, on her Italian experience
and her discovery of la Mazzei in Florence.

Drawing from Staël's recently published correspondence
with Don Pedro de Souza, Hoog relates her discovery of
Rome--of the temple of the Sybilla, in particular, "[et]
les inspirations de tous les genres dont [son] âme à été
remplie ..."--with the conception of Corinne as Sybilla,
and the metamorphosis of Germaine into Corinne. Corinne,
in sum, "marque la véritable prise de la parole féminine
dans sa forme la plus pure, l'improvisation" (44). (D.J.C.)

Hrbata, Zdenek. "*De la Littérature* de Madame de Staël.
(Quelques remarques sur l'héritage des Lumières et les
problèmes de la littérature romantique naissante)."
Philologica Pragensia 25 (1982): 1-12.

Lecherbonnier, Bernard, coord. With the collaboration of
Bernard and Jacqueline Cerquiglini, Fernand Egéa, Bernard
Lecherbonnier, Bernard Lehembre, and Jean-Jacques Mougenot.
Histoire de la littérature française. (Coll. Beaux Livres.)
Paris: Nathan, 1984. Pp. 240. Fr. 260.00.

Mansau, Andrée, ed. *Réflexions sur le suicide* [1815]. Paris:
Editions de l'Opale, 1984. Pp. 90. Fr. 45.00.

Mühlemann, S. "Staël." Pp. 2195-205 in Jean-Pierre de Beaumarchais, et al., eds., *Dictionnaire des littératures de
langue française*, T. III. Paris: Bordas, 1984. Pp. 2638.
Fr. 340.00.

Everything that is worth knowing and that one ought to know
about Mme de Staël, her life and work--in ten pages. In a
remarkably balanced, unbiased *essai de synthèse*, Mühlemann
accurately seizes up his subject, her importance in the
immediate historic circumstances, as well as her intellectual
contribution to politics, literature, and the history of
ideas in general. With a two-and-a-half-page synoptic "life
and work" chart; several selective bibliographies and a
general bibliography. A *tour de force--vraiment*. (D.J.C.)

Mülinen, Pascale de, Mme. "Madame de Staël et la Suisse."
Schweiz/Suisse/Svizzera/Switzerland (April 1975).

A special issue devoted to Coppet and Mme de Staël.

Scaiola, Anna Maria. "'Je suis curieuse de l'Italie.' Sulla
fortuna, oggi, di Madame de Staël." *Micromégas* (Jan.-Aug.
1982): 277-85.

Schwarz, Waltraut. "Bologna aus der Sicht der Frau von Staël
und ihrer deutschen Reisebegleiter, Berater und Übersetzer:
August Wilhelm, Friedrich und Dorothea Schlegel." *Franco-*
fonia 2 (Spring 1982): 57-70.

Solovieff, Georges. "A propos des choix, omissions et repentirs
dans 'De l'Allemagne' de Madame de Staël." *SFr* 28 (1984):
53-74.

Taxis-Bordogna, Olga, Gräfin von. *Madame de Staël*. Hildesheim
(W. Germany): Georg Olms, 1984. Pp. 382. Subs. price DM
56.00; other DM 68.00.

In this biography in novel form, first published in 1939,
the author endeavors to understand the emotions, actions,
and reactions of Germaine de Staël as woman and writer.
Following an extensive account of Mme de Staël's childhood
and youth, overshadowed by the conflict between Germaine's
passionate and exuberant character and her mother's stringent
nature, Countess von Taxis-Bordogna retraces the individual
stages of Staël's eventful and enormously active life.
Contains a critical and evaluative analysis of Staël's
two main works, *De la littérature ...* and *De l'Allemagne*.
(Adapted from publisher's slip.)

Vallois, Marie-Claire. "Les voi(es) de la Sibylle: Aphasie
et discours féminin chez Madame de Staël." *SFr* 26 (1982):
35-48.

See also Meregalli ("General 3. Criticism"); Delon, Naudin
("French 1. General"); Herrmann ("Sand"); Gutjahr ("German
3. Heine").

Reviews of books previously listed:

Annales Benjamin Constant 2 (1982) (see *RMB* for 1982, pp.
198-202), rev. by Paul Delbouille in *RHL* 84 (1984):
286-87; BALAYE, Simone, *Madame de Staël, Lumières et liberté*
(see *RMB* for 1982, p. 261), rev. by Henri Grange in *RHL* 84
Benjamin Constant 2 (1982): 123-28; HOFMANN, Etienne, ed.,

Benjamin Constant, Madame de Staël et le Groupe de Coppet
(see *RMB* for 1982, p. 261), rev. by Henri Grange in *RHL* 84
(1984): 968-73; OMACINI, Lucia, ed., *Des circonstances
actuelles qui peuvent terminer la Révolution* (see *RMB* for
1979, p. 229), rev. by Carlo Cordié in *Paideia* 39 (1984):
138-42; by Jacques Godechot in *AHRF* 54 (1982): 153-56.

STENDHAL

Andrieu, René. *Stendhal ou le bal masqué.* Paris: Jean-
Claude Lattès, 1983. Pp. 260.

   Rev. by V. Del Litto in *SC* 26 (1983-84): 199-200.

Bailbé, Joseph-Marc. "Stendhal et Champfleury: du réalisme
à l'intimité." *RHL* 84 (1984): 231-44.

   Compares Stendhal and Champfleury on the following points:
the depiction of the provincial woman, the discourse of
love, and the writer and his characters. Concludes that
"du naturel de Stendhal à la bonhomie de Champfleury la
distance ne semble pas très grande."

Barzun, Jacques. "Shaw versus Stendhal." *Partisan Review* 50
(1984): 613-19.

Berthier, Philippe. "Julien Gracq en Stendhalie." *RHL* 84
(1984): 271-84.

   On Gracq's lifelong fascination for Stendhal. Gracq's
knowledge of Stendhal was limited to *Le Rouge et le noir*
and *La Chartreuse de Parme* but he was attracted by the style,
rhythm, and climate of Stendhal's work.

Bokobza, Serge. "*Armance*: contribution à la titrologie
stendhalienne." *SC* 26 (1983-84): 233-39.

   The choice of *Armance* as the title of a novel in which
Octave is the main character could be explained as stressing
Octave's incapacity. Octave's absence from the title is in
accord with his character in the text. Suggestive. (E.J.T.)

Bolster, Richard. "Les *Mémoires d'un touriste* et la France
de Louis-Philippe." *SC* 26 (1983-84): 152-60.

   On Stendhal's assessment of conditions in France and his
views on international politics.

Bottacin, Annalisa. "L'adaptation de *la Chartreuse de Parme*
par Mauro Bolognini: les réactions de la presse italienne."
SC 26 (1983-84): 189-93.

On the extensive and highly favorable press commentary on Bolognini's adaptation of *La Chartreuse* for television.

Bravo Castillo, Juan. "Stendhal: autobiografía y novela." *CHA* 402 (Dec. 1983): 105-16.

Brotherson, Lee. "'L'intimité singulière' dans *Armance.* *SC* 26 (1983-84): 179-83.

Brief discussion of nonsexual intimacy in *Armance.* Nothing new. (E.J.T.)

Caramaschi, Enzo. "Paul Valéry face à *Lucien Leuwen.*" *SC* 26 (1983-84): 355-64.

On Valéry's preface to the 1926 Debraye edition of *Lucien Leuwen.* Valéry shows his interest in the biography and psychology of Stendhal and treats him more as a *moraliste* than a novelist.

Chantreau, Alain. *Stendhal et Nantes.* Nantes: Société Nantaise d'Etudes Littéraires, 1983. Pp. 131.

Rev. by V. Del Litto in *SC* 26 (1983-84): 287-88.

Chantreau, Alain. "La *Vie de Henry Brulard*: du roman à l'autobiographie." *RHL* 84 (1984): 206-16.

Suggests that in writing *La Vie de Henry Brulard* Stendhal used novelistic structures that he had utilized previously in *Le Rouge et le noir*, particularly the symbolic colors: black (God, religion, his father, his teachers, Grenoble) and red (his Jacobinism, his precocious anti-religious feelings, his enthusiasm for the republican armies).

Colesanti, Massimo. *Stendhal: le regole del gioco.* Milan: Garzanti, 1983. Pp. 361. L. 22,000.00.

Rev. by Graziano Benelli in *Letture* 39, no. 406 (April 1984): 373-74.

Collet, Annie. "Une lettre inédite d'Henri Beyle, consul de France." *SC* 26 (1983-84): 217-20.

Stendhal writing to the pontifical authorities to seek better conditions for a French prisoner.

Coulont-Henderson, Françoise. "Remarques sur la mémoire et les croquis dans la *Vie de Henry Brulard.*" *SC* 26 (1983-84): 141-51.

A first-rate discussion of the functions of the *croquis*
in *Vie de Henry Brulard*. According to Coulont-Henderson,
the *croquis* serve: (1) to locate memory in space; (2)
to supplement or replace description; (3) to analyze memories
from different points of view; (4) to evoke sensations of
the past. She demonstrates further that the *croquis* sometimes compete with the text and represent a priority given
to the visual. Lucid and rewarding. (E.J.T.)

Croce, Elena. "Stendhal e l'Italia." *NA* 2147 (July-Sept.
1983): 208-32.

Crouzet, Michel. "A propos de *Racine et Shakespeare*: tradition, réforme, et révolution dans le Romantisme." *NCFS*
12 (1983-84): 1-35.

An intelligent presentation of *Racine et Shakespeare*
which could serve as an introduction to the work. Crouzet
argues, correctly, that Stendhal is not proposing a new
poetics in *Racine et Shakespeare* but rather a non-poetics.
As Stendhal espouses freedom from rules, it is not classicism that he attacks as much as it is the *idea* of a literary
school. Stendhal calls for an internal poetics which would
render rules useless. Crouzet also comments perceptively
on Stendhal's treatment of the problems of language and
illusion. Recommended. (E.J.T.)

Crouzet, Michel. "Sur la topographie de *La Chartreuse de
Parme* et sur le rapport des lieux et des lieux communs."
Pp. 99-139 in Michel Crouzet, ed., *Espaces romanesques*.
Paris: P.U.F. et Université de Picardie, 1982. Pp. 248.
Fr. 70.00.

Del Litto, V. "Bibliographie stendhalienne. 1983 Année
Stendhal." *SC* 27 (1984-85): 63-107.

Del Litto, V. "Une note inédite sur *Rome, Naples et
Florence*." *SC* 27 (1984-85): 1-5.

A brief, previously unpublished piece by Stendhal in
which he notes the reactions of friends and acquaintances
to *Rome, Naples et Florence*.

Del Litto, Victor, and Hermann Harder, eds. *Stendhal et
l'Allemagne* (Actes du XIIIe Congrès International Stendhalien). Paris: Nizet, 1983. Pp. 238. Fr. 149.80.

Rev. in *BCLF* 463 (July 1984): 910.
Contains: Victor Del Litto, "Stendhal et l'Allemagne:

état des recherches et perspectives" (9-19); O.C. Römer,
"Le milieu éclairé de Brunswick au temps du royaume de
Westphalie" (21-30); Pierrette Bourdanton-Neaud, "Stendhal
et Mozart" (31-41); Francis Claudon, "Le séjour de Stendhal
en Allemagne" (43-56); Fabienne Gégou, "L'amour en Allemagne
d'après certaines réflexions éparses dans *De l'amour*"
(57-64); Jean-Jacques Labia, "Brunswick, le *Chasseur Vert* et
la temporalité stendhalienne" (56-78); Wolfgang Milde,
"Stendhal et la Bibliothèque de Wolfenbüttel" (79-84);
Marguerite Arnautovic, "Stendhal et Goethe" (85-102); Kurt
Ringger, "Vittoria Accorambona entre Stendhal et Tieck"
(103-24); Henri-François Imbert, "La notion d'affinité
élective chez Goethe et Stendhal" (125-33); Gisela Moinet,
"Stendhal et la comédie" (135-52); Anthony Purdy, "Stendhal
et Werther: du secret à la publicité" (153-67); Jean
Théodoridès, "Beyle, von Born et Broussonet" (169-76);
Guy Weill-Goudchaux, "Winckelmann et Stendhal" (177-89);
René Bourgeois, "*Rot und Schwarz*: quelques remarques sur
la traduction de Friedrich von Oppeln-Bronikowski" (191-96);
Alfred Guth, "Nietzsche et Stendhal" (197-204); Hermann
Hofer, "Christian Sénéchal et les stendhaliens allemands
(avec des documents inédits)" (205-16); Hermann Harder,
"Stendhal et Heinrich Mann" (217-27).

Del Litto, Victor, and Kurt Ringger. *Stendhal et le Romantisme*
(Actes du XVe Congrès International Stendhalien, Mayence
1982). (Collection Stendhalienne, 25.) Geneva: Droz, 1984.

Denier, Renée. "Reprenons à Stendhal: à propos de deux
articles du *Globe*." *SC* 26 (1983-84): 130-40.

Convincingly argues that two articles published in *Le
Globe* in 1824 and attributed to Stendhal by Daniel Muller
in 1919 and thereafter by a long list of scholars are
actually re-translations into French of an essay by Stendhal
translated into English and published in the *New Monthly
Magazine*. Denier further establishes that the re-translation
into French was the work of an inexperienced translator whose
knowledge of English was sometimes faulty. (E.J.T.)

Dentan, Michel. "Le lecteur idéal de *Henry Brulard*." *EdL*
3 (1984): 39-46.

Shows how Stendhal in writing *Henry Brulard* makes no
effort to furnish his future readers with the information
that they would need to understand his text. His ideal
readers of the future are those who have confidence in him,
who understand his needs, obsessions, and tastes.

Devos, Willy. "Stendhal en néerlandais. Bibliographie 1982-
    1983." *SC* 27 (1984-85): 61-62.

    Dutch translations of Stendhal and articles in Dutch on
    Stendhal.

Didier, Béatrice. "Roman et autobiographie chez Stendhal."
    RHL 84 (1984): 217-30.

    Argues that in writing his autobiography Stendhal con-
    sciously attempted to avoid novelistic structures and devices.
    In order to do this, he had recourse to a systematic dis-
    ruption of narration, imposing on himself the disorder of
    memory rather than the order of chronology. Paradoxically,
    in inventing a new autobiographical writing, Stendhal became
    a precursor of modern novelistic techniques. Closely
    argued. (E.J.T.)

Douchin, Jacques-Louis. "Esquisse de numérologie stendhalienne."
    SC 26 (1983-84): 240-48.

    Numerological study of dates in Stendhal's life. Silly.
    (E.J.T.)

Finch, Alison. *Stendhal: La Chartreuse de Parme.* (Studies
    in French Literature, 34.) London: Edward Arnold, 1984.
    Pp. 72.

    Rev. by V. Del Litto in *SC* 26 (1983-84): 375-76.
    A good introduction to the novel for non-specialists.
    Finch gives a clear, lucid account of the tone of *La Chartreuse*,
    discusses the various forms of humor, touches on structural
    harmony and diffusiveness, and takes up the problems of
    narrative uncertainty and the narrator's interventions.
    Finch also gives appropriate attention to the geographical
    and political background of the novel. Recommended for
    undergraduate students. (E.J.T.)

Fischer, Jan O. "Précis bibliographique des traductions
    tchèques et slovaques de Stendhal." *SC* 27 (1984-85): 59-60.

    Translations since World War II.

Francillon, Roger. "Mais où ont donc passé les millions de la
    Sanseverina: Réflexions sur le rôle de l'argent dans *la
    Chartreuse de Parme.*" *EdL* 3 (1984): 79-89.

    An original analysis of the function of money in *La
    Chartreuse.* Money is a negative value only in two cases:
    when it is used to produce capital and when it serves personal
    vanity. Otherwise, money is seen positively, permitting

aesthetic pleasures, brilliant receptions, and generosity toward the poor, and serving as an instrument of personal passions and follies. (E.J.T.)

Geninasca, Jacques. "Le dialogisme intratextuel chez Stendhal." *EdL* 3 (1984): 13-26.

Semiotic analysis of a passage from *Rome, Naples et Florence*.

Greschoff, C.J. "'Julianus Bifrons' ou le double dénouement du *Rouge et noir*." *RHL* 84 (1984): 255-70.

Explains the "double ending" of *Le Rouge et le noir* as a result of Julien's being a "double character": both ambitious and sensitive. The two endings respond to the two sides of Julien's character. Greshoff's interpretation is clear and closely argued, but not new. (E.J.T.)

Hamm, Jean-Jacques. "Un laboratoire stendhalien: les *Chroniques italiennes*." *RHL* 84 (1984): 245-54.

Sees the *Chroniques italiennes* as occupying an intermediate position in Stendhal's practice of writing, between plagiarism (as in *Vie de Haydn*) and the complete rewriting of an original text (as in *La Chartreuse de Parme*).

Houbert, Jacques. "Un portrait inédit de Stendhal par Devéria?" *SC* 26 (1983-84): 365-68.

On the possibility that an unidentified crayon portrait by Devéria might be of Stendhal.

Ifri, Pascal. "Les techniques narratives dans l'autobiographie et le roman autobiographique: l'exemple de Stendhal et de Musset." *Neophil* 68 (1984): 355-64.

An analysis of *La Confession d'un enfant du siècle* and *Souvenirs d'égotisme* which seeks to disprove Lejeune's affirmation that on the level of the internal analysis of the text, there is no difference between autobiography and the autobiographical novel. Ifri contends, to the contrary, that the point of view of the hero is dominant in the auto-biographical novel while that of the narrator is dominant in autobiography. The autobiographical novel maintains a chronological continuity and a developing plot while auto-biography is prone to digressions which scramble the chronology and prevent the development of a plot. Dialogues and monologues are important in the autobiographical novel but virtually absent from autobiography. A useful discussion. (E.J.T.)

Imbert, Henri-François. "Fonction de *Lucien Leuwen* dans
l'oeuvre romanesque de Stendhal." *SC* 26 (1983-84): 165-78.

   Proposes that in writing *Lucien Leuwen* Stendhal was
attempting to adjust his own writing habits (which owe a
great deal to the Ideologues and to La Bruyère) to meet
the novelistic tendencies of his time (as practiced by
Balzac and Scott).

Imbert, Thérèse. "Henri Beyle et l'inventaire du Musée
Napoléon (Documents inédits)." *SC* 27 (1984-85): 9-20.

   Letters by Daru, Vivant Denon, and the Duc de Cadore
relating to the inventory of the Musée Napoléon, which
Stendhal had been charged to supervise.

Jackson, John E. "Les silences de Stendhal." *EdL* 3 (1984):
27-38.

   Dealing primarily with *Armance*, Jackson attempts to
explain why Stendhal is silent on the origins of the psychology of his characters. He concludes that the trauma
which Stendhal experienced at the death of his mother is in
part responsible. Octave's unexplained melancholy is
related to Stendhal's own incestuous passion and its origin
must therefore be repressed. Stimulating. (E.J.T.)

Jacobs, Helmut C. *Stendhal und die Musik. Forschungsbericht
und kritische Bibliographie 1900-1980.* (Bonner Romanistische Arbeiten, 17.) Frankfurt-am-Main: Peter Lang,
1983. Pp. 258.

   Rev. by Kurt Ringger in *SC* 26 (1983-84): 196-97.

Landry, François. "Des âmes tendres aux happy few: vers une
religion stendhalienne." *EdL* 3 (1984): 63-77.

   Solid essay on the meaning of religion in Stendhal.
His critical attitude notwithstanding, Stendhal postulates
a link between the perfection of the heart and soul on the
one hand and religion on the other. For him, religion
would be a reunion of sensitive souls united in their
struggle against cruelty and death. (E.J.T.)

Laurens, Gilbert. "Le mythe d'Hérodiade chez Stendhal."
SC 26 (1983-84): 344-54; 27 (1984-85): 21-28.

   Establishes Stendhal's fascination for painting of
Hérodiade, and links it to childhood obsessions relating to
blood and death.

Laurent, Jacques. *Stendhal comme Stendhal, ou le mensonge ambigu.* Paris: Grasset, 1984. Pp. 288. Fr. 79.00.

Rev. by Dominique Fernandez in *L'Express* (March 2-8, 1984): 97-98; by Béatrice Didier in *QL* 415 (April 16-30, 1984): 19; in *Europe* 664-65 (Aug.-Sept. 1984): 217-18.

This is a highly personal reflection on Stendhal. Laurent recounts his own relationship to Stendhal as it has developed through reading his books and then launches an attack on critics who "colonize" Stendhal in the interest of fashionable critical schools. Béatrice Didier is singled out for harsh ridicule. Laurent says that he wants to *débarbouiller* Stendhal, to free him from the domination of Freud and Marx. While Laurent does score some points, his own presentation of Stendhal is biographical in approach and thereby as limited as the approaches he criticizes. (E.J.T.)

Le Yaouanc, Moïse. "*Julia ou l'amour à Naples* et *La Chartreuse de Parme.*" *RHL* 84 (1984): 179-98.

While there is no evidence that Stendhal knew Guy d'Agde's *Julia ou l'Amour à Naples* (1835), some striking resemblances between some scenes in Agde's novel and scenes in *La Chartreuse* (Ernest V's deal with la Sanseverina for her favors, Fabrice and Clélia's scene of passion in the jail cell) lead the author to conclude that Stendhal knew Agde's novel and drew on it for some episodes.

Luneau-Hawkins, Annick. "Le style de *la Chartreuse de Parme*: esquisse d'étude syntaxique." *SC* 26 (1983-84): 249-62.

Demonstrates that Stendhal's use of coordinating conjunctions (*et* and *mais*) is rich and complex.

Mansau, Andrée. "Stendhal et ses ancêtres médecins de Montpellier: la thèse de Louis-Joseph Gagnon." *SC* 27 (1984-85): 36-42.

Reminds us that Stendhal's family included a number of medical doctors and briefly describes the doctoral thesis of his great-uncle.

Maquet, Albert. "Kochnitzky." *SC* 26 (1983-84): 186-88.

On Stendhalian themes (dandyism, cosmopolitanism, passion for music, love of Italy) found in the poet, journalist, and critic Kochnitzky.

Maquet, Albert. "Un des grands enthousiasmes de Stendhal: 'L'Elefante,' satire en dialecte vénitien de Pietro Buratti."

Pp. 739-59 in Jean-Marie d'Heur and Nicoletta Cherubini, eds.,
*Etudes de philologie romane et d'histoire littéraire offertes
à Jules Horrent*. Liège: GEDIT, 1980. Pp. 853.

Mariani, Giovanna. "L'incompiutezza del *Lucien Leuwen* di
Stendhal: alcuni atteggiamenti della critica." *SFr* 27
(1983): 477-86.

A survey of the various critical explanations for the
inachèvement of *Lucien Leuwen*. Critics surveyed include
Thibaudet, Blin, Bardèche, Giraud, Maranini, Prévost, Durand,
Felman, Alain, Blum, Hemmings.

Marin, Louis. "Images dans le texte autobiographique: sur le
chapitre XLIV de la *Vie de Henry Brulard*." *Saggi* 23 (1984):
197-231.

A probing discussion of the chapter in *Vie de Henry Brulard*
in which Stendhal narrates his first crossing of the Alps
into Italy. Marin is particularly concerned with the
function of images as interferences in retelling what "really"
happened (Stendhal is conscious that stories he has been
told and engravings he has seen are coloring his depiction)
and as graphic aids for narration. (E.J.T.)

Martonyi, Eva. "L'année Stendhal en Hongrie. Bibliographie."
SC 27 (1984-85): 57-58.

Annotated bibliography for 1983.

McWatters, K.G., ed. *Chroniques pour l'Angleterre*, tome II
(1823-1824). Publications de l'Université des Langues et
Lettres de Grenoble, 1982. Pp. 320.

Rev. by P. Berthier in *SC* 26 (1983-84): 197-99.
Volume II of the first scholarly, critical edition of
Stendhal's writings for the British press. This edition
replaces Martineau's faulty *Courrier anglais*.

McWatters, K.G., ed. *Chroniques pour l'Angleterre*, tome III
(1825-1826). Publications de l'Université des Langues et
Lettres de Grenoble, 1983. Pp. 344.

Rev. by P. Berthier in *SC* 26 (1983-84): 197-99.
Continuation of the above.

Méras, Mathieu. "Deux nouveaux portraits inédits d'Alberthe
de Rubempré et d'Adolphe de Mareste." *SC* 26 (1983-84):
161-64.

Previously unknown portraits of Stendhal's lover,
Alberthe, and his friend and confidant, Mareste.

Méras, Mathieu. "Trois portraits inédits d'Adolphe de
Mareste et d'Alberthe de Rubempré." *SC* 27 (1984-85): 6-8.

A photograph (the only one found to date) of Mareste plus
a drawing and a miniature painting of Alberthe.

Mossman, Carol A. *The Narrative Matrix: Stendhal's Le Rouge
et le noir*. (French Forum Monographs, 53.) Lexington, Ky.:
French Forum Publishers, 1984. Pp. 177. $12.50.

An insightful, intelligent, and fresh reading of *Le Rouge
et le noir*, which Mossman treats as a fantasy construct
whose ending is strongly overdetermined. Stendhal's ending
is no longer justified according to the "logic of the
character" but rather through articulations of the oedipal
myth and a *regressus ad uterum* wish. This permits Mossman
to rethink the novel as framed by twin blades (that of the
sawmill and that of the guillotine), one of which is associated with birth, the other with death. A first-rate
psychoanalytical study. (E.J.T.)

Muller-Kotchetkova, Tatiana. "Stendhal en U.R.S.S. Bibliographie 1979-1983." *SC* 27 (1984-85): 52-56.

Pascal, Gabrielle. "Stendhal: la naissance d'*Henry Brulard*,
ou à la recherche du moi perdu." *ELit* 17 (1984): 283-309.

A probing discussion of *Vie de Henry Brulard* and particularly of Chapter III, which Pascal sees as putting into place
the principal themes of the autobiography, especially the
rejection of the father and the choice of maternal filiation.
Pascal discusses a number of other issues such as the problem
of self-revelation, the mistrust of language, and the function of the ironic mode. A rewarding essay. (E.J.T.)

Pérez Gállego, Cándido. "La pasión creadora de Stendhal."
CHA 402 (Dec. 1983): 116-23.

A wide-ranging article emphasizing the role of creative
passion in Stendhal as it relates to characters in a particular socio-political situation.

Pérez Gállego, Cándido. "Stendhal: El amor como género
literario." *Arbor* 458 (Feb. 1984): 29-40 [173-84].

Poliaghi, Nora Franca. *Stendhal e Trieste*. (Biblioteca dell'
Archivum Romanicum, Serie I, vol. 184.) Florence: Leo S.
Olschki, 1984. Pp. vi+202. L. 28,000.00.

Porter, Dennis. "Reinventing Travel: Stendhal's Roman
Journey." *Genre* 16 (1983): 467-76.

A solid essay on the *Promenades dans Rome* as an anti-guide
book. Porter argues that the *Promenades* reinvented travel
literature as a privileged genre for the expression of the
libertarian dream. Rome is rearticulated in such a way
that "it ceases to signify power, the Law, and duty, and
is transformed instead into the maternal place of powerlessness and pleasure." (E.J.T.)

Ringger, Kurt, and Rolf Klein. "Lucien le lion: à propos
d'un patronyme stendhalien." *SC* 27 (1984-85): 29-35.

Argues that Lucien's family name, Leuwen, might be a
French spelling for the German word for "lion" (Löwe-Löwen).
The argument is supported by the fact that at the time the
term "lion" was used as a synonym for "dandy." The choice
of Leuwen as Lucien's family name would thereby stress the
dandy in Lucien.

Robida, Michel. "Stendhal et l'Europe." *RDM*, Jan. 1984,
pp. 184-85.

On an exposition at the Bibliothèque Nationale.

Rosa, George M. "The Tempest and the Rock: An Intertextual
Study of Two Images in Stendhal's *De l'amour*." *RomN* 24
(1983-84): 161-67.

On Stendhal's use of verses from Canto I of Byron's
Don Juan.

Rousset, Jean. "Les échanges à distance." *EdL* 3 (1984):
3-12.

Studies the ways in which Stendhalian lovers communicate
indirectly. Stendhal is seen as a master creator of messages
with two (sometimes three!) intended receivers but containing a message destined for one receiver only, the lover.
Solid. (E.J.T.)

Rude, Fernand. *Stendhal et la pensée sociale de son temps.*
Nouvelle édition augmentée. Brionne: Gérard Montfort,
1983. Pp. 362.

Rev. by V. Del Litto in *SC* 26 (1983-84): 386-87.
A reprint of a major work, published in 1967, with
appendices including an important survey of scholarship
on the subject since the first edition. (E.J.T.)

Salamand, Georges. "Romain Rolland et Stendhal." *SC* 26 (1983-84): 121-29.

Reproduces (1) excerpts from a paper which Romain Rolland wrote when he was a student at the Ecole Normale Supérieure (Rolland criticizes, among other things, Stendhal's psychological descriptions) and (2) a page of Rolland's *Journal* of 1943 in which he is rather lyrical about *La Chartreuse de Parme*.

Schork, R.J. "Mann and Stendhal." *GR* 59 (1984): 63-67.

Starting from evidence of Mann's high regard for *Le Rouge et le noir*, Schork proposes that some intertextual verbal parallels argue that Mann used passages from *Le Rouge* to impart "a muted Stendhalian sheen" to his novel *Der Erwählte*.

Schuerwegen, Franc. "Le détective défaillant ou l'instance du policier dans les *Chroniques italiennes*." *OL* 39 (1984): 213-29.

A suggestive reading of the *Chroniques italiennes*, especially "Trop de faveur tue," as *récits policiers*. (E.J.T.)

Sgard, Jean. "L'explicit de la *Vie de Henry Brulard*." *RHL* 84 (1984): 199-205.

The quotation from Villemain which comes at the end of the work is linked to a number of themes developed in *Vie de Henry Brulard*: the impossibility of expressing passion and happiness in 1835, the divorce between the writer and the bourgeois public, and the gap between the real and the ideal which leads to a "fiasco d'imagination."

Simons, Madeleine A. "Stendhal et les métamorphoses du sacré. Le décor gothique: 'scena tragica' et 'scena comica.'" *SC* 26 (1983-84): 329-43.

An excellent discussion of the role of the sacred in Stendhal's fiction, particularly in *Le Rouge et le noir*. For Stendhal, *amour-passion* is identical to religious feeling, being a transfer to the lover of the sentiments which the Christian has for God. The imagery which surrounds the woman loved is often associated with the Madonna, and chapels and churches play a prominent part in Julien's destiny. (E.J.T.)

Teissier, Philippe. "*Armance* ou la genèse de l'univers stendhalien." *SC* 26 (1983-84): 221-32.

Argues that *Armance*, through its characterization, its depiction of socio-historical reality, and its reflection of its author's existential situation, foretells Stendhal's great novels.

Thompson, C.W. *Le Jeu de l'ordre et de la liberté dans la Chartreuse de Parme.* (Collection stendhalienne, 24.) Aran: Editions du Grand-Chêne, 1982. Pp. 245. Sw.Fr. 45.00.

Rev. by F. Landry in *RHL* 84 (1984): 291-92; by G. Strickland in *FS* 38 (1984): 350-51; in *BCLF* 463 (July 1984): 911.

Listed last year without comment. Clearly the best discussion yet of *La Chartreuse* by a critic who is alert to the differences and discontinuities among Stendhal's novels and who emphasizes this novel's differences from Stendhal's other novels. *La Chartreuse*, which is concerned with the relationship between order and freedom, is seen as oriented toward synthesis and reconciliation. The importance that the novel gives to the notion of play (Roger Caillois's definitions and distinctions serve as a theoretical base here) is crucial to bringing about an equilibrium among freedom, rules, and chance. The three major characters, Gina, Mosca, and Fabrice, are closely analyzed from this perspective. The discussion of Gina is particularly original. Thompson de-romanticizes the character and stresses that much of her subversive activity is aimed at maintaining her own psychic freedom. Mosca's political attitudes are discussed with lucidity and precision as is Fabrice's itinerary toward spirituality. (E.J.T.)

Thompson, Patrice. "La musique et les idées de génie." *EdL* 3 (1984): 47-62.

On the manner in which musical sensations combine with other recurring elements in Stendhal's writing.

Vita di Rossini. Città di Castello: Passighi, 1984. Pp. 314. L. 12,000.00.

Rev. by Marta Morazzoni in *Lettura* 39 (June-July 1984): 534-36.

Weiand, Christof. "'Ernestine': prototype de la narration stendhalienne." *SC* 26 (1983-84): 263-79.

Detailed narratological study of "Ernestine," a short narrative which is part of *De l'amour.*

Woolen, Geoff. "Un 'pilotis' de *Rouge et Noir*: Benjamin Appert." *SC* 26 (1983-84): 305-28.

Detailed discussion of the career and activities of the prison reformer Benjamin Appert, who appears briefly as a character in *Le Rouge et le noir*.

See also André, Bailbé, Bolster, Coquillat, Knapp-Tepperberg ("French 1. General"); Joseph ("Chateaubriand"); *H.B.* ("Mérimée"); Ifri ("Musset").

Reviews of books previously listed:

BERTHIER, Philippe, *Stendhal et la sainte famille* (see *RMB* for 1983, p. 262), rev. by J.-J. Hamm in *SC* 26 (1983-84): 383-85; CROUZET, Michel, *Stendhal et l'italianité* (see *RMB* for 1982, p. 266), rev. by P. Berthier in *RHL* 83 (1983): 947-50; CROUZET, Michel, *La Vie de Henry Brulard ou l'enfance de la revolte* (see *RMB* for 1983, p. 266), rev. by V. Brombert in *RHL* 84 (1984): 634-35; DEL BO, Dino, *Le Iscrizioni di Stendhal* (see *RMB* for 1982, p. 267), rev. by C. Cordié in *SFr* 27 (1983): 573; DEL LITTO, Victor, *Essais stendhaliens* (see *RMB* for 1981, pp. 245-46), rev. by C. Cordié in *SFr* 27 (1983): 573; DEL LITTO, Victor, ed., *OEuvres intimes*, *vol. II* (see *RMB* for 1983, pp. 267-68), rev. by G. Moinet in *SFr* 28 (1984): 176; by E. Talbot in *NCFS* 12 (1983-84): 217-18; DEL LITTO, V., ed., *Le Rose et le vert* (see *RMB* for 1982, p. 267), rev. by I. Simon in *NCFS* 12 (1983-84): 218-20; GUERIN, Michel, *La Politique de Stendhal* (see *RMB* for 1982, p. 268), rev. by K.G. McWatters in *MLR* 79 (1984): 460-62; MAGNANI, Luigi, *L'Idea della Chartreuse* (see *RMB* for 1980, p. 250), rev. by C. Cordié in *SFr* 27 (1983): 572-73; by C. Dédéyan in *RHL* 84 (1984): 290-91; MEININGER, Anne-Marie, ed., *Lucien Leuwen* (see *RMB* for 1983, p. 272), rev. by G. Dethan in *SC* 26 (1983-84): 285-87; by K. Ringger in *RHL* 84 (1984): 288-90; RINGGER, Kurt, *L'Ame et la page* (see *RMB* for 1983, p. 274), rev. by A. Chantreau in *RHL* 84 (1984): 292-93; by G. Moinet in *SFr* 28 (1984): 176-77; by Eileen Mullady in *RR* 74 (1983): 499-500; *Stendhal e Milano* (see *RMB* for 1983, pp. 275-77), rev. by Mario Pozzi in *GSLI* 161 (1984): 154.

SUE

Brunetti, Bruno. "La forma del racconto ne *Les Mystères de Paris* di Eugène Sue e ne *I Misteri di Napoli* di Francesco Mastriani." Pp. 201-15 in *Letteratura popolare di espressione francese dall'"Ancien Régime" all'ottocento. R. Barthes e il suo metodo critico.* Atti del X Convegno della Società

universitaria per gli studi di lingua e letteratura francese.
Bari, 6-10 maggio 1981. (Quaderni, 4.) Fasano: Schena, 1983.

Le Juif errant. (Bouquins.) Paris: Robert Laffont, 1983.
Pp. 1114. Fr. 89.00.

Silve de Ventavon, Jean. "Eugène Sue et la droite." *Ecrits
de Paris* 435 (May 1983): 77-82.

Svane, Brynja. "Structures narratives et tendances idéologiques.
Une étude d'Eugène Sue, *Mathilde*." Pp. 341-49 in *Actes du
VIIIe Congrès des Romanistes Scandinaves (Odense 17-21 août
1981).* (Etudes romanes de l'Université d'Odense, 13.)
Odense University Press, 1983. Pp. 399.

   Rev. by F.-J. Haussmann in *ZRP* 99 (1983): 555-62.

See also Angenot, Krakovitch, Wolfszettel ("French 1. General").

TÖPFFER

Candaux, Jean-Daniel. "Le 'scrapbook' töpfférien d'Edmond
Chenevière." *Bulletin de la Société d'Etudes Töpffériennes*
8 (May 1980): 2-8.

   Chenevière (1862-1932), a Geneva banker and bibliophile
specializing in Geneva writers and especially Töpffer, compiled
an album of Töpffer's drawings which is now in the Bibliothèque
publique et universitaire de Genève.

Paccaud, Antoine, and Bernadette Pilloud, eds. *En zigzag
avec Rodolphe Töpffer et la bande dessinée.* Yverdon-les-
Bains: Service des Expositions des Affaires culturelles,
1983. Pp. 36.

   The catalogue of a show devoted to Töpffer and the comic
strip given at the Hôtel de Ville of Yverdon-les-Bains,
accompanied by the following articles: Jean-Daniel Candaux,
"Rodolphe Töpffer a-t-il inventé les 'voyages en zigzag'?"
(7-12); Jacques Droin, "De l'importance des 'Voyages en
zigzag' dans la vie de Rodolphe Töpffer" (13-17);
Manuela Busino-Maschietto, "L'oeuvre graphique du peintre
genevois Rodolphe Töpffer (1799-1846)" (18-23).

TRISTAN

Michaud, Stéphane, ed. *Flora Tristan (1803-1844)*. Préface
de Frédéric Lescure. (Aux Sources du Socialisme.) Paris:
Les Editions ouvrières, 1984. Pp. 140. Fr. 50.00.

Rev. by Fernand Rude in *QL* 423 (Sept. 1-15, 1984): 17-18.
A useful anthology of some sixty extracts, mostly rather
brief, from the published works and the letters of the great
feminist. Michaud summarizes her career and importance in
a good introduction (9-27) and provides, also, a "Chronologie:
biographie et histoire mêlées" (28-32). The explanatory
footnotes, although not numerous, are adequate for this
popularizing presentation. (J.S.P.)

Tholoniat, Richard. "Jules Vallès et Flora Tristan, face à
l'Angleterre victorienne." *L'Information Historique* 4 (1983):
30-37.

See also Aron ("French 1. General").

VEUILLOT

Hesbert, dom René-Jean, ed. *Çà et là dans les oeuvres de
Louis Veuillot*. Paris: Nouvelles Editions Latines, 1981.
Pp. 199. Fr. 48.00.

Forty-five brief extracts from Veuillot's works.

Léger, Xavier. "Un écrivain méconnu: Louis Veuillot (1813-
1883)." *Le Club Français de la Médaille*. *Bulletin* 78-79
(1er trimestre 1983): 48-51, 55.

Le Roux, Benoît. *Louis Veuillot: un homme de combat*. Paris:
Téqui, 1984. Pp. 294. Fr. 64.00.

Rev. by Willy de Spens in *NRF* 382 (Nov. 1, 1984): 86-87.

VIGNY

Association des Amis d'Alfred de Vigny. Bulletin No. 13:
1983-84. Pp. 58.

Contents: Floriane Forster, "Compte rendu d'activité"
(3-5); Simone Pirard, "Voyage en Charente du 23 avril
1983" (6-7); Jacques-Philippe Saint-Gérand, "Où donc est la
Beauté que rêve le Poète?" (8-20); Simon Jeune, "Au secours

des jeunes talents: un billet inconnu de Vigny" (21-27);
Christiane Lefranc, "Les mystères de Loches en 1777 ..."
(28-34); Claude Dietschy-Picard, "Les officiers du roi
dans la famille paternelle d'Alfred de Vigny" (35-44);
Michel Cambien, "Alfred de Vigny, philosophe et poète"
(45-55); "Bibliographie" (57-58).

Saint-Gérand reconstructs the list of rhetorical treatises,
dictionaries, grammars, and critical writings against which
Vigny's esthetic theories fought, in particular those giving
pride of place to painterly metaphors. Jeune publishes
the text of Vigny's recommendation of the statue "Abelard
and Heloise" sculpted by Emile Chatrousse. From a handful
of letters, Lefranc fleshes out an unhappy love story whose
heroine may have been Vigny's mother. Dietschy-Picard
gives biographical sketches of Vigny's military relatives:
great-grandfather, uncles, and cousins. Cambien discerns
a problematic tension between analysis and synthesis in
Vigny's work as well as a successful resolution of that
dialectic in *Les Destinées*.

Becq, Annie. "Le discours idéologique à l'épreuve du poème:
   La Sauvage d'Alfred de Vigny." *Romantisme* 39 (1983): 119-
   26.

Bouvet, Alphonse. "Julien selon Vigny: Julien, Daphné
   et la deuxième tentation du Docteur Noir." Pp. 187-205
   in *L'Empéreur Julien: de la légende au mythe*, vol. 2.
   Paris: Les Belles Lettres, 1981.

Buss, Robin. *Vigny: Chatterton*. (Critical Guides to French
   Texts, 34.) London: Grant and Cutler, 1984. Pp. 78.
   £2.25.

   Brief rev. in *FMLS* 20 (1984): 369.

Conem, Francis. "H. Ryner et Alfred de Vigny." *Les Messages
   de Psychodore* 5 (Feb. 1983): 7-8.

Denommé, Robert T. "'Chatterton' ou le dilemme du héros
   dans un monde non-héroïque." *CAIEF* 35 (1983): 141-54.

   In order to become a hero in the eyes of a society of
   which he disapproves and in the face of history, which refuses
   to acknowledge the value of heroism, Chatterton strives to
   overcome obstacles in his personal life. Yet because Vigny
   associates his poet-protagonist too closely with a thesis,
   Chatterton doesn't seem to have a sufficiently complex,
   coherent personality to attain the heroism for which he
   seeks.

Jarry, André. "Les lieux de l'écriture chez Alfred de Vigny: étude de quelques manuscrits." *Littérature* 52 (Dec. 1983): 81-111.

Legrand, Yolande. "Alfred de Vigny, poète et peintre." *Eidôlon* 24 (1983): 79-107.

LeHir, Yves. "Sur des citations d'Alfred de Vigny dans *Stello*." *TLL* 20 (1982): 227-32.

Majewski, Henry F. "The Second Consultation of the 'Docteur Noir': Vigny's *Daphné* and the Power of Symbols." *SiR* 20 (1981): 461-74.

Roloff, Volker. "*Torquato Tasso, Chatterton, Um auto de Gil Vicente*: Überlegungen zum romantischen Schriftstellardrama." *Arcadia* 19 (1984): 34-51.

Saint-Gérand, Jacques-Philippe. "Remords et contrition." *La Licorne* (1980): 189-91.

Steiner, George. "Suffering in Silence." *TLS*, Sept. 16, 1983, p. 1000.

See also Coquillat, Daniels, Grossir, Krakovitch ("French 1. General").

Reviews of book previously listed:

VIALLANEIX, Paul, ed., *Les Destinées* (see *RMB* for 1983, p. 282), rev. by Claude Duchet in *Romantisme* 43 (1984): 123-24; by J.C. Ireson in *MLR* 79 (1984): 943.

VILLEMAIN

Melavié, Jean. "Abel Villemain en verve: malices et sourires d'un universitaire du siècle passé." *Aevum* 57 (1983): 450-62.

A collection of Villemain's witticisms, including those he pointed out in others.

Malavié, Jean. "Politique de Villemain." *L'Information Historique* 4 (1983): 181-87.

VINET

La Vérité n'a point de couture. Réflexions et aphorismes
  tirés des agendas. (Symbolon.) Lausanne: L'Age d'Homme,
  1984. Pp. 240. Fr. 90.00.

WEILL

Reviews of book previously listed:

  FRIEDMANN, Joë, *Alexandre Weill écrivain contestataire et*
  historien engagé, 1811-1899 (see *RMB* for 1980, p. 265), rev.
  by Alain Nabarra in *FR* 58 (1984-85): 293-94; by Nelly
  Wilson in *FS* 38 (1984): 473-74.

GERMAN

(Compiled by Konstanze Bäumer, Syracuse University;
Christopher R. Clason, University of California,
Davis; William Crisman, University of California,
Berkeley; Roger Crockett, Texas A & M University;
John F. Fetzer, University of California, Davis;
Bernd Fischer, Ohio State University; Michael Jones,
Ohio State University; Wulf Koepke, Texas A & M
University; Scott McLean, University of California,
Davis; Robert Mollenauer, University of Texas, Austin;
Jeffrey L. Sammons, Yale University; Steven P. Scher,
Dartmouth College; Leonard Schulze, University of
Texas, Austin)

1. BIBLIOGRAPHY

Allen, Robert T., and Paul J. Korschin, gen. eds. *The
Eighteenth Century: A Current Bibliography*. N.S. 6, for
1980. New York: AMS Press, 1984. Pp. 643. Eds. for
German: John A. McCarthy and Barbara Becker-Cantarino.

"Annotierte Auswahlbibliographie germanistischer Dissertations-
schriften." *ZG* (Leipzig) 5 (1984): 126, 254-55, 375-78,
502-05.

*Deutsche Bücher: Referatenorgan germanistischer, belletristischer
und deutschkundlicher Neuerscheinungen* (vorm. *Het Duitse
Boek*) 14 (1984). Amsterdam: Editions Rodopi N.V.

Broad, selective coverage of recent critical works. Each
number begins with an interview of a contemporary new writer.
Survey reviews in the concluding "Kurz berichtet."

"Doctoral Dissertations" [U.S. and Canada]. *Monatshefte* 76
(1984): 304-06.

*Germanistik: Internationales Referatenorgan mit bibliographischen
Hinweisen*. Jahrgang 25. 4 Hefte: 1, 2/3, 4. Tübingen:
Niemeyer, 1984-85.

For Romanticism see "II. Allgemeines"; XVII. Allgemeines
zur Literaturwissenschaft"; "XXI. Deutsche Literaturgeschichte,
Allgemeines"; "XXIX. Goethezeit (1770-1830)"; "XXX. Von der
Spätromantik bis zum Realismus (1830-1880)." Books but not
articles are reviewed. Articles and independent chapters
within *Sammelbände* are cross-listed by epoch and author.
Heft 3/4 includes the annual index of authors and topics.

Hagen, Waltraud, et al., eds. *Handbuch der Editionen:
Deutschsprachige Schriftsteller. Ausgang des 15. Jahrhunderts
bis zur Gegenwart.* München: C.H. Beck (Lizenzausgabe, Volk
und Wissen Volkseigener Verlag Berlin DDR), 1979. Pp. 608.

   Index arranged by periods (e.g., 1789-1830, 1830-1900);
authors arranged alphabetically throughout. A judiciously
selective, well-annotated handbook ("Ratgeber") that brings
together the best editions and reference works produced by
Eastern and Western scholarship. (R.M.)

Hartke, Werner, ed. *Deutsche Literaturzeitung für Kritik der
internationalen Wissenschaft: Herausgegeben im Auftrage der
Akademie der Wissenschaften der DDR (=DLZ).* Vol. 106, 1985.
Berlin: Akademie-Verlag, 1984.

   The monthly installments include a small section for
Germanistik.

Hohnholz, J., ed. *Literature--Music--Fine Arts: A Review of
German-Language Research Contributions on Literature, Music,
and Fine Arts (=LMFA).* (German Studies, Section III, edited
by the Institute for Scientific Co-Operation.) Vol. 18,
Nos. 1 and 2: 1985.

   English-language reviews of German-language studies in the
three named fields, each section accompanied by a "Selected
Bibliography."

Koch, Hans-Albrecht, and Uta Koch, eds. *Internationale
Germanistische Bibliographie 1980 (IGB).* New York, London,
and Paris: K.G. Saur, 1981. Pp. 855.

   This is the opening volume of the *IGB*, which will be produced
annually and which will attempt a reporting comprehensiveness
that is to extend eventually beyond Europe and America. Listings only, no review evaluations, index by name (including
the person written about) and by subject. In areas relating

to literary scholarship this work will duplicate somewhat
the coverage offered by *Germanistik* (see above). However,
the target is "German Studies"--including linguistics, literary
history, and literature by period--and the topical arrangement is categorical rather than chronological. The *IGB*
should thus complement rather than compete with *Germanistik*.
(R.M.)

Kossmann, Bernhard, and Monika Richter, eds. *Bibliographie der
deutschen Sprach- und Literaturwissenschaft.* Vol. 23, 1983.
Frankfurt a.M.: Vittorio Klostermann, 1984. Pp. 795.

"XI. Goethezeit," pp. 274-326; "XII. Romantik," pp. 327-
47; "XIII. 19. Jahrhundert," pp. 348-97. A continuation of
the Eppelsheimer/Köttelwesch bibliography, integrated with
the holdings and new acquisitions of the Stadt- und Universi-
täts bibliothek Frankfurt a.M.

Lederer, Herbert. "American Doctoral Dissertations on Austrian
Authors: Degrees Granted in 1983." *Modern Austrian Literature*
17,2 (1984): 123-24.

O'Neill, Patrick. *German Literature in English Translation:
A Select Bibliography.* Toronto, Buffalo, and London: University of Toronto Press, 1981. Pp. 242.

The author has chosen to serve the interests of "the
teaching scholar in the humanities, the student of comparative literature, and the educated general reader rather than
the literary statistician" (vii). In contrast to the critical,
evaluative, and exhaustive listings by B.Q. Morgan, for
example, this bibliography is purely enumerative and reflects
the serious literature that is available in modern translation.
This is a finding list, not a "springboard ... for a discussion
of translation trends during the twentieth century ..." (x).
(R.M.)

Richardson, Larry L. *Introduction to Library Research in German
Studies: Language, Literature, and Civilization.* (Westview
Guides to Library Research.) Boulder, Colo.: Westview Press,
1985. Pp. 227.

Compiled with the librarian as well as the scholar in mind.
The critical evaluations of specific reference works make this
a useful research aid. Modern search procedures are well
presented. (R.M.)

Zeller, Otto, and Wolfram Zeller. *Internationale Bibliographie der Zeitschriftenliteratur aus allen Gebieten des Wissens (IBZ).* Vol. 20 (Pars 1 and 2, each in 6 vols.), 1984. Osnabruck: Felix Dietrich, 1984.

The article listings for each half-year are arranged in: A. Index of periodicals consulted (Periodica); B. Classified subject index of articles (Index rerum); C. Index of articles arranged by the names of authors (Index autorum); and D. Systematic index of key words (Index systematicus).

2. GENERAL

Bahti, Timothy. "Fate in the Past: Peter Szondi's Reading of German Romantic Genre Theory." *Boundary 2* 11 (1983): 111-25.

Szondi's reconstruction of Romantic genre poetics, as expressed in his articles and published lectures, reveals a recurrent and characteristic employment of prefiguration or anticipation on the one hand, fulfillment on the other. Fulfillment of prefigurations is found for Szondi in Hegel. But if his historical account leads up to and ends with Hegel, how would Szondi regard his own anterior writing of that dialectical history? "... I would like to ask of Szondi, as the *historian* of idealist *Gattungspoetik*, what it means for him likewise to go beyond the end of this history in Hegel by going back behind it in order to write that history as a history of the prefiguration and fulfillment of the successful mediation of history and system" (117). The problem of writing a history "when one is thoroughly self-conscious of standing not before some threshold, but long after it" (119) is the problem of belatedness *vis à vis* the ideal, the situation of the post-idealist historian searching for hope in the past. (M.J.)

Berman, Antoine. *L'Epreuve de l'étranger: Culture et traduction dans l'Allemagne romantique.* (Les Essais.) Paris: Gallimard, 1984.

Boehme, Hartmut. "Kosmos und Leib bei Kant und Schelling." *EG* 39 (1984); 251-67.

The dialectic of Self and Other takes many forms. Boehme follows one form—body and cosmos—of one kind of self-other formulation, the ontogeny-phylogeny parallel. In contrast to the natural sciences, the philosophy of nature as "natura naturans" from Bruno through Spinoza to Schelling conceived of "living nature" as a model of the unity of art and science. On the other hand, Kant, in his later theory of the sublime

but also in the early "Theorie des Himmels" (1755), developed
a theory of the cosmos that transcends mechanics and physics,
viewing it "als grandiose Projektion dessen, was er am eigenen
Leib findet" (258). This foreshadows Novalis ("ist denn das
Weltall nicht in uns?"). The homogeneity of microcosm and
macrocosm parallels "die imaginäre Identität phylo- und onto-
genetischer Frühzustände" (262) characteristic of early
Romanticism. Schelling's emphasis on the "sympathy" between
nature and the subject, however, allows him to define philosophy
as "Erinnern des Zustandes, in welchem wir eins waren mit der
Natur," as memory of symbiotic unity with "Mother Nature."
Kant's notion of sublimity was impelled by both narcissistic
self-aggrandizement and by its concomitant fear of the empti-
ness of the Copernican universe. Schelling, by contrast,
proposes a view of the identity of subject and nature in art.
This "symbiotische Verschmelzung" is the mother. "Kunst ist
darum das ausgezeichnete Medium jener grossen Einheit mit Natur,
die verborgen die Sehnsucht nach dem leiblichen Verschmelzen
mit dem allmächtigen und vollkommenen Objekt in sich aufnimmt"
(266). (M.J.)

Brinkmann, Richard. "Geschichte und Geschechten in der Romantik."
Seminar 20 (1984): 157-87.

Offers an unnecessarily wordy discussion of historical and
narratological questions--of "Geschichte" and "Geschichten"--
with reference to Romanticism, particularly to Novalis and
Arnim. Primary points include the double aspect of "Geschichte"
as both past events and their later description, notions of
history as "Heilsgeschichte," supplementary reference to the
future within the context of past and present, and the accompanying aesthetic dimension. Such texts occupy a "gray zone"
between fictional and expository texts and have been studied by
both post-structuralism and analytic philosophy. Concern
with the aesthetic dimension of historiography is already
evident in Novalis's and Arnim's opinions about historical
"facts" and their poetic rendition. In *Ofterdingen* stands the
significant sentence: "so scheint es mir, als wenn ein
Geschichtsschreiber notwendig auch ein Dichter seyn
müsste ...," which Novalis goes on to connect with partial
history's relation to total history. (M.J.)

Deeney, Noel. "The Romantic Science of J.W. Ritter." *The
Maynooth Review* 8 (1983): 43-59.

Deeney's article on Ritter's "Romantic Science" pursues
several goals with varying success. The short sketch of
Ritter's life and the blend of solid and sometimes ingenious
experimentation with highly speculative, often fantastic,

philosophical extrapolations is well presented. His assessment of a good sampling from Ritter's *Fragmente aus dem Nachlasse eines jungen Physikers* is refreshingly sober. By merely citing a few examples and adding a few caustic words of characterization, the author demonstrates a truth about which one seldom reads--namely, that a good number of these Romantic fragments are downright silly. On the other hand, Deeney characterizes the fragments about time-space relations, the unity of all forces in nature, and the relationship between magnetism and electricity as remarkable, speculative anticipations of things to come. Here, I think, he is on treacherous ground because the context of such speculations and his sweeping analogies do not offer a plausible extrapolation from experience. Rather, such insights or foresights appear to be the result of a free, often fantastic play of the imagination with certain scarcely accredited phenomena of nature. While such mental activity belongs very much to the many ways of "Romanticizing" the world, it should not be confused with genuine scientific imagination. The evocation by Deeney of the spectre of Feyerabend's *Against Method*--subtitled *Towards an Anarchistic Theory of Knowledge*--toward the end of the article is of questionable value as a rehabilitation or reexamination of "Romantic Science." It is fairly predictable that this approach, while probably shedding new light on some characteristics of German *Naturphilosophie* and the semi-scientific endeavors it engendered, will in all likelihood also confirm the belief that "Romantic Science" could not have any future as a science. I am also afraid that the author's hints at affinities between genuinely scientific insights and mysticism are not very useful in explaining the role of imagination and intuition in modern science. One unknown can hardly explain another unknown. And a resurrection of Jacob Böhme won't gain German *Naturphilosophie* scientific respectability, irrespective of what other intellectual respectability it has. As a final point it should be mentioned that some of the scientific discoveries which Deeney attributes to Ritter (the voltaic pile, Ohm's work on electricity--which, I suppose, is a reference to Ohm's law--the first "dry" cell, and Koch's work on infectious diseases) are either not correct or at best debatable. (See the work by A. Hermann on Ritter, or the *Proceedings of the Electrochemical Society of America*, 1978.) (Walter Wetzels, University of Texas at Austin.)

Jaeschke, Walter. "Early German Idealist Reinterpretation of the Quarrel of the Ancients and Moderns." *Clio* 12 (1983): 313-31.

"Early German Idealist" refers in this instance primarily to Schelling and Hegel. Their response to the *Querelles des Anciens et des Modernes* is emblematic of the central importance of art and religion for the definition of modernity in the idealist period. The unity of art and religion makes possible knowledge of the Absolute; but this claim assumes two forms. Schelling drew the consequences from the historicization of the Absolute implicit in aesthetics; the mode of appearance of the Absolute is thus contained in a history of its *Darstellung*: identical (natural) in antiquity, diremptive (historical) in the modern period, dominated by Christianity. This opposition becomes prominent in the claim of the "new mythology." Hegel complicates the stark dichotomy of ancient and modern by introducing intermediate stages: only Protestantism is "modern," "subjective" (Descartes), leaving "destroyed this alien consecration of Nature established by Catholicism and thereby de-divinized Nature" (326-27). Both art and religion are unsuitable for overcoming modern diremption; Hegel's solution in philosophy frees modernity from the burden of the scheme of origin, loss, and return; modernity must avoid the "temptation of an ideal of unity void of differences," because it consists in "recognizing itself and realizing its freedom through opposition" (330). (M.J.)

Koppen, Erwin, and Rüdiger von Tiedemann, eds. *Wege zur Komparatistik: Sonderheft für Horst Rüdiger zum 75. Geburtstag. Arcadia* (Sonderheft 1983): 1-160.

This collection of 22 essays by such scholars as Wellek, Weisstein, and H.H.H. Remak is a combination of *testimonial* ("Why I became a Comparatist") and *avowal* of a rather German-style, non-theoretical school of comparative literature. Comparison for its own sake and a personal appreciation of literature rather than critical theory are the prevailing themes. Romanticism and Romanticists are touched upon frequently and with appreciation, e.g.: "In Germany, then, the Romantic centre of hermeneutics is still visible (though Gadamer depicts it with a certain disapproval), and Peter Szondi has restored the eighteenth-century context of Hölderlin's hermeneutic insights" (Elinor Schaffer, "Voyaging on Strange Seas of Thought Alone: or How I Became a Comparatist," p. 114). (R.M.)

Lange, Victor. *The Classical Age of German Literature 1740-1815*. New York: Holmes & Meier, 1983. Pp. x+275. $26.00.; paper $17.50.

Rev. by C.A.M. Nobel in *QQ* 91 (1984): 1019-22, along with
Eric A. Blackall, *The Novels of the German Romantics* (see
RMB for 1983, pp. 289-91).

McVaugh, Robert. "A Revised Reconstruction of the Casa
Bartholdy Fresco Cycle." *ArtB* 66 (1984): 442-52.

On the Nazarenes.

Röder, Petra. *Utopische Romantik: Die verdrängte Tradition
im Marxismus. Von der frühromantischen Poetologie zur
marxistischen Gesellschaftstheorie.* Würzburg: Königshausen & Neumann, 1982. Pp. 267.

By means of an inflationary usage of the concept of utopia,
Röder traces the similarities between early Romantic thinking and the early Marx. This is an important topic,
addressed recently by others--e.g., Leonard Wessell in
Karl Marx, Romantic Irony, and the Proletariat (1979)--
not mentioned here. Röder touches on many aspects of the
topic, on its dichotomies and their supercession in both
modes of thought. The traditional idealist mechanism of
unity, diremption, and renewed (potentiated) unity is shown
to be common to both; and the principle receives diverse
expressions: spirit and nature, man and woman, etc. Unfortunately, although the author claims to discuss the
"Jenaites," that does not prevent her from including under
that rubric Hölderlin, Brentano, Schelling, Baader, and
Arnim (as well as current critics--she is particularly
fond of Manfred Frank and Jochen Hörisch) in her veritable
orgy of indiscriminate quotation: the *Berufskrankheit* of
German dissertationese. More scepticism and critical
distance regarding both the dangers of frenetic and context-
ignoring citation as well as the utopian fantasies she
adduces would have been appropriate. (M.J.)

Roloff, Volker. "Torquato Tasso, Chatterton, Um auto de Gil
Vicente: Überlegungen zum romantischen Schriftstellerdrama." *Arcadia* 19 (1984): 34-51.

Roloff sees in the genre of the *Schriftstellerdrama*
an exemplification of the unity of European Romanticism,
and to demonstrate this thesis he adopts a comparative
approach--with Goethe's *Tasso* as paradigm--which emphasizes
the development of the dramatic conflict as a result of
the protagonist's very function as a *writing* person. The
drama develops out of the dialectic situation, but in particular out of the "possibility of dialogue." Vigny and

the Portuguese writer Almeida Garret are used to argue the continuity of the thesis. (R.M.)

Sayre, Robert, and Michael Löwy. "Figures of Romantic Anti-Capitalism." *NGC* 32 (1984): 42-91.

The key section (pp. 60-87) is a "typology" of the figures of Romantic anti-capitalism.

Sullivan, Henry W. *Calderón in the German Lands and the Low Countries: His Reception and Influence, 1654-1980*. (Cambridge Iberian and Latin American Studies.) Cambridge University Press, 1983. Pp. 510.

An exhaustive reception-study of the wide-ranging influence of Calderón in German theater and intellectual life. The entry of Calderón through the Lowlands and then his establishment as the model for comedy in the German-speaking countries (Germany avoided the tragedies and religious plays) are documented extensively. Sullivan argues convincingly that the significance of Calderón as a European writer has been underestimated and also that the Romantic penchant for comparing Calderón unquestioningly with Shakespeare while seeing only the latter as "naturalizable" on the German stage is a double disservice to Calderón. The author documents the ease with which German intellectuals--with their penchant for the transcendent--looked to Calderón rather than to Shakespeare as a model for the merging of Christian ethic and tragic aesthetic. Calderón sought in drama a Symbolic Order, a confrontation with "cultural obligation."
   The Idealist period receives particular attention in Sullivan's book. Although Goethe and the Romanticists (especially the Schlegels, E.T.A. Hoffmann, and Eichendorff) are focused upon, more attention could have been paid to the (Classical) *health*-vs.-(Romantic) *sickness* issue. This substantial study is a solid documentation of 300 years of Calderón influence in Germany, and in addition it surveys the cultural and philosophical trends of that 300-year period. In many instances the influence of this conservative intellectual has gone undetected in German letters, and Sullivan's work is thus a major contribution to a better understanding of that idea of tragedy developed by Calderón and espoused so extensively by German thinkers. (R.M.)

Wittmann, Reinhard. *Buchmarkt und Lektüre im 18. und 19. Jahrhundert: Beiträge zum literarischen Leben 1750-1880*. Tübingen: Max Niemeyer Verlag, 1982. Pp. xii+252. DM 58.00.

Rev. by Hannelore Heckmann-French in *JEGP* 83 (1984): 276-77.

See also Whitmore, Daniel ("English 4. Scott"); Kipperman ("German 3. Fichte); Chase (German 3. Hegel"); Gutjahr ("German 3. Heine"); Brion ("German 3. Hölderlin"); Sütterlin ("German 3. Jean Paul"); Kreutzer ("German 3. Kleist"); Kurzke ("German 3. Novallis"); Frühwald ("German 3. Schlegel, A.W."); Behler, Kurz, Peters, Pikulik, Schreiber ("German 3. Schlegel, Fr."); Morlang, Pikulik ("German 3. Tieck"); Köhler, Oeser ("German 3. Varnhagen von Ense, Rahel").

Review of book previously listed:

BLACKALL, Eric A., *The Novels of the German Romantics* (see *RMB* for 1983, pp. 289-91), rev. by C.A.M. Noble in *QQ* 91 (1984): 1019-22, along with Victor Lange, *The Classical Age of German Literature 1740-1815* (see above).

The "German 2. General" section will be reviewed and brought up to date next year.

3.   STUDIES OF AUTHORS

ARNIM, ACHIM VON

Frye, Lawrence O. "Textstruktur als Kunstauffassung: Achim von Arnim und die Ästhetik Schillers." *LJGG* 25 (1984): 131-54.

Unfamiliar perhaps with either Arnim's poetological texts or the relevant scholarship, Frye attempts to understand Arnim with the help of Schiller's "ästhetische Erziehung," which certainly has no more in common with Arnim's work than any other poetological text of the idealistic period. Those arbitrarily selected passages in which Frye believes he finds similarities between Arnim and Schiller (and even Winckelmann) have long been recognized as Arnim's point of departure from the classicistic aestheticization of nature. According

to Arnim artistic reality in particular should not be embel-
lished--as attributed to him by Frye according to Schiller's
arguments. Unaware of Arnim's central aesthetic category,
the "getäuschte Täuschung," the author is unable to reach an
historically acceptable understanding of Arnim's specific
aesthetic. Within Frye's theoretical framework the conclusion
that Arnim is more sceptical than Schiller seems redundant.
One of Frye's closing statements best characterizes his rather
vague analysis: "In jedem Werk sieht es anders aus...." (B.F.)

Hoermann, Roland. "Achim von Arnims Erzählung 'Melück Maria
Blainville: Die Hausprophetin aus Arabien': Eine romantische
Heldin als Schauspielerin, Geliebte und Heilige." *Aurora*
44 (1984): 178-95.

Hoermann bases his interpretation of the story upon an
understanding of Melück's development as a tragic character.
Such an analysis neglects the allegorical aspects of Melück's
figure, which have been pointed out in previous scholarship.
·According to Hoermann, Melück's downfall is her need to avenge
herself for Saintree's deception. Arnim, however, clearly
shows that this is indeed a misunderstanding on the part of
the character Frenel. Melück's sorrow over her betrayed
love is in fact a magic catalyst by which the truth of
Saintree's and the French nobility's grandeur, appearance
without substance, love without heart, is unveiled. This
is the reason Melück's sorrow eats away at Saintree's heart.
The story is less concerned with individual loss of identity
or conscience and religion than with a social allegory of the
French aristocracy shortly before its fall. Herein lies
the significance of Melück's prophecy of the approaching
revolution. (B.F.)

Werner, Hans-Georg, ed. *Ludwig Achim von Arnim: Die Erzählungen und Romane*. Vol. 4. Leipzig: Insel, 1984. Pp. 645.

The fourth volume of this Arnim collection presents an
untarnished edition of the *Kronenwächter* as well as an
impressive afterword on the origination of the novel. Werner
convincingly places the literary classification of Arnim's
image of the Middle Ages within its contemporary historical
situation. It reflects above all Arnim's disappointment with
Prussia's course after 1815 as well as his scepticism toward
the French Revolution. Werner successfully shows how Arnim's

fantastic-historical novel differs from the traditional
concept of the historical novel (e.g., Lukács's treatment
of Scott) and how it actually negates supposed laws of
historical necessity. With this understanding the restoration attempts by the guards of the crown prove to be a
destructive force without a future. This insight is due
largely to Arnim's narrative technique, which magnifies
rather than conceals historical contraditions. Hence the
Kronenwächter stands as one of the few counter-examples of
the Romantics' glorification of the Middle Ages. (B.F.)

Wolf, Gerhard, ed. *Achim von Arnim "Mir ist zu licht zum
   Schlafen"*: *Gedichte, Prosa, Stücke, Briefe.* (Märkischer
   Dichtergarten.) Frankfurt: Fischer Verlag, 1984. Pp. 319.

   Wolf's collection gives a good first impression of the
many facets of Arnim. His selection of poems, however,
cannot disguise the fact that the lyric is not one of Arnim's
strengths. Also, there are surely more interesting letters
than those exchanged between Arnim and Bettina during the
Wiepersdorfer years. In contrast, Arnim's true talent--
narrative prose--is represented by only one story, "Die
Einquartierung im Pfarrhaus." The four political and
aesthetic essays may be new to many readers. The drama
fragment and the shadow-play are refreshing reminders of
Arnim's almost forgotten experiments with folk drama. Even
though Wolf's afterword brings little that is new to light,
it does point out parallels between the situation of today's
writer in the GDR and that of Arnim as a Prussian aristocrat
and a politically and socially conscious author. (B.F.)

See also Brinkmann, Röder ("German 2. General"); Fink ("Eichendorff").

Reviews of books previously listed:

   FISCHER, Bernd, *Literatur und Politik: Die "Novellensammlung
   von 1812" und das "Landhausleben" von Achim von Arnim* (see
   RMB for 1983, pp. 305-06), rev. by Paul Michael Lützeler
   in *GQ* 58 (1984): 125-26; STERNBERG, Thomas, *Die Lyrik Achim
   von Arnims* (see *RMB* for 1983, p. 309), rev. by Bernd Fischer
   in *GQ* 58 (1984): 126-27.

ARNIM, BETTINA VON

Craig, Gordon A. "Romance and Reality: Bettina von Arnim
   and Bismarck,." Pp. 27-47 in Craig, *The End of Prussia.*
   University of Wisconsin Press, 1984.

This article is one of the series of lectures in honor
of the historian Merle Curti which Craig delivered in 1982
at the University of Wisconsin. Craig draws attention to
the fact that Bismarck explicitly mentioned Bettina von
Arnim in his memoirs, *Gedanken und Erinnerungen*, with--as
Craig interprets it--affectionate overtones. Apparently,
Bismarck never met von Arnim, though we know that her second
son, Siegmund, who later became a Prussian diplomat, was a
supporter of Bismarck and his politics. Despite obvious
differences between the historical figures of Bettina von
Arnim and Bismarck, Craig argues that there are also striking
similarities in character as well as in goals. Both of them
were "irreverent," "capricious," "self-centered," and
"energetic" human beings who attracted and demanded a lot
of attention in their time. Both tried to influence Frederick
William IV, the so-called Romantic king of Prussia. Craig
briefly compares their different ways and means in pursuit
of this goal. He argues that Bismarck's success and von
Arnim's failure to influence the king contributed to the
"end of Prussia." (K.B.)

See also Wolf ("Arnim, Achim von"); Oellers ("Schlegel-
Schelling, Caroline").

BAADER

See Röder ("German 2. General").

BÖRNE

See Bech, Espagne ("Heine").

BONAVENTURA

Askedal, John Ole. "*Bonaventuras Nachtwachen*--en kilde til
Henrik Ibsens *Peer Gynt*." *Edda*, No. 5 (1983): 299-304.

Askedal exhibits parallels between *Peer Gynt* and the
Nachtwachen, as dark anti-Romantic satires; but though he
suggests that the latter might have been a source for Ibsen,
he gives no evidence and it seems unlikely, given the work's
obscurity in the 1860s. (J.L.S.)

Gulyga, A. "Kto avtor romana 'Nochnye bedeniia'?" *Voprosy
    Literatury*, No. 9 (Sept. 1982): 203-16.

   While Western scholars constantly come up with new authorship candidates, one in the Soviet Union has returned to
the oldest of all: Schelling. Gulyga's method, which for
some reason he considers decisive, is to demonstrate that it
cannot be proved that Schelling cannot have written the
novel. By and large he strings together the old, in some
cases hoary arguments on behalf of Schelling, with rhetorical
questions, hypothetical suppositions, and tenuous associations,
some quite improbable. We are obliged to believe, not only
that the work is not nihilistic--a claim made with reference
to the first night-watch only--but that Schelling would have
at that time used his own scandal-ridden wife's name in a
satire of adultery. Gulyga has not thought carefully about
the text and has an incomplete knowledge of the history of
the discussion, though what he does know he judges reasonably.
Of some interest is his reference to a letter of Paulus
of Nov. 17, 1803, in which it is said that Schelling is
secretly working on a novel that will pursue "extravagant
medical phantasies," first published in E. Klessmann,
*Caroline: Das Leben der Caroline Michaelis-Böhmer-Schlegel-
Schlelling* (1975; p. 250). (J.L.S., with thanks to Emilia
Hramov)

Habersetzer, Karl-Heinz. "Bonaventura aus Prag und der Ver-
    fasser der *Nachtwachen*." *Euphorion* 77 (1983): 470-82.

   After expressing himself rather scornfully about all other
treatments of the *Nachtwachen* problem, Habersetzer comes
forward with his own candidate. His method is to discover
several other items under the pseudonym Bonaventura in
periodical literature through the 1840s, as well as an 1811
translation of Italian fairy tales; this last Bonaventura
is identifiable with Adolf Wolfgang Gerle (1781-1846), a
minor Prague writer known to literary history. Despite the
supposititious argument there is no reason whatever to believe
that any of the Bonaventuras is identical with any other.
All the other evidence adduced is attenuated and the
proposal depends upon a low qualitative evaluation of the
text as a Jean Paul imitation. Habersetzer would have done
well to study the history of the question more thoroughly
and learn some humility and caution from it.

Meyer, Karl-Heinz. "Johann Karl Wezel und die 'Nachtwachen
    von Bonaventura.'" *Neues aus der Wezel-Forschung* 2 (1984):
    62-86.

One of the newest authorship candidates is Johann Karl
Wezel (1747-1819), an Enlightenment author with fierce
proto-Jacobin views and a tendency to the pessimistic
and the grotesque; he is supposed to have been mentally
ill in his late years, though Meyer disputes this. It
would be futile in this space to reproduce and criticize
the argument; it is the usual farrago of speculation,
attenuated probabilities, greater or lesser similarities
in themes and interests. Nowhere is there a trace of what
one might regard as evidence. The argument, moreover,
is very difficult to understand: disorderly, punctuated
by apparently weighty rhetorical questions, burdened by
scraps of learning of dubious relevance, and unburdened
by usable references to other sources. Meyer ascribes the
suppression of Wezel's authorship to an "idealistic"
conspiracy against the "materialist" author; here one
begins, I fear, to hear the voice of the cuckoo. Parts of
the argument may be more intelligible to the band of Wezel
experts, and it is said to be only the first part of a
projected proof, but I must say I see no promise here so
far. (J.L.S.)

Mielke, Andreas. *Zeitgenosse Bonaventura*. (Stuttgarter
    Arbeiten zur Germanistik, No. 132.) Stuttgart: Akademischer
    Verlag Hans-Dieter Heinz, 1984. Pp. iv+304.

The intense and learned study has two major thrusts: a
methodological critique of approaches to the authorship
problem by means of parallel passages or stylistic comparisons, and an ingenious argument that stops just short of
ascribing the *Nachtwachen* to Jean Paul. The critique is
carried out in the form of a relentless, perhaps too relentless, but certainly effective demolition of Schillemeit's
Klingemann thesis (see *ELN* 12, Supp., 128). Mielke's view
is that the text is a satire on writers like Klingemann,
perhaps even on Klingemann himself, while he also offers
the suggestion that the footnotes do not belong to the text
proper, but were added by an editor, possibly Klingemann.
The implied ascription to Jean Paul is supported by a number
of ingenious and in some cases debatable interpretive positions: that the text cannot be nihilistic because of the
presence of satirical elements, indicating allegiance to
surviving values; that an author can alter his style at
will, with the corollary that the author must have masked
his style if he wished to remain anonymous; that the text
is to be understood philosophically, as an attack on Schelling
and Fichte; that the author "Bonaventura" is to be distin-
guished from the narrator Kreuzgang, who himself is one of

the objects of the satire, in that he carries Fichte's ego-
philosophy *ad absurdum*. None of this persuades me that
Jean Paul is to be taken seriously as an author candidate,
but the originality of some of these interpretive initiatives
should animate and enrich the discussion. Most impressive
is Mielke's command of other texts in the environment, not
only of Jean Paul, of whom he has total mastery, but also
of the journal literature and public debate between Romantic
and anti-Romantic positions, showing that many of the
themes and motifs of the *Nachtwachen* were widely shared (thus
making arguments from parallels nugatory) and that the text
is more firmly rooted in the contemporary context than many
of us have previously seen. (J.L.S.)

See also Hunter-Lougheed ("Hoffmann, E.T.A."); Kuzniar ("Jean
Paul").

Review of book previously listed:

PFANNKUCHE, Walter, *Idealismus und Nihilismus in den "Nachtwachen" von Bonaventura* (see *RMB* for 1983, p. 313), rev. by
Andreas Mielke in *Aurora* 44 (1984): 232–34.

BRENTANO

Brandstetter, Gabriele. "Hieroglyphik der Liebe: Überlegungen
zu Brentanos 'Fortsetzung von Hölderlins Nacht.'" *JFDH*
(1983): 213–66.

The complete text of Brentano's continuation of Hölderlin's
"Nacht" (finished most likely in 1836 as a gift for Emilie
Linder) is preceded by a thorough *explication de texte* and
followed by a copious critical apparatus including the
description of manuscripts, dating problems, and highly
informative explanatory notes. The analysis of the "hiero-
glyphics of love" provides a captivating continuation of the
pioneering efforts in this direction by Frühwald and others,
and makes some helpful distinctions in the often confused
and confusing Romantic terminology between allegory, symbol,
and arabesque. The discussion of the "double language"
(not to mention the duplicity of the verbal idiom) through
which Brentano could both speak of and yet remain silent
about his desperate love affair is truly first rate. The
protean quality of such words as "heimlich" sheds new light
even on poems of earlier vintage. (J.F.F.)

Catholy, Eckehard. "Clemens Brentano *Ponce de Leon*. Die
'Bildungs-, Entwicklungs- und Erziehungs-Komödie." Pp. 241-
68 in *Das deutsche Lustspiel: Von der Aufklärung bis zur
Romantik*. (Sprache und Literatur, 109.) Stuttgart: Kohlhammer, 1982. Pp. 342.

An absolutely brilliantly conceived and clearly structured
analysis of how Brentano, in trying to fulfill the requirements set forth by Goethe and Schiller in their competition
for a comedy based on "action," scrupulously avoided the
character comedy of the eighteenth century by concentrating
on verbal effects, but in the process also bungled any
requisite plot development. Very intriguing is the well-
documented thesis that the play constitutes an "anti-Godwi"
(Ponce as a contrafacture of this prose protagonist who was
conceived contemporaneously) to the extent that the play
of masks and masquerades throughout serves as a means for
the various figures to evolve into real human beings. A new
classification--that of the comedy of development or of
education--is proposed, something which should elicit a
barrage of pros and cons from Brentano scholars as well as
from devotees of the theater and/or stage. (J.F.F.)

Erpenbeck, John. "Szenarium einer Flucht." *NDL* 30:12 (1982):
73-84.

This is an impressionistic piece--rather than a piece of
scholarship--full of rhetorical devices such as chiasmus
and framed by an imaginary dialogue between writer and readers.
The year of Brentano's initial visit to Dulmen, 1818, becomes
the fulcrum point for discussion of the conflicting progressive
and regressive tendencies of this age (the former represented
by the Wartburg festival, Hegel's philosophy of reason in his
Encyclopedia, and, of all things, Karl Marx's birth!, while
the latter is embodied in the Karlsbad Decrees, Schopenhauer's
philosophy of the will and its fatalistic undermining of
reason). More interesting than any obligatory party-line
dogma are the off-beat asides, such as the linking of the
magnetic forces of galvanism with the influx of divine forces
in the sacraments. (J.F.F.)

Jung, Wolfgang. "'Es ist Gebrauch seit langer Zeit': Ein un-
bekanntes Gelegenheitsgedicht Clemens Brentanos für die
'Gesellschaft aus dem Strobelkopf' in Wien." *JFDH* (1983):
171-212.

Even though the poem in question is of marginal literary
merit or little intrinsic interest, its initial publication
together with the explanatory notes supplied by the critic do

help dispel some mysteries and mystiques surrounding
Brentano's affiliations with the literary circle meeting
weekly at the inn "Zum Strobelkopf" during his short-lived
stay in Vienna (1813-1814). In a somewhat tedious, positivistic manner, allusions to various members are expanded into
detailed accounts of the real personages. The two manuscript
versions of the poem printed here give indications of the
actual activities of the group which, according to the
evidence at hand, was not the "militant Catholic circle"
that it was purported to be by critics previously. (J.F.F.)

Küppers, Kurt. "'So werde die Emilia ein Vorbild für Othilia':
Untersuchungen zum Gedicht 'Sieh ich bin eine Magd des Herrn'
von Clemens Brentano." *JFDH* (1983): 147-70.

Brentano's innate pedantic streak and his penchant for
teaching younger people through lyric poetry provoke the
critic to call into question this occasional poem which
Enzensberger labeled a "literarily insignificant" work.
Clarification of the personages alluded to in this poem may
not excite too many readers, but the analysis of such concepts
as "maiden of love" does, when Küppers demonstrates how
Brentano applied this epithet to a variety of women in his
life. Likewise enlightening are the analyses of the image
of the pheasant and its roots in the *Physiologus* or the
symbol of the lily among the thorns. (J.F.F.)

Mathes, Jürg. "Zur Druckgeschichte der Emmerick-Biographie
Brentanos." *JFDH* (1983): 267-82.

As the editor of the volumes of the historical-critical
edition dealing with A.K. Emmerick, Mathes is highly qualified
to give an account of the genesis of the biography of the
stigmatic. In a kind of mini-*Forschungsbericht*, he draws
attention to the merits and shortcomings in scholarly assess-
ments of Brentano's biographical resumé, including some
errors of his own, but focusing primarily on Schmöger's
often arbitrary editing of the Emmerick *vita*, especially when
material in the text went against the grain of his extremely
orthodox views. (J.F.F.)

Peter, Maria. "Spuren Dantes und anderer italienischer Dichter
in Clemens Brentanos *Romanzen vom Rosenkranz*." *Arcadia* 19
(1984): 130-52.

Short on interpretation but long on information, this article provides a catalogue of interesting parallels between
Dante's *Divine Comedy* and Brentano's diffuse epic poem--some-
thing long suggested in theory, but only now investigated in

practice. This compendium includes matters of form (rhetorical devices) as well as content (amplification of sources,
the biographical introduction in terza rima, the time and
place of the action, the rose and other central symbols,
etc.). Especially helpful is the explanation of why Dante
and not some other precursor served as model, based on such
common features as their fascination for the triadic principle
or biographical correlations--living in an age of transition
or radical and rapid change. (J.F.F.)

Rölleke, Heinz. "Eine Quelle zu Brentanos *Geschichte vom
braven Kasperl und dem schönen Annerl*." *WW* 34 (1984): 341-
43.

Clever speculation--but solidly founded--that Brentano's
story owes a greater literary debt to Friedrich Kind's tale
of 1813, *Das Schmetterlings-Cabinett*, than has, up to now,
been suspected. This link to the story of Weber's librettist
for the *Freischütz* is, as is always the case with Rölleke,
undergirded by striking motif and content resemblances based
on close reading and careful research. (J.F.F.)

Tunner, Erika. "Lore Lay--Loréley: Romantique ou décadente?"
Romantisme 13 (1983): 167-75.

In spite of a dearth of evidence that the French poet of
the Decadent school, Jean Lorrain, either knew or ever read
a single line of Brentano, Tunner uncovers remarkable similarities between the former's prose poem "Loréley" (1892)
and the latter's femme fatale "Lore Lay" from *Godwi*. The
critic, via some astute detective work, traces these resemblances to elective affinities in taste and sensibility,
as well as to their mutual insecurity, nervousness, and tor-
mentingly complex psyches. (J.F.F.)

Ward, Mark, and Robert Wylie. "The Tale Is Not in the Telling:
On Brentano's *Geschichte vom braven Kasperl und dem schönen
Annerl*." *NGS* 11 (1983): 123-43.

An insightful analysis of the complex narrative structure
of the novella, showing how the reader's desire for coherence
is thwarted by such devices as the triumvirate of narrating
voices--Kaspar, the old peasant woman, and the anonymous
narrator proper. Particularly convincing is the shift in
focus on the part of the latter from a view of the poet as
an aloof and idiosyncratic individual to that of a person
who tries to intervene directly in the course of human affairs
and who, by an unfortunate confluence of events, fails.
Clear, commonsense approach with refreshing results, espe-

cially with regard to the function of the perplexing allegorical monument at the close. (J.F.F.)

See also Röder ("German 2. General").

Reviews of books previously listed:

BEHRENS, Jürgen, *Clemens Brentano: Sämtliche Werke und
Briefe*, Vol. 28: Part II (see *RMB* for 1982, pp. 303-04),
rev. by Helene M. Kastinger Riley in *CG* 16 (1983): 70-71;
BLACKALL, Eric, *The Novels of the German Romantics* (see *RMB*
for 1983, pp. 289-91), rev. by Hans Eichner in *JEGP* 83 (1984):
602-04; FETZER, John, *Clemens Brentano* (see *RMB* for 1981, p.
277), rev. by Helene M. Kastinger Riley in *CG* 16 (1983):
68-69; HAYER, Horst, *Brentanos 'Godwi'* (see *ELN* 17, Supp.,
189), rev. by Henning Boetius in *Germanistik* 24 (1983): 737;
MATHIAS, Ursula, *Kontextproblem der Lyrik Clemens Brentanos*
(see *RMB* for 1982, pp. 306-07), rev. by Stephan Berning in
Germanistik 25 (1984): 161-62; REINDL, Nikolaus, *Die
poetische Funktion des Mittelalters in der Dichtung Clemens
Brentanos* (see *ELN* 16, Supp., 147), rev. by Helene M.
Kastinger Riley in *CG* 16 (1983): 250-51.

CHAMISSO

Walach, Dagmar, ed. *Erläuterungen und Dokumente: Adelbert
von Chamisso: "Peter Schlemihls wundersame Geschichte."*
Stuttgart: Reclam, 1982. Pp. 112.

With this small volume the Reclam series of "Erläuterungen
und Dokumente" once again provides a valuable tool for the
interpretation of a major work of German literature, authored
by a leading scholar. Walach supplies detailed notes to the
text, a history of *Schlemihl*-reception, interpretive examples,
a usefully limited bibliography, and various other aids to
the teacher or student in understanding this important
novella. The reproductions of illustrations lend the volume
a fine visual "finishing touch." (C.R.C.)

See also Oeser ("Varnhagen von Ense, Rahel").

EICHENDORFF

Bönisch, Anna. "Die Auffindung der Handschriften des Dichters
Joseph von Eichendorff im Seldnitzer Schlosse." *Eichendorff
Nachrichten* 9 (1983): 1-7.

Eichendorff, Rudolf Freiherr von. "Meine Lebensschicksale."
Aurora 44 (1984): 147-52.

The first printing of a fragmentary autobiography of
Eichendorff's uncle illuminates details of Eichendorff
family life. (W.C.)

Feilchenfeldt, Konrad. "Eichendorffs Freundschaft mit Benjamin
Mendelssohn und Philipp Veit." *Aurora* 44 (1984): 79-99.

As the preface says, the purpose of the article is to
"illuminate a piece from the student-and-soldier life of
the poet." Besides printing correspondence, Feilchenfeldt
discusses, with little interesting interpretation, the
poems "An Philipp" and "Soldatenlied." (W.C.)

Fink, Gonthier-Louis. "Pygmalion und das belebte Marmorbild:
Wandlungen eines Märchenmotivs von der Frühaufklärung bis
zur Spätromantik." *Aurora* 43 (1983): 92-123.

Fink locates Eichendorff's "Marmorbild" and "Die Zauberei
im Herbst" in the developing use of the Pygmalion motif from
Condillac, Bodmer, and Rousseau, to Winckelmann and Herder,
to late Romanticism. Enlightenment thinkers saw in the
Pygmalion story a metaphor for the birth of consciousness;
Winckelmann, Herder, and the Sturm und Dränger saw in it an
allegory of art's power on the observer, and of the artist's
creative power; and the late Romantics saw the birth of
seductive beauty from stone as a sign of the world's "moral
dualism," in which the Venus statue is a "symbol of the
perversity and danger" of material nature. A thorough
account, the article sometimes interprets the Pygmalion motif
so broadly that it subsumes any occurrence of vivification
to the point of blurring important distinctions, e.g.,
between Eichendorff's Venus statue, Hoffmann's robots, and
the Alräunchen from Arnim's *Isabella*. (W.C.)

Heiduk, Franz. "Zur Selbstbiographie Rudolf von Eichendorffs."
Aurora 44 (1984): 153-58.

A textual history of the newly printed autobiography
(listed above). Contains a useful index to proper names of
Eichendorff family members and acquaintances. (W.C.)

Holtmeier, Irmela. "Eichendorff-Bibliographie." *Aurora* 43
(1983): 235-39.

Holtmeier, Irmela. "Eichendorff-Bibliographie." *Aurora* 44
(1984): 224-27.

Iehl, Dominique. "Über einige Aspekte der Landschaft bei
Friedrich und Eichendorff." *Aurora* 43 (1983): 124-33.

Iehl establishes the typical "dimensions" of space that
unify C.D. Friedrich's and Eichendorff's work: fullness
(often ambiguously confusing), tragic depth, and attractive
distance. In her view, neither painter nor poet is a
Romantic pantheist. Rather, they place human figures across
from nature in attitudes of humbleness, admiration, and
astonishment, so that distance becomes the "Ursituation."
The article concludes by lengthily, but hardly surprisingly,
showing that Eichendorff and Friedrich both use religious
symbols originally rather than flatly and traditionally.
(W.C.)

Köhnke, Klaus. "Flucht in die Innerlichkeit? Zu Eichendorffs Novelle 'Die Glücksritter.'" *ActaG* 15 (1982): 17-40.

Krahé, Peter. "Eichendorffs 'Meerfahrt' als Flucht vor dem
'praktischen Abgrund.'" *Aurora* 44 (1984): 51-70.

Krahé discusses the fragmentary novella in the context
of European voyage-and-escape literature, and in light of
Eichendorff's usual treatment of Venus and gold motifs.
Eichendorff's presentation shows equal opposition both to
"the confusion of the times and their utilitarian tendencies,
which ... must lead to spiritual impoverishment," and to
the escapism that tries to elude those tendencies. The
novella's characters are left in "a twilight world of
illusion, attraction, and danger." (W.C.)

Ohff, Heinz. *Joseph Freiherr von Eichendorff*. Berlin: Stapp,
1983. Pp. 151.

A short biography that breaks very little new ground.
(W.C.)

Pikulik, Lothar. "Abendliche Erfahrung. Zu einem Gedicht
Eichendorffs und seinem Zusammenhang mit der Tradition."
Aurora 44 (1984): 7-15.

The poem in question is "Der Abend." Pikulik interprets
the poem as presenting a variation of Wackenroder's "language
of nature," "language of art," and "language of words,"
which are respectively provinces of God, poets, and everyday
people. In Eichendorff, the language of nature awakens
the inner life, as in Pietism and *Empfindsamkeit*, primarily
through language's approach to music. Unlike in Pietism,
however, the inner life is "the structure of language" in
a Lacanian sense: by writing a poem the speaker is reaching

"the poem in all things," which itself refers only to a
deeper poem, *ad infinitum.* So the outer world becomes a
reflection of the inner world, and vice versa. A good
description of syntactic problems in the poem, but much
free association is going on here. For instance, with very
little justification Pikulik takes every noise in the poem
to symbolize language. (W.C.)

Polheim, Karl Konrad. "Neues vom 'Taugenichts.'" *Aurora*
43 (1983): 32-54.

As the opening confesses, the article is a "necessarily
fragmentary account" whose purpose is not to present a
"single theme" but to bring up "several problems" related
to the novella's textual history. These are: (1) that
the manuscript shows Strophes 2 and 3 of the song "Wem
Gott will rechte Gunst erweisen" are reversed in all printed
editions; (2) that the "schöne gnädige Frau," who only appears deceptively to be a married noblewoman in the final
published copy, actually *is* a married noblewoman in the
novella's first (partial) draft, a figure Polheim takes to
be drawn from the Minnedienst tradition; and (3) that the
commonly accepted date for the novella's conclusion (1817)
is right, despite complications that arise from the first
periodical printing and from a previously unknown sketch
of Chapter 2. (W.C.)

Post, Klaus-Dieter. "Hermetik der Häuser und der Herzen:
Zum Raumbild in Eichendorffs Novelle 'Das Schloss Dürande.'"
Aurora 44 (1984): 32-50.

Post ties into attempts to re-historicize Eichendorff by
finding "unmistakable" symbols of the French Revolution in
the novella. In Part 1 of the fairy tale, the castle,
which appears as threatening from without, is actually more
threatening to itself because of its static, constrictive
lack of human connections to the world. Part 2 replaces
stasis with dynamic motion, and human isolation with human
connectedness. This dialectic of open and closed spaces
also characterizes the novella apart from the fairy tale
and parallels the situation of people in revolutionary
times. Unlike many readings that purport to discuss the
"space" of works, this article contains many exemplary
close readings and traces each observation down to fine
details. (W.C.)

Riley, Thomas A. "Die Allegorie in *Ahnung und Gegenwart.*"
Aurora 44 (1984): 23-31.

Riley wants to see the novel as a reflection of Eichendorff's reading the *Divine Comedy* and "possible" readings of commentaries on it. Much far-fetched guesswork here, including such odd conclusions as that mad Rudolf "could" represent "Reason." (W.C.)

Rowland, Herbert. "Überwindung des Irdischen bei Eichendorff und Mathias Claudius: Betrachtungen über eine Stelle im 'Marmorbild' und 'Ein Lied hinterm Ofen zu singen.'" *Aurora* 44 (1984): 124-29.

After acknowledging Eichendorff's interest in Claudius's "positive" Christianity, which avoided strict orthodoxy, worldly Pietism, and Rationalism, Rowland goes on to discuss the "obvious" and "unmistakable" relation between Claudius's image of winter in the title's poem and Fortunato's image of morning from "Marmorbild." Besides presenting images common to both works, Rowland established that both use humor and irony to "surmount the merely earthly and allow a happy glimpse of the godly." (W.C.)

Scheitler, Irmgard. "'... Aber den lieben Eichendorff hatten wir gesungen.' Beobachtungen zur musikalischen Rezeption von Eichendorffs Lyrik." *Aurora* 44 (1984): 100-23.

A thorough, well-documented chronicle of the folk, choral, and solo songs inspired by Eichendorff's lyrics, the article adds little to an interpretation of the poems. (W.C.)

Schwering, Markus. "Eichendorff und C.D. Friedrich: Zur Ikonographie des romantischen Landschaftsbildes." *Aurora* 44 (1984): 130-46.

Schwering announces his essay as an attempt to develop the results of Dominique Iehl's 1983 essay on the same subject (reviewed above). Starting from Oskar Seidlin's observation that Eichendorff's landscapes present a "sichtbare Theologie," the article shows that both painter and poet station observers in an elevated foreground with an often ominous middle ground and an ideal high horizon in the background; the situation parallels man's state of having to cross a spiritual danger-zone to reach salvation. Both artists also transport Christian iconography into the landscape, but in a way that often allows no one, clear meaning, since both are undecided about the extent to which God transcends or appears in nature. Complementarily, the figures in the writings and paintings are caught in an existence between identity with, and more distant, mere analogy to, nature. (W.C.)

Schwering, Markus. "Künstlerische Form und Epochenwandel:
Ein Versuch über Eichendorffs Roman *Ahnung und Gegenwart*."
Aurora 43 (1983): 7-31.

    Schwering sees the novel as a product of European thought
midway between Hegelian universal-historical time sense and
the particularizing of late nineteenth-century positivism,
a development the author feels reflected novelistically in
the shift from *Bildungsromane* to *Zeitromane*. *Ahnung und
Gegenwart* is like early Romantic novels in being a counter-
type to Goethe's *Meister*: it rejects resigned integration
back into bourgeois society for a view of triadic world
history in which poetry sometimes prefigures world unity.
However, the novel is unlike early Romantic novels because
it pays particular attention to details of the historical
moment and often projects a traditional Christian view of
a God-nature dichotomy in which salvation is not immanent
in history. (W.C.)

Steinsdorff, Sibylle von. "'Das Gantze noch einmal umarbei-
ten!': Notizen Eichendorffs zur geplanten Überarbeitung
seiner Novella 'Eine Meerfahrt.'" *Aurora* 44 (1984): 71-78.

    Contains a photo, description, and transcript of a
previously unpublished page, on whose front side Eichendorff
discusses plans to rework "Meerfahrt," and on whose back side
he answers questions from Adolf Schöll about the novella.
The sheet suggests that the first printed edition of the
story is based on the 1835 manuscript. Beyond this, the
obtuseness of Schöll's questions leads Steinsdorff to
speculate that the "anti-Romantic" reading tastes of 1835
were the prime cause of Eichendorff's not finishing the
novella. (W.C.)

Stöcklein, Paul. *Joseph von Eichendorff in Selbstzeugnissen
und Bilddokumenten*. Reinbek bei Hamburg: Rowohlt, 1983.
Pp. 177.

    A biography that shows all the standard strengths and
weaknesses of the Rowohlt monograph series, the book contributes little to the understanding of Eichendorff's works.
(W.C.)

Verweyen, Theodor. "Eine verschollene Eichendorff-Handschrift."
Aurora 44 (1984): 16-22.

    Contains a photo and description of the manuscript for
"Die Sperlinge." An appended interpretation of the poem
seeks to supplement Ansgar Hillach's view that Eichendorff's
poems are organized like emblems with *inscriptio* (title),

pictura (early poem), and *subscriptio* (end of poem). The
simple "Sperlinge" shows that Eichendorff used a variety
of models—in this case, Verweyen feels, the *sermo humilis*.
(W.C.)

See also Sullivan ("German 2. General").

FICHTE

Kipperman, Mark. "Fichtean Irony and Some Principles of
Romantic Quest." *SiR* 23 (1984): 223-36.

Fichte's role in the German Romantic period is analyzed
in view of Bloom's description of the "quest romance." His
analysis of the mutual interdetermination ("Wechselwirkung")
of I and not-I becomes the starting point for a self-
affirmation that can be applied to a psychological subject
(Novalis), particularly when summarized as *Einbildungskraft*
(imagination). Thus "the world is an other that discloses
itself to me, becomes real to me, only through my own
creative act ..." (230). Romantic imagination can surpass
itself in "striving," in the quest. Kierkegaard, despite
his critique of Fichtean irony, "knew his debt to Fichte"
(235); he recognized the negative and the redemptive movement in the quest—the necessary interaction of both.
(M.J.)

See also Kipperman ("General 3. Criticism"); Mielke ("Bona-
vantura"); Fischer ("Kleist"); Oellers ("Schlegel-Schelling,
Caroline").

FOUQUÉ

De Bruyn, Günter. "Ein Märkischer Don Quijote." Pp. 267-
301 in Günter de Bruyn, ed., *Friedrich de la Motte Fouqué:
Ritter und Geister: Romantische Erzählungen*. (Märkischer
Dichtergarten.) Frankfurt am Main: Fischer, 1981.

In an essay which constitutes the "Nachwort" to an edition
of ten Fouqué stories, de Bruyn entertainingly summarizes
the Romantic author's life and works. Fouqué's complete
literary output reflects many low points; de Bruyn's realistic view of his subject is refreshing, and he does not flinch
while pointing out a lack of quality in much of Fouqué's
work. (C.R.C.)

Max, Frank Rainer. "Fouqués 'Parcival': Romantische Renova-
tion eines poetischen Mittelalters." Pp. 541-55 in Jürgen
Kühnel, Hans-Dieter Mück, Ursula Müller, and Ulrich Müller,
eds., *Mittelalter-Rezeption II: Gesammelte Vörtrage des
2. Salzburger Symposions "Die Rezeption des Mittelalters in
Literatur, Bildender Kunst und Musik des 19. und 20. Jahrhunderts."* (Göppinger Arbeiten zur Germanistik, Nr. 358.)
Göppingen: Kümmerle, 1982.

Max furnishes interesting background information on the
composition of Fouqué's late (1832) epic, a little-known
"Nacherzählung" of Wolfram's masterpiece. Fouqué's once-
popular view of the transfigured, beautified Germanic Middle
Ages had become unfashionable; Max demonstrates that Fouqué
remained faithful to his ideal, although he was obliged to
suffer greatly. This epic contains an intensely personal
tone with the self-awareness that the time for such works
has long ago passed, and Max concludes therefore that the
epic was not meant for public viewing. This essay provides
an introduction to Fouqué's reworking of medieval materials,
and it documents the shift in popular attitudes toward the
Middle Ages which occurred from 1810 to 1830. (C.R.C.)

Rautenberg, Ursula. "Parzivals Bildungs- und Entwicklungs-
stufen: Zu Friedrich de la Motte Fouqués 'Parcival.'"
Pp. 557-72 in Jürgen Kühnel, Hans-Dieter Mück, Ursula Müller,
and Ulrich Müller, eds., *Mittelalter-Rezeption II: Gesammelte Vorträge des 2. Salzburger Symposions "Die Rezeption
des Mittelalters in Literatur, Bildender Kunst und Musik
des 19. und 20. Jahrhunderts."* (Göppinger Arbeiten zur
Germanistik, Nr. 358.) Göppingen: Kümmerle, 1982.

Rautenberg's paper traces Fouqué's knowledge of an interest
in the Parzival materials to Karl Rosenkranz's work on Wolfram, and describes exemplary "Rezeptionssituationen" in
the epic, which set the various scenes of the tale into a
narrative context. This study yields an interesting account
of a very important period of reception history, during
which the interest in medieval sources blossomed rapidly,
making lines of influence very difficult to trace. (C.R.C.)

See also Oeser ("Varnhagen von Ense, Rahel").

FREILIGRATH

See Freund-Spork ("Heine").

FRIEDRICH, C.D.

Mitchell, Timothy. "Caspar David Friedrich's *Der Watzmann*:
German Romantic Landscape Painting and Historical Geology."
ArtB 66 (1984): 452-64.

See also Iehl, Schwering ("Eichendorff"); Paulin ("Tieck").

GOETHE

See Flax ("General 3. Criticism"); Roloff, Sullivan, Ziemke
("German 2. General"); Catholy ("Brentano"); Fairley,
Heinrich-Heine-Institut, Düsseldorf, ed., Peters ("Heine");
Fritz, Köpke ("Jean Paul"); Raiser, Sembdner, Wittkowski
("Kleist"); Kurz, Schulz ("Schlegel, Fr."); Oellers
("Schlegel-Schelling, Caroline"); Köhler, Oeser ("Varnhagen
von Ense, Rahel").

GRILLPARZER

See Kozielek ("Werner").

HEBBEL

See Kozielek ("Werner").

HEGEL

Chase, Cynthia. "Getting Versed: Reading Hegel with
Baudelaire." *SiR* 22 (1983): 241-66.

   "'Le Soleil' does without those articulations as the mind
in memorization forgets the meanings linking the words
it cites. This is what it is, Baudelaire shows us, Hegel
tells us, to get versed" (255-56). Baudelaire's poem is
thus regarded as a poetic "versification" of the philosophical movement adumbrated in Hegel's discussion of the sign--
and the concomitant moments of "sign-creating fantasy"
and of memory--in the *Encyclopedia*. The aticle continues
and elaborates on the poststructuralist valorization of
the *sign* in Hegel's text, an emphasis begun by the (never
mentioned) precursors Derrida and de Man. (M.J.)

See also Bahti, Jaeschke ("German 2. General"); Erpenbeck
("Brentano"); Schwering ("Eichendorff"); Heise ("Heine");
Carmagnola, Warminski ("Hölderlin").

HEIDEGGER

See de Man, Heller, Kleinschmidt ("Hölderlin").

HEINE

Aregger, Agnes J. *Heine und Larra: Wirkungsgeschichte eines
deutschen Schriftstellers in Spanien.* Zurich: Verlag Reihe
W, 1981. Pp. 333. DM 24.00.

Studies of Heine's influence in Spanish literature have
in the past concentrated on the delayed effect of his poetry
on "modernismo" near the end of the nineteenth century.
Aregger wishes to show that Heine's activist prose had an
effect much earlier. But since this seems to be, on Heine's
side, exlusively a matter of *De l'Allemagne* and, on the
Spanish side, a few scattered echoes among critics and a
single 1836 essay by Larra (supplied here in German translation), Aregger fills out the study with a history of nineteenth-century Spanish literature and criticism, a social
and political comparison of Spain and Germany, and a great
many parallel quotations to demonstrate the congeniality
of Heine and Larra on a wide variety of political and
literary-sociological issues. The overlong, sometimes repetitious study is not very interesting, largely because the
author's view of Heine is uncritical, naive, and conventional,
especially in regard to her dismissal of his poetry. She
does not show a trace of originality, and, while I am not
competent to judge her perceptions of Larra and Spanish
literary history, this looks to me like one more minimally
competent dissertation whose publication in book form might
have been spared us. (J.L.S.)

Bech, Françoise. *Heines Pariser Exil zwischen Spätromantik
und Wirklichkeit: Kunst und Politik.* (Europäische Hochschulschriften, Series 1, Vol. 728.) Frankfurt am Main, Bern,
and New York: Peter Lang, 1983. Pp. 330. DM 106.00.

There continues to be a need to examine Heine's exile from
an internal French perspective, but this intermittently intelligent, undisciplined study does not meet it. Indeed,
its overall point is difficult to determine. The main body
of the book consists of explications of *Religion und Philoso-*

phie, *Börne*, and *Lutezia*; of these, only the *Börne* chapter
is reliably perspicacious. The volume is otherwise padded
with unintegrated material: an irritatingly inaccurate
biographical account of Heine, potted biographies of Balzac
and of Saint-Simon (whom Bech incorrectly says Heine never
mentions); a review of the 1830 Revolution; an essay on the
urban experience with references to Baudelaire apparently
derived from the fantasies of Dolf Oehler, etc. Everything
has the appearance of an unedited first draft. The author
seems to be seeking aperçus, which are sometimes well for-
mulated, sometimes arbitrary to the point of eccentricity;
the effect is not improved by the frequent evidence that
German is not her native language. She does not quote consistently from a standard edition, and quotations are not
always marked. The skimpy and sloppy bibliography shows
little awareness of current work on Heine and France; there
is much dependence on dated sources such as J. Dresch,
L. Betz, and L. Marcuse. The atrocious price of the crudely
printed product contributes to an impression of its super-
fluousness in this form. (J.L.S.)

Bianchi, Danilo. *Die unmögliche Synthese*: *Heines Frühwerk
im Spannungsfeld von petrarkistischer Tradition und frühromantischer Dichtungstheorie*. (Europäische Hochschulschriften, Series I, Vol. 716.) Bern, Frankfurt am Main, and
New York: Peter Lang, 1983. Pp. 301. DM 106.00.

   Manfred Windfuhr's influential argument of 1966 that Heine's
early poetry is Petrarchist is here pursued in extensive
detail. With constant reference to the theoretical arguments of A.W. Schlegel, of which Heine is supposed to have
been a follower, Bianchi pursues with dogged persistence
Petrarchan motifs and techniques in the early poetry, while
postulating the influence of Calderón on both the poetry
and *Almansor* and of *Macbeth* on *William Ratcliff*; Calderón
and Shakespeare are both seen in a Petrarchan–Baroque
succession. There is much interesting and pertinent learning in this study, and the Petrarchan tradition was undoubtedly
a segment of the Romantic system with which Heine wrestled.
But the concept of Petrarchism blocks the view into Heine's
originality and contributes to the conventional devaluation
of his poetry; Bianchi seems convinced that it is nothing
more than a pastiche of borrowed motifs and techniques.
The insistent argument, with its rather old-fashioned hunt
for sources and influences, masks the element of speculation
in it. There is no real evidence that Heine was strongly
focused on Petrarchism or that he paid much attention to
Calderón; Bianchi spends much time with a comparison to a
Calderón drama that Heine cannot have known, since it was

not translated into German in his time. Heine's rather
dismissive remarks on Calderón and quite hostile one toward
Petrarchism are explained by a total shift of values in the
1830s that repudiates the early work, a view that fore-
shortens the continuity in Heine's poetic dilemmas. The
argument requires not only a disparagement of the early
poetry as wholly derivative, but denies that *Almansor* can
have anything to do with Heine's Jewish feeling or that
Ratcliff is a Gothic drama, positions eccentric enough to
cast doubt on the fundamental assumptions of the exercise.
(J.L.S.)

Bichsel, Peter. "Heinrich Heine: Ein Brief an George Sand."
  Freibeuter, No. 7 (1981): 129-33.

  A subjective, skeptical capriccio on Heine's letter to
Sand of Aug. 17, 1838 (which Bichsel improbably claims
was dictated to a secretary); unconcerned with the old
dispute about its meaning, Bichsel concludes that it could
have been written to any woman and shows a passionate man
with little courage for passion. (J.L.S.)

Bockelkamp, Marianne. "Heine et 'sa' ponctuation." Pp. 182-
  93 in *Edition und Interpretation*. *Edition et Interprétation
  des Manuscrits Littéraires*, ed. Louis Hat and Winfried
  Woisler. (*JIG*, Series A, Vol. 11.) Bern, Frankfurt am
  Main, and Las Vegas: Peter Lang, 1981. Pp. 301.

  Examples of Heine's insistently idiosyncratic punctuation,
often altered by printers. (J.L.S.)

Brandon, Wallace Reid. "Heine--the Sword and Flame of the
  1830's." *U[niversity of] S[outh] F[lorida] Quarterly* 22:
  1-2 (Fall-Winter 1983): 39-43.

  A general account of Heine as a liberal freedom-fighter,
of indifferent accuracy in regard to facts, chronology,
and the sense of texts. (J.L.S.)

Calvié, Lucien. "Une procession religieuse à Sète vue par
  Henri Heine." *EG* 38 (1983); 328-41.

  Defines the political implications of a passage in *Lutezia*
contrasting the populist, sensualist naivety of Rossini's
music to the spiritualist artificiality of Mendelssohn's.
(J.L.S.)

Derré, Jean-René. "Heine écrivain français? Examen de la
  question d'après quelques-uns de ses manuscrits." Pp. 58-
  68 in *Edition und Interpretation*. *Edition et Interprétation*

des Manuscrits Littéraires, ed. Louis Hay and Winfried Woesler. (*JLG*, Series A, Vol. 11.) Bern, Frankfurt am Main, and Las Vegas: Peter Lang, 1981. Pp. 301.

A close examination of Heine's French manuscripts shows that he was very insecure in orthography and usage, and depended a great deal on his (subsequently dismissed) secretary Reinhardt to clean things up, but it also shows the verve and thoughtfulness with which he reedited his ideas into French. (J.L.S.)

Escoffier, Françoise. "Henri Heine et 'La Revue des Deux Mondes.'" *RLM* (Oct. 1982): 130-37.

A casual accumulation of texts by and about Heine from the *Revue des Deux Mondes*, in no chronological order and without references. (J.L.S.)

Espagne, Michel. "La bosse de Victor Hugo: Manuscrits de H. Heine et historie littéraire de la France." *Romanistische Zeitschrift für Literaturgeschichte/Cahiers d'Histoire des Littératures Romanes* 6 (1982): 322-37.

Extracts from the genetic variants of a note on Hugo are taken as evidence of a crisis in Heine's late philosophy and aesthetics; his opposition to Hugo is a "quest for his own identity." Possibly overingenious, especially as Heine's shifting characterizations are more plausibly explained by personal motives. (J.L.S.)

Espagne, Michel. "La parabole des souris. Itinéraire d'un fragment textuel." Pp. 202-12 in *Edition und Interpretation. Edition et Interprétation des Manuscrits Littéraires*, ed. Louis Hay and Winfried Woesler. (*JIG*, Series A, Vol. 11.) Bern, Frankfurt am Main, and Las Vegas: Peter Lang, 1981. Pp. 301.

A passage relativizing differing philosophies of history in a comprehensive pantheism, originally dropped from *Religion und Philosophie*, was revised for *Shakespeares Mädchen und Frauen*, arguably as part of Heine's defense against Börne. (J.L.S.)

Espagne, Michel. "Übersetzung und Orientreise: Heines Handschriften zum *Loeve-Veimars-Fragment*." *Euphorion* 78 (1984): 127-42.

In a study of the manuscript variants of Heine's late memoir on his early French translator, Espagne shows how Heine's own preoccupations are woven in, especially aesthetic freedom and aristocratic self-stylization in Oriental costume versus repressive bourgeois morality and republican frugality. (J.L.S.)

Espagne, Michel; Almuth Grésillon; and Catherine Viollet, eds. *Cahier Heine 3: Écriture et contraintes*. Paris: Editions du Centre National de la Recherche Scientifique, 1984. Pp. 143.

The third *Cahier Heine* is almost entirely given over to genetic analyses, that is, detailed examinations of manuscript variants in order to reconstruct the motives of creation. Jean-Pierre Lefebvre tries to recover the inhibitions with which Heine struggled in composing his necrologue of Ludwig Marcus. Almuth Grésillon examines the generation of Heine's numerous portmanteau words. Jean-Louis Lebrave applied speech-act theory to one episode in Heine's duplicitous effort to seize control of Meyerbeer's public relations. In one of the most interesting articles, Michel Espagne delineates the conflict between the objective, generalizing constraints of the moribund genre of the animal fable revived by Heine late in life with his subjectivity, ambiguity, and ideological specificity. Also valuable is Michael Werner's analysis of the alterations Heine made in the French version of *Lutezia* with an eye to a different national public, though in my opinion Heine's perceptions of his public, German or French, were at worst opportunistic and at best imaginary. In conclusion, Marianne Bockelkamp presents Jules Laforgue as translator of an early poem of Heine not included in *Buch der Lieder*. This French group is engaged in some of the most refined scholarship on Heine being produced today; the results, however, are intensely specialized. Microphilology combined with contemporary French discourse theory does not make for easy reading, and the concentrated intellectual effort may sometimes lead to overingenuity. Many misprints, incidentally. (J.L.S.)

Fairley, Barker. "Heine's Vaudeville"; "Heine and the Festive Board"; "Heine, Goethe, and the *Divan*." Pp. 211-32; 232-45; 246-52 in Fairley, *Selected Essays on German Literature*, ed. Rodney Symington. (Canadian Studies in German Language and Literature, Vol. 29.) New York, Berne, Frankfort/M, and Nancy: Peter Lang, 1984. Pp. 378. $35.80.

These familiar papers were originally published in 1934, 1967, and 1956 respectively, but they are worth noting here both on account of Fairley's importance in the modern history of English-language Heine scholarship and in acknowledgment of the very welcome project of making the old master's

essays on Goethe, Heine, Kleist, Raabe, and other topics
available in book form. (J.L.S.)

Freund-Spork, Walburga. "Individuelles Leid und solidarisches
Bewusstsein. Die soziale Problematik der Weber in Gedichten
von Freiligrath, Heine und Weerth." *Grabbe-Jahrbuch* 1 (1982):
99-109.

Example of a plan for teaching tenth-graders about politically activist poetry with three poems on the Weavers'
Revolt of 1844. (J.L.S.)

Giesemann, Gerhard. "Zu einigen Aspekten der Rezeption Heinrich Heines im slovenischen Realismus." Pp. 233-49 in
*Obdobje realizma v slovenskem jeziku, krijiževnosti in
kulturi: Tipoloska problematika ob jugoslovanskem in
šivšem europskem kontektstu*, ed. Boris Paternu et al.
Ljubljana: Filozofska fakulteta, 1982. Pp. 538.

Not seen.

Goebel, Gerhard. "Apoll in Hameln. Ein Nachtrag zu den
'Göttern im Exil.'" *GRM* N.S. 32 (1982): 286-99.

A folkloric attempt to identify the Pied Piper of Hamelin
with a demonized Apollo touches in passing on Heine's
legend of Apollo disguised in exile. (J.L.S.)

Grésillon, A., and J.-L. Lebrave. "Manuscrits, linguistique
et informatique." Pp. 177-89 in *Avant-texte, texte,
après-texte*, ed. Louis Hay and Péter Nagy. Paris and
Budapest: Editions du CNRS and Akadémiai Kiadó, 1982.
Pp. 217.

"Automatic edition" of variants, a method drawn from information theory and linguistics, is demonstrated on a
Lutezia text, and purports to be able to distinguish between
levels of historical reportage and subjective utterance.
(J.L.S.)

Gutjahr, Herbert. *Zwischen Affinität und Kritik: Heinrich
Heine und die Romantik.* (Analysen und Dokumente: Beiträge
zur Neueren Literatur, ed. Norbert Altenhofer, Vol. 12.)
Frankfurt am Main, Bern, and New York: Peter Lang, 1984.
Pp. 194. DM 68.00.

At first this study looks like another conventional exercise paraphrasing and explicating Heine's views of Romanticism; in fact, it is more limited than some, restricting
itself almost entirely to a contrast with the theories of

August Wilhelm and Friedrich Schlegel. But it becomes
more interesting when it touches upon the "affinities" to
Romanticism: Gutjahr finds them in the conviction of the
exceptional role of the poet; the linkage of all things in
unremitting symbolism; the obsolescence of classical objectivity in favor of a modern subjective, lyrical, and re-
flective poetry; the recognition that literature is not
wholly mimetic but that its source is inward. Gutjahr
also rightly criticizes Heine's indifference to Lessing's
distinctions between the literary and visual arts and at
least touches upon the problems thrown up by the fact that
Heine's aesthetics are most commonly expressed in connection
with the visual arts, and he suggests that the Romantics
saw the illusionary content of poesy in a more differentiated way than Heine. But these are only highlights in
a competent but rather ordinary performance; Gutjahr's
conclusion that Heine exhibited affinity to Romanticism
in aesthetic questions but opposition in regard to the
social effect of literature does not seem to me to penetrate to the depth of his perplexity about Romantic poesy.
The study is quite derivative of recently fashionable
trends, especially reception theory and neo-Marxism; Altenhofer (the dissertation director, I presume) is dutifully
quoted at length and Freud is dragged in at the end. As
becomes increasingly noticeable these days, no non-German
titles are listed in the bibliography; even Madame de Staël
is quoted in German. (J.L.S.)

Heinrich-Heine-Institut, Düsseldorf, ed. *Heine-Jahrbuch 1984*
(= *HeineJ 1984*). Hamburg: Hoffmann und Campe, 1984. Pp.
232; 8 pls.

There are six major essays. Jochen Hörisch finds Heine's
outlook permanently shaped by the academic, social, and
emotional traumas he suffered at the University of Göttingen.
With an extensive knowledge of and responsiveness to the
lyrical environment of the 1820s, Michael Perraudin places
Heine into an "epigonal" pattern of allusion, echo, and
imitation of other poems, illustrated in regard to one model
poem of Goethe's. The (English) essay, in the spirit of
Sengle's rehabilitation of Biedermeier literary practice,
is a stimulating and perhaps controversial contribution.
Another significant contribution is Susanne Zantop's thoughtful, well-written demonstration that Heine's historiographical principles in *Französische Zustände* are aimed specifically at Ranke, whose alleged objectivity and ideological indifference are to be exposed as conservative allegiance.
Not least valuable is the evidence that Heine's view of

Ranke was not wholly precise and that they shared certain
idealistic and utopian tendencies. In yet another of his
genetic manuscript studies, Michel Espagne attacks the
traditional text of "Bimini" as an ideological falsifica-
tion, rearranging it to reduce its metaphysical pessimism
in favor of a satirical, political, materialistic meaning
stressing the aesthetic of the ugly. Jocelyne Kolb, expanding further (in English) on her thesis of Heine's
"lack of affinity for music," shows that his references to
music always mean something other than music, which is
especially a metonymy for poetry, and she compares Hoffmann's successful and Balzac's unsuccessful verbal evocations of music. Using as an example the literary and
often evasively diplomatic stylization of Heine's letters
to members of his family, Ursula Roth mounts a justified
warning against the unmediated employment of his correspondence as a biographical source.

Among shorter items, Ulrich Pongs submits a note on
Heine's use of the Bibliothèque Royale; Margaret A. Rose
shows (in English) that the young Friedrich Engels imitated
Heine's travel writings; and Rolf Nagel discusses mentions
of Heine in a novel of the modern Brazilian writer Erico
Verissimo, who chronicled the settlement of Brazil, in
substantial part by Germans. There is an account of the
difficulties overcome in restoring Salomon Heine's garden
house in Hamburg-Ottensen and an eloquently outraged report
on an unsuccessful action to prevent the erection on the
island of Norderney of a sculpture depicting the young
Heine by the former Nazi cultural official Arno Breker.
Heine society business, including a ten-year retrospect
by retiring president Wilhelm Gössmann, book reviews,
running bibliography, and chronicle of Heine events as
usual. (J.L.S.)

Heise, Wolfgang. "Heine und Hegel." Pp. 254-87 in Heise,
*Realistik und Utopie: Aufsätze zur deutschen Literatur
zwischen Lessing und Heine*. Berlin: Akademie-Verlag,
1982. Pp. 317.

    Rev. by G. Laudin in *EG* 39 (1984): 73-75; by Ingrid
Pepperle in *ZG* 5 (1984): 217-21.
    Republication of the essay published in 1973 in *WB* (see
ELN 12, Supp., 137-38), and in the proceedings of the 1972
Weimar Heine conference (see *ELN* 14, Supp., 121.) (J.L.S.)

Heissenbüttel, Helmut. "Karl Kraus und die Folgen: Heinrich
Heine als Journalist." Pp. 75-86 in Heissenbüttel, *Von
fliegenden Fröschen, libidinösen Epen, vaterländischen
Romanen, Sprechblasen und Ohrwürmern*. Stuttgart: Klett,
1982. Pp. 189.

In a radio address of 1979, Heissenbüttel defends Heine
against Kraus's charge of having betrayed literature to
journalism, on the grounds that Heine reunited rhetoric
and aesthetics in a modern search for truth. Heissenbüttel misunderstands the unease at Heine's "character"
as resistance to his progressive message, distorted by
censorship, so that the finely crafted essay misses the
point in important ways. (J.L.S.)

Kaiser, Gerhard. "Doktor Faust, sind Sie des Teufels? Eine
Notiz zu Heinrich Heines *Seegespenst*." *Euphorion* 78 (1984):
188-97.

A comparative study of the poem "Seegespenst" shows
Heine's awareness of the preformation of emotions and
perceptions through literature; even the prosaic captain
unconsciously utters a literary quotation. The poet's
liberation to reality is only apparent, for in subsequent
poems of *Nordsee I* he lands again in literary dreams.
(J.L.S.)

Kinder, Hartmut. "Heinrich Heine: Der Rabbi von Bacherach
(1840)." Pp. 295-313 in *Romane und Erzählungen zwischen
Romantik und Realismus: Neue Interpretationen*, ed. Paul
Michael Lützeler. Stuttgart: Reclam, 1983. Pp. 463.
DM 42.80.

A largely paraphrasing explication stresses the contrast
in tone between the earlier and the later parts of the
Rabbi; Kinder argues, dubiously, to my mind, that the
Romanticism of the earlier part is motivated by an effort
to bridge the Jewish and Gentile worlds, and he asserts
the literary quality of the work without an effort to
demonstrate it. (J.L.S.)

Kortländer, Bernd, ed. Heinrich Heine, *Atta Troll: Ein
Sommernachtstraum*. (insel taschenbuch 748.) Frankfurt
am Main: Insel, 1983. Pp. 219; 32 illus. DM 8.00.

The solid, well-informed afterword to this both attractive and inexpensive edition actually constitutes one of
the best contemporary essays on *Atta Troll*, a work which, as
Kortländer points out, has been left on the margin of
Heine criticism. While Kortländer is perhaps a little in-
dulgent of Heine's political position here, he at least
suggests that posterity might evaluate the contemporary
political poets rather more positively than Heine did.
Kortländer rightly stresses attention to the parallels
to the caricatures of Grandville, made plausible in

several of the illustrations, and points out, as no one has
before, the use of Heine's bear figure in a photo-montage
of 1934 by John Heartfield. (J.L.S.)

Kraft, Werner. *Heine, der Dichter.* Munich: edition text +
    kritik, 1983. Pp. 168. DM 24.00.

    Rev. by Karlheinz Fingerhut in *Germanistik* 25 (1984):
    194-95.

    Any book in German devoted to Heine's poetry is an event,
although this one was, of course, not composed in Germany
but in Israel. It consists of essays on the contemporary
reception of Heine, on Platen, and on metrics, followed by
twenty-six poem interpretations, mostly very brief. Two or
three of these items have, to my knowledge, been published
before, and I suspect others may also have been in newspapers.
Kraft probes the effect of Heine's art down to phonetic and
metrical details; his approach is genuinely critical in the
sense of judging and evaluating, not always positively.
Unfortunately the volume does not do much toward restoring
the prestige of literary criticism of Heine's poetry. Kraft
is a singularly unclear writer, not in syntax or diction,
but in the association of ideas. His model appears to be
Karl Kraus, to whom he alludes repeatedly; these references,
along with others to Borchardt, George, Kafka, and Rilke,
generate an oddly archaic stylistic atmosphere of the 1920s.
The sparing references to other scholars are mostly of
ancient date, and no contemporary non-German criticism is
acknowledged; there are also some odd errors of fact. Poems
are not identified by cycle or number and are treated in isolation, without regard to the clusters in which they appear.
A recurrent concern with identifying genuine experience in
the poetry seems especially old-fashioned. The interpretations sometimes exhibit much curious literary learning but
strike me as diffuse, as a form of intellectual causerie.
Despite an occasional illuminating insight, I cannot judge
this volume to be a contribution to the comprehension of
Heine's poetry. (J.L.S.)

Kruse, Joseph A. *Heinrich Heine: Leben und Werk in Daten und
    Bildern.* (insel taschenbuch 615.) Frankfurt am Main:
    Insel Verlag, 1983. Pp. 352. DM 18.00.

    A biographical sketch with sixteen color and 225 black-and-
white annotated illustrations, a chronicle, and a bibliography.
(J.L.S.)

Mende, Fritz. "Heinrich Heine und das historische Lehrbeispiel
    eines 'Bürgerkönigs.'" *WB* 30 (1984): 357-80.

With his customary precision and thoroughness, Mende
traces the stages of Heine's flexible attitude toward Louis-
Philippe, finding consistency in a persistent allegiance to
the cause of the people and a recognition of socio-historical necessity. The argument is lucid and exact, but over-
looks Heine's mythifying identification of poetry and power,
with its consequent authoritarian Caesarism. Heine's ideal
of the monarch as "incarnation of the popular will" is a
great deal less democratic than Mende takes it to be. (J.L.S.)

Moss, Laurence. "Text and Context in *Dichterliebe*." *Ars
Lyrica* 2 (Fall–Winter 1983): 23–38.

Nobis, Helmut. "Heines Krankheit zu Ironie, Parodie, Humor
und Spott in den *Lamentationen* des *Romanzero*." *ZDF* 102
(1983): 521–41.

Close readings with the purpose of showing irony, parody,
humor, and scorn in the *Lamentationen*, leading to a total
destruction of literature and poetry. Debatable in places;
also isolated from non-German criticism. (J.L.S.)

Oellers, Norbert. "Friedrich Wilhem Krummachers Gedicht 'Am
Lurleifelsen'--eine Quelle für Heine? Mit einer methodolo-
gischen Vorbemerkung." Pp. 283–93 in *Sammlung und Sichten:
Festschrift für Oskar Fambach zum 80. Geburtstag*, ed.
Joachim Krause, Norbert Oellers, and Karl Konrad Polheim.
(Mitteilungen zur Theatergeschichte der Goethezeit aus der
Sammlung Oskar Fambach am Germanistischen Seminar der
Universität Bonn, ed. Norbert Oellers and Karl Konrad Polheim
with Joachim Krause, Vol. 4.) Bonn: Bouvier, 1982. Pp. 344.

Discovery of a previously unnoticed Loreley poem that
Heine is likely to have known, since it appeared in an
almanach published by his friend J.B. Rousseau that also
contained poems by Heine. (J.L.S.)

Peters, George F. "Heines Spiel mit dem Erlebnismuster Liebes-
lyrik im Schatten Goethes." *Neophilologus* 68 (1984): 232–
46.

Argues that the real experience behind the love poetry
is not one or another love affair but Goethe's poetry, which
Heine confronts and debunks. The demonstration is persuasive
but the reasons given--e.g., love is no longer possible in
capitalist society--are not. (J.L.S.)

Peters, George F. "Memory and Myth: The Narrator's Salvation
in Heine's *Ideen. Das Buch Le Grand*." *Rocky Mountain Review*
38 (1984): 169–78.

A thoughtful analysis of *Buch Le Grand* as fictionalized childhood memories reorganized in adult consciousness stresses discontinuity and the break with the organic sense of self represented by Goethe's model. Peters rightly sees the transformation of memory into myth as Heine's device for escaping his own biography. His reasons for this forced disjunction from his own past self remain obscure. (J.L.S.)

Petrowski, M. "Wladimir Majakowski in 'Heines Manier.'" *KuL*
    32 (1984): 194-208. Originally as Miron Petrovskiĭ.
    "Vladimir Maiakovskiĭ i Genrikh Geine." *Voprosy Literatury*
    (July 1983): 154-80.

Taking as a starting point Mayakovsky's poem "In Heine's Manner," the interesting article details affinities and similarities to Heine of the Russian poet, who learned German from Heine's poems. (J.L.S.)

Pinkert, Ernst-Ullrich. "Die Realität der fiktiven 'Piazza di
    San Marco' in Heines *Reise von Munchen nach Genua.*" *Text &
    Kontext* 12 (1984): 31-42.

The piazza is not in Ala, where Heine places it, but is borrowed from the nearby town of Rovereto. Pinkert tries to give a political interpretation to this conflation, but it is just as likely a mistake, owing to Heine's relative subordination of external reality to its imaginative re-creation. (J.L.S.)

Prater, Donald. "Stefan Zweig et Heinrich Heine. Quelques
    Refléxions." Pp. 45-50 in *Stefan Zweig 1881-1942. Actes
    du Colloque tenu à l'Université de Metz (decembre 1981)
    Département d'Allemand*, ed. Pierre Grappin. Paris: Didier,
    1982. Pp. 68.

Although Zweig barely mentioned Heine and their personalities were very different, Prater believes he can identify similarities in various coincidental aspects of their lives, most notably in the exile situation. It seems that to place Heine on a level with Zweig it is necessary to regard him with something less than awe. (J.L.S.)

Prawer, S.S. *Coal-Smoke and Englishmen: A Study of Verbal
    Caricature in the Writings of Heinrich Heine.* (The 1983
    Bithell Memorial Lecture.) London: Institute of Germanic
    Studies, University of London, 1984. Pp. vi+37.

With his customary elegance and as much indulgence as one might hope for from a British citizen, Prawer analyzes Heine's "grotesque denunciations of England and the English," arguing

that they are "deconstructed" by the exceptions he made and
his own exhibits of awareness that they were prejudiced.
One might as easily argue that these "deconstructions" are
characteristic rhetorical gestures of Heine's habit of appeal
for acceptance of his faults by seemingly ingenuous confession of them. Heine's Napoleonism, though mentioned in
passing, might have been stressed more as a central motive
of his Anglophobia. (J.L.S.)

Rose, Paul Lawrence, ed. Heinrich Heine, *History of Religion
and Philosophy in Germany.* [Townsville]: James Cook University of North Queensland, 1982. Pp. xx+133. $10.00.

Rev. by Ronald H. Nabrotzky in *GSR* 7 (1984):   580-81.
Rose's text of *Religion und Philosophie* presents itself
as a revised version of the old Leland translation, though
I cannot see that the revision has done much to relieve
Leland's late-Victorian stiffness. Added as a "fourth part"
on Hegel are a page from the *Briefe über Deutschland* (without
indicating that this is an unpublished text) and excerpts
from the *Geständnisse.* The generally encomiastic introduction,
which puts great stress on Heine's late repudiation of some
of the basic ideas of the work after his religious "return,"
is not very analytic and is marked by imprecise and in places
misleading formulations. The annotation will be helpful to
the less-informed reader, but it makes no pretense to
thoroughness and is marred (p. 35) by a serious and, for the
reader, confusing error misapplying to Metternich an allusion
to Friedrich Wilhelm III. An opportunity to produce a good,
modern English version of *Religion und Philosophie* of value
to the more than casual reader has been missed here. (J.L.S.)

Sammons, Jeffrey L. "Heinrich Heine: Reception in the World's
Strangeness." Pp. 1245-64 in *Literary Theory and Criticism:
Festschrift Presented to René Wellek in Honor of His Eightieth
Birthday*, ed. Joseph P. Strelka. Bern, Frankfurt am
Main, and New York: Peter Lang, 1984. Pp. 1462. $80.00.

Complaints about the way Heine's vast reputation has
generated myth, legend, and misinformation that often appear
impervious to fact and learning, and an appeal for balancing
our presentist allegiance to Heine with factual accuracy,
unbiased judgment, and responsible criticism.

Schoenemark, Erna. "Heinrich Heine im November 1933." *DU*
(East) 36 (1983):   585-86.

A schoolteacher discovers to her surprise that Heine
praised Luther. Trivial. (J.L.S.)

Schusky, Renate. "Heine, England und die Engländer." Pp.
139-48 in *Der curieuse Passagier": Deutsche Englandreisende
des achtzehnten Jahrhunderts als Vermittler kultureller und
technologischer Anregungen*, ed. Marie-Luise Spieckermann.
Heidelberg: Carl Winter, 1983. Pp. 159; 24 pls.

A review of Heine's reactions to his English journey of
1827 brings nothing new, and indeed is rather useless,
since it makes the easily refuted claim that his view of
England was positive before he was disillusioned by direct
experience and asserts that he was not dependent on sources,
though in fact his images of England and the English are
cliché-ridden and very dependent on the Napoleonic legends
he uncritically absorbed. (J.L.S.)

Straschek, G.P. "Stalin, Heinz Goldberg und Genrich Geine."
Exilforschung 1 (1983): 147-58.

The sad story of Heinz Goldberg, invited to the Soviet
Union in 1936 to write a film on Heine, who just managed
to escape the terror against German exiles, allegedly
because Stalin loved Heine. (J.L.S.)

Werner, Michael. "Heinrich Heine--über die Interdependenz
von jüdischer, deutscher und europäischer Identität in
seimen Werk." Pp. 9-28 in *Juden im Vormärz und in der
Revolution von 1848*, ed. Walter Grab and Julius H. Schoeps.
Stuttgart and Bonn: Burg Verlag, 1983. Pp. 400.

An observant, expert, though necessarily cursory review
of Heine's Jewish problem argues for the political relevance
of each of its stages, including the "Return." This view
of the matter is justified but partial. (J.L.S.)

Werner, Michael. "Noch einmal: Heines 'Wanderratten.' Zur
Interpretation einer Handschrift." Pp. 286-301 in *Edition
und Interpretation. Edition et Interprétation des Manu-
scrits Littéraires*, ed. Louis Hay and Winfried Woesler.
(*JIG*, Series A, Vol. 11.) Bern, Frankfurt am Main, and
Las Vegas: Peter Lang, 1981. Pp. 301.

A close examination of the manuscript variants in an
effort to solve the difficult question of the ideological
point of view in the poem. (J.L.S.)

Windfuhr, Manfred, ed. Heinrich Heine, *Historisch-kritische
Gesamtausgabe der Werke*. Vol. II: *Neue Gedichte*, ed.
Elisabeth Genton; Vol. XII/2: *Französische Maler; Franzö-
sische Zustände; über die französische Bühne: Apparat*, ed.
Jean-René Derré and Christiane Giesen. Hamburg: Hoffmann

und Campe, 1983; 1984. Pp. 986, 8 pls.; pp. 794 (505–1298),
continuously paged from Vol. XII/1), 24 pls. DM 96.00;
98.00 (subscription price).

Rev. of Vol. II by Werner Bellmann in *WW* 34 (1984): 228–30.
Volume II contains *Neue Gedichte* and the poetic paralipomena
of the middle period, including the French translations. The
commentary covers in elaborate detail the long, complicated
genesis of Heine's second volume of poetry and provides
extensive examples of contemporary reception. Apart from the
conscientious philological material, there is little here
that is new. The characteristic discipleship to Heine in
this case rather inhibits critical insight, and the somewhat
pedestrian commentary exhibits no intelligible principle of
poetic evaluation. It is, however, very learned and suggests
some interesting echoes of other poets in Heine's political
verse.
Vol. XII/2, the huge commentary to the early writings on
France, explicates the text literally line by line. Drawing
on a mass of contemporary and subsequent historical materials,
including the French press on which Heine himself was so
dependent, the commentary not only stresses Heine's vision
and insight, but also his errors of judgment and limits of
perception. It is thus a most significant contribution toward
locating Heine more accurately in the context of French
history and current events. Of the 24 plates, 15 are color
reproductions of paintings discussed in *Französische Maler*,
a particular blessing, since they are rarely to be found
anywhere in color. (J.L.S.)

Woesler, Winfried. "Des modifications textuelles prises comme
interaction entre auteur et public." Pp. 205–14 in *Avant-
texte, texte, après-texte*, ed. Louis Hay and Péter Nagy.
Paris and Budapest: Éditions du CNRS and Akadémiai Kiadó,
1982. Pp. 217.

Endeavors to show that Heine's self-censoring revisions of
the *Wintermärchen* manuscript are the consequence of submission
to the wishes or expectations of others as representatives
of a public that is, in a sociological sense, co-author of
the text. (J.L.S.)

See also Avni, Mende ("French 2. Hugo").

Reviews of books previously listed:

ARNOLD, Heinz Ludwig, ed., *TuK* No. 18/19 (see *RMB* for 1983,
pp. 340–41), rev. by Karlheinz Fingerhut in *HeineJ 1984*, pp.

182-85; BEHAL, Michael, et al., *Heinrich Heine Epoche--Werk--Wirkung* (see *RMB* for 1980, pp. 296-97), rev. by Peter Branscombe in *MLR* 79 (1984): 981-82; by Robert C. Holub in *Monatshefte* 75 (1983): 445-47; by Hartmut Kircher in *Germanistik* 24 (1983): 777; BOCKELKAMP, Marianne, *Analytische Forschungen zu Handschriften des 19. Jahrhunderts* (see *RMB* for 1983, p. 342), rev. by Volkmar Hansen in *HeineJ 1984*, pp. 175-76; by Karl Pörnbacher in *Germanistik* 24 (1983): 775; BRIEGLEB, Klaus, ed., *Heinrich Heine, Sämtliche Schriften* (see *ELN* 7, Supp., 102; 9, Supp., 129-30; 10, Supp., 150; 11, Supp., 130-31; 14, Supp., 122; 15, Supp., 160-61), rev. of the 12-volume paperback reprint (Frankfurt am Main, Berlin, and Vienna: Ullstein, 1981) by Rainer Hoffmann in *WW* 32 (1982): 297-99; DRAPER, Hal, *The Complete Poems of Heinrich Heine* (see *RMB* for 1982, pp. 307-08), rev. by Gabriele Annan in *NYRB*, Feb. 16, 1984, pp. 11-13; by Henry Hatfield in *SiR* 22 (1983): 647-48; by Robert C. Holub in *GQ* 57 (1984): 485-87; FÜLLNER, Bernd, *Heinrich Heine in deutschen Literaturgeschichten* (see *RMB* for 1983, pp. 346-47), rev. by Jeffrey L. Sammons in *Germanistik* 24 (1983): 775-76; GALLEY, Eberhard, and Alfred Estermann, eds., *Heinrich Heines Werk im Urteil seiner Zeitgenossen*, Vol. I (see *RMB* for 1982, pp. 308-09), rev. by Robert C. Holub in *GQ* 57 (1984): 324-26; GÖSSMANN, Wilhelm, and Joseph A. Kruse, eds., *Der späte Heine* (see *RMB* for 1984, pp. 348-49), rev. by Frauke Bartelt in *HeineJ 1984*, pp. 176-81; GRAB, Walter, *Heinrich Heine als politischer Dichter* (see *RMB* for 1983, pp. 349-50), rev. by Hartmut Kircher in *Germanistik* 24 (1983): 776; by Fritz Mende in *Germanistik* 24 (1983): 778; by Fritz Mende in *HeineJ 1984*, pp. 181-82; by Harry Zohn in *GSR* 7 (1984): 352-53; GRANDJONC, Jacques, and Michael Werner, *Wolfgang Strähls "Briefe eines Schweizers aus Paris"* (see *RMB* for 1980, p. 299), rev. by Fritz Mende in *Germanistik* 24 (1983): 776; HOLUB, Robert C., *Heinrich Heine's Reception of German Grecophilia* (see *RMB* for 1982, p. 313), rev. by Jocelyne Kolb in *GQ* 57 (1984): 662-64; KRUSE, Joseph A., et al., *Heinrich Heine und seine Zeit* (see *RMB* for 1981, p. 297), rev. by Karlheinz Fingerhut in *Germanistik* 25 (1984): 194; MENDE, Fritz, *Heinrich Heine: Chronik seines Lebens und seiner Werke* (see *ELN* 9, Supp., 134), rev. of the 2nd ed. of 1981 by Helmut Koopmann in *Arbitrium* 2 (1984): 193-95; NATIONALE FORSCHUNGS- UND GEDENKSTAETTEN, ETC., ed., *Heinrich Heine Säkularausgabe*, Vols. I, I K, II, IV, VII K, IX, X, XI, XV, XVI, XVII, XXV K, XXVI, XXVI K, XXVII K (see *ELN* 14, Supp., 126; 15, Supp., 164; 17, Supp., 207; *RMB* for 1979, p. 286; for 1980, p. 305; for 1981, p. 298; for 1983, pp. 358-59), rev. by Helmut Koopmann in *Germanistik* 25 (1984): 190-94; NETTER, Lucienne, *Heine et la peinture de la civilisation*

parisienne (see *RMB* for 1980, p. 306), rev. by Bernd
Kortländer in *HeineJ 1984*, pp. 190-91; PRAWER, S.S.,
Heine's Jewish Comedy (see *RMB* for 1983, p. 360), rev. by
Gabriele Annan in *NYRB*, Feb. 16, 1984, pp. 11-13; by anon.
in *AB Bookman's Weekly* 73 (1984): 4914; by Martin Bollacher
in *Germanistik* 25 (1984): 195; by Harry Zohn in *GSR* 7
(1984): 581-82; ROSENTHAL, Ludwig, *Heinrich Heines Erb-
shaftsstreit* (see *RMB* for 1982, pp. 316-17), rev. by
M. Werner in *EG* 38 (1983): 501-02; SAMMONS, Jeffrey L.,
Heinrich Heine: A Modern Biography (see *RMB* for 1979,
p. 288), rev. by Victor G. Doerksen in *MGS* 7 (1981): 319-
20; by Rüdiger von Tiedemann in *Arcadia* 19 (1984): 68-74;
SAMMONS, Jeffrey L., *Heinrich Heine: A Selected Critical
Bibliography of Secondary Literature 1956-1980* (see *RMB*
for 1982, p. 317), rev. by George F. Peters in *Rocky
Mountain Review* 38 (1984): 266-67; by Rüdiger von Tiedemann
in *Arcadia* 19 (1984): 68-74; SCHNEIDER, Manfred, *Die
kranke schöne Seele der Revolution* (see *RMB* for 1980, p.
309), rev. by Waltraud Wiethölter in *Germanistik* 24 (1983):
763-64; SPENCER, Hanna, *Heinrich Heine* (see *RMB* for 1982,
p. 318), rev. by Ronald Heinz Nabrotzky in *GSR* 7 (1984):
156-57; by Gerhard Weiss in *HeineJ 1984*, pp. 192-93; UEDING,
Gert, *Hoffmann und Campe* (see *RMB* for 1981, p. 300), rev.
by Konrad Kratzsch in *Germanistik* 24 (1983): 927; VOIGT,
Jürgen, *Ritter, Harlekin und Henker* (see *RMB* for 1982, pp.
338-39), rev. by Joseph A. Kruse in *Germanistik* 24 (1983):
779; by Ludwig Rosenthal in *HeineJ 1984*, pp. 196-200;
WEHNER, Walter, *Heinrich Heine: "Die schlesischen Weber"*
(see *RMB* for 1981, p. 301), rev. by Roy C. Cowen in *Monatshefte* 75 (1983): 433; WINDFUHR, Manfred, ed., *Heinrich
Heine: Historisch-kritische Gesamtausgabe der Werke*, Vol.
VIII/2 (see *RMB* for 1981, pp. 301-02), rev. by Norbert
Oellers in *Germanistik* 25 (1984): 189-90; by Jeffrey L.
Sammons in *Arbitrium* 2 (1984): 191-93; ZAGARI, Luciano,
and Paolo Chiarini, eds., *Zu Heinrich Heine* (see *RMB* for
1981, pp. 302-04), rev. by Gerd Heinemann in *HeineJ 1984*,
pp. 186-87; ZLOTKOWSKI, Edward A., *Heinrich Heine's Reise-
bilder* (see *RMB* for 1980, p. 312), rev. by Robert C. Holub
in *Monatshefte* 75 (1983): 445-47.

HÖLDERLIN

Abusch, Alexander. "Holderlins poetischer Traum von einem
  Vaterland des Volkes." Pp. 98-117 in Abusch, *Ansichten
  über einige Klassiker*. Berlin-Ost: Aufbau Verlag, 1982.

Adler, Jeremy, trans. "Friedrich Hölderlin on Tragedy: 'Notes
on the Oedipus' and 'Notes on the Antigone.'" Pp. 205-44 in
E.S. Schaffer, ed., *Comparative Criticism 5.* Cambridge
University Press, 1983. Pp. 371.

   Included with the translation of these extremely difficult
   texts is a useful introduction. (S.M.)

Adler, Jeremy. "Philosophical Archaeology: Hölderlin's 'Pindar
Fragments.' A Translation with an Interpretation." Pp. 23-
46 in E.S. Schaffer, ed., *Comparative Criticism 6.* Cambridge University Press, 1984. Pp. 375.

Beck, Adolf. *Hölderlins Weg zu Deutschland: Fragmente und
Thesen.* Stuttgart: Metzler, 1982.

   Rev. by Christoph Jamme in *Hegel-Studien* 18 (1983): 432-
   41.

   This volume collects Beck's four masterful essays on
   Hölderlin's relationship to Germany, a series of essays which
   appeared originally in the *JFDH* (see *RMB* for 1978, p. 211;
   for 1980, p. 314; for 1981, p. 306). (S.M.)

"Bibliographische Hinweise und Zitate zur Frankfurter Hölder-
lin-Ausgabe." *Le Pauvre Holterling* 6 (1983): 68.

Binder, Wolfgang. "Äther und Abgrund in Hölderlins Dichtung."
Pp. 349-69 in Christoph Jamme and Otto Pöggeler, eds., *Frank-
furt aber ist der Nabel dieser Erde.* (Deutscher Idealismus:
Philosophie und Wirkungsgeschichte in Quellen und Studien,
Vol. 8.) Stuttgart: Klett-Cotta, 1983. Pp. 402.

   A detailed analysis of the images of *Äther* and *Abgrund*
   in Hölderlin's poetry, with "Vom Abgrund nemlich" forming
   the central text of the discussion. Binder traces these
   concepts in Hölderlin's earlier poetry and notes in the late
   fragment a reversal of meaning in the terms' configurations.
   (S.M.)

Böschenstein, Bernhard. "Das Bild der Schweiz bei Ebel,
Boehlendorff und Hölderlin." Pp. 58-72 in Christoph Jamme
and Otto Pöggeler, eds., *Frankfurt aber ist der Nabel dieser
Erde.* (Deutscher Idealismus: Philosophie und Wirkungsge-
schichte in Quellen und Studien, Vol. 8.) Stuttgart: Klett-
Cotta, 1983. Pp. 402.

   Böschenstein discusses Ebel's *Anleitung auf die nützlichste
   und genussvollste Art in der Schweiz zu reisen* (1793) and his
   Schilderung der Gebirgsvölker der Schweiz (1798/1802) as well
   as Boehlendorff's *Geschichte der Helvetischen Revolution,*

setting these works into the context of Hölderlin's image
of Switzerland. The study adds considerable depth to our
understanding of the historical dimensions of Switzerland
in Hölderlin's work. (S.M.)

Boschenstein, Bernhard. "Les derniers poèmes de Hölderlin."
(Trad. par John E. Jackson en collab. avec l'auteur.)
Romantisme 11 (1981): 3-16.

Brion, Marcel. "Hölderlin et ses dieux." *Les Études
Philosophiques* 1 (1983): 1-10.

Hölderlin's conception of the gods is discussed in the
context of European Romanticism. (S.M.)

Carmagnola, Fulvio. "Hölderlin e Hegel: Il tragico e il
logos." *ACME* 35 (1982): 251-70.

Corngold, Stanley. "Hölderlin and the Interpretation of
the Self." Pp. 187-200 in E.S. Schaffer, ed., *Comparative
Criticism 5.* Cambridge University Press, 1983. Pp. 371.

A rigorous and insightful treatment of the self in Hölderlin's work in light of current reevaluations of Romanticism
and with reference to contemporary critical theory. (S.M.)

de Man, Paul. "Heidegger's Exegeses of Hölderlin." Pp. 246-
66 in de Man, *Blindness and Insight.* 2d rev. ed. Intro.
by Wlad Godzich. University of Minnesota Press, 1983.
Pp. 308.

Reprint and translation (by Wlad Godzich) of "Les exégès
de Hölderlin par Martin Heidegger," an essay that first
appeared in *Critique* (Paris, 1959/62). De Man notes that
Hölderlin and Heidegger both "speak of the same thing" and
that Heidegger's commentaries "have brought out precisely
the central concern of Hölderlin's work," how to speak
Being experienced in the absolute temporal present and how
to then say Being itself. But de Man pursues here rigorously
what he sees as the central paradox of Heidegger's exegeses:
that "Hölderlin says exactly the opposite of what Heidegger
makes him say." De Man sees in Hölderlin's work a reversal
(*Kehre*) but not a reconciliatory turn as this has most often
been read, but rather a reversal that "manifests itself in
a radical turnabout that takes [Hölderlin] away from a
philosophy of reconciliation toward a philosophy of
necessary separation." (S.M.)

Franz, Michael. "September 1806." *Le Pauvre Holterling* 6
(1983): 9-53.

Gaskill, Howard. "Some Recent Trends in Hölderlin Criticism."
  GL&L 36 (1982-83): 166-81.

  A generally level-headed and well-considered review of
  recent Hölderlin scholarship. Gaskill argues that the work
  written in English by such scholars as Cyrus Hamlin has been,
  in the main, ignored by most Hölderlin scholars, and cites
  Hamlin's neglected study of Wordsworth's *Prelude* and
  Hölderlin's *Hyperion* (which appeared in *Genre* in 1973).
  While Hamlin's above-mentioned analysis is a particularly
  fine study, one has difficulty agreeing with Gaskin's
  assessment of other works, notably Constantine's *Locality
  in Hölderlin* and Unger's *Hölderlin's Major Poetry*; the former
  hardly yields the insights Gaskill claims for it, and Unger's
  study, while providing an introduction for the English reader, does not offer new contributions to Hölderlin scholarship. (S.M.)

Hamburger, Michael. "'Und mich leset o/ Ihr Blüthen von
  Deutschland.' Zur Aktualität Hölderlins." *Le Pauvre Holterling* 7 (1984): 29-40.

Heller, Erich. "Thinking about Poetry, Hölderlin and Heidegger."
  Pp. 63-83 in Heller, *In the Age of Prose*. Cambridge University Press, 1984.

  The essay first appeared in a *Festschrift* for Oskar Seidlin
  in 1976. A fine consideration of Heidegger's readings of
  Hölderlin's poetry and poetics. Heller's essay should
  provide a nice counterpoint to de Man's discussion of Hölderlin and Heidegger listed above. (S.M.)

Hölderlin, Friedrich. *Werke: Geschenkausgabe in 4 Bänden.*
  Frankfurt: Insel Verlag, 1983. Vol. 1: *Gedichte.* Pp.
  195; Vol. 2: *Gedichte.* Pp. 210; Vol. 3: *Hyperion.* Pp.
  174; Vol. 4: *Der Tod des Empedokles. Briefe. Anhang.*
  Pp. 281.

  The publisher has made the selection of texts for this
  edition, based on its *Werke und Briefe* of 1969, edited by
  Friedrich Beissner and Jochen Schmidt (see rev. by Wolfgang
  Hecht, *Germanistik* 11 [1970]: 547). The selection and
  arrangement of the poems by Beissner and Schmidt have been
  retained, and the whole of the major lyric poetry is given
  with selections from the earliest and the latest poems.
  Hyperion and the "Fragment von Hyperion" are printed together in the third volume; the fourth volume contains the
  three versions of *Empedokles* as well as Hölderlin's most
  important letters. The type of the *Geschenkausgabe* is

considerably smaller than that of the 1969 *Werke und Briefe*, but one nice innovation is that the shorter poems and the two-line epigrams are printed separately on individual pages.

As a *Lese- und Studienausgabe* the edition of 1969 had many advantages: the selection and arrangement of the poetry were intelligent, and in addition to *Hyperion* and the versions of *Empedokles* the editors included the essays and Hölderlin's translations of Sophocles's *Antigone* and *Oedipus* as well as selections from the Pindar and other translations, and they printed a good selection of important letters to Hölderlin, most notably those of Susette Gontard. The 1969 edition had, further, an admirable section of detailed notes that provided excellent background and orientation for the texts.

While the *Geschenkausgabe* has, as noted, been drawn from the Beissner/Schmidt edition, what has been left out will confound: all translations and essays as well as all letters to Hölderlin have been deleted and the *Anmerkungen* have been dropped. In short, much of what made the earlier Beissner/Schmidt edition such an admirable *Studienausgabe* is missing, and the failure to reprint the notes is particularly unsettling. (S.M.)

Jakobson, Roman, and Grete Lübbe-Grothues. "The Language of Schizophrenia. Hölderlin's Speech and Poetry." Trans. by Susan Kriton. *Poetics Today* 2 (1980-81): 137-44.

Jamme, Christoph. "Liebe, Schicksal und Tragik. Hegels 'Geist des Christentums' und Hölderlins 'Empedokles.'" Pp. 300-24 in Christoph Jamme and Otto Pöggeler, eds., *Frankfurt aber ist der Nabel dieser Erde*. (Deutscher Idealismus: Philosophie und Wirkungsgeschichte in Quellen und Studien, Vol. 8.) Stuttgart: Klett-Cotta, 1983. Pp. 402.

A detailed and carefully argued analysis of points of convergence and disagreement between the figures of Christ and Empedokles in the respective works. Jamme sees both Christ and Empedokles not as figures of mediation but as individuals who offer radical breaks with their respective traditions. (S.M.)

Jens, Walter. "Kein eigenes Leben." *Frankfurter Anthologie* 7 (1983): 63-66.

An individual analysis of Hölderlin's "Der Frühling." (S.M.)

Kleinschmidt, Erich. "Die Hermeneutik der heroischen Dekakenz:
Zur Ausdrucksproblematik von Martin Heidegger's Hölderlin-
Interpretation." *LiLi* 13 (1983): 303-17.

    A sharp critique of Heidegger's interpretations of Hölder-
lin, in which Kleinschmidt traces the dangers of a criticism
that allows the poetic text and the analysis to merge.
(S.M.)

Martens, Gunter. "Textkonstitution in Varianten: Die Bedeutung
der Entstehungsvarianten für das Verständnis schwieriger
Texte Hölderlins." Pp. 69-96 in *Edition und Interpretation*.
Berlin and Las Vegas: Peter Lange, 1981.

Menze, Clemens. "Hölderlins pädagogische Entwürfe aus seiner
Hofmeisterzeit 1794/1795." Pp. 261-83 in Christoph Jamme
and Otto Pöggeler, eds., *Frankfurt aber ist der Nabel dieser
Erde*. (Deutscher Idealismus: Philosophie und Wirkungs-
geschichte in Quellen und Studien, Vol. 8.) Stuttgart:
Klett-Cotta, 1983. Pp. 402.

    Discusses Hölderlin's pedagogical theories, as these
emerged in his years as *Hofmeister*, in the context of the
history of pedagogy and in light of Rousseau's influence on
education. (S.M.)

Merkel, Ingrid. "Zwischen Klassik und Revolution: Friedrich
Hölderlin." Pp. 228-44 in Walter Hinderer, ed., *Geschichte
der deutschen Lyrik*. Stuttgart: Reclam, 1983.

    Merkel seeks to locate Hölderlin's work in that tricky
region between Romanticism and Classicism, but she offers
no really new observations that would help resolve the by-now
tired debate as to whether Hölderlin's work can best be
considered Romantic or Classic. Merkel wants to "reclaim"
Hölderlin for a more loosely defined concept of Classicism,
a poetry defined by the poets' practical and theoretical
concerns for "Klassizität"--but this "Klassizität" is never
really defined by Merkel with any rigor. (S.M.)

Müller-Seidel, Walter. "Hölderlins Ode 'Dichterberuf': Zum
schriftstellerischen Selbstverständnis um 1800." Pp. 191-
208 in Müller-Seidel, *Die Geschichtlichkeit der deutschen
Klassik*. Stuttgart: J.B. Metzlersche Verlagsbuchhandlung,
1983.

    A very fine analysis of Hölderlin's ode "Dichterberuf"
that examines Hölderlin's concept of poetic vocation and
places it firmly within the historical context. Müller-
Seidel cogently refutes grandiose conceptions of Hölderlin's
poetry as a kind of prophecy. (S.M.)

Nancy, Jean-Luc. "La joie d'Hyperion." *Les Études Philosophiques* 1 (1983): 177-94.

A lucid and far-ranging consideration of "Das Eine in sich selber unterschiedene" for Hölderlin's thought. (S.M.)

Pöggeler, Otto. "Ist Hegel Schlegel? Friedrich Schlegel und Friedrich Hölderlins Frankfurter Freundeskreis." Pp. 325-48 in Christoph Jamme and Otto Pöggeler, eds., *Frankfurt aber ist der Nabel dieser Erde*. (Deutscher Idealismus: Philosophie und Wirkungsgeschichte in Quellen und Studien, Vol. 8.) Stuttgart: Klett-Cotta, 1983. Pp. 402.

Pöggeler extends here his study of individual relationships within Hölderlin's circle of friends (see *RMB* for 1982, p. 374). Pöggeler pursues here Haym's thesis that Romantic theory is aufgehoben in Hegel's *Phänomenologie des Geistes* (and in that sense at one point had to have shared Friedrich Schlegel's positions, was thus at one point Schlegel ...). Pöggeler offers detailed glimpses of the interactions between Hölderlin's friends and the reflection of those interactions in their works. (S.M.)

Prignitz, Christoph. "Hölderlins Konfrontation mit den Reichsstädten." Pp. 42-57 in Christoph Jamme and Otto Pöggeler, eds., *Frankfurt aber ist der Nabel dieser Erde*. (Deutscher Idealismus: Philosophie und Wirkungsgeschichte in Quellen und Studien, Vol. 8.) Stuttgart: Klett-Cotta, 1983. Pp. 402.

Analyzes the political value of the *Reichsstädte* in Hölderlin's thought, with reference to his comments on Nürnberg and his experiences in Frankfurt. Prignitz traces Hölderlin's sympathy for the radical pronouncements of the lower classes as well as for their actions. (S.M.)

Sattler, D.E. "Al rovescio: Hölderlin nach 1806." *Le Pauvre Holterling* 7 (1984): 17-28.

Sattler, D.E. "Leonoren I." *Le Pauvre Holterling* 7 (1984): 5-6.

Sattler, D.E. "Rekonstruktion des Gesangs." Pp. 259-70 in *Edition und Interpretation*. Berlin and Las Vegas: Peter Lang, 1981.

Sattler, D.E., ed. *Friedrich Hölderlin: Sämtliche Werke*. Vols. 4: Oden I (Manuscript Facsimiles) & 5: Oden II (Text). Frankfurt: Stroemfeld Roter Stern, 1984. Pp. 384; 468.

Rev. by Marleen Stoessel in *Die Zeit*, March 29, 1985.
The continuing publication of the volumes of the *Frank-
furter-Ausgabe* remains the most exciting development in
Hölderlin scholarship during the last ten years.   (S.M.)

Seifert, Albrecht. *Untersuchungen zu Hölderlins Pindar-
Rezeption.* Munich: Fink, 1982.

> Rev. by H. Stefan Schultz in *ZDP* 102 (1983):   282-85.
> A detailed and exacting study that substantially contributes
> to our understanding of Hölderlin's profound debt to Pindar.
> (S.M.)

Steiner, George. "On Hölderlin's Translation of Sophocles'
Antigone." Pp. 66-106 in Steiner, *Antigones.* Oxford
University Press, 1984. Pp. 316.

> Rev. by Terrence Des Pres in *The Nation*, March 2, 1985.
> Steiner's commentaries on translation in *After Babel* (1975)
> contain some of the best thinking that has been done on
> translation, and he continues that work here in a detailed
> consideration of Hölderlin's translation of *Antigone.*   (S.M.)

Szondi, Peter. "Holderlin's Overcoming of Classicism." Trans.
by Timothy Bahti. Pp. 251-70 in E.S. Schaffer, ed., *Comparative Criticism 5.* Cambridge University Press, 1983. Pp.
371.

> A translation (with introductory remarks) of Szondi's
> landmark essay. (S.M.)

Thomasberger, Andreas. "Mythos, Religion, Mythe: Hölderlins
Grundlegung einer neuen Mythologie in seinem 'Fragment
philosophischer Briefe.'" Pp. 284-99 in Christoph Jamme and
Otto Pöggeler, eds., *Frankfurt aber ist der Nabel dieser
Erde.* (Deutscher Idealismus: Philosophie und Wirkungs-
geschichte in Quellen und Studien, Vol. 8.) Stuttgart:
Klett-Cotta, 1983. Pp. 402.

> Thomasberger's point of departure is provided by the
> arrangement of theoretical texts given in the fourteenth
> volume of the *Frankfurter-Ausgabe, Entwürfe zur Poetik* (see
> *RMB* for 1981, p. 310). The fragment "Über Religion,"
> usually seen as belonging to the Homburg years and dated
> at 1799, is hypothetically dated in the *Frankfurter-Ausgabe*
> as belonging to the winter of 1796/97 and is seen thus as
> a part of Hölderlin's proposed plan for a series of
> philosophical letters, the "Neue Briefe über die aesthetische
> Erziehung des Menschen" (see *Stuttgarter Ausgabe*, 6:2).
> This is an important study in the reevaluation of Hölderlin's

fragmentary essays and it gives a detailed reading of the "Fragment philosophischer Briefe." (S.M.)

Thurmair, Gregor. "Des Gesetz der Dichtung. Hölderlins Rezeption der greichischen Poesie." Pp. 254-71 in Karl Richter and Jörg Schönert, eds., *Klassik und Moderne.* Stuttgart: J.B. Metzlersche Buchhandlung, 1983.

Thurmair offers a careful analysis of Hölderlin's later work and sees in the poetological essays and the late poetry not a "später Widerruf" (as Schmidt has characterized Hölderlin's late work) but rather the logical conclusion of Hölderlin's study of Greek literature. (S.M.)

Unger, Richard. *Friedrich Hölderlin.* (Twayne's World Authors Series, 738.) New York: Twayne Publishers, 1984. Pp. 155.

In comparative literature courses on European Romanticism, Hölderlin is now being taught with some regularity, and a solid introduction in English to Hölderlin's life and works would be a welcome reference volume. One would hesitate, however, to send students to Richard Unger's *Friedrich Hölderlin.* Ideally the Twayne volumes offer both an introduction to the author for the beginning reader and, in the context of that introduction, allow the scholar to present a series of interpretative analyses. Unger's volume on Hölderlin will, unfortunately, tend to confound the uninitiated while it will leave scholars questioning points of analysis, statements of fact, and turns of phrase all along the way. (S.M.)

Wais, Kurt. "Jean-Jacques Rousseau verstanden durch Hölderlin." Pp. 35-62 in Wais, *Europäische Literatur im Vergleich.* Tübingen: Max Niemeyer Verlag, 1983.

Warminski, Andrzej. "Hölderlin in France." *SiR* 22 (1983): 173-97.

Warminski has written some of the best philosophically grounded articles on Hölderlin published in the last five years. Here he confronts our often unexamined notions of Greek culture and art and their impact on our interpretations of Holderlin's work. Discussing Holderlin's late letters to Boehlendorff, Warminski makes fine distinctions between Hölderlin's and Hegel's aesthetics, and the essay offers, with reference to contemporary critical theory, a rigorous line of argument that pursues fundamental distinctions between rhetorical and representational readings of Hölderlin's poetics. (S.M.)

See also de Man ("General 3. Criticism"); Des Allemagnes
("French 1. General"); Jouve ("French 2. Nerval"); Koppen
and von Tiedemann, Röder ("German 2. General").

Reviews of books previously listed:

CONSTANTINE, David J., The Significance of Locality in the
Poetry of Friedrich Hölderlin (see RMB for 1981, pp. 306-07),
rev. by Johannes Mahr in Germanistik 25 (1984): 516-17;
DANNHAUER, Heinz-Martin; Hans Otto Horch; and Klaus Schuffels,
eds., Wörterbuch zu Friedrich Hölderlin: Auf der Text-
grundlage der Grossen Stuttgarter Ausgabe (see RMB for 1983,
p. 367), rev. by David Constantine in MLR 80 (1985): 217-19;
FINK, Markus, Pindarfragmente: Neun Hölderlin-Deutungen (see
RMB for 1983, p. 368), rev. by Howard Gaskill in CG 17 (1984):
143-44; by Glenn W. Most in Germanistik 24 (1983): 748-49;
JAMME, Christoph, "Ein ungelehrtes Buch": Die philosophische
Gemeinschaft zwischen Hölderlin und Hegel in Frankfurt 1797-
1800 (see RMB for 1983, p. 370), rev. by Alice Kuzniar in
GQ 58 (1985): 285-86; PETERS, Uwe Henrik, Hölderlin: Wider
die These vom edlen Simulanten (see RMB for 1983, p. 374),
rev. by Christoph Jamme in Hegel-Studien 18 (1983): 442-43;
by Jürgen Söring in Germanistik 18 (1984): 171; SATTLER,
D.E., Friedrich Hölderlin: Sämtliche Werke, Vol. 9 (see RMB
for 1983, p. 375), rev. by Jochen Hieber in FAZ, Nr. 271,
November 22, 1983; SATTLER, D.E., Friedrich Hölderlin:
Sämtliche Werke, Vols. 10 and 11 (see RMB for 1983, p. 375),
rev. by Jochen Hieber in FAZ, Nr. 150, July 2, 1983; by
Christoph Jamme in Hegel-Studien 18 (1983): 442-43; THOMAS-
BERGER, Andreas, Von der Poesie der Sprache: Gedanken zum
mythologischen Charakter der Dichtung Hölderlins (see RMB
for 1983, p. 376), rev. by Lawrence Ryan in Germanistik 25
(1984): 172; WACKWITZ, Stephan, Trauer und Utopie um 1800:
Studien zu Hölderlins Elegienwerk (see RMB for 1983, p. 378),
rev. by Gerhard Kurz in Germanistik 25 (1984): 172-73;
ZUBERBÜHLER, Rolf, Die Sprache des Herzens: Hölderlins
Widmungsdichtung (see RMB for 1983, p. 379), rev. by Gerhard
Kurz in Germanistik 25 (1984): 173.

HOFFMANN, E.T.A.

Castein, Hanne. "Christa Wolfs Neue Lebensansichten eines
Katers: Ein Beitrag zur Hoffmann-Rezeption in der DDR."
MHG 29 (1983): 45-53.

Castein's illuminating comparison of Christa Wolf's story
with Kater Murr also calls attention to other recent Hoffmann-

inspired texts such as Johanna and Günter Braun's *Allein im Weltraum* and Hermann Kasack's *Mechanischer Doppelgänger*. (S.P.S.)

Ellis, John M. "Über einige scheinbare Widerspruche in Hoffmanns Erzählungen." *MHG* 29 (1983): 31–35.

Drawing on examples from *Das öde Haus*, *Rat Krespel*, and *Meister Floh*, Ellis convincingly argues that occasional inconsistencies and contradictions in Hoffmann's narratives are only seemingly unintentional; in fact they are instances of his subtle reader manipulation. (S.P.S.)

Fritz, Horst. "*2. Kapitel*: Verdinglichung als kollektiver Verblendungszusammenhang. E.T.A. Hoffmann: 'Klein Zaches.'" Pp. 58–78 in Fritz, *Instrumentelle Vernunft als Gegenstand von Literatur: Studien zu Jean Pauls "Dr. Katzenberger," E.T.A. Hoffmanns "Klein Zaches," Goethes "Novelle" und Thomas Manns "Zauberberg."* (Literaturgeschichte und Literaturkritik. Schriften zur Deutschen und Allgemeinen und Vergleichenden Literaturwissenschaft, Bd. 4.) München: Fink, 1982. Pp. 236.

Rev. by Ernst Ribbat in *MHG* 29 (1983): 67–69.

Harper, Anthony, and Norman Oliver. "What Really Happens to Anselmus? 'Impermissible' and 'Irrelevant' Questions about E.T.A. Hoffmann's *Der goldne Topf*." *NGS* 11 (1983): 113–22.

Yet another inconclusive speculation about Anselmus's end, this time prompted by Structuralist premises, to reach the hackneyed conclusion: the ironic stance of Hoffmann's narrator is all-pervasive. (S.P.S.)

Hunter-Lougheed, Rosemarie. "'Bonaventura' und E.T.A. Hoffmann, unter besonderer Berücksichtigung des Plozker Tagebuches." *GRM* 32 (1982): 345–63.

Hunter-Lougheed's case for Hoffmann's authorship continues to lack conclusive evidence (see reviews of her earlier speculations in *ELN* 17, Supp., 214 and in *RMB* for 1983, pp. 312–13). (S.P.S.)

Kaulbach, Friedrich. "Das perspektivische Wirklichkeitsprinzip in E.T.A. Hoffmanns Erzählung 'Der Sandmann.'" *Perspektiven der Philosophie. Neues Jahrbuch* 6 (1980): 187–211.

Rev. by Franz Loquai in *MHG* 29 (1983): 84.

Köhler, Ingeborg. "Richard Wagner und E.T.A. Hoffmann."
MHG 29 (1983): 36-40.

Inconclusive recapitulation of well-known biographical
references to Wagner's life-long admiration for Hoffmann's
narratives. (S.P.S.)

Mitteilungen der E.T.A. Hoffmann-Gesellschaft. Sitz in Bamberg.
29. Heft 1983. Bamberg: E.T.A. Hoffmann-Gesellschaft
e.V., 1983 [=MHG].

In addition to the articles listed by author in this
section, the 1983 volume contains pictures, portraits,
facsimiles, reports on commemorative celebrations, announce-
ments, and other miscellany of interest to Hoffmann scholars.
The separate review section, expertly edited by Wulf
Segebrecht, continues to bring extensive reviews of recent
Hoffmann editions, criticism, and selected dissertations.
An additional review section by Franz Loquai offers concise
commentary on selected recent articles and other bibliographical items not reviewed in detail. (S.P.S.)

Peters, Jochen-Ulrich. "Die Entthronung des romantischen
Kunstlers: Gogols Dialog mit E.T.A. Hoffmann." Pp. 155-
67 in Dialogizität, ed. Renate Lachmann. München: Fink,
1982.

In the theoretical framework of Bachtin's, Žirmunsky's,
Mukařosky's, and Durišin's studies of the "concept of
dialogicity," Peters analyzes the creative assimilation
of Hoffmann's narrative model in four Gogol stories:
The Portrait, Nevsky Prospekt, Notes of a Madman, and The
Nose. Peters shows how Gogol gradually distanced himself
from Hoffmann and concludes that in assessing the affinity,
divergences from the model are just as significant as
parallels. (S.P.S.)

Schmidt, Hans-Walter. "Der Kinderfresser: Ein Motiv in
E.T.A. Hoffmanns Ignaz Denner und sein Kontext." MHG 29
(1983): 17-30.

Schmidt's focus on the fascinating "Kinderfresser-Motiv"
sheds new light on the interpretation of Ignaz Denner.
(S.P.S.)

Steinecke, Hartmut. "Probleme der Hoffmann-Edition." MHG
29 (1983): 11-16.

Steinecke, co-editor (with Wulf Segebrecht) of the forthcoming E.T.A. Hoffmann: Das Gesamtwerk (Deutscher Klassiker-

Verlag), offers here a cogent and informative discussion of the basic premises, projected principles, and practical difficulties of editing Hoffmann today. (S.P.S.)

Toggenburger, Hans. *Die späten Almanach-Erzählungen E.T.A. Hoffmanns.* Bern: Lang, 1983. Pp. 261. SwFr. 57.90.

   Rev. by Friedhelm Anhuber in *MHG* 29 (1983): 71–73.

Wörtche, Thomas. "Demonstriertes Erzählen: Zu E.T.A. Hoffmanns *Klein Zaches genannt Zinnober.*" Pp. 271-91 in *Germanistik in Erlangen: 100 Jahre nach der Gründung des Deutschen Seminars,* ed. Dietmar Peschel. Erlangen: Universitätsbibliothek Erlangen-Nürnberg, 1983.

   Wörtche promises an informed and up-to-date discussion of *Klein Zaches* and the considerable body of criticism devoted to it. In fact his article is an interminable compilation of unnecessarily cumbersome formulations lacking coherence and clear critical focus. Wörtche's tortuous presentation obscures rather than illuminates; he offers hackneyed interpretative details as new critical insights. Surely *Klein Zaches* deserves better! (S.P.S.)

Wurl, Paul-Wolfgang. "Was sich am Morgen meines 50. Geburtstags ereignete: Heinrich Seidel huldigt E.T.A. Hoffmann." *MHG* 29 (1983): 41–44.

See also Milner ("French 1. General"); Liganos ("French 2. Sand"); Sullivan ("German 2. General"); Fink ("Eichendorff"); Heinrich-Heine-Institut, Düsseldorf, ed. ("Heine"); Fritz ("Jean Paul"); Hilzinger ("Wackenroder").

Reviews of books previously listed:

FÜHMANN, Franz, *Fräulein Veronika Paulmann aus der Pirnaer Vorstadt oder Etwas über das Schauerliche bei E.T.A. Hoffmann* (see *RMB* for 1981, p. 316), rev. by Ulrich Helmke in *MHG* 29 (1983): 76-77; LOECKER, Armand De, *Zwischen Atlantis und Frankfurt: Märchendichtung und Goldenes Zeitalter bei E.T.A. Hoffmann* (see *RMB* for 1983, p. 382), rev. by Wulf Segebrecht in *MHG* 29 (1983): 77; McGLATHERY, James M., *Mysticism and Sexuality: E.T.A. Hoffmann. Part One: Hoffmann and His Sources* (see *RMB* for 1983, p. 382), rev. by Friedrich Kittler in *MHG* 29 (1983): 69-71; by Kenneth G. Negus in *Seminar* 19 (1983): 297-98; by Ulrich Stadler in *Germanistik* 24 (1983): 749-50; MAGRIS, Claudio, *Die andere Vernunft: E.T.A. Hoffmann* (see *RMB* for 1981, pp. 320-31), rev. by Wulf Segebrecht in *MHG* 29 (1983): 61-66; SCHER, Steven Paul, *Interpretationen*

zu *E.T.A. Hoffmann* (see *RMB* for 1981, p. 324), rev. by
Jürgen Walter in *MHG* 29 (1983): 66-67; SCHNAPP, Friedrich,
ed., *Der Musiker E.T.A. Hoffmann: Ein Dokumentenband* (see
RMB for 1983, pp. 383-84), rev. by Uwe Schweikert in *MHG*
29 (1983): 79-80.

JEAN PAUL

Fritz, Horst. "1. *Kapitel*: Ein Modell instrumenteller
Vernunft. Jean Paul: 'Dr. Katzenbergers Badereise.'"
Pp. 19-57 in Fritz, *Instrumentelle Vernunft als Gegenstand
von Literatur: Studien zu Jean Pauls "Dr. Katzenberger,"
E.T.A. Hoffmanns "Klein Zaches," Goethes "Novelle" und
Thomas Manns "Zauberberg."* (Literaturgeschichte und
Literaturkritik. Schriften zur Deutschen und Allgemeinen
und Verleichenden Literaturwissenschaft, Bd. 4.) München:
Fink, 1982. Pp. 236.

Jahrbuch der Jean Paul-Gesellschaft (=JJPG). Im Auftrag der
Jean-Paul-Gesellschaft, Sitz Bayreuth, ed. Kurt Wölfel,
18. Jg. Munich: C.H. Beck, 1983. Pp. 233.

The 1983 issue of the *Jahrbuch* offers the third collection
of contemporary reviews of Jean Paul's works. Nine different
journals are presented here. Most important are probably
the reviews in the *Neue allgemeine deutsche Bibliothek*, in
the *Morgenblatt für gebildete Stände* and its "Beilage,"
and in the *Journal des Luxus und der Moden.* The very mixed
reception of Jean Paul's work will be evident from this
collection. Kurt Wölfel's collection of reviews is to be
concluded in a fourth volume. (W.K.)

Knowlton, James. "Erbe and Its Vicissitudes: Günter de
Bruyn's Reexamination of Jean Paul." *Studies in GDR
Culture and Society* 4 (1984): 213-25.

Köpke, Wulf. "Jean Pauls Auseinandersetzung mit Werther und
Wilhelm Meister im 'Titan.'" *Goethe im Kontext: Kunst
und Humanität, Naturwissenschaft und Politik von der Aufklärung bis zur Restauration*, ed. Wolfgang Wittkowski.
Tübingen: Max Niemeyer, 1984. Pp. 69-82 + discussion pp.
82-88.

A discussion of the reception of Goethe's novels by Jean
Paul, both in his *Vorschule der Ästhetik* and in the fictional context of *Titan.* Jean Paul's implicit criticism
is directed against Goethe's seeming acquiescence in the
existing social conditions. (W.K.)

Kuzniar, Alice A. "The Bounds of the Infinite: Self-Reflection in Jean Paul's 'Rede des todten Christus." *GQ* 57 (1984): 183-96.

A critical reading of Jean Paul's *Rede* starting from its reception by "Bonaventura" in the *Nachtwachen*. With the help of deconstructionist methods, the self-referentiality problem of the narrator and the text are elucidated. (W.K.)

Montandon, Alain. "L'imaginaire du livre chez Jean Paul." *Romantisme* 44 (1984): 35-48.

Oehlenschläger, Eckart. "Jean Paul." Pp. 104-14 in Karl Konrad Pohlheim, ed., *Handbuch der deutschen Erzählung*. Düsseldorf: Bagel, 1981. Pp. 653.

An examination of the shorter narrative works by Jean Paul. Since experience never reveals more than disjointed fragments of reality, imagination has to supply the vision of the whole. The "fool's" perspective in the short narratives proves this in a special way. (W.K.)

Ortheil, Hanns-Josef. *Jean Paul mit Selbstzeugnissen und Bilddokumenten dargestellt.* (Rowohlts Monographien, Vol. 329.) Reinbek: Rowohlt, 1984. Pp. 158.

A general introduction into the life of Jean Paul with many illustrations. There is surprisingly little analysis of the major works, which Ortheil had offered in his *Der poetische Widerstand im Roman* (1980), but this little volume seems to be intended for the casual reader. Details are not always correct. (W.K.)

Pierre, Roland, trans. and ed. *Biographie conjecturale (1799).* (Palimpseste.) Paris: Aubier-Montaigne, 1981. Pp. 181.

Rev. by Jean Mondot in *Dix-Huitième Siècle* 15 (1983): 481-82.

Pietzcker, Carl. *Einführung in die Psychoanalyse des literarischen Kunstwerks am Beispiel von Jean Pauls "Rede des toten Christus."* Würzburg: Königshausen & Neumann, 1983. Pp. 214.

Rev. by Sander L. Gilman in *GR* 49 (1984): 166-67; by Waltraud Wiethölter in *Germanistik* 25 (1984): 76-77.
Pietzcker uses Jean Paul's provocative *Rede* about the death of God to prove the validity of psychoanalytical methods for the understanding of literary texts. Jean Paul's text is used as an example for a more general statement. Neverthless, Pietzcker offers at the same time a very provocative reading of Jean Paul's most famous text. (W.K.)

Pross, Wolfgang. "Fälbels und Siebenkäs' Wanderungen und Johann
Michael Füssels 'Fränkische Reise': Empirismus, Ästhetik und
soziale Wirklichkeit im Werk Jean Pauls." Pp. 352-70 in Wolf-
gang Griep and Hans-Wolf Jäger, eds., *Reise und soziale
Realität am Ende des 18. Jahrhunderts.* (Neue Bremer Beiträge,
Vol. 1.) Heidelberg: Carl Winter, 1983.

Pross discusses Füssel's travel account as a likely source
for Jean Paul's descriptions of his native region. More
generally, Pross analyzes the conflict between accurate render-
ing of social reality in travel books and the expression of
the experience of scenic beauty. This very problem has entered
into the work of Jean Paul. (W.K.)

Sütterlin, Christa. *Wasser der Romantik: Eine Studie zu den
Zeit-Raum-Beziehungen bei Jean Paul und J.M.W. Turner.*
(Europäische Hochschulschriften, Series 1, Vol. 564.) Bern,
Frankfurt, and New York: Peter Lang, 1983. Pp. 263.

A comparison of Jean Paul's water metaphors and the description of landscape with water in Turner's painting is most
intriguing. This is a very fruitful area of investigation.
The dissertation by Christa Sütterlin suffers from two problems:
a somewhat narrow view of Jean Paul influenced by Emil Staiger
and too little actual comparison of Jean Paul and Turner. It
is also questionable whether *Titan* should have been her only
source for Jean Paul. (W.K.)

Wölfel, Kurt. "Hahenschrei: Über das Widmungsschreiben vor
Jean Pauls 'Titan': 'Der Traum der Wahrheit.'" Pp. 221-
30 in Dietmar Peschel, ed., *Germanistik in Erlangen: Hundert
Jahre nach der Gründung des Deutschen Seminars.* (Erlanger
Forschungen, Reihe A. Band 31.) Erlangen: Universitäts-
bund Erlangen-Nürnberg, 1983. Pp. 655.

Wölfel discusses this preface to *Titan* both as poetic dream
and as a rare example of Jean Paul's dedicating a work to
princes. The attempt to give this dedication a poetic sensibility had to fail since it contradicted Jean Paul's very
principles of aesthetics. Jean Paul should have returned to
his customary form of prefaces instead. (W.K.)

Zimmermann, Werner. *Jean Paul: "Siebenkäs," Frauenbild und
Geschlechterkonstellation: Beitrag zu einer psychoanalytischen
Interpretation.* Phil diss. Freiburg/Br., 1982. Freiburg:
Weber Druck, 1982. Pp. 231.

An examination of the woman figures in *Siebenkäs* and
Siebenkäs's two marriages, seen in the context of eighteenth-
century social history and Jean Paul's relations to his

parents and his presumed or documented sexual problems. An interesting perspective that needs to be explored further. (W.K.)

See also Vijn ("General 3. Criticism"); Habersetzer, Mielke ("Bonaventura"); Fritz ("Hoffmann, E.T.A.").

Reviews of books previously listed:

JAHRBUCH DER JEAN-PAUL-GESELLSCHAFT, 1980 ed. (see *RMB* for 1981, p. 331), rev. by Dennis F. Mahoney in *Monatschefte* 76 (1984): 218-19; MAURER, Peter, *Wunsch und Maske: Eine Untersuchung der Bild- und Motivstruktur von Jean Pauls Flegeljahren* (see *RMB* for 1982, p. 329), rev. by Dennis F. Mahoney in *Monatshefte* 76 (1984): 100-01; SPEIER, Hans-Michael, *Die Ästhetik Jean Pauls in der Dichtung des deutschen Symbolismus* (see *RMB* for 1981, p. 333), rev. by Jürgen Söring in *Germanistik* 25 (1984): 210-11.

KANT

Makkreal, Rudolf. "Imagination and Temporality in Kant's Theory of the Sublime." *JAAC* 42 (1984): 303-15.

See also Kelley ("English 4. Wordsworth"); Boehme ("German 2. General"); Arens ("Kleist"); Johnston ("Schiller").

KERNER

Jennings, Lee Byron. *Justinus Kerners Weg nach Weinsberg (1809-1819): Die Entpolitisierung eines Romantikers.* Columbia, S.C.: Camden House, 1982. Pp. x+133. $17.00.

Rev. by Donald P. Haase in *JEGP* 83 (1984): 410-12.

KLEIST

Adam, Wolfgang. "Gewaltlosigkeit, Gewalt: Ein Vergleich der Gestaltung dieser Thematik in Kleists *Prinz Friedrich von Homburg* und in der indischen Dichtung *Bhagavadgeetha*. Zu einem Hinweis Walther Muschgs in seiner *Tragischen Literatur-geschichte*." *German Studies in India* 8 (1984): 1-8.

Arens, Katherine M. "Kleist's 'Bettelweib von Locarno': A
Propositional Analysis." *DVJS* 57 (1983): 450-68.

Argues that most literary critical practice describes
only surface structure, and that "propositional analysis" of
the kind here offered has access to a deep structure of
logical necessity. Not grammar or style, but the logical
structure of events, as thoroughly manipulated by the author,
constitutes the communicated, exhaustive meaning of the text.
Such thorough manipulation on Kleist's part, Arens argues,
sets the text up as a coherent, delimited universe, "valid
and verifiable" (455) in its own logical terms. Evocation
and hermeneutic conjecture have no place in this model of
reading. Cites some secondary work on the alleged Kant-
crisis (since the essay concludes that "Kleist was able to
undertake an extension of Kant's work into language" [468]),
but resolutely disregards all previous work on Kleist's
language, as well as his own provocative statements concerning the process of articulation (in, for example, "Über
das allmähliche Verfertigung der Gedanken beim Reden").
(L.S.)

Bachmeier, Helmut, and Thomas Horst, eds. *Heinrich von Kleist:
Amphitryon. Erläuterungen und Dokumente.* (Universal-Bibliothek,
Nr. 8162.) Stuttgart: Reclam, 1983. Pp. 160. DM 4.40.

Bogdal, Klaus-Michael. *Heinrich von Kleist: Michael Kohlhaas.*
(Text und Geschichte: Modellanalysen zur deutschen Literatur.)
Munich: Wilhelm Fink Verlag, 1981. Pp. 125.

A fine essay on strategies of reading *Kohlhaas*. Bogdal
takes the obvious--that much of the text's continuing appeal
lies in its tenacious presentation of the heroic and paradoxical pursuit of justice--and situates it in cultural and
historical contexts that help articulate the meaning of both
the quest and the text. He places the novella in a tradition
reaching from Defoe's *Robinson Crusoe* to Peter Schneider's
Messer im Kopf, but the "model analysis" offered her is
genuinely eclectic, managing to deal convincingly and concisely with philosophical, historical, and stylistic issues.
The dominant motif is that of a conflict in eighteenth-century
legal theory (say: Rousseau *contra* Adam Müller), to which
the text is a literary monument. Includes close readings of
key scenes (Luther's study, the market in Dresden), historical
documentation (e.g., excerpts from the *Brandenburgische
Halsgerichtsordnung* of 1516), and a good bibliography. (L.S.)

Brown, Hilda M. *Kleist and the Tragic Ideal: A Study of
Penthesilea and Its Relationship to Kleist's Personal and*

Literary Development 1806-1808. (European University Papers,
Ser. 1, Vol. 203.) Bern, Frankfurt, and Las Vegas: Peter
Lang, 1977. Pp. 149. SwFr. 33.00.

Rev. by Ruth Angress in *Germanistik* 24 (1983): 753-54.

Clouser, Robin A. "Heroism in Kleist's 'Das Erdbeben in
Chili.'" *GR* 58 (1983): 129-40.

De Leeuwe, H.H.J. "Warum Heisst Kleists 'Marquise von O...'
von O...?" *Neophil* 68 (1984): 478-79.

Attacks what he considers speculative interpretations of
the significance of the initial (advanced by Steven Huff;
see below). Claims to remain with the "facts": a tradition
of using such initials was started in German literature by
Gellert (in imitation of Richardson). Kleist is supposed
to have derived his initials from "Schwedische Gräfin von
G ..." and from Schiller's "Der Geisterseher" (*O*, *F*). Hardly
demonstrated, and even if true, not necessarily contradictory
to Huff's argument. (L.S.)

Fischer, Bernd. "Fatum und Idee: Zu Kleists *Erdbeben in Chili*."
DVJS 58 (1984): 414-27.

Correctly sees that the story is more than an anti-clerical
tirade; more fundamentally, it is an ironization and trivialization of literary-philosophical motifs of the time, motifs
which propose, collectively, to reconcile conflict under
the healing rubric of Idealism (hence the "Idee" of Fischer's
title). Kleist resists this Idealism, without, however, offering us much in the way of an alternative. A good start, but
doesn't go very far. (L.S.)

Fischer, Bernd. "Wo Steht Kleist im *Amphitryon*?" *SN* 56 (1984):
61-68.

Argues that previous criticism of the play falls into
three main categories, stressing (1) the victory of *Gefühl*,
(2) the dramatizing of the idealistic *Identitätsproblematik*
(e.g., Fichte), and (3) the existential conflict of man with
his gods. Declares that what *all* interpretations share is
a search for a *positive* reading of the play. While most of
Fischer's insights concerning the play itself are interesting
and defensible, he is setting up straw men; he seems unaware
that much recent Kleist criticism has stressed what he would
call the "negative." More significantly, he does not really
engage points of contact between idealistic philosophy and
social questions. He simply declares the play to be about
the latter. Seems to have been written primarily as a provo-
cation. (L.S.)

Gebhart, Peter. "Notizen zur Kunstanschauung Heinrich von
   Kleists." *Euphorion* 77 (1983): 483–99.

   A tour-de-force summary of Kleist's challenging aesthetics,
which cannot be aligned with the heuristic programs of
either Classicism or Romanticism. It is rather an "Aesthetik
der Irration," which substitutes "Energien und Wirkungen"
for the mimetic reproduction of meaning (496). Gebhart ranges
freely and succinctly across both Kleist's works and the
secondary literature, including a number of striking sources
often neglected (e.g., Lou Salomé). Must reading. (L.S.)

Gelus, Marjorie, and Ruth Ann Crowley. "'Kleist Conquers New
   York': Kleist Reception in the U.S., 1975-76." *CLS* 18
   (1981): 459-74.

   A benign catalogue of reviews given by journalists of
Rohmer's film (*The Marquise of O...*) and Robert Kalfin's
Off-Broadway production of *The Prince of Hamburg*. Although
the authors nod in the direction of *Rezeptionsaesthetik*,
they do not analyze any of the cultural paradigms underlying
the reception of Kleist. They conclude that the Kleist
perceived here is "faded, or superficial, or lacking in
vitality and differentiation" (472), but that, in any case,
"at least a beginning has been made toward creating a new
audience for Kleist" (473).

Göttler, Fritz. *Handlungssysteme in Heinrich von Kleists "Der
   Findling": Diskussion und Anwendung narrativer Kategorien
   und Analyseverfahren.* (Europäische Hochschulschriften, Reihe
   1, Nr. 584.) Frankfurt/Main and Bern: Peter Lang, 1983.
   Pp. 267.

   An ambitious project to bring to literary studies some of
the methodological structures of related fields such as
cybernetics, system theory, and sociology. Originally a
Munich dissertation (1981) written for Klaus Kanzog, the
book takes Clause Brémond's structuralism to be the best
literary-theoretical representative of these related fields.
Göttler takes previous Kleist criticism to task for failing
to recognize that *any* aspect of a text (theme, motif, narrator, etc.) must be seen as a function within a system, and
can have meaning only within such a structure. He is careful
to point out that he is offering only an "analysis," and not
an "interpretation," but the implication is clear: he believes
that the latter can be based only on the *kind* of structuralism
he is outlining. A good three-fourths of the book is
devoted to discussion of the complex of theoretical concerns
Göttler has; only 33 pages are actually concerned with "die

narrative Struktur des 'Findling.'" These contain some 59
"narrative interactions," schematically represented in
terms of "System-input, Regelung, Kosten, Output." The book
abruptly ends without a concluding summary of its import.
It would seem that structuralist *études* are alive and well
in Munich. (See Renner, below.) (L.S.)

Heller, Erich. "The Dismantling of a Marionette Theatre, or,
Psychology and the Misinterpretation of Literature. A
Lecture." Pp. 193-213 in *In the Age of Prose: Literary
and Philosophical Essays.* Cambridge University Press, 1984.
Pp. xii+268.

One has to admire the verve of Heller's ringing defense of
the humanistic imagination, his resolute refusal to contami-
nate it with methodological overdeterminations derived from
the "physiological, biological, chemical, biochemical, elec-
trophysical, libidinous, economical, measurable" (212). He
is offended by Margret Schaefer's psychoanalytical reading
of the puppet dialog (*American Imago* 32 [Winter 1975]: 365-
88). But he is really after bigger game: *all* readings that
do not do justice to the "immeasurable life of the mind"
(212). In his polemic, though, he perpetuates one of the
most dubious, overdetermined readings of the "Marionettentheater," namely that it is a "story" (rather than a
dialog) whose meaning "is transparently clear to any intelligent reader" (207). He makes Kleist into the epitome of
Romantic *perfectibilité.* His argument, like that of his
target, winds up parodying itself. (L.S.)

Horn, Peter. *Kleist-Chronik.* (Athenäum Taschenbücher, Nr.
2161.) Königstein: Athenäum, 1980. Pp. x+140. DM 18.00.

Rev. by Hilda M. Brown in *Germanistik* 25 (1984): 174.
A combination of annalistic biography and *Kulturfahrplan,*
listing in chronological order (under annual headings)
"significant events" from October 18, 1773 (Kleist's birthday) to 1826 (when Tieck published the *Gesammelte Schriften*).
Especially thorough toward the end (the years 1810 and 1811
comprise about one-third of the volume), but also manages
intriguing configurations during the earlier years (e.g.,
Schröder performs *Hamlet* for the first time in Germany in
Hamburg in the year of Kleist's birth). Extremely useful
for awakening the mind to new connections. (L.S.)

Horst, Falk. "Kleists Michael Kohlaas." *WW* 33 (1983): 275-
85.

Renews the old question concerning Kohlhaas's "authentic"
motivation: genuine *justice* or an affect-based need for

revenge? Consists mainly of a plot summary and a few
sparse references to secondary literature. Contributes
nothing new to the question. (L.S.)

Huff, Steven R. "Kleist and the Expectant Virgins: The
Meaning of the 'O' in *Die Marquise von O....*" *JEGP* 31
(1982): 367-76.

   Contends that the name alludes to the Virgin Mary, via
the Iberian tradition of representing her as pregnant:
the Madonna de la O. Sees confirmation of the thesis in
the opening interjection (expressing joy and hope) of
antiphonic chants sung during Advent: "O...." (L.S.)

Kreutzer, Hans Joachim, ed. *Kleist-Jahrbuch 1980*. Berlin:
Erich Schmidt, 1982. Pp. 167.

   Rev. by John Gearey in *GR* 59 (1984): 124-25; by Hermann
F. Weiss in *CG* 57 (1984): 483-85; by Wolfgang Wittkowski
in *Deutsche Bücher* 14 (1984): 142-43.
   The inauguration of a "new series" of annual reports by
the Heinrich-von-Kleist Gesellschaft, replacing the older
"new series" begun in 1962 by Walter Müller-Seidel and
edited since 1971 by Wieland Schmidt, which in turn had
revived the original *Jahrbuch der Kleist-Gesellschaft*,
published from 1921 to 1941. Several editorial policies
are announced: the yearbook is to be interdisciplinary
and genuinely international (although only German-language
contributions are accepted); it is to be accessible to the
general public (hence eschewing narrow issues and jargon);
and it is to include a spectrum of forms, from essays to
colloquia to book reviews. The volume is, thus, supposed
to represent a microcosm of Kleist studies, a somewhat
hubristic notion, considering the proliferation of work on,
and interest in, its subject. This edition manages tolerably
well, however, to range widely: it includes essays on "the
crisis of the Prussian state around 1800," on historiography,
on philosophy, on perception theory, and on European Romanticism. All contributions, however (except book reviews),
are from Germans. (L.S.)

Kreutzer, Hans Joachim, ed. *Kleist-Jahrbuch 1984*. Berlin:
Erich Schmidt Verlag, 1984. Pp. 176.

   This year's volume contains two major essays: Carl
Dahlhaus on the relationship between music and literature,
and Peter K. Jansen on Monk Lewis (who visited Wieland in
Weimar ten years before Kleist did) and the significance
of *Trivialliteratur* for an understanding of Kleist. Most

of the remaining essays stem from a November 1983 colloquium on theater and the staging of Kleist. The one theme
that emerges with any clarity is that the reception of
Kleist in contemporary theater tends to stress the irrational, whereas professional literary criticism stresses
idealism. There are also reviews of recent work (e.g.,
James McGlathery's *Desire's Sway*). Despite claims that
the "new" *Kleist-Jahrbuch* is supposed to be international,
by far most of the contributions are by professors in the
Federal Republic. (L.S.)

Leistner, Bernd. "Heinrich von Kleists 'Der zerbrochne
Krug.'" *WB* 30,12 (1984): 2028-47.

A sensitive and close reading of the political structures
at stake in the play; links them convincingly to aesthetic
issues, in particular to genre questions. Argues that
Schiller and Kleist both failed to revitalize Sophoclean
tragedy (in *Die Braut von Messina* and *Robert Guiskard*,
respectively), but that Kleist recognized the failure
and learned from it, being thus enabled to complete *Krug*.
Sees Kleist's critique of state ideology permeating the
piece, embodied particularly in the figure of Frau Marthe.
(L.S.)

Lixl, Andreas. "Utopie in der Miniatur: Heinrich von
Kleists Aufsatz 'Über das Marionettentheater.'" *GQ* 56
(1983): 257-72.

Loose, Hans-Dieter. *Kleists "Hermannsschlacht": Kein Krieg
für Hermann und seine Cherusker. Ein paradoxer Feldzug
aus dem Geist der Utopie gegen den Geist besitzbürgerlicher
und feudaler Herrschaft.* Karlsruhe: von Loeper, 1984.
Pp. 291.

A 1983 Karlsruhe dissertation which takes up the old
question concerning Kleist's alleged Prussian chauvinism,
and resituates it in what Loose sees as the proprietary
implications of bourgeois society around 1800. Kleist's
resistance to the French is not so much pro-Prussian as
it is a function of his conviction that Napoleon was the
"Inkarnation besitzbürgerlicher Weltsicht." Kleist emerges
as a utopian humanist in a line of social critics stretch-
ing from Rousseau to Brecht, striving to get his readers
and audiences to reflect on the constraining conditions
of social order. A meager bibliography, which nevertheless gives a firm sense of Loose's own intellectual roots.
(L.S.)

Parry, Idris. "Kleist on Puppets." Pp. 9-12 in *Hand to Mouth
and Other Essays*. Manchester: Carcanet New Press, 1981.
Pp. 173.

    Rev. by Theodore Ziolkowski in *CG* 16 (1983): 369-70.
Originally broadcast as an introduction to a reading
of the translated dialog (also printed here) on BBC, this
little essay is an attempt to capsulize Kleist for British
audiences. In his enthusiasm, Parry claims too much: he
sees in Kleist "an explanation for the conscious naivety of
phenomena like the Dada movement ... a philosophical foundation for the experiments in language and material which
characterize our time ... the [establishment of] the 'point
of view' which led Cubism to present a face seen from all
aspects at once ..." (11). A lot, for a six-page dialog
(which Parry, like so many others, insists on seeing as an
"essay"). (L.S.)

Peck, Jeffrey M. "The Politics of Reception and the Poetics
of Reading: The Hermeneutic Text. Heinrich von Kleist's
Die Marquise von O...." *CREL* 2 (1982): 130-37.

Preuss, Werner. "Kein anderer K.: Anmerkungen zu Kleist-
Interpretationen." *Kürbiskern* 1 (1981): 87-94.

    The immediate instigation for this energetic essay was
Günter Kunerts 1977 radio play, "Ein anderer K." But Preuss
takes literally everyone—scholars and literati alike—to
task for reducing Kleist to their small(er) worlds. Kleist
remains a "permanent Herausforderung" (87), whose reception-
history shows how pitifully limited his readers are. While
Preuss's views of Kleist are themselves sometimes reductive
(as in his bald statement that Kleist's "Gesellschaftskritik ...
im Grunde restaurativ ist" [93], his sortie is provocative.
(L.S.)

Raiser, Robert. "Heinrich von Kleists 'Penthesilea'—Eine
Uraufführung?" *NDH* 29 (1982): 196-200.

    The title of this fine little essay suggests Raiser's
opinion that a production of *Penthesilea* worthy of the name
has yet to be mounted. He discusses Hans Neuenfels's 1981
staging in the Schillertheater, Berlin, a "Mischung aus
Multi-Media-Show, Bildungstheater und psychoanalytisch
gefärbtem Surrealismus" (196). The main point is that contemporary directors, audiences, and reviewers are no more
able to hear the Dionysian greatness of the play than were
Kleist's own contemporaries, foremost among them the repressive Goethe. (L.S.)

Reeve, William C. "Ein dunkles Licht: The Court Secretary
in Kleist's *Der zerbrochene* [sic] *Krug*." *GR* 58 (1983): 58-
65.

Renner, Karl Nikolaus. *Der Findling: Eine Erzählung von
Heinrich von Kleist und ein Film von George Moorse. Prinzi-
pien einer adäquaten Wiedergabe narrativer Strukturen.*
(Münchener Germanistische Beiträge, Nr. 31.) Munich: Wilhelm
Fink Verlag, 1983.

A Munich dissertation (1981) written under the direction of
Klaus Kanzog. The film version of "Findling," originally
done for German television by the American director Moorse,
and released for theatrical showing in 1969, allegedly
differs from Kleist's story in the following fundamental way:
"Die Erzählung thematisiert ein in der Goethezeit weit
verbreitetes Theorem: die letzlich metaphysisch begründete
Vorstellung eines allgemeinen sozio-kulturellen Verfalls.
Der Film demonstriert hingegen die Unmöglichkeit, den Genera-
tionenkonflikt in einer Gesellschaft zu lösen, die soziale
Interaktion ausschliesslich als Realisierung von Besitzverhält-
nissen begreift" (284). The investigation of these differences
is based on a revised version of Juri Lotman's neo-formalist
narrative theory, in which "occurrences" (*Ereignisse*) are
defined as "the violation of textually developed semantic
orders." Renner turns to Lotman's structuralism in order to
provide a theoretical underpinning for the idea of "adequa-
tion," which must underlie any comparison of film and story.
He claims that increased "objectivity" is gained by breaking
both works down into their constituent narrative components,
and then comparing the narratology inherent in the two works.
The resulting characterization of the story is dubious, of
the film banal. What emerges with most clarity is the as-
tonishing health of structuralism in Bavaria. (L.S.)

Seeba, Hinrich C. *"Overdraɣt der Nederlanden in't Jaar 1555*:
Das historische Faktum und das Loch im Bild der Geschichte
bei Kleist." Pp. 409-43 in Martin Bircher, Jörg-Ulrich
Fechner, and Gerd Hillen, eds., *Barocker Lust-Spiegel:
Studien zur Literatur des Barock. Festschrift für Blake
Lee Spahr.* (Chloe. Beihefte zum Daphnis, Vol. 3.) Amster-
dam: Rodopi, 1984. Pp. 456.

A fascinating article which argues that Simon Fokke's
etching ("Overdragt der Nederlanden in't Jaar 1555") was
the "original" of the etching that inspired Kleist's play.
But there is more at stake here, as Seeba and Frau Marthe
know. Seeba ranges widely in the historiography and legal
theory of the age, and concludes that Pufendorf's radical

claims concerning the necessity for *original facts* in
history-writing constitute the true theoretical background
of the issue of evidence-reading dramatized in the play.
There never was an "*unzerbrochner Krug*"--it has to be recon-
stituted, like history, in artistic representations. A fine
blend of scholarship and theoretical concerns, which
challenges the still-dominant positivism of many of Seeba's
fellow Baroque scholars. (L.S.)

Sembdner, Helmut. *In Sachen Kleist: Beiträge zur Forschung*.
Second (revised) edition. Munich and Vienna: Hanser, 1984.
Pp. 382. DM 68.00.

    Reprint of the eighteen essays that appeared in the first
edition (1974), supplemented by eight more recent contributions. Many of them reveal concerns traceable to Sembdner's
work as editor of the standard edition of Kleist's works:
tracking down unknown letters and manuscripts, reviewing
Kleist's personal relationships with family members and
contemporaries, elucidating the vagaries of Kleist's punctuation. The most significant among the new essays is a 1982
piece (first delivered as a lecture in the Rudolf-Steiner-
Haus in Stuttgart) on "Goethes Begegnung mit Kleist." (L.S.)

Sembdner, Helmut, ed. *Heinrich von Kleists Nachruhm: Eine
Wirkungsgeschichte in Dokumenten*. (Dokumente zu Kleist, 2.)
Frankfurt/Main: Insel, 1984. Pp. 606.

    Substantially revised reissue of the 1967 edition, although
this volume is not labeled "second edition"; the "2" indicates
that it is a companion volume to Sembdner's *Heinrich von
Kleists Lebensspuren: Dokumente und Berichte der Zeitgenossen* (see *RMB* for 1978, p. 232). *Lebensspuren* ends
with the police reports of Kleist's death; *Nachruhm* begins
with the newspaper reports of the event, followed by extracts
from private correspondence. The numbering of the entries
in the 1967 edition has been retained, with additions
designated by supplemental letters (e.g., 375*a*: Cosima
Wagner an Houston S. Chamberlain. Wahnfried, 2. Febr.
1894: "Wir lasen 'Die Hermannsschlacht' von Kleist. Die
Bitterkeit gegen Deutschland, die sich darin ausspricht,
stimmt zu unserer Empfindung. Und er hat die echte german-
ische Natur grossartig in Hermann gestaltet" [294]). There
is a thorough list of precise sources, and an index of names
as well as of Kleist's works. The book is divided into five
major sections: "Kleists Tod und die Öffentlichkeit," "Im
Gedanken der Freunde und Verwandten," "Editoren und Bio-
graphen," "Kleist und sein Werk im Urteil der Nachwelt,"
and "Zur einzelnen Werken." Sembdner chose not to extend

the collection past 1960, the cut-off point for the first edition. Even so, this volume is a delight for Kleist scholars, cultural browsers, and anyone interested in *Rezeptionsgeschichte*. (L.S.)

Silberman, Marc. "The Ideology of Re-Presenting the Classics: Filming *Der zerbrochene* [*sic*] *Krug* in the Third Reich." *GQ* 57 (1984): 590-602.

A brief but convincing analysis of interpretive gestures perpetrated on Kleist's text by Emil Jannings and Gustav Ucick in the 1937 film. Silberman argues that Kleist's darkness and irony are converted into slapstick humor that is ultimately nonthreatening to the status quo. Thus the film is an example of what Goebbels called for, a propaganda which "niemals als gewollt in Erscheinung tritt" (594). Shows a firm and differentiated understanding of both film and play. (L.S.)

Thieberger, Richard. "La Marquise d'O...." Pp. 23-33 in Alain Faure, Yvon Flesch, and Armand Nivelle, eds., *Gedanken über Dichter und Dichtungen: Essays aus fünf Jahrzenten (Les textes et les auteurs: Cinquante années de réflexions sur la littérature)*. Bern and Frankfurt/Main: Peter Lang, 1982. Pp. 587.

Rev. by André Drijard in *Seminar* 20 (1984): 69-71.
The first entry in a collection presented to Austrian-born French Germanist Thieberger on his retirement, this essay was delivered as a lecture at a 1978 conference in Louvain. He points to "sources" (Montaigne and Cervantes) and "parallels" (Mme Gomez's *Cent Nouvelles nouvelles*), but the real contribution of the essay is to consider the behavior of the "other hero" of the story, the Russian officer, as duplicitously reinforcing the Marquise's search for affirmation of repressed knowledge. The novella emerges "presque sous forme d'un petit roman d'éducation" (33). (L.S.)

Wells, George A. "The Basis and the Effectiveness of the Tragic Outcome in Kleist's *Penthesilea*. *NGS* 11 (1983): 99-112.

Wells, George A. "Der Kurfürst gegen den Prinzen: Recht und Unrecht in Kleists Schauspiel *Prinz Friedrich von Homburg*." *WW* 33 (1983): 286-95.

Declares that *Homburg* is "Kleists erfolgreichst[es] Bühnenstück" (has he forgotten *Der zerbrochne Krug*?), and that the tendency among modern commentators is to view the

prince "von Anfang an als moralisch einwandfrei" (286). He
attacks these readings (and those that would stress the
irony in the play) as revisionist, and allies himself with
older criticism, which, he says, stresses the moral *development* of the prince, and sees the political didactics of the
Kurfürst as totally justified.   (L.S.)

Wittkowski, Wolfgang.   "Goethe und Kleist: Autonome Humanität
und religiöse Autorität zwischen Unbewusstsein und Bewusst-
sein in *Iphigenie, Amphitryon, Penthesilea*."   Pp. 205-09 in
Wittkowski, ed., *Goethe im Kontext: Kunst und Humanität,
Naturwissenschaft und Politik von der Aufklärung bis zur
Restauration. Ein Symposium.* Tübingen: Niemeyer, 1984.
Pp. xxiv+396.

The volume presents the papers read at the 1982 Albany
symposium *Goethe Compared.* Wittkowski depicts the three
plays as involved in the same agonistic struggle for a
definition of "autonomous humanity," a liberation not only
from their classical literary models, but from the authority of religion and state in the Age of *Bildung.* Claims
that Goethe's position only seems to be more authoritarian
and conservative, and that Kleist misunderstood how much
they had in common: "dass Goethe in diesem prometheischen
Ringen um Durchsetzung der autonomen Ethik und menschlich-
ethischen Autonomie gegen die Autorität der kirchlichen und
weltlichen Gewalten gar nicht sein Gegner war, sondern
sein Vorläufer" (221).   It would seem that it was Goethe
who refused to see in Kleist a perpetuator of his concerns!
(L.S.)

See also de Man, Flax ("General 3. Criticism"); Fairley ("Heine").

Reviews of books previously listed:

HINDERER, Walter, ed., *Kleists Dramen: Neue Interpretationen* (see *RMB* for 1981, p. 337), rev. by Marjorie
Gelus in *Monatshefte* 76 (Fall 1984):   363-64: KREUTZER,
Hans Joachim, ed., *Kleist-Jahrbuch 1981/82* (see *RMB* for
1983, pp. 392-93), rev. by Peter Goldammer in *WB* 30,9
(1984); 1576-80; MAASS, Joachim, *Kleist: A Biography,*
trans. Ralph Manheim (see *ELN* 17, Supp., 230; also *RMB*
for 1983, pp. 393-94), rev. by S.S. Prawer in *TLS*, Jan.
27, 1984, p. 91; by Anthony Vivis in *Drama* 153 (1984):
50; McGLATHERY, James M., *Desire's Sway: The Plays of
Heinrich von Kleist* (see *RMB* for 1983, p. 394), rev. by
Linda Hill in *GSR* 7 (1984):   577; by Valentine C. Hubbs
in *Kleist-Jahrbuch 1984* (see Kreutzer, above), pp. 162-63;

RESCHKE, Karin, *Verfolgte des Glücks: Findebuch der Henriette Vogel* (see *RMB* for 1983, p. 396), rev. by Marlies Janz in *Arbitrium* 3 (1984): 215-18; by Ernst Osterkamp in *Kleist-Jahrbuch 1984* (see Kreutzer, above), pp. 163-75; SAMUEL, Richard H., and Hilda M. Brown, *Kleist's Lost Year and the Quest for "Robert Guiskard"* (see *RMB* for 1982, p. 336), rev. by Ilse-Marie Barth in *Arbitrium* 3 (1983): 283-87; by Dirk Grathoff in *Monatshefte* 76 (1984): 219-21; by Wolfgang Wittkowski in *CG* 16 (1983): 245-47; SEIDLIN, Oskar, *Von erwachendem Bewusstsein und vom Sündenfall: Brentano, Schiller, Kleist, Goethe* (see *RMB* for 1981, p. 339), rev. by James F. Hyde, Jr., in *Monatshefte* 76 (1984): 93-94; SEMBDNER, Helmut, *Das Detmolder "Käthchen von Heilbronn": Eine unbekannte Bühnenfassung Heinrich von Kleists* (see *RMB* for 1981, pp. 339-40), rev. by Penny Milbouer in *GSR* 7 (1984): 151-52; UGRINSKY, Alex, ed., *Heinrich von Kleist Studies* (see *RMB* for 1982, pp. 338-39), rev. by Wolfgang Nehring in *Kleist-Jahrbuch 1984* (see Kreutzer, above), pp. 156-60.

LESSING

See Mitchell ("General 3. Criticism").

MARX

See Röder ("German 2. General"); Erpenbeck ("Brentano").

NOVALIS

Ekman, Björn. *Novalis Hymnen an die Nacht: Kommentierte Studienausgabe*. Kopenhagen: Gyldendal, 1983. Pp. 212.

  Rev. by A. Nivelle in *EG* 39 (1984): 453-54.

Fischer, Karl-Heinz. *Wertform und Dichtung: Grundzüge einer ideologiekritischen Literaturtheorie erläutert an Texten von Novalis*. Bern: Lang, 1982. Pp. 189.

  Rev. by Klaus Weissenberger in *GQ* 57 (1984): 480-81.

Glorieux, Jean-Paul. *Novalis dans les lettres française a l'époque et au lendemain du symbolisme (1885-1914)*. Presses universitaires de Louvain, 1982. Pp. 528.

  Rev. by Rosemary Lloyd in *YCGL* 32 (1983): 150-51.

Kurzke, Hermann. *Romantik und Konservatismus: Das "politische" Werk Friedrich von Hardenbergs (Novalis) im Horizont seiner Wirkungsgeschichte.* München: Fink, 1983. Pp. 292.

Rev. by Björn Ekmann in *Text und Kontext* 12 (1984): 167-70.

Kurzke's impressive book reads like a summary and critical revision of the numerous historical studies of the last 20 years concerning the political stance of the Romantics. He approaches the central question as to the conservatism versus the modernism of the Romantic Movement as a problem of exactness in historical scholarship. In order to understand how Novalis confidently employs a great degree of rationality toward an irrational goal it is crucial to take into consideration that his transcendental-philosophical suppositions remain unquestioned and utopian. Novalis is a philsopher, not a politician; metaphors such as monarchy, Christianity, philosophy of nature and art, are merely fields of experimentation for an open utopianism. His placement in the conservative movements of the nineteenth and twentieth centuries can be explained by his problematic reception which followed the young Hegelians' understanding of Romanticism. Kurzke does not shy away from analyzing today's conception of conservatism as an affirmative and technocratic ideology, and he distinguishes it from the utopian and oppositional (against the mechanized state) conservatism of the Romantics. Whether, however, Novalis could serve as a prophet of today's peace movements, as Kurzke suggests in his epilogue, seems to be a different question. (B.F.)

Monroe, Jonathan. "Novalis' *Hymnen an die Nacht* and the Prose Poem *avant la lettre.*" *SiR* 22 (1983): 93-110.

Nischik, Traude-Marie. "'Himmlisches Leben im blauen Gewande ...': Zum poetischen Rahmen der Farben- und Blumensprache in Novalis' 'Heinrich von Ofterdingen.'" *Aurora* 44 (1984): 159-77.

This detailed study attempts to give some structure to Novalis's complex imagery of flowers and colors. Central to the analysis is of course the unravelling of the metaphor of the "blaue Blume" in *Heinrich von Ofterdingen.* Nischek poses the following two theses: (a) Novalis's language of flowers and colors serves as the main poetic medium by which his program of progressive "Universalpoesie" is to be realized; (b) the problem of translating the metaphor of the blue flower at the same time marks the limits which are imposed upon Novalis's poetic program by language itself. The mystical word cannot be whispered to Ofterdingen until his death. The supposed poetic salvation remains a mystery to the reader, for even the poet is unable to name it. (B.F.)

Schreiber, Jens. *Das Symptom des Schreibens: Roman und Absolutes Buch in der Romantik (Novalis/Schlegel)*. Frankfurt: Lang, 1983. Pp. 281.

Rev. by Dennis F. Mahoney in *Aurora* 44 (1984): 229-32.

Seidel, Margot. *Novalis' Geistliche Lieder*. Frankfurt: Lang, 1983. Pp. 335.

Seidel evaluates Novalis's hymns against the background of his biography, the tradition of the hymn, and the clerical lyric in the eighteenth century. In addition to uncovering many individual influences and levels of interpretation she also poses a quite plausible periodization of these hymns which retraces the anacreontic and pietistic beginnings, the "Sophia" experience, the longing for an "unio mystica" (à la Zinzendorf), and, finally, the "Todeslyrik." Seidel's findings, however, remain within the realm of traditional Christian imagery and ideas. She is unable to suggest a connection between the hymns and Hardenberg's religious-speculative, poetological, and philosophical program. (B.F.)

See also Boehme, Brinkmann ("German 2. General"); Kippermann ("Fichte"); Schreiber ("Schlegel, Fr.").

Reviews of books previously listed:

SENCKEL, Barbara, *Individualität und Totalität: Aspekte zu einer Anthropologie des Novalis* (see *RMB* for 1983, p. 402), rev. by A. Nivelle in *EG* 39 (1984): 454-55; STRACK, Friedrich, *Im Schatten der Neugier: Christliche Tradition und kritische Philosophie im Werk Friedrichs von Hardenberg* (see *RMB* for 1983, p. 403), rev. by Donald P. Haase in *GQ* 57 (1984): 659-60; by Raymond Immerwahr in *Seminar* 20 (1984): 304-06.

PLATEN

See Kraft ("Heine").

RAABE

See Fairley ("Heine").

RITTER

See Deeney ("German 2. General").

SCHELLING

See Boehme, Jaeschke, Röder ("German 2. General"); Gulyga,
Mielke ("Bonaventura"); Oellers ("Schlegel-Schelling,
Caroline").

SCHILLER

Bolten, Jürgen, ed. *Schillers Briefe über die ästhetische
Erziehung.* (st 1984.) Frankfurt: Suhrkamp, 1984.

The collection includes a lengthy introduction by the
editor, the "Augustenburger Briefe," letters that refer
to the treatise, the "Ankündigung der Horen," and a number
of essays published in recent years (none before 1967)
by Rudolf Vierhaus, Rolf Grimminger, Wolfgang Düsing,
Jeffrey Barnouw (excerpt), and Günter Rohrmoser. There
are also original contributions by Wolfram Hogrebe and
Hans-Georg Pott. The volume offers an excellent overview
of recent work on the aesthetic letters and on Schiller's
aesthetics as a whole. (M.J.)

Johnston, Otto W. "Mirabeau and Schiller on Education to
Freedom." *Monatshefte* 76 (1984): 58-72.

Public education was a central issue in post-revolutionary
France as well as in neighboring Germany. But the central
importance of Mirabeau's writings and public statements
for the genesis and further formulation of Schiller's program of aesthetic education had been insufficiently realized.
A Kantian in method, Schiller derived much of the socio-
political content of his treatise from Mirabeau: specifically the linking of education with liberty, education's
basis in pleasure, and the crucial role of artists. But
Schiller modified Mirabeau's radicalism by "seeking to
reconcile bourgeois progressive thinking with those
privileges and prerogatives established over generations
by the German nobility" (69). (M.J.)

Middell, Eike. "Schillers Klassizität und seine Stellung
in der deutschen Klassik." *WB* 29 (1983): 1247-70.

"Classical perfection," as a goal set forth in the preface
to the *Thalia* fragment of *Don Carlos*, means fulfilling an
absolute standard. This entailed a rejection of political
bourgeois tragedy and its replacement by an abstract ideal
in the guise of an aesthetic form. To grasp the entire
Schiller with all his contradictions would be to emphasize
not only his critique of early bourgeois capitalism under
the influence of the French Revolution, but also to investi-
gate the problematics of a notion of totality and harmony
to be found in art where none exists in reality. The goal:
"Klassik nicht als das normativ Festgeschriebene, sondern
dialektisch zu begreifen in ihrem philosophischen Utopismus
und ästhetischen Avantgardismus als einen bewussten poetischen und politischen Konstruktionsversuch ..." (263).
(M.J.)

Sharpe, Lesley. *Schiller and the Historical Character:
Presentation and Interpretation in the Historiographical
Works and in the Historical Dramas.* (Oxford Modern
Languages and Literatures Monographs.) Oxford University
Press, 1982. Pp. 211. $29.50.

   Rev. by Wulf Koepke in *JEGP* 83 (1984): 282-84.

Wessell, Leonard, P., Jr. *The Philosophical Background to
Friedrich Schiller's Aesthetics of Living Form.* Frankfurt
a.M. and Bern: Peter Lang, 1982. Pp. 174.

   Rev. by Harold Osborne in *BJA* 23 (1983): 362-63.

See also Frye ("Arnim, Achim von"); Catholy ("Brentano");
De Leeuwe, Leistner ("Kleist"); Oellers ("Schlegel-
Schelling, Caroline"); Kozielek ("Werner").

SCHLEGEL, A.W.

Frühwald, Wolfgang. "Der Zwang zur Verständlichkeit: August
Wilhelm Schlegels Begründung romantischer Esoterik aus
der Kritik rationalistischer Poetologie." Pp. 129-48 in
Die literarische Frühromantik, ed. Silvio Vietta.
Göttingen: Vandenhoeck und Ruprecht, 1983. Pp. 222.

   Frühwald sees Schlegel's importance as that of mediating
early Romantic ideas through his popular lectures, whose
history the article traces. In particular, he popularized
the polar distinction of "Enlightened" and "Romantic" and
contributed to the paradoxical Romantic position of trying
to obtain "Verständlichkeit" through "Unverständlichkeit."

A disappointingly unoriginal and incidental essay from an
otherwise well-conceived anthology. (W.C.)

Schlaffer, Heinz. "Der Charakter des Interpreten: August
Wilhelm Schlegel." *Literatur und Erfahrung* 12/13 (1983):
32-34.

Schlaffer seeks to redeem Schlegel's translation work
from his own and others' charges of being "derivative,"
"second-class literature." The internationalism of the
translations accords with the Jena circle's concept of
"genial criticism" and furthers the idea that understanding
must be pluralistic to be universal. (W.C.)

See also "Des Allemagnes," Schwarz ("French 2. Staël");
Bianchi, Gutjahr ("Heine"); Behler, Behrens, Schulz
("Schlegel, Fr."); Oellers ("Schlegel-Schelling, Caroline");
Meregalli ("Spanish 2. General").

SCHLEGEL, FR.

Behler, Ernst. *Die Zeitschriften der Brüder Schlegel: Ein
Beitrag zur Geschichte der deutschen Romantik.* Darmstadt:
Wissenschaftliche Buchgesellschaft, 1983. Pp. 192.

Behrens, Klaus. *Friedrich Schlegels Geschichtsphilosophie
(1794-1808): Ein Beitrag zur politischen Romantik.*
Tübingen: Niemeyer, 1984. Pp. 280.

Beginning from Schlegel's claim that "every ahistorical
theory disgusts me," Behrens traces Schlegel's historical
thought up to his Catholic conversion and move to Vienna.
Instead of stressing final historical causes outside
history, Schlegel took history's direction to be immanent
in the heterogeneous historical "tendencies" of the
present and emphasized the future rather than the past.
Within this system, Revolution comes to be understood less
as a political event than as "an arbitrary act of historical
discontinuity, the break-through of a new time whose content and goal are unknown."
Lucidly written with extensive attention to both primary
and secondary sources, Behrens's book is important as a
first attempt to bring Schlegel's political ideas and
experiences into one unified presentation. The book is
also a good source for the political thoughts of many
Schlegel contemporaries. (W.C.)

Bohrer, Karl Heinz. "Utopie 'Kunstwerk': Das Beispiel von
   Friedrich Schlegels *Rede über die Mythologie*." Pp. 303-32 in
   *Utopieforschung: Interdisziplinäre Studien zur neuzeitlichen
   Utopie*, Vol. 3, ed. Wilhelm Vosskamp. Stuttgart: Metzler,
   1982. Pp. 468.

   Bohrer studies the *Rede* as an early example of a modern
tendency he calls the "utopia of the moment," the reduction
of traditional utopian ideals to an artistic/imaginative
instant. Earlier, Schlegel had accepted the historical view
that people would reach a conventional perfection through
aesthetic experience, parallel to--but instead of--political
perfection through the French Revolution. Later, in place
of human perfectibility comes the progressive artwork, an
artwork which through fantasy leads back into "the original
chaos of human nature" in an extensionless "now-time," as
art history becomes independent of history itself. Such an
ahistorical artistic absolute becomes social/utopian rather
than merely personal through assuming a transcendental subject. A good defense against any charge that Schlegel's
absolutizing of art is motivated by political conservatism.
(W.C.)

Kurz, Gerhard. "Friedrich Schlegels Begriff der 'symbolischen
   Form' und seine literaturtheoretische Bedeutung." Pp. 30-43
   in *Aspekte der Romantik: Vorträge des Kolloquiums am 25.
   und 26. April 1983*, ed. Sven-Aage Jørgensen, Per Øhrgaard,
   and Friedrich Schmöe. Munich: Fink, 1983.

   In one of the anthology's better essays, Kurz starts by
showing that the Goethean distinction of "allegory" and
"symbol" did not characterize the Romantics, who took allegory and symbol interchangeably as "having the same function:
the mediation of the finite with the infinite, the particular
with the whole." Schlegel extended to literary criticism
the idea of "characteristica universalis," which Leibniz
articulated to describe the infinite applicability of finite
mathematical signs; in the "Lessing Charakteristiken,"
Schlegel tried to establish analogous features which, while
particular, are infinitely variable in Lessing's "spirit,"
each subsequent re-reading of his works, and ultimately all
literature. The "symbolic form" of a work is that which
makes all these characteristica coalesce into a unity; "modern
formulas for what Schlegel called 'symbolic form' are 'poly-
functionality,' 'ambiguity' and 'polyvalence.'" A by-product
of this notion is to give the reader constitutive power over
the text and to take much intentional control away from the
writer. (W.C.)

Peters, Günter. "Das tägliche Brot der Literatur: Friedrich
Schlegel und die Situation des Schriftsstellers in der
Frühromantik." *JDSG* 27 (1983): 235-82.

Pikulik, Lothar. "Die Frühromantik in Deutschland als Ende
und Anfang: Über Tiecks *William Lovell* und Friedrich Schlegels
Fragmente." Pp. 112-28 in *Die literarische Frühromantik*, ed.
Silvio Vietta. (Kleine Vandenhoeck-Reihe, 1488.) Göttingen:
Vandenhoeck & Ruprecht, 1983. Pp. 222. DM 20.80.

The article's general intent is to ask whether early
Romanticism is the end of the Enlightenment or the beginning
of mainstream Romanticism. Pikulik admits early on that he
can touch on Schlegel "only in passing" as a subject "too
complex for more precise analysis in this context," and indeed
only three pages concern Schlegel. Pikulik sees Schlegel's
use of irony in the *Philosophische Lehrjahre* as analogous
to the use of poly-perspectivism in Tieck's novel, a device
caught half-way between eighteenth-century skepticism and
"true" Romantic longing for the Endless. (W.C.)

Pizer, John. "Friedrich Schlegel's Comparative Approach to
Literature." *Selecta* 3 (1982): 31-36.

Schreiber, Jens. *Das Symptom des Schreibens: Roman und
Absolutes Buch in der Frühromantik (Novalis/Schlegel)*.
Frankfurt a. M.: Peter Lang, 1983. Pp. 281.

Rev. by Dennis Mahoney in *Aurora* 44 (1984): 29-32.
The title is deceptive in that Schlegel's novel, *Lucinde*,
never even comes up in the book. Schlegel appears, in
scattered references, primarily as a minor side-figure in a
Lacanian study of Novalis, whose reaction to Schlegel's
encyclopedism helps Schreiber distinguish Enlightenment
systematism from early Romantic novel theory. (W.C.)

Schulz, Gerhard. "Theater um Goethe und die Brüder Schlegel:
Bemerkungen zu Demarkationslinien der Literaturgeschichte."
Pp. 194-204 in *Goethe in Kontext: Kunst und Humanität,
Naturwissenschaft und Politik von der Aufklärung bis zur
Restauration: Ein Symposium*, ed. Wolfgang Wittkowski.
Tübingen: Niemeyer, 1984. Pp. 396.

Spuler, Richard. "*Lucinde*: Roman des Romans." *CG* 16 (1983):
166-76.

Spuler's intention is to illuminate the structural principles of *Lucinde* on the basis of Esther Hudgin's 1975 model
in her *Nicht-epische Strukturen des romantischen Romans*, to

give "a series of observations" in greater support of the
model, and finally to analyze the "Lehrjahre der Männlich-
keit" section more thoroughly than usual. The novel reveals
three structural principles: dialectic (of chaotic feminine
with systematic masculine), reflexion (or self-parody), and
ambiguity. Using these principles as tools, Spuler reads the
"Lehrjahre" section as an allegory about writing novels, in
which Lisette becomes a symbol for the pre-Lucinde novel-
writing that Julius has to outgrow: like Julius himself
before Lucinde, she speaks in the third person, she has an
unproductive pregnancy in contrast with Lucinde's productive
pregnancy, etc. An interesting reading of the "Lehrjahre"
section, but one that self-confessedly adds only one more
small touch to the traditional reading of the novel. (W.C.)

See also Röder, Sullivan ("German 2. General"); Gutjahr
("Heine"); Pöggeler ("Hölderlin"); Meregalli ("Spanish
2. General").

Reviews of books previously listed:

BLANCO UNZUÉ, Ricardo, *Die Aufnahme der spanischen Literatur
bei Friedrich Schlegel* (see *RMB* for 1983, p. 409), rev. by
Hans Eichner in *Arbitrium* 2 (1984): 184-86; DIERKES, Hans,
*Literaturgeschichte als Kritik: Untersuchungen zu Theorie
und Praxis von Friedrich Schlegels frühromantischer Literatur-
geschichtsschreibung* (see *RMB* for 1983, pp. 410-11), rev.
by Michael T. Jones in *GQ* 57 (1984): 482-83; by Hannelore
Scholz in *ZG* (Leipzig) 3 (1984): 365-67.

SCHLEGEL-SCHELLING, CAROLINE

Oellers, Norbert. "Caroline Schelling: gesch. Schlegel,
verw. Böhmer, geb. Michaelis." Pp. 168-96 in Benno von
Wiese, ed., *Deutsche Dichter der Romantik: Ihr Leben und
Werk.* 2nd ed. Berlin: E. Schmidt, 1983.

A thoroughly researched and detailed article about Caroline
Schlegel-Schelling's life (part I) and literary endeavors
(part II). Since her life has already been dealt with in
several recent publications, the second part of this article
proves to be the more interesting. Oellers points out that
Caroline admired Goethe--Rahel Varnhagen's and Bettina von
Arnim's Goethe adoration comes immediately to mind here--
but did not think very highly of Schiller. Besides her
numerous witty and brilliantly written letters, Caroline left
a first draft for an autobiographical novel. She also wrote

some poetry, for instance, a satirical poem about Fichte's
Romantic philosophy of science, as well as a substantial
number of literary reviews and essays, which were published
in respected journals such as the *Athenaeum*, *Allgemeine
Literatur-Zeitung*, and *Die Horen*. Some of these reviews
appeared under A.W. Schlegel's name and are still wrongly
believed to have been written by him, rather than by her.
At times it proves hard to separate Caroline's share of the
articles clearly from A.W. Schlegel's and later on from
Schelling's. More basic research in this field is needed.
(K.B.)

See also Gulyga ("Bonaventura").

SCHOPENHAUER

See Erpenbeck ("Brentano").

TIECK

Calinescu, George. "Ludwig Tieck." *Revista de Istorie si
    Teorie Literara* 32 (1983): 27-39.

Galaski, Lisa. "Romantische Ironie in Tieck's *Die verkehrte
    Welt*." *RG* 14 (1984): 23-57.

    Scholars have not given *Die verkehrte Welt* its due because
they have measured it against its better-known forerunner
Der gestiefelte Kater, Galaski contends. Romantic irony
is the play's governing principle, and the work must be
interpreted from the toal perspective, which neither the
actors nor the fictional audience possess. Structurally
the play is on two levels. In the fictional reality of the
theater, the audience, director, and actors interact and
the play continually calls attention to itself: "Das
Theater stellt ein Theater vor." In the fictional reality
of the stage play actors strive for self-representation
within their given roles. Naive characters like the stranger
strive only for self-representation, while others, like the
fool Pierrot, are conscious of their roles, expand them,
and reflect upon them, often with parodistic intent. The
two characters who direct the action, Scaramuz from within
the stage fiction and Apollo on a higher level from behind
the scenes, are examined in great detail which is a bit
desultory at times, like the play being interpreted. Never-

theless the article effectively explores the numerous avenues
by which Tieck uses Romantic irony in the structure of the
work in connection with the fundamental problem of the irreconcilable contradiction between reality and the ideal.
(R.C.)

Grunewald, Eckhard. "Die 'Heldenbilder' der Brüder Tieck."
Aurora 43 (1983): 134-50.

Grunewald cites a previously unpublished letter from Ludwig
Tieck to Friedrich Heinrich von der Hagen in support of his
contention that the "Heldenbilder," designed by Ludwig and
sketched and painted by his brother Christian Friedrich,
were not intended as serious representations of heroes of
German antiquity and legend. The lithographs, harshly
criticized because of their anachronistic costumes and unusual proportions, were actually a simple card game, designed
for Ludwig's entertainment during a lengthy illness in 1809.
As such they belonged to a popular tradition at the turn of
the century. That they have long been misunderstood is a
result of von der Hagen's intentional misrepresentation of
the cards as a "Heldengalerie." (R.C.)

Härtl, Heinz. "Tieck und Lessing." Pp. 526-38 in Hans-
Georg Werner, ed., *Lessing-Konferenz Halle 1979*. Vol. 2.
(Kongress- und Tagungsberichte der Martin-Luther-Universität
Halle-Wittenberg.) Halle-Wittenberg: Martin-Luther-Universi-
tät, 1980.

Tieck's "contradictory" relationship to Lessing the dramatist is examined. Though both men were striving for a German
national theater, and though both saw in Shakespeare a legitimate model, Tieck was, according to Härtl, repulsed by
the "Verbürgerlichung" of German theater in the course of
the eighteenth century in which Lessing had taken part without foreseeing the trivialization and mannerism into which
it would fall by 1800. Tieck's love for and proximity to
the folk theater are discussed, although Härtl is careful
not to make a revolutionary of him. (R.C.)

Horton, David. "'Verwirrung' in *Der blonde Eckbert*." *GL&L*
37 (1984): 322-35.

Horton discusses the fairy tale's narrative structure
rather than taking the psychological route so popular today.
He argues that the mystification of the reader was Tieck's
intention in writing the work, and that "critics' determination to identify a single, unifying sense" goes against this
original intention. Rather, the reader is caught in the

same hermeneutic uncertainty as the characters and is consciously deprived by the author of any higher perspective
than the characters enjoy. Tieck's skillful intertwining
of narrative perspectives increases the reader's disorienta-
tion. The story's concluding revelation is defended against
Raymond Immerwahr's criticisms as being a real strength of
the narrative, because, while it answers a major question
it poses several others. This plunges the reader into a
hermeneutic vicious circle in which he must continually
reinterpret certain elements of the tale in light of insights
gained from others. (R.C.)

Morlang, Werner. *Die Problematik der Wirklichkeitsdarstellung
   in den Literaturessays von Arno Schmidt.* (Europäische Hochschulschriften, Series I, Vol. 514.) Bern and Frankfurt
   am Main: Peter Lang, 1982. Pp. 207. Sw.Fr. 46.00.

   In compiling a Tieck bibliography one could easily overlook this book, because there is nothing in the title to
indicate that half of it is devoted to Tieck's preeminent
position in Arno Schmidt's less than orthodox theory of
Romantic Realism. Morlang argues convincingly that Schmidt
identified with Tieck and projected his own childhood experiences onto the Romanticist, interpreting and emphasizing
certain aspects of the latter's life based upon his own.
Further, Schmidt sought to give the theories which he created
for his own literary production historical legitimacy by
projecting them onto "realistic" authors of the past. Tieck's
importance to Schmidt as a foil to the German Classical
Movement, which the latter detested, and to the Germanists
who defend it, is discussed at length. However, Tieck owes
his first position among Schmidt's canon of "genuine"
Romanticists to his alleged realization of the inherently
chaotic, evil nature of all creation, and his overcoming
of this pessimistic attitude in his works by means of a
"längeres Gedankenspiel"--through his poetic imagination the
writer alienates and transcends this uninhabitable world.
   Morlang by no means comes across as an apologist for
Schmidt's method, though at times he seems to soften justifiable criticism. He may be a bit too diplomatic in his
discussion of Schmidt's annoying habit of bastardizing
quotations in order to make them fit snugly into his theories.
In general, however, he fairly points out the inconsistencies
in Schmidt's arguments where he finds them, taking him particularly to task for his denial of the religiosity of the
Romanticists, especially Tieck. In trying to demonstrate
how certain scenes from Tieck's works are directly traceable
to experiences in his life, Schmidt fails increasingly, Morlang

concludes, the farther the literary scenes have been alienated from objective reality through the poet's imagination. (R.C.)

Paulin, Roger. "Tiecks Empfindungen vor Caspar David Friedrichs Landschaft." *Aurora* 43 (1983): 151-59.

Although Tieck appears not to have sought Caspar David Friedrich's acquaintance during the time they both lived in Dresden, a passage in a Tieck novella from 1834, *Die Sommerreise*, demonstrates that he understood and appreciated Friedrich's successful melding of composition and sentiment: "die Ruhe, Kontrolle, Festigkeit der Linie bei höchster Symbolkraft des Gegenstandes." (R.C.)

Pikulik, Lothar. "Die Frühromantik in Deutschland als Ende und Anfang: Über Tiecks *William Lovell* und Friedrich Schlegels *Fragmente*." Pp. 112-28 in *Die literarische Frühromantik*, ed. Silvio Vietta. (Kleine Vandenhoeck-Reihe, 1488.) Göttingen: Vanderhoeck & Ruprecht, 1983. Pp. 222. DM 20.80.

For comment, see listing above under "Schlegel, Fr."

Piru, Al. "O precizare in marginea unui text despre Tieck." *Revista de Istorie si Teorie Literara* 32 (1983): 26-27.

Stanguennec, André. "Ontologie et pathologie du symbole dans trois contes de Ludwig Tieck." *Revue Philosophique de la France et de l'Etranger* 109 (1894): 3-26.

Weigand, Karlheinz. "Zu Tiecks *Der blonde Eckbert* anhand der Deutung durch Ernst Bloch." *Bloch Almanach* 3 (1983): 115-22.

Review of book previously listed:

NAHREBECKY, Roman, *Wackenroder, Tieck, E.T.A. Hoffmann, Bettina von Arnim: Ihre Beziehung zur Musik und zum musikalischen Erlebnis* (see *RMB* for 1982, p. 349), rev. by Ann Clark Fehn in *GQ* 57 (1984): 339.

VARNHAGEN VON ENSE, RAHEL

Köhler, Lotte. "Rahel Varnhagen." Pp. 290-316 in Benno von Wiese, ed., *Deutsche Dichter der Romantik: Ihr Leben und Werk*. 2nd ed. Berlin: E. Schmidt, 1983.

In comparison to Norbert Oellers's article about Caroline Schlegel-Schelling in the same book, Köhler's essay lacks depth and conviction and is not on top of modern research about Rahel. On the whole, Köhler stays on safe but now

well-known biographical ground. In contrast to prevailing
scholarly opinion, she does not think of Rahel Varnhagen
as a Romantic but rather views her as indebted mainly to the
philosophy of Enlightenment and to Goethe. Köhler points
out that Rahel's writings can be compared with Goethe's
inasmuch as the work of both is based on the principles of
truth and justice. In fact, Rahel admired Goethe as "den
grossen Wahrheitsfreund." Noteworthy also is the high
esteem in which Rahel held her own skillfully written letters.
As early as 1800, she thought them important enough to be
collected and edited as a contribution to "Originalgeschichte."
(K.B.)

Oeser, Hans-Christian. "'Wilhelm Meisters Lehrjahre' als
    Thema eines romantischen Romans: Kritik und Bewunderung
    Goethes in 'Die Versuche und Hindernisse Karls.'" *Archiv*
    220 (1983): 27-52.

    This article draws attention to the relatively unknown
fragmentary novel *Die Versuche und Hindernisse Karls: Eine
deutsche Geschichte aus neuerer Zeit*. Published in 1808,
it was written collectively by a circle of anti-French
Romantics in Berlin: Fouqué, Chamisso, Bernhardi, Varnhagen
von Ense, and Neumann. Together with Neumann, Varnhagen had
a leading influence on this literary project. *Karl* stands
clearly in the wake of Goethe's *Wilhelm Meisters Lehrjahre*
and so far has also been of interest to researchers because
of its "multi-author" narrative structure. Apart from this
dimension, Oeser views the work as a significant literary
contribution to the central Romantic debate about the novel
as a truly universal literary form. He discusses at length
the aesthetic means employed by the individual authors to
differentiate their own literary product from Goethe's work.
At the same time, Oeser argues that *Karl* can be read as a
persiflage of other Romantic novels that imitated Goethe's
Lehrjahre and also as a satirical attack on the early Romantic
concept of individuality. Thus, Oeser concludes, *Karl* is an
example of the Romantics' ironizing and criticizing themselves in a unique literary way. (K.B.)

See also Oellers ("Schlegel-Schelling, Caroline").

WACKENRODER

Hilzinger, Klaus Harro. "Die Leiden der Kapellmeister: Der
    Beginn einer literarischen Reihe im 18. Jahrhundert."
    Euphorion 78 (1984): 95-110.

The specifically bourgeois sonata and symphony, "absolute"
artforms because--unlike earlier instrumental music--they are
not bound to any ideological purpose, represent the freedom
of the autonomous subject against an authoritarian society.
They are also examples of how the abstracting of an artform
into the ideal can obscure its foundations in reality. Such
is the case with Joseph Berglinger. His internalization of
the music which should free him mires him even more in
conventionality. He cannot differentiate between art and
religion and develops an elitist arrogance. Reacting to
the misery of his family, he tries to escape his ethic
responsibility by fleeing into the ideal. His flight fails
with the realization that his physical existence depends upon
satisfying that society he detests. Berglinger is forced
to realize that the harmony between the real and the ideal,
life and art, to which the Monk's idealized renaissance
bore ample witness, is no longer possible under the aesthetic
and historical contradictions of present society. Hilzinger
also briefly discusses J.F. Reichardt's novel fragment from
1779: *Leben des berühmten Tonkünstlers Heinrich Wilhelm
Gülden* and Hoffmann's *Kreisleriana*. (R.C.)

WAGNER

See Köhler ("Hoffmann, E.T.A.").

WERNER

Barasch, Monique. "Schicksal und Willensfreiheit in Zacharias
   Werners Tragödie *Der Vierundzwanzigste Februar*." *USF
   Language Quarterly* 21 (1982): 5-6.

   This clearly written, brief essay offers a concise statement of Werner's religious formulation of the "Schicksal"
concept. According to Barasch, Werner maintained that one
could escape the consequences of a curse (an integral component of such dramas) if one resisted temptation through
free will. Werner presents us here with the negative
aspect of this struggle. In Barasch's interpretation,
Werner's linking of fate with Christian freedom of choice
differentiates *Der Vierundzwanzigste Februar* from other
fate dramas. (C.R.C.)

Fiandra, Emilia. "Il mito di Phosphoros: Utopia e misticismo
   in Werner." Pp. 125-43 in Marino Freschi, ed., *Mito e
   utopia nel romanticismo tedesco: Atti del seminario inter-*

nazionale sul romanticismo tedesco. Naples: Instituto
Univ. Orientale, 1984.

Koziełek, Gerard.   "Friedrich Ludwig Zacharias Werner." Pp.
485-504 in Benno von Wiese, ed., *Deutsche Dichter der
Romantik: Ihr Leben und Werk.* 2nd ed. Berlin: E. Schmidt,
1983.

   In this newly revised and expanded encyclopedia of Romantic
artists, Koziełek summarizes Werner's life and works as he
attempts to set straight much of the misinformation which
has been spread concerning this dramatist. Koziełek suggests
that the German public saw Werner as the successor to
Schiller, and that his plays greatly influenced both Grillparzer and Hebbel. While one may not agree with some of
the conclusions drawn in this article, Koziełek's style is
lively and compelling, and his writing becomes a pleasure
for the reader. The brief bibliography provides some useful
suggestions for study. (C.R.C.)

WIELAND

Schelle, Hansjorg, ed. *Christoph Martin Wieland.* (Wege der
   Forschung, vol. 421.) Darmstadt: Wissenschaftliche Buchgesellschaft, 1981. Pp. 493.

   Rev. by Herbert Rowland in *ECS* 17 (1983-84): 218-21.

ITALIAN

(Compiled by Daniela Bini, University of Texas,
Austin; Augustus Pallotta, Syracuse University)

1. BIBLIOGRAPHY

"Bibliografia manzoniana." *ON* 8, Supplement (1984): 99-115;
126-45; 160-79.

Much of the bibliography included here pertains to interest in Manzoni reflected in the *terza pagina* of Italian
newspapers, in regional publications as well as popular
magazines and cultural reviews.

Fasano, Pino. "Primo Ottocento." *RLI* 88 (1984): 286-96.

Urbancic, Ann. "Ottocento." *RSI* 2 (1984): 224-28.

2. GENERAL

*Il Facchino. Giornale di scienze, lettere, arti e varietà
(1839-1845).* A cura di Alfredo Cottignoli. Parma: La
Pilotta, 1982. Pp. 271.

Cottignoli's selection of representative articles from
this important organ of mid-Ottocento cultural life points
to a clear transition in the review from socio-political
concerns to literary matters. (A.P.)

Kimbell, D.R.B. "Neo-Classical Counter-Currents in Italian
Romantic Opera." *IS* 34 (1984): 67-78.

Minor, Vernon Hyde. "Tommaso Righi's Roman Sculpture: A
Catalogue." *BM* 126 (Nov. 1984): 668-74; 12 illus.

Funerary sculpture and stucco church decorations.

Paladino, Vincenzo. "'Meraviglioso' romantico: le proposte
del *Conciliatore*." *CL* 12 (1984): 29-52.

The *meraviglioso* or *wunderbar*, not to be confused with
the "sublime," is treated here as a literary topos which
drew considerable attention in Italian Romantic circles
between 1816 and 1819. Visconti traced its origin to Middle

Eastern sources which were assimilated to European literature
as a result of the Crusades and Arab influence in Spain.
Paladino singles out two categories of the *meraviglioso*:
an irrational-metaphysical vein with religious connotations
present in some of Berchet's works; and a realistic, historically grounded vein apparent in Manzoni's *Fermo e Lucia*. In
I promessi sposi Manzoni is said to have toned down the
meraviglioso, heeding Visconti's advice contained in the
postille to the first draft of the novel. Stimulating
and well researched. (A.P.)

Raimondi, Ezio. "Language and the Hermeneutic Adventure in
Literature." *Forum Italicum* 18 (Spring 1984): 3-25.

A penetrating essay in which the author, advocating new
modes of critical inquiry, points to Leopardi's "Infinito"
and the introductory passage of *I promessi sposi* as projec-
tions of "the artistic and thus not necessarily mimetic
space" in which "different spatial and non-spatial relationships can be expressed in the correspondence with the
modeling structure of the universe" (15). (A.P.)

Springer, Carolyn. "The Classical Landscape in the Risorgimento." *StIR* 3 (1983): 235-40.

Composite review:

Middleton, Robin. *BM* 126 (Dec. 1984): 790-91.

A review of the following: Amadeo Belluzzi et al., *Mantova
nel settecento: Un ducato ai confini dell'impero*; Giovanni
Mezanotte, *L'architettura della Scala nell'età neoclassica*;
Antonella Doria, *Piermarini disegni*; Dante Cesarini, *Giuseppe
Piermarini: Architetto neoclassico, Saggio bibliographico*.

3. STUDIES OF AUTHORS

ALFIERI

See Real Ramos ("Spanish 2. General").

BERCHET

Mazziotti D'Ambrosio, Anna Maria. "L'apprendistato poetico
di Giovanni Berchet." *CL* 12 (1984): 237-63.

An intelligent outline of Berchet's literary career
including his youthful attraction to Parini and Porta,
Berchet's activity as a translator of Gray and Goldsmith,

and his contribution to the ideological coherence of Italian
Romanticism. As regards the latter aspect, Mazziotti
exaggerates somewhat Berchet's collaboration to *Il Conciliatore*, claiming that it was instrumental in affording the
journal "una fisionomia decisamente romantica che non era
all'inizio nelle intenzioni dei promotori" (252). Berchet's
work is seen as marked by a harsh criticism of society and
an anti-classical, but also anti-humanistic, conception of
literature. (A.P.)

FOSCOLO

Chemotti, Saveria. "Il tempo 'svelato': in margine a una
originale interpretazione dell' esilio di Ugo Foscolo."
CL 12 (1984): 53-80.

A prolix re-elaboration of S. Aglianò's study on Foscolo's
exile published in *Argomenti* in 1941. Chemotti widens
the scope of the subject matter, drawing extensively from
Foscolo's works merely, however, to reiterate Aglianò's
thesis that, unlike other political exiles who longed to
return to Italy, Foscolo saw his departure as a final break
with his adopted land, a break caused, in Aglianò's words,
by "il dissolversi totale di ogni speranza per la redenzione
degli italiani, negati a ogni ragione di concordia e di
vitalità." (A.P.)

Frare, Pierantonio. "L'endecasillabo dei sonetti del Foscolo."
ON 8 (1984): 163-80.

A chapter from Frare's undergraduate thesis on "La
metrica dei sonetti del Foscolo." The article dwells on
linguistic and formal matters often in a quantitative
fashion; peripheral attention is given to aesthetic considerations. (A.P.)

Limentani, Uberto. "Foscolo's Farewell to Lady Dacre." *IS*
34 (1984): 63-66.

Unpublished letter dated June 1827 from Foscolo to Lady
Dacre, a friend and patron of the poet. In it Foscolo
comments on his *Discorso sul testo di Dante* and refers
to his plans to write a similar work on Petrarch. The
plans remained just that, since Foscolo died three months
later. (A.P.)

Macchioni Jodi, Rodolfo. *Itinerari della lirica foscoliana.*
Rome: Bulzoni, 1983. Pp. 170.

Rev. by Maryse Jeuland-Meynaud in *REI* 29 (1983):   251-53.

Miller-Isella, Rita. *La poetica del tradurre di Ugo Foscolo
nella versione del "Viaggio sentimentale."* Bern: Peter
Lang, 1982. Pp. 375.

Rev. by Pino Fasano in *RLI* 88 (1984):   289.

Santi, Victor A.   "The Image of the Sun in *Le ultime lettere
di Jacopo Ortis*, the *Sepolcri*, and the *Grazie* of Ugo Foscolo."
Italian Culture 3 (1983):   63-70.

Solar and night images are studied as antithetical and
characteristically Romantic tropes which in Foscolo's
writings assume vital symbolical meaning. Thus, in the
Sepolcri the sun stands for fertility, love, and hope
whereas in *Le Grazie* the same image qualifies the portrait
of Venus as a symbol of eternal femininity. (A.P.)

Sole, Antonino.   "La sublimità malinconica di Jacopo Ortis."
RLI 88 (1984):   52-79.

Begins with the premise that Foscolo was led to pattern
his *Jacopo Ortis* on Goethe's *Werther* because of its structural simplicity and the presence of a single major character.   There follows an extensive comparative study of the
two works focused on such common elements as autobiographical strains, the theme of solitude, the tension between
the self and society.   The originality of *Jacopo Ortis*
"si dispiega ... in un momento di crisi nel passaggio dalla
cultura illuministica al romanticismo" (73).   Unduly prolix
but instructive and, in some respects, very perceptive.
(A.P.)

LEOPARDI

Bini, Daniela.   *A Fragrance from the Desert. Poetry and
Philosophy in Giacomo Leopardi.*   (Stanford French and
Italian Studies 27.)   Saratoga, Calif.: ANMA Libri, 1983.
Pp. 188.

Sensitive to the need to correct the division in Leopardi's
work between philosophy and poetry singled out by other
critics, Bini undertakes a careful and systematic study of
this matter to show "the presence in Leopardi of a dialectical inner relationship" in which the two elements in
question are seen not "as separate moments which exclude
each other, but as mutually necessary" (6).   The work consists of three chapters, each devoted to a philosophical
category and its subordinate or complementary expressions.
Thus in Chapter I Bini analyzes the function of sensationalism in Leopardi, dwelling on such subjects as the pheno-

menology of human faculties, imagination and language, action and thought. Chapter II deals with Leopardi's materialistic view of the world treated here as a complementary aspect of sensationalism. Chapter III, the central part of the book, focuses on idealism both as philosophical category and as a vital component of Leopardi's poetry. The study also takes into account the works of Condillac, La Mettrie, and Schiller, among others, as important points of reference that delineate the sources or the parameters of Leopardi's thought. Bini's skillful and organic treatment of the dialectical interaction in Leopardi between philosophy and poetry constitutes a scholarly contribution of singular value and interest. (A.P.)

Caesar, Michael. "Leopardi Unnamed." *RSt* 5 (1984-85): 143-48.

Argues that the main line of Leopardi criticism in the last twenty years, following Walter Binni's example, has dwelled excessively on "a notion of completeness or totality" of the self. This orientation has proved highly problematical in the light of Lacanian psychoanalysis and its influence on current critical discourse. Caesar does not object to the dominance of the self in Leopardi studies but to "its asphyxiation of other critical categories that might rival it" (146). He suggests reconsideration of what K. Foster called the "provisional" character of Leopardi's thought together with a potentially productive effort to study Leopardi's work in the context of European Romanticism. (A.P.)

Caesar, Michael. "Poet and Audience in the Young Leopardi." *MLR* 77 (1982): 310-24.

In Leopardi's youthful verse Caesar finds a noteworthy transition from eloquence and imagination to interpretation and reflection. This "inwardness" can be legitimately linked with the philosophical conversion of 1820 and with the observations in *Zibaldone* on the self as a poetic subject. In the two "canzoni patriottiche" the critic finds stylistic evidence in support of his argument. (D.B.)

Capanna, Francesco. "Il Leopardi e la critica crociana." *RSCr* 20 (April-June 1983): 130-39.

Carannante, Antonio. "Leopardi e Mario Fubini." *Belfagor* 86 (1982): 198-207.

Discusses Fubini's long-standing contribution to Leopardi scholarship, especially his reevaluation of the *Operette* and his criticism of those who saw in Leopardi only the poet of the *Idylls*. One of Fubini's limitations: his under-

estimation of polemical and negative themes in Leopardi's
work. (D.B.)

Cărcăleanu, Eleonora. *Leopardi în România.* Bucuresti:
Editura Minerava, 1983. Pp. 229.

Rev. by G. Carageani in *EL* 9 (April–June 1984): 123–28.
Examines Romanian translations of Leopardi's work from
1874 to the present, critical assessment of Leopardi, and
his influence on Romanian writers and poets, especially
Eminescu. According to Carageani, the work is not free
of serious flaws and omissions. Not seen. (A.P.)

De Sanctis, Francesco. *Giacomo Leopardi.* Roma: Editori
Riuniti, 1983. Pp. 313.

Reprint of De Sanctis's influential study published first
in 1885 and widely regarded as "atto di fondazione della
critica leopardiana." Contains an introduction by E.
Ghidetti and a brief biography of De Sanctis called "biog-
raphy-autobiography" in the sense that the famous critic
found his place in the world of literature through a keen
understanding of Leopardi. (D.B.)

Leopardi, Giacomo. *Canti.* A cura di A. Tartaro. Bari:
Laterza, 1984. Pp. 234.

The author of several outstanding essays on Leopardi,
Tartaro offers a school edition of all thirty-six Canti
based on the Naples 1835 edition. Also included are five
poetic fragments. The poems are preceded by a lucid
introduction in which Tartaro discusses structure, ideology,
and language in the *Canti*. The critic rightly emphasizes
the connection between Leopardi's ideology and his choice
of an appropriate language. Short biography and a good
bibliography. (D.B.)

Leopardi, Giacomo. *Diario del primo amore e prose autobio-
grafiche.* Genova: Il Melangolo, 1981. Pp. 81.

Includes five youthful pieces by Leopardi together with
a few autobiographical pages modeled after Alfieri's *Vita.*
In the introduction G. Amoretti notes that youth exalts
Leopardi's narcissistic fantasies of omnipotence and represents the first movement of liberation from the contingen-
cies of nature ("autonoma produzione di simboli") whereas
in his mature years the poet reduces eros to a verbal entity.
The linguistic symbol becomes the only possible gratifica-
tion. (D.B.)

Leopardi, Giacomo. *Operette morali.* Milano: Garzanti, 1984.
Pp. 421.

Rev. by M. Mazzocca in *LI* 35 (1983): 279-82.

Contains a long introductory essay by P. Ruffilli patterned on Galimberti's reading of the *Operette* whose foundation is said to rest on "un materialismo assolutamente negativo." Ruffilli also remarks that the positive aspect of the text is found in Leopardi's philosophical language which, being at once creative and exegetic, produces a new prose with philosophic and poetic attributes. This prose represents the prototype of a literature grounded on antiphrasis. Includes a biography of Leopardi and a carefully detailed bibliography. (D.B.)

Leopardi, Giacomo. *Pensieri.* A cura di C. Galimberti. Milano: Adelphi, 1982. Pp. 187.

Rev. by M. Mazzocca in *LI* 35 (1983): 283-85.

Appended to the text is a short essay ("Fanciulli più che uomini") which illuminates the relationship between *Pensieri, Operette,* and *Zibaldone.* According to Galimberti, Leopardi's thought broadens Machiavelli's observations on man as a political being and as a social and psychological animal. The modernity of Leopardi's insights (the economy-generated wisdom that rules the world today, the reduction of all values to those of commerce and money, the irony about our faith in industrialization) is underlined together with the cruel truth that the noble soul has nothing to teach but "la certezza del male di esistere." (D.B.)

Leopardi, Giacomo. *Storia di un'anima.* A cura di Ugo Dotti. Milano: Rizzoli, 1982. Pp. 575.

Rev. by N. Bellucci in *RLI* 88 (1984): 294-95.

The "story" Leopardi began but never finished was developed instead in his letters, of which Dotti offers a large selection in chronological order. The introduction discusses the significance of Leopardi's friendship with Giordani, seen as instrumental in fostering Giacomo's struggle for intellectual freedom. In Dotti's view, the letters show a rapid transition from a personal to a universal message carrying the sense of "una missione illuminatrice." (D.B.)

Leopardi, Giacomo. *La vita e le lettere.* A cura di N. Naldini. Milano: Garzanti, 1983. Pp. VII+589.

Rev. by N. Bellucci in *RLI* 88 (1984): 295.

A collection of 323 letters chronologically arranged, with notes and a biographical sketch of the poet. The preface by F. Baldini dwells on the theme of illness as a central element in the *Epistolario.* (D.B.)

Martina, Franco. "Leopardi, l'adolescenza filosofica."
   Belfagor 38 (1983):   377-94.

   Martina examines Leopardi's philosophical writings from
1813 to 1815. He points out that Leopardi's main ideas
were inspired by the philosophical debates of the time but
they took a different course. Starting with a positive
view of reason (Leibniz, Algarotti) in the "Dialogo filosofico," Leopardi quickly discovers the negative force of
reason and attempts to correct prevailing misconceptions.
Even at an early stage his thought cannot be reduced to a
particular model. He assimilated, reflected upon everything
he read, and developed original ideas which proved more advanced than the sources of his inspiration. (D.B.)

Mazzocca, Stella. "Ripetizione ed alterità da Cicerone a
   Leopardi." *LI* 34 (1982):   74-84.

   The "Coro dei morti," "L'infinito," and "Il tramonto della
luna" are examined vis-à-vis Cicero's *De Natura Deorum*.
The religious and philosophical syncretism of Cicero's times
pointed to "la vita beata." In Leopardi, on the other hand,
the presence of influential doctrines (Stoicism, Epicureanism,
the Academy) documents only the insolubility of a search,
whose end is Nothingness. Not only the "harmonia mundi"
is impossible; impossible is also its dream. (D.B.)

Nava, Giuseppe. "Pascoli e Leopardi." *GSLI* 160 (1983):   507-
   23.

   Leopardi's constant presence in Pascoli's poetry, traced
here in detail, appears in a substantial form in 1890 and
centers on two major themes: the memory of youth, and the
relationship man-nature. Juxtaposing Leopardi's and Pascoli's
verse, Nava shows that similar and often identical images
are used by Pascoli with different and often opposite aims.
Whereas Leopardi looks to the past to meditate on the present,
for Pascoli the past is a means to escape the present.
Leopardi is equally present in the *Canti di Castelvecchio*,
but here too the borrowing of individual images results in
a whole which is antithetical to Leopardi's thought. (D.B.)

Santagata, Marco. "I confini dell'idillio: 'La sera del dí
   di festa.'" *SCr* 1-2 (1982):   34-63.

   A structural and linguistic analysis of the poem aimed at
explaining and justifying the abrupt change in tone and
the resulting stylistic incoherence of the poem's middle
stanza. Working with three different manuscripts, Santagata
tries to prove that Leopardi's revisions in the course of

fifteen years were aimed not at erasing the internal diversi-
ties but at clarifying them through a process of self-
awareness. Three are the points of view in the text: the
objective, external description of nature in the first
stanza; the dramatic intervention of the protagonist "I"
who struggles for reconciliation with the "I" of the narrator in the second stanza; and the philosophical objectivity
of the last stanza. Two contrasting models of composition
are present: the open and closed structure appropriate
respectively to idylls and *canzoni*. The text reveals a
moment of transition in Leopardi's work: the end of the
idyll as a coherent continuum. (D.B.)

Scuderi, Ermanno. "Leopardi poeta d'amore." *RC*, n.s. 13-16
(1983): 12-16.

A superficial treatment of the concept of love in Leopardi
which adds nothing to our understanding and appreciation
of his poetry. On the contrary, by attributing the source
of the poet's suffering to love, Scuderi clearly impoverishes
its existential meaning. (D.B.)

Simonelli, Luciano. "Quei bei versi di Leopardi scritti nel
Quattrocento." *Domenica del Corriere*, June 9, 1984, pp. 42-
51.

An interview with Mario Pincherle, author of *Fantastico
diario di G. Leopardi*, in which he claims that Leopardi's
"Appressamento della morte" was inspired by the "Canzone
della morte" of the fifteenth-century poet Pandolfo Collenuccio. The assertion seems valid enough, for in his research at the Leopardi library Pincherle found the issue
of the *Biblioteca italiana* (Sept. 1816) in which G. Perticari
published an essay on Collenuccio together with the poem
in question. (D.B.)

Timpanaro, Sebastiano. "Prosaiche meschinità intorno a
Giacomo Leopardi." *Belfagor* 88 (1984): 103-10.

Timpanaro defends himself against various accusations by
Corti and Buscaroli, among others, prompted by his provocative piece, "Come nel 1983 si può impedire la pubblicazione
di importanti inediti leopardiani," published in *Il Ponte*
(April 1983). What Timpanaro says in his defense is essentially of journalistic, not scholarly, interest. (D.B.)

Bàrberi Squarotti, Giorgio. "La letteratura come fine: le
'morali' dei *Promesi sposi.*" *CL* 12 (1984): 219-35.

The article seeks to address various objections raised
by Marxist critics with regard to Manzoni's alleged conservative ideas. Bàrberi Squarotti defends the function of
didacticism in the novel exemplified, among other instances,
by Renzo's moralizing in the last chapter. He views Renzo's
conservative attitude not as a *terminus a quo* but as an
evolving process of maturation grounded on the experiences
of living. Moreover, "oltre ad essere un romanzo di esperienze, *I promessi sposi* sono anche un romanzo che
intende proporre una lezione di vita" (233).

The difficulty with this form of "reading" lies in the
exercise of the same reductivist approach used by detractors
of Manzoni, albeit with different conclusions. Manzoni's
work eschews reductivism *tout court.* Renzo's (and other
characters') moral consciousness takes form as a result of
individual rational choice, not as the expression of pro-
grammatic authorial intervention. (A.P.)

Bo, Carlo. "Manzoni: la parole come scienza." *ON* 8 (1984):
21-30.

Reason, individual freedom, and responsibility are seen
as the essential tenets of Manzoni's work. In elucidating
their import, Bo finds it necessary to defend Manzoni
against present-day detractors. To this critic, the essence
of Manzoni "sta nella luce profonda della sua parola, nel-
l'aver riportato la parola alla sua funzione di scienza"
(30). (A.P.)

Bonora, Ettore. "Da Don Valeriano a Don Ferrante: il
rifiuto dei modelli." *GSLI* 161 (1984): 185-208.

Argues that Don Valeriano and Don Ferrante are distinct,
autonomous characters. The former is seen essentially as
a comic figure inspired by Molière (possible sources:
L'avare and *Le bourgeois gentilhomme*). In *I promessi sposi*
Don Ferrante's prototype is subjected to a consummate
process of abstraction as a result of which the comic vein
disappears and the character is reduced to a functional,
ancillary entity complementing, in a contrasting fashion,
the figure of Donna Prassede. The transformation is said
to underline Manzoni's resistance to literary models.
Though well argued, Bonora's study tends to diminish the
scope of Don Ferrante's characterization, which takes on

greater nuances and complexity precisely by virtue of the revision process illustrated here. (A.P.)

Caturegli Fochi, Anna. "Il primo traduttore inglese dei *Promessi sposi.*" *CL* 12 (1984): 133–42.

On Charles Swan's translation, *The Betrothed Lovers*, published in Pisa in 1828. The critic points out that, in translating *I promessi sposi*, Swan, a Protestant minister, "fa della propria fede e ministero la chiave di lettura e metro di giudizio" (133). A valid statement, but one that explains only in part the inadequacy of the English version. Other drawbacks: Swan's limited knowledge of Italian and his unfamiliarity with Italian customs reflected in the original. (A.P.)

Colombo, Umberto. "I primi biografi del Manzoni." *ON* 8 (1984): 45–64.

Discusses three bio-critical studies on Manzoni published in 1873: G. Rovani, *La mente di A. Manzoni*; G. Carcano, *Vita di A. Manzoni*; and F. Venosta, *A. Manzoni, Cenni sulla sua vita e le sue opere*.

Dell'Aquila, Michele. *Manzoni. La ricerca della lingua nella testimonianza dell'epistolario ed altri saggi linguistici.* Bari: Adriatica, 1984. Pp. 315.

De Rienzo, Giorgio. "*I promessi sposi* al computer. Analisi del lessico e della fraseologia di Lucia." *ON* 8 (1984): 77–102.

Partial account of the computer-generated lexical analysis of the novel undertaken by De Rienzo. As regards Lucia, we learn that she uses "un vocabolario di 485 parole sul totale di 3360 pronunciate" (79). The critic attempts a systematic study of statistical findings but the end results offer few, if any, fresh discoveries. For instance, we are reminded that Lucia's lexicon is that of everyday speech, rich in religious denotations yet essentially informal and repetitive. One salient point: "Il linguaggio sentimentale di Lucia nei confronti di Renzo è un linguaggio di separazione, più che di comunicazione; un soliloquio più che un dialogo" (85). (A.P.)

Di Nepi, Piero. "*I promessi sposi* e la geometria dei sentimenti." *Il Veltro* 27 (1983): 668–71.

On Manzoni's equilibrium in depicting human sentiments, discernible especially in the portrait of Gertrude.

Di Ricco, Alessandra. "Il Manzoni nei giudizi della *Civiltà cattolica*." *RiLI* 1 (1983): 271-310.

　　The scant attention devoted to Manzoni by the *Civiltà cattolica* is attributed to the fact that the Jesuit conservative review looked upon the author of *La morale cattolica* as a problematic writer whose stature and importance could not be ignored. Accordingly the few articles on Manzoni are said to reflect gross distortions and, worse, a manipulating effort to integrate Manzoni's thought to the reactionary ideology professed by the review. (A.P.)

Fido, Franco. "*I promessi sposi* come sottotesto in alcuni romanzi dell'Ottocento." *Italica* 61 (1984): 96-107.

　　Manzoni's influence on Italian fiction during the second half of the nineteenth century, though pervasive, takes the form of an ambivalent and problematic process of attraction-rejection vis-à-vis *I promessi sposi*. Such a process attests to the affirmation of a narrative model that could hardly be ignored; the striving, among better writers, for individual expression; and, implicitly, the evolving perception of Manzoni's art. In this context, Fido examines De Marchi's *Demetrio Pianelli*, Nievo's *Confessioni di un Italiano*, Rovani's *Cento anni*, and Fogazzaro's *Piccolo mondo antico*. From these works, the critic selects narrative nuclei whose structural, stylistic, and intellectual characteristics confirm the closeness to or the divergence from the original model. (A.P.)

Filippi, Paola. "Il manzoniano Alexander Lernet-Holenia." *ON* 8 (1984): 65-70.

　　Examines both *Die Verlobten*, a free translation of *I promessi sposi* (Zurich, 1950) by Lernet-Holenia, and his essay, "Manzoni und das Christentum" motivated by the translation and published in 1955 in the Austrian review *Wort in der Zeit*.

Forgacs, David. "Manzoni and the Discourse of History and Fiction." *RSt* 5 (Winter 1984-85): 128-42.

　　The division between history and fiction is examined first, though briefly, in the light of the ambiguities of poetic discourse advanced by Jakobson and, more extensively, in the context of a historiographic tradition which, in the eighteenth century, was marked by a sharp distinction between history and literature and, in the early Ottocento, by the convergence of history and narrative. To Forgacs, Manzoni's position proved ambivalent: it assented to the fusion of

history and fiction represented by Thierry and Scott, as it
was supportive of the historiography of Voltaire, Muratori,
and Verri. The ambivalence was resolved when Manzoni "em-
braced the discipline of history to the disadvantage of
poetry" (139).

Fully instructive in its delineation of the traditional
dichotomies between historiography and literature, Forgacs's
essay falls short as an accurate assessment of the central
questions inherent in Manzoni's position, questions which
pertain to philosophy and aesthetics as theoretical factors
underlying the hybrid texture of historical narrative. The
weakness of Forgacs's article lies less in the validity of
its arguments than in the choice of the *Discorso* on Lombard
history and the *Colonna infame* as exemplary evidence of Manzoni's position. Virtually omitted from the discussion are
the key works, *Del romanzo storico* and *I promessi sposi*,
where the question of history and fiction is tested on the
grounds both of critical theory and narrative elaboration.
(A.P.)

Grechi, Gian Franco. "Stendhal e Manzoni: momenti per dei
confronti." *ON* 8 (1984): 31-43.

Contrived and unconvincing comparison between *I promessi
sposi* and Stendhal's *Abesse de Castro* based on the premise
that the French writer knew Manzoni's work and that the
Abesse "si presta con immediatezza ad un confronto," being
"l'unico romanzo storico del Beyle" (23). (A.P.)

Illiano, Antonio. "Tecnica e sintassi del racconto ironico
in Manzoni." *Italica* 61 (1984): 85-95.

Counters the traditional perception of *Fermo e Lucia* as
merely a draft of *I promessi sposi* with a discerning study
of the work's autonomous, innovative structure and its
narrative forms which prove to be totally new in Italian
fiction--such forms as the interaction author-narrator,
the author's ironical-polemic rapport with the reader, the
function of digression in the organizing process of narration. The textual illustrations chosen by Illiano not only
confirm the value of his analysis, they bring to light
the freshness and sophistication of Manzoni's narrative.
(A.P.)

Jones, Verina R. "Illiteracy and Literacy in *I promessi sposi*."
RiLI 1 (1983): 527-52.

A valuable study devoted mainly to the presence of illiteracy in the novel, its historical causes, and sociological
ramifications. Whereas literacy is associated with the power

structure, is socially restricted and the product of social
stratification, illiteracy identifies the condition of
humble characters like Renzo who are painfully cognizant
of the consequences of illiteracy. Manzoni, who "displays
a perception of the issue which is historically accurate"
and consistent with his ideological stance, holds "a pessimistic view of the role of literacy in a society where
the poor are excluded from its control" (544).   (A.P.)

Lazzaro-Weis, Carol. "The Providential Trap: Some Remarks
    on Fictional Strategies in *I promessi sposi.*" *StIR* 4
    (Spring 1984): 93-106.

    In the elaboration of *I promessi sposi*, Manzoni is said
to follow, in many areas, the tradition of ancient Greek
romances which, beginning in the Seicento, were revived through
numerous French and Italian translations. Despite modifications and obvious changes in the treatment of history, religion, and character psychology, Manzoni's work reflects
the integration of the "basic romance techniques of realistic plot construction, external causality, and character
portrayal" (97). The supportive arguments, which readily
bring to mind the contributions of Getto and Raimondi,
are tenable as indicators of broad structuring principles
underlying Western narrative tradition. Beyond this level,
and particularly in the more tangible area of textual analysis, the archetypal structures studied here bear but tenuous
affinities with Manzoni's narrative; indeed, they raise more
questions than they satisfy. For instance, examining the
entity of Manzoni's characters with the meter of fixed
personality traits inherent to the romances can hardly do
justice to the richness and complexity of Manzoni's art.
(A.P.)

Mambretti, Silvana. "Aspetti linguistici della componente
    milanese del *Fermo e Lucia.*" Pp. 747-63 in *Studi di lingua
    e letteratura lombarda offerti a Maurizio Vitale.* Pisa:
    Giardini, 1983. Pp. 824.

    Considerable attention is attached here to the role played
by Milanese dialect in the gestation of *Fermo e Lucia.* In
documenting the presence of two linguistic registers in the
work (Italian and Milanese), Mambretti cites dialectical
and colloquial expressions together with phonological and
lexical forms adopted from the Milanese. The resulting
evidence prompts the critic to note that the first draft is
written in Italian but "è certo pensato in milanese." A
very good complement to T. Matarrese, "Lombardismi e tos-
canismi nel *Fermo e Lucia*," *GSLI* 154 (1977): 380-427 (rev.
in *ELN* 17, Supp., 255). (A.P.)

Manzoni, Alessandro. *On the Historical Novel*. *Del romanzo storico*. Trans., with an Introduction, by Sandra Bermann. University of Nebraska Press, 1984. Pp. 134.

Rev. by S.B. Chandler in *Italica* 61 (1984): 272-74.

Clearly a major contribution to Manzoni studies in this country, Bermann's faithful version of *Del romanzo storico*, a work virtually unknown to English-speaking critics, and her discerning Introduction leave one with a sense of optimism about the prospect of greater interest in Manzoni outside Italy. Following a careful review of Manzoni's formative years in Paris and his eventual attraction to Scott and Shakespeare, Bermann traces the development of the traditional distinctions between history and poetry from Aristotle and Cicero to Vico and Muratori. More than a useful excursus in literary history, this retrospective investigation exemplifies the thoroughness, precision, and incisiveness of Bermann's mode of analysis as she examines Manzoni's ambitious effort to effect a synthesis of history and fiction together with the aesthetic and ethical factors that led to a reassessment of such an undertaking. Most valuable in Bermann's essay is the section (35-49) in which the timeliness of Manzoni's ideas reflected in *Del romanzo storico* is treated in the light of twentieth-century critical concerns. Thus the nominalist view of language shared by structuralist critics which "reduces to man-made linguistic constructs, and therefore to the arbitrary, anything that might otherwise pass for truth" (51) is rightly seen as extraneous to Manzoni's thought. Closer to Manzoni are the distinctions drawn by Ricoeur between philosophy and poetry as well as Lukacs's position regarding history as "the primary index of the reality that literature should strive to represent" (54). Finally Bermann calls to our attention the fact that in *The Nature of Narrative* Scholes's and Kellog's concerns with the problematic posed by the fusion of history and narrative document "at a distance of one hundred years what Manzoni seems largely to have foreseen" (58). Bermann's contribution lends full credence to F. Jameson's characterization of *Del romanzo storico* as "the most comprehensive statement" on the historical novel written by a novelist in the nineteenth century. (A.P.)

Milani, Este. "In margine ad una lettera inedita di Manzoni al figlio Pietro." *ON* 8 (1984): 71-76.

Text of a letter dated November 1849 not included in the *Epistolario* edited by Cesare Arieti.

Ragonese, Gaetano. *Da Manzoni a Fogazzaro. Studi sul-
l'Ottocento narrativo.* Palermo: Società Grafica Artigiana,
1983.

   In the essay "Manzoni tra illuminismo e romanticismo,"
published first in 1978, Ragonese studies the legacy of
the Enlightenment in Manzoni in terms of his outlook on life
and the interplay between faith and reason. As a contrast
to Manzoni, the critic examines the erosion of religious
faith as a dominant aspect of Fogazzaro's narrative. Includes
articles on Verga, Capuana, and D'Annunzio. (A.P.)

Sansone, Mario. "I due volti di Alessandro Manzoni." *ON* 8
(1984): 5-20.

   Examines two prevalent currents in Manzoni studies today:
manzonismo, a largely positive orientation identified with
Catholic culture, and *anti-manzonismo,* represented by critics
who are receptive to Marxist ideology. Sansone argues that
the problem boils down to the inability of the second group
to accept Manzoni's religious faith, the coherence and rationality of his ethical values, and the fact that, whether
one likes it or not, the Church has authority in matters of
faith. Such are the reflections of an established scholar
who, by his own admission, is neither Catholic nor a believer.
(A.P.)

Spinazzola, Vittorio. "*I promessi sposi*: l'io narrante e il
suo doppio." Pp. 841-60 in *Studi di lingua e letteratura
lombarda offerti a Maurizio Vitale.* Pisa: Giardini, 1983.

   The first-person narrative is treated, with uncommon perception, as an ideological presence that mediates the two
historical planes (Seicento and Ottocento) in Manzoni's novel
and, through a selective omniscience, projects the prospect
of a liberal bourgeois society anchored to the value system
of progressive Catholicism. (A.P.)

Stoppelli, Pasquale. "Manzoni e il tema di Don Giovanni."
Belfagor 34 (1984): 501-16.

   Da Ponte's libretto of Mozart's *Don Giovanni* is called
"una delle grandi fonti del romanzo manzoniano" (502).
Following Segre's semiological definition of literary
sources as a critical inquiry to be conducted along the lines
of intertextual analogies, Stoppelli fashions a comparative
frame involving Don Giovanni > Don Rodrigo/Egidio on one
hand, and Lucia/Gertrude, on the other, posited in the role
of innocent victims: "Gertrude è l'innocente traviata dal
seduttore; Lucia è l'innocente che resiste al seduttore"

(511). The Gertrude/Egidio subtext is thus seen as "una
storia parallela a quella degli sposi promessi" (513). An
enriching alternative approach to the traditional study
of literary sources. (A.P.)

Trombatore, Gaetano. *Saggio sul Manzoni. Parte prima. La
giovinezza.* Vicenza: Neri Pozza, 1983. Pp. 251.

In addition to five essays on Manzoni's youthful poetry
published in various journals, the book includes a new and
comprehensive study on Manzoni's sojourn in Paris, "Il
quinquennio parigino," pp. 143-223. Trombatore's sensitive
reconstruction of Manzoni's intellectual formation is based
on wide-ranging corroboration and an enlightening exegesis
of factual evidence, never on the facile psychological
speculations cultivated by other biographers. A second
dimension of this work that merits attention is the bio-
critical portrait of Claude Fauriel, a portrait that goes
well beyond the Manzoni-Fauriel relationship studied by
other scholars. The latter part of the essay offers an
extensive analysis of "Urania" and "Parteneide" which complements individual articles on other youthful poems by Manzoni
included in the volume. (A.P.)

See also Jeronimidis and Wren ("French 2. Hugo").

PELLICO

Pellico, Silvio. *Breve soggiorno in Milano di Battistino
Barometro.* A cura di Mario Ricciardi. Napoli: Guida,
1983. Pp. V+179.

New edition of Pellico's short novel, published first in
two installments in *Il Conciliatore.* Left incomplete because
the Austrian government in Milan discontinued its publication, the work sketches three aspects of Milanese bourgeois
life. Political undertones are present, but the novella
holds interest as a special document modeled, according to
Ricciardi, on Voltaire's *Candide.* (A.P.)

SALUZZO

Costa-Zalessow, Natalia. "Le novelle romantiche di Diodata
Saluzzo Poerio." *IQ* 25 (Winter 1984): 5-13.

Discusses three of Saluzzo's eight novellas (published
in a single volume in 1830) in terms of plot structure,
lyrical qualities, and historical frame. Saluzzo's narra-

tive merits a reevaluation "perché documenta una fase di
trapasso della narrativa italiana dal preromanticismo al
Romanticismo vero e proprio" (11). (A.P.)

TOMMASEO

Missori, Virgilio, ed. *Carteggio inedito tra N. Tommaseo e*
   G.P. Vieusseux (1835-39). Firenze: Olschki, 1981. Pp. 683.

   Rev. by Umberto Carpi in *RiLI* 1 (1983): 215-21.

VERRI

Cicoira, Fabrizio. *Alessandro Verri. Sperimentazione e auto-*
   censura. Bologna: Pàtron, 1982. Pp. 178.

   Rev. by Gilberto Pizzamiglio in *LI* 36 (1984): 450-54.

SPANISH

(Compiled by Brian J. Dendle, University of Kentucky)

1. BIBLIOGRAPHY

Zubatsky, David S. "An International Bibliography of Cumulative Indices to Journals Publishing Articles on Hispanic Languages and Literatures: First Supplement." *Hispania* (Los Angeles) 67 (1984): 383-93.

A supplement to the bibliography published in *Hispania* 58 (1985): 75-101; contains some nineteenth-century items.

2. GENERAL

Alfageme Ruano, Pedro. "Murillo y la escuela romántica sevillana." *ArH*, No. 198 (Jan. 1982): 85-95.

Murillo was considered "la última evolución del arte en la historia" in nineteenth-century Seville. The teaching of art was based on imitation; Valeriano Bécquer escaped from the stifling artistic ambience of Seville. Six plates of Valeriano Bécquer's paintings.

Alvarez Pantoja, María José. "La vida cotidiana de una ciudad provincial (Sevilla 1814-1820)." *ArH*, No. 192 (Jan. 1980): 9-65.

Angles, Enrique Arias. "Landscape Painting in Spain During the Romantic Period." *Arts Magazine* 59,ii (1984): 110-18.

Landscape painting flourished in Spain in the Romantic period, deriving ideas from other continental schools, and from the history of Spanish painting.

Arnaiz, José Manuel. "Another Giaquinto Source for Goya." *BM* 126 (Sept. 1984): 561; 2 illus.

Goya's "St. Luke" was derived from Giaquinto's "Martyrs of Portus Romae."

Braojos Garrido, Alfonso. "El *Semanario de Agricultura y Artes* (1832-1833), un periódico fisiócrata en la Sevilla

de fines del Antiguo Régimen." *ArH*, No. 192 (Jan. 1980):
67-106.

The *Semanario*, which was originally published in Spanish
in London (1829-31), was strongly Anglophile.

Burgo, Jaime del. *Para la Historia de la Primera Guerra Car-
lista*. Pamplona: Institución Príncipe de Viana, 1981.
Pp. 374; illus.

The annotated text of the diary of Florencio Sanz y Baeza
(the secretary to the Real Junta Gubernativa de Navarra),
who offers a detailed account of the activities and intrigues
of the Carlist court, 1834-39. Lengthy onomastic index.
Invaluable.

Caldera, Ermanno. "Calderón desfigurado. (Sobre las represen-
taciones calderonianas en la época prerromantica)." *Anales
de Literatura Española* (University of Alicante) 2 (1983):
57-81.

Provocative essay, in which Caldera analyzes *refundiciones*
by Bretón, Gorostiza, Solís, and others, including that of
La vida es sueño. Theater audiences in the second and third
decades of the nineteenth century preferred the *comedias de
enredo*. Calderón's plays were rewritten to conform to
literary theory (the unities), changed taste (linguistic
simplification), and morality (in which the censors also had
their part).

Camacho Rueda, Eduardo. "Reparto de tierras y agitaciones
campesinas. Pilas, 1821-1839." *ArH*, No. 198 (Jan. 1982):
133-53.

Dérozier, Claudette. "La caricatura en la prensa satírica
ilustrada de la Regencia de Espartero a través de algunos
periódicos: *El Cangrejo* (1841), *La Posdata* (1842-1843) y
La Guindilla (1842-1843)." Pp. 117-31 in *Revisión de Larra
(¿Protesta o revolución?)*. (Centre de Recherches d'Histoire
et Littérature en Europe au XVIIIe et au XIXe Siècles, Vol.
14; Annales Littéraires de l'Université de Besançon, No.
283.) Paris: Les Belles Lettres, 1983.

The use of political caricature in the right-wing *El
Cangrejo* and *La Posdata* and the republican *La Guindilla*;
all three journals launched harsh (and often antisemitic)
attacks on Mendizábal.

Escobar, José, and Anthony Percival. "Viaje imaginario y
sátira de costumbres en la España del siglo XVIII: Los
Viajes de Enrique Wanton al país de las monas." Pp. 79-94
in Michael Rössner and Birgit Wagner, eds., *Aufstieg und*

und Krise der Vernunft. (Festschrift für Hans Hinterhäuser.) Wien, Köln, and Graz: Böhlau, 1984.

Taut discussion of Zaccaria Seriman's imaginary voyage and of the continuation by the Spanish translator Joaquín Vaca de Guzmán (a work which, if we are to believe Galdós, enjoyed a certain popularity during the Romantic period).

Fuentes, Juan Francisco. "Madrid, en vísperas de la sublevación de Bessières." Pp. 99-113 in *Revisión de Larra (¿Protesta o revolución?).* (Centre de Recherches d'Histoire et Littérature en Europe au XVIIIᵉ et au XIXᵉ Siècles, Vol. 14; Annales Littéraires de l'Université de Besançon, No. 283.) Paris: Les Belles Lettres, 1983.

An atmosphere of permanent conspiracy, the unrest of the Madrid populace, rumors of foreign invasion, and the presence of the mysterious Paraguayan intriguer José Fort form the background to the abortive ultra rising of August 1825.

Gil Novales, Alberto. "El movimiento juntero de 1835 en Andalucía." *Cuadernos de Filología* (University of Valencia) 3,3 (1983): 85-118.

The *juntas* opposed both Carlism and the Estatuto Real (which they considered illegitimate); they served to channel and contain popular revolutionary fervor. A lucid overall presentation.

Gil Novales, Alberto. "Prensa satírica de la época de Larra: *El Matamoscas.*" Pp. 133-40 in *Revisión de Larra (¿Protesta o revolución?).* (Centre de Recherches d'Histoire et Littérature en Europe au XVIIIᵉ et au XIXᵉ Siècles, Vol. 14; Annales Littéraires de l'Université de Besançon, No. 283.) Paris: Les Belles Lettres, 1983.

The *exaltado* journal *El Matamoscas* (1836-37) gave short shrift to Spain's rulers.

Gil Novales, Alberto. "Repercusiones españolas de la Revolución de 1830." *Anales de Literatura Española* (University of Alicante) 2 (1983): 281-328.

Numerous details of liberal conspiracies, 1830-33.

Glendinning, Neil. "Goya's Letters to Zapater." *BM* 126 (Nov. 1984): 706-07.

Reviews the following: José Camón Aznar, *Goya* (Instituto Camón Aznar)--vol. I (1980; pp. 175; 118 illus., 52 col. pls.), vol. II (1981; pp. 136; 108 illus., 44 col. pls.); *Diplomatario de Francisco de Goya*, ed. Angel Canellas López (Zaragoza: Institución "Fernando el Católico," 1981; pp. 589); *Francisco de Goya, Cartas a Martín Zapater*, ed. Mercedes Agueda and Xavier de Salas (Madrid: Turner, 1982; pp. 244; 16 illus.).

Hamnett, Brian R. "Liberal Politics and Spanish Freemasonry,
    1814-1820." *H* 69,ccxxvi (1984): 222-37.

Heredia Soriano, Antonio. *Política docente y filosofía ofi-*
    cial en la España del siglo XIX. Salamanca: Ediciones de
    la Universidad, 1982. Pp. 440.

    The teaching of philosophy in Spain, 1833-1868: educa-
tional reforms, the neo-Catholic counterreaction, textbooks,
political ramifications. Comprehensive bibliography;
onomastic index.

Ilie, Paul. "Goya's Teratology and the Critique of Reason."
    ECS 18 (1984): 35-56.

    An extended consideration of how "El sueño de la razón
produce monstruos" should be read. "Either Goya depicts the
dream of reason, thus conferring upon reason the active power
of producing monsters, or else he depicts the *sleep* of reason,
thus exonerating reason from responsibility for what happens
during its inactivity." Ultimately but in more specific terms,
the first alternative is favored. (I.H.C.)

Leblon, Bernard. *Les Gitans dans la littérature espagnole.*
    Toulouse: Institut d'Etudes Hispaniques et Hispano-Améri-
    caines, Université de Toulouse-Le Mirail, 1982. Pp. 251.

    Pp. 44-52 offer the barest mention of the role of gypsies
in Romanticism and the mid-nineteenth-century *zarzuela.*

Mainer, José Carlos. "Del romanticismo en Aragón: *La Aurora*
    (1839-1841)." II, 303-15 in *Serta Philologica F. Lázaro*
    Carreter. Madrid: Cátedra, 1983.

    The role of Aragón in Romantic mythology; the young mili-
tant liberal Romantic editors of *La Aurora* (who included
Borao y Clemente, Braulio Foz, and Guillén Buzarán); their
reviews of Romantic dramas performed in Zaragoza; the activities of the *Liceo* of Zaragoza; their moralistic treatment
of the novel.

Martínez García, Francisco. *Historia de la literatura leonesa.*
    León: Editorial Everest, 1982. Pp. 1151.

    Pp. 317-429 provide a summary of the cultural background
to nineteenth-century Leonese literature and offer details
of numerous writers, including comprehensive treatments of
Gil y Carrasco, Modesto Lafuente, and Julián Escudero (el
"labriego poeta").

Meregalli, Franco. "Sobre el Teatro español en la crítica
    de Voltaire a los hermanos Schlegel." Pp. 239-52 in Americo
    Bugliani, ed., *The Two Hesperias. Literary Studies in*
    Honor of Joseph G. Fucilla on the Occasion of His 80th
    Birthday. Madrid: José Porrúa Turanzas, 1977.

Meregalli draws attention to the grossly neglected work
of Werner Brüggemann, *Die Spanienberichte des 18. und 19.
Jhs. und ihre Bedeutung ...* (Münster, 1956), and touches
on the reappraisal of the theaters of Shakespeare and Calderón in the eighteenth century, Durán's role in introducing
the new German theories to Spain, and the politicization
of Calderonian criticism.

Nadal, Jordi. *El fracaso de la revolución industrial en
España, 1814-1913.* Barcelona: Editorial Ariel, 1975.
Pp. 315.

Ortiz, Fernando. "Manuel Paso, poeta anticolonialista."
Pp. 48-58 in Fernando Ortiz, *La estirpe de Bécquer.* Jérez
de la Frontera: Libros Fin de Siglo, 1982.

Paso (1864-1901) was greatly influenced by Bécquer and
Zorrilla.

Paradissis, A.G. "Una versión contemporánea española de
Mercadet de Balzac: traducción y arte dramático."
Thesaurus 38 (1983): 139-52.

Francisco del Villar's adaptation (1851) of Balzac's·
play.

Pegenaute Garde, Pedro. "*La Abeja Madrileña* de 1814: datos
para su estudio." *Hispania* (Madrid), No. 155 (1983): 599-
621.

A description of *La Abeja Madrileña*, one of the leading
liberal journals. Pegenaute proposes that Regato, and not
Gallardo, was its editor.

Pujols, Esteban. "Lord Byron en Andalucía (verano de 1809)."
ArH, No. 196 (May 1981): 85-91.

Includes identification of Byron's lodgings. Illustrated.

Real Ramos, César. "De los 'desarreglados monstruos' a la
estética del fracaso (Prehistoria del drama romántico)."
Anales de Literatura Española (University of Alicante) 2
(1983): 419-45.

General observations on Romantic features in the eighteenth-
century *comedia de teatro*, the lachrymose drama, and the
melodrama. Descriptions of seven translated plays: Alfieri's
Bruto (1820), D'Arnaud's *Los amantes desgraciados* (1791),
Melesvilles' *¡Está loca!* (1835), D'Aubigny's *Les deux
sergents* (1830), Ducange's *Treinta años* (1829), and Scribe's
Bertran et Raton (1835) and *Le Solliciteur* (1831).

Rees, Margaret A. "Un refugiado agresivo: Nicolás Santiago
de Rotalde y el Gobierno francés de los años 1830."

Hispania (Madrid), No. 150 (1982):   207-19.

Rotalde (the editor of *El Dardo*) strenuously protested the humiliations which the *emigrados* suffered at the hands of the French authorities.

Ringrose, David R. *Madrid and the Spanish Economy, 1560-1850.* University of California Press, 1983. Pp. 405.

The Spanish interior was isolated both geographically and economically and enjoyed slow population growth. Madrid's function was political, not industrial or commercial. In the nineteenth century, a Castilian agro-commercial oligarchy (the *moderados*) inherited power. A centralized bureaucracy was insulated from economic problems; Madrid exploited and depended upon the rest of Spain; the population of Madrid consisted of a few thousand affluent families and a mass of urban poor; the Madrid élite was divided geographically from the "liberal" periphery. Ringrose discerns little structural change between the eighteenth and mid-nineteenth centuries in the role of Madrid. "Thus nineteenth-century Madrid remained functionally elitist, dominated by a small, wealthy upper class and populated by rural and urban masses no better off than 100 or 200 years before." Comprehensive bibliography. A most useful study.

Rodríguez Rodríguez, Luis. *Los liberales lucenses (1808-1854).* La Coruña: Ediciós do Castro, 1981. Pp. 241.

Rudat, Eva M. Kahiluoto. "'Lo prerromántico': una variante neoclásica en la estética y literatura españolas." *Ibero*, No. 15 (1982): 47-69.

Taking as her departure point the combination of reason and feeling in the esthetic theories of Azara and Arteaga, Professor Rudat levels a reasoned criticism against recent attempts to seek Romantic traits in neoclassical art and literature. "Dentro de la continuidad neoclásica, en la cual se funden el concepto de arte como *mímesis* (razón) y como expresión (sentimiento) el equilibrio de razón y sentimiento permite caracterizar la literatura y el arte de los años de transición del siglo dieciocho al diecinueve como una variante neoclásica."

Scari, Robert M. "Unamuno: fruto tardío del romanticismo español." *Hispano*, No. 81 (May 1984): 51-70.

A rather pedestrian attempt at proving that Unamuno, above all in *Del sentimiento trágico de la vida*, exemplifies Romantic values, as defined by Alex Comfort. Edmund King's essay on a similar topic receives no mention.

Zulueta, Carmen de. "George Borrow: el sorprendente éxito de *La Biblia en España*." Pp. 255-65 in Sylvia Molloy and

Luis Fernández Cifuentes, *Essays in Hispanic Literature in Honor of Edmund L. King*. London: Támesis, 1983.

British interest in Romantic Spain--an exotic land of bandits, cholera, and Papists--explains in part the success of Borrow's work. Ford's advice encouraged Borrow to produce a lively text.

3. STUDIES OF AUTHORS

AMADOR DE LOS RIOS

See Arboleda ("Bécquer").

ASSAS

See Arboleda ("Bécquer").

AYGUALS DE IZCO

Reglin, Renate. *Wenceslao Ayguals de Izco: kleinbürgerliche Socialkritik im Folletin-Roman des 19. Jahrhunderts*. Frankfurt: Vervuert, 1983. Pp. 192.

The Spanish publishing industry ca. 1850; Ayguals's political message.

BÉCQUER

Arboleda, José R. *Historia de los templos de España*. Barcelona: Puvill, 1979. Pp. 416.

Bécquer's *Historia de los templos* (1857) was a financial disaster and never completed, being limited to the churches of Toledo. Arboleda discusses Bécquer's precursors in the genre (Piferrer, Amador de los Ríos, Manuel de Assas, Parro, Chateaubriand), and briefly analyzes the *Historia*, establishing its relationship to the *Rimas*. The annotated text of the *Historia*. Bibliography.

Havard, Robert G. "Meaning and Metaphor of Syntax in Bécquer, Guillén and Salinas." *Ibero*, No. 19 (1984): 66-81.

Bécquer's insistence on form leaves us with a contradiction: "the random, spiritual and evanescent quality, which is the object of Bécquer's quest, is antithetical to the densely structured world of the *Rimas*."

Mansour, George P. "The Poetization of Experience: An Explication of Bécquer's *Rima XXIX*." *HisJ* 2,2 (1981): 95-101.

 Statement of the obvious.

Ortiz, Fernando. "Bécquer y la tradición poética andaluza."
Pp. 37-46 in Fernando Ortiz, *La estirpe de Bécquer*. Jérez
de la Frontera: Libros Fin de Siglo, 1982.

 The influence on Bécquer of Lista, Rodríguez Zapata,
Mármol, Dacarrete, and above all Arístides Pongilioni.

See also Ortiz ("Spanish 2. General").

BLANCO WHITE

Cross, Tony. *Joseph Blanco White. Don José María Blanco y
Crespo. Stranger and Pilgrim*. London, 1984. (Obtainable
from The Essex Hall Bookshop, 1-6 Essex St., London WC2R
3HY.) Pp. 47. £1.20.

 A sympathetic general introduction to Blanco, based in
large part on manuscript sources. Cross summarizes Blanco's
religious development. He also refers to Blanco's hypo-
chondria and emotional lability.

Garnica, Antonio. "En busca de Blanco White." *ArH*, No. 198
(Jan. 1982): 25-40.

 Garnica transcribes a lecture given by the late Vicente
Llorens in Seville in 1975, in which Llorens resumes his
researches and discusses Blanco's correspondence and reviews
of Llanos's *Don Esteban*. For Llorens, Blanco was, in the
breadth of his knowledge, one of the leading West European
critics of his day. Blanco preached conciliation at a time
when Spain was dividing into warring bands.

Murphy, G. Martin. "España perseguidora. Irlanda perseguida."
ArH, No. 200 (Sept. 1982): 115-38.

 Blanco White's ancestors settled in Seville to escape the
English persecution of Irish Catholics. Blanco's rancorous
Practical and Internal Evidence Against Catholicism (1825)
lent support to those who opposed Catholic emancipation.
Disillusioned with Oxford conservatism, Blanco in 1832
accompanied to Dublin his friend Archbishop Whately, whose
tolerant outlook offended Irish Protestants and left Blanco
socially isolated. Thomas Moore's lightweight *Travels of an
Irish Gentleman* inspired Blanco to reply with *Second Travels*

of an Irish Gentleman in Search of a Religion, in which
theological arguments are employed against Catholicism.
A fascinating exploration of Blanco's role in the religious
controversies of the United Kingdom.

Ortiz, Fernando. "Blanco White: el exilio, no el reino." Pp.
15-35 in Fernando Ortiz, *La estirpe de Bécquer*. Jérez de
la Frontera: Libros Fin de Siglo, 1982.

   Sympathetic general presentation.

BORAO Y CLEMENTE

See Mainer ("Spanish 2. General").

BRETON DE LOS HERREROS

See Caldera ("Spanish 2. General").

CASTRO

Corona Marzol, Gonzalo. "Una lectura de Rosalía." *RL* 44,87
(1982): 25-62.

   La flor (1857), Rosalía's first work, and later collections
are examined for autobiographical elements; *La flor* is clearly
related to Rosalía's later works. A crisp analysis.

Davies, Catherine. "Rosalía de Castro's Later Poetry and Anti-
Regionalism in Spain." *MLR* 79 (1984): 609-19.

   The note of bitter resentment and the theme of persecution
in *En las orillas del Sar* are Rosalía de Castro's reaction
to the incomprehension and hostility with which her work was
received. She was attacked, or ignored, by Pardo Bazán,
clericals, middle-class moralists, and "the Establishment."
Competently argued.

Havard, Robert G. "'*Saudades*' as Structure in Rosalía de
Castro's *En las orillas del Sar*." *HisJ* 5,1 (Fall 1983):
29-41.

   The "inbuilt structural mode" of *En las orillas del Sar*
is based on the complexity of *saudades* (a paradigm of Galicia,
love, religion).

Palley, Julian. "Rosalía de Castro: Two Mourning Dreams."
Hispano, No. 82 (Sept. 1984): 21-27.

   Dream encounters in "A mi madre" and "En sueños te di un
   beso...."

DACARRETE

See Ortiz ("Bécquer").

DURAN

See Meregalli ("Spanish 2. General").

ESCUDERO

See Martínez García ("Spanish 2. General").

ESPRONCEDA

Badessi, Alessandra. "Uomo vs donna nella visione letteraria
   ed esistenziale di José de Espronceda." *Cuadernos de
   Filología* (University of Valencia) 3,3 (1983): 33-60.

Espronceda, José de. *Teatro Completo*. Ed. de A. Labandeira
   Fernández. Madrid: Editora Nacional, 1982. Pp. 521.

   The neoclassical and Romantic theatrical background,
   biographies of Espronceda and of his collaborators Ros de
   Olano and Eugenio Moreno López, bibliography of the three
   writers. Texts of *Blanca de Borbón*, *Ni el tío ni el sobrino*,
   Amor venga sus agravios.

Fey, Catherine L. "*El estudiante de Salamanca*: oscilaciones
   en un poema fantástico." *ExTL* 12,1 (1983-84): 51-58.

   A pedestrian treatment, which adds nothing to Casalduero
   who, incidentally, is not mentioned.

Gies, David T. "Visión, ilusión y el sueño romántico en la
   poesía de Espronceda." *Cuadernos de Filología* (University
   of Valencia) 3,3 (1983): 61-84.

   The role of dream (nightmare, evasion, illusion) in Espronceda's universe.

Lewis, Thomas E. "Contradictory Explanatory Systems in
Espronceda's Poetry: The Social Genesis and Structure of
El Diablo Mundo." *I&L* 4,17 (1983): 11-45.

    A heavily theoretical discussion, covering the *canciones*,
"A Jarifa en una orgía," and *El Diablo Mundo*. For Lewis,
Espronceda realized the disjunction between liberal bourgeois theory and social practice; the subsequent appeal
to metaphysics was intellectually sterile.

Paulino, José C. "La aventura interior de don Félix de Monte-
mar." *RL* 44,88 (1982): 57-67.

    The inner dynamics of don Félix's mythical journey.

See also Romero Tobar ("Larra").

FOZ

See Mainer ("Spanish 2. General").

GALLARDO

See Pegenaute Garde ("Spanish 2. General").

GIL Y CARRASCO

See Martínez García ("Spanish 2. General"); Fontanella ("Quintana").

GOROSTIZA

See Caldera ("Spanish 2. General").

GUILLEN BUZARAN

See Mainer ("Spanish 2. General").

LAFUENTE

Alonso Cabeza, María Dolores. "Costumbrismo y realismo social."
  RL 44,88 (1982): 69-96.

  Modesto Lafuente's satirical *costumbrismo*.

See also Martínez García ("Spanish 2. General").

LARRA

Aymes, Jean-René. "Mariano José de Larra: Ensayo bibliográ-
  fico." Pp. 45-95 in *Revisión de Larra (¿Protesta o revolución?)*. (Centre de Recherches d'Histoire et Littérature
  en Europe au XVIIIe et au XIXe Siècles, Vol. 14; Annales
  Littéraires de l'Université de Besançon, No. 283.) Paris:
  Les Belles Lettres, 1983.

  Selected, descriptive (but not critical) bibliography.

Dérozier, Albert. "¿Porqué una revisión de Larra?" Pp. 13-34.
  in *Revisión de Larra (¿Protesta o revolución?)*. (Centre de
  Recherches d'Histoire et Littérature en Europe au XVIIIe
  et au XIXe Siècles, Vol. 14; Annales Littéraires de l'Université de Besançon, No. 283.) Paris: Les Belles Lettres,
  1983.

  Taking as his starting point the obituaries published at
  the time of Larra's death, Dérozier challenges the moral
  condemnation (nineteenth century) and sentimentality (twentieth century) with which critics have treated Larra's
  works. Larra's originality lies in his "inquietud dinámica,"
  his spontaneous reaction to events; he deserves rigorous
  scholarly investigation. A useful introduction to the study
  of Larra.

Durnerin, James. "Fascinación y repulsa por Dumas en el
  Larra crítico y creador." Pp. 143-57 in *Revisión de Larra
  (¿Protesta o revolución?)*. (Centre de Recherches d'Histoire
  et Littérature en Europe au XVIIIe et au XIXe Siècles, Vol.
  14; Annales Littéraires de l'Université de Besançon, No. 283.)
  Paris: Les Belles Lettres, 1983.

  Larra's dramatic theories; the influence of Dumas's
  Henri III et Sa Cour on *El Doncel de Don Enrique el Doliente*
  and *Macías*.

Escobar, José. "Larra durante la ominosa década." *Anales de Literatura Española* (University of Alicante) 2 (1983): 233-49.

Larra's enlistment in the Voluntarios Realistas reflected financial need rather than ideological commitment; Larra's attitude at the time suggests a reformer (Enlightened, even liberal), not a reactionary. Well argued.

Escobar, José. "El sombrero y la mantilla: moda e ideología en el costumbrismo romántico español." Pp. 161-65 in *Revisión de Larra (¿Protesta o revolución?)*. (Centre de Recherches d'Histoire et Littérature en Europe au XVIIIe et au XIXe Siècles, Vol. 14; Annales Littéraires de l'Université de Besançon, No. 283.) Paris: Les Belles Lettres, 1983.

Escobar contrasts the *costumbrismo nacionalista* of Carnerero's journals (which rejected foreign ways) and the *costumbrismo "contestario"* of Larra. For Larra, changes in fashion reflect the progress of society. An illuminating article.

Gil Novales, Alberto. "Notas en torno a lecturas de Larra." Pp. 35-42 in *Revisión de Larra (¿Protesta o revolución?)*. (Centre de Recherches d'Histoire et Littérature en Europe au XVIIIe et au XIXe Siècles, Vol. 14; Annales Littéraires de l'Université de Besançon, No. 283.) Paris: Les Belles Lettres, 1983.

The irreverent spirit of the Enlightenment penetrated Spain during the *trienio*, in translations of the Baron d'Holbach and of Dulaurens (whose *Le Compère Mathieu* is mentioned by Larra). "De la lectura de Larra sale siempre un amargor nacional, terrible acumulación de conciencia, que anuncia ya angustias machadianas, desesperaciones de nuestro siglo XX."

Lorenzo-Rivero, Luis. "Afinidades de Galdós con Larra." *SN* 56 (1984): 85-97.

Lorenzo-Rivero indicates thematic parallels between Galdós and Larra. Galdós's direct debt to Larra (for example, in *La desheredada* and certain of the *episodios*) could profitably have been explored.

Morange, Claude. "Visión de la estructura social en los artículos de Larra." Pp. 185-216 in *Revisión de Larra (¿Protesta o revolución?)*. (Centre de Recherches d'Histoire et Littérature en Europe au XVIIIe et au XIXe Siècles, Vol.

14; Annales Littéraires de l'Université de Besançon, No. 283.) Paris: Les Belles Lettres, 1983.

Larra's treatment of social questions has *costumbrista* (descriptive), moral (critical), and political components; the political vision predominates by far.

Pélorson, Jean-Marc. "El humor de Larra o la descortesía de la esperanza." Pp. 167-74 in *Revisión de Larra (¿Protesta o revolución?)*. (Centre de Recherches d'Histoire et Littérature en Europe au XVIIIe et au XIXe Siècles, Vol. 14; Annales Littéraires de l'Université de Besançon, No. 283.) Paris: Les Belles Lettres, 1983.

Analysis of the function (above all ideological) of humor in the "Tercera carta de un liberal de acá."

Perry, Leonard T. "Larra: una evaluación de la literatura española en su 'Don Candido....'" *MSpr* 77 (1983): 57-63.

Uncritical summary of the literary views expounded in "Don Cándido Buenafé."

Robin, Claire-Nicolle. "Larra y el 'mal du siècle.'" Pp. 175-81 in *Revisión de Larra (¿Protesta o revolución?)*. (Centre de Recherches d'Histoire et Littérature en Europe au XVIIIe et au XIXe Siècles, Vol. 14; Annales Littéraires de l'Université de Besançon, No. 283.) Paris: Les Belles Lettres, 1983.

Larra regretted the absence in Spain of a Napoleonic man of genius; his concept of society was aristocratic; he believed that nations were engaged in a "struggle of life."

Romero Tobar, Leonardo. "Circunstancias y alusión en un artículo de Larra ('El Siglo en blanco')." Pp. 639-47 in *Homenaje a Gonzalo Torrente Ballester*. Salamanca: Biblioteca de la Caja de Ahorros, 1981.

A lucid exposition of the background to Larra's witty article. *El Siglo*, edited by Espronceda, Ros de Olano, Núñez de Arenas, and Ventura de la Vega, advocated radical liberal policies and was frequently censored.

Varela, José Luis. *Larra y España*. Madrid: Espasa-Calpe, 1983. Pp. 342.

A well-documented study, in which Varela touches on Larra's education, character, marital problems, suicide, posthumous role as tragic or national symbol, Azorín's cult of Larra, and Larra's style, politics, and sources. The Appendix discusses Larra's service with the *Voluntarios realistas*, his candidacy for deputy for Avila in 1837, and his relations with Dolores Armijo. Comprehensive bibliography; onomastic index.

Wyler, Jacqueline. "La evolución del concepto de patriotismo en la obra de Larra." Pp. 217-24 in *Revisión de Larra (¿Protesta o revolución?)*. (Centre de Recherches d'Histoire et Littérature en Europe au XVIIIe et au XIXe Siècles, Vol. 14; Annales Littéraires de l'Université de Besançon, No. 283.) Paris: Les Belles Lettres, 1983.

   Larra's vision of *patria* is at times ill-defined; its source is in the liberal enlightened philosophy of such thinkers as Quintana. Larra regretted the lack in Spain of social cohesion; he believed in the need to educate "the people."

See also Durnerin ("French 2. Scribe"); Aregger ("German 3. Heine").

LISTA

See Ortiz ("Bécquer").

LLANOS

See Garnica ("Blanco White").

LLORENTE, JUAN ANTONIO

Dufour, Gérard. *Juan Antonio Llorente en France (1813-1822)*. Geneva: Librairie Droz, 1982. Pp. 375.

   A clearly written comprehensive account of Llorente's life in exile. In France, Llorente achieved celebrity with his *Histoire critique de l'Inquisition d'Espagne*, became a "liberal" Christian (rather than *afrancesado*), and defended an autonomous national church. An index of names would have been helpful.

MADOZ

Paredes Alonso, Francisco Javier. *Pascual Madoz 1805-1870.*
Pamplona: Ediciones Universidad de Navarra, 1982. Pp. 574.

   Paredes Alonso's study covers in exhaustive detail Madoz's
political and administrative career. Madoz edited the
progresista journal *El Catalán*, 1834-35; in 1849, he defended
the cause of protectionism on behalf of Catalan interests.
Regrettably, the preparation of the *Diccionario* (1845-50)
is but briefly treated. Bibliography; onomastic index.

MARTÍNEZ DE LA ROSA

See Fontanella ("Quintana").

MELENDEZ VALDES

Junquera, Mercedes. "Meléndez Valdés: un romántico intelec-
tual." *REH* 18 (1984): 293-312.

   The mature Meléndez Valdés was aware of the sufferings of
the lower classes, was religious in Encyclopaedist fashion,
and possessed a pre-Romantic sensibility and love of nature.

MESONERO ROMANOS

Mesonero Romanos, Ramón de. *Manual de Madrid.* Madrid:
Fareso, 1982. Pp. 412; illus. Ptas. 900.00.

   Facsimile of the 1833 edition.

MIÑANO

Castañón, Jesús. "Sebastián de Miñano: un periodista del
período liberal." *Anales de Literatura Española* (University
of Alicante) 2 (1983): 83-102.

   Competent presentation of Miñano's journalism during the
trienio.

MOR DE FUENTES

Mor de Fuentes, José. *Bosquejillo de la vida y escritos de D. José Mor de Fuentes*. Introducción, edición y notas de Manuel Alvar. Zaragoza: Guara Editorial, 1981. Pp. 167.

In the sensitive introduction, Alvar discerns in Mor de Fuentes (the translator of *Werther*) a fundamental timidity, moralizing tendency, devotion to nature, and a conflict between neoclassical and Romantic attitudes. Mor de Fuentes was Romantic in his subjectivity and rapidity of writing. Alvar reproduces the text of the 1836 edition of the *Bosquejillo*.

MORENO LÓPEZ

See Espronceda ("Espronceda").

NÚÑEZ DE ARENAS

See Romero Tobar ("Larra").

PARRO

See Arboleda ("Bécquer").

PIFERRER

See Arboleda ("Bécquer").

PONGILIONI

See Ortiz ("Bécquer").

PRÍNCIPE

Buesa Oliver, Tomás. "Miguel Agustín Príncipe, primer paraninfo zaragozano en lengua española (1837)." II, 113-26 in *Serta Philologica F. Lázaro Carreter*. Madrid: Cátedra, 1983.

Príncipe's inaugural speech for the 1837 courses at the
University of Zaragoza was in Castillian and referred to
the Romantic-classical polemic; his literary collaboration
in *El Entreacto.*

QUINTANA

Fontanella, Lee. "Pelayo and Padilla in Reformist and Revolutionary Spain." Pp. 61-72 in Sylvia Molloy and Luis
Fernández Cifuentes, *Essays in Hispanic Literature in Honor
of Edmund L. King.* London: Támesis, 1983.

Discusses above all Quintana's treatment of Pelayo;
passing mentions of Gil y Carrasco's and Martínez de la
Rosa's treatment of Padilla.

See also Wyler ("Larra").

REGATO

See Pegenaute Garde ("Spanish 2. General").

RIVAS

Caldera, Ermanno. "De *Aliatar* a *Don Alvaro.* Sobre el
aprendizaje clasicista del Duque de Rivas." *Cuadernos
de Filología* (University of Valencia) 3,3 (1983): 5-31.

Stylistic devices reveal Rivas's gradual evolution from
neoclassicism to a Romantic sensibility.

RODRÍGUEZ ZAPATA

See Ortiz ("Bécquer").

ROS DE OLANO

Amusco, Alejandro. "La poesía de Antonio Ros de Olano."
Anales de Literatura Española (University of Alicante)
2 (1983): 25-56.

Detailed description of the poems, which were carefully
revised by Ros de Olano, published in *Poesías* (1886).
Amusco indicates Romantic and grotesque features.

See also Espronceda ("Espronceda"); Romero Tobar ("Larra").

SELGAS

Aranda, Eusebio. *José Selgas*. Murcia: Academia Alfonso
X el Sabio, 1982. Pp. 217; illus.

Selgas's biography, works, collaboration in *El Padre
Cobos* (1854-56), poetic style (his use of parallelism,
word play, cliché). Aranda notes Selgas's failure as a
novelist and his seeming lack of interest in Murcia. The
bibliography includes description of the journals in which
Selgas collaborated.

VENTURA DE LA VEGA

See Romero Tobar ("Larra").

VICETTO

Alberich, José. "Valle Inclán y Benito Vicetto: en torno
a *Los Hidalgos de Monforte*." Pp. 9-24 in Giuseppe Bellini,
ed., *Aspetti e Problemi delle Letterature Iberiche*. Rome:
Bulzoni, 1981.

Valle Inclán read Vicetto's *Los Hidalgos de Monforte*;
he shares with Vicetto a grotesque mixture of eroticism
and religion and also folletinesque elements.

VILLAR

See Paradissis ("Spanish 2. General").

ZORRILLA

Dowling, John. "Traditional Spain in the Works of José
Zorrilla: The Poet and His Father." *CH* 2 (1980): 97-108.

Dowling argues that a guilt-ridden Zorrilla wrote at a
furious pace between 1837 and 1849 in a fruitless attempt to
regain the favor of his conservative father. Intriguing and
plausible.

Llorens, Vicente. "El oportunismo de Zorrilla." Pp. 359-69
in *Homenaje a José Manuel Blecua*. Madrid: Gredos, 1983.

Succinct overall view of Zorrilla's dramas.

See also Ortiz ("Spanish 2. General").